WHAT IS WORLD BAND RADIO?

It is no secret why world band radio is now such popular entertainment. Thanks to advanced technology, it allows us to enjoy a generous slice of life from every corner of the world. Television and VCRs can't begin to equal the wealth of news, music and entertainment available on world band radio. There's nothing else quite like it, and it's all there at the touch of a button.

Passport to World Band Radio provides you with everything you need to enjoy these shows from around the world. Program schedules . . . ratings of world band radios . . . how to get started. It's all there, right to the point.

Share in the thrill of eavesdropping on distant lands and peoples. Tune into world band, and tune in the world.

The "other" Venice.

Kurt Kroszner

1990 PASSPORT TO

CONTENTS

WORLD BAND RADIO

1990 BUYER'S GUIDE TO WORLD BAND RADIO

WORLDSCAN

GLOSSARIES AND GUIDES

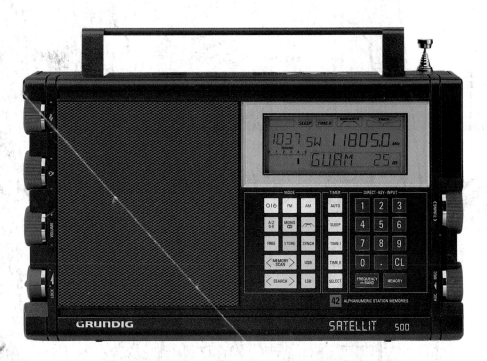

RADIO DREAMS

GRUNDIG WORLD RECEIVER

ISSN 0897-0157

International Broadcasting Services, Ltd.

PASSPORT TO WORLD BAND RADIO

1990

Editor-in-Chief	Lawrence Magne
Editor	Tony Jones
Features Editor	Elizabeth Macalaster
Contributing Editors	Tim Akester (Zimbabwe), Alex Batman (U.S.), Geoff Cosier (Australia), Jock Elliott (U.S.), Noel Green (England)
Consulting Editors	John Campbell (England), Don Jensen (U.S.)
Special Contributors	Rogildo Fontenelle Aragão (Brazil), James A. Conrad (U.S.), Gordon Darling (Papua New Guinea), Antonio Ribeiro da Motta (Brazil), DXFL/Isao Ugusa (Japan), Joe Hanlon (U.S.), Ruth M. Hesch (U.S.), Robert J. Hill (U.S.), Edward J. Insinger (U.S.), Konrad Kroszner (U.S.), Toshimichi Ohtake (Japan), Robert R. Palmer (U.S.), RNM/Tetsuya Hirahara (Japan), Jairo Salazar (Venezuela), Don Swampo (Uruguay), Craig and Shelda Tyson (Australia), David L. Walcutt (U.S.)
Database Software	Richard Mayell
Laboratory	J. Robert Sherwood
Marketing & Production	Mary W. Kroszner
Administration	J. M. Brinker
Communications	Consultech Communications, Inc.
Graphic Preparation	The Bookmakers, Incorporated, Wilkes-Barre, Pennsylvania
IBS—North America	Box 300, Penn's Park, Pennsylvania 18943 USA
IBS—Latin America	Casilla 1844, Asunción, Paraguay

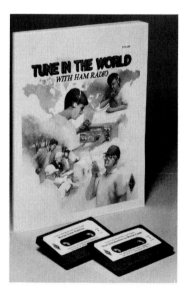

WORLD TIME
−1
0
+1
+2
+3
+4
+5
+6
+7
+8
+9
Tallinn, U.S.S.R.
Riga, U.S.S.R.
Pori, Finland
Minsk, U.S.S.R.
Vilnius, U.S.S.R.
Karlsborg, Sweden
Reykjavik, Iceland
Hörby, Sweden
Kvitsøy, Norway
Copenhagen, Denmark
Flevoland, Netherlands
Skelton, United Kingdom
Daventry, United Kingdom
Dublin, Ireland
Jülich, West Germany
Rampisham, United Kingdom
Wavre, Belgium
Leipzig, East Germany
Allouis, France
Berne, Switzerland
Vienna, Austria
Szekésfehérvár, Hungary
Lisbon, Portugal
Algiers, Algeria
Tangier, Morocco
Rabat, Morocco
Tunis, Tunisia
Canary Islands
Leningrad, U.S.S.R.
Sverdlovsk, U.S.S.R.
Moscow, U.S.S.R.
Kenga, U.S.S.R.
Krasnoyarsk, U.S.S.R.
Novosibirsk, U.S.S.R.
Irkutsk, U.S.S.R.
Chita, U.S.S.R.
Yakutsk,
Warsaw, Poland
Prague, Czechoslovakia
Tula, U.S.S.R.
Kiev, U.S.S.R.
Krasnodar, U.S.S.R.
Armavir, U.S.S.R.
Belgrade, Yugoslavia
Bucharest, Romania
Alma-Ata, U.S.S.R.
Frunze, U.S.S.R.
Altai, Mongolia
Ulan Bator, Mongolia
Khabarovsk, U.S.S.
Harbin, China
Tirana, Albania
Sofia, Bulgaria
Tbilisi, U.S.S.R.
Baku, U.S.S.R.
Tashkent, U.S.S.R.
Urumqi, China
Vatican City
Rome, Italy
Forli, Italy
Noblejas, Spain
Istanbul, Turkey
Kavalla, Greece
Yerevan, U.S.S.R.
Ashkhabad, U.S.S.R.
Dushanbé, U.S.S.R.
Hohhot, China
Beijing, China
Peshawar, Pakistan
Islamabad, Pakistan
Rawalpindi, Pakistan
Xi'an, China
Athens, Greece
Ankara, Turkey
Caltanissetta, Sicily
Tel Aviv, Israel
Mashhad, Iran
Tehrān, Iran
Kabul, Afghanistan
Kathmandu, Nepal
Sfax, Tunisia
Tripoli, Libya
Benghazi, Libya
Baghdad, Iraq
Amman, Jordan
Zāhedān, Iran
Quetta, Pakistan
New Delhi, India
Lhasa, Tibet (China)
Fuzhou, China
Kunming, China
Cairo, Egypt
Riyadh, Saudi Arabia
Doha, Qatar
Dubai, U.A.E.
Sib, Oman
Karachi, Pakistan
Thimpu, Bhutan
Dhaka, Bangladesh
Taipei,
Jiddah, Saudi Arabia
Abu Dhabi, U.A.E.
Masīrah, Oman
Muscat, Oman
Calcutta, India
Hanoi, Vietnam
Nouakchott, Mauritania
Bamako, Mali
N'Djamena, Chad
Thamarīt, Oman
Bombay, India
Vientiane, Laos
Iba, Phi
Manila
San'a, Yemen A.R.
Hydarabad, India
Rangoon, Burma
Niamey, Niger
Aden, Yemen P.D.R.
Bangkok, Thailand
Madras, India
Ouagadougou, Burkina Faso
Kaduna, Nigeria
Conakry, Guinea
Moundou, Chad
Bangalore, India
Phnom Penh, Cambodia
Kara, Togo
Garoua, Cameroon
Omdurman, Sudan
Monrovia, Liberia
Hargeisa, Somalia
Parakou, Benin
Addis Ababa, Ethiopia
Abidjan, Ivory Coast
Mogadishu, Somalia
Accra, Ghana
Bangui, Central African Republic
Kuala Lumpur, Malaysia
Lomé, Togo
Bunia, Zaire
Kampala, Uganda
Cotonou, Benin
Yaoundé, Cameroon
Nairobi, Kenya
Padang, Indonesia
Lagos, Nigeria
Bukavu, Zaire
Seychelles Islands
Samarinda, Indonesia
Jos, Nigeria
Kinshasa, Zaire
Zanzibar
Jakarta, Indonesia
Enugu, Nigeria
Malabo, Equatorial Guinea
Dar es Salaam, Tanzania
Ujung Pandang, Indonesia
Buea, Cameroon
Batá, Equatorial Guinea
Bujumbura, Burundi
Darwin, Australia
Libreville, Gabon
Lubumbashi, Zaire
Katherine, Australia
Cabinda, Angola
Blantyre, Malawi
Tennant Creek, Australia
Brazzaville, Congo
Antananarivo, Madagascar
Luanda, Angola
Beira, Mozambique
Benguela, Angola
Alice Springs, Australia
Malange, Angola
Gweru, Zimbabwe
Carnarvon, Australia
Windhoek, Namibia
Maputo, Mozambique
Harare, Zimbabwe
Johannesburg, South Africa
Gaborone, Botswana
Maseru, Lesotho
Pietersburg, South Africa
Umtata, South Africa
Perth, Australia
Capetown, South Africa
Melbourne, Austr
THE WORLD
OF WORLD BAND RADIO
WORLD TIME
−1
0
+1
+2
+3
+4
+5
+6
+7
+8
+9

+11
+12
−11
−10
−9
−8
−7
−6
−5
−4
−3
−2
Nuuk, Greenland
Anchor Point, Alaska
Ottawa, Canada
Montreal, Canada
Calgary, Canada
Toronto, Canada
Vancouver, Canada
Magadan, U.S.S.R.
Petropavlovsk-Kamchatskiy, U.S.S.R.
Choybalsan, Mongolia
Sapporo, Japan
Vladivostok, U.S.S.R.
Pyongyang, North Korea
Tokyo, Japan
Seoul, South Korea
Hiroshima, Japan
Scotts Corners, ME, U.S.A.
Halifax, Canada
Olamon, ME, U.S.A.
Chicago, IL, U.S.A.
Salt Lake City, UT, U.S.A.
New York, NY, U.S.A.
Red Lion, PA, U.S.A.
Washington, DC, U.S.A.
Noblesville, IN, U.S.A.
Cincinnati, OH, U.S.A.
San Francisco, CA, U.S.A.
Redwood City, CA, U.S.A.
Delano, CA, U.S.A.
Los Angeles, CA, U.S.A.
Nashville, TN, U.S.A.
Greenville, NC, U.S.A.
Cypress Creek, SC, U.S.A.
Atlanta, GA, U.S.A.
Dallas, TX, U.S.A.
New Orleans, LA, U.S.A.
Okeechobee, FL, U.S.A.
Miami, FL, U.S.A.
Havana, Cuba
México City, Mexico
Saipan, Northern Mariana Islands
Guam
Bonaire, Netherlands Antilles
Caracas, Venezuela
Managua, Nicaragua
Maturín, Venezuela
Georgetown, Guyana
Maracaibo, Venezuela
Mérida, Venezuela
Paramaribo, Surinam
Majuro, Marshall Islands
Bogotá, Colombia
Cayenne, French Guiana
Cali, Colombia
Montsinéry, French Guiana
Biak, Indonesia
Belem, Brazil
Quito, Ecuador
Iquitos, Peru
Manaus, Brazil
Bougainville, Papua New Guinea
Recife, Brazil
Pucallpa, Peru
Pôrto Velho, Brazil
Port Moresby, Papua New Guinea
Lima, Peru
Salvador, Brazil
Cuzco, Peru
Cuiabá, Brazil
Brasília, Brazil
Tahiti, French Polynesia
Arequipa, Peru
La Paz, Bolivia
Goiânia, Brazil
Santa Cruz, Bolivia
Belo Horizonte, Brazil
Sucre, Bolivia
Rio de Janeiro, Brazil
Calama, Chile
São Paulo, Brazil
Asunción, Paraguay
Curitiba, Brazil
Foz do Iguaçú, Brazil
Florianópolis, Brazil
Brisbane, Australia
Pôrto Alegre, Brazil
Santa Fé, Argentina
Santiago, Chile
Montevideo, Uruguay
Buenos Aires, Argentina
Auckland, New Zealand
Córdoba, Argentina
Wellington, New Zealand
Viedma, Argentina
Christchurch, New Zealand
Coyhaique, Chile
Base Esperanza, Antarctica
Murdo, Antarctica
+11
+12
−11
−10
−9
−8
−7
−6
−5
−4
−3
−2

Kurt Kroszner

GETTING STARTED WITH WORLD BAND RADIO

by Harry L. Helms

You finally did it. You're the proud new owner of a world band radio!

You unpack the unit and admire its styling and design. You examine the controls and array of functions. You flip through the owner's manual, seemingly written by and for Tibetan engineers. Suddenly, you find yourself thinking, *How am I ever going to figure out how to use this thing?*

Today's world band radios do indeed look complicated at first glance. But, then, so do many other everyday electronic devices, such as VCRs and compact disc players. A world band radio is no more mysterious to use than these, and is often a lot more interesting.

What is World Band Radio?

World band is really just another broadcasting range, like the AM band and the FM band you're already used to. In fact, world band is located right between the AM and FM bands.

World band radio uses thirteen groups of frequencies that lie within the shortwave portion of the radio spectrum. These permit music, news and entertainment to be heard throughout the world on a regular basis, although with only Spartan audio fidelity. With a world band radio, it's possible—in fact, common—at the same moment to have the choice of listening to stations from London, Moscow, Beijing, Paris, Boston or Jerusalem.

This same shortwave spectrum, like a train that includes both passenger and freight cars, includes more than world band radio. It also is home to amateur radio and specialized segments for what's commonly called *utility* stations. Amateur and utility stations—the "freight cars"—are not intended to be heard by the general public and often require relatively sophisticated equipment to decipher. However, some radio enthusiasts—*shortwave listeners*—can and do tune to these special signals, in addition to world band broadcasts. (For more on this, see "Eavesdropping on Disaster," found elsewhere in this edition of *Passport*.)

But even if you're only tuning around the shortwave spectrum just outside the world band segments, don't be surprised if you hear the mysterious beeps and myriad other sounds that these stations make.

Finding Your Way Around

The frequencies used by world band stations are measured in either *kiloHertz*

Left, The choice among world band receivers is vast. Shown are just some that are currently being offered.

(kHz) or *MegaHertz* (MHz). A MegaHertz is equal to 1000 kiloHertz, so 9.58 MHz is the same as 9580 kHz.

You'll hear world band stations announce their operating frequencies using both methods, but in *Passport to World Band Radio* only kHz are used, to avoid confusion. Some advanced radio sets can display the frequency to one-tenth or even one-hundredth of a kHz, but that sort of tuning accuracy is not necessary for world band listening.

If you flip through the Blue Pages of *Passport to World Band Radio*, you'll notice that most world band stations operate within certain ranges of frequencies, and that those frequencies are spaced exactly 5 kHz apart. For example, look at the listings for the 15100 to 15600 kHz range. Most stations use frequencies ending in 0 or 5 and are spaced at least 5 kHz from other stations. You will find that this pattern holds in all the other ranges, too, such as 5950 to 6200, 7100 to 7300, 9500 to 9900, 11650 to 12050 and 13600 to 13800 kHz.

Advanced technology world band receivers have a digital readout display—something like a TV channel display—showing the exact frequency tuned. Here, we'll assume your receiver is such a digital-readout type.

However, your radio might have, instead, an old-style slide rule tuning arrangement. If so, finding the station you want will be something of a trial-and-error proposition. With practice, you'll be able to tune such a receiver reasonably near a desired frequency, but a digital-readout receiver is much easier to use. There are, after all, some *1,100* world band channels from which to choose. This makes it pretty hard to find a station if you can't even tell where you're tuning.

Understanding Those Controls

Today's world band radios often manage to pack numerous knobs, sliders, switches and buttons into a tiny area. The owner's manual should describe the exact operation of your set's controls. However, the following are found on most world band radios, although many will not have them all and some will have even more.

-Digital frequency display. If your radio has a digital readout, this will show

Passport's Lawrence Magne with three sizes of world band receivers.

the exact frequency the radio is tuned to, either in kHz or MHz. Some displays show the frequency to the nearest kHz—as in 9580 kHz—while some others display fractional frequencies, such as 9580.5 kHz.

-Tuning knob. No mystery about this control! Simply turn it until the frequency of the station you want to hear is shown on the display, or use it in conjunction with *Passport's* Blue Pages to "go fishing" for whatever is on the airwaves.

A few radios come equipped only with *slewing* controls—elevator-like up/down tuning buttons—in lieu of a tuning knob. Slewing buttons are fine for operating a TV or VCR, where the number of channel choices is reasonably limited. But for the vastness of choice that is world band radio, these buttons are a mediocre substitute for a conventional tuning knob.

-Tuning keypad. This works much like the keypad on a Touch-Tone telephone or a calculator. Just press the buttons for the frequency you want, tap the (usually) *enter* or *execute* key, and the radio is instantly tuned for you. For example, if you want tune in 9580 kHz, you would typically press 9-5-8-0 and the execute key.

Not all keypads operate the same way, however. As most world band stations are on frequencies ending in either 0 or 5, a few keypads allow you to enter only frequencies ending in 0 or 5. If you try to enter a frequency such as 9582 kHz, you'll either get an error message on the digital display, or else a truncated frequency, such as 9580 kHz, will be tuned. A handful of models confuse matters by requiring you to manipulate an *AM* key or some other control before entering a frequency.

-BFO or SSB control. Single sideband (SSB) is a method of transmission used by amateur radio operators and utility stations. If you tune an SSB signal with your radio's BFO or SSB control set to *off*, you'll hear grossly distorted audio that sounds like Daisy Duck in heat. Almost no world band stations use SSB, so leave this control off—or, on some models, set to AM.

-Bandwidth (Wide-Narrow) control. For best audio, leave this in the *wide* position. If there's annoying interference from other stations, try setting the control to *narrow*. A few top-class radios have more than two bandwidths, which allows you to move from wide to intermediate to narrow, instead of just from wide to narrow.

-Sensitivity, or attenuator, control. When set to *high*—or *normal* or *DX*, depending on the manufacturer's nomenclature—you can hear weak stations better, and even strong stations may sound less "hissy." However, under certain conditions the high position may cause strong stations to *overload* the radio, resulting in a babble of false signals that decreases listening pleasure. In such cases—which with better radios are not common—the *local* position can help.

For best results, leave this control switched to the high position. However, feel free to experiment with the local position if you hear a mishmash of stations that sound as though they're piled atop each other on the same channel.
(*continued on page 116*)

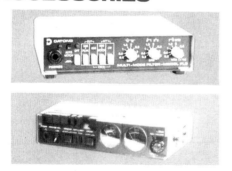

Yaesu has serious listeners for the serious listener.

Yaesu's serious about giving you better ways to tune in the world around you.

And whether it's for local action or worldwide DX, you'll find our VHF/UHF and HF receivers are the superior match for all your listening needs.

The FRG-9600. A premium VHF/UHF scanning communications receiver. The 9600 is no typical scanner. And it's easy to see why.

You won't miss any local action with continuous coverage from 60 to 905 MHz.

You have more operating modes to listen in on: upper or lower sideband, CW, AM wide or narrow, and FM wide or narrow.

You can even watch television programs by plugging in a video monitor into the optional video output.

Scan in steps of 5, 10, 12½, 25 and 100 KHz. Store any frequency and related operating mode into any of the 99 memories. Scan the memories. Or in between them. Or simply "dial up" any frequency with the frequency entry pad.

Plus there's more, including a 24-hour clock, multiplexed output, fluorescent readout, signal strength graph, and an AC power adapter.

The FRG-8800 HF communications receiver. A better way to listen to the world. If you want a complete communications package, the FRG-8800 is just right for you.

You get continuous worldwide coverage from 150 KHz to 30 MHz. And local coverage from 118 to 174 MHz with an optional VHF converter.

Listen in on any mode: upper and lower sideband, CW, AM wide or narrow, and FM.

Store frequencies and operating modes into any of the twelve channels for instant recall.

Scan the airwaves with a number of programmable scanning functions.

Plus you get keyboard frequency entry. An LCD display for easy readout. A SINPO signal graph. Computer interface capability for advanced listening functions. Two 24 hour clocks. Recording functions. And much more to make your listening station complete.

Listen in. When you want more from your VHF/UHF or HF receivers, just look to Yaesu. We take your listening seriously.

YAESU

Yaesu USA
17210 Edwards Road, Cerritos, CA 90701
(213) 404-2700

Dealer inquiries invited.

Prices and specifications subject to change without notice.
FRG-9600 SSB coverage: 60 to 460 MHz.

TEN OF THE BEST SHOWS FOR 1990

Several dozen countries reach out to us every day with thousands of programs over world band radio. Their hope is that you come to know better their lands, their peoples, and how they view things from perspectives you might otherwise never encounter.

To help you sift through this potpourri of choices, we've picked ten of what we feel are among the best programs on world band radio. Nearly all are easy to hear in most places on at least one frequency, and they include news, music, current affairs—even short stories.

So, pack your bags with this *Passport* list and enjoy your electronic journey into the elite ranks of world band programming.

Newshour
BBC World Service

If there is any one thing that listeners expect from world band radio, it is up-to-the-minute, interesting news. The BBC's incomparable *Newshour* provides just that—and how!

Newshour is a recent addition to world band radio, having just emerged from its electronic womb in November, 1988,

Left, Eiger, Moench and Jungfrau as seen from Bernese Oberland, Switzerland. Right, The Rhine River valley, south of Bonn, West Germany.

West German Embassy

Swiss Tourist Office

when the BBC revamped portions of its programming. *Newshour's* high card is its broad international appeal, as so many of the stories broadcast are of worldwide—rather than purely regional or national—concern.

The program begins with ten minutes of up-to-the-hour headline news from a variety of different locales, including the United States, China, Armenia—or wherever significant news is breaking. This is followed by about twenty minutes of in-depth features and reports from correspondents on various of the lead stories in the headlines. This, in turn, is followed by five minutes of financial news. Strictly British news is limited to approximately ten minutes in the second half hour, after which the program closes with special features and analysis, such as on the subject of the tenth anniversary of the Iranian revolution.

What distinguishes the BBC's *Newshour* from Radio Canada International's *The World At Six* and *As It Happens* that we picked last year?

> If there is any one thing that listeners expect it is up-to-the-minute, interesting news. The incomparable *Newshour* provides just that—and how!

It is that much of Radio Canada's programming—top-drawer though it may be—is, by design, devoted to strictly Canadian concerns, while the "Beeb's" *Newshour*—aired only once daily, at 2200 World Time—is much broader in its outlook. In the Americas, tune to *Newshour* on 5975, 6175, 9915 or 15260 kHz. In Europe, try 3955, 6195, 7325, 9410 or 12095 kHz. In East Asia and the Pacific, best bets include 9570, 11955 or 15140 kHz.

Random Selection
Deutsche Welle

If you've wondered what happened to Larry Wayne's popular daily feature *Germany Today*, this is it. The same kind of lighter stories from the news, along with Wayne's whimsical presentation, have been condensed into a fresh new weekly feature that airs three times each Saturday. Precious few programs give such a complete sense of what life is like in another country.

> Instead of robbing her, they apologized for the intrusion and left a donation of twenty Deutsch Marks.

Random Selection typically begins with a bit of information about the weather in Cologne . . . plus whatever else may be of seasonal interest, such as the celebration of Christmas. It then moves rapidly through a number of interesting stories from the German papers, any of which will almost certainly never make a single international headline.

A few seem straight out of a Peter Sellers' movie. For example, two burglars in a German town broke into an old woman's house, looked around, and found that she had nothing worth stealing. Indeed, she was, herself, an invalid. So, instead of robbing her, they apologized for the intrusion and left her a donation of twenty Deutsch Marks.

Another told of an unlucky fellow who had been arrested for a bank robbery he hadn't committed. The reason: his description fitted that of the real robber. Witnesses confirmed that the suspect wasn't the robber. However, further investigation revealed that he, too, had been planning the same holdup . . . but that the other guy had beaten him to the punch.

Perhaps the best thing about *Random Selection* is Wayne's presentation. It is light and airy, when appropriate, and his puns are enough to make a nun groan. Wayne's closing is traditional, and includes well-wishes from Jezzy, the family feline. It may well be the second best fifteen minutes you can spend on a Friday night.

There is a rub in all this: This show is beamed only to North America. However, it still can be enjoyed in Europe, and elsewhere to some extent, because of world band radio's stubborn and fortuitous propensity to propagate beyond where it is aimed.

So, on Saturdays (that is, Friday evenings in the Americas) at 0100 World Time try 6040, 6085, 6145, 9565, 9735, 11865 or 15105 kHz. At 0300, tune to 6085, 9545, 9605, 11810 or 15205 kHz. The final repeat is audible at 0500 on 5960, 6130, 9670, 9700, 11705 or 11845 kHz.

As a postscript, Deutsche Welle is particularly effective in keeping its listeners informed as to what's on, when, and on what frequencies. Drop them a note at Deutsche Welle Public Relations Department, Postfach 10 04 44, D-5000 Cologne 1, Federal Republic of Germany, and ask to be placed on the mailing list for their free bimonthly magazine, *tune in*. As a bonus, at the end of each year you will also receive a colorful German calendar.

Embassy of Japan

Japanese children celebrate the Shichigosan festival.

Down Our Way
Radio RSA

A propaganda station from a nation in which human beings of different colors are disallowed from having normal relationships with each other would hardly seem to be the place to discover excellence in programming. But, withal, Radio RSA's *Down Our Way* does a commendable job in spotlighting the vibrant entertainment scene in South Africa. There are interviews with singers, songwriters and actors, and the show plays plenty of good—albeit presumably "approved"—music. It conveys a wonderful sense of how at least some South Africans amuse themselves in their leisure time.

One part of the program plays songs currently popular within the black community, while another runs down the South African Top Thirty. There are also vignettes on South African performers who have emigrated to make their splash abroad.

All in all, this is arguably the best program on world band radio devoted to entertainment as an industry. There should be more shows like it.

In Europe, try *Down Our Way* Saturdays at 1100 World Time on 21590 kHz; 1500 on 15270, 17755, 21535, 21590, 21670 or 25790 kHz; and 2000 on 17795 or 21590 kHz. In Asia and the Pacific, it's at 1300 on 21590 kHz.

Interestingly, *Down Our Way* is not included in Radio RSA's evening transmissions to North America. However, it is heard there Saturday mornings much of the year at 1500 World Time on 21590, 21670 or 25790 kHz.

"Documentary Series"
Radio Nederland

This program has no official title—or, rather, it has several of them, since on Wednesdays Radio Nederland runs a series of varied documentaries. Some last only one night, some extend for weeks.

Take, for example, one of the better one-night shows: *What the Tourist Saw.* This had a Radio Nederland reporter accompanying a tour bus around Holland to give the listener a real tourist's view of the country . . . a verbal view, of course—tulips being especially appropriate in the country. Another discussed the Prince of the Netherlands' involvement in environmental and wildlife issues.

Extended series have included *The Savage Breast*. Rather than being a National Geographic-type special, it turned out to be an examination of music in the (*continued on page 119*)

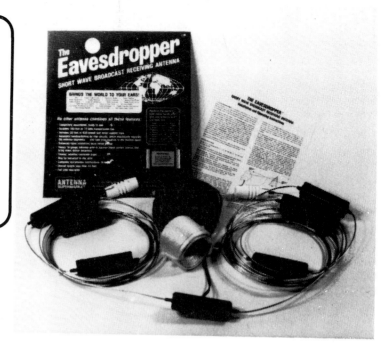

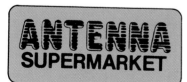

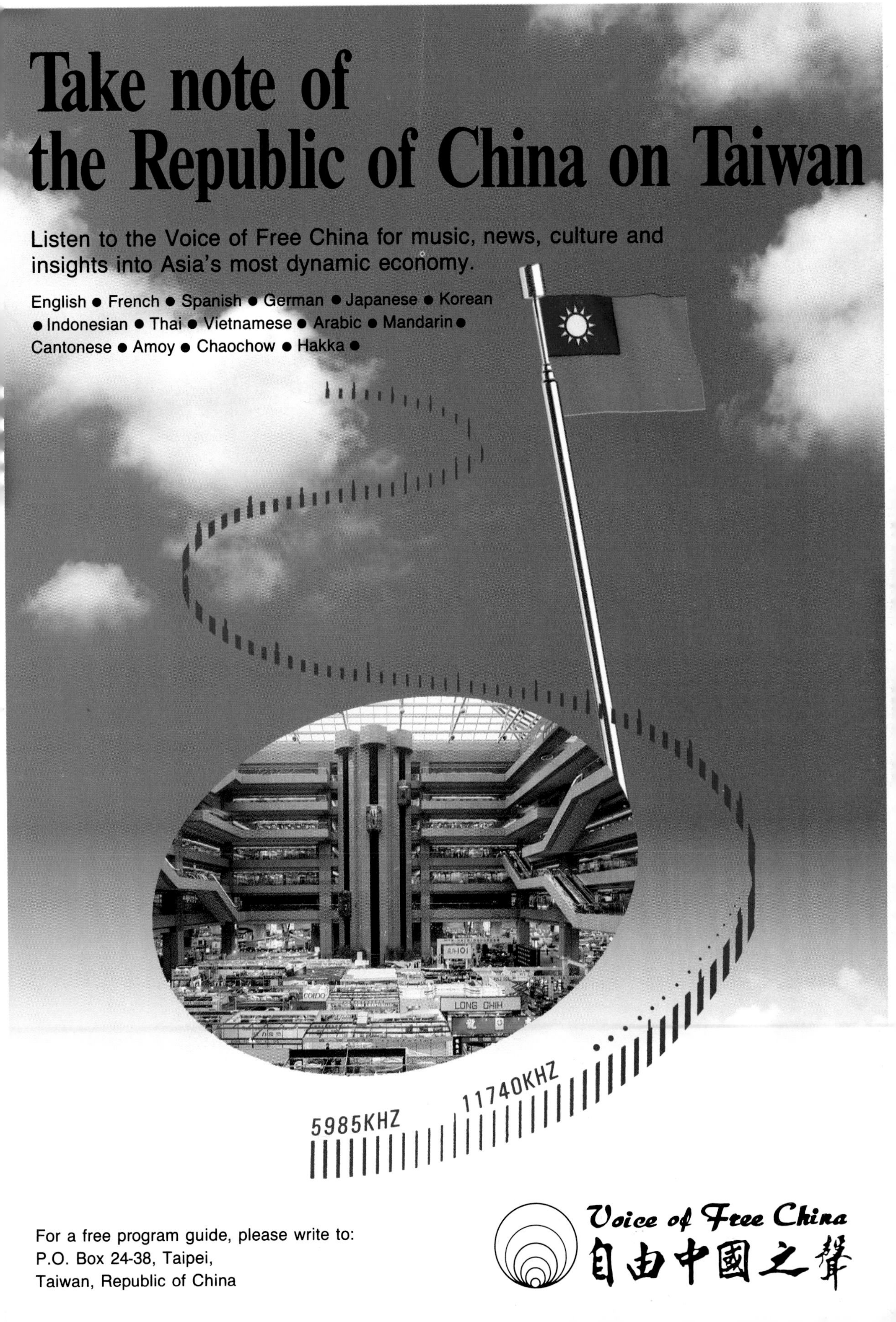
Take note of
the Republic of China on Taiwan
Listen to the Voice of Free China for music, news, culture and insights into Asia's most dynamic economy.
English ● French ● Spanish ● German ● Japanese ● Korean ● Indonesian ● Thai ● Vietnamese ● Arabic ● Mandarin ● Cantonese ● Amoy ● Chaochow ● Hakka ●
LONG CHIH
5985KHZ
11740KHZ
For a free program guide, please write to:
P.O. Box 24-38, Taipei,
Taiwan, Republic of China
Voice of Free China
自由中國之聲

The U.S.S. John F. Kennedy on patrol in the Persian Gulf.

Photo–U.S. Navy

BBC: DISPATCHES FROM THE FRONT LINES

by Jock Elliott

July 3, 1988. The U.S. Navy shoots down an Iranian civilian jetliner.

1100 World Time. Before U.S. broadcasters can repeat the American government's *pro forma* denials, before Radio Moscow can complain of "United States adventurism in the Gulf," the smart money is already tuning to the BBC for the real facts:

> "An Iranian airliner has crashed in the sea at the western end of the Strait of Hormuz. All 229 people on board are feared dead. The Iranian news agency says the plane was brought down by the United States fleet in the Gulf. There has so far been no word from the Americans. The plane—an Airbus A-300 of Iranair—was on its way from the port of Bandar Abbas in Iran to Dubai in the United Arab Emirates . . ."

The subject was extraordinary, but the broadcast itself was nothing unusual. It was a typical BBC World Service news report—accurate, dispassionate and factual. That straightforward formula helps explain why the BBC World Service is the most respected international news organization in the world.

Every week 160 countries pump thousands of hours of programming into the international world band airwaves. Of this, the BBC World Service broadcasts just over 767 hours—less than a third of the time of either the United States or the Soviet Union. Yet, the BBC brings in the largest audience: at least 120 million people around the world each week. That's one consequence of its hard-won reputation for integrity.

That integrity has won the "Beeb" respect which crosses nearly all the lines of contention that otherwise fracture the human race. This includes the prominent and the mighty. For example, during a state visit to Britain in 1987, King Fahd of Saudi Arabia requested that the BBC's Arabic Service be fed directly to his chambers in Buckingham Palace. And more than a few world leaders have been known to call affairs of state to a halt to absorb the BBC news on the hour.

The BBC's audience is at least 120 million each week.

Not only pro-Western heads of state recognize the impact of the BBC's broadcasts. "All the Arab radio stations rave from dawn to noon, but nobody listens to them because everyone switches to London." Who said that? None other than Libya's President Gadafi.

The BBC has also won the hearts of the meek and the oppressed. An Afghan listener to the BBC's Pashto Service, along with his daughter, were blown off their feet while trying to escape a Soviet bombing attack on their village. The seven-year-old girl, although unhurt, was distraught because their world band radio had been destroyed. Her father reassured her, "Do not worry about the radio." But, she cried out, "If it is broken, you will not be able to listen to the BBC news!"

Even professional reporters not affiliated with the BBC regard it with uncommon respect. During a briefing on the Gulf War called by the Iraqi government, scores of international journalists suddenly trooped out of the room. The reason? It was time for the BBC World Service news. The *Washington Post* correspondent explained, "The BBC is the only way we can be sure of what's going on."

BBC

Prime Minister Thatcher makes a historic phone-in broadcast to the Soviet Union.

BBC listeners are equally ardent. Indeed, their enthusiastic response seems designed to insure full employment for the world's postal services. For example, take these figures:

- Half a million letters in countless tongues pour into the BBC's headquarters at Bush House in London each year.
- More than 80,000 people a year write to the World Service in English alone, and *Passport's* own mini-survey of readers shows that the BBC World Service is the overwhelming favorite among the swelling ranks of U.S. world band listeners.
- When South African newspaper advertisements announced the inauguration of a BBC transmission facility in Lesotho, 5,000 letters arrived requesting information and a copy of the BBC's program guide, *London Calling*.
- Prior to the bloody ending of the 1989 "Beijing Spring," the BBC's mailbag

from China brought in 4,000 requests each month for information.

A steadfast commitment to excellence and integrity prompts a wordy, but fitting, response from the BBC itself. By its own account, the BBC World Service's objectives include "making programmes that are of high professional standard, relevance, and interest, to attract and retain audiences, and, above all, to provide a credible, unbiased, reliable, accurate, balanced and independent service of news covering international and national developments."

The BBC World Service is highly regarded, in part because it is not an organ of propaganda. Although funded by the British government, the World Service is not editorially responsible to it. As a result, there is no "party line" to be adhered to. There is only the World Service's own resolute standard of impartiality and accuracy.

That standard has drawn fire from the beginning. On January 3, 1938—the first day of broadcasting for Britain's new international radio service—a news bulletin reported that a Palestinian Arab, found in possession of arms, had been executed by British authorities. The Foreign Office complained.

The Director of the Overseas Service snapped back, "The omission of unwelcome facts of news and the consequent suppression of truth runs counter to the Corporation's policy laid down by appropriate authority." In other words, pack it in your old kit bag—the BBC broadcasts the genuine article.

As Sir William Haley, former BBC Director-General, neatly put it, "The BBC does not attempt to have one story for its own people and another for the rest of the world."

BBC

The BBC's Peter Goodwin, left, interviews Martin Brown on veterinary techniques.

The BBC continues to resist attempts to compromise its integrity. During the 1982 Falklands War, the British military—and Prime Minister Thatcher—roundly criticized the BBC for reporting the unvarnished truth. Later surveys found, however, that Argentineans listened to the BBC simply because its broadcasts about the war could be believed. If even the enemy believes you, then you must be doing something very worthwhile.

At the heart of the BBC news-gathering machine is the World Service newsroom. More than 120 journalists, working three shifts, man it around the clock. They select stories, check facts and prepare the ten score daily news programs.

Additionally, a far-flung network of foreign correspondents, freelancers and news agencies—along with the BBC's own Monitoring Service, which listens to the broadcasts of other countries, plus the CIA's similar Foreign Broadcast Information Service and its West German counterpart—feed the beast with a million words of information each day. At virtually any time, news bulletins are going out in at least one of thirty-seven languages—and sometimes as many as six at once.

Most weekdays, the BBC World Service transmits about forty news programs in English. These newscasts include dispatches from areas all but ignored by U.S. news agencies except during a crisis. Among these are Latin America, Asia, Africa, Northern Europe and the Indian sub-continent. When rioting broke out in Rangoon, Burma, U.S. news sources paid short shrift to the story—implying, in effect, that nothing much was happening.
(*continued on page 123*)

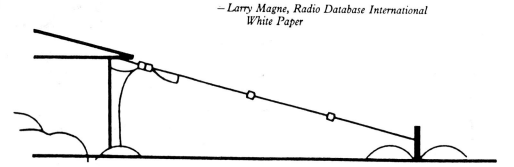

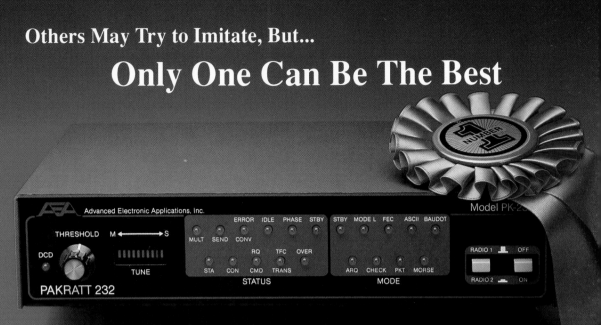

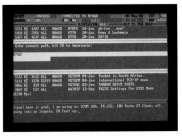

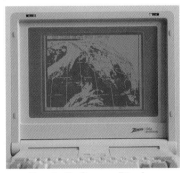

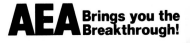

EAVESDROPPING ON DISASTER

by Larry Van Horn

The night sky was barren of cloud and moon. The cold sea, calm as glass, reflected pinpricked meadows of starlight.

The horizon was all but impossible to make out. One seaman murmured ominously that he had never seen the ocean look so . . . flat.

Jack Phillips, in the ship's radio room, was busy transmitting messages to the radio communications station at Cape Race, Newfoundland. The station had just come into range. The traffic had stacked up all day. Phillips was hard pressed to get all the messages sent. In fact, the radio operator on another ship, the *California*, was roundly scolded by Phillips for interrupting his transmissions to Cape Race. "Shut up, shut up," said Phillips. "I'm busy. You are jamming my signals and I'm working Cape Race!"

Phillips ignored his ship's last chance to avert disaster. The *California* was trying to send a message that could have prevented what was to happen 45 minutes later—a warning that large concentra-

Icebergs create perils near commercial shipping lanes.

Photo—Will Gould, NOAA

tions of dangerous icebergs were being spotted in the vicinity. That message was never heard.

At 11:40 p.m. the unthinkable happened.

The impact, although jarring to the crew, was not noticed by many of the passengers. Within twenty minutes, Captain Smith saw the hopelessness of his situation. He ordered Phillips in the radio room to send out the standard CQD distress call for assistance.

The ship's estimated position:

41 Degrees 46 Minutes North
50 Degrees 14 Minutes West

The ship was doomed.

Two hours and twenty minutes later on April 15, 1912, the *R.M.S. Titanic*, with over 1500 souls on board, sank to the bottom of the North Atlantic Ocean.

Several ships heard the distress pleas of the *Titanic* early that morning, but none could get there in time. In fact, the *Titanic* even tried using a new Morse code distress call—SOS—but to no avail. Nothing

(*continued*)

could be done to save the sinking ship.

Since its early days, radio has played an important part in all sorts of disasters and rescues. Listeners have also been a part of these dramas. Their radios have brought rescue operations across continents and oceans right into their own homes. It is listening excitement at its finest.

There are many frequencies on which listeners can hear rescues. Knowing these is important but, even then, a lot of luck is involved. Being at the right place at the right time is the "name of the game."

A prime channel for listening to aircraft and ship distress calls is 500 kHz. This is right below the AM (mediumwave) band, but many tabletop world band radios offer frequency coverage this low.

At 11:40 p.m. the unthinkable happened. The ship was doomed.

The mode of communication used on this frequency is Morse code, but listeners will not have any problems hearing a distress call. Just listen for the letters SOS sent as one word. The letters in Morse code would sound like "dah-dah-dah-di-di-di-dah-dah-dah," or three long characters, three short characters, then three long characters again. If you hear an SOS, this means an emergency has arisen on a ship or aircraft and they are asking for assistance. Further Morse code transmissions will usually contain the ship or aircraft's callsign, the ship's name, and the location of the stricken vessel or aircraft.

Morse code is due to be replaced by more advanced modes in the coming years. However, once that change is fully implemented you will still be able to tune in distress calls with an add-on accessory.

Another good frequency to tune is 2182 kHz. This frequency has a lot of traffic on it, and ships in trouble can sometimes be heard here calling the U.S. Coast Guard or other maritime rescue agencies.

A couple of years ago, the cruise liner, *Scandinavian Star*, caught fire off the coast of the Yucatán Peninsula of Mexico. A radio listener, listening to 2182 kHz, got a blow-by-blow account of the fire and rescue. He heard this as it happened, via his world band radio.

Another good channel to monitor is the Coast Guard air channel on 5696 kHz. While monitoring this channel, a Houston, Texas listener eavesdropped on the rescue of a Caribbean island hopper airplane. He heard the entire operation of the Coast Guard searching for the aircraft.

All twenty passengers and crew of the aircraft were rescued, but the next story didn't have such a happy ending.

An offshore oil rig is a very dangerous place to work. This point was really brought home when a rig caught fire and exploded in the North Sea a couple of years ago. A listener using his world band radio tuned to 5680 kHz—a search and rescue frequency—and heard the disaster and rescue operation. Some of what he heard . . .

Naval vessel: "We are in receipt of SOS for oil platform fire. We can respond with five helicopters, if needed."

Rescue Coordinator: "We request the help and it would be appreciated. What type of aircraft do you have to assist in the rescue?"

Naval vessel: "We have SH3F helos available. What is the status of the rescue?"

Rescue Coordinator: "There has been an explosion on an oil platform rig. There were 250 people on the rig; only forty have been recovered. Helos on the scene now."

Later, more descriptive reports were received describing lifeboats, fire and many casualties.

Ocean rescues aren't the only ones that can be heard via shortwave radio. After the crash of Pan Am Flight 103 over Lockerbie, Scotland, one monitor reported hearing the rescue operation firsthand. While monitoring 5680 kHz shortly after Flight 103 disappeared from air traffic control radars, he heard airborne rescuers describing what the Scottish countryside looked like following the bombing and crash of the Pan Am jumbo jet. These were essentially the first reports received anywhere—long before any network television reports or pictures became available. (*continued on page 125*)

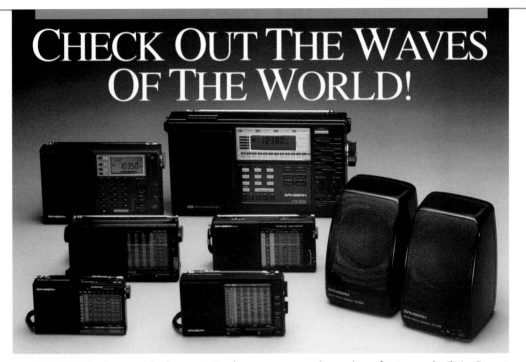

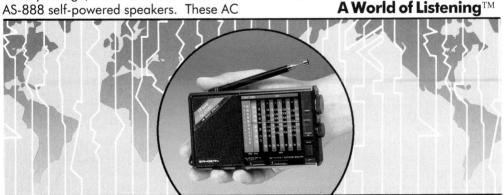

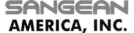

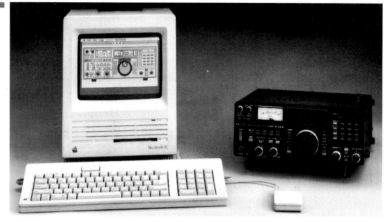

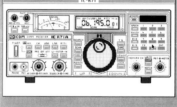

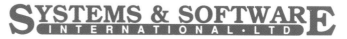

POWER
METER
AGC
ICOM
1999.800.00
SPECTRUM SCOPE
MEMORY BANK
FILTER WIDTH
IF SHIFT
NOTCH

EEB

THE NATION'S LARGEST SHORT WAVE RADIO DEALER

ICOM R9000

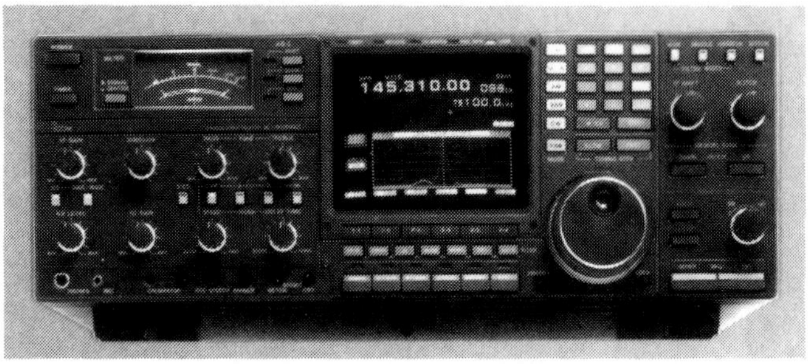

- 0.1 to 2000 MHz continuous
- CRT display
- 1000 memory channels
- Most advanced receiver
- Priced under $5000! Call.

ICOM R71A

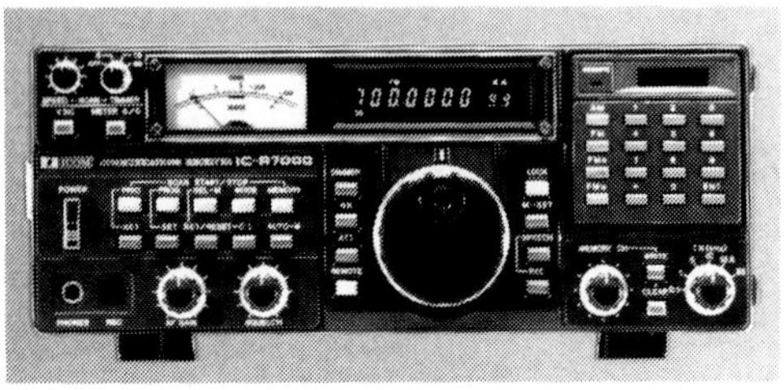

- 0.1 to 30 MHz all-mode (FM optional)
- 32 memory and 3 filter positions
- Our best seller
- Many EEB modifications
- Priced under $850! Call.

ICOM R7000

- 25 to 2000 MHz, multimode
- 100 memory channels
- Nothing else like it under $4000
- Many EEB modifications
- Priced under $1050! Call.

EEB—THE ICOM EXPERTS

Some folks say EEB is number one in the world. We've been growing and expanding for eighteen years.

- **Service** Our customers deserve the best. We deliver it!
- **Pricing** It's our goal to provide the best products at the best possible prices.
- **People** We have a team of seasoned pros to process your orders. Our technical and marketing staff are amateur radio operators with many years of experience.
- **Product** We're constantly searching the world for new products. Only those products that pass our rigorous tests appear in our catalog.
- **Location** EEB is just minutes from Washington, D.C. In our new retail store, you can see and compare all the items from our catalog.
- **Expertise** Our *technical team* has developed modifications to optimize receiver performance, many NOVEX items for the SWLer, and CRIS—the Computer-Radio Interface System.
- **Dedication** We test, evaluate, and demonstrate all the high-tech items we sell in our retail store.

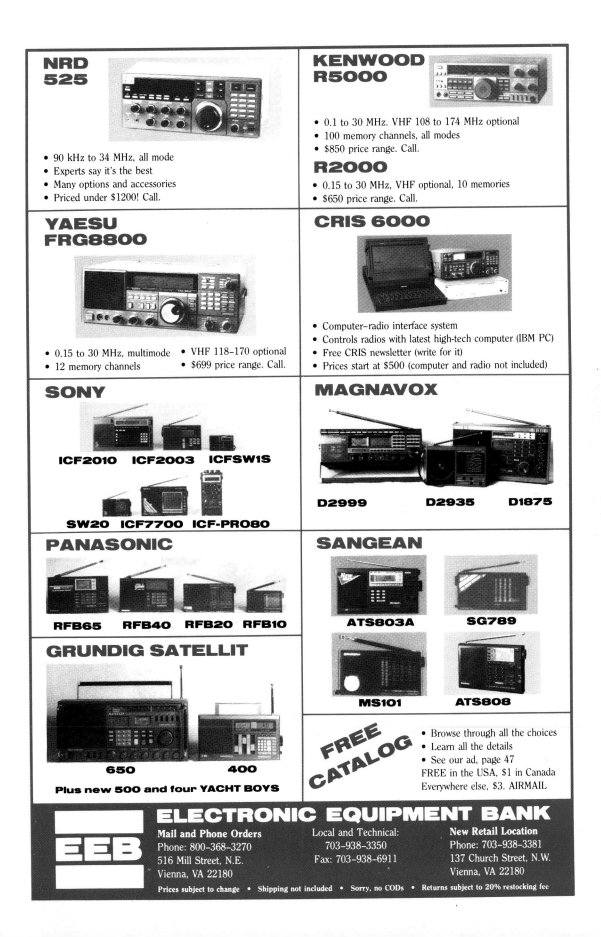

Reederij Boekel
RONDVAARTEN

TWENTY EASY-TO-HEAR STATIONS

Local AM and FM stations are loud and clear as soon as you turn your radio on. Not so with world band. Hearing a station clearly depends on a number of factors . . . including luck.

A few of these factors: Some stations use superpower transmitters that launch radio signals like rockets. Others use overseas relay facilities to extend the bounce of their signals. And some operate on clearer channels than others.

Add another factor: World band radio disperses its signals exceptionally broadly. This means that even though a particular station is not directing its signal your way, you may still be able to hear it well enough to enjoy its programs.

And a little luck: Unlike local AM, FM or TV, world band stations are affected by seasonal and daily changes in reception conditions. Radio signals can be better some days than others, depending on what's happening in the heavens.

Of the many countries broadcasting on the world bands, we've put together twenty or so that bring together pretty much the right combination of factors to broadcast signals that tend to be heard loud and clear, in English, within North

Left, A tourist's-eye view of Holland. Right, Bush House, London serves as worldwide headquarters for the BBC World Service.

BBC

Netherlands Embassy

America and Europe. In many cases, listeners in Asia and the Pacific can also hear these stations, as well.

Regardless of where you are, world band stations tend to be especially well received when it is evening at your location. Complete times and channels are in the "Worldwide Broadcasts" and "The Blue Pages" sections.

Remember that during the summer some stations shift their schedules by one hour. All hours and days of the week are listed in *World Time*—please see "Getting Started with World Band Radio" in this edition should you want further details.

EUROPE

France

Radio France Internationale is easily heard in Europe from its transmitters located in France. It's heard almost as well in North America, both from those same transmitters and from additional transmitters located in French Guiana.

RFI's programs cover many aspects of life in France. In its two half-hour transmissions, the station concentrates on news and press reviews, with one or two feature programs halfway through.

> Its World Service programming carries an impact on the progress of humankind that is beyond measure.

The hour-long 1600 transmission was once called *Paris Calling Africa*. Although the station has dropped that title, the broadcast still contains a good bit of juicy information on Africa that you're not likely to hear anywhere else.

Most of RFI's programs are in French, but three times daily its broadcasts in English can be heard in the Americas. Best reception is at 0315-0345 on 6045, 7135, 7280, 9790, 9800, 11670 or 11995 kHz. The other times, which are less well-heard, are 1245-1315 on 15365, 17720, 21635 or 21645 kHz; and 1600-1700 on 15360, 17620 or 17795 kHz.

In Europe, best bets are 0315-0345 and 1600-1700 on 3965 or 6175 kHz. For Asia and the Pacific, try RFI's new transmission at 1400-1430 on 21780 kHz.

Germany

Deutsche Welle, the official station of the Federal Republic of Germany, is also an easy catch in both Europe and North America. This powerful, technically excellent station broadcasts in English to North America in the evenings at 0100-0150 on 6040, 6085, 6145, 9565, 9735 and 11865 kHz. There are also repeat broadcasts at 0300 on 6085, 9545 and 9605 kHz, and again at 0500 on 5960, 6130 and 9700 kHz—this last period being destined for the West Coast.

Deutsche Welle can be heard "off the beam" in Europe at various times. Among the best-heard in the United Kingdom, if you're an early riser, is 0500-0550 on 6130 kHz. In the evening, try 1900-1950 on 11785, 11810 or 13790 kHz.

Deutsche Welle also has brought into operation a relay facility at Trincomalee in Sri Lanka. Listeners in Asia and the Pacific can now hear Deutsche Welle at 0900-0950 on 6160, 11945, 17780, 21650 and 21680 kHz; and again at 2100-2150 on 9670, 9765, 11785 or 15435 kHz.

Pretty much no matter where you live, Deutsche Welle comes in loud and clear. Its programs range from news and the European economy to music and the popular *Random Selection*.

Holland

Radio Nederland, in addition to its modern transmitter facility at Flevoland in Holland, also operates from relay sites in the Netherlands Antilles and Madagascar. Radio Nederland specializes in news and features on European affairs. It also boasts *The Happy Station*, an enjoyable treat for the entire family, and the *Documentary Series* shows.

This station is heard well throughout much of North America at 0030-0125 on 6020, 6165 and 15315 kHz; 0330 on 6165 and 9590 kHz; 0730 on 9630 and 9715 kHz; and 1830 on 17605 and 21685 kHz.

Radio Nederland beams to Europe at 1130-1225 on 5955 and 9715 kHz; and 1430 on 5955 kHz. To Asia at 0830 on 17575 and 21485 kHz; 1130 on 17575,

21480 and 21520 kHz; and 1430 on 13770, 15150, 17575 and 17605 kHz. To the Pacific at 0730 on 9630 and 9715 kHz; 1030 on 9675 kHz; plus a briefer transmission weekdays only at 0830–0855 on 9770 kHz.

Switzerland

Swiss Radio International airs half-hour broadcasts in English. On Monday through Saturday, there's *Dateline*, plus on Saturday there's also the *Swiss Shortwave Merry-Go-Round*. All days there's the news, plus current events and special human interest features. Be sure to catch the hilarious *The Grapevine* with Rob Brooks and Paul Sufferin, on the first and third Sundays of each month.

In North America, listen at 0200 on 6095, 6135, 9725, 9885, 12035 or 17730 kHz; and again at 0400 on 6135, 9725, 9885 or 12035 kHz. In Europe, SRI may be heard at 0730, 1300 and 1830—one hour earlier summers—on 6165 or 9535 kHz; and again at 2230 (2130 summers) on 6190 kHz. Best bets for Asia and the Pacific are 0830 on 9560, 13685, 17670 or 21695 kHz; plus 1100 and 1330 on 13635, 15570 or 17830 kHz.

United Kingdom

The British Broadcasting Corporation, fondly known by its vast worldwide listenership as the "Beeb," operates one of the most extensive networks of relay transmitters anywhere, rivaled only by the Voice of America. Using its own transmitters, as well as those of other broadcasters, located in the United Kingdom, Hong Kong, Singapore, Cyprus, the Seychelles, Lesotho, Canada, the US, Brazil, and Ascension and Antigua Islands, the BBC blankets the globe. Its World Service programming, both in English and a variety of other tongues, carries an impact on the progress of humankind that is beyond measure.

Mornings, the BBC World Service is best heard in Eastern North America at 1100–1330 on 5965, 6195, 9515 or 11775 kHz; and again at 1600–1745 on 9515, 11775 or 15260 kHz. In Western North America mornings, try 1100–1615 on 9740 kHz, and 1600–1745 on 15260 kHz.

Early evenings, Eastern North Americans can tune in at 2000–2200 on many frequencies, including 5975 or 15260 kHz. An interesting aside is that there's a special *Caribbean Report* at 2115–2130 Monday through Friday on 5975—but not 15260—kHz. It's one of the few ways to keep in touch accurately with events in and concerning this region.

Later in the evening, North Americans can hear the Beeb at 2200–0815 on a wide variety of frequencies. Best bets are 5975 (to 0730), 6175 (to 0330 or 0430), 9640 (0545 to 0815), and 9915 (to 0430). The BBC broadcasts a plethora of different programs, many of which are superb, but is especially recognized for its incomparable news and current events programs.

USSR

Radio Moscow is one of the easiest stations to hear anywhere. Not only are its transmitters powerful, but the Soviet Union covers so much of the globe that it is near to both European and Asian audiences. Not at all uncommon, even for the veteran radio buff, is to spend an hour listening to a fairly weak signal in some exotic language only to hear Radio Moscow's interval signal at the top of the hour!

No other station broadcasts more than Radio Moscow. Regardless of where you are, you can hear it throughout much of the day and night.

Broadcasts to North America and Europe are virtually continuous over a twenty-four-hour period. They are divided into two separate networks: the North American Service, which operates from early to mid-evening, and the World Service, which operates at all other times of the day, with different programs for both services.

No other station broadcasts in more languages than Radio Moscow. Regardless of where you are in the world, you

(*continued on page 127*)

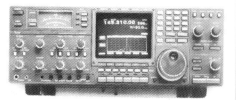

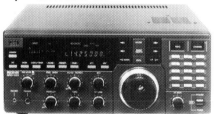

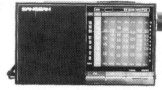

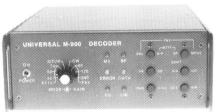

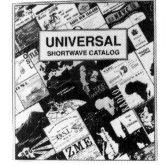

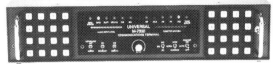

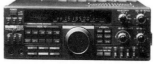

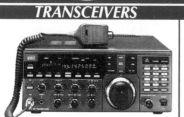

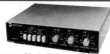

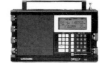

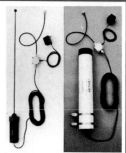

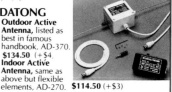

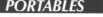

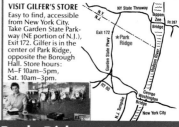

"Listening is only half the fun. Popular Communications is the other half."

Published Monthly Since 1982

Far and way the best and most widely read magazine for the listening enthusiast. See for yourself. Send check or money order for $2.40 postage and receive two recent issues of Pop'Comm by First Class Mail. (Sorry, no choice of issues in this special sampling offer. Offer void outside U.S.A.) Mail to:

Popular Communications Sampler
76 North Broadway
Hicksville, New York 11801

Be sure to include your name and address!

U.S.A. Subscription Rates:
1 year 12 issues $18.00
2 years 24 issues $35.00
3 years 36 issues $52.00

Canada/Mexico—One year $20.00, two years $39.00, three years $58.00; Foreign—one year $22.00, two years $43.00, three years $64.00. Foreign Air Mail—one year $75.00, two years $149.00, three years $223.00.

MUSIC: THE BEAT OF THE WORLD

Throughout the world, people make music in myriad ways, and for reasons ranging from celebration to ritual. Just about all of it—the entire planet's wealth of songs—can be heard on world band radio. Some, you are unlikely to hear anywhere else. And, because music is the universal language of man, you can enjoy programs in any tongue.

To make your selection of music easier, the best times and frequencies to listen are shown. Hours and days of the week are listed in *World Time*—please see "Getting Started with World Band Radio" in this edition should you want further details.

Folk Music

Folk music—the term "native music" vanished with Charles Boyer's Casbah—is as varied as the folks who sing it. Ballads tell stories, true events, legends. There are love songs and work songs and nursery rhymes.

Popular music, especially of the folk-rock and country variety, owes much to Celtic and Elizabethan folk songs. Too, a good deal of classical music is based on folk tunes and dance rhythms from nearly every corner of the globe. Our musical heritage has broad roots.

Perhaps the most extensive program of folk music on world band radio is **Radio Moscow's** *Folk Box*, which airs Fridays at 1730, Thursdays at 2030 and 0030, and Wednesdays at 0730 on a wide assortment of frequencies. It is a compendium of folk music from the various republics that constitute the Soviet Union, and the program also describes national musical instruments and folklore. All in all, it's probably the best program of folk music on world band radio.

Direct from the Soviet republics come **Radio Kiev** and **Radio Vilnius**. Kiev airs stunning tenor solos and beautiful Ukrainian choral singing, while Vilnius features Lithuania's unique, melodic style of choir music.

In North America, Radio Kiev can be heard at 0030-0100 and 0300-0330 on a wide variety of frequencies, including 7400, 13645, 15180 and 15455 kHz. In Western Europe, Kiev is easily heard at 1900-1930 on many frequencies that change seasonally. Among these are 6010, 6090, 6165, 7115, 7330, 9560, 9600 and 11780 kHz. All times are one hour earlier summers.

Radio Vilnius is beamed to North America at 2300-2330 on such frequencies as 7400, 9765, 11790, 13645, 15180 and 15455 kHz. In Western Europe, tune (*continued on page 132*)

Left, Gypsy flamenco dancers bring out the soul of Spain.

Joe Viesti

... tuned in and up to date with MONITORING TIMES

That's because every month **Monitoring Times** brings everything you need to know to make world band listening even more rewarding: the latest information on international broadcasting schedules, frequency listings, station profiles, program commentary, personality interviews, international DX reports, propagation charts, reviews of world band radio products, and tips on how to hear the rare stations.

But **Monitoring Times** doesn't stop there. It also keeps you up to date on what's happening on the airwaves between the international broadcasting bands: information on government, military, police and fire networks; action on the ham bands; and tips on monitoring everything from air-to-ground and ship-to-shore signals to radioteletype, facsimile and space communications.

Jammed with up-to-date information and concisely written by the top writers in the field, **Monitoring Times** belongs next to your receiver.

Order your subscription today before another issue goes by: only $18 per year in the U.S.; $26 per year for foreign and Canada. For a sample issue, send $2 (foreign, send 5 IRCs). For MC/VISA orders, call 1-704-837-9200.

MONITORING TIMES

Your authoritative source, every month.

P.O. Box 98
Brasstown, N.C. 28902

Myles Mustoe

Left, London's Big Ben, standing majestically over the Houses of Parliament. Right, Students in a geography class tune into World Band Radio on a daily basis.

GEOGRAPHY THAT STAYS TUNED IN

by Ian McFarland

Ask any primary school children what their favorite subject is, and the odds are pretty good that you won't hear geography mentioned very often. It's one subject that kids have traditionally disliked—until now.

Myles Mustoe, of Washington state in the U.S. Pacific Northwest, is one teacher who may just turn the tide for beleaguered geography teachers everywhere. Mustoe teaches at the elementary and secondary school levels.

What makes him special? He uses world band radio to tune kids in to lifestyles and cultures of countries everywhere.

He credits his mother and a ham radio neighbor with sparking an early interest in world band radio when he was in the third grade. His mother, who emigrated from East Germany, listened regularly to stations from her home country for news. Mustoe just got interested by osmosis.

The genesis of Mustoe's use of world band radio as a teaching tool was a graduate studies project at Central

Kurt Kroszner

Washington University. Mustoe combined an interest in geography with his interest in international broadcasting to come up with a sure fire way to breathe life into a mummified subject.

The project, which involved working with elementary and high school students in the classroom, proved that world band radio is an excellent means of whetting students' interest in geography.

It was the human element, Mustoe says, that attracted him to geography in the first place. He feels that radio is an ideal way to get a feel for this human element and the cultures of different countries.

World band radio is a sure-fire way to breathe life into a mummified subject.

Mustoe likes to think of classroom use of world band radio as an "electronic field trip." "International radio is an ideal means of showing the students that geography isn't strictly a science," he adds.

Mustoe isn't one to keep his successful teaching methods a secret. Several years ago he formed IMAST, the International Monitoring Association for Students and Teachers, which is basically a forum for the exchange of ideas on the use of world band radio as a teaching tool. And it can be a most successful tool indeed, as Mustoe has discovered since he started livening up his geography classes by introducing his students to world band radio.

In recent years Mustoe has managed to spread the word about world band radio to any number of his fellow teachers throughout North America. He's received a wealth of enthusiastic feedback about the positive results which have followed.

Mustoe recounts the story of one seventh-grade teacher in California. He had watched a last-place student do a complete turnaround following the introduction of world band radio in the classroom. From goat to gold: That's the success story that's been repeated many times over with other students.

Charles Faris, a fifth-grade teacher at the Osborne Elementary School in Pittsburgh, Pennsylvania, and Freddy Curtis, a sixth grade teacher at the West Side Elementary school in Readyville, Tennessee, also boast that their students love geography. Like Myles Mustoe, the secret of their success is looking beyond the textbooks.

Faris' and Curtis' approach to using world band radio in the classroom takes particular advantage of the fact that a great many international broadcasting stations have a "mailbag" program in their lineup. This means that listeners can send in questions, and the broadcaster will answer them over the air.

At a radio convention, Charles Faris explained how he uses programs on world band radio as a teaching aid in his geography class. The class had already taken an active part in special programs broadcast on Radio Beijing and Radio Finland. In fact, the broadcast with Radio Beijing had become an annual event in Faris' class.

Prior to actually formulating the questions they'd like answered, the children actually listen to a selection of programs from a particular country. Then they come up with their own questions about the country they're studying. The questions are forwarded to the appropriate world band station, which answers them on the air. Faris records the programs, then plays back the tapes in class so that everyone can hear the program, in a peer-group environment, at the same time.

Classroom use of world band radio is an "electronic field trip."

That convention encounter led to a similar project set up between Faris' class and the *Bonsoir Africa* program which I produced and hosted on Radio Canada International's African service back in 1984. It may sound like a strange choice of programs on which to answer a host of questions from a school in the United States; but because of back radiation, the program probably had more listeners in various parts of the United States than it did in Africa. Back radiation, by the way,

Myles Mustoe

Myles Mustoe points out location of a world band station.

occurs when a portion of a radio signal comes off the back of the antenna, rather than the front. Often this phenomenon allows listeners to hear a program clearly, even though it's not beamed to their location.

The twenty-five students in Faris' class had quite an amazing variety of questions. Eleven-year-old Michael Reismeyer wanted to know if Calgary was ready for the 1988 Olympics. Ben Rogers, on the other hand, was interested in the types of aircraft in the Canadian Armed Forces. Ben Tomon was interested in knowing what the most popular television show was amongst kids in Canada. Jennifer Wright's question reflected the typical eleven-year old's preoccupation with eating. She wanted to know what Canada's favorite food was, and was, no doubt, relieved to hear that it wasn't broccoli or peas. The number one favorite is french fries.

In the spring of 1988, Freddy Curtis' sixth-grade Social Studies class was studying the landscape and lifestyle of the world's second largest country—you know, the one the U.S. claims it gets all its cold weather from. As any Canadian will tell you, though, all the cold Arctic air really sweeps down from Alaska, not Canada.

Curtis contacted me to see if it would be possible for the kids to have their questions answered on the RCI mailbag program, *Listeners' Corner*. I jumped at the chance to repeat the very enjoyable radio experience I had had with Charles Faris' class four years earlier.

Questions about sports and pop music figured prominently in the list of questions sent in, but almost one third of the children had questions about the school systems in various parts of Canada. Twelve-year-old Sherry Burdick focused on schools in the Ontario, while David Smithson wanted to know about sixth-grade classes in Quebec, the country's predominantly French province. Tracey Mathews was interested in knowing if Canadian classes are as large as those in the United States, and Jamie Reed was curious about how much snow had to fall before students were able to miss school.

To help spread the word about the success of world band radio in the classroom, Mustoe recently put his concepts and world band radio teaching methods into a book, *Shortwave Goes To School*. The book's 60 pages include a basic primer in world band radio and details on the kinds of programs that can be heard from around the world. Most importantly, it includes a number of sections pertaining to world band radio activities in the classroom. For any teacher interested in adding zip to geography classes, this book is a "must."

With any luck, Myles Mustoe's findings will change the face of geography teaching far and wide, as well as make children more aware of the diverse and interesting world around them. They'll also discover through world band radio that children and adults the world over have more similarities than is generally recognized.

And, let's face it—getting to know your neighbors around the world is a darned sight more likely to strengthen international friendship and understanding than is a building filled with politicians.

Ian McFarland is Announcer-Producer of English Weekend Programming at Radio Canada International.

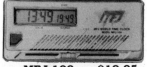

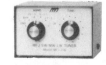

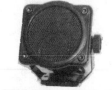

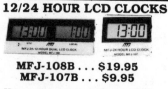

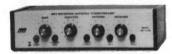

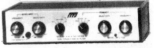

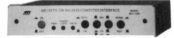

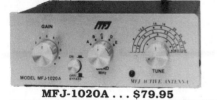

FAMOUS BEST QUALITY VOILE

I DON'T LEAVE HOME WITHOUT IT!

by Dan Robinson

On a street in downtown Khartoum, I was running for my life. Behind me, about a hundred Sudanese security troops were pursuing a crowd of banner-waving demonstrators. *Thud, pop*—the sound of tear gas exploding above our heads, and then the burning of eyes.

Suddenly, the strap of my correspondent's bag snapped in the middle of the street. In that leather satchel were my notebooks, an extra microphone, batteries . . . and a Sony ICF-2002, my lifeline to the outside world. Should I run back toward the advancing security force, into the thick cloud of gas to retrieve the bag, or leave it?

It was April 1985, and this was the scene as the Sudanese military took control of Khartoum in a coup against President Gaarfari Mineiri.

Only a few days before, two of my colleagues had been beaten by security forces and interrogated for several hours after taking photos of a similar street demonstration. The prospect of similar treatment did not thrill me. Also, what was being described in some news ac-

Left, A smile hints at the warmth of the Senegalese, who are among the friendliest people in Africa. Right, Kenya is taking increasingly strong action to protect elephants from poaching.

Dan Robinson

John Isaac, United Nations

counts as a "bloodless" rebellion didn't exactly convince those of us who had seen several bodies in the city's hospital.

But, holding a handkerchief to my mouth and nose, I ran the twenty paces back, retrieved the bag, and made a beeline for the doors of the Acropole Hotel.

It was a good thing I went back for that bag and its contents. In the rough and tumble world of foreign news gathering, being without your world band radio is like losing one of your hands. When telexes and satellite facilities are shut down—often deliberately—and airports closed, as was the case in Khartoum, an eerie vacuum descends. Out of touch with your office for days, your deadlines and those of your competitors don't stop. You continue to report, write, record, and attempt to send on a daily basis. All this is just so that when communication is restored, you'll be ready with the latest information. Make no mistake about it—in such situations information is like gold.

In the rough and tumble world of foreign news gathering, being without your world band radio is like losing one of your hands.

For three years, I covered the news of Africa as a foreign correspondent for the Voice of America. Never once did I travel without a world band radio. In fact, during my time covering events across the continent, I never knew a single foreign correspondent—radio, news agency, newspaper or television—who left home without one.

World band radios—both tabletops and portables—are tools of the trade, a standard feature of the equipment bags carried today by foreign correspondents. News bureaus have depended on them for years. In the old days, beefy Zenith Trans-Oceanics or massive, deskbound Hallicrafters or Hammarlund receivers did the trick. Today, the incredible advances in receiver technology allow foreign correspondents to leave their overseas base carrying the world around in their shirt pockets.

Along with one or two tape recorders, microphones, batteries, cassettes, patch cords, alligator clips, and the ever-present portable computer—small, compact receivers are tucked away. And the smaller the better. Traveling light is more important to reporters overseas than anything else. On the road, it's crucial to be mobile at a moment's notice.

When necessary, you've also got to be able to conceal your equipment when you're out of the hotel room. Leaving funny looking computers, phone-feed wires, and radios sitting on desks is an invitation to theft and suspicion. Trying to explain to a soldier or customs' officer at a small border crossing point or an airport that your digital Sony is just a radio—and nothing more—can be a frustrating and comical experience. "Do not worry sir," they coo. "Your things will be safe here until we confirm the nature of their contents."

You would probably expect that portable radios get a lot of rough treatment in the course of all this action, and you're right. I have seen portable world band receivers with half their antennas gone, with heavy tapes wrapped around their battery compartments, with broken or replacement knobs.

It's also been amusing to see the various ways reporters try to coax the best signal from their precious little boxes. It's one thing to be out in the open tuning in a signal, and quite another to be inside a hotel room or large conference hall constructed like a fortress. At the height of the famine coverage in Ethiopia in 1984 and 1985, the echoes of the VOA, BBC, Radio France and Deutsche Welle could be heard from numerous balconies of the Addis Ababa Hilton. And, if you looked real hard, the outlines of thin wire antennas could be seen dangling down the side of the hotel facing the swimming pool. Anything to get that signal!

But what does a world band radio do for a correspondent overseas? Most importantly, it can help make sure that what you are reporting is as accurate and realistic as possible.

Sometimes it's too realistic. For example, following the overthrow of Uganda's military government in early 1986, thousands of former troops fled from the capital, Kampala, northward to Sudan.

Along the way, they looted not only weapons and vehicles, but also food and medicine from missionary and aid stations.

At the international press center in Nairobi, I monitored this drama using my '2010 radio. I heard desperate people at the small aid station talking frantically on two-way radios to their headquarters in Kampala, begging for help. I heard shots ring out. I heard cries.

By memorizing regional emergency communications channels used by the United Nations and other agencies, I was able to tune in this scene. In turn, the VOA and other press agencies were able to report the looting as it happened from one of the smallest outposts imaginable in Africa. A world band radio brought this drama to the press's attention.

> Incredible advances in receiver technology allow foreign correspondents to carry the world around in their pockets.

In Ethiopia in 1984, the Marxist government was celebrating the 10th anniversary of the coup against the late Emperor Haile Selassie. I stood in Revolution Square watching hundreds of thousands of people parade past. As I jotted my observations on paper and recorded a few on-scene reports, I was simultaneously listening to my '2002 radio.

This set has ten memory positions. So, if you know the frequencies of the stations you want to hear, you can punch them into the memory, then call them up simply by pressing one of the buttons. This enabled me to monitor local Ethiopian radio on an FM frequency. It also allowed me to hear the latest version of the event I was witnessing as it was being broadcast over world band by the BBC and by my own station, the VOA.

Why listen to the news when you're right there observing it? Well, simply because the news is not controllable. Foreign correspondents cooperate, but they also compete. One rule learned early on is that you're not always on top of the story even while watching it with your own eyes.

Indeed, the main political drama unfolding in Ethiopia that day was only part of a larger story that would be gripping the world in the months to come. Information about the shocking human tragedy of widespread famine was beginning to make its way out—via other correspondents, through news leaks, and by way of official and off-the-record interviews.

For these reasons, it was important to hear how my own newsroom in Washington was "playing" my story on the Ethiopian situation. Were there other developments—perhaps a statement by the White House . . . by the Soviet government . . . by a relief organization in Geneva . . . by a rebel organization—that I needed to consider in preparing my report for the day?

> I heard desperate people on the radio begging for help. I heard shots ring out, I heard cries.

Indeed, was the BBC or Radio France correspondent four rooms down the hall in my hotel reporting the same story? Did they have different figures? The only way to know, other than through the cooperative journalistic process, was to flip on the world band radio whenever possible. No correspondent can be expected to cover all the news, but one way to integrate and reflect it into your own report is to stay tuned.

World band radios are also used by foreign news bureaus to supplement their existing sources. Following one of Africa's military coups in 1984, a malfunction in the studio of the Voice of Nigeria resulted in police and military barracks communications being aired over the international frequencies of that radio station. Along with millions of surprised listeners across the continent, several foreign news agencies in Nairobi heard this communication and were able to follow developments much, much more closely!

During an aircraft hijacking in Mogadishu, Somalia in 1984, the foreign press stationed in Nairobi kept a constant ear on Radio Mogadishu—both its Somali and English newscasts—for the latest developments in that drama.

And news offices in Nairobi also monitor the broadcasts of opposing sides in civil conflicts, such as with the rebel Sudan Peoples Liberation Army radio in Sudan—which is actually broadcast from neighboring Ethiopia.

During her coverage of the Seoul Olympics in 1988, VOA correspondent Paula Wolfson recalled tuning in the news on her world band portable. Journalists covering the Olympics had access to American television network programming, of course. But for the latest news about South Korean political protests and other regional developments, it was wise to stay tuned to the world band airwaves.

You might think that reporters from major American networks have little use for world band radios while on assignment in this country. But remember, these same people are often assigned at a moment's notice to breaking stories, or to "reaction" pieces connected to world news stories.

So it always helps to stay in touch. Indeed, as the presidential campaign of 1988 churned along, a few correspondents from commercial radio and television networks stayed in touch by using world band portables—just to get the big picture.

Needless to say, correspondents for international broadcasters the world over have had similar experiences with world band radio. Whether in the middle of the African bush, in Lima, Peru, or in Warsaw, Poland—portable world band receivers are our ticket to staying in touch, staying ahead, and bringing to worldwide audiences the most accurate news possible.

VOA Foreign Correspondent Dan Robinson currently hosts Nightline Africa. *He has been with the Voice since 1979.*

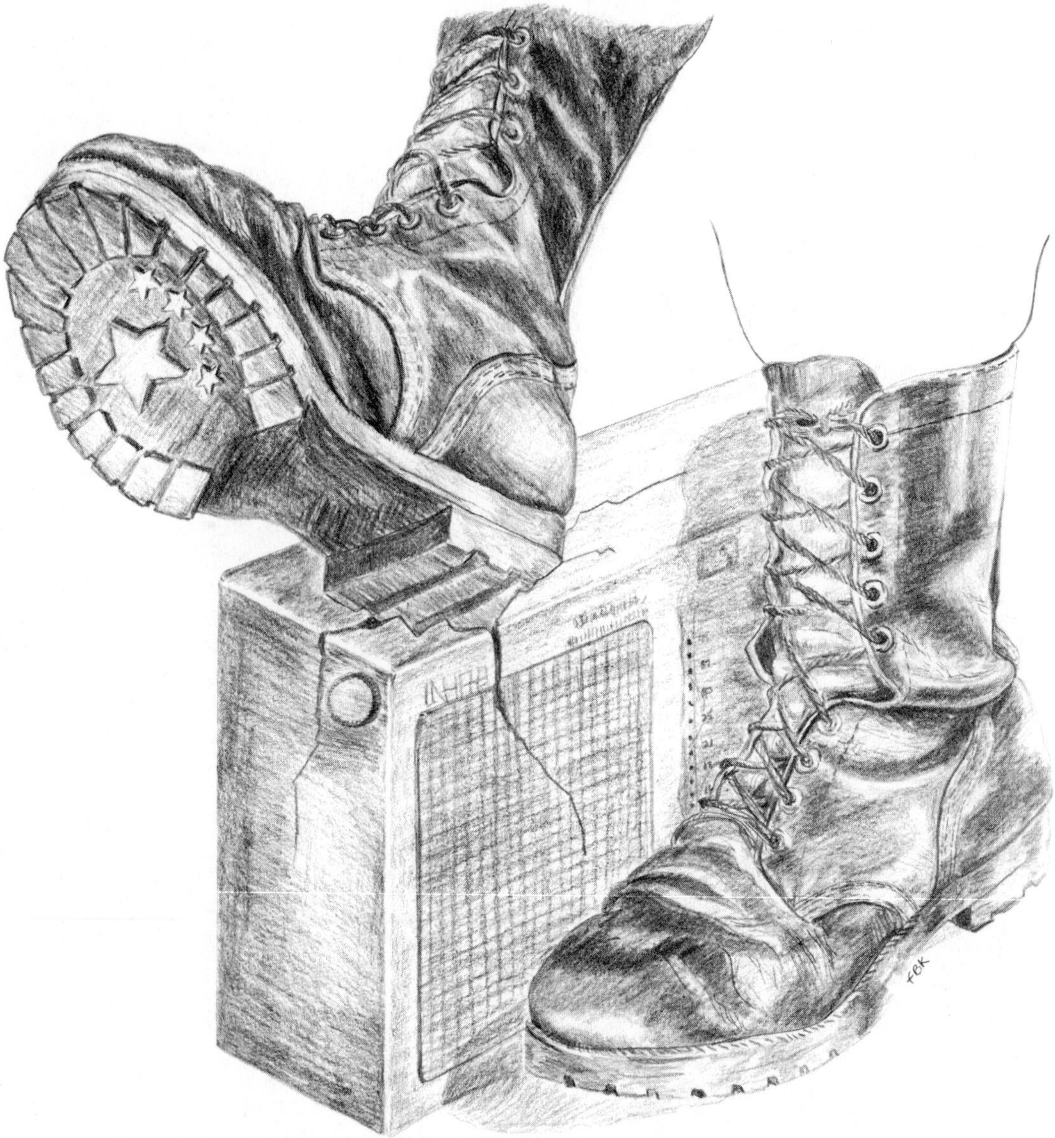

Florence B. Kolvites

WHEN RADIO IS FORBIDDEN

by Don Jensen

Don't take too casually your freedom to listen. Tuning in international broadcasts may be safe and enjoyable . . . but not always, not everywhere.

"I remember when I started to remember," a young Chinese world band listener revealed to *Passport to World Band Radio* just before the 1989 "Beijing Spring." "My father dared, on some stifling steam bath summer nights, to tune in to certain stations on his old wireless to hear some different news."

"Every time he listened," C— Litang recalls in his letter, "my father wore a look of nervousness and excitement."

"One night, while he was at the wireless, a knock came at the door. The uninvited 'guests' intruded in and came directly over to my dad's wireless. One of them felt it with his hand and it was still warm!"

"The wireless was taken away. My dad was brought to a 'political study class,' where he suffered a lot. For years after, he was labeled as one who tuned in to 'enemy' broadcasts.

"Later we came to know," C— writes, "that the 'reporter' was our neighbor. The puzzle then was clear. My dad, the 'eavesdropper,' had neglected to consider the existence of a real eavesdropper next door!"

This was China in the late 1960s, the time of the Great Proletarian Cultural Revolution and the fearsome Red Guards. Mao Zedong had unleashed students in a campaign against "cultural contamination" from Western and bourgeois ideas. It became *Lord of The Flies* with an Asian twist, a precursor to the unspeakable events to come in Cambodia.

Millions of Chinese were caught up in the fury of the rampaging armies of teenagers. Mao's efforts to "purify" communist society fell heaviest on the educated, like Litang's father—those who sought knowledge beyond the world around them.

The Chinese were not the first to try to shut off free access to world band listening. Almost as early as broadcasting began, countries from autocratic Iran to democratic Great Britain have tried to stop people from hearing other points of view, particularly during war or civil unrest.

During the Spanish Civil War in the late 1930s, radio received its first real wartime tryout. Franco's fascist rebels captured powerful shortwave transmitters, and soon were bombarding Republican Spain with propaganda. The programming, together with Franco's battlefield successes, forced the Madrid government to react. Prime Minister Juan Negrin banned the use of radio receivers by Republican civilians for the duration of the war.

In Nazi Germany, Hitler tried to discourage listening to foreign broadcasts in the mid-1930s by introducing a three-tube "People's Radio." It was cheap enough for everyone to afford—they were sold or given away by the millions. However, it was also, purposefully, only capable of bringing in signals from powerful nearby home service stations.

Hitler tightened the screws as only a totalitarian regime can. The Nazis decreed that any German who published, or even repeated, information from foreign stations would be punished by up to five years in prison. Soon after the outbreak of war, a total ban on listening to foreign broadcasts was imposed throughout Germany.

The Nazis fumed about the "insidiously lying rumors broadcast by the (shortwave) radio." But, despite savage persecution of violators, Germans continued to listen.

Some paid a terrible price. One wartime source discovered that in 1940, early in the War, nearly 1,500 Germans had already been sent to concentration camps or been executed for listening to foreign broadcasts. The final figure of German radio victims during the War has never been fully determined.

Russians, Poles, Slovaks and other Europeans living under the yoke of Nazi rule also were forbidden by the Germans to own radios. In occupied France, possession of radio equipment was punishable by immediate execution.

One clandestine letter from a French veteran of World War I reached the BBC in 1941. Wrote the elderly listener, "Although I am in occupied France, with the invaders in our very house, we listen to your transmissions, which are, of course, forbidden!"

In the village of La Coquille, near Limoges, France, Maquis resistance leader Edouard Brunet and his comrades listened to forbidden radio transmissions from Russia and England in the relative safety of the local graveyard.

In 1940, as world band expert Al Quaglieri's family still recalls, the American government confiscated or rendered inoperative those shortwave radios possessed by German or Italian nationals residing in the United States. In the case of Quaglieri's grandparents, the family shortwave set was disabled by a neighbor—a radio repairman hired for this purpose by the Government.

"Possession of radio equipment was punishable by immediate execution."

Also during this period, Germany and Italy were trying to create pro-Axis sentiment in the United States not only by the use of direct world band propaganda, but also through foreign-language "ethnic" broadcasts within the U.S. As Arnold Hartley, a pioneer in ethnic American broadcasting, recalls, "Many station owners didn't even speak the broadcast language, and so had no idea what was going out over their transmitters. This allowed a number of announcers, who were being paid secretly by the German and Italian consulates in New York, to turn out pro-Axis propaganda."

The Federal Communications Commission brought this "world band radio without world band" to a quiet end in 1940. Foreign language broadcasts within the United States were purged of pro-Axis announcers, some of whom eventually were rehabilitated during the War and allowed to come back on the air. Multilingual censors also were hired and paid for by the stations.

A more subtle approach to discourage listening to hostile shortwave voices was

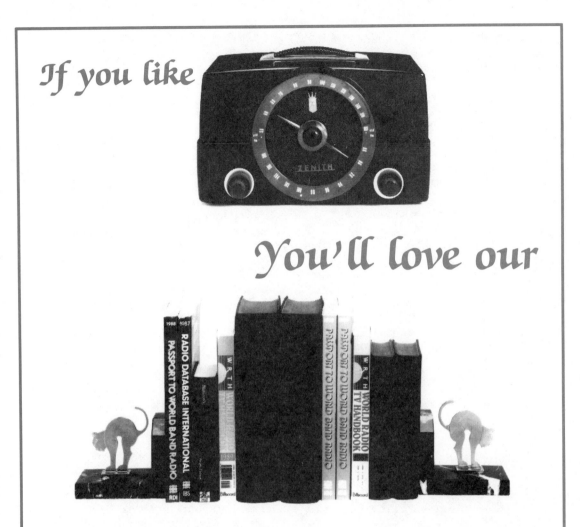

initiated by the South African government in the early 1960s, according to British author Julian Hale. The Pretoria government committed all domestic broadcasts for blacks to limited-range FM. In addition, they made it difficult for black South Africans to buy receivers able to tune shortwave.

The South African government also announced that fines and up to seven years in prison awaited anyone caught taking part in broadcasts from foreign radio stations which were deemed to be "hostile." While not directly banning world band listening, the law discouraged South African world band listeners from writing to proscribed stations, lest that be seen as offering aid to the enemy—in this case, anti-apartheid viewpoints.

In a similar vein, in the early Sixties the United States intercepted mail from abroad that was deemed to be "communist propaganda." The intended recipient was sent a notice from the Government to this effect, indicating that if he wished to receive his mail he would have to specifically request it and sign for it.

> "He listened to forbidden radio in the relative safety of the local graveyard."

This all took place while the McCarthy era and its blacklists remained fresh in people's minds. Consequently, until struck down by the Supreme Court, this practice had a chilling effect on listener communication with at least some world band stations.

A few world leaders want international broadcasts only for themselves. For example, Iran's late Ayatollah Ruhollah Khomeini obsessively listened to radio news from foreign nations, but tried to prevent his people from doing the same.

"He listens to news at all hours except when sleeping or praying." Khomeini's daughter, Zahra Mustafavi, told the *Washington Post*. "He has a portable radio, which he carries even during the fast—believe me—and even during meals.

"He's careful that he himself hears the news, rather than hearing it from others."

Attempts to prevent shortwave listening by law or dictate have been universally ineffective, even when ruthlessly enforced.

But electronic jamming—deliberate interference with radio signals—has been somewhat more successful. The first recorded jamming attempt occurred in 1932, when Romania tried, unsuccessfully, to electronically block Soviet propaganda broadcasts.

Then, in 1934, Chancellor Engelbert Dollfuss of Austria, desperate to combat Nazi propaganda aimed at incorporating Austria into the Third Reich, jammed German broadcasts.

The Italians, at war with Ethiopia, jammed programs from Addis Ababa and those of the BBC's Arabic Service, as well. Rival factions in the Spanish civil bloodshed jammed each other. By the time World War II began, jamming had already become widespread.

Great Britain was, then, the notable exception. The BBC, in a 1940 declaration, stated, "Jamming is really an admission of a bad cause. The jammer has a bad conscience . . . is afraid of the influence of the truth. In our country we have no such fears . . ."

Jamming has many sounds, all ear-rending: a growl, a warble, a rotary whine, an oscillating *woo-woo*, a bubble-machine bubbling. In the past, the Soviets, who practiced jamming more extensively than any other nation over the decades, used diesel engine-type roaring noises interspersed with Morse code signals that presumably identified the jamming transmitter.

Sometimes the interference has been musical, a non-stop playing of a single recording, such as Santana's "Soul Sacrifice," or the relaying of regular broadcast programs—notably China's CPBS-1 and Moscow's "Mayak" networks—distorted so as to enhance the masking effect.

Recent electronic attacks on foreign broadcasters have taken more subtle forms—confusing listeners or ridiculing the offending programs, rather than blocking them with noise.

For example, in Central America today, a tame phony "Radio Venceremos" often operates side-by-side with the real clandestine station of the same name, presumably to mislead listeners trying to

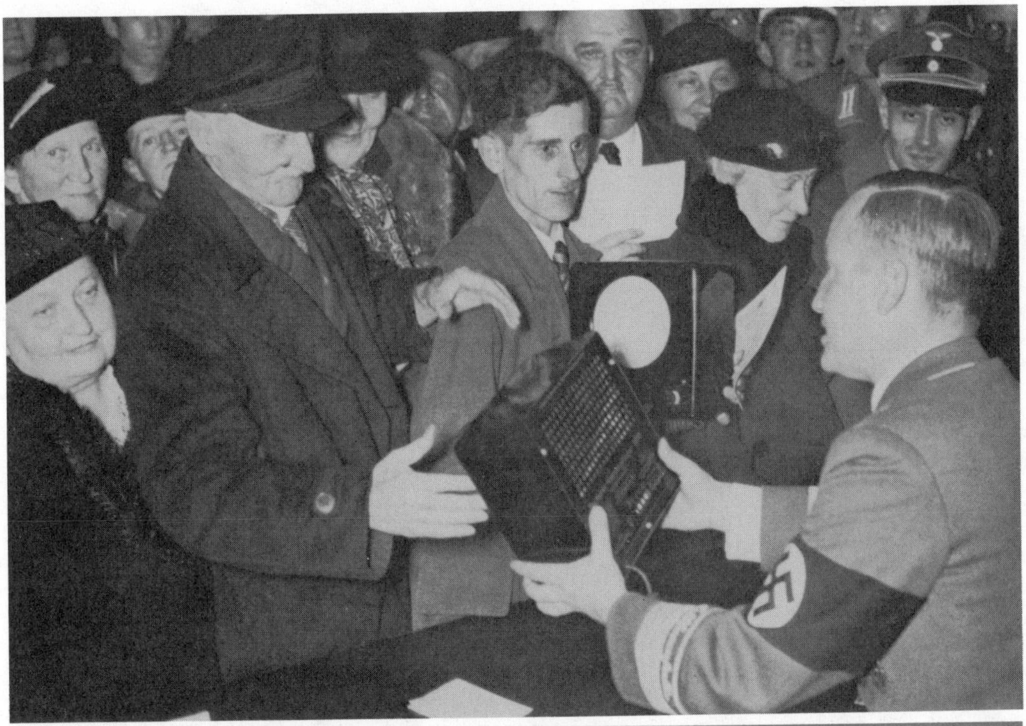

People's Radios were used by Nazis to discourage listening to foreign broadcasts.

hear the real Salvadorean revolutionary broadcaster.

During World War II, the Russians placed a powerful radio signal precisely atop that of a German broadcaster, allowing a mystery voice, dubbed "Ivan the Terrible," to interrupt and answer the enemy announcer with devastating sarcasm.

But attacks on radio waves have a price: jamming is incredibly expensive. In 1962, intelligence sources put the number of Russian jamming stations at 2,000, with another 500 in use in eastern Europe. The annual operating costs were estimated at $100 to $186 million. Before Soviet jamming ended in late 1988, it was estimated that between 2,000-3,000 jammer stations were pouring out 60 million watts worth of electronic noise daily. The shutdown reportedly saved Moscow between $750 million and $1 billion a year!

There is yet another price to be paid by the jamming country: the bestowing of credibility upon the jammed broadcaster. As surveys have shown, the same broadcasts tend to have higher credibility among listeners when they are jammed than when they are not jammed.

Shortwave signals come skipping into the target zone by skywave. To jam them requires a number of noise-generating shortwave transmitters located close to the listeners. So, to get the most bang from the jamming buck, the U.S.S.R. saturated its major population centers with groundwave jamming transmitters to block incoming broadcasts. In less populated areas, only skywave—not the more effective groundwave—jamming was economical. Therefore, it was never too difficult for rural Soviet listeners to hear Western programming. Creative urbanites also cashed in on this loophole by taking weekend picnics to the countryside, transistor radios in tow.

In the postwar years, Soviets jammed Western programming until the early 1970s, when Moscow's view of foreign shortwave broadcasting began to soften. Jamming continued, but it was more selective, focusing on certain stations and language services.

But jamming cannot be laid only on

communist doorsteps. For a time, Rhodesia—today's Zimbabwe—jammed British broadcasts. Spain devoted much effort to blocking clandestine Radio España Independiente and Radio Euzkadi, a Basque clandestine. At one point, Greece opted to jam some Greek-language broadcasts of Germany's Deutsche Welle. After the overthrow of President Salvador Allende, Chile became an active jammer of certain Spanish-language broadcasts the Pinochet regime considered too far to the left, including those of Radio Sweden.

Jamming often follows in the wake of conflict—such as the "Beijing Spring"—and the volatile Middle East is no exception. Israel, using "woo-woo" oscillating heterodynes, interfered with Radio Cairo and other Arab transmissions during the October War and again during the invasion of Lebanon. More recently, the Israelis have been jamming the clandestine Al Quds Radio, while various Arab countries have sometimes disrupted Kol Israel's popular Arabic Service.

The same "woo-woo" oscillating heterodyne technique—basically, moving an open carrier back and forth over the target signal—is also used by today's second-most active jamming country, Iraq, which also has "bubble" jammers, so-called because of the sound they make. Iran has engaged in jamming both during and after the Shah's rule, but to a far lesser extent.

Even the democratic West has not been immune from the jamming virus. Back in 1956, Great Britain broke its own no-jamming rule, disrupting Greek transmissions to strife-torn Cyprus, then under British rule.

"The U.S. has never seriously contemplated jamming," an American official declared in the early 1970s. That may be true for English language broadcasts directed to the United States. But in various parts of the world, even today, clandestine broadcasts aimed at countries which the U.S. supports are being jammed. It would be surprising if at least some of that has not been supported, financially or technically, by the United States.

Indeed, such assistance is known to have taken place at least once, although it may have been inadvertent. Harris shortwave transmitters provided to Pinochet's Chile by a U.S. government assistance program wound up being used not only for broadcasting, but also to jam Radio Moscow and other stations.

Even today, the American military maintains a jamming apparatus in place to be used against broadcasts in the event of war, according to one responsible official. "Anything goes during war," he declares, citing a clause in the international radio regulations that allows those regulations to be suspended in times of armed conflict.

That jamming apparatus is known to have been used on at least two occasions, including during the American invasion of the Dominican Republic. However, claims by the Nicaraguan government that the U.S. National Security Agency has jammed broadcasts from ships off Central America don't appear to be plausible, given the interceptive nature of the NSA's mandate.

As we enter a new decade, we can take pleasure in knowing that there is less deliberate noisemaking on world band radio now than at any other time in the past forty years. The Soviet Union, the primary source of jamming since the Cold War, is no longer disrupting foreign broadcasts. Gorbachev and his policy of *glastnost* have opened the doors of the Soviet Union to world band radio—a world full of music, ideas and pleasures.

"It is a world we've lost for so long!" says C—— Litang in his letter, "A world my father tried very hard to forget—a world I'm trying to find!"

Don Jensen, a veteran writer on radio topics, is Consulting Editor to Passport to World Band Radio.

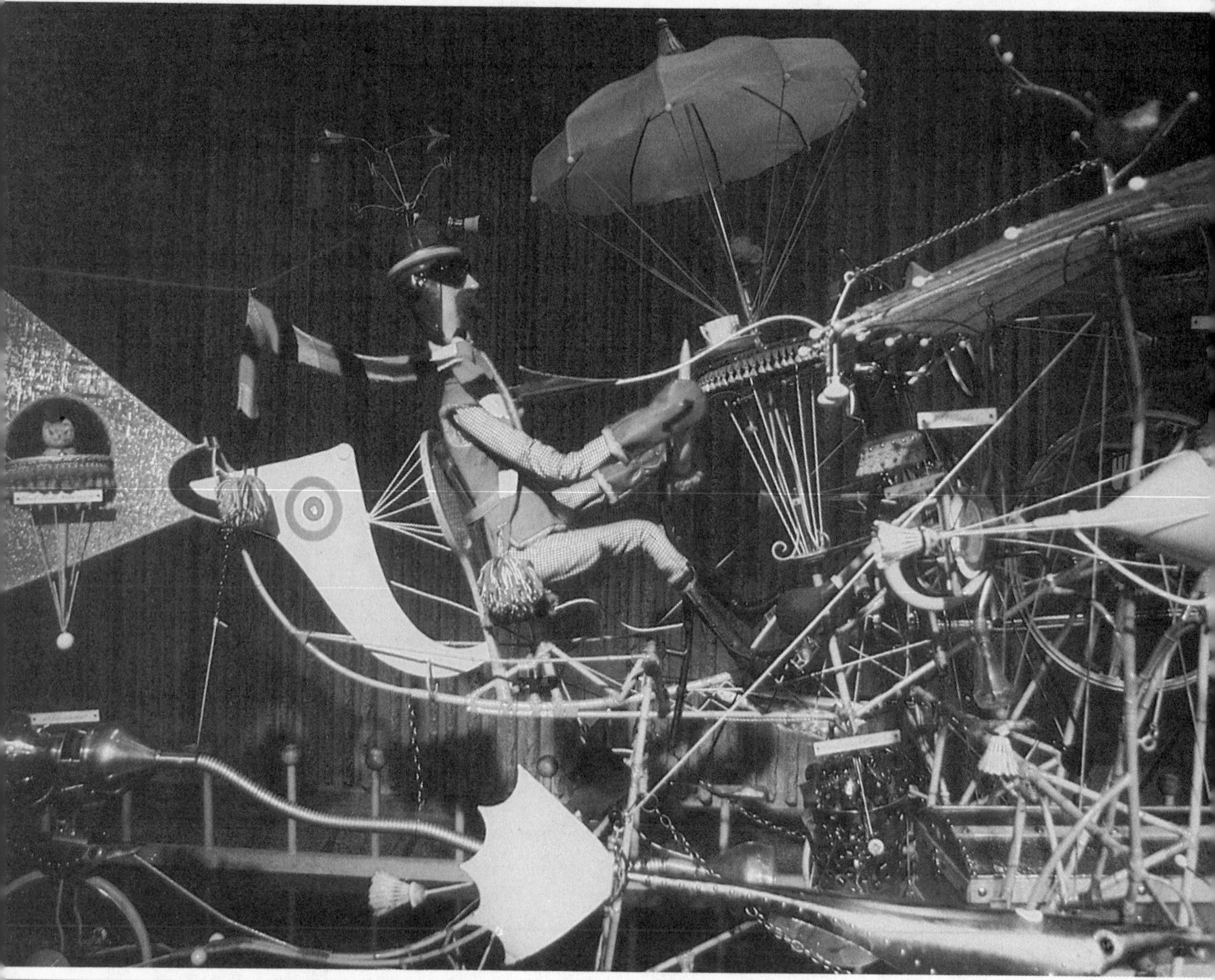

Ontario Science Center in Toronto pays homage to the creative spirit. Pierre St. Jacques

THE WIDE, WIDE WORLD OF SCIENCE

by Jock Elliott

World band radio tends to be embraced by the curious among us. So it's hardly surprising that it offers a wide variety of programs covering all sorts of new developments in science, technology, medicine and nature—and how they affect our lives.

Here are just some of the science and technology programs currently being presented on the international airwaves. Remember that not only times, but also days of the week are given in World Time—see "Getting Started with World Band Radio" in this edition for details. Also, *Passport's* "Worldwide Broadcasts in English" provides you with the best times and frequencies for your location.

Canada

Radio Canada International has two programs of real interest. *Spotlight On Science* covers the full range of basic and applied science in Canada, including such diverse fields as astronomy, chemistry, medicine, genetics and ecology. Recent topics have included acid rain, the "greenhouse effect," depletion of the ozone layer, gene mapping, fish farming, stress on the farm, the effect of female hormone fluctuations on task performance, and epileptic chickens. *Spotlight On Science* is broadcast Thursdays at 1200 and 1900; Fridays at 0400; Saturdays at 0000 and 1800; and Sundays at 2200. All World Time, of course.

Innovation Canada, broadcast in both English and French, focuses on developments in Canadian trade, as well as news in science and technology. Topics that have been covered include the appearance of a device for detecting the theft of plutonium from a nuclear reactor, a solar-powered water pump designed for use in the third world, and a look at how Canadian Customs uses technology to combat drug trafficking. *Innovation Canada* can be heard in English Mondays at 1200 and 1900 World Time; Tuesdays at 0400; Saturdays at 0100, 0300, 2100, 2200, and 2300; and Sundays at 1300. Both of these programs are usually heard one hour earlier during the summer.

Germany

The West German **Deutsche Welle** offers *Science and Technology* during its English language broadcasts on Fridays at 0100, 0300 and 0500 World Time; Saturdays at 0400 and 0600; and Sundays at 2100. It covers developments in a wide variety of scientific and technical disciplines, ranging from medicine to the exploration of space. *Man and Environment*, which covers environmental topics in advanced and developing countries, is broadcast Fridays at 2100; and again on Saturdays at 0200, 1500 and 1900.

Holland

Radio Nederland covers news of the environment and technology—including medicine, computers and astronomy—in *Research File*, broadcast Mondays in English to North America at 0030 and 0330 World Time, and at other times for the rest of the world. A recent, and typical, program topic: the pros and cons of biotechnology.

Israel

Kol Israel broadcasts *Spectrum* on Mondays at 2000 and 0000 World Time, and on Tuesdays at 0200. *Spectrum* deals with science and technology in Israel. It includes the latest in basic and applied scientific research and engineering in such fields as medicine, biology, industrial science, nature, ecology and agriculture. Past programs have covered such diverse topics as earthquake rescue techniques used by the Israeli rescue mission to Armenia; research into asthma; immunology; the effects of classical music on chickens; aging; lasers; sleep patterns; and pesticides.

Norway

Radio Norway International broadcasts a regular half-hour English language program, *Norway Today*, every Sunday. Once a month, fifteen minutes of this program are devoted to *Science Notebook*, which not only covers traditional science and technology, but also looks at environmental questions and the general debate around research policies and future development. The first transmission is broadcast at 0600 World Time Sundays, and is repeated at 0800, 0900, 1200, 1300, 1400, 1600, 1700, 1800, 1900, 2200, 2300 and (early Monday World Time) 0000.

South Africa

Radio RSA presents *Our Wild Heritage*, a ten-minute program which covers everything from entomology to climatology, and often features reports from the field—literally—by host Dave Holt-Biddle. Programs include talks on endangered flora and fauna; developments in endangered-species breeding programs; game reserves and natural areas; and interviews with environmental newsmakers. *Our Wild Heritage* is broadcast Sundays at 1700, 2000, and 2100 World Time; Mondays at 0400; Tuesdays at 2100; and Fridays at 1600.

Research RSA—broadcast Sundays at 2000, Mondays at 1600, and Thursdays at 1600 World Time—concentrates on just about all aspects of scientific and industrial research in South Africa. Some examples: the development of alternative fuels and the use of volcanic ash in building bricks.

Switzerland

Swiss Radio International frequently focuses on problems relating to nature, ecology and science on its *Dateline* program, heard Monday to Saturday, and on *Supplement*, broadcast the second Sunday of each month. English language programs are broadcast on SRI at 0200, 0400, 0630, 0830, 1000, 1100, 1330, 1530, 1830 and 2100 World Time.

> While noshing on your favorite oat bran and frozen yogurt, give a listen to Health Matters, which reveals all manner of useful–rather than merely trendy–tips.

United Kingdom

No listing of distinguished programs would be complete without the myriad offerings of the **BBC World Service.** Heading its broad scientific program roster is *Science in Action*, which covers the gamut of applied science, from linear accelerators to orthopedic medicine. It is heard Fridays at 1615 World Time, with repeats Sundays at 1001 and Mondays at 0230.

Basic science is covered in *Discovery*, which is broadcast year-around, except summer. It can be heard Tuesdays at 1001 and 1830 World Time, and again on Wednesdays at 0330. During the summer, the breezy show *Pop Science*, complete with musical requests, is hosted by Janice Long at those same times.

Friends of the environment can enjoy *Nature Now*, which is heard Fridays at 1445 World Time, with repeats Sundays at 0915 and Mondays at 0445. Aggies can tune in *The Farming World* Wednesdays at 1225, as well as on Thursdays at 0640 and 1940.

Just about all of us are interested in being healthy and fit. While noshing on your favorite oat bran and frozen yogurt, give a listen to *Health Matters*, which reveals all manner of useful—rather than merely trendy—tips on just about everything from how to keep your face free from wrinkles to avoiding clogged arteries. It is heard Mondays at 1115 and 1630 World Time, Tuesdays at 0815, and Wednesdays at 0215.

> Recent topics have included the effect of female hormone fluctuations on task performance, and epileptic chickens.

From time-to-time, the BBC also airs special science and nature programs, such as 1988's excellent environmental series, *Global Concerns*. These are effective in providing an in-depth look at a single issue or discipline.

United States

The **Voice of America** discusses science and technology on several of its programs, the foremost among them being *New Horizons*, broadcast to the Americas on Mondays at 0110 World Time, and to other parts of the World Sundays at 1110, 1510 and 2110. This is a weekly science documentary covering a broad range of subjects, from physics and chemistry through biology, medicine and the social sciences. Recent programs have dealt with research into superconductivity, the biological basis of schizophrenia and manic depression, and efforts to map the human genome.

Other scientific issues can be heard on *Science Notebook*, *Medicine Today* and *Science in Our Lives*, which are parts of the VOA's various magazine-format programs.

Jock Elliott is Contributing Editor to Passport to World Band Radio.

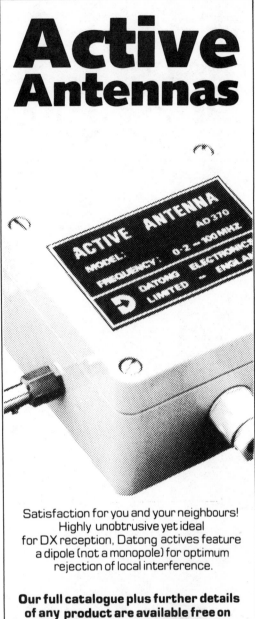

THE BASEBALL FAN'S CAPSULE GUIDE TO CRICKET

by John Campbell

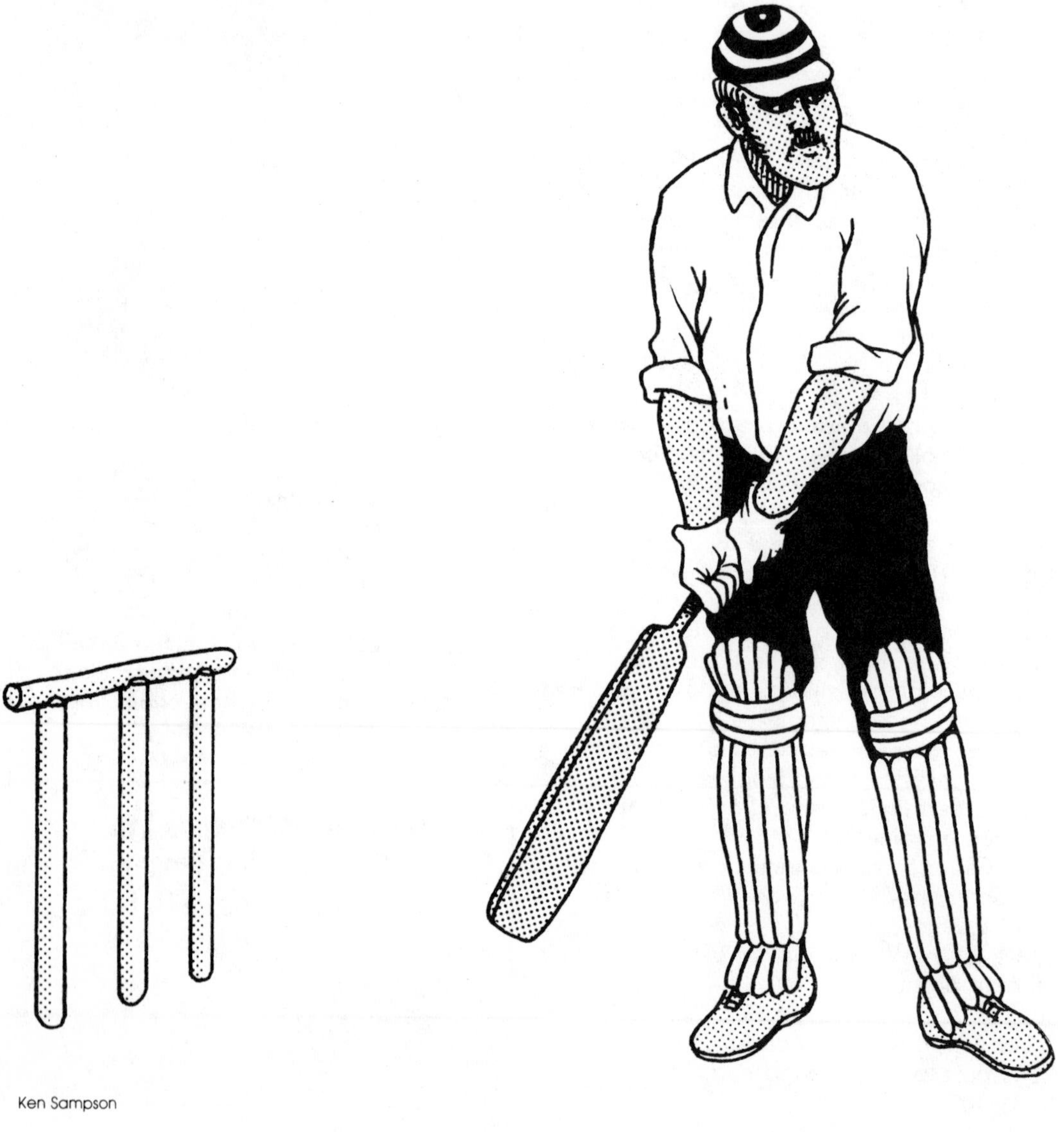

Ken Sampson

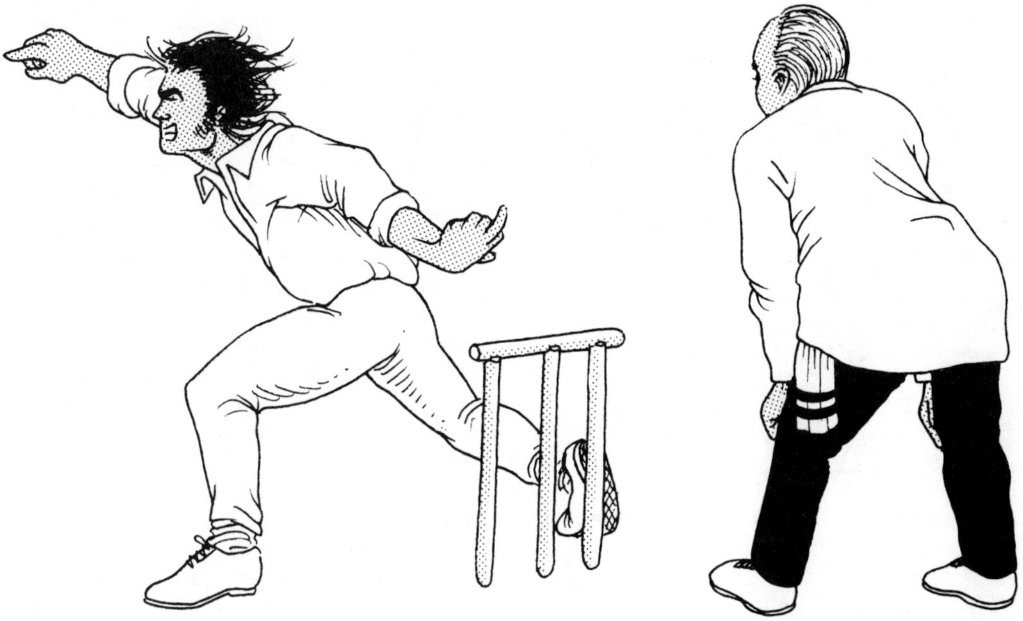

Ken Sampson

Not done yet? Not after five days? A five-day game of cricket, an English form of baseball, is not unusual. The English are masters of slow sports, but five-day games can be dramatic. They have to be. Otherwise, places whose citizens have less patience—the West Indies, Australia, Pakistan, India, New Zealand, to name a few—would probably have taken up hours-long baseball instead of days-long cricket.

This timing can make the broadcast of one solitary cricket game more like the coverage of an entire Olympics. So, what most world band stations do is broadcast only bits and pieces of a game, or else they assign special transmitters and frequencies for "ball-by-ball" coverage. This allows normal programming to continue unmolested on the usual frequencies.

Cricket—no relation to croquet—is played with *two* bats and a hardball. Two 11-man teams play on a field of grass, with the action centering around two "wickets"—each with three wooden dowels, called "stumps," that are stuck into the ground near each other. These dowels hold up two sideways sticks, called "bails."

In front of each wicket is a base, called the "crease." For those weaned on baseball, it's easiest to think of the two wickets as home plate and the pitcher's mound, respectively.

The pitcher is called a "bowler," and for good reason. Unlike in baseball, in cricket pitches can and usually do bounce, like a tennis serve, off the ground, or even roll on like a bowling ball, before getting to the hitter. The batter—"batsman" in cricketese—can be slicing away at the ball like Greg Norman one moment, then reaching for the sky like Boris Becker the next.

A bowler delivers only six balls in a row, called an "over." He is supposed to pitch the ball so it knocks one of the bails off the batsman's wicket. This is where the batsman comes in. He's there not only to hit runs for the usual reason, but also to clobber the ball before it can get to the wicket and knock off a bail.

A "square leg" isn't weird anatomy; it's where one of the two umpires normally stands.

The batsman uses a long, flat-sided bat that looks for all the world like an elongated pledge paddle from Jolly Green Giant U. If he misses the ball and it knocks off a bail, he is struck out, or "bowled." It's as if, in baseball, the pitcher could put out the batter only if the batter missed a swing and the ball hit one of the catcher's kneecaps!

If the batsman gets a hit, he can just stand there and wait for the next pitch—he doesn't have to run. But if he runs, it's not a one-way trip around a diamond, as in baseball, but *back and forth* between the two wickets. In fact, there are always two runners, since there has to be a man on base whenever somebody's up to bat. When there's a hit, these two run in opposing directions, like human pistons in a two-cylinder engine, passing each other somewhere between the two wickets.

Each dash between the wickets is worth a run. So, if the runners both can go from one wicket to the other, say, three times—that's one-and-a-half round trips—his team scores three complete runs. If the defending team throws the ball so it knocks the bail off one of the wickets while running is in progress, the runner who is closest to the "broken" wicket—the wicket with the fallen bail—is out: "run out."

Cricket has its own version of home runs. Here's how it works. Following a hit, running stops if the ball goes out of the field. If the ball hasn't touched the ground, the hit scores six runs. If it has, it's worth four. A "six" is as impressive as a home run in baseball, and probably rarer; a "four" is more like a triple.

The field is carved up into "off," "leg," and "on" sections. So, if a position has "off," "leg" or "on" in its name, you know where that player is supposed to stand. Playing positions beginning with "long" are on the boundary—outfielders. "Mid" players are a bit closer in, and "short" positions are infielders. A "square leg" isn't weird anatomy; it's where one of the two umpires normally stands.

A game is over after only two innings or a designated number of days—three to five—whichever comes first. An "innings" (no, not an inning) is completed either when ten men are out or if the offensive captain says it's over, whichever comes first.

Each game takes so long because a batsman has no fixed maximum number of pitches he has to face, and he can succeed himself as hitter again and again. He is out only when the defending team can get him out—for example, by a catch in the field, as in baseball. There are no strikes or balls in cricket. There aren't even any crickets in cricket.

Even in England, not everybody is keen on watching games that take as long as some wars to complete. So there's now also one-day cricket.

Most world band stations broadcast only bits and pieces of a game, or else they assign special transmitters for "ball-by-ball" coverage.

Cricket also has its own World Series called, appropriately enough, the Cricket World Cup. There are also numerous "test matches." These are of comparable importance to the Cricket World Cup, except that there's no worldwide winner at the end. Either way, you're hearing the finest the cricket world has to offer.

John Campbell is Professor of Computer Science at University College London.

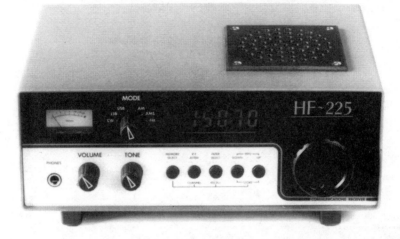

LONDON BUSES
RM 395
BBC
RM395

WHAT'S ON TONIGHT?

Passport's Hour-by-Hour Guide to World Band Shows

Nothing can quite match the variety of programs on world band radio—every hour there's something going on. At 0000 World Time, which for North Americans is the start of evening prime time, there are at least a dozen stations to be heard broadcasting news and feature programs in English.

The same holds true in virtually every other part of the world, as well. News, music, comedy, plays, language courses, cooking, science, travel, economics, history . . . it goes on and on. Prime time television, cable and all, has a way to go to top that.

Keep in mind that some operations, notably the World Service of Radio Moscow, are on the air twenty-four hours a day in English on a variety of channels. On many radios these may be heard much of the day or night simply by dialing about until a clear channel is found.

All shows are listed in World Time (UTC), which is announced by many stations at the start of transmission or at the top of the hour. "Repeat" programs usually start with fresh news, but include the same features aired earlier.

Key channels are given for North America, Western Europe, East Asia and the Pacific—including Australia and New Zealand. Information on secondary and seasonal channels, as well as channels for other parts of the world, may be found in the "Worldwide Broadcasts in English" and "The Blue Pages" sections.

Evening Prime Time–North America
0000

BBC World Service. First, there's the half-hour *Newsdesk*, which includes both international and national news. Then there are such variety programs as *Megamix* and *Omnibus*, as well as various serialized programs. Continuous to North America on 5975, 6175, 9590, 9915 and 15260 kHz; to East Asia until 0030 on 11945, 11955, 15360 and 17875 kHz; and to the Pacific until 0030 on 9570 and 11955 kHz.

Christian Science Monitor World Service, USA. *News*, news analysis and news-related features, with emphasis on

London bus driver points out directions to tourist passenger.

London Regional Transport

international developments. Excellent, if somewhat dry. To North America and Europe for eight hours Tuesdays through Sundays (Mondays through Saturdays, local American date) on 7400, 9850 and 13760 kHz.

Kol Israel. *News*, followed by a variety of feature programs—some of which are aired now, others of which can be heard an hour later or, in summer, an hour earlier. Depending on the time of year, features include *Israel Sound* (Israeli pop songs), *Studio Three* (arts in Israel), *Shabbat Shalom* (with music requests), *Calling All Listeners* (replies to questions), *DX Corner* (for radio enthusiasts), *Spotlight* (current events), *Spectrum* (science and technology), *With Me in the Studio* (guest interviews), *Thank Goodness It's Friday* (Sabbath eve program), *Faith to Faith* (religious affairs), *Israel Mosaic* (variety of topics), *Letter from Jerusalem*, *Jewish News Review*, *Living Here*—and a Hebrew language lesson, *Ulpan of the Air*. Half hour to Eastern North America and Europe on 7460, 9385, 9435, 11605, 15615 or 15640 kHz.

Spanish National Radio. *News*, followed most weekdays by *Panorama*, which features current events, music, literature, science, the arts and more. The broadcast closes with the five-minute language course, *Learn Spanish*. On weekends, different features, usually on a serial basis, are followed by sports news. Fifty-five minutes to Eastern North America on 9630, 11880 or 15110 kHz.

Radio Moscow. The second hour of a two-hour cyclical broadcast to Eastern North America. *News*, followed by feature programs, including *Top Priority, Moscow Mailbag, Home in the USSR, Science and Engineering*, and *Sidelights on Soviet Life*. Just dial around—you'll find it.

Radio Yugoslavia. Summers only at this time. *News*, followed by features (see 2100). Forty-five minutes to Eastern North America on 5980, 7215, 9620, 11735 or 15105 kHz.

Radio Sofia, Bulgaria. Winters only at this time. *News*, followed by commentary in *Events and Developments* or *Balkan Panorama*. This, in turn, is followed by such features as *Time Out For Sports, Popular Music, DX Corner*, and *Across the Map of Bulgaria*. One hour to Eastern North America on 9700, 11660 or 11720 kHz.

Voice of America. First hour of VOA's separate two- hour broadcasts to the Caribbean and Latin America. *News*, followed some days by *Caribbean Report*, and then either *Music USA* or Special English news and features—all depending on which target zone is being served. An excellent way to keep in touch with events in the western hemisphere. The service to the Caribbean is on 6130, 9455 and 11695 kHz; the service to the Americas is on 5995, 9775, 9815, 11580, 11740 and 15205 kHz.

Radio Beijing. *News*, followed by *News About China*, then *Current Affairs*. There are then various feature programs, such as *Culture in China, Listeners' Letterbox*, or *In the Third World*. One hour to Eastern North America winters on 9665, 9770 and 11715 kHz; summers on 15130, 17715 and 17855 kHz.

Belgische Radio en Televisie, Belgium. Winters only at this time; see 2330 for program details. To Eastern North America for twenty-five minutes on 9925 kHz.

Radio Habana Cuba. *News*, followed by such feature programs as *Spotlight on Latin America, DXers Unlimited, Be My Guest*, or *Life in Cuba*. Lots of good Cuban and Caribbean music. To Eastern North America on 9665 kHz winters, 11820 kHz summers.

WRNO, USA. This station plays mostly rock music and some jazz, plus religious programs. Offerings to date have included *Cousin Brucie's Crusin' America, Rock Over London, Profiles of Rock Stars*, and NBC's *The Jazz Show*. To North America throughout much of the evening on 7355 kHz.

Armed Forces Radio & Television Service, USA. Around- the-clock news, sports and features from the various American radio networks. See 1400 for details.

0030

Radio Canada International. Winters only at this time. Relays the excellent CBC domestic service news program, *As It Happens*, which features international stories, Canadian news and general human interest features. One hour on 5960 and 9755 kHz.

Netherlands Embassy

Holland's size and environmental consciousness makes it a natural setting for bicycling.

Radio Nederland. *News*, followed by *Newsline*, a current affairs program. There is then a different feature each night, including *Rembrandt Express, Images* (arts in Holland), or *Shortwave Feedback*—a listener response program. Mondays (Sunday nights local time in North America) are devoted to *The Happy Station*, an eclectic program of chat, letters and light music. This has the distinction of being the longest-running program on radio—even longer than CBS's venerable *World News Roundup*—having begun in the 1920s. Fifty-five minutes to Eastern North America on 6020, 6165 and 15315 kHz.

Radio Budapest, Hungary. This time Tuesdays through Sundays, winters only. *News*, followed by interviews, features and music. Unlike most stations, Radio Budapest's regularly scheduled feature programs are aired several times a month, rather than on a weekly basis. Reception is usually better in the summer and spring than in the winter. To Eastern North America on 6110, 9585, 9835, 11910 and 15160 kHz.

Radio Kiev, Ukrainian SSR. Winters only at this time. Similar to the 1900 transmission, but directed to Eastern North America on various frequencies, including 7400, 11790, 13645, 15180 and 15455 kHz.

0050

Vatican Radio. Each weekday at this time, this Curia-run station looks at issues in the news and how they affect Catholics around the world. It also analyzes the role of the Church in coping with events, as well as the involvement of the Church, priests and the laity in these matters. Different programs are aired on the weekends. Twenty-five minutes to Eastern North America on 6105 or 15180 kHz, plus 9605 and 11780 kHz.

0100

BBC World Service. *News Summary*, followed most days by *Outlook*, a program of news and human-interest stories, and *Financial News*. These are succeeded by one or more of a variety of feature programs, including *Society Today, Profile, New Ideas* and *Europe's World*—plus drama, music and book reviews. Continuous to North America on 5975, 6175, 9590, 9915 and 15260 kHz.

Christian Science Monitor World Service, USA. Continuation of 0100 broadcast to North America and Europe Tuesdays through Sundays on 7400, 9850 and 13760 kHz.

Kol Israel. *News* at the top of the hour, then various feature programs (see 0000). A half hour to Eastern North America and Europe on 7460, 9385, 9435, 11605, 15615 or 15640 kHz.

Radio Japan. At this time to Eastern North America summers only on 5960 kHz, but is year-around at this time to Western North America on 17810 and 17845 kHz. See 0300 for program details.

Spanish National Radio. Repeat of the 0000 transmission. To Eastern North America on 9630, 11880 and 15110 kHz.

Radio Moscow. *News*, followed by *Outlook*, a series of editorial features and commentary. There are then various *ad hoc* features, such as *Daily Talk, Home in the USSR, People*, and *Science and Engineering*. Just dial around to find a clear frequency.

Radio Prague, Czechoslovakia. *News*, then *Newsview*, a series of editorial comments. This is followed by a number of feature programs, including *Introducing Czechoslovakia, Economics, Cultural Program, Folk Music*, and a special feature on trade-union activities in *The WFTU Calling*. Usually well-heard in Eastern North America on 5930, 7345, 11990 and 15540 kHz.

Radio Habana Cuba. *News*, followed by feature programs that differ from those at 0000. There are also healthy doses of Latin American, Cuban and Caribbean music. Great reception in North America winters on 9655 kHz, and summers on 11820 kHz.

Radio Luxembourg. *News*, then the latest rock music hits. Heard well in much of Europe, but reception much poorer in North America (best bet is along the East Coast). On 6090 kHz.

Radio Yugoslavia. Winters only at this time. *News*, with concentration on events in Eastern Europe. This is followed by commentary and one of several feature programs, including *Sidewalk Rock* (popular music in the Third World), *Science and Technology Report*, and *Spotlight on Culture*. Usually good reception in North America. Forty minutes to Eastern North America on 5980, 7215, 9620, 11735 or 15105 kHz.

Voice of America. *News*, then *Report to the Americas*, a program of news features involving the United States and Latin American countries. To the Americas on 6130 and 9455 kHz, plus 5995, 9775, 9815, 11580, 11740 and 15205 kHz.

HCJB, Ecuador. Latin American *news* at 0100, usually followed by *Passport*, which includes music and special features on Ecuador and the world at large. To North America on 9745, 11775 and 15155 kHz.

Deutsche Welle, West Germany. *News*, followed by *Newsline Cologne*, which includes commentary, in-depth news features, press review, and a spot

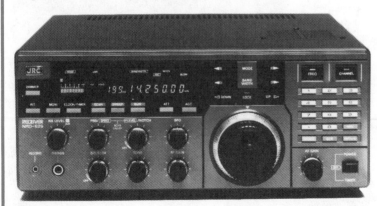

recalling important events for that date in history. These are succeeded by various feature programs, including *Economic Notebook, Living in Germany*, and *Random Selection*. Very good reception in North America on 6040, 6085, 6145, 9565, 9735 and 11865 kHz.

KUSW, USA. Mostly popular music and regional weather reports, plus *news* five minutes before the hour. Well-heard throughout the evening in North America on 11695 kHz.

0130

Radio Baghdad, Iraq. Summers only at this time. See 2100 for program details. To Eastern North America on 9515 or 11945 kHz. If these fare poorly, try the Asian frequencies of 11810 and 11880 kHz.

Radio Austria International. Summers only at this time; see 0230 for program details. To Eastern North America on 9870, 9875 and 13730 kHz.

Voice of Greece. Preceded, and to a lesser extent followed, by gobs of delightful Greek music, plus news and features in Greek. There's a ten-minute English *newscast*, more or less at 0130, heard at least most days except Mondays (Sunday nights local North American date). To Eastern North America on 7430 or 11645 kHz, plus 9395 and 9420 kHz.

Radio Budapest, Hungary. Repeat of the 0030 transmission. To Eastern North America on 6110, 9585, 9835, 11910 and 15160 kHz.

0145

BBC World Service for Asia. See 1115, which is usually better heard. In Asia and North America, until 0230 try 5965, 7235, 9580, 11955, 15310, 15380 or 17875 kHz.

0200

BBC World Service. *News*, followed by *British Press Review*. These are succeeded by a cornucopia of features, including *Network UK, Andy Kershaw's World of Music, People and Politics, Album Time*, a dramatized novel, *Science in Action, Sports International*, and *Assignment*. Continuous to North America on 5975, 6175, 9590, 9915 and 15260 kHz.

Christian Science Monitor World Service, USA. Continuation of 0000 broadcast to North America and Europe Tuesdays through Fridays on 9455 kHz, and Monday through Fridays on 9850 and 13760 kHz.

Radiobras, Brazil. Brazilian *news*, followed by *The Best in Brazilian Popular Music*, which features some of the most melodious sounds on world band radio, accompanied by occasional critical commentary on the music or biographies of the composers. This program takes an intermission for short features on Brazilian folklore, cultural events, contemporary Brazil, tourist attractions, and so forth. The musical feature is then resumed for the rest of the broadcast. A pleasant fifty minutes to North America on 11745 kHz.

Radio Cairo. Begins with Egyptian music, followed by a feature program, more sultry music, then *news* and commentary. The news is succeeded by more feature programs, including *Quiz of the Month, Cultural Life in Egypt, Focus, Reader's Corner* and *Mailbag*. All programs are interlaced with exotic Egyptian songs. One and a half hours of fair reception in North America on 9475 and 9675 kHz.

Voice of Free China, Taiwan. *News* and commentary focusing on events in China, then three different features. The last is *Let's Learn Chinese*, which has a

Kurt Kroszner

Alabaster Sphinx at Memphis, Egypt

South African Embassy

Umblanga Rocks Lighthouse continues to steer ships from harm's way.

series of segments for beginners, intermediate and advanced learners. Other features include the *Republic of China Today*, *Chinese Old Songs* and *Journey Into Chinese Culture*. One hour to North America on 5950 or 5985 kHz.

Radio Kiev, Ukrainian SSR. Summers only at this time. Repeat of 2330 transmission. To North America on various frequencies, including 11790, 13645, 15180 and 15455 kHz.

Kol Israel. Winters only at this time. *News*, followed by various features (see 0000). A half hour to North America on 7460, 9385 and 9435 kHz.

Radio Moscow. Continuation of the evening transmission to North America. On numerous frequencies—simply dial about.

Radio Habana Cuba. Repeat of the 0000 transmission. To North America winters on 6140 and 9655 kHz; summers on 9710 and 11820 kHz.

Swiss Radio International. *News*, followed by human interest features. On Sundays, the last fifteen minutes airs *Swiss Shortwave Merry-go-Round*, which answers technical questions sent in by listeners; Mondays are devoted alternately to *Supplement*, a feature on Swiss life, and *The Grapevine*, a listeners' contact program with a unique sense of humor. A half hour to North America on 6135, 9725 and 9885 kHz.

Radio RSA, South Africa. World and African *news*, followed by *Africa South*, a collection of special features focusing on the African continent, particularly South Africa. Fairly good reception in much of North America on 9580 and 9615 kHz.

HCJB, Ecuador. Begins with *Call of the Andes, Saludos Amigos*, or *Radio Reading Room*—depending on the day of the week. These programs are, in turn, followed by various features, such as *DX Party Line, Música del Ecuador, Ham Radio Today, Musical Mailbag*, or *Unshackled*. Excellent reception throughout North America on 11775 and 15155 kHz.

KUSW, USA. Continuous with popular music, *news* and weather to North America on 11695 kHz.

Radio Bucharest, Romania. *News*, then commentary. This is followed by several feature programs, including *Youth Club, Friendship and Cooperation*, and *The Skylark*—a charming selection of Romanian folk songs. To North America on 5990, 9510, 9570, 11830 and 11940 kHz.

0230

Radio Austria International. Winters only at this time. *News*, followed by a series of current events and human interest stories, including interviews with newsmakers. Monday's program features *Postfach 700*, a listener contact or mailbag show. A half hour to North America on 9870, 9875 and 13730 kHz.

Radio Tirana, Albania. *News*, followed by commentary and different feature programs for each day of the week. These include *Sports Report* and *Leafing Through the Marxist-Leninist Press*. To North America on 9500 or 9760 kHz.

Radio Portugal. National *news*, followed by feature programs. Tuesdays and Thursdays bring *Sun and Sea*, a tourist program; Wednesdays feature *Our choice of Music*; and Saturdays either *DX Corner, Mailbag* or *Philately*. Unfortunately, there are no broadcasts on Sundays or Mondays (Saturday and Sunday nights local North American dates). Only fair reception in Eastern North America—worse to the west—on 9600, 9635, 9680, 9705 and 11840 kHz.

Radio Sweden. Each broadcast is called *Weekday, Saturday* or *Sunday*, and begins with world and Nordic *news*, followed by human interest features and interviews. Occasionally, documentaries are offered—Scandinavian emigrees to New Zealand in the late 19th and early 20th centuries, for example. A half hour of variable reception to North America on 9695 and 11705 kHz.

Radio Finland International. Summers only at this time. Repeat of the 0630 transmission. To North America on 11775 and 15185 kHz.

0300

BBC World Service. *News*, then *News About Britain*, followed at 0315 most days by news analysis on *The World Today* or From Our Own Correspondent. At the half hour are feature programs, such as *Discovery* or *Pop Science*—and music, quiz shows or religion. Continuous to North America on 5975 and 9915 kHz; to early risers in parts of Western Europe on 6195, 9410 and sometimes 12095 kHz; and to East Asia on 15280 and 17815 kHz.

Christian Science Monitor World Service, USA. Continuation of transmission to North America and Europe Tuesdays through Fridays on 9455 kHz, and Mondays through Fridays on 9850 and 13760 kHz.

Radio Five, South Africa. Designed for South African listeners, which makes this interesting listening—if your radio can pick it up—as South Africa tries to resolve its problems. Programs include pop songs, traffic reports, contest announcements and advertisements, as well as weather reports. There's also *news headlines* later in the transmission. Two hours of fair-to-poor reception—summer is worst—on 4880 kHz.

Voice of Free China, Taiwan. Repeat of the 0200 transmission. To North America on 5950 or 5985 kHz.

Radio Beijing. Repeat of the 0000 transmission. To North America on 9690, 11715, 15130, 15455 or 17855 kHz.

Deutsche Welle, West Germany. Repeat of the 0100 transmission. To North America on 6085, 9545 and 9605 kHz.

Radio Moscow. Continuous to North America throughout the evening on numerous frequencies.

Radio Habana Cuba. Repeat of the 0100 transmission. To North America

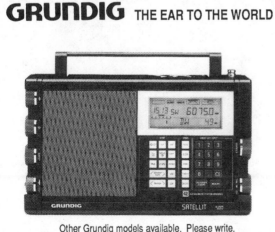

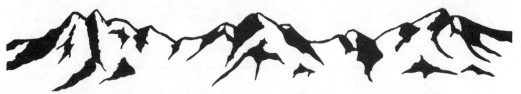

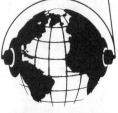

winters on 6140 and 9655 kHz; summers on 9710 and 11820 kHz.

KUSW, USA. Continuous with popular music, *news* and music to North America on 9815 or 11695 kHz.

HCJB, Ecuador. *News*, then *Guidelines for Family Living, Rendezvous, Grace Worship Hour*, and other Protestant religious programming. To North America on 11775 and 15155 kHz.

Radio Japan. Winters only at this time. *News*, followed by commentary—both oriented to Japanese and Asian affairs. These are succeeded by one of several feature programs, including *Cross Currents* or *Let's Learn Japanese*. At the end of the hour there is more commentary, followed by *Tokyo Pop In*, with Japanese popular music. One hour to Eastern North America on 5960 kHz.

Voice of Turkey. Summers only at this time. *News* and press reviews, followed by such arcane offerings as *The Kemalist Reforms and Religion, Turkish Panorama* and *The Western Thrace Question*. Then there's some pleasant Turkish music, followed by more features and music. Fifty minutes to North America on 9445 kHz.

0315

Radio France Internationale. *News*, then a review of the French press, followed by such feature programs as *Land of France, Drum Beat, Science Notes* and *Economic Issues*. Thirty minutes on 9800 or 11670 kHz.

0330

Radio Finland International. Winters only at this time. Repeat of the 0730 transmission. To North America on 9635 and 11775 kHz.

Radio Tirana, Albania. *News* and commentary, then features from the 0230 broadcast, including *Songs of Our Lives, Musical Pages*, and *The Cultural and Historical Traditions of the Albanian National People*. To North America on 9500 or 9760 kHz.

United Arab Emirates Radio, Dubai. Similar to the transmission at 1330, but on 11940 and 15435 kHz. Heard best in North America during the warm-weather months. See 1330 transmission for program details.

All the world's a stage on world band radio.

Radio Nederland. Repeat of the 0230 transmission. Fifty-five minutes to North America on 6165 and 9590 kHz.

BBC World Service for Africa. The BBC World Service for Africa airs excellent special programs for and about that continent, which otherwise tends to be poorly covered by the international media. Although this special BBC service is beamed only to Africa, it can sometimes be heard in other parts of the world, as well. Try 6005, 11750, 11730, 11845 or 15420 kHz.

Voice of Greece. Repeat of the 0130 transmission. Ten minutes of English, surrounded by long periods of Greek music and programming, to North America, except Mondays (Sunday nights local American date), on 7430, 9395 and 9420 kHz.

0400

BBC World Service. Kicking off the hour is *Newsdesk*, which airs world news, British news and press reviews. This is usually followed by a first-rate musical or drama-reading feature program, such as Saturday's *Here's Humph* jazz show and *Andy Kershaw's World of Music* on Thursdays. Continuous to North America and the Pacific on 5975 kHz; to Western Europe on 3955, 6195, 9410 and 12095 kHz; and to East Asia on 15280 and 17815 kHz.

Christian Science Monitor World Service, USA. Continuation of 0000 transmission to North America and Europe Tuesdays through Sundays on 9455 kHz, and daily on 9870 and 13760 kHz.

Radio Habana Cuba. *News* and propaganda, along with some interesting Latin American information, followed by fine Cuban, Caribbean and Latin American music, plus popular and traditional music, salsa and jazz. A short sports program follows. Heard for some hours throughout the evening to North America winters on 5965, 6140, 9655, 9710, 11760 or 11820 kHz.

Swiss Radio International. Repeat of the 0200 transmission. To North America on 6135, 9725, 9885 and 12035 kHz.

Voice of America. Directed to Africa and Europe 0400–0700, but widely heard elsewhere. *News*, then *VOA Morning*—a conglomeration of popular music, interviews, human interest stories, science digest, sports news, and so on, with news summaries at the half-hour. To Africa at 0300–0600 on 9575 kHz; to Europe at 0400–0700 on 5995 kHz, among many other frequencies.

Radio Bucharest, Romania. An abbreviation of the 0200 transmission, beginning with national and international *news* and commentary, then the feature program from the first half-hour of the 0200 broadcast. To North America on 5990, 9510, 9570, 11830 and 11940 kHz.

Kol Israel. Summers only at this time. *News* for fifteen minutes from Israel Radio's domestic network. To Europe and North America on 11585, 11655, 15640 and 17575, and to Asia and the Pacific on 17630 kHz.

KUSW, USA. Continuous, usually with popular music, *news* and weather, to North America on 9815 or 11695 kHz.

Voice of Turkey. Winters only at this time. See 0300 for program details. To North America for fifty minutes on 9445 kHz.

HCJB, Ecuador. *Music in the Night*, with the rest of the hour-long transmission devoted to *Happiness Is*, a religious discussion between the station staff and visitors. To North America on 11775 and 15155 kHz.

Radio Moscow. *News*, then a continuation of Moscow's evening transmissions to North America. Reception good on the West Coast of North America on a broad variety of frequencies.

0430

BBC World Service for Africa. See 0330. Try 6005, 9515, 9600 or 15420 kHz.

0500

BBC World Service. *News*, then *Twenty-Four Hours*, which is one of many of the BBC's in-depth news analysis programs. This is followed by *Financial News*, *Words of Faith*, and another news-analysis program—*The World Today*. Continuous to North America and the Pacific on 5975 kHz; to Western Europe on 3955, 6195, 7120, 9410 and 12095 kHz; and to East Asia on 15280 and 17815 kHz.

Christian Science Monitor World Service, USA. Continuation of 0000 transmission to North America and Europe Tuesdays through Fridays on 9455 kHz, and Mondays through Fridays on 9870 and 13760 kHz.

Deutsche Welle, West Germany. Repeat of the 0100 transmission to North America, but on 5960, 6130 and 9700 kHz.

HCJB, Ecuador. Part of a continuous transmission starting at 0030. To North America on 6230, 9720, 9745 or 11775 kHz.

Spanish National Radio. Repeat of the 0000 and 0100 transmissions to North America, but on 9630, 11880 or 15110 kHz.

Voice of Nigeria. Usually clearer in winter than in summer, but never a barn burner. First, *Jamboree* (African popular music and mailbag), followed by *news*, editorials and commentary until 0600, when the station begins its broadcast in other languages. One hour on 7255 kHz.

Kol Israel. Winters only at this time. *News* for fifteen minutes from Kol Israel's domestic network. To Europe and North America on 7460, 9435, 9455, 11588 and 11605 kHz, and to Asia and the Pacific on 15650 or 17630 kHz.

Radio Moscow. Clearly heard on the west coast of North America. Tune around to find it on any of the numerous and

Tugboats ply their trade in the port of Hamburg.

ever-changing Moscow frequencies.

Radio Habana Cuba. Well heard throughout North and Central America on 5965, 9655, 11760 or 11820 kHz.

KUSW, USA. Weekends only at this time. Similar programming—popular music, *news* and weather—as on weekdays. To North America on 6175 kHz.

0530

HCJB, Ecuador. Continues to North America on 6230, 9720, 9745 or 11775 kHz.

Evening Prime Time– East Asia and the Pacific 0600

BBC World Service. *Newsdesk*, followed by such diverse features as *Meridian* (an arts show), *Jazz for the Asking*, dramatized novels, *Rock Salad, Time for Verse* and *The Farming World*. Continuous to North America on 5975 and 9640 kHz; to Western Europe on 3955, 6195, 7120, 9410 and 12095 kHz; to East Asia on 15280, 15360 and 17815 kHz; and to the Pacific on 5975, 7150, 9640, 11955 and 15360 kHz.

Christian Science Monitor World Service, USA. Continuation of 0000 transmission to North America and Europe Tuesdays through Fridays on 9455 kHz, and Mondays through Fridays on 9870 and 13760 kHz.

Radio Korea, South Korea. *News*, followed by commentary. Then there's *Seoul Calling*—a magazine program of interviews, pop music and human interest segments—and *Let's Learn Korean*. The remainder of the broadcast offers a variety of one-day-a-week features, including *KBS Salon* (interviews with visitors to South Korea), *Sports Report* and *Inside North Korea*. Heard in Europe, but reception iffy in North America. One hour to North America on 6060 and 9570 kHz; and to East Asia on 7275 kHz.

Radio Habana Cuba. Repeat of the 0000 transmission. To Western North America winters on 9525 kHz; summers on 11835 kHz.

Radio Moscow. This is the World Service of Radio Moscow, rather than the North American Service. *News*, followed by *Focus on Asia and the Pacific*, then a special musical program for the last part of the hour. Tune around—it's on numerous channels that change periodically.

Voice of the Mediterranean, Malta. This relatively new station, reportedly with Libyan connections, starts off with *Thought for the Day*, then follows with

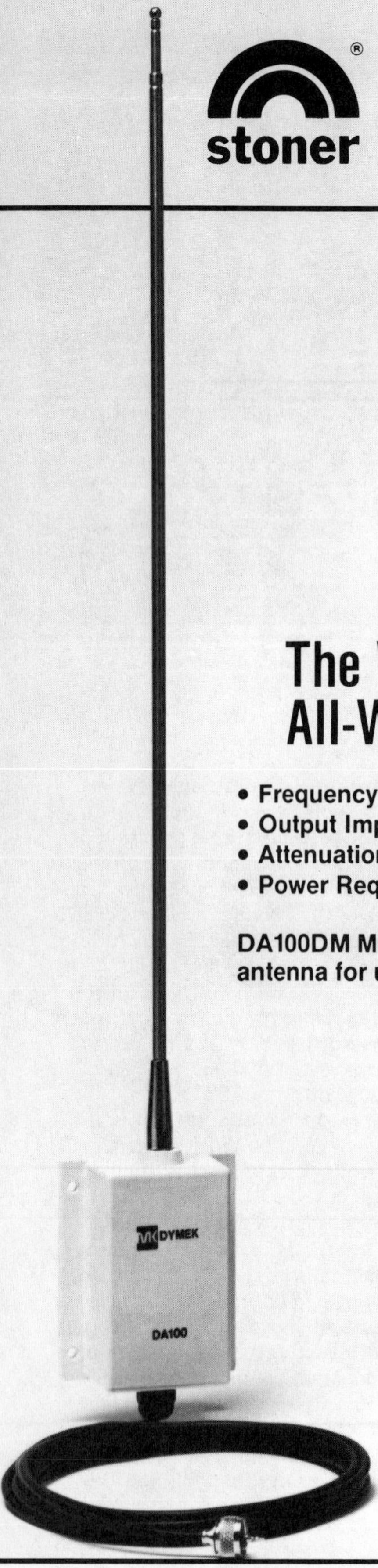
DYMEK
DA100

DYMEK DA100D
ATTENUATION
DC OFF AC

such features as *Discussion Program, Sugar and Spice*, or *Musical Tour*. Audible in Europe and North America on 9765 kHz.

KUSW, USA. Part of the evening-long broadcast to North America, but featuring at this time *Music and the Spoken Word*, which reportedly is the longest running continuous program in the U.S. Too, the Mormon Tabernacle choir sings classic songs, as well as religious favorites. Heard Sundays only on the winter frequency of 6175 kHz.

HCJB, Ecuador. Continues to North America on 6230, 9720, 9745 or 11775 kHz.

0630

BBC World Service for Africa. See 0330. Try 6005, 9515, 9600 or 11940 kHz.

Radio Finland International. Summers only at this time. See 0730 winter transmission for program details. Twenty-five minutes to Europe on 6120, 9560 and 11755 kHz.

Radio Sofia , Bulgaria. Summers only at this time. An abbreviated version of the 2300 broadcast, concentrating on *news* and commentary. To Europe on 9700 and 11720 kHz.

0645

Ghana Broadcasting Corporation. Designed for Ghanaian listeners, rather than foreigners, so reception is marginal—especially during the warm months. African music begins the program, followed by *news*. At 0730, more traditional African music is played. On 6130 kHz.

0700

BBC World Service. *News*, followed by the in-depth news program *Twenty-Four Hours*. Shows that are usually oriented to current events follow at 0730—an exception being the listener-correspondence show *Write On . . .* , hosted by Britain's popular sportscaster Paddy Feeny, on Thursdays. Continuous to North America on 9640 kHz summers, but winters on 5975 and 9640 kHz only until 0730. To Western Europe continuously on 7150, 9410, 12095 and 15070 kHz; to East Asia on 15280, 15360 and 17815 kHz; and to the Pacific on 7150, 9640, 11955 and 15360 kHz.

Christian Science Monitor World Service, USA. Continuation of transmission to North America and Europe Tuesdays through Fridays on 9455 kHz, and Mondays through Fridays on 9870 and 13760 kHz.

Radio Australia. *News*, then a variety of feature programs, including *You Asked for It* (answers to listeners' questions), *Window on Australia, Health Report* and *Communicator*, as well as interludes of popular music. Continuous on 9655 kHz (plus 11720 kHz from 0730), but try the 0800 transmission for even better reception. Underfunded operation—with a weak signal, to boot—but still great listening.

Voice of Free China, Taiwan. Repeat of the 0200 transmission. To North America on 5950 or 5985 kHz.

HCJB, Ecuador. Latin American *news*, followed by *Shalom*. Other programs include *World of Science, Call of the Andes, Kaleidoscope*, and *Guidelines for Family Living* at 0720. To Europe on 6210, 9610 or 9655 kHz; to the Pacific on 6130 and 9745 kHz.

0730

Radio Finland International. Winters only at this time. Finnish and Nordic *news*, followed by a press review. Monday through Friday there's "Northern Report." Feature programs include *Science Horizon, Backgrounder* and *Learning Finnish*. A half hour on 6120, 9560 and 11755 kHz.

Radio Sofia, Bulgaria. Winters only at this time. An abbreviated version of the 0000 broadcast, concentrating on *news* and commentary. To Europe on 9700 and 11720 kHz.

Radio Prague, Czechoslovakia. Mostly *news* and political commentary. To the Pacific—Australia and New Zealand—on 11685, 17840 and 21705 kHz.

BBC World Service for Africa. See 0330. Try 9600, 11860 or 15105 kHz.

0800

BBC World Service. *News*, generally followed by religious and entertainment features—except on Tuesday, when there's *Health Matters*, and Wednesday, when *Business Matters* is aired—both for a quarter hour at 0815. For night owls, this is heard, summers only, until 0815 in North America on 9640 kHz. Continuous to Western Europe on 7150, 9410, 12095 and 15070 kHz; to East Asia on 15280, 15360 and 17815 kHz; and to the Pacific on 7150, 9640, 11955 and 15360 kHz.

Christian Science Monitor World Service, USA. *News*, news analysis and news-related features, with emphasis on international developments. Excellent, if somewhat dry. Mondays through Fridays for two hours to North America on 9455 kHz, and to the Pacific on 17855 kHz.

KYOI, Saipan, Northern Marianas. Sometimes audible in North America and Europe. Part of the World Service network of Christian Science Monitor, with excellent *news*, plus good current and oldies light rock and pop. Religious programming is minimal. Two hours on 17780 kHz.

Radio Australia. Begins with *news* summary, followed by *International Report*—a current affairs program that looks at two or three major stories in detail. The second part focuses on sports results and popular music. Heard in North America continuously on 9580 kHz until shortly after local sunrise. Sometimes audible in Europe on 9655 kHz; heard well in East Asia on 17715 and 17750 kHz.

Radio Finland International. Summers only at this time; see 0730 for program details. To East Asia and the Pacific on 17795 and 21550 kHz.

0815

BBC World Service for Africa. See 0330. To 0845 on 11860 kHz.

0830

Radio Finland International. Summers only at this time; see 0730 for program details. To East Asia on 11855, 15245 or 17800 kHz.

0900

BBC World Service. *News*, news analysis, including *The World Today*, plus financial and sports news most days to 0945. These are usually succeeded by drama, music or a peek at life in Britain. Of these, for most listeners *Andy Kershaw's World of Music* on Mondays will be the pick of the litter. Continuous to Western Europe on 5975, 6045, 7325, 9410, 9750, 9760, 12095, 15070 and 17640 kHz; to East Asia on 15360 kHz, plus until 0945 on 15280 and 17815 kHz; and to the Pacific on 11750 and 15360 kHz.

Christian Science Monitor World Service, USA. Continuation of two-hour service Mondays through Fridays to North America on 9455 kHz, and to the Pacific on 17855 kHz.

Radio New Zealand International. Continuation of the relay of domestic service programs, usually concentrating on easy listening and classical music. Continuous during summers on 6100 and 9850 kHz—sign on is later winters. Difficult to receive well outside the Pacific region.

ABC, Brisbane, Australia. Service of the Australian Broadcasting Corporation, designed for listeners in Australia, but also heard in North America. Programming includes *news*, interviews and music. Continuous, but quite weak outside the Pacific region, on 4920 and 9660 kHz.

Radio Australia. Begins with international and Australian *news*, then music and one of several feature programs, including *Smith's weekly, Time B'Long Master* (about Papua New Guinea under Australian administration), or *Agrinews*. To North America on 9580 kHz; to East Asia on 15415 kHz.

Radio Finland International. Winters only at this time; see 0730 for program details. To East Asia and the Pacific on 11795 and 21550 kHz.

0930

Radio Finland International. Winters only at this time; see 0730 for program details. To East Asia on 11855, 15245 or 17800 kHz.

1000

BBC World Service. *News Summary*, followed by religion, "oldies," *Sports International, Jazz for the Asking*, entertainment personality profiles, classical musical analysis, Alistair Cooke's popular *Letter from America*, and *People and Politics* or other material on the British political scene. Continuous to Western

Konrad Kroszner

Ancient windmills continue to grace the Dutch countryside.

Europe on 5975, 6045, 7325, 9410, 9750, 9760, 12095, 15070 and 17640 kHz; and to East Asia and the Pacific on 15360 kHz.

Christian Science Monitor World Service, USA. *News*, news analysis and news-related features, with emphasis on international developments. Excellent, if somewhat dry, for four hours Mondays through Fridays to North America on 9495 kHz and two hours on 9455 kHz.

Radio Australia. *News*, followed by *International Report*—an in-depth news analysis that concentrates on the Asian and Pacific regions. This is succeeded by one of several feature programs, including *Pacific Sunrise, Australian Country Style, Try to Remember*, or *Interaction*. Heard well in North America on 9580 kHz; in East Asia on 15415 kHz.

Voice of Vietnam. Better heard in Europe than in North America. Begins with *news*, then political commentary and Vietnamese music. Omnidirectional on 9840 and 15010 kHz.

Swiss Radio International. For program details, see 0200, which is a repeat of this transmission. To East Asia and the Pacific on 9560, 13685 and 17670 kHz.

All India Radio. *News*, then interviews, subcontinental music, and such feature programs as *Hindi by Radio, DX Corner, Mailbag*, and *Panorama of Progress*. To the Pacific on 11860 and 15335 kHz; to East Asia on 11925 and 15155 kHz.

HCJB, Ecuador. *Happiness Is*, followed on the half-hour by such features as *Saludos Amigos, DX Party Line*, or *Música del Ecuador*. To the Pacific on 6130, 9745 and 11925 kHz.

Kol Israel. Summers only at this time. *News* from Israel Radio's domestic network, followed by various features: *Mainstream* (consumer and community affairs, Spectrum (science and technology), *With Me in the Studio* (guest interviews), *Israel Mosaic* (variety of topics), *Studio Three* (arts in Israel), and *Spotlight* (current events). A half hour to Europe—occasionally audible in Eastern North America—on 11585, 17578, 17590 and 21760 kHz. To Asia and the Pacific on 15650 or 17630 kHz.

Armed Forces Radio & Television Service, USA. National Public Radio's excellent newscast, *Morning Edition*, summers for two hours. See 1400 for frequency and other details.

1030

Radio Nederland. To the Caribbean on 6020 kHz; to the Pacific on 9675 kHz.

1100

BBC World Service. *News*, followed by *News About Britain*, then such feature programs as *Health Matters, Sportsworld, Meridian* and *The Ken Bruce Show*. Continuous to North America on 5965, 6195, 9515, 9740 or 11775 kHz; to Western Europe on 5975, 6045, 7325, 9410, 9750, 9760, 12095, 15070, 17640 and 25750 kHz; and to East Asia and the Pacific on 9740 kHz (except 1115-1130, see below).

Christian Science Monitor World Service, USA. Continues to North America Mondays through Fridays on 9455 and 9495 kHz.

Radio Australia. *News*, followed by music. At 1130, there is *Soundabout*, the latest in rock releases, except on Fridays and Sundays, when *International Top Hits airs*. To North America clearly on 9580 kHz; to East Asia on 11800 kHz.

An Ecuadorian corn vendor displays her grain.

Radio Moscow. *News*, then editorial commentary. This followed by such feature programs as the excellent *Folk Box, Music and Musicians, The Jazz Show*, or *Yours for the Asking*. Heard on a wide variety of frequencies.

Voice of Vietnam. Repeat of the 1000 transmission. To Asia on 7430 and 9730 kHz.

HCJB, Ecuador. Continues to the Pacific until 1130 on 11925 kHz.

Deutsche Welle, West Germany. Repeat of the 0900 transmission.

Radio Japan. To North America on 6120 kHz; to East Asia on 11815 or 11840 kHz.

Radio Beijing. Repeat of the 0000 transmission. To North America winters on 9665 kHz; summers on 17855 kHz.

Radio RSA, South Africa. *News*, followed by *South Africa*. To Europe on 21590 kHz.

Radio Pyongyang, North Korea. *News*, much of it devoted to the "great leader, Kim Il-Sung." This is followed by Korean patriotic music and such features as *Korea Today*. A plethora of political commentary throughout. To Asia on 7200, 7230 and 9540 kHz.

Kol Israel. Winters only at this time. *News* from Israel Radio's domestic network, followed by various features (see 1000). A half hour to Europe—sometimes heard in Eastern North America—on 11585, 15095, 17578, 17590, 21625 or 21760 kHz. To Asia and the Pacific on 15650 or 17630 kHz.

Armed Forces Radio & Television Service, USA. National Public Radio's excellent newscast, *Morning Edition*, at this time. See 1400 for frequency and other details.

1115

BBC World Service for Asia. The BBC World Service airs some special programs for and about Asia. Although beamed only to Asia, this service can sometimes be heard in other parts of the world—notably the Pacific and North America—as well. Until 1130, try 6195, 9740, 11750 and 15360 kHz.

1130

Radio Austria International. Summers only at this time; see 1230 for program details. To North America on 15450 kHz; to Europe on 6155 and 13730 kHz; and to East Asia on 13730 kHz.

Radio Berlin International, East Germany. Summers only at this time; see 1230 for program details. To Asia on 15440, 17880, 21465 and 21540 kHz.

1145

BBC World Service for Asia. See 1115. In Asia and North America, try 5995, 7180 or 15280 kHz.

Evening Prime Time— Asia and Western Australia 1200

BBC World Service. **Newsreel** (except Sundays), followed by *Multitrack, Brain of Britain, The Farming World, In a Nutshell* (explanation of various "isms") and other political analysis, *Novel Ideas* or drama. *Sports Roundup* follows at forty-five minutes past the hour. Continuous to North America on 5965, 6195, 9515, 9740 or 11775 kHz; to Western Europe on 5975,

6045, 7325, 9410, 9750, 9760, 12095, 15070, 17640 and 25750 kHz; and to East Asia and the Pacific on 9740 kHz.

Christian Science Monitor World Service, USA. *News*, news analysis and news-related features, with emphasis on international developments. Excellent, if somewhat dry. To North America for two hours Mondays through Fridays on 9455 and 9495 kHz.

Radio Canada International. Summers only at this time; see 1300 for program details. Mondays through Fridays to North and Central America on 9635, 11855 and 17820 kHz.

Radio Tashkent, Uzbek SSR. *News* and commentary, followed by such features as *Life in the Village, Youth Program, On the Asian Continent* and *Muslims of the Soviet East*. Heard better in Asia, the Pacific and Europe than in North America. Half hour on 9540, 9600, 9715, 11785 or 15460 kHz.

Radio Australia. *News*, then *International Report*. These are followed at the half hour by such features as *Interaction, Business Horizons*, and the excellent *International Country Music*. To North America on 9580 kHz; to East Asia on 9710 and 11800 kHz.

Kurt Kroszner

An enclosed courtyard provides a haven from the streets in Salzburg, Austria.

Radio Moscow. *News*, followed by *Update*—an in-depth analysis of news features. Heard on many frequencies.

HCJB, Ecuador. Starts with a half hour of *Sound Words*, followed at 1230 by *Happiness Is*. One hour on 11740 and 17890 kHz to North America, where reception is usually quite good.

Radio Beijing. *News* and various features—see 0000 for specifics. To North America winters on 9665 and 17710 kHz; and summers on 17855 kHz. To East Asia and the Pacific on 11600 and 11660 kHz.

Vatican Radio. Twenty-five minutes Mondays through Saturdays to Asia and the Pacific on 15190, 17685 or 21515 kHz. A daily transmission to Africa on 17840 and 21485 kHz carries different programming.

Radio Yugoslavia. Summers only at this time. *News*, followed by various features (see 2100). Forty-five minutes to Asia, the Pacific and Eastern North America on 17740, 21555 and 25795 kHz.

Armed Forces Radio & Television Service, USA. National Public Radio's excellent newscast, *Morning Edition*, winters. See 1400 for frequency and other details.

1215

Radio Cairo. To East Asia on 17595 kHz.

1230

Radio Austria International. Winters only at this time. Mondays through Fridays feature *Report from Austria*. On Saturdays, there's *Austrian Coffee Table*—which consists of light chat and different kinds of music, including classical, popular, jazz, or German and Austrian popular songs from the Twenties and Thirties. On Sundays, it's *Shortwave Panorama* for radio enthusiasts. One half hour Monday through Saturday, one hour on Sunday, to North America on 17870 kHz; to Europe on 6155 and 13730 kHz; and to East Asia on 15430 kHz.

Radio Berlin International, East Germany. Winters only at this time. *News*

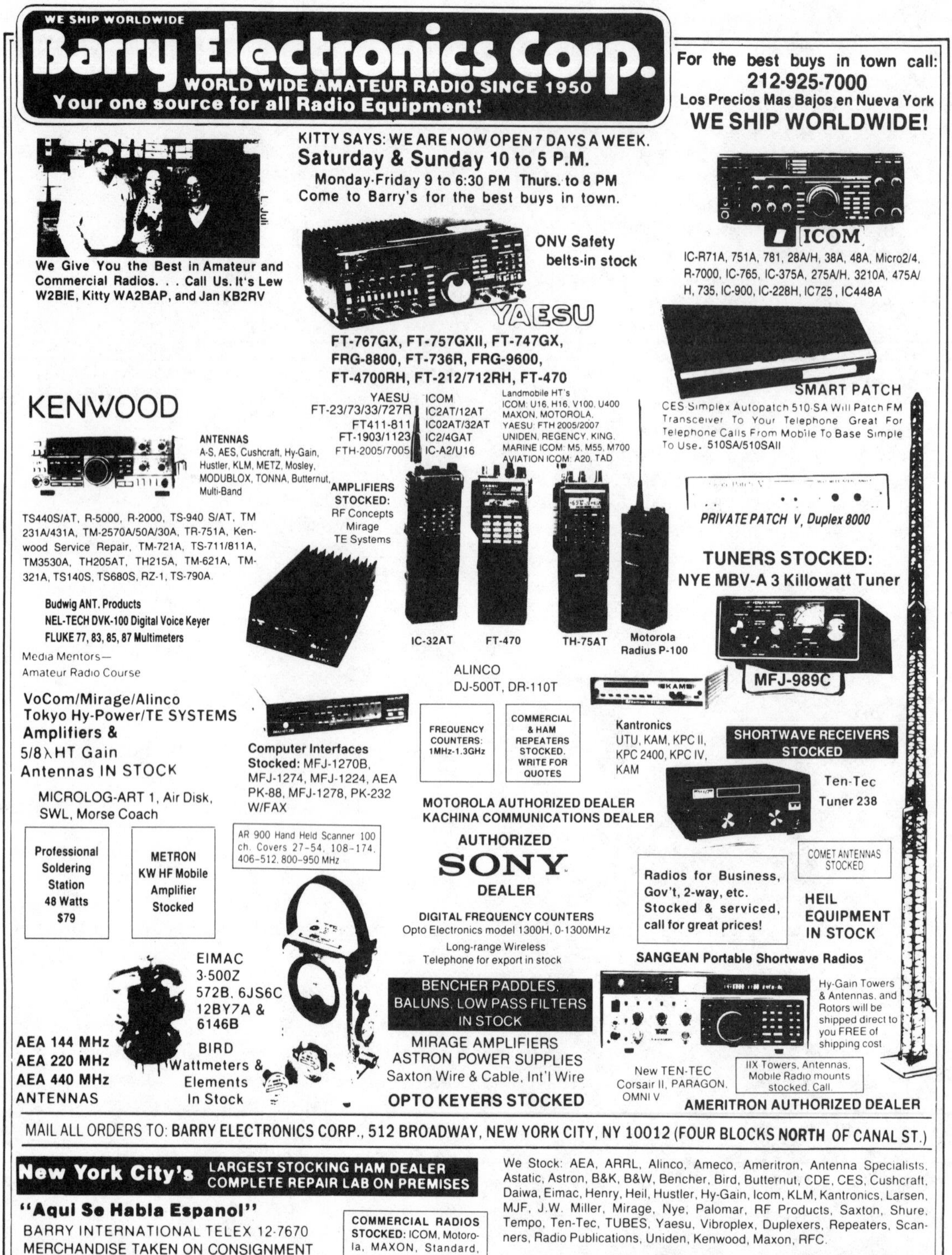
WE SHIP WORLDWIDE
Barry Electronics Corp.
WORLD WIDE AMATEUR RADIO SINCE 1950
Your one source for all Radio Equipment!
For the best buys in town call:
212-925-7000
Los Precios Mas Bajos en Nueva York
WE SHIP WORLDWIDE!
KITTY SAYS: WE ARE NOW OPEN 7 DAYS A WEEK.
Saturday & Sunday 10 to 5 P.M.
Monday-Friday 9 to 6:30 PM Thurs. to 8 PM
Come to Barry's for the best buys in town.
We Give You the Best in Amateur and Commercial Radios. . . Call Us. It's Lew W2BIE, Kitty WA2BAP, and Jan KB2RV
ONV Safety belts-in stock
YAESU
FT-767GX, FT-757GXII, FT-747GX, FRG-8800, FT-736R, FRG-9600, FT-4700RH, FT-212/712RH, FT-470
ICOM
IC-R71A, 751A, 781, 28A/H, 38A, 48A, Micro2/4, R-7000, IC-765, IC-375A, 275A/H, 3210A, 475A/H, 735, IC-900, IC-228H, IC725, IC448A
SMART PATCH
CES Simplex Autopatch 510-SA Will Patch FM Transceiver To Your Telephone Great For Telephone Calls From Mobile To Base Simple To Use. 510SA/510SAII
KENWOOD
ANTENNAS
A-S, AES, Cushcraft, Hy-Gain, Hustler, KLM, METZ, Mosley, MODUBLOX, TONNA, Butternut, Multi-Band
YAESU
FT-23/73/33/727R
FT411-811
FT-1903/1123
FTH-2005/7005
ICOM
IC2AT/12AT
IC02AT/32AT
IC2/4GAT
IC-A2/U16
Landmobile HT's
ICOM: U16, H16, V100, U400
MAXON, MOTOROLA,
YAESU: FTH 2005/2007
UNIDEN, REGENCY, KING,
MARINE ICOM: M5, M55, M700
AVIATION ICOM: A20, TAD
PRIVATE PATCH V, Duplex 8000
TS440S/AT, R-5000, R-2000, TS-940 S/AT, TM 231A/431A, TM-2570A/50A/30A, TR-751A, Kenwood Service Repair, TM-721A, TS-711/811A, TM3530A, TH205AT, TH215A, TM-621A, TM-321A, TS140S, TS680S, RZ-1, TS-790A.
AMPLIFIERS STOCKED:
RF Concepts
Mirage
TE Systems
TUNERS STOCKED:
NYE MBV-A 3 Killowatt Tuner
Budwig ANT. Products
NEL-TECH DVK-100 Digital Voice Keyer
FLUKE 77, 83, 85, 87 Multimeters
Media Mentors—
Amateur Radio Course
IC-32AT
FT-470
TH-75AT
Motorola Radius P-100
MFJ-989C
ALINCO
DJ-500T, DR-110T
VoCom/Mirage/Alinco
Tokyo Hy-Power/TE SYSTEMS
Amplifiers &
5/8λ HT Gain
Antennas IN STOCK
FREQUENCY COUNTERS: 1MHz-1.3GHz
COMMERCIAL & HAM REPEATERS STOCKED. WRITE FOR QUOTES
Kantronics
UTU, KAM, KPC II, KPC 2400, KPC IV, KAM
SHORTWAVE RECEIVERS STOCKED
Computer Interfaces Stocked: MFJ-1270B, MFJ-1274, MFJ-1224, AEA PK-88, MFJ-1278, PK-232 W/FAX
Ten-Tec
Tuner 238
MICROLOG-ART 1, Air Disk, SWL, Morse Coach
MOTOROLA AUTHORIZED DEALER
KACHINA COMMUNICATIONS DEALER
AR 900 Hand Held Scanner 100 ch. Covers 27-54, 108-174, 406-512, 800-950 MHz
AUTHORIZED
SONY
DEALER
COMET ANTENNAS STOCKED
Professional Soldering Station 48 Watts $79
METRON KW HF Mobile Amplifier Stocked
Radios for Business, Gov't, 2-way, etc. Stocked & serviced, call for great prices!
HEIL EQUIPMENT IN STOCK
DIGITAL FREQUENCY COUNTERS
Opto Electronics model 1300H, 0-1300MHz
Long-range Wireless Telephone for export in stock
SANGEAN Portable Shortwave Radios
EIMAC
3-500Z
572B, 6JS6C
12BY7A &
6146B
BENCHER PADDLES, BALUNS, LOW PASS FILTERS IN STOCK
Hy-Gain Towers & Antennas, and Rotors will be shipped direct to you FREE of shipping cost
AEA 144 MHz
AEA 220 MHz
AEA 440 MHz
ANTENNAS
BIRD
Wattmeters & Elements In Stock
MIRAGE AMPLIFIERS
ASTRON POWER SUPPLIES
Saxton Wire & Cable, Int'l Wire
New TEN-TEC Corsair II, PARAGON, OMNI V
IIX Towers, Antennas, Mobile Radio mounts stocked. Call.
OPTO KEYERS STOCKED
AMERITRON AUTHORIZED DEALER
MAIL ALL ORDERS TO: BARRY ELECTRONICS CORP., 512 BROADWAY, NEW YORK CITY, NY 10012 (FOUR BLOCKS NORTH OF CANAL ST.)
New York City's LARGEST STOCKING HAM DEALER COMPLETE REPAIR LAB ON PREMISES
"Aqui Se Habla Espanol"
BARRY INTERNATIONAL TELEX 12-7670
MERCHANDISE TAKEN ON CONSIGNMENT FOR TOP PRICES
Monday-Friday 9 A.M. to 6:30 P.M. Thursday to 8 P.M.
Saturday & Sunday 10 A.M. to 5 P.M. (Free Parking)
IRT/LEX-"Spring St. Station". Subways: BMT-"Prince St. Station". IND-"F" Train-Bwy Station"
Bus: Broadway #6 to Spring St. Path-9th St./6th Ave. Station.
COMMERCIAL RADIOS STOCKED: ICOM, Motorola, MAXON, Standard, Yaesu. We serve municipalities, businesses, Civil Defense, etc. Portables, mobiles, bases, repeaters...
ALL SALES FINAL
We Stock: AEA, ARRL, Alinco, Ameco, Ameritron, Antenna Specialists, Astatic, Astron, B&K, B&W, Bencher, Bird, Butternut, CDE, CES, Cushcraft, Daiwa, Eimac, Henry, Heil, Hustler, Hy-Gain, Icom, KLM, Kantronics, Larsen, MJF, J.W. Miller, Mirage, Nye, Palomar, RF Products, Saxton, Shure, Tempo, Ten-Tec, TUBES, Yaesu, Vibroplex, Duplexers, Repeaters, Scanners, Radio Publications, Uniden, Kenwood, Maxon, RFC.
WE NOW STOCK COMMERCIAL COMMUNICATIONS SYSTEMS
HAM DEALER INQUIRES INVITED PHONE IN YOUR ORDER & BE REIMBURSED
COMMERCIAL RADIOS stocked & serviced on premises.
Amateur Radio Courses Given On Our Premises, Call
Export Orders Shipped Immediately. TELEX 12-7670
FAX: 212-925-7001

and commentary, then specific untitled features, followed by the *Round About the GDR, GDR Report, Sports Round-Up* and *RBI DX Club*. Forty-five minutes to East Asia on 15445, 17880, 21465 and 21540 kHz.

Belgische Radio en Televisie, Belgium. Summers only at this time, Mondays through Saturdays. See 1330 for program details. Twenty-five minutes to North America on 17555 kHz; to Asia on 21815 kHz.

1245

Radio France Internationale. *News*, which gives in-depth coverage of French politics and international events. This is then usually followed by a short feature. A half hour to North America on 15365, 17720 and 21635 kHz; to Central America on 21645; and to Europe on 9805 and 11670 kHz.

Radio Berlin International, East Germany. Summers only at this time; see 1345 for program details. Repeat of the 1130 transmission. To Asia on 15440, 17880, 21465 and 21540 kHz.

Bruce Paton

Britain's influence continues to be strongly felt in Canada's maritime provinces.

1300

BBC World Service. *News*, then news analysis on *Twenty-Four Hours*. These are followed by a number of features, including *Network UK, Development*, or sports. Until 1330 (1345 weekends) to North America on 5965, 6195, 9515, 9740 or 11775 kHz. Continuous to Western Europe on 5975, 7325, 9410, 9750, 9760, 12095, 15070, 17640 and 25750 kHz; to East Asia on 5995, 7180 and 9740 kHz; and to the Pacific on 9740 kHz.

Christian Science Monitor World Service, USA. Continues to North America Mondays through Fridays on 9455 and 9495 kHz.

Radio Canada International. Winters only at this time. *North Country* opens with *news*, then interviews, human interest stories and current events. One hour Mondays through Fridays to North and Central America on 9635, 11855 and 17820 kHz.

Radio Moscow. Part of an earlier segment of the World Service beginning at 1200 and extending to 2200; for example, on 11840 kHz. *News*, followed by *Inside Report*, then a series of interviews and features designed to give a picture of life in the Soviet Union. Focus is on the effects of *perestroika* and the increased openness now underway in the USSR. One hour on a vast number of channels—simply tune around the 11, 15 or 17 MHz band segments for best reception. *Glasnost* has greatly improved this station.

Radio Pyongyang, North Korea. Repeat of the 1100 transmission. To Europe on 9325 and 9345 kHz; to the Americas on 9600 kHz; to East Asia on 11735 kHz.

Radio Yugoslavia. Winters only at this time. *News*, followed by various features (see 2100). Forty-five minutes to Asia, the Pacific and Eastern North America on 11735, 15325 and 15380 kHz.

Radio Australia. *News*, followed by *Window on Australia*—interviews with local correspondents around the country. At the half hour, there's *Sports Report*. To North America on 9580 kHz.

Radio Moscow. *News*, then *Inside Report*—an analysis of events in the USSR. On numerous frequencies audible worldwide.

Kurt Kroszner

Graceful arches line arcade off Rue Boucher in Brussels, Belgium.

HCJB, Ecuador. *Stories of Great Christians*, followed by *Our Daily Bread*, with *news* at twenty-five minutes past the hour. To North America on 11740 and 17890 kHz.

Radio Canada International. Summers only at this time; see 1400 for program details. To North and Central America weekends only on 11955 and 17820 kHz.

1330

United Arab Emirates Radio, Dubai. *News*, then a documentary feature which runs in a series from beginning to end. This often centers around traditional Arab fables, with titles that have included *Follow the Wind* (a history of music), *Arab Women and the Koran* and *Arabic Music*. A half hour to Europe on 15435, 17775 and 21605 kHz.

Belgische Radio en Televisie, Belgium. Winters only at this time, Mondays through Saturdays. *News*, press review, and such features as *Belgium Today, Europe, The Arts, Cooking* and *Musical Roundabout*. To North America on 17555 kHz; to Asia on 21815 kHz.

Radio Tashkent, Uzbek SSR. Repeat of the 1200 transmission. Heard in Asia, the Pacific, Europe and North America on 9540, 9600, 9715, 11785 and 15460 kHz.

Swiss Radio International. See 0400, which is a repeat of this transmission, for program details. To East Asia and the Pacific on 9620, 11695, 13635 and 15570 kHz.

1345

Radio Berlin International, East Germany. Winters only at this time. Repeat of the 1230 transmission. To Asia on 17880, 21465 and 21540 kHz.

1400

BBC World Service. *News Summary*, followed weekdays by *Outlook*. On the half hour, there's *Business Matters* or special *ad hoc* features, such as *Off the Shelf*. On weekends after the news summary, you can hear *Sportsworld* or *Anything Goes*. Continuous to Western North America on 9740 kHz; to Western Europe on 5975, 7325, 9410, 9750, 9760, 12095, 15070, 17640 and 25750 kHz; to East Asia on 5995, 7180 and 9740 kHz; and to the Pacific on 9740 kHz.

Christian Science Monitor World Service, USA. *News*, news analysis and

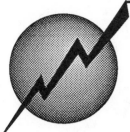

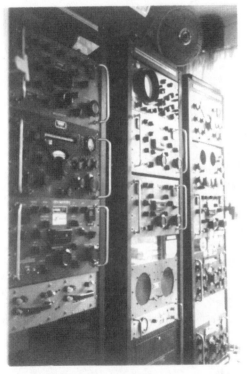

news-related features, with emphasis on international developments. Excellent, if somewhat dry, for two hours Mondays through Fridays to North America on 13760 and 17555 kHz, and to Europe on 21780 kHz.

Armed Forces Radio & Television Service, USA. From a small military transmitter in England, this 24-hour service is intended as a backup to a satellite that feeds U.S. Naval personnel in and around the Azores. Some days it's on, while others it is nowhere to be found. Too, it moves about from one frequency to another with abandon. If, after all this, you finally succeed in finding it, you need a radio that can process its signals, which are in the lower-sideband mode. The reward for your persistence and wise choice of a radio is a delightful mix of around-the-clock news, sports, finance, weather and commentary from all the U.S. radio networks—CBS, NBC, Mutual, ABC, NPR, USA Today . . . you name it, it's there. Without a single commercial. Especially notable is CBS' *World News Roundup* at 1430 summers. When this popular station is on the air, it's audible in Europe, the Americas and beyond on any one or two of the following frequencies: 9239.3, 9242.3, 9244.3, 13651.3, 16041.3 or 16454.3 kHz.

Radio Korea, South Korea. Repeat of the 0600 transmission, but to East Asia and North America on 9570, 9750 and 15575 kHz.

Radio France Internationale. A new transmission to Southeast Asia, this latest offering from Paris opens with *news*, then goes into various brief features, for a total of a half hour. On 21770 kHz.

Voice of the Mediterranean, Malta. See 0600 for program details. Heard in Europe on 11925 kHz.

Radio Moscow. Repeat of the 1100 broadcast. Audible on many frequencies.

Radio Australia. *News*, followed by *International Report* and, on the half hour, special feature programs. To North America on 9580 kHz.

HCJB, Ecuador. Begins with *Morning in the Mountains*, then *news* at 1425, followed by *Through the Bible* at 1430. To North America on 11740 and 17890 kHz.

Radio RSA, South Africa. *News*, then the *Woman's Page* and *Yours and Mine*—a musical request show spotlighting South African popular music. To North America on 17745 or 21670 kHz; to Europe on 21590 kHz.

Radio Canada International. Winters only at this time. *News*, followed by *Sunday Morning*—a program from the CBC domestic network. Sundays only to North and Central America on 11955 and 17820 kHz.

1500

BBC World Service. *Newsreel*, followed by sports, music or the arts. Continuous to Western North America on 9740 kHz; to North America weekends on 9515, 11775 or 15260 kHz; to Western Europe on 6195, 7325, 9410, 9760, 12095, 15070 and 17640 kHz; and to East Asia on 5995 and 7180 kHz. Also, until 1515, to the Pacific on 9740 kHz.

Christian Science Monitor World Service, USA. Continues Mondays through Fridays to North America on 13760 and 17555 kHz, and to Europe on 21780 kHz.

Afrique Numero Un, Gabon, West Africa. Commercially, rather than nationally, sponsored world band broadcaster. Although almost entirely in French, much air time is devoted to hi-life and jeje music—two enjoyable forms of African popular rhythms. For those who know French, and can afford it, the station frequently accepts telephone requests. To 1600 on 15200 or 17630 kHz, then to 2130 on 15475 kHz.

BBC World Service for Africa. See 0330. Try 11860, 15420, 17740, 21550 or 21660 kHz.

Radio RSA. *News*, followed by *Africa South*. To North America on 17745 or 21670 kHz; to Europe on 21590 kHz.

Radio Japan. *News* and various features. To North America winters on 5990 kHz, summers on 11865 kHz; to Europe on 21700 kHz; to East Asia on 11815 kHz.

HCJB, Ecuador. Continues to North America on 11740 and 17890 kHz.

1530

Belgische Radio en Televisie, Belgium. Summers only at this time, Mondays through Saturdays. Repeat of the 1230

South African Embassy

Tradition continues to be reflected in rural South Africa.

transmission, but on 17595 and 21810 kHz. Although beamed to Africa, these frequencies are often audible in Europe and Eastern North America.

Armed Forces Radio & Television Service, USA. Continuous news and sports news, with CBS' *World News Roundup* winters at 1430. See 1400 for frequency and other details.

1600

BBC World Service. *News*, followed by *News About Britain*. Feature programs that follow include sports, drama, science and examinations of topics. At 1645, on Sundays there's the popular *Letter from America*, and on weekdays at the same time you can hear a news analysis program, *The World Today*. Continuous to North America on 9515, 11775 or 15260 kHz; and to Western Europe on 6195, 7325, 9410, 12095 and 15070 kHz. Also, to East Asia until 1615 on 5995 and 7180 kHz.

Christian Science Monitor World Service, USA. *News,* news analysis and news-related features, with emphasis on international developments. Excellent, if somewhat dry. Six hours Mondays through Fridays to North America and Europe on 21640 kHz.

Radio France Internationale. The program formerly called *Paris Calling Africa*, is heard quite well in North America and Europe. Begins with world and African *news*, followed by feature programs, including the *Land of France, Turntable, Mailbag, Drumbeat* (African arts), *Spotlight on Africa* and, perhaps surprisingly, *Latin American Magazine*. One hour, audible in Europe and North America, on 6175, 15360, 17620 and 17795 kHz.

United Arab Emirates Radio, Dubai. Comparable to the 1330 transmission, but on 11790, 15320 and 15435 kHz.

Radio Portugal. *News* of Portugal, plus feature programs and Portuguese music. Mondays through Fridays to Asia on 15210 kHz.

Radio Korea, South Korea. *News* and features to Asia and beyond on 5975 and 9870 kHz.

Radio Moscow. Continues on many frequencies.

HCJB, Ecuador. Continues to North America until 1630 on 11740 and 17890 kHz.

Voice of America. *News*, followed by *Nightline Africa*—special news and features on African affairs. Heard beyond Africa, such as in Europe and North America, on many frequencies, including 15410, 15580, 17785, 17800 and 17870 kHz.

Armed Forces Radio & Television Service, USA. News, sports and features from American domestic radio networks. See 1400 for frequency and other details.

1615

BBC World Service for Africa. See 0330. Until 1730, you can try 9595, 11940, 15400 or 17880 kHz.

1630

Belgische Radio en Televisie, Belgium. Winters only at this time. Repeat of the 1330 transmission, but on 17595 and 21810 kHz. Beamed to Africa, but often audible in Europe and Eastern North America.

1700

BBC World Service. *News* and *Commentary*, followed by such features as *Book Choice, Just a Minute, Sportsworld* and *Sports Roundup*. Until 1745 to North America on 9515, 11775 or 15260 kHz. Continuous to Western Europe on 6195, 7325, 9410, 12095 and 15070 kHz.

Christian Science Monitor World Service, USA. Continues Mondays through Fridays to North America and Europe on 21640 kHz.

Radio Moscow. *News*, then such features as *Mailbag, Culture and the Arts, Science and Engineering, Round About the USSR* and *Jazz Show*. Around-the-clock on countless frequencies—dial around to find the best channel.

Voice of America. Produced for Africa. *News*, then *African Panorama*, interviews, current affairs, music and human interest features. Audible in many parts of the world on 15410, 15445, 15580, 15600, 17785, 17800 and 17870 kHz.

Radiobras, Brazil. For program details, see the 0200 broadcast, which is a repeat of this transmission. To Europe on 15230 kHz.

Radio Beijing. Similar to the 0000 transmission, but directed to Africa—and heard elsewhere—on 9570 and 11575 kHz.

KUSW, USA. Continues to North America on 15650 kHz.

Kol Israel. Summers only at this time. *News* from Israel Radio's domestic network. To Europe—sometimes audible in Eastern North America—for fifteen minutes on 11585 and 11655 kHz.

Radio Sweden International. *News*, followed by features; see 0230 for program details. To Europe on 6065 and 9615 kHz.

1730

Radio Prague, Czechoslovakia. *News*, Czech and Slovak folk music, plus a wide variety of political and cultural feature programs. To Asia and Africa, but audible in other parts of the world, on 9605, 11685, 11990, 13715 and 21505 kHz.

Radio Berlin International, East Germany. Summers only at this time. African-oriented *news* and feature programs on 9665, 13610, 15145 and 15340 kHz. Often audible in Europe and Eastern North America.

Exotic flowers are offered at market in Ecuador.

Radio Bucharest, Romania. *News*, features and Romanian folk music to Europe on 7105 and 9690 kHz.

Evening Prime Time–Europe 1800

BBC World Service. *Newsdesk* for a half hour, followed most days by pop and classical music, plus the arts. Continuous to Western Europe on 6195, 7325, 9410, 12095 and 15070 kHz; and to the Pacific on 11750 kHz.

Christian Science Monitor World Service, USA. Continues Mondays through Fridays to North America and Europe on 21640 kHz.

Radio Canada International. Targeted to Africa, but heard quite well in North America. *News*, weather and sports—as well as *Spectrum*. Expands to an hour on weekends, and includes *Canada Rocks* and *Spotlight on Science*. Half hour weekdays, one hour weekends on 13680, 15260 and 17820 kHz.

Radio Kiev, Ukrainian SSR. Summers only at this time; see 1900 for program details. To Europe on 7330, 9560, 9600 and 11780 kHz.

Radio Kuwait. Popular and rock music, plus such occasional features as *The Study of the Mosque* and *Kuwait, Our Beloved Homeland*. Heard in Europe and Eastern North America for three hours on 11665 kHz.

Radio Prague, Czechoslovakia. *News*, followed by folk music, and on Sundays by *Christian Comment from Czechoslovakia*. A half hour to Europe on 5930 and 7345 kHz.

Voice of America. *News*, followed by *Focus* on weekdays, *Encounters* on Sundays, and *American Viewpoints* on Saturdays. The second half hour is devoted to news and features in "special English"—that is, simplified talk in the American language for those whose mother tongue is other than English. To Europe on 6040, 9760, 11760 and 15205 kHz; to Africa, but often heard elsewhere, on 15410, 15580, 17785 and 17800 kHz.

Radio Moscow. Repeat of the 0800 transmission. On many frequencies.

Radio Jordan. *News* from an Arab perspective, followed by vintage pop music, interrupted occasionally by a radio drama. Heard in Europe and Eastern North America on 9560 kHz, with 13655 kHz as an alternative.

West German Embassy

Cologne Cathedral, the city's symbol, dates from the 12th century.

Kol Israel. Winters only at this time. *News* from Israel Radio's domestic network. To Europe—sometimes audible in Eastern North America—for fifteen minutes on 7405, 9455, 9930 or 11585 kHz.

Radio RSA, South Africa. *News* and commentary, followed on weekdays by *Africa South*. Weekends bring an interesting variety of features, including *Saturday RSA, Conversation Corner, Touring RSA*, and the nature show *Our Wild Heritage*. To Europe on 17795, 21535 or 21590 kHz.

Radio Korea, South Korea. *News*, followed by features; see 0600 for program details. To Europe—sometimes also heard in North America—on 15575 kHz.

KUSW, USA. Continues to North America on 15650 kHz.

Armed Forces Radio & Television Service,, USA. Around the clock with news, sports and features from the various American domestic radio networks. See 1400 for details.

1830

Radio Yugoslavia. Summers only at this time. *News*, followed by various features (see 2100). Forty-five minutes for Europe on 7215, 9660 and 11735 kHz.

BBC World Service for Africa. See 0330. Wherever you are in the world, try 6005, 9630, 15400 or 17880/17885 kHz.

1900

BBC World Service. Begins on weekdays with the *news*, followed by *Outlook, Financial News*, and such feature programs as *Network UK* and *How It All Began*. Continuous to Western Europe on 6195, 7325, 9410, 12095 and 15070 kHz; and to the Pacific on 11750 kHz.

Christian Science Monitor World Service, USA. Continues Mondays through Fridays to North America and Europe on 21640 kHz.

Radio Algiers, Algeria. *News*, then rock and popular music. Also some occasional brief features, such as *Algiers in a Week*, which covers the main events in Algeria during the past week. One hour of so-so reception on 9509, 9640, 9685, 15215 and 17745 kHz.

Radio Kiev, Ukrainian SSR. Winters only at this time. *News*, followed by commentary. Monday through Friday, features *The Ukraine Today*, a show about Ukrainian life. On Saturday, the feature after commentary is *The Dialogue*, a listener contact program, and on Sundays it's *Music From the Ukraine* and *The Stamp Collector*. The high point of any broadcast from Kiev is the beautiful Ukrainian choral music that's often played. A half hour to Europe on 6010, 6090, 6165 and 7115 kHz.

Kol Israel. Summers only at this time. *News*, followed by various features (see 0000). A half hour to Europe—often audible in Eastern North America—on 11605, 13750, 15640 and 17590 kHz.

Radio Prague, Czechoslovakia. *News*, delightful Czech and Slovak folk

South African Embassy

Grain basket in Ndebele village is to hold the harvest.

music, and a variety of features—see 0100 for more program details. Fifty-five minutes to Europe on 5930 and 7345 kHz.

HCJB, Ecuador. The first evening transmission for Europe. This evangelical station, operated by American missionaries, broadcasts Latin American *news*, often followed by *Passport*, which includes music and special features on Ecuador and the world at large. On 15270 and 17790 kHz.

Deutsche Welle, West Germany. This African-oriented transmissions includes *Newsline Cologne* and *African News*, along with such features as *Man and Environment* and Living in Germany. To West Africa, but heard elsewhere, on 11785, 11810, 13790 and 15390 kHz.

Radio Japan. Mainly *news* and commentary, with a four-minute music slot just before the end of the transmission. To North America—Western North America, as a practical matter—on 5990, 9505 or 11865 kHz. To the Pacific on 9640, 11850 or 15270 kHz.

Radio Portugal. Summers only at this time, Mondays through Fridays. *News* about Portugal, plus features and beautiful Portuguese music. To Europe on 11740 kHz.

Spanish National Radio. *News*, followed by features and Spanish music; see 0000 for program details. To Europe on 9765, 11790 or 15280 kHz.

Radio Kuwait. Continues being heard in Europe and Eastern North America on 11665 kHz.

Radio Jordan. Continues being heard in Europe and Eastern North America on either 9560 or 13655 kHz.

Radio Moscow. Continues on a wide variety of frequencies.

Voice of America. *News*, followed by *African Panorama*. The *Sound of Soul*, with entertaining host George Collinet, airs on the half hour. To Europe on 6040, 9760, 11760 and 15205 kHz; to Africa, but often heard elsewhere, on 15410, 15580, 17785 and 17800 kHz.

1920

Voice of Greece. Comparable to the 0130 English transmission, but to Europe on 7430, 9395, 9425 or 11645 kHz.

1930

Voice of the Islamic Republic of Iran. One full hour of *news*, religion and commentary. To Europe on 9022 kHz.

Radio Yugoslavia. Winters only at this time. *News*, followed by various features (see 2100). Forty-five minutes to Europe on 5980, 9620 and 9660 kHz.

2000

BBC World Service. *News*, followed by news analysis weekdays on *The World Today*. Saturdays, there's *From Our Own Correspondent*, and Sundays you can hear *Worldbrief*. There are then various features, such as *Meridian, Brain of Britain, Words of Faith, The Vintage Chart Show, Science in Action* and *Assignment*. Continuous to most of Eastern North America on 5975 and 15260 kHz; to Western Europe on 3955, 6195, 7325, 9410, 12095 and 15070 kHz; to East Asia on 5965, 7180, 11715 or 15140 kHz; and to the Pacific on 9570, 11750 and 15140 kHz.

Christian Science Monitor World Service, USA. Continues Mondays through Fridays to North America and Europe on 21640 kHz, plus the additional frequency of 17555 kHz.

Radio Damascus, Syria. Actually starts at 2005. *News*, followed by lots of Syrian music and a daily press review, then a different feature for each day of the week. These include *Portrait from Our Country, Around the World in a Week* and *Syria in a Week*. Most of the transmission, however, airs Syrian and some Western popular music. One hour to Europe, often also audible in Eastern North America, on 12085, 15095 or 17710 kHz.

Radio Baghdad, Iraq. Summers only at this time. See 2100 for program details. To Europe, often also audible in Eastern North America, on 13660 kHz.

Radio Pyongyang, North Korea. Repeat of the 1100 transmission. To Europe and beyond on 6576, 9345, 9640 and 9977 kHz.

Radio Portugal. *News* about Portugal, followed by Portuguese music and various features; see 0230 for details. To Europe Mondays through Fridays for a half hour on 11740 kHz.

Kol Israel. Winters only at this time. *News*, followed by various features (see 0000). A half hour to Europe—often also audible in Eastern North America—on 7355, 7462, 9435, 9855 or 11605 kHz.

Voice of America. Continues to Europe on 6040, 9760, 11760 and 15205 kHz; to Africa, but often heard elsewhere, on 15410, 15580, 17785 and 17800 kHz.

Radio Moscow. Continuous on many frequencies audible in Europe, North America and elsewhere.

Radio Jordan. Continues to be audible in Europe and Eastern North America on 9560 or 13655 kHz.

Radio Kuwait. Continues to be audible in Europe and Eastern North America on 11665 kHz.

2045

All India Radio. Indian music, regional and international *news*, and interviews on

Doranne Jacobson, United Nations

Young Rajastani folk dancers entertain in Jaipur, India.

current events. Continuous, with fairly good reception in Europe, but mediocre in North America. To 2230 on 7412, 9910 and 11620 kHz.

2100

BBC World Service. *News*, then *Sports Roundup*. These are followed by various features, including *Europe's World, Sports International, Business Matters, The Pleasure's Yours, Megamix* and *Recording of the Week*. Continuous to most of Eastern North America on 15260 kHz, plus (except 2115–2130 weekdays, see below) on 5975 kHz; to Western Europe on 3955, 6195, 7325, 9410 and 12095 kHz; to East Asia summers on 11750 and 15140 kHz, plus winters until 2115 on 5965 and 7180 kHz; and to the Pacific on 9570, 11750 and 15140 kHz.

Christian Science Monitor World Service, USA. Continues Mondays through Fridays to North America and Europe on 17555 and 21640 kHz.

Radio Yugoslavia. Summers only at this time. *News*, followed by well-prepared accounts of events in Eastern Europe, and features on East-West relations—all interspersed by pleasant Yugoslav popular and folk music. This station provides the least-biased information from Eastern Europe, and may be heard for forty-five minutes in Europe and Eastern North America on 5980, 7130, 9620 and 9660. However, for mid-summer these change to 7215, 9660, 11735 and 15105 kHz.

Radio Baghdad, Iraq. *News*, then a generous helping of Iraqi music, and a press review just prior to the second hour of transmission. A few brief features, including *Guests in Baghdad* and *The Song of Today*, with some *ad hoc* interviews and current events. Two hours to Europe—sometimes also heard in Eastern North America—winters on 7295 or 9770 kHz; summers on 13660 kHz.

Radio Canada International. Summers only at this time. See 1800 for program details, but this transmission includes *SWL Digest* on Saturdays. To Western Europe—also well-heard in North America—at 2100–2130 weekdays, 2100–2200 weekends, on 15325 and 17875 kHz.

Fishing is a major industry at Terrence Bay, Nova Scotia.

Radio Sweden International. Repeat of the 1700 transmission, but directed to Europe and West Africa on 6065, 9655 or 11705 kHz.

Belgische Radio en Televisie, Belgium. Summers only at this time. Similar to the 1330 transmission, but twenty-five minutes daily to Europe on 5910 and to Eastern North America on 9925 kHz.

Radio Beijing. *News*, then various feature programs; see 0000 for details. To Europe winters on 9710 and 6860 kHz, summers on 9820 and 11500 kHz.

Deutsche Welle, West Germany. *News*, followed by such features as *Morning Magazine, Science and Technology, Asia in the German Press*, and *Mailbag Asia*. To Asia and the Pacific winters on 7130, 9650, 9765 and 11785 kHz; summers on 9670, 9765, 11785 and 15435 kHz.

Radio Moscow. Continuous to most parts of the world on numerous frequencies.

Radio Japan. Repeat of the 1900 transmission. A half hour to Europe on 11800 kHz; to East Asia winters on 6025 kHz, summers on 9695 kHz; to the Pacific winters on 9640 and 11850 kHz, summers on 15270 and 17890 kHz.

Radio Bucharest, Romania. *News*, followed by various features and delightful folk music. To Europe on 9690, 9750 or 11940 kHz.

Swiss Radio International. For program details, see 0400, which is a repeat of this transmission. To Africa, but audible in much of the rest of the world, on 9885, 13635, and either 15525 or 15570 kHz.

KUSW, USA. Continuous to North America on 15650 kHz.

Radio Jordan. Heard continuously in Europe and Eastern North America on either 9560 or 13655 kHz.

Voice of America. *News*, followed on weekdays by *World Report* and on Sundays by *New Horizons* and *Issues in the News*. On Saturdays the hour also features *Weekend Magazine*. To Europe on 6040, 9760, 11760 and 15205 kHz; to Africa, but often heard elsewhere, on 15410, 15580, 17785 and 17800 kHz.

All India Radio. Continues to Europe on 7412, 9910 and 11620 kHz. In Eastern

North America, try 11620 kHz.

BBC World Service for Africa. See 0330. Regardless of where you are located, try tuning to 15400 kHz.

2115

BBC World Service for the Caribbean. Only just inaugurated in 1988, the BBC World Service for the Caribbean airs *Caribbean Report* to the Caribbean basin. Fortunately, it is often clearly heard throughout much of North America, as well. This brief soup-to-nuts show provides experienced, British-oriented coverage of Caribbean economic and political affairs which, except for East-West clashes, otherwise tend to be given short shrift by the international media. Too, there's the all-important news of sports, including cricket, for which Barbadian and other island players are justifiably renowned. Mondays through Fridays only on 5975 kHz.

2200

BBC World Service. *Newshour*, inaugurated late in 1988, is simply the finest newscast to be found anywhere on the airwaves—radio, TV or tom-tom. Aired only once each day at this relatively awkward time—early for North America, Asia and the Pacific; late for Europe—*Newshour* is nonetheless a "must." To Eastern North America on 5975, 6175, 9915 and 15260 kHz; to Western Europe on 3955, 6195, 7325, 9410 and 12095 kHz; to East Asia on 11955 kHz; and to the Pacific on 9570, 11955 and 15140 kHz.

Christian Science Monitor World Service, USA. *News*, news analysis and news-related features, with emphasis on international developments. Excellent, if somewhat dry. Two hours Mondays through Fridays to North America 9465 and 17555 kHz.

Radio Yugoslavia. Winters only at this time. *News,* followed by features (see 2100). Forty-five minutes heard in Europe and Eastern North America on 5980, 7130, 9620 and 9660 kHz.

Radio Australia. Best heard in Asia, the Pacific and —mainly in the warm months—the West Coast of North America. *News summary*, followed by such features as *Australian Country Style* and popular music. Roughly continuous on 15160, 15240, 15320 and 17795 kHz.

Voice of Free China, Taiwan. See 0200. For Western Europe, but on 9852.5, 9955, 11805, 15345 or 17612.5 kHz.

Voice of Turkey. Summers only at this time. See 2300 for program details. To North America on 9445 kHz; to Europe on 9685 kHz; to East Asia on 17760 kHz.

Radio Vilnius, Lithuanian SSR. Summers only at this time. See 2300 for program details. To Europe and Eastern North America on 6100, 7400, 11790, 13645 and 15455 kHz.

Belgische Radio en Televisie, Belgium. Winters only at this time. Similar to 1330 transmission, but daily for twenty-five minutes to Europe on 5910 and to Eastern North America on 9925 kHz.

Radio Canada International. Winters only at this time. See 1800 for program details, but this transmission includes *SWL Digest* on Saturdays. To Western Europe—also well-heard in North America—weekdays at 2200-2230, weekends at 2200-2300, on 9760 and 11945 kHz.

Radio Moscow. Continuous to many parts of the world on numerous frequencies.

Radio Prague, Czechoslovakia. *News* and folk music for 15 minutes to Europe on 6055 kHz.

KUSW, USA. Continuous to North America on 15650 kHz.

Voice of United Arab Emirates, Abu Dhabi. Begins with *Readings from the Holy Koran*, in which verses are chanted in Arabic, then translated into English. Then there is a documentary series, such as *Palestine Under the Muslims*. The last half hour is a relay of Capital Radio in Abu Dhabi, complete with rock music and local contests. To Eastern North America and Europe winters on 6170, 9595 and 11965 kHz; summers on 9595, 11985 and 13605 kHz.

KVOH, USA. *News*, then *Good News for Today* (scriptures). The remainder of the broadcast is devoted to such programs and religious commentary as *Marilyn Hickey* and *Today With Derek Prince*. World news and *Good News for Today* are repeated on the half hour, and there is also a sports news program at

United Nations

Worshippers praying inside the Badhshahi Mosque in Lahore, Pakistan.

twenty-five minutes after the hour. To North and Central America on 17775 kHz.

Radio Baghdad, Iraq. Winters only at this time; see 2100 for program details. To Europe, and sometimes also audible in Eastern North America, on 7295 or 9770 kHz.

2230

Radio Mediterranean, Malta. *News*, then such features as *Welcome to Malta, Industrial and Economic Report*, and *Great Personalities*. The second half hour consists of popular music. One hour to Europe—sometimes also audible in Eastern North America—on 6110 kHz.

2300

BBC World Service. *News*, followed by *Commentary*. These are succeeded by a variety of features, including *Multitrack, Write On, The Farming World* and *From the Weeklies*, plus programs on drama, books, music and the other arts. However, the main treat at this time is Alistair Cooke's *Letter from America*, heard Sundays at 2315. Continuous to North America on 5975, 6175, 9590, 9915 and 15260 kHz; to East Asia on 11945, 11955 and 17875 kHz; and to the Pacific on 9570 kHz.

Voice of Turkey. (2200 summer) *News*, Turkish music, along with features that tend to be on the dry side. To Eastern North America on 9445 kHz; to Europe on 7250 kHz; to East Asia on 9680 kHz.

Radio Vilnius, Lithuanian SSR. Winters only at this time. *News*, followed by such features as *The Way We Live, Musical Panorama, Youth Club, Letterbox, Lithuanian by Radio* and some very pleasant Lithuanian music. A half hour to Europe and Eastern North America on 6100, 7165, 7400, 13645, 15180 and 15455 kHz.

Radio Japan. *News*, commentary, and such features as Cross Currents, Asia Now, Business and Science, and *This Week*. One hour to Europe on 11800 kHz; to East Asia on 15195 kHz.

Radio Pyongyang, North Korea. See 1100 for program details.

Radio Moscow. The North American service begins with world and national *news*, followed by *Outlook* (editorial com-

Netherlands Embassy

Dutch girls promenade in the traditional Marken costume.

mentary). The remainder of the broadcast is devoted to any of numerous features, such as the standard *Home in the USSR, Science and Engineering*, and *Daily Talk*. On numerous frequencies—dial about for the clearest channel.

Radio Sofia, Bulgaria. Summers only at this time; see 0000 for program details. One hour on 9700, 11660, 11720 or 15330 kHz.

KVOH, USA. *News*, then *Good News for Today*, followed by special features and a sports roundup. To North and Central America on 17705 kHz.

Voice of the United Arab Emirates, Abu Dhabi. The first half hour is a review of articles and editorials from the Arab press. The closing half hour is devoted to such features as *Those Who Embrace Islam*. This second hour heard in Eastern North America and Europe is aired winters on 6170, 9595 and 11965 kHz; summers on 9595, 11985 and 13605 kHz.

Kol Israel. Summers only at this time. *News*, followed by various features (see 0000). A half hour beamed to Eastern North America and Europe on 11605, 15615 and 15640 kHz.

2305

Radio Polonia, Poland. *News* and commentary, followed by a variety of feature programs, including *Focus*, *Panorama*, and *Postbag*. To Europe and North America on 5995, 6175, 7125 and 7270 kHz, but hard to hear in North America.

2330

Belgische Radio en Televisie, Belgium. Summers only at this time. *Brussels Calling* begins with the *news*, followed by press reviews and *Belgium Today*—a feature on an item of national interest. Other features are on economics, Third World development efforts, arts, and listeners' questions. To Eastern North America for twenty-five minutes on 9925 kHz.

Radio Canada International. Summers only at this time; see 0030 for program details. To Eastern North America on 5960, 9755 and 11905 kHz.

Radio Kiev, Ukrainian SSR. Summers only at this time. Similar to the 1900 transmission, but to North America on 7400, 11790, 13645, 15180 and 15455 kHz.

Radio Tirana, Albania. See 0230 and 0330 for program details. To Eastern North America on 9500 or 9760 kHz.

Radio Korea, South Korea. See 0600 for program details. To Eastern North America for one hour on 15575 kHz.

Radio Budapest, Hungary. This time Mondays through Saturdays, summers only. See 0030 for program details. To Eastern North America on 6110, 9585, 9835, 11910 and 15160 kHz.

Prepared by Alex Batman and the staff of Passport to World Band Radio.

ITU SUSPENDS WORLD BAND EXPANSION

by Lawrence Magne

In 1979, after years of planning and negotiation, the governing body for radio worldwide, the International Telecommunication Union (ITU), met and agreed to expand those portions of the high frequency radio spectrum commonly known as the shortwave broadcasting bands, or world band radio. This was met with joy by listeners and broadcasters, alike. At last, this popular communications medium would be relieved from much of the overcrowding that has made reception, at times, downright unpleasant.

In fact, arguably the primary accomplishment of that 1979 ITU conference was to acknowledge what had been—and still is—taking place all along. For years, international broadcasters, frustrated in their attempts to provide signals of acceptable quality to their listening audiences, have been operating outside the radio "neighborhoods" set aside for them by the ITU. This *out-of-band* broadcasting is legal, provided certain procedures—as once specified under ITU Regulation No. 115 and associated Regulations, and now under Regulation No. 342—are followed. Chief among these is that a new out-of-band frequency can generate no harmful interference to a *bona fide* primary (non-broadcasting) user.

However, in addition to providing for expanded shortwave broadcasting spectrum space, the 1979 ITU Conference also mandated that a planning procedure for the use of world band channels be drawn up and approved.

Here is the rub. As of 1989, no such procedure had been agreed upon. So, at a meeting in Nice, France, in the summer of 1989, the ITU simply pulled the plug—at least for now—by resolving that the 1979 expansions not be used for high frequency broadcasting.

What does all this mean for world band listeners?

On one hand, not much. The expansions that were supposed to have taken place in 1989 and beyond have, to a large extent, already become *faits accompli* (see box). Something like sixty countries already broadcast legally out of band, and they're hardly likely to relinquish their hard-won turf.

However, while sixty countries is a lot, there are numerous others that are not operating out-of-band. Many of these may never do so.

For listeners, this is a real drawback, as it means that only some countries—usually economically advanced—will be heard clearly. Others will have to tough it out inside the overcrowded *de jure* shortwave broadcasting allocations.

Some broadcasters in advanced countries may be hurt, as well. For example, Radio Canada International, facing a possible budget cutback, is now fighting for its economic life. RCI, like many other international broadcasters, is prohibited by its national radio regulatory body—*not* the ITU—from operating out-of-band except between 13600–13800 kHz. So RCI can't really exploit this option to allow it to reach more listeners for the same cost of transmission, or the same number of listeners with a lower-cost transmission schedule.

> Out-of-band broadcasting is, by default, increasingly becoming "the rule of the road."

Finally, it suggests that out-of-band broadcasting is, by default, increasingly becoming "the rule of the road." This is well within the pale of ITU regulations. However, it also serves to diminish interest in a truly workable structure that would allow for virtually all international broadcasting to take place successfully within portions of the radio spectrum set aside exclusively for that purpose.

Lawrence Magne is Editor-in-Chief of Passport to World Band Radio.

The World Band Spectrum: How It Looks Now

(5.8–22 MHz only)

Existing ITU Allocations (kHz)	WARC-79 Allocations (kHz)	Actual Usage (kHz)
5950–6200	5950–6200	5850–6250
7100–7300	7100–7300	7100–7600
9500–9775	9500–9900	9300–9995
11700–11975	11650–12050	11500–12100
—None—	13600–13800	13600–13800
15100–15450	15100–15600	15005–15700
17700–17900	17550–17900	17550–17900
21450–21750	21450–21850	21450–21850

WHO ELSE IS LISTENING?

There's an upsurge in world band listening in the United States. This we know, but it's rather like seeing the tracks of an elephant, but not the elephant itself. We know something is going on, but haven't been able to see the beast itself clearly.

Who else is listening? At last, we seem to have the outline of an answer.

Unfortunately, even though statistics cover nearly every iota of human activity, world band radio has traditionally been shrouded in mystery. Advertisers, who care passionately about their listening audiences, are a rarity on world band radio. This reduces the incentive to undertake Arbitron and similar types of audience measurements.

Instead, government officials rule the roost. Some care a great deal about how they are faring with their audiences. But in some cases, international broadcasters' lack of interest in their audiences is so extreme that they will not supply schedule details to listeners—or even the news media. Only a few years ago, one station functionary went so far as to refuse to give out a program schedule because "it might fall into the hands of the communists."

Give us this day our daily bread, for with or without listeners we'll still be fed.

Aggravating this indifference is the international nature of shortwave coverage. It's one thing for CBS to study its U.S. audience; quite another for Radio Pakistan to study its listenership in thirty different countries.

There are exceptions, of course. A scattering of broadcasters and academics have made noble attempts to determine the audience size in the United States, and perhaps somewhere there is buried a quiet study of the Canadian listening audience. But these surveys suffer from flaws, most of which result from meager funding. Consequently, none can be depended upon to give dependable information on the size of the total North American listening audience—much less who listens to what stations, when, and for what reasons.

At International Broadcasting Services, where our research funding is about 1% of the size of the mosquito eradication budget of Pinellas County, Florida, we haven't undertaken any lofty studies to ascertain how many Americans are huddled evenings around their world band radios.

What we have done, though, is to undertake some uncomplicated research into the motives and demographics of the *Passport* readership. We now know, for example, that *Passport* readers are overwhelmingly male, non-black and non-immigrants. It also appears that people seem to acquire an interest in world band radio after they have reached forty—due, one supposes, either to the wisdom of maturity or to the foolishness of middle age.

Newcomers tell us that are attracted to world band radio not so much because they are electronics buffs as they are by what the programs have to offer. Additionally, what listeners like most about world band radio is that it gives a fresh perspective. Other attractions cited include program content and the large number of available stations.

The favorite type of program? News—no surprise here—with music being a distant second. A miscellany of politics, weather, sports and regional information brings up the rear.

> The favorite type of program? News, with music being a distant second.

Favorite station? The BBC World Service, succeeded by Radio Moscow, Radio Canada International, Radio Australia and the Deutsche Welle. These are followed by Radio Habana Cuba, Radio Luxembourg, Radio France Internationale, Kol Israel, Radio Austria International, the Voice of Free China and the Voice of America.

Interestingly, while in the world of private broadcasting audience popularity is a key measure of success, among the five top world band broadcasters three are facing fiscal pressures. Two—the BBC World Service and Radio Australia—have had to cope with significant budget cutbacks, while a third—Radio Canada International—may yet have its plug pulled in 1990 by its own government. It's hard not to conclude that at least some governments do not fully appreciate the effectiveness of their own stations.

One unexpected finding is that turnover—the dropout rate—among newcomers is minuscule. Squeaks, squawks, propaganda and all—people who try world band radio seem to stick with it . . . at least those who read *Passport*. Perhaps those who buy *Passport to World Band Radio* are already predisposed to a long-term relationship with world band radio. Or possibly they remain as world band listeners because *Passport* gives them the radio-buying and schedule information necessary to enjoy world band fully. We just don't know yet.

So, while cheap and quick polling techniques do tell us something about the characteristics of existing listeners, they don't really answer the big questions: How many people are listening, who are they, and why do they listen? Perhaps more importantly, why are those who don't listen not listening?

We tried a different tack—receiver sales. The U.S. government reportedly only keeps track of "multiband" devices—a catchall rubric which lumps together world band and umpteen other categories, including scanners.

Receiver manufacturers aren't of much help, either. Many keep their sales figures under wraps, and there are no statistics prepared by the industry as a whole, such as the Electronic Industries Association. Indeed, it's been over a dozen years since a manufacturer had a survey firm make a study of the world band market in the U.S. (One finding: The highest degree of interest in world band listening in the U.S. in 1977 was among Polish-Americans.)

In principle, with some study and adjustments, valid receiver sales could lead to the Promised Land of certain accurate audience statistics. At the very least, we would have some idea of the order of magnitude of the audience as a whole.

So, at IBS we have been reaching into our mosquito-swatting budget to try to nail down receiver sales for 1988 in the U.S. Here's what we've found, based largely on actual sales figures, by place of *manufacture*:

• Japan & Europe—quality world band portables and tabletops, branded.	145,000–195,000
• Japan—oem multiband portables with shortwave.	Unknown
• Hong Kong—quality world band portables, branded and oem.	20,000–30,000
• Hong Kong—low-cost oem multiband portables with shortwave (usually made by subcontractors in the People's Republic of China).	544,000
• People's Republic of China—low-cost world band portables, branded.	2,000
• Taiwan—quality world band portables, branded and oem.	30,000–45,000
• Taiwan—low-cost oem portables.	Unknown
• Malaysia, Singapore and South Korea.	Unknown

Annual unit sales increases for quality models has been between 20-25% for the past couple of years, whereas sales of low-cost multiband portables, while vacillating from year-to-year, have been relatively stable or growing slightly overall. While the reasons for this are complex and not entirely clear, it appears that the demand for cheap multiband sets is motivated at least as much by factors other than the wish to listen to world band broadcasts. These non-world band markets, such as citizens band, have been on the decline for some time, now. World band, on the other hand, has been on the rise.

Our own casual research suggests something else: that turnover among those using quality radios is quite low, whereas turnover among those attempting to hear world band broadcasts on multiband portables appears to be quite high. This is hardly surprising. Low-cost, low-technology multiband portables sound so awful and are so clumsy to tune that, as one listener put it, "there's no point in my wasting my time with this."

Thus, the relative shift away from multibands to quality sets suggests that world band listening is acquiring a more stable base of listeners.

Getting back to the original premise concerning the size of the U.S. listening audience, extrapolating these incomplete receiver sales figures into audience figures is simply not possible without knowing a great deal more concerning several variables— the average listening cycle of each receiver, to name but one.

So, who else is listening? Precise figures continue to elude us. Nevertheless, it would be surprising, given the level of receiver sales, if the total number of world band listeners in the U.S. were less than a million, or more than three million. That is, very roughly 1%—maybe 2%—of the adult population.

Prepared by Jock Elliott and Lawrence Magne.

GETTING STARTED

(*continued from page 13*)

RF (or IF) Gain control. In practice, this control performs no useful function for world band listening. However, if set improperly, it can make your radio seem unresponsive, or even "dead." So, leave it at, or even taped permanently to, the maximum setting—*high* or *DX*. With Grundig Satellit series receivers, leave the setting at *AGC*.

Tuning in Stations

Now that you know what the main buttons and switches are for, it's time to put them to work. Let's try tuning in an easily heard station.

If you're in North America and it's daytime, turn to the listing for 15000 kHz in the Blue Pages in the back of this edition of *Passport*. You'll see that stations WWV in Colorado and WWVH in Hawaii both operate there. These are run by the US National Bureau of Standards and transmit the precise official time and a station identification once each minute. Since they are easily heard throughout North America, they're good stations to try for first.

If you're in Europe, try instead the BBC on 9410 or 12095 kHz; in Asia or the Pacific the BBC on 15360 kHz is a good bet. The Blue Pages show the times when these are on.

Before doing any tuning, turn the BFO or SSB control to off, set the sensitivity to high, and choose the wide bandwidth position. If there is an RF gain control, set it to the maximum setting. Fully extend the telescopic antenna of your radio, if it has one, or attach an antenna wire to the antenna terminals. If you're in a metal-framed building, such as a high-rise or a mobile home, try placing your radio near a window, as metal tends to keep out radio waves before they reach your antenna.

Ready to go?

1. **Turn your radio on.** (A few travel portables require two switches to be turned on so as to keep the radio from coming on accidentally in transit.)
2. **Turn the tuning knob, or punch in 1-5-0-0-0 on the keypad, to tune in 15000 kHz.** (On some sets a band selector or "AM" button may have to be used first.)
3. **Adjust volume to the desired level.** On WWV or WWVH, you will hear a time tick each second. On the BBC, you will hear English-language programming.

That's it! In most cases, operating a world band radio requires only these three straightforward steps.

Now that you know how to use your world band radio, try tuning in some other stations. You might want to take a crack at some of the easiest-to-hear stations, or perhaps a few of the ten best programs for 1990. Both are described elsewhere in this edition of *Passport*.

World Time Prevents Confusion

You'll notice that the operating times of various stations are given, both in *Passport* and over the air, in World Time—a 24-hour clock system which is also known as *UTC*, *GMT* or *"Zulu."* To convert World Time to your local time, subtract five hours if you're in the Eastern North American time zone, six hours in the Central, seven hours in the Mountain and eight hours in the Pacific. Subtract one hour less if daylight saving time is in effect.

In Continental Western Europe, add one hour—two hours summer. In the UK, World Time is the same as local time except during the summer, when you add one hour. In Japan add nine hours year around, and in Western Australia add eight.

For example, suppose you're in Ohio and it's January—that is, five hours behind World Time. You want to hear the BBC news scheduled for 1300 World Time. You would listen for it at 8:00 am Eastern time.

By the way, World Time also applies to the date. If a BBC drama program is scheduled for 0215 World Time Sunday, in Ohio you would listen at 9:15 pm *Saturday*.

Reception Varies with Time of Day and Season

As you use your radio, you'll soon notice that reception on different world band frequencies varies with the time of day.

The 5950 to 6200 kHz range is loaded with stations at night, but you'll hear very little there at your local noon. By contrast, you can hear plenty of stations at noon in the 15100 to 15600 kHz range, but few at your local midnight.

Too, signals are often strongest during your local prime-time evening hours. This is because stations try to beam their signals so they are audible when most people are at home to listen.

Nevertheless, there is still a wealth of choices during the day, even though signals tend to be weaker. This means that for the most fruitful daytime results a better-than-average radio can be a real plus.

There are some notable exceptions, though. For example, in much of North America the best time to hear Radio Australia is not in the evening, when its signals are weak and noisy. Rather, it's in the early hours of the morning—on 9580 kHz.

As a very general rule of thumb, reception is choicest below 10000 kHz during the evening and at night, best above 15000 kHz during the day and early evening, with the 10000 to 15000 kHz range having mixed characteristics. There are specific tips on this under "World Band Spectrum" within the glossary in the back of this book.

Add to this the schedule information in *Passport*, plus a little experience, and soon you will know exactly which frequencies and times are best for the stations you want to hear.

Because world band radio uses the earth's own "natural satellite"—the *ionosphere*—there is a tendency for what can be heard to vary, like the weather, not only daily, but also seasonally. This means that at certain times of the year you can listen to smaller, weaker stations that you otherwise might not be able to hear.

For example, frequencies beginning with threes, fours, fives, sixes and sevens are at their most vigorous during or near the hours of darkness in winter. That's why winter is the best time for North Americans and Europeans to try for stations in Latin America and Africa, as

most of these are found in the "low ranges" below 8 MHz.

Spring and fall, on the other hand, are usually the best times to try for exceptionally distant signals that traverse the Equator, such as from New Guinea to New York. Summertime evenings are especially good for long-distance reception above 15000 kHz.

Most broadcasters maintain pretty much the same frequency usage year-around. However, some—especially the largest—tailor their schedules to be different during the summer from what they are during the winter. These seasonal schedules are indicated in *Passport* by a "J" ("June") for" summer and a "D" ("December") for winter. All other schedules are adhered to year-around, so don't have either a (J) or (D).

Another way in which world band stations differ from local stations is that any number of broadcasters—even a dozen or more—may make use of a given channel. Fortunately, you usually hear only one station at a time, but sometimes an unwanted station will make listening less pleasant by penetrating through from underneath to bother the station you're trying to hear.

While listening to specific stations and programs is interesting, be sure not to miss out on the fun of using *Passport's* Blue Pages to tune around to see what you can hear. While most major stations are heard pretty regularly, there are at least as many that come in only every now and then. Too, new stations come on the air, and old ones change frequencies and schedules. This dynamism is a real part of the allure of world band listening.

Communication doesn't have to be one-way, as is evidenced by the listener-participation programs detailed in "Ten of the Best Shows for 1990," found elsewhere in this book. Should you wish to write some of the stations that broadcast shows you particularly like—or dislike—by all means do so. If it's an official government station, simply address your letter to the capital of the station's home country—no street, postal code or other local details are necessary. Some will provide you with their latest program schedules, calendars, souvenirs and information on their country. Most especially, nearly all are eager to hear what you have to say about their programs.

Harry Helms is Senior Editor at Academic Press, Harcourt Brace Jovanovich, Inc. His most recent radio guide, the Shortwave Listening Handbook, *is published by Prentice Hall.*

TEN OF THE BEST
(*continued from page 19*)

Netherlands and elsewhere. It included a wonderful segment with a synthesizer composer who came up with a novel Latin American pop song right there on the air. Another extended feature, *The Australian Connection*, focused on the Netherlands' relations with Australia over the 200 years of European settlement on that continent.

Each episode is fairly long—no trendy "bites" here. They are thoroughly researched, and include informative interviews with people who are experts on the night's topic. It's probably the best documentary series on world band radio, and the format allows for a welcomed flexibility in the topics covered.

In North America, tune in Thursdays (Wednesday nights your local time) at 0050 World Time on 6020, 6165 or 15315 kHz; with a repeat at 0350 on 6165 or 9590 kHz. In Europe, it's heard Thursdays at 1150 on 5955 or 9715 kHz; repeated at 1450 on 5955 kHz. In Australia and New Zealand, try it at 0750 on 9630 or 9715, with a repeat at 1050 on 9675 kHz. In East Asia, best bets are at 0850 on 17575 or 21485 kHz; 1150 on 17575, 21480 or 21615 kHz; and 1450 on 13770, 15150, 17575 or 17605 kHz.

Short Story
BBC World Service

Andy Warhol used to say that every person is a star for fifteen minutes in his life. *Short Story* affirms this in a very special and constructive way.

This is because almost all the drama aired on *Short Story* is created not by professional playwrights or authors, but by ordinary listeners to the BBC World Service. It's the sort of thing that could come off as an exercise in mediocrity, but instead achieves the opposite. By opening the doors to literally a world of potential artistic talent, *Short Story* brings a wealth of fresh talent to the public eye. And you, the listener, are right there for the debut.

Appropriate to Warhol's notion, the time limit for these radio premieres is but fifteen minutes, so the scripts are brief—around 2,000 words—and are tightly constructed. Most of the stories usually have some sort of novel twist . . . like the one about the gent who was driving in a snowstorm and found a live body in a hearse parked alongside the road.

Each story is entertaining and is impeccably read by BBC pros. If you're impressed enough with the program—and your own literary talents—you might try your hand at composing a script for the airwaves. Remember, though: Competition is keen. At the BBC, they usually select only the very best.

Andy Warhol used to say that every person is a star for fifteen minutes. Short Story affirms this in a very special way.

In North America, you can hear *Short Story* Tuesdays (Monday nights your local time) at 0130 World Time on 5975, 6175, 9590, 9915, 12095 or 15260 kHz; with a repeat Fridays (Thursday nights your local time) at 0430 on 5975, 9510 and 9915 kHz. In Europe, best bets are Sundays at 0945, with a repeat Mondays at 1945, on 9410, 12095 or 15070 kHz.

In East Asia and the Pacific, try Sundays at 0945 World Time on 9740, 11750, 15360 or 17830 kHz; with repeats Mondays at 1945 on 7275, 9570 or 11750 kHz, Tuesdays at 0130 on 11955 kHz, and Fridays at 0430 on 5975, 15280 and 17815 kHz.

Cross Currents
Radio Japan

Innovation: It's alive and well on *Cross Currents*—Asian radio's answer to the "Letters to the Editor" page.

Here's how it works. Once each month the program solicits letters on a topic—say, "Preparing for Old Age," or "The World's Population Reaching Five Billion"—from its listeners throughout the world. The idea works because so many well-written letters are received.

Each topic lasts for one full month. The first week's responses come mainly from listeners in Japan, since the mail time is so short. But subsequent weeks feature letters from listeners from all over: Asia, South America, North America, Africa, Australia and New Zealand.

As with the BBC's *Short Story*, it's the unleashed talent of the world's lay writers that makes the program sparkle. Although not necessarily experts on the subject at hand, *Cross Current's* contributors obviously give the topic serious thought and respond in ways that reflect their own personal and national perspectives.

In North America, catch *Cross Currents* Tuesdays (Monday nights your local time) at 0320 World Time (0120 summer) on 5960 kHz. In Europe, tune in Mondays at 0720 on 15325 or 21500 kHz. In the Pacific, try 0520 Mondays on 15270 kHz.

Letter from America
BBC World Service

If Britain is every American's spiritual motherland, then Alistair Cooke is every American's spiritual uncle. Like a kindly latter-day de Tocqueville, he patiently explains the grand and foolish aspects of America not just to non-Americans—nearly everybody else does this—but also, without peer, to Americans themselves.

> If Britain is every American's spiritual motherland, then Alistair Cooke is every American's spiritual uncle. The show is Cooke at his best.

So, for those who have cherished Alistair Cooke's learned introductions to *Masterpiece Theater* and countless other video plums, here's something very special. Each week on *Letter from America*, the veteran BBC correspondent and scholar "writes home," publicly, about the latest goings-on in America. Topics include politics, social trends, the arts, and just about anything else, blended into a wonderful melange. The show is Cooke at his best: fifteen minutes, *a cappella*, that seem to pass like five.

Letter From America is both erudite and entertaining, and one could hardly find a more mellifluous voice for radio than that of Alistair Cooke. If any program—news aside—is a "must" on world band radio, this is it.

In North America, tune in Sundays (Saturday nights your local time) at 0545 World Time on 5975 or 9640 kHz; with repeats Sundays at 1645 on 11775, 15260 or 25750 kHz, and again at 2315 on 5975, 6175, 9590, 9915, 12095 or 15260 kHz. In Europe, try Saturdays at 1015, with repeats Sundays at 0545 and 1615, on 9410, 12095 or 15070 kHz. In East Asia and the Pacific, the best bet is at 1015 on 9740, 11750, 15360 or 17830 kHz.

The Best In Brazilian Popular Music
Radiobras

There are any number of good music programs on world band radio. But *The Best In Brazilian Music* plays some of the most beautiful and melodic music on radio. It is smooth and mellow, yet spiced with light-hearted Latin rhythms. While some songs are contemporary, many go back to popular goodies from the post-World War II era. These vintage recordings represent the transition in Brazilian popular music from the sambas of the Forties to the contemporary beat of the Eighties and emerging Nineties.

Not all songs are sambas, of course. There are romantic ballads, jazz—even rock and roll, Brazilian style.

The program airs right after the news, then continues until nearly the half hour. After some talk, the music resumes until sign-off at ten minutes to the hour. The program not only includes the wonderful music itself, but also brief, encapsulated information about the composers and performers. You're not likely to come across the likes of this anywhere else!

It's best heard in North America at 0210 World Time on 11745 kHz. In Europe, give it a try at 1810 on 15265 kHz.

The Grapevine
Swiss Radio International

This may be the best mailbag program on world band radio, and it's a pity that it hasn't been given more air time. As it stands now, the program is broadcast only fortnightly, every other Monday. Something this good deserves to be on at least once a week.

In general, *The Grapevine* does what a typical mailbag program is supposed to

Few hosts get along better on the air than do Paul Sufrin and Robert Brooks. They can be heard on Swiss Radio International's delightful show, *The Grapevine*.

do—answers listeners' questions about life in Switzerland: What is the Swiss railway system like? How do the Swiss go about sport fishing? The hosts, Rob Brookes, a Brit, and Paul Sufrin, a Canadian, also respond to listeners' requests for Swiss folk music.

What makes the show so special is the banter between Brookes and Sufrin: It is full of atrocious puns and similar verbal wit. And it flows with aplomb. Brookes and Sufrin have that natural, easy rapport that so many programs with dual hosts try to create, but rarely succeed at. In Brookes and Sufrin's case, the congeniality never seems forced, but comes naturally—as if two old pals had gotten together to have a ball leafing through listeners' letters. And they do.

Brookes and Sufrin are not the only funny part of the show. Sometimes listeners' mail, including long comic poems or satires of popular song lyrics, can be almost as good as the banter between Brookes and Sufrin itself.

The spirit is contagious. If you have a good joke that you want read on the air, send it to *The Grapevine*. If it's good, it probably has a better chance of being read and appreciated there than anywhere else.

In North America, this program is best heard alternate Mondays (Sunday nights your local time) at 0210 and 0410 World Time on 6135, 9885 and 12035 kHz. In Europe, it's on at 0740, 1310 and 1840 on 6165 and 9535 kHz.

In East Asia and the Pacific, try 0840 and 1010 on 9560, 13685 and 21695 kHz; and at 1110 on 13635, 15570 and 17830 kHz.

The Week In Review
Kol Israel

News and current events have always been a mainstay of world band radio, and practically no area of our tired planet gets quite so much coverage as the Middle East.

Unfortunately, the collective outcome of all these news reports is to oversimplify the Middle Eastern conflict into one between "the Arabs" *versus* "the Israelis."

Kol Israel's *The Week In Review* helps dispel such notions.

The Week in Review, aired Sundays, looks at the major stories in the Israeli press over the past week, often excerpting from editorial commentary as well as news writeups. From this extensive overview of the Israeli press, listeners receive a clearer notion of just how diverse public opinion is in a country that's so tiny, you can drive from one end of it to the other in an hour. Whether the subject be the *intifada*, relations with Israel's allies, or moss growing on the Western Wall, opinions almost always vary.

> Its highest achievement is that it helps us understand why solutions that might seem obvious to those who only watch The Evening News haven't been cheerfully adopted.

The Week in Review makes for more than interesting listening. Its highest achievement is that it helps us understand why solutions that might seem obvious to those who only watch The Evening News haven't been cheerfully adopted by the Israelis long ago.

The Week In Review is well heard in Eastern North America Mondays (Sunday nights your local time) at 0100 World Time on 9435, 11605, 15615 and 15640 kHz. For Europe, as well as Eastern North America, it's found Sundays at 2240 on most of those same channels. In summer, it's heard one hour earlier.

Prepared by Alex Batman and the staff of Passport to World Band Radio.

BBC: FRONT LINE DISPATCHES

(*continued from page 25*)

However, listeners to the World Service were electrified by the BBC's warning to British subjects to flee the country. Obviously, something important was going on.

While international news is the BBC's staple, there are specialized newscasts, as well. Three times daily, you can hear about goings-on in the United Kingdom on *News about Britain*. Twice a day, there's also a survey of editorial opinion from the British press on *British Press Review*. If you're into political debate, there's *People and Politics*, that covers British Parliamentary affairs, and which includes juicy excerpts from speeches in the House of Commons.

> World leaders call affairs of state to a halt to absorb the BBC news.

Talking From . . . offers profiles from Northern Ireland, Scotland, and Wales. One *Talking From . . .* show featured an audio tour of a manufacturing plant in the Midlands, complete with machinery pounding in the background. In another, listeners were taken on a visit to the Isle of Lewis, in the Hebrides off the rocky coast of Scotland. The show revealed how Harris tweed has been painstakingly hand-loomed for generations by island craftsmen.

Programs like these provide a regional counterpoint to the world news. They also remind us that the BBC is, after all, British. Other world band broadcasters, even when they try to imitate the BBC World Service, tend to be so oriented to international diplomatic concerns that they rarely include much in the way of regional programming in their broadcast mix.

John Tusa, Managing Director of BBC World Service, explains why this broader approach is taken. "The ambition of the Service," he points out, "is to reflect the whole of life and to offer this mirror to the whole world."

Through a tradition of integrity and excellence, the BBC World Service comes very near, indeed, to achieving those goals. In so doing, it sets the standard by which all others are measured.

WGBH, Boston

Alistair Cooke's weekly "Letter from America" is one of the finest programs to be heard.

What's ahead? The BBC, for years thought of as an institution in the loftiest sense of the term, has made clear that it isn't about to rest on its laurels. "When you are regarded as an institution," the head of the World Service points out, "you are already halfway downhill." Already, the news operation has been expanded, enlivened and freed from vestiges of its imperial past.

> If even the enemy believes you, then you must be doing something very worthwhile.

This tampering with a sacred formula for success has disturbed more than a few traditionalists, but the result has been a healthy mandate for change and vigor. And there's more to come in the months ahead.

Jock Elliott is Contributing Editor to Passport to World Band Radio.

When the News Is Over . . .

For listeners to the World Service in English, there is more to the BBC than just newscasts. From *Andy Kershaw's World of Music* to *Words of Faith,* the BBC covers nearly the entire range of possibilities in radio broadcasting. Although the letters *BBC* are not an ironclad guarantee of excellence, most non-news shows are among the best that the English language has to offer. Some plums:

• Numerous musical presentations, including country, rock, jazz, folk and classical styles—along with the eclectic request show *Anything Goes.*

• Two programs on books: *Good Books,* in which a celebrity recommends a favorite book; and *Book Choice,* which consists of short reviews of recent publications.

• *Meridian*, which covers the full range of the arts.

• Three sports programs: *Sports International, Sports Roundup* and *Sportsworld.* Taken together, these encompass a broad variety of athletic activities, including soccer, cricket and motorcycle racing.

• *Health Matters,* for the latest developments in medicine and ways to stay fit and well.

• *Business Matters* and *Financial News*—"musts" for the latest on worldwide commercial and financial activities.

• *Letter from America,* Alistair Cooke's incomparable analysis of the goings-on at the west side of "The Pond."

• *Farming World*, with "how-to"information and news of technological developments in agriculture.

• Science and nature programs (see box in "What's On Tonight?" in this book).

• Heads-up quiz shows, including *Brain of Britain, Quote . . . Unquote, My Word!* and *My Music.*

Finally, the BBC World Service capitalizes on radio as the "theater of the mind," with dramatized short stories and plays. Two recent productions featured Sir John Gielgud in *The Tempest,* and Dame Peggy Ashcroft and Sir Anthony Quayle in *The Lovers of Viorne.* This is world-class drama—the good stuff—available at no cost and without commercials.

In addition to its excellent programming, the World Service also sets a standard of excellence with its program guide, *London Calling.* This monthly magazine gives complete details on programs, schedules and frequencies of the BBC World Service. As a bonus, it also includes lively and informative articles. You can obtain a free copy and subscription form by writing to *BBC London Calling* at:

PO Box 76, Bush House Strand, London WC2B 4PH United Kingdom	or	630 Fifth Avenue New York, NY 10020 USA

J.E.

Will Gould, NOAA

Powerful Hurricane Gilbert is tracked by NOAA's satellite network.

EAVESDROPPING ON DISASTER

(*continued from page 30*)

Following the Challenger space shuttle disaster, the best available information about the ongoing rescue came from shortwave radio listeners who tuned in and heard hundreds of ships and aircraft participating in a large search for the debris of the Challenger and its crew. In fact, the search for the debris lasted several weeks, and the whole operation could be followed via shortwave radio frequencies—even when NASA was trying to keep details of the tragedy under wraps.

Natural disasters can also be heard on shortwave radio. Mother Nature sometimes can provide her own brand of problems for mankind in the form of hurricanes, floods, and earthquakes. The best place to follow these events is on the amateur radio ("ham") frequencies. Usually in major disasters of these kinds, communications are the first things to go. When this happens, often the only way to get information into, or out of, the affected area is via amateur radio.

During the rampage of Hurricane Gilbert throughout the Caribbean in 1988, amateur radio operators provided the first reports from the island nation of Jamaica. I monitored this eyewitness report of the storm's fury, sent from a ham operator on the western coast:

> ". . . people were crawling on their hands and knees trying to get inside . . . some people were just carried away by the wind and sea and disappeared . . . cars were strewn around . . . these little sailboats on the beach were driven into cars like spears . . . ".

Shortly after Gilbert left the Cayman Islands, I received the following report from an amateur radio operator on those islands:

> ". . . all citizens on Little Cayman, Grand Cayman and Cayman Beach have been accounted for . . . there are no

here has been considerable . . ."

any major disaster, her normal means of ...tion, as well as electrical ...er, will fail. Amateur radio operators prepare for these sorts of disasters, and offer their assistance to local and federal governments free of charge. They send emergency information to friends and relatives around the world, plus they handle official traffic for governmental agencies. The ham frequencies are the place to go when a major disaster strikes, and many world band radios can receive these.

In fact, some of the more unusual rescues I've heard have been on the ham bands. During the American military invasion of the island of Grenada, an amateur radio operator was in the school where American students on the island resided. These were the same American students the U.S. military was trying to rescue. The operator was providing the State Department, via radio, eyewitness accounts of the fighting between American troops and Cuban soldiers.

As this fellow was transmitting, gunfire could be heard in the background. The clatter of helicopters carrying the American troops also vibrated the loudspeaker. The radio operator continued through it all, transmitting his reports to the Department of State in Washington, D.C.—and to sharp-eared listeners throughout the rest of the listening world.

Electricity had been cut, so the amateur radio station was operating on batteries. As day sank into night at my listening post, I could still hear this tireless ham on the air, providing invaluable feedback.

As the night progressed, his battery weakened. By around midnight, I could no longer hear his communications.

I never found out what happened to our bold amateur radio reporter. But this was a day I shall not forget—a day spent in my easy chair, in my radio room, sharing firsthand in the stuff of history.

Larry Van Horn is an electronics and computer specialist with the U.S. Navy.

Passport's Guide to Selected Rescue Frequencies

500 kHz	International Distress and Calling Frequency (Morse Code)
2141 kHz	U.S. Coast Guard Air Rescue Operations Channel (USB)
2182 kHz	International Distress and Calling Frequency (USB)
2261 kHz	U.S. Coast Guard Air Rescue Operations Channel (USB)
3023 kHz	Calling/Distress/Safety Frequency (USB)
3123 kHz	U.S. Coast Guard Air Rescue Operations Channel (USB)
4125 kHz	Calling Supplemental Worldwide Distress and Calling Frequency (USB)
5680 kHz	Calling/Distress/Safety Frequency (USB)
5692 kHz	U.S. Coast Guard Air Rescue Ops Channel—Helicopters (USB)
5696 kHz	U.S. Coast Guard Air Rescue Operations Channel (USB)
8980 kHz	U.S. Coast Guard Air Rescue Ops Channel—Helicopters (USB)
8984 kHz	U.S. Coast Guard Air Rescue Operations Channel (USB)
11195 kHz	U.S. Coast Guard Air Rescue Operations Channel (USB)
11198 kHz	U.S. Coast Guard Air Rescue Ops Channel—Helicopters (USB)
11201 kHz	U.S. Coast Guard Air Rescue Operations Channel (USB)
15081 kHz	U.S. Coast Guard Air Rescue Operations Channel (USB)
15084 kHz	U.S. Coast Guard Air Rescue Ops Channel—Helicopters (USB)
15087 kHz	U.S. Coast Guard Air Rescue Operations Channel (USB)

Amateur Radio Frequency Allocations

1800–2000 kHz	160 meters	18068–18168 kHz	17 meters
3500–4000 kHz	80 meters	21000–21450 kHz	15 meters
7000–7300 kHz	40 meters	24890–24990 kHz	12 meters
10100–10150 kHz	30 meters	28000–29700 kHz	10 meters
14000–14350 kHz	20 meters		

L.V.H.

TWENTY EASY

(*continued from page 39*)

can hear it throughout much of the day and night on a wide and ever-changing variety of frequencies throughout the world band spectrum.

Radio Moscow broadcasts a variety of programs including news, interviews, political commentary, music, and features on life in the Soviet Union. Its *Folk Box* is one of the best music programs on world band radio. Just tune around, especially in the evening, and you'll find it.

Belgium

Belgische Radio et Televisie (BRT) is the voice of the Dutch-speaking portion of Belgium's population. Although all broadcasts originate from transmitters located in Belgium, the BRT's signal is adequate to be reasonably well heard in Eastern North America, Europe and even beyond.

BRT's 25-minute broadcasts in English are a mixture of Belgian news, current events, and special features—all of high quality. These are heard in Eastern North America at 1330 Monday through Saturday on 17555 or 21815 kHz; plus daily at 2200 and 0030 on 9925 kHz. The 0030 transmission is usually the easiest-to-hear of the three.

BRT broadcasts to Europe daily at 1830 on 5910 or 5915 and 11695 kHz, and again at 2200 on 5910 or 5915 kHz. In Asia and the Pacific, try Monday through Friday at 0800 on 11695 or 21815 kHz, and again Monday through Saturday at 1330 on 21815 kHz.

All broadcasts are one hour earlier during the summer.

AFRICA

South Africa

Radio RSA uses no relay transmitters, but its signal is usually fairly well heard in Europe and North America, anyway. Radio RSA broadcasts are audible daytime in North America and Europe at 1400–1600 on 17745, 21590 or 25790 kHz. In the evenings in North America, the station can be heard at 0200–0300 on 6010, 9580 or 9615 kHz.

Radio RSA also broadcasts to Europe at 1100–1200 and 1800–1900 on 21590 kHz. Asian listeners might try tuning in at 1300–1400 on 17730, 17755 or 21590 kHz.

Over the past couple of years, Radio RSA has changed its program format a number of times, trying to attract a larger, more sympathetic audience. At present, programs include profiles of newsmakers, round-table discussions of politics, features on entertainment in South Africa, and music.

MIDDLE EAST

Egypt

Radio Cairo is one of those stations that is a bit tenuous to include in a list of easy-to-hear stations, even though it is unquestionably powerful enough to reach both Europe and North America.

The problem is audio quality. Radio Cairo's announcers frequently sound as if they were speaking with a mouthful of mush. This makes it an easy station to pick up, but a difficult one to enjoy.

Radio Cairo broadcasts to North America at 0200–0330 on 9475 and 9675 kHz. It also transmits to Europe at 2115–2245 on 9900 kHz. News of the Middle East is presented, as well as Egyptian history and enjoyable music. If you're in Asia, try for Cairo at 1215–1330 on 17595 kHz.

Israel

Like Radio RSA and Radio Cairo, **Kol Israel** uses no relay transmitters, but its signal is mighty enough to be heard clearly in Europe and much of North America. And, unlike Radio Cairo, it does not have a problem with audio quality.

Kol Israel can be heard three times daily with half-hour broadcasts to North America in English at 0000, 0100 and 0200 on 9385, 9435, 11605, 15615 or 15640 kHz. Its transmission to Europe and Eastern North America at 2230 on such frequencies as 9435, 11605, 13750, 15640, 17575 or 17630 kHz is usually clearly audible in both places. European listeners can also tune in at 2000 on those same frequencies.

Kol Israel's programming structure is interesting in itself. The transmission to North America at 0100 is more or less a repeat of the 2230 transmission, but the 0000 and the 0200 broadcasts carry different programs than do the 0100 and 2230 transmissions. Nevertheless, all four carry ten minutes of regional news, followed by various feature programs.

Kol Israel also airs an English-language relay of a domestic-service network. This is beamed to Europe and North America for fifteen minutes each day at 1800 on 9930, 11585 or 11655 kHz. A similar newscast appears at 0500, and may be heard on such frequencies as 11585, 11605, 15640 or 17575 kHz. This is the same newscast that many foreign journalists in Israel start off the day by listening to.

Yet another domestic-service program segment, but with features after the news, is heard in Europe at 1100–1130 on 11585, 17575, 21625 or 21760 kHz, and in Asia and the Pacific on 15650 kHz. It was this midday newscast that allowed world band listener Henry Kissinger, then in Beijing, to learn of the Pope's death. The 0500 newscast is also beamed that way on 17630 kHz.

All transmissions are one hour earlier during the summer.

ASIA
India

North American listeners will be surprised to find **All India Radio** listed as an easy-to-hear station, since it is often a difficult catch in the western hemisphere. But it comes in quite clearly evenings in Europe on 11620 kHz, the frequency which has traditionally been best for North America, as well. The programming begins at forty-five minutes after the hour with a press review, followed by Indian music, news on the hour, commentary, more Indian music—both traditional and popular—and a few feature programs, such as *Hindi by Radio*, around 2130.

Perhaps the most notable thing about All India Radio is the high percentage of subcontinental music the station plays. Listening to AIR can put you in a mood flashback to the late Sixties, with evenings spent enjoying forbidden herbs and the music of Ravi Shankar.

The station has hinted at a future North American service. This presumably would be a relay, or a "swap" arrangement with another broadcaster, as the ongoing upgrade of transmitter facilities in India does not include configurations explicitly intended for the Americas.

All India Radio broadcasts in English to Europe at 1845–1945 on 7412 and 11620 kHz; and at 2045–2230 on 7412, 9910 and 11620 kHz. In Eastern North America, 11620 kHz can sometimes be heard weakly at 2045–2230.

Listening to AIR can put you in a mood flashback to the late Sixties, with evenings spent enjoying forbidden herbs and the music of Ravi Shankar.

To East Asia and the Pacific, AIR is audible at 1000–1100 on 11860, 11925, 15155, 15355, 17387 or 17740 kHz. For East Asia only, try 2245–0115 on 7215, 9535, 9910, 11715, 11745 or 15110 kHz. For the Pacific only, it's audible at 2000–2045 on 7265 kHz; and at 2045–2230 on 7265, 9550, 9910 or 11715 kHz.

China

Radio Beijing, the official voice of the People's Republic of China, was once an iffy catch in North America, depending largely on propagation conditions. Now, however, Radio Beijing has relay agreements with Canada, Mali, France (including French Guiana), Spain and Switzerland. These allow the station to be audible clearly throughout North America. Unfortunately, the channels presently used by Radio Beijing suffer from heavy interference, making listening difficult.

During the historic events of June, 1989, Radio Beijing was notable in that on June 4th, the station broadcast a stirring condemnation of the Tien'anmen Square massacre (see box). This announcement was one of the clearest signs that the demonstrations were not just restricted to students. Rather, as it turned out, they were a more broad-based expression of pent-up outrage that included trusted members of the government apparatus.

As we go to press, Radio Beijing continues to broadcast seven times a day to North America in English, with each new one-hour transmission being a repeat of

Radio Canada International

Li Dan, right, Head of Radio Beijing's English Department, is toasted at a reception in his honor at Radio Canada International.

the first. Radio Beijing may be heard at 0000 on 9665, 9770, 11715, 15130, 17715 or 17855 kHz; 0300 on 9690, 9770, 11715, 15130, 15455 or 17855 kHz; 0400 on 11685, 11840 or 15195 kHz; 1100 and 1200 on 9665 or 17855 kHz (11600 and 11660 kHz, although beamed elsewhere, may also be audible); plus 1300 and 1400 on 11855 kHz.

Europeans can hear Radio Beijing at 2000–2055 and 2100–2155 on 9710, 9820 or 11500 kHz, and via Switzerland at 2200–2230 (2100–2130 summers) on 3985 kHz. In much of Asia, listeners can tune in at 1200–1255 and 1300–1355 on 11660, 15280 or 15400 kHz. In Australia and New Zealand, the one-hour broadcasts are heard at 0830 and 0930 on 9700, 11755, 15440 or 17710 kHz; 1200 on 11600 or 15450 kHz; and 1300 on 11600 kHz.

A rare catch for many years, the **Voice of Free China** in Taiwan is now clearly heard throughout North America, but less so in Europe. Several years ago, the Voice of Free China signed a reciprocal agreement with Family Radio, a North American evangelical broadcaster, for use of their shortwave transmitters in Okeechobee, Florida, in return for Family Radio's use of Taiwanese facilities. Now, Taiwan blankets North America with a clear, powerful signal, but still remains questionable in Europe. An interesting note about the station's programming is that the 0200 broadcast on one evening is repeated the next evening at 0300. So if you miss it one night, you can catch it the next.

A Moment of Courage at Radio Beijing

From time-to-time, world band listeners are treated to a special and poignant broadcast, usually made as democratic forces are about to be overrun by the armed might of tyranny. 0300 World Time, in the opening hours of June 4, 1989, brought one such moment:

"This is Radio Beijing. Please remember June the 3rd, 1989. The most tragic event happened in the Chinese capital, Beijing. Thousands of people, most of them innocent civilians, were killed by fully armed soldiers when they forced their way into the city. Among the killed are our colleagues at Radio Beijing.

"The soldiers were riding on armored vehicles and used machine guns against thousands of local residents and students who tried to block their way. When the Army convoys made the breakthrough, soldiers continued to spray their bullets indiscriminately at crowds in the street. Eyewitnesses say some armored vehicles even crushed foot soldiers who hesitated in front of the resisting civilians.

"Radio Beijing English Department deeply mourns those who died in the tragic incident, and appeals to all its listeners to join our protest for the gross violation of human rights and the most barbarous suppression of the people. Because of the abnormal situation here in Beijing, there is no other news we could bring you. We sincerely ask for your understanding, and thank you for joining us at this most tragic moment."

The announcer—who apparently was not, as was widely reported, Mr. Li Dan—has not been heard since over Radio Beijing.

L.M.

Both the 0200 and 0300 broadcasts are on either 5950 or 5985 kHz. The Voice of Free China also broadcasts to Asia at 0200 on 15345 and 11860 kHz, and to Europe at 2200 on 9955, 15345 and 17612.5 kHz.

Japan

Like the Voice of Free China, **Radio Japan** was, until fairly recently, a hit-and-miss proposition on the East Coast of North America—although it has always been well received on the West Coast. A few years ago, the station signed a reciprocal agreement with Radio Canada International to use RCI's Sackville, New Brunswick facilities in return for RCI's using Radio Japan's transmitters in Tokyo. Now, Japan's signal is loud and clear.

Radio Japan's transmission of its General Service from Canada to North America airs at 1100 on 6120 kHz and at 0300 (0100 summers) on 5960 kHz, but broadcasts of the General Service to Europe from the Gabon facility can also be heard quite clearly in North America at 1500 on 21700 kHz and at 2100 on 11800 kHz. Reception of these transmissions is usually best in Eastern North America.

Radio Japan transmits its Regional Service to Western North America direct from newly constructed transmitters in Tokyo. The Regional Service for the Americas is aired at 0100 on either 11905 or 17825 kHz; and again at 0300 on 17825 kHz and either 11870 or 15195 kHz.

Listeners in Australasia can hear Radio Japan's Regional Service at 0900 on 11885, 15270 or 17890 kHz. The General Service is aired at 0500 and 0700 on 15270 kHz; 1900 on 9640, 11850 or 15270 kHz; and 2100 on 9640, 11850, 15270 or 17890 kHz.

PACIFIC

Australia

Radio Australia is on the air around the clock with "down under" programs that range from news to the popular *Smith's Weekly*. The best time to hear the station, if you live in Eastern North America, is between 0800 and 1500 in the morning on 9580 kHz, but you can also try 6060 kHz at 1130-1400. If you live on the West Coast—or even on the East Coast, if it's summer or spring—you can hear Radio Australia on 17795 kHz in the evenings, beginning at 2200 and broadcasting continuously in English until 0400.

LATIN AMERICA

Ecuador

One of the oldest South American broadcasters is the evangelical station, **HCJB**, in Quito, Ecuador. This friendly operation broadcasts to North America, one of its prime target areas, at 1130-1600 on 11740 and 17890 kHz, and at 0030 in the evenings on 11775 and 15155 kHz. It also is beamed to Europe, where it is less clearly heard, at 0700 on 6205, 9610 or 11835 kHz; 1900 on 15270 and 17790 kHz; and once again at 2130 on 15270 and 17790 kHz. HCJB also broadcasts to the South Pacific at 0700 on 6130 and 9745 kHz.

Some people are put off by evangelical broadcasts. There is, after all, quite a lot of religious commentary on HCJB, since that is the station's main mission. But there are also some fairly interesting programs that are only loosely tied to the religious message, including *Música del Ecuador*, *DX Party Line* and *Call of the Andes*. Of all the religious broadcasts encountered on world band radio, HCJB is far and away the best.

Cuba

As one might expect, **Radio Habana Cuba** is clearly heard throughout North America, but is less well heard in Europe. The station broadcasts in English to North America in the evenings at 0000-0200 on 9655 or 11820 kHz; 0200-0450 on 6140 and 9655, or 9710 and 11820 kHz; 0450-0600 on 9655 or 11820; and 0600-0800 on 9525 or 11835 kHz. Its European broadcasts are severely curtailed to a two-hour-long transmission in the afternoon at 1900 on 11800 kHz. The 0000-0100 hour broadcast is repeated again at 0200 and 0400, and the 0100-0200 broadcast is re-aired at 0300 and 0500.

Radio Habana Cuba has revamped its programming several times since its inception under Fidel Castro. Originally, it was a lively, almost extemporaneous, operation that was arguably the most interesting of all the Marxist stations. Its technical standards were reasonably high, as well.

But after "The Year of The Seven Million Tons," in which nearly all Cubans, including station personnel, "volunteered" to help with the sugar cane harvest, the programming became colorless, while frequency usage deteriorated to a seemingly hit-and-miss exercise. Radio Habana even began appearing on the same channels as Radio Moscow's American services—each drowning out the other.

Still, a typical transmission continued to dispense with all but a few brief feature programs and concentrate on a lively and varied menu of Caribbean, Cuban and Latin American music. Indeed, during this period Radio Habana was considered to be one of the best sources of this kind of music. However, more recently the station has expanded such feature programs as *Be My Guest*, and *Life In Cuba*, and Latin music now seems limited to the last five or ten minutes of the show—although the excellent *Jazz Place* continues to grace the airwaves.

NORTH AMERICA

Canada

Because it is so near, **Radio Canada International** is heard clearly throughout Eastern and Central North America. However, RCI has been less successful in Europe, even with relay facilities being put to use.

The broadcasts to North America are at 1300–1400 Mondays through Fridays on 9635, 11855 and 17820 kHz; 1400–1700 Sundays on 11955 and 17820; and 0000–0130 daily, plus 0130–0200 Sundays and Mondays, on 9755 and 5960 kHz. The 0000–0130/0200 transmission features such current events programs as the Canadian Broadcasting Corporation's excellent *The World at Six* and *As It Happens*.

The morning broadcast features a number of special interviews, and such regular programs as *Innovation Canada*, *Spectrum* and *SWL Digest*. The afternoon transmission to Africa, heard fairly well in North America, begins at 1800 on 13680, 17820 and 15260 kHz, and follows a slightly different program format—only running for a half hour, with another half hour of transmission at 1900 Mondays through Fridays to Africa.

Although RCI in English produces a spotty signal in Europe, for Asia and the Pacific, it be heard at 1300–1330 on 15270 and 15385 or 17810 kHz (supplementary frequencies that may be reactivated in 1990 include 11955 and 15435 kHz); and at 2200–2230 on 11705 or 15440 kHz.

Most of RCI's English-language transmissions are one hour earlier during the summer.

United States

With relay stations all over the world, there is probably no place where the **Voice of America** cannot be heard. The two best times to hear it in North America are at 0000–0200 on 5995, 6130 and 9455 kHz, when the VOA broadcasts to the Caribbean and South America, and at 1600–2200 on 15410 and 17800 kHz for its broadcast to Africa. For Europeans, programs may be heard at 1700–2200 on 6040, 9760, 11760 or 15205 kHz.

The new VOA Pacific Service, inaugurated in 1989, may be heard at 1900–2000 and 2100–2200 on 9525, 11965 and 15185 kHz. In East Asia, good bets for the regular VOA English Service include 1000–1100 on 11720 kHz; 1100–1330 on 9760, 11720 or 15160 kHz; 1330–1500 on 9760 or 15160; 2200–2400 on 15205, 15290, 17735 or 17820 kHz; and 0000–0100 on 15290, 17735 or 17820 kHz.

Prepared by Contributing Editor Alex Batman and the staff of Passport to World Band Radio.

(*continued from page 45*)

in at the late hour of 2230-2300 on 6100 kHz. Its transmissions, like those of Radio Kiev, are heard one hour earlier summers.

A wide variety of music also emanates from Western Europe. **Radio Portugal International**, heard weekday evenings, offers its choice of Iberian music. This sometimes focuses on melancholy Portuguese *fados*, made famous in the 1830s by the young gypsy prostitute Maria Severa, and in this century by supreme *fadista* Amália Rodrigues.

Fados are the Portuguese equivalent of the blues. But, as one observer put it, "you ain't really been blue till you've felt the *fado*." With the *fado*, suffering is delicious.

In North America, Radio Portugal International can be heard Tuesdays through Saturdays (remember, this is the equivalent of Mondays through Fridays local evenings) at 0200-0230 on 9600, 9635, 9680, 9705 or 11840 kHz. The best bet in Western Europe is Mondays through Fridays at 2000-2030 on 11740 kHz, and in Asia Mondays through Fridays at 1600-1630 on 15210 kHz. Music, when aired, is usually towards the end of the half-hour transmission period.

> Fados are the Portugese equivalent of the blues. With the fado, suffering is delicious.

Neighboring Spain also airs folk songs. Although the **Spanish National Radio** has no particular program set aside for music in its 55-minute English transmissions to the Americas—at 0000, 0100 and 0500 on 9630, 11880 or 15110 kHz—the station occasionally plays impassioned *flamencos* and other types of music from the Spanish provinces. Europeans can tune in at 1900 and 2100 on 9765, 11790 or 15280 kHz.

Northward to the rugged Alps, **Swiss Radio International** also plays traditional music. There are generous doses of lively tunes with a distinctive *Schweizer* twist. In North America, tune in on Tuesdays and Fridays at 0115 and 0315 on 6135, 9725, 9885 and 12035 kHz. In Western Europe, listen daily at 1700 (1600 summers) on 3985, 6165 and 9535 kHz. In East Asia and the Pacific, try Mondays and Thursdays at 0745 on 9560, 13685, 17830 and 21695 kHz, and again on 1045 on 13635, 15570 and 17830 kHz. For East Asia, there's yet another transmission Mondays and Thursdays at 1315 on 9620 and 11695 kHz.

If you prefer folk music with a lacy East European flavor, try **Radio Prague**. It's delightful music is heard in North America, amidst the various features, between 0115 and 0155 on 5930, 7345 and 11990 kHz. Czech and Slovak folk music can also be heard in the European Service, which is aired at 1530 and 2200 on 6055 kHz, and again at 1800 and 1900 on 5930 or 7345 kHz. In Australia and New Zealand, try Prague at 0730 and 0830 on 11685, 17840 or 21705 kHz.

Another especially pleasant offering from East Europe is Romania's **Radio Bucharest**, which features *The Skylark*, aired to North America Fridays at about 0225 on 9510, 9570, 11830 or 11940 kHz. Listeners in Western Europe can hear the program within the 1930-2030 transmission on 9690, 11810 or 11940 kHz.

From tiny Albania in the Balkans comes **Radio Tirana**, the last voice of Stalinist orthodoxy still on the international airwaves. For North America, at 2345, 0245 and 0345 it features both older and newer Albanian patriotic and love songs on 9500 or 9760 kHz. Although some songs bear such ringing titles as "Long Live the Party," they are nonetheless enjoyable to hear . . . especially if you don't understand Albanian. Although Radio Tirana's schedule is fluid, in Western Europe it can be heard clearly in English at various times, including 0630-0655 on 9500 kHz.

Radio Polonia's *Folk Spot*—heard adequately in Western Europe, but poorly, usually in the winter, in Eastern North America—is aired sporadically at various times, including around 2320 on 6135, 7125 and 7270 kHz. It's worth hearing if you can pick it up.

Like a soup kitchen that mixes religious instruction with food, **Radio Sofia** intersperses its relatively uninteresting feature programs with a scattering of delightful Bulgarian folk songs. Reception is usually fairly good, thanks to the station's powerful transmitters. In North America, try Sofia at 0000–0100 on 9700 or 11720 kHz, and again at 0400–0500 on 7115 kHz. In Western Europe, it is audible at many times, including when it's beamed overseas. A good time to tune in is at 1930–2000, 2130–2200 and 2230–2330 on 9700 and 11720 kHz.

Even better is the delightful mix of folk and classical music aired over Bulgaria's **Horizont** domestic service. Although it is in Bulgarian, there's so much music played that the talk hardly counts. Horizont is aired from 0100 on 11660 kHz, and is well heard in various parts of the world, including much of the day in Western Europe and evenings in the Americas, when the channel is clear and propagation is suitable.

Jewish folk music, once found throughout Europe, all but vanished in the ashes of World War II. Lamenting this, a visitor to Jerusalem once remarked to a **Kol Israel** producer that the station doesn't seem to air much in the way of traditional music. The producer explained that Israel is a modern industrial nation, and that the station is there to convey this fact in both speech and music.

Nevertheless, vestiges of cantorial and other traditional Jewish music still manage to tiptoe past the doyens of modernism and take to the airwaves, usually as relays of domestic-service programs intended for recent Israeli immigrants. Try the Bukharian and Georgian Services of Kol Israel at 1455–1525 on 13750, 15615, 15640, 15650, 17575 or 17630 kHz; the Hungarian Service at 1745–1800 on 9010, 9435, 11605, 13750 or 15615 kHz; the Romanian Service at 1800–1825 on 9010, 11605 or 12077 kHz; and the relatively powerful Persian Service at 1530–1625 on 11605, 15650, 17575 or 17630 kHz. Reception is best in Western Europe, although it's also sometimes audible with good equipment in Eastern North America. Too, all programs are heard one hour earlier summers.

Even the **BBC** has its share of folk music programming. *Andy Kershaw's World of Music* is a five-star potpourri of everything from a police band in Mali to festival music in Martinique . . . from a Vietnamese lullaby to a Saharan lament. A real treat, heard for fifteen minutes to North America Mondays at 0215 and Thursdays at 0445 on 5975 and 9915 kHz; to Western Europe Mondays at 0945 on 5975, 6045, 7325, 9410, 9750, 9760, 12095, 15070 and 17640 kHz; to East Asia Mondays at 0945 on 9740, 15360 and 17830 kHz; and to the Pacific Mondays at 0945 on 11750 and 15360 kHz.

Belly Ballet

If you listen to Middle Eastern music on a world band radio, you'll typically hear uncomplicated tunes, with the melody being varied by interspersing extra notes among the main ones. This makes the music sound as if it is sliding about the scale. Often, you'll hear wailing, plaintive sounds—the Arab equivalent of the "She Done Me Wrong Song"—that depend heavily on stringed instruments, drums and flutes.

Either you like this sort of thing, or you don't. It's not the type of music to cheer you up, but its romantic allure is, for many, hard to resist. Too, it makes excellent, low-profile background music—especially if you can't understand the chitchat, which in Arabic and Persian tends to be muted and unobtrusive.

A five-star potpourri of everything from a police band in Mali to festival music in Martinique . . . from a Vietnamese lullaby to a Saharan lament.

Because virtually all these stations transmit from the Middle East and lack relay facilities, long-distance reception is best, with some exceptions, in Europe, Africa and Eastern North America. However, with good equipment, reception of sorts is possible in nearly any other part of the world.

Arab music, interspersed with English commentary, is beamed to the world by mighty **Radio Damascus.** Interestingly, this station includes more music than it does feature programs—a rarity among world band broadcasters. Radio Damascus broadcasts in English to Western Europe at 2005–2105 on 9550 and 12085 kHz winters, 15095 and 17710 kHz summers. This transmission is often audible in Eastern North America, as well, at 2105–2205 on 12085 kHz winters and 17710 kHz summers.

In the evenings, **Radio Cairo** plays a high percentage of music in its broadcast in English to North America at 0200–0330 on 9475 and 9675 kHz. Radio Cairo also broadcasts to Western Europe at 2115–2245 on 9900 kHz, with pretty much the same programming.

The quality of reception of these stations can vary. Cairo is consistently audible, but Damascus is more sporadic, usually being better during the summer months. **Radio Baghdad** in English is also a hit-and-miss proposition, as that station has had trouble finding a clear frequency over the years. For the moment, Baghdad broadcasts to Western Europe at 2100–2300 on 9770 kHz winters, and at 2000–2200 on 13660 kHz summers. In North America, try 0230–0430 winters, 0130–0330 summers, on 9515 or 11945 kHz, and if these are not satisfactory try 7280, 11810 or 11880 kHz.

If you don't care whether you hear English, **Radio Cairo** plays a good bit of music—on rare occasion including the late, legendary Om Kalsoum—throughout much of the day in its General Arabic domestic service. This is often audible in Eastern North America and Western Europe on such frequencies as 12050 and 17670 kHz.

Another station in Arabic that plays high-quality Middle Eastern music is **Radio Baghdad**. This station changes channels often, but throughout much of the day and night you can try such established frequencies as 7225, 7280, 9730, 11750, 11760, 11825, 11840, 12025, 15110, 15150, 15310, 15400, 15415 or 17830 kHz.

With less music and more commentary is the Arabic Service of the **Voice of the United Arab Emirates**, beamed to different parts of the world at 0215-2130, but which is especially well-received in North America from 1300 to 1600--and even earlier in Western Europe—on 17645, 17705, 17820, 21515, 21580, 21735, 25670 and 25900 kHz. There's also an English Service for North America at 2200–2400, followed at 0000–0200 by Arabic, on seasonally changing frequencies, including 6170, 9595, 11965, 11985 and 13605 kHz.

To stir your blood, the **Voice of the Islamic Republic of Iran** broadcasts intervals of Persian music throughout much of the day and night on 15084 kHz. With even less music and a lot more diatribe, **Radio Jamahiriya** from Libya broadcasts at 1745–0440, with the best chances of reception being on such channels as 6120, 7245, 15235, 15415 or 15450 kHz.

If modern Israeli music is your cup of *butz*, **Kol Israel** relays its Reshet Bet domestic service at 0400–2300 (0300 to 2200 summers) at different times on various frequencies, including 9385, 11585, 11655, 13750, 15095, 15615, 17545, 17590 and 21555 kHz. If you're lucky, you might hear Ofra Haza, a musician who mixes traditional and popular music.

> Day and night, the musical voices east of Europe are almost always there, ready to entertain at your command.

Finally, there is the **Voice of Turkey**, which broadcasts in English to North America at 2300–2350 and, again, at 0400–0450 with good music between feature programs. Sans English, Turkey can be found with large doses of appealing village and other indigenous music at various times, day and night, on 9445, 9460, 9685, 11775, 11925, 11955, 15160, 15200, 15405 or 17760 kHz.

One nice thing about Middle Eastern music is that so much of it graces the airwaves—much more than can possibly be covered here. But you can use *Passport's* Blue Pages to dial about the bands to see what strikes your fancy. Day and night, the musical voices east of Europe are almost always there, ready to entertain at your command.

African Rhythms

The rhythm and beat of African music is more highly developed than those of any other traditional music in the world. Its strong, driving pulsations are generated by such instruments as the balafon, cora,

United Nations

Village men performing a folk dance of the Punjab.

simple flutes and drums. The antithesis of melancholy Middle Eastern songs, it's the king of music for dancing and good times.

Unfortunately, there are precious few stations audible in North America and Western Europe that play a healthy percentage of African songs. Of the scattering of high-powered stations, perhaps the best is **Afrique Numero Un** from Gabon, which broadcasts mostly in French, but which also plays styles of African popular music called *ju-ju* and *high-life*. King Sunny Ade from Nigeria is the king of ju-ju.

The music is melodious and the rhythms are intoxicating—it's some of the best dance music to be found on world band radio. Afrique Numero Un is best heard in Eastern North America and Western Europe at 0500–0600 on 4830 or 9580; 0800–1600 on 15200 or 17630 kHz; 1600–2100 on 4830, 9580 or 15475; and 2100–2300 on 4830 or 9580 kHz.

Another African station audible in Western Europe and North America is the **Voice of Nigeria**, which plays a request-line program of African popular music at 0500–0530 on 7255 kHz. Signing on at 0400 on 4850 kHz is **Cameroon RTV Corporation** with popular African music, and at 0430 on 4904.5 kHz is **Radio Chad**—both of which are difficult to hear. A bit more reliable is Niger's **La Voix du Sahel** on 5020 kHz, which signs on at 0530 with the call of the Koran. It then goes on to play traditional African music until a newscast in French at 0600. Yet another Francophone African station with good music is **Radiodiffusion Télévision Malienne**, sometimes audible at 0800–1800 on 11960 kHz.

If you don't care whether your music comes directly from an African station, but is simply good African music, the **Voice of America's** *Music Time in Africa* is devoted to traditional African music on

Sundays at 1730-1800, and to popular African music in its second edition at 1930-2000. Both editions can be found on such frequencies as 15410, 15445, 15580, 15600, 17785, 17800 or 17870 kHz. Listen for Senegal's superb Youssou N'Dour, who in Africa is fully as popular as Michael Jackson, and Nigeria's Fela Anikulapo Kute. You won't be disappointed!

Asian Music

The South Asian voices of **All India Radio** and **Radio Pakistan** bridge Middle Eastern and Oriental music. The music they play is at once similar to, and yet different from, Middle Eastern music.

India has a venerable tradition of both folk and classical songs. The basis of this music is the art of improvisation—the musicians make up the music as they go along. Singers and flutes are both popular, but stringed instruments, such as the sitar, are more commonly heard, often in conjunction with the tabla drum. Indians use many more notes than do Western musicians, so to a neophyte the music may sound slightly out of tune. Of course, it's anything but.

Both stations are fairly well heard in Western Europe. AIR is audible there in English at 1845-1945 on 7412 or 11620; and 2045-2230 on 7412, 9910 or 11620 kHz. The best chance in Western Europe for Radio Pakistan in English is 1720-1800 on 9400, 11570 or 15545 kHz.

In Eastern North America reception of India is spotty and weak, although new transmitters coming on stream shortly may help, even though they won't be beamed to North America. For now, the best bet for AIR is at 2045-2230 on 11620 kHz, and Radio Pakistan can sometimes be heard with music in its Urdu Service at 1315-1545 on 11615, 13675, 15605, 17660, 21580 or 21740 kHz.

To East Asia and the Pacific, AIR is audible from 1000-1100 on 11860, 11925, 15155, 15355, 17387 or 17740 kHz. For East Asia only, try 2245-0115 on 7215, 9535, 9910, 11715, 11745 or 15110 kHz. For the Pacific only, AIR is audible from 2000-2045 on 7265 kHz; and from 2045-2230 on 7265, 9550, 9910 or 11715 kHz.

Traditional, as well as more modern, tunes make the radio voyage from the Far East. Unlike Indian music, the established music of China and Japan is composed, not improvised. Often, a wide range of instruments is played together in an orchestra to get a great variety of sounds. Both countries use their music in stylized theater productions, such as the Kabuki Theater in Japan. But the world band listener will hear quite a difference between the two, mainly because Japanese music builds its melodies with different notes, creating a more haunting sound.

In general, Far Eastern music is relaxing, with a gentle pulse. You will hear a profusion of flutes and stringed instruments, plus the exclamatory presence of cymbals and occasional bells.

Regrettably, **Radio Beijing** plays very little Chinese music, although during the suppression of the 1989 "Beijing Spring" the station often substituted various types of music for regular programming. Indeed, during the Cultural Revolution only a handful of revolutionary compositions, created in league with Mao Zedong's wife, were even allowed on the air.

For the moment, Radio Beijing still features *Music Album*, broadcast to North America on Sundays at 1130 and 1230 on 9665 or 17855 kHz; 0030 on 9665, 9770, 11715, 15130, 15455, 17715 or 17855 kHz; and 0330 on 9690, 9770, 11715, 15130, 15455 or 17855 kHz; and 0430 on 11685, 11840, 11980 or 15195 kHz. In Western Europe, try 2030 and 2130 on 9710, 9820 or 11500 kHz.

Off the coast of the People's Republic of China is Taiwan, whose **Voice of Free China** features music with a little more variety than Radio Beijing's. Traditional Chinese music is aired on *Jade Bells and Bamboo Pipes* at 0230-0245 on Fridays, and repeated at 0330-0345 on Saturdays. The Voice of Free China also offers *New Record Time*, featuring the latest hits on the Taiwan pop scene, at 0230 on Thursdays, repeated at 0330 on Fridays. There's also *Chinese Old Songs*, which features hits from before the 1950s, from 0230 on Saturdays, repeated at 0330 on Sundays. Even when the Voice of Free China is not broadcasting in English—after 0400 to North America on 5985 kHz, for example—you can still hear a good number of current Chinese hits from Taiwan.

Radio Korea's music output is limited to Sundays in *Echoes of Korean Music*, which airs at 1415-1430 on 9570, 9750

West German Embassy

Bavarians, Germany's friendliest people, need little excuse to celebrate.

and 15575 kHz, and is repeated at 2345–2400 on 15575 kHz. One week the show features traditional Korean music; the next, South Korean popular music. Korean pop songs also can be heard most days in *Seoul Calling*, Radio Korea's magazine show, which airs at 1420–1440 on 9570, 9750 and 15575 kHz, and is repeated at 2350–0010 on 15575 kHz.

Island Dances

The most romantic music found over world band radio has always been that aired over **Radio Tahiti**. For years, listeners have strained to hear the soft, sensual sounds sung by Tahiti's South Pacific islanders.

Some of this music lives on, but to some extent Tahitians have abandoned it in favor of foreign or domestic rock music. To make matters worse, reception has deteriorated.

Still, it's worth a try—especially late evenings at 0320 and 0420 onwards on 11824 and 15171 kHz—during the warmer seasons in North America.

The Latin Beat

When listening to Latin American music on world band radio, you can often hear songs with a Spanish-Indian origin, and dance to their lively, driving rhythms. The influence of African music is strong in several countries—Brazil and Cuba, for example—which has given rise to such well-known Latin American dances as the samba, rumba and conga.

Like African music, much Latin music is for dancing. But unlike the African variety, Latin dances—the tango, in particular—are more stylized than improvised.

Perhaps the best taste of Latin American music can be had daily on **Radiobras's** *Best In Brazilian Popular Music*, beamed to North America at 0210-0230 and 0235-0250 on 11745 kHz; and to Western Europe at 1810-1830 and 1835-1850 on 15265 kHz.

Less reliable reception comes from **Radio Argentina al Exterior**, heard in English to North America at 0200-0300 and 0400-0500 on 9690 or 11710 kHz, to Western Europe at 1730-1830 on 15345 kHz, and to Asia in Japanese at 1000-1100 on 11710 kHz. Interspersed with the station's feature programs are numerous tangos—a passion going back decades in Argentina.

In Central America, there are two worthy stations in Costa Rica, **Radio Reloj** on 6005.5 kHz, which broadcasts twenty-four hours a day, and **Radio Impacto** on 5030 and 6150 kHz, which airs most of its music on Sundays. Reception of both is usually satisfactory during the hours of darkness in North America, with Radio Impacto playing more of a soft-rock variety of Latin American music and Radio Reloj—thankfully playing the more traditional.

For music with a more indigenous twist, *Música del Ecuador* may be heard in North America Wednesdays after 0200 and Sundays around 0100 over evangelical station **HCJB** on 9720, 9745, 11775, 11910 or 15155 kHz; and in Western Europe after 2130 Tuesdays on 15270 and 17790 kHz. The music on this program tends toward Ecuadorian folk tunes that are difficult to find reliably anywhere else.

Radio Habana Cuba plays a high percentage of Cuban songs on its North American broadcast, which airs nightly at 0000-0200 and 0450-0600 on 9655 or 11820 kHz; 0200-0450 on 6140 and 9655, or 9710 and 11820; and 0600-0800 on 9525 or 11835 kHz. Unfortunately, reception of Habana outside the Americas is spotty. Warning: 0200-0300 is a repeat of 0000-0100, and 0300-0400 is a repeat of 0100-0200. So you'll hear the same music again if you stay tuned all night.

Although Latin American stations are best heard winters in the Western Hemisphere and East Asia, with good equipment and patience they can also be heard in more distant parts of the world, especially in the 4750-5100 kHz range. Radio aficionados from Melbourne to Helsinki devote long hours each winter to trying to flush out these faint prized catches.

Western Popular Music

Rock and jazz are staples on countless local stations, so why tune them in on world band?

For many, there is no good reason. But for forward-looking music buffs, there can be found the leading edges of musical trends. World band listeners can also scour the airwaves for that which doesn't appear on local playlists. With world band, there is a constant churning of fresh groups and playing styles unheard of outside the confines of MCI.

> With world band, there is a constant churning of fresh groups and playing styles unheard of outside the confines of MCI.

World band radio airs no small amount of jazz and rock. Born of American blacks, jazz and rock and roll have long since swept across North America and Europe to the point where even non-Western stations now feature "Western" popular music, sometimes of local origin.

Radio Kuwait on 11665 kHz and **Radio Jordan** on 9660 kHz, both audible in Eastern North America and Western Europe from around 1800, play almost nothing but pop music until sign off at 2100 and 2200, respectively. Also on the air from that part of the world with popular hits is **Radio Algiers**, heard poorly at 1900-2000 in English on 9509, 9680, 15215 or 17745 kHz. Radio Kuwait does sometimes interrupt the run of music with a feature program, but that only lasts about fifteen minutes, then the music is once again back on the air.

For music from the USA, powerful **KUSW** in Salt Lake City alternates current hits with "oldies" and weather forecasts for various cities throughout the U.S. It also airs music from the famed

Mormon Tabernacle Choir. KUSW is heard much of the day and night on such frequencies as 6130, 6135, 6175, 9815, 9850, 11695, 15580 or 15650 kHz. **WRNO** in New Orleans—heard at various times on 6185, 7355, 9715, 11965, 13760 or 15420 kHz—plays the usual roster of everyday rock hits. KUSW is heard well through the Western Hemisphere, while WRNO's signal excels only in North America.

More limited coverage of pop and rock comes from the **BBC's** *Multitrack*. In Western Europe, it's heard Mondays, Wednesdays and Fridays at 1830 on 6195 and 7325 kHz; and again Tuesdays, Thursdays and Saturdays at 1215 on 7325, 9750 and 12095 kHz.

In North America, *Multitrack* is found Mondays, Wednesdays and Fridays at 2330 on 5975, 6175, 7325, 9590, 9915 and 15260 kHz. It's also beamed to North America Tuesdays, Thursdays and Saturdays at 1215 on 5965, 9915 and 11775 kHz.

In East Asia and the Pacific, tune in on Mondays, Wednesdays and Fridays at 1830 on 11750 kHz; and also Tuesdays, Thursdays and Saturdays at 1215 on 9740 kHz.

The BBC brings a first-rate menu of C&W to fans so far removed from rural America that they think a two-holer is part of a golf game.

The **Voice of America**, headquartered in Washington, carries pop and rock music, as well. *Music USA* airs at 0030 weeknights on 6130, 9655 and 11695 kHz. Although these frequencies are beamed to the Caribbean, they are heard clearly throughout much of North America.

If you go for country and western music, **Radio Australia's** *International Country Music* plays a good variety at 1230 on Saturdays, heard well in North America on 9580 kHz. It can sometimes also be heard in Western Europe Mondays at 1530, and again on Tuesdays at 1730 on 6035 and 7205 kHz.

The **BBC's** *Country Style*, hosted by the award-winning David Allan, brings a first-rate menu of C&W to fans so far removed from rural America that they think a two-holer is part of a golf game. In North America, tune in Wednesdays at 0145 and 0445 on 5975 and 9915 kHz; in Western Europe try the same day at 1115 on 5975, 6045, 7325, 9410, 9750, 9760, 12095 and 15070 kHz; to East Asia at 0445 on 15280 and 17815 kHz; and to the Pacific at 0445 on 5975 kHz.

Closer to the roots of country music is the **Canadian Broadcasting Service's Northern Quebec Service.** Pleasant country music is heard at various times of the day, often when the language of transmission is other than English. In North America—and sometimes Australia and New Zealand, as well—tune in 6195, 9625 or 11720 kHz at different times of the day and night.

The birthplace of country music can also be heard once each week. The **Voice of America's** *Music, U.S.A.* includes a portion—*Country Music, U.S.A.*—aired to the Americas Saturdays after 0030 on 6030, 6165 and 9590 kHz; to Western Europe Fridays after 1730 on 6040, 9760, 11760 and 15205 kHz; to North East Asia Fridays after 1130 on 9760, 11720 and 15160 kHz; and to the Pacific Fridays after 1130 on 5985, 6110, 11720, 15160 and 15425 kHz, and again after 1930 on 9525, 11965 and 15185 kHz.

Although jazz isn't fully appreciated in the continent of its birth, in many parts of the world it continues to be popular and to evolve into new styles. The **Voice of America's** famous *Jazz Hour*, hosted by the venerable Willis Conover, features the best in jazz. In Western Europe, it's heard Saturdays at 2010–2100 on 6040, 9760, 11760 and 15205 kHz. For East Asia, it's on Saturdays at 1410–1500 on 9760 and 15160 kHz. Some of these frequencies are audible in parts of North America, as well.

Jazz also can be heard on the **BBC's** *Here's Humph*. It's audible in North America Saturdays at 0430 on 5975 and 9510 kHz. In Western Europe, tune in Fridays at 1945 on 3955, 6195 and 7325 kHz; and Saturdays at 1001 on 7325, 9760 and 12095 kHz. In East Asia and the Pacific, the program is aired Saturdays at 0430 on 5975, 15280 and 17815 kHz; and 1001 on 15360 kHz. To the Pacific only, there is a transmission Fridays at 1945 on 11750 kHz.

The BBC also features *Jazz for the Asking*. It's heard in North America Sundays at 0630 on 5975 and 9640 kHz. For Western Europe, it is aired Saturdays at 1830 on 3955, 6195 and 7325 kHz; Sundays at 0630 on 3955 and 6195 kHz; and again Wednesdays at 1030 on 7325, 9760 and 12095 kHz. For East Asia and the Pacific, try Sundays at 0630 on 15360 kHz, and Wednesdays at 1030 on 9740 and 15360 kHz. For the Pacific only, there's also a transmission Saturdays at 1830 on 11750 kHz.

> Some you may grow to love, while others may sound like cats in heat.

Even **Radio Moscow** features jazz—highly popular in the Soviet Union, notwithstanding that it used to be banned from the state airwaves—on the *Jazz Show* at 0030 and 2030 on Mondays, 1730 on Tuesdays, 1430 on Wednesdays, 1130 on Thursdays, 1530 on Fridays, and 0730 and 1730 on Saturdays. Numerous frequencies are available—just dial around.

For a Caribbean twist, try **Radio Habana Cuba's** *Jazz Place* on Mondays at 0030, 0230 and 0430. Frequencies are given above in "The Latin Beat."

Share in the Diversity

This roster of music is far from exhaustive, but at least it provides a sense of the musical variety that awaits you within the world band spectrum. Some you may grow to love, while others may sound like cats in heat. But it's impossible not to find something that will move you one way or another. All you need are ears, a world band radio, and a desire to share in the beat of the world.

Prepared by Alex Batman and the staff of Passport to World Band Radio.

Passport Updates on Radio Canada International

Radio Canada International's *SWL Digest* is dedicated to your enjoyment of world band radio. Hosted by Ian McFarland, it includes monthly updates to *Passport's* Buyer's Guide by Lawrence Magne, as well as contributions from *Passport* editors Tony Jones and Don Jensen. Here's when to tune in:

World Time

Winter	Summer	
1330	1230	Tuesday on 9635, 11855 and 17820 kHz
2137	2137	Saturday on 11880, 13670, 15150 and 17820 kHz
2208	2108	Saturday on 9760 and 11945 kHz.
2307	2307	Sunday on 9755 and 11730 kHz
0109	0009	Sunday (Saturday night in North America) on 5960 and 9755 kHz.
0109	0109	Sunday (Saturday night in North America) on 9535, 11845, 11940 and 13720 kHz.
0337	0337	Saturday (Friday night in North America) on 9645 or 11730 kHz
0409	0409	Wednesday (Tuesday night in North America) on 11790 or 15275 kHz

1990 BUYER'S GUIDE TO WORLD BAND RADIO

HOW TO BUY A WORLD BAND RADIO

World band radios have to receive signals battered by long journeys from afar. So it's not surprising that at least some models are on the leading edge of technology.

That's the good news. Less encouraging is that there is no shortage of low-technology clunkers on the market. When you're shopping for a world band radio, you have to be on your toes.

Specialized Tests for Evaluating Radios

That's why, starting in 1977, we commenced testing world band radios. These tests, which have nothing to do with advertising, include "hands on" evaluations and specialized laboratory analysis. The results form the basis of *Passport's* "Buyer's Guide," as well as the detailed findings made available in the *RDI White Paper* series of publications.

Best-Value Performers Start at $200

One thing these tests have shown is that while cheap world band radios serve little good purpose except for occasional use on trips, it's usually not necessary to spend hefty sums to obtain a pleasant radio.

The best values in portables are usually found in the $200–400 range. These perform surprisingly well, and are more than adequate for most listeners' needs. Too, they can be used both in the home and on trips, and they don't require a special antenna.

What Do You Want to Hear?

In the final analysis, it's what you're trying to hear that should determine the type of purchase you make. If you're interested only in the strong, clear stations, then there's no need to spend a king's ransom on equipment designed to hear a fly scratch its back in Pago Pago.

On the other hand, if you listen to weaker signals, a more costly receiver may be justifiable. Too, if you live where world band signals tend to lack strength—Western North America or New Zealand, for example—a tabletop receiver with a sophisticated antenna will usually provide more satisfactory results.

Most of these premium models command premium prices—usually around $1,000 in the U.S., and somewhat more in Europe. However, this isn't always the case. The British-made Lowe receiver, for example, provides superior performance and top-notch quality of construction for about two-thirds as much.

Ratings of Overall Performance

★★★★★ Superb
★★★★ Excellent
★★★ Good
★★ Fair
★ Poor

Classement Général

★★★★★ Superbe
★★★★ Excellent
★★★ Bon
★★ Moyen
★ Médiocre

Clasificación General

★★★★★ Magnífico
★★★★ Sobresaliente
★★★ Bueno
★★ Regular
★ Mediocre

Einteilung in Klassen

★★★★★ Ausgezeichnet
★★★★ Vorzüglich
★★★ Gut
★★ Nicht Sehr Gut
★ Schlecht

COMPARATIVE RATINGS OF WORLD BAND PORTABLES

World band portables—at least those that are worth considering—can be a delight. Some are even versatile enough not only for travel, but also for listening around the home. Others, though, can be real dogs. You see, selecting a world band radio isn't like buying, say, a television set. Most TVs perform similarly, but model-to-model differences among world band portables can be profound.

How Much?

With world band radios, often the more you pay, the more you get. But not always.

Look at *Passport's* ratings—each one the result of exhaustive laboratory and hands-on testing—and you will see a number of models that outperform competitors costing nearly twice as much.

Also, consider what you want the radio for. If you're looking strictly for a world band radio—not a world band radio that's also a facsimile machine and a satellite receiver—there's no point in purchasing a $6,500 unit whose world band performance is essentially the same as other models costing a fraction as much. So, as a general rule of thumb, buy a world band radio—and nothing more—unless you have a real need for the non-world-band features.

Finally, it's best to avoid going for the cheapest radio you can lay your hands on—especially if it's a "multiband portable" (see box). While the novelty of hearing stations from afar may be ample reward for the short haul, it can get tiring pretty fast if the receiver is unpleasant to the ear. Remember, world band signals usually traverse continents, and the international radio spectrum is overcrowded with too many stations fighting over too few frequencies. To cope with all this calls for a certain threshold of performance . . . and cost.

So, figure to spend $190 or more for a radio you'll listen to with any regularity. Equally, if you're thinking of spending large sums on a portable, you may wish to consider a tabletop model, instead. These are evaluated and rated elsewhere in this "Buyer's Guide."

Models are listed in order of suitability for listening to world band radio broadcasts. For the U.S., "list"—suggested retail—prices are quoted. Unless otherwise noted, in the U.S. discounts of 10–15% are common, whereas in Canada prices tend to run higher than U.S. list.

Prices in Asia vary widely, with those in Japan being among the highest and those in such places as Singapore among the lowest. As list prices are largely an American phenomenon, the observed *selling* price parameters, expressed in dollars for the sake of comparison, are cited for the European Economic Community.

Finally, German radio regulations require that world band receivers sold in the Federal Republic do not cover the shortwave spectrum above 26.1 MHz. However, travelers to Germany are routinely allowed to bring in receivers covering the "forbidden" 26.1–30 MHz portion of the shortwave spectrum.

MINI-PORTABLES

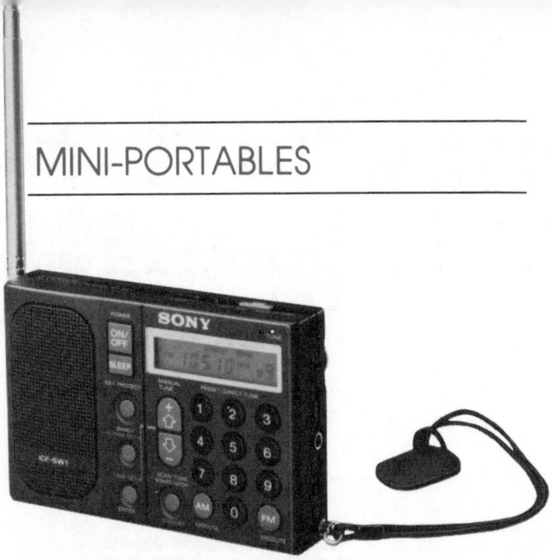

Sony's ICF-SW1S and new ICF-SW1E pack high performance in a miniature package.

★ ★ ★ ★ *Editor's Choice*

Sony ICF-SW1S

Prices: $349.95 in U.S., $370–480 in Europe.

Advantages: Superb high-quality, low-distortion audio when earpieces, which come standard with the set, are used. Various helpful tuning features. Unusually straightforward to operate for a high-tech model. World Time clock. Alarm/sleep facilities. Quality-audio FM stereo with earpieces. Comes standard with amplified outboard antenna, in addition to the usual built-in antenna, to enhance reception of weak signals. Comes standard with AC power adaptor that adjusts automatically to local current level anywhere in the world. Night light for LCD.

Disadvantages: Tiny speaker provides mediocre audio quality. Lacks tuning knob. Tunes only in coarse 5 kHz increments, making for substandard reception of the relatively small number of "off-channel" broadcasts. World Time clock can be read only when radio is switched off. Volume control located at rear, making it easy to change accidentally. Substandard rejection of certain spurious signals ("images") for price class. Comes with earpieces, rather than headphones.

Overall: Although relatively costly, the new Sony ICF-SW1—the closest thing to a world band "Walkman" available—is, hands down, the best mini-portable on the market.

★ ★ ★ ★ **New for 1990** *Editor's Choice*

Sony ICF-SW1E

Prices: $260–340 in Europe.

Identical to Sony ICF-SW1S, preceding, but lacking the carrying case and most accessories. Not available in North America.

★ ★ ★ **New for 1990** *Editor's Choice*

Sony ICF-SW20

Prices: $99.95 in U.S., $110–150 in Europe.

Advantages: Superior adjacent-channel rejection, comparable to that of pricier ICF-SW1S and ICF-SW1E siblings, for size and class.

Disadvantages: Tiny speaker produces mediocre audio quality. Limited coverage of world band spectrum includes omission of important 13 MHz segment. Lacks digital frequency display.

Comments on New Model: This tiny offering from Sony is the latest of a number of world band radios that have been designated as "new models," but which are really discontinued models with new styling. Simply the earlier ICF-4920 and ICF-5100 *in mufti*, the 'SW20 is old tea in new bags. All the pluses, such as

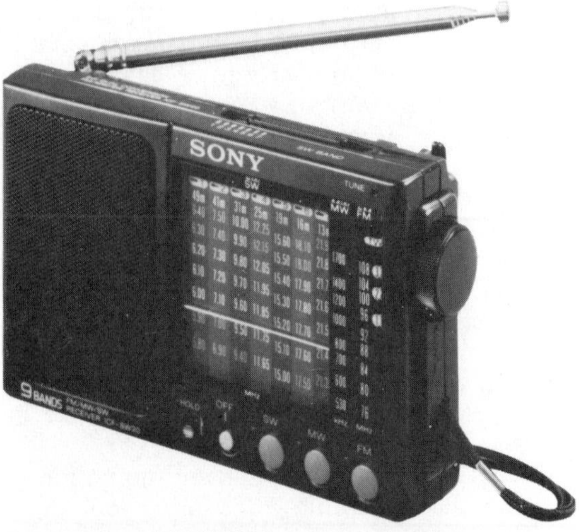

The new Sony ICF-SW20 is merely an earlier model with a new cabinet. Still, it performs quite well for its price and size.

good selectivity, and minuses, such as limited coverage of the world band spectrum, are present.

Withal, this tiny set remains a good performer for the money. It's a pity that Sony couldn't have gone one step further and provided coverage of the important 13 MHz segment.

★ ★ **New for 1990**

Sangean MS-103
Sangean MS-103L

Prices: *MS-103:* $114.95 in U.S.; *MS-103L:* $75–150 in Europe.
Advantages: Better coverage of world band spectrum than otherwise-identical sibling model MS-101. FM stereo through headphones.
Disadvantages: Mediocre rejection of adjacent-channel signals. Mediocre rejection of certain spurious signals ("images"). Slightly limited coverage of world band spectrum. Lacks digital frequency display. Inferior audio quality.
Overall: Although preferable to its MS-101 sibling, the Sangean MS-103 is nonetheless a modest mini-portable of interest almost exclusively to the weight-and price-conscious traveler. Also sold under a wide and ever-changing variety of brand names, including Emerson, Goodmans and Siemens.
Comment: The MS-103 includes world band coverage from 2.3–5.2 MHz, but has no longwave coverage. The MS-103L covers 2.3–5.2 MHz, but receives longwave broadcasts.

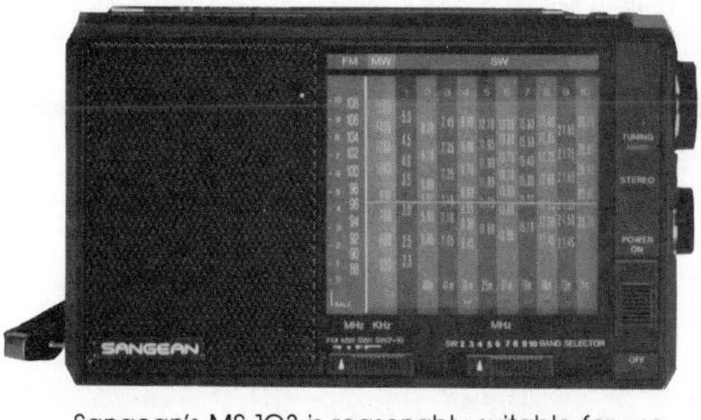

Sangean's MS-103 is reasonably suitable for use on travels.

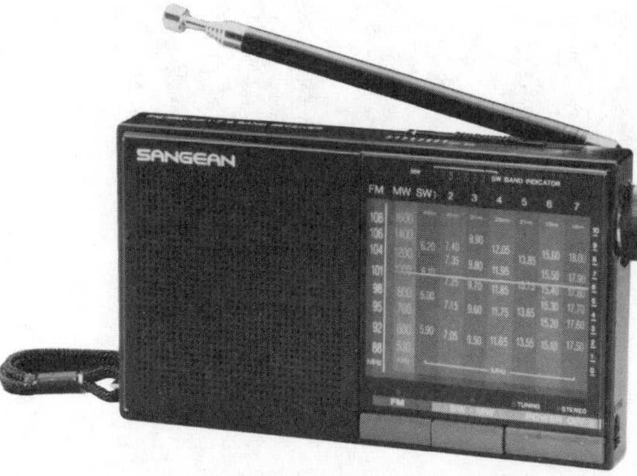

The Sangean MS-101 performs less well than some other mini models in its price class, but is sometimes heavily discounted.

★ ★

Sangean MS-101

Prices: $99.95 in U.S., $65–125 in Europe.
Advantages: Inexpensive. FM stereo through headphones.
Disadvantages: Mediocre rejection of adjacent-channel signals. Mediocre rejection of certain spurious signals ("images"). Limited coverage of world band spectrum. Lacks digital frequency display. Inferior audio quality.
Overall: A low-priced, modest mini-portable of interest almost exclusively to the weight- and price-conscious traveler. Also sold under a wide and ever-changing variety of brand names, including Emerson, Goodmans and Siemens.

Sangean SG-789 is widely available under various brand names and is inexpensive.

★ ★

Sangean SG-789
Emerson PSW4010
Sangean SG-789L

Prices: *SG-789/PSW4010:* $79.95 in U.S.; *SG-789L:* $60–95 in Europe.

Advantages: Inexpensive. FM stereo through headphones.

Disadvantages: Mediocre rejection of adjacent-channel signals. Mediocre rejection of certain spurious signals ("images"). Somewhat limited coverage of world band spectrum includes omission of important 13 MHz band. Lacks digital frequency display. Inferior audio quality.

Overall: Similar to the Sangean MS-101, but with less complete coverage of the world band spectrum.

Comment: SG-789 covers world band from 2.3–5.2 MHz, but has no longwave coverage. SG-789L has no 2.3–5.2 MHz coverage, but receives longwave broadcasts.

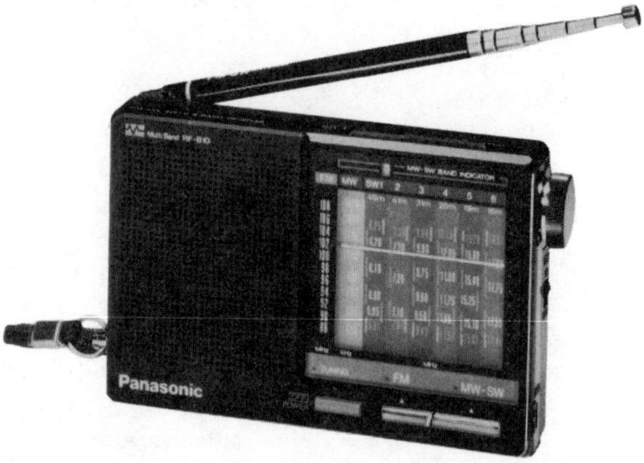

Panasonic's tiny RF-B10 is outclassed by a number of competing models.

★ ★

Panasonic RF-B10
National B10

Prices: *Panasonic:* $99.95 in U.S., $95–135 in Europe.

Advantages: Relatively inexpensive. Two-year warranty.

Disadvantages: Substandard overall performance includes mediocre rejection of adjacent-channel signals and certain spurious signals ("images"). Limited coverage of world band spectrum includes omission of important 13 MHz segment. Mediocre audio quality. Lacks digital frequency display.

Overall: Better, more advanced choices available at same or lower prices.

RADIOS TO AVOID

For most, especially in North America, world band radio or shortwave listening is something unfamiliar. Indeed, judging from receiver sales figures (see "Who Else Is Listening?" in this *Passport*), most who eventually learn of the field do so when they purchase a "multiband portable," likely from a mail-order catalog.

Multiband portables, such as the large Alconic Series 2959 or smaller Realistic DX-360 (see this "Buyer's Guide") are just that: radios that cover not only the usual AM and FM bands, but also any of a number of other bands, such as weather, TV audio, aeronautical . . . and the shortwave spectrum—usually calling it "SW1," "SW2," and so forth—that includes world band broadcasts. Sometimes exotic-looking antennas, public-address systems, bright cabinet trim, padded leatherette cases, and other features are added to make the radio more attractive to the undecided consumer.

These sets, many of which come from five manufacturers in Hong Kong, have obvious appeal. They are usually affordable, and because they perform so many tasks, they almost seem like dream machines. After all, if you get so much for so little, how can you possibly go wrong?

Alas, if you're looking for world band performance, you will go wrong. World band, which consists of thousands of weak signals packed within slivers of congested radio spectrum space, suffers dearly on these glitzy non-performers. Their outdated technology and dime store circuitry simply can't cope with the rigors of the medium.

To begin with, most of these models give you no meaningful indication of where the set is tuned. Like an old AM radio, they require that you slip and slide a needle around the dial until you hear the station you want. Unlike AM, however, world band contains *hundreds* of channels. Finding a foreign station you want amidst all this confusion becomes a tiresome hit-and-miss chore.

Additionally, these sets contain circuitry designed to cope not only with world band, but also other media. The end result is something like having a golf cart serve as the family automobile. Mixed in with the station you're trying to hear—if, indeed, you can hear it at all—is a cacophony of howls, squeals, extraneous chitchat and teletype sounds. It's pretty hard to take once the novelty has worn off.

The new Panasonic RF-B65 is a delightful radio—easy to use, affordable and a reasonable performer.

★★★★ New for 1990 *Editor's Choice*

Panasonic RF-B65
Panasonic RF-B65L
National B65

Prices: *RF-B65:* $279.95 in U.S.; *RF-B65L:* $300–450 in Europe.

Advantages: Very easy-to-operate advanced-technology radio. Pleasant audio quality. Various helpful tuning features. World Time clock. Alarm/sleep facilities. Two-year warranty. One of the few lightweight portables capable of receiving single-sideband signals, used by hams and utility stations (see "Eavesdropping on Disaster"). In U.S., attractively priced for a superior performer within its size class.

Disadvantages: Tuning knob cumbersome to turn rapidly.

Overall: A very nice, easy-to-use portable for listening to noncritical favorite programs.

Comments on New Model: Panasonic has taken its earlier model RF-B60—already the best in its size class—and made it capable of demodulating single-sideband signals by adding not only the appropriate electronic circuitry, but also a fine-tuning control to interpolate between the 1 kHz increments of the primary tuning controls. In the "L" version, there is also coverage of longwave broadcasts.

If you live in Europe or Eastern North America, where world band signals tend to be fairly strong, and wish to listen to the major international broadcasters, the 'B65 makes an excellent choice.

★★★★

Sony ICF-2003
Sony ICF-7600DS

Prices: *ICF-2003:* $299.95 in U.S.; *ICF-7600DS:* $260–400 in Europe.

Advantages: Various helpful tuning features. Separately displayed World Time clock. Alarm/sleep facilities. One of the few lightweight portables capable of receiving single-sideband signals, used by hams and utility stations (see "Eavesdropping on Disaster").

Disadvantages: Sensitivity to weak signals slightly below par with built-in antenna. Pedestrian audio quality. Lacks tuning knob.

Overall: Similar to the new Sony ICF-SW1, but a bit larger and lacking accessories and high-quality earpiece audio, the Sony ICF-2003/ICF-7600DS is a worthy portable for air travel.

Sony's ICF-2003 continues to make a good showing, but its years-old design makes it less attractive than Panasonic's RF-B65.

The Sony ICF-PRO80 offers reception of much more than world band, but at a relatively steep price.

★★★★

Sony ICF-PRO80
Sony ICF-PRO70

Prices: $449.95 in U.S., $550–700 in Europe.

Advantages: Comes equipped with versatile VHF scanner (reduced coverage in 'PRO70 version). Above average at bringing in weak world band stations. One of the few lightweight portables suitable for reception of "utility" signals (see "Action Between The Bands").

Disadvantages: Awkward to operate. Operation of outboard scanner module especially cumbersome, as it requires removal and replacement of battery pack and antenna. Mediocre audio quality. Lacks tuning knob and most travel features.

Overall: Of value mainly to DX radio enthusiasts in need of a small world band portable with a VHF scanner.

★★★

Panasonic RF-B40
Panasonic RF-B40L
National B40

Prices: *RF-B40:*$229.95 in U.S.; *RF-B40L:* $220–320 in Europe.

Advantages: Very easy to use. Two-year warranty.

Disadvantages: Tunes only in coarse 5 kHz increments, which leads to sub-optimal adjacent-channel rejection. Lacks tuning knob.

Overall: Although lacking in any strong pluses or minuses, the 'B40 is a pleasant, easy-to-operate portable for noncritical listening. However, for relatively little more, the Panasonic RF-B65 is well worth the extra money.

Comment: The RF-B40L includes coverage of longwave broadcasts.

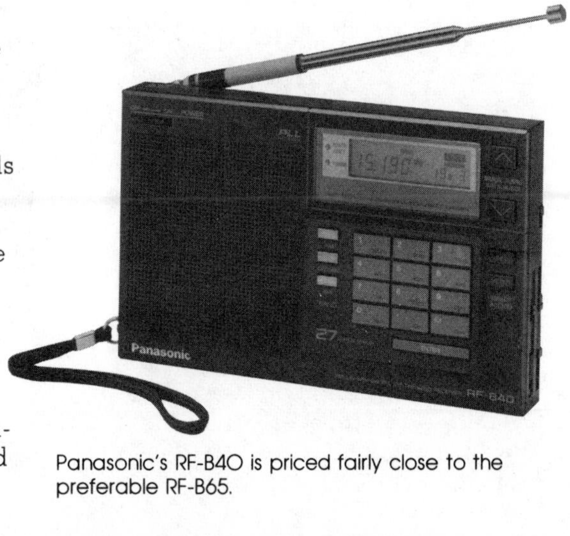

Panasonic's RF-B40 is priced fairly close to the preferable RF-B65.

The Sony ICF-7700 makes use of an innovative frequency readout.

★★★

Sony ICF-7700
Sony ICF-7600DA

Prices: *ICF-7700:* $199.95 in U.S.; *ICF-7600DA:* $230–300 in Europe.

Advantages: Very easy to use. World Time clock. Alarm/sleep functions.

Disadvantages: Coarse 5 kHz tuning increments create performance shortcomings—notably mediocre adjacent-channel rejection. Slightly limited coverage of world band spectrum.

Overall: A much better bet for the technically timid is the Panasonic RF-B65.

★★★ *Editor's Choice*

Sony ICF-7601

Prices: $129.95 in U.S., $125–170 in Europe.

Advantages: High sensitivity aids in reception of weak stations.

Disadvantages: Lacks digital frequency display. Slightly limited coverage of world band spectrum. Adjacent-channel rejection, although reasonable, not equal to that of some other Sony models.

Overall: This latest entrant in the popular ICF-7600 series—well over a million have been sold—represents a slight, but noticeable, improvement over earlier versions. This is a proven performer within its price range.

Sony's ICF-7601 continues to provide good value.

Toshiba's RP-F11, a good choice for the money, is one of the few low-cost portables with a genuine signal-strength meter.

★★★ *Editor's Choice*

Toshiba RP-F11

Prices: $119.95 in U.S., $170–200 in Europe.

Advantages: Analog signal-strength meter, a rarity at this price. More likely than most models to be discounted.

Disadvantages: Limited coverage of world band spectrum. Lacks digital frequency display. Mediocre adjacent-channel, adjacent-band and first-IF rejection. Not widely available.

Overall: A reasonable performer that, after discounts, can be an above-average value.

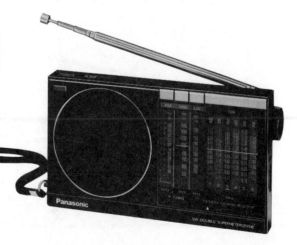

★★

Panasonic RF-B20
Panasonic RF-B20L
National B20

Prices: *RF-B20:* $149.95 in U.S.; *RF-B20L:* $120–195 in Europe.

Advantages: Unusually good audio for such a small radio. Two-year warranty.

Disadvantages: Limited coverage of world band spectrum includes omission of important 13 MHz segment. Mediocre adjacent-channel rejection. Lacks digital frequency display.

Overall: A reasonable performer that would be much better were it able to sort stations out more successfully.

Comment: The RF-B20L includes coverage of longwave broadcasts.

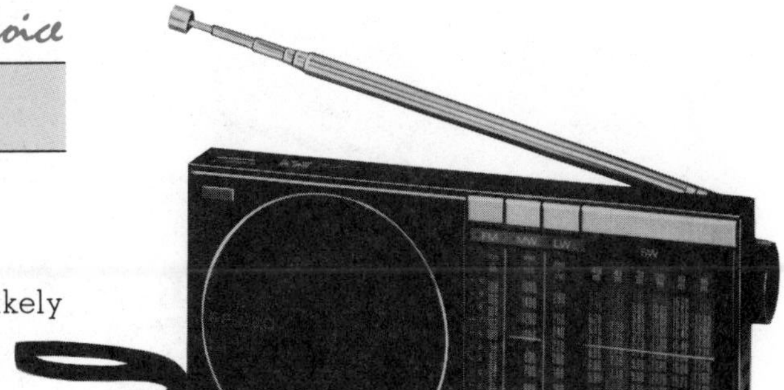

The Panasonic RF-B20 has little to offer.

★ ★ **New for 1990**

Grundig Yacht Boy 230

Prices: $149.00 in U.S., $120–175 in Europe.

Advantages: Relatively wide coverage of world band spectrum for compact analog portable. Includes World Time and worldwide multi-country clock/alarm/sleep timer with electronic map. Dial light. Stereo FM with earphones.

Disadvantages: Mediocre rejection of certain spurious ("image") signals. Mediocre rejection of adjacent-channel signals. Lacks digital frequency display. On-off switch tricky to turn on. Pushbutton volume control increases or decreases sound in relatively large increments.

Overall: A reasonable, but undistinguished radio made relatively attractive by its unusually handy world clock.

Comments on New Model: Grundig's Asian-made Yacht Boy series has never provided much in the way of world band performance. This latest entry is no exception, providing performance that is only adequate, what with excessive adjacent-channel interference, poor rejection of "image" interference, and annoying backlash when tuning the lower end of a given band.

However, the world clock is a delight to use. At the push of a button, it gives you the local time in the major cities of the world—as well, of course, as World Time.

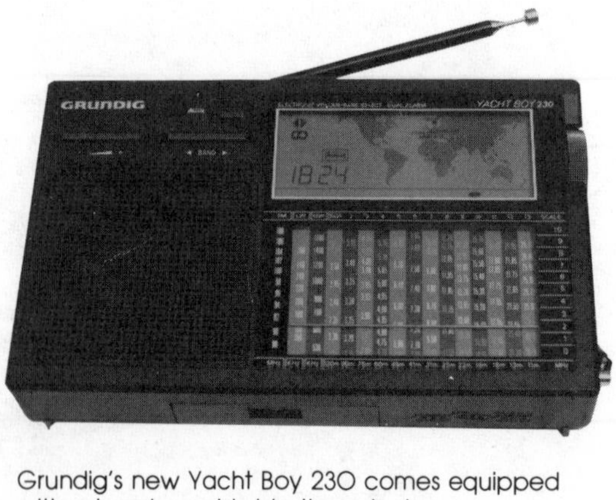

Grundig's new Yacht Boy 230 comes equipped with a handy worldwide time clock.

The new Magnavox D1875 is essentially the earlier D1835 with a new cabinet. It still provides worthy performance for the money.

★ ★ **New for 1990** *Editor's Choice*

Magnavox D1875 / Philips D1875

Prices: *Magnavox:* $99.95 in U.S.; *Philips:* $85–125 in Europe.

Advantages: Fairly sensitive to weak signals. Relatively inexpensive. More likely than most models to be heavily discounted in the U.S.

Disadvantages: Mediocre rejection of adjacent-channel signals. Mediocre rejection of certain spurious signals ("images"). Limited coverage of world band spectrum. Lacks digital frequency display.

Overall: A so-so performer, the D1875 is nonetheless one of the better low-cost portables.

Comments on New Model: As with Sony's ICF-SW20, the "new" D1875 is essentially the former D1835 with a new cabinet. The '1875 is also more costly than the discontinued '1835, which makes it something less than the hands-down bargain the earlier model was. Nevertheless, the D1875 is still the model of choice where price is the chief consideration.

The Grundig Yacht Boy 220 is new for 1990.

★ ★ **New for 1990**

Grundig Yacht Boy 220

Prices: $119.00 in U.S., $95–150 in Europe.

Advantages: None.

Disadvantages: Mediocre rejection of adjacent-channel signals. Mediocre rejection of certain spurious ("image") signals. Lacks digital frequency display. Pushbutton volume control increases or decreases sound in relatively large increments. Limited coverage of world band spectrum.

Overall: An uninspiring, but adequate, travel radio.

Comments on New Model: This offering performs comparably to the more costly Yacht Boy 230, but lacks some of the '230's "bells and whistles"—notably the interesting world clock, timer facilities and dial light.

Nevertheless, overall performance between 5.8 and 22 MHz is similar to it, but with one plus: The '220 does not have the degree of dial backlash found on the '230. Too, the '220's on/off switch is easier to use.

★ ★

Sony WA-6000

Prices: $170–230 outside North America.

Advantages: Built-in cassette recorder and microphone.

Disadvantages: Limited coverage of world band spectrum includes omission of important 13 MHz segment. Mediocre overall performance. Lacks digital frequency display. Not available in North America.

Overall: Worth considering if you need a world band radio and recorder in one small, not-too-costly package.

★ ★ **New for 1990**

Cougar H-88

Prices: $49.95 in U.S., $40–70 in Europe.

Advantages: Inexpensive.

Disadvantages: Limited coverage of world band spectrum. Mediocre rejection of adjacent-channel signals. Mediocre rejection of certain spurious signals ("images"). Modest sensitivity to weak signals. Lacks digital frequency display. Tuning knob somewhat stiff to turn. Power switch easily activated by accident, such as when radio packed on trips.

Overall: A passable radio for the price.

Comments on New Model: Although the subassemblies for a number of widely sold multiband radios come from China, most of these radios' final assembly is in Hong Kong. The Cougar goes a step further—this is a truly Chinese product. Otherwise, the chief characteristics of this model are low price and lackluster performance.

China's Cougar H-88 gives basic performance at a basic price.

Opal's OP-35 is a great clock, but a not-so-great radio.

★ ★

Opal OP-35
Siemens RK 702

Prices: *OP-35:* $99.95 in U.S.; *RK 702:* $75–160 in Europe.

Advantages: Relatively inexpensive, especially after discounts. Includes handy World Time and worldwide multi-country clock/timer. Available duty free for about $70 on Lufthansa flights.

Disadvantages: Very limited coverage of world band spectrum. Mediocre rejection of adjacent-channel signals. Mediocre rejection of certain spurious signals ("images"). Modest sensitivity to weak signals. Drifts off frequency when held. Lacks digital frequency display. Not widely available.

Overall: A clock that comes with a radio, rather than *vice versa*. A better bet for this type of clock/radio combination is Grundig's new Yacht Boy 230, but the '230 is somewhat more costly.

★

Sangean ATS-802

Prices: $134.95 in U.S., $90–150 in Europe.

Advantages: Digital frequency display, an exceptional feature in this price class. FM stereo through headphones.

Disadvantages: Dreadful overall performance, especially adjacent-channel rejection. Tortoise-slow tuning. Limited coverage of world band spectrum.

Overall: This model, which sounds so intriguing in the promotional description, in reality has only its digital frequency display to commend it.

MID-SIZED PORTABLES

★ ★ ★ ★ *Editor's Choice*

Sony ICF-2010
Sony ICF-2001D

Prices: *ICF-2010:* $429.95 in U.S.; *ICF-2001D:* $500–690 in Europe.

Advantages: High-tech synchronous detector circuit with selectable sideband; this results in superior reduction of adjacent-channel interference and selective fading distortion with world band signals, as well as within the longwave and mediumwave AM broadcasting bands. Two bandwidths allow for superior tradeoff between audio fidelity and adjacent-channel rejection. Numerous helpful tuning features, including 36 memories with handy individual pushbuttons. Separately displayed World Time clock. Alarm/sleep/timer facilities. Some reception of air band signals. The best travel-weight

A favorite in recent years is Sony's innovative ICF-2010, which features genuine synchronous detection.

portable for reception of utility and ham signals (see "Eavesdropping on Disaster"). Available at extra cost with AN-1 amplified antenna as model ICF-2001DS in Europe, or with the AN-1 as two separate components elsewhere.

Disadvantages: Audio quality below par for price class. Lacks meaningful tone controls. Proliferation of controls and high-tech features may intimidate or confuse some. Memories and time setting sometimes erase when set is jostled, causing "AA" computer batteries to lose contact. Wide bandwidth somewhat broad for world band reception (remediable by various specialty firms, such as Radio West). Synthesizer chuffs somewhat.

Overall: Except for audio quality and ease of operation, Sony's established offering continues to be the best performing travel-weight portable. Although it looks more complicated to operate than it really is, the recent introduction of Grundig's Satellit 500 highlights the '2010/'2001D's aesthetic and ergonomic shortcomings. Although Sony's ICF-2010/ICF-2001D is in need of an ergonomic and cosmetic redo, for traveling radio enthusiasts it will remain the portable of choice until something better comes along.

★★★★ **New for 1990**

Grundig Satellit 500

Prices: $599.00 in U.S., $375–500 in Europe.

Comment on Testing: Our initial tests of the Grundig Satellit 500 were made on a pre-production prototype which performed quite well. The findings that follow are based not on this but, rather, on our tests of a production unit, s/n 801458, which generally performed more poorly. According to the manufacturer, units from serial number "2000 upwards"—presumably 802000 upwards—will be better-constructed.

Advantages: High-tech quasi-synchronous detector circuit, which behaves as a synchrophase circuit, with selectable sideband via off-tuning; this results in superior reduction of adjacent-channel interference with world band signals,

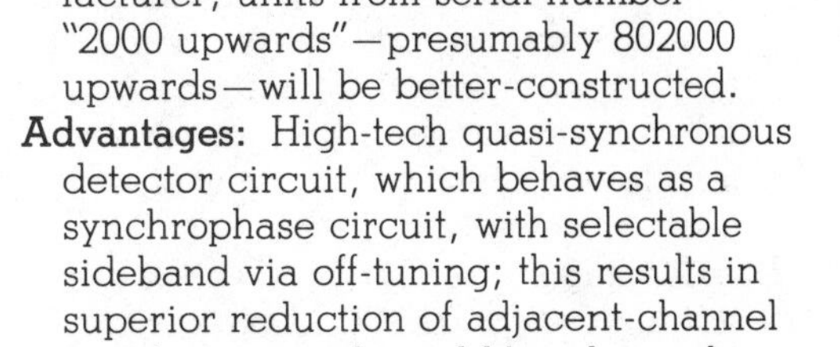

The new Grundig Satellit 500 is Germany's answer to Sony's ICF-2010.

as well as within the longwave and mediumwave AM broadcasting bands. Two unusually well-chosen bandwidths allow for superior tradeoff between audio fidelity and adjacent-channel rejection. Excellent ultimate rejection, remarkable for a portable. Relatively easy to operate, with superior ergonomics for a feature-laden high-tech receiver. Numerous helpful tuning features, including 42 channel memories. Large, easy-to-read LCD shows not only tuned frequency, but also station name when memory call-up is used. Separate bass and treble tone controls. Two World Time clocks, displayed separately from frequency readout. Alarm/sleep/timer facilities, including two-event timer that also turns certain models of tape recorders on and off. Unusually effective night light illuminates LCD and keypad. Stereo FM with headphones; in Europe, reportedly also with optional outboard speaker. Generally superior FM and mediumwave AM performance. Worldwide 110–127/220–240V AC power supply. In North America, comes with two-prong North American and European plug types—in Europe, only European-type plug is provided. Comes equipped with a built-in NiCd battery charger (see *Disadvantages*). Mounting (metric) screw holes for securing radio in mobile environments, such as on board boats or ships.

Disadvantages: Tendency to spurious interference to world band broadcasts from nearby AM, FM and television stations. Mediocre sensitivity to weak signals in lower world band frequency ranges—especially 60, 75 and 90 meters. Nominal synchronous detector circuit behaves as a quasi-synchronous, or synchrophase, circuit in that it does not correct selective-fading distortion. That same circuit, which reduces interference via off-tuning of the received signal, sometimes generates a weak spurious heterodyne (whistle), variable with the tuned frequency, when station is off-tuned. High overall distortion—10 to 12%—in single-sideband mode at audio frequencies of 1 kHz and below. Dynamic range poor at 5 kHz channel spacing. Outboard AC power supply sometimes causes faint hum (50 dB down). Quality control difficulties present in initial production; manufacturer states these will be cleared up as of "serial number 2000 upwards" (see Comment on Testing, above). Use of built-in NiCd battery charger in early production samples reportedly causes overheating of certain makes of cells. According to industry sources, manufacturer no longer wishes to promote the NiCd charger as a feature; however, our unit's battery cavity states, somewhat ambiguously, "DON'T CHARGE BATTERIES! ONLY NI-CD-ACCU." Pushbuttons require relatively high finger pressure. Synthesizer chuffs considerably, and also "clunks" at certain switchover points.

Overall: In many ways quite different from Sony's ICF-2010 and ICF-2001D models, this new entry from Grundig is noteworthy for its attention to ergonomics and appearance. Its performance, however, is a mixed bag—excellent in certain respects, mediocre in others. *Do not use this set as a NiCd charger without first checking with the manufacturer.*

Comments on New Model: While costlier Japanese world band radios have tended to appeal to radio aficionados, they have rarely stirred the interest of the general public. Grundig's new Satellit 500 portable, on the other hand, is a sleek set that looks—and is—both exciting and relatively easy to operate.

There are all kinds of small touches to make operation straightforward and pleasant. For example, the channel memories store not only frequencies and the like, but also station names of up to four characters each (for example, "KUSW" or "BBC"). And while you expect the LCD, with its wealth of operating information, to be illuminated at night, you don't expect to find the keypad lit, as well. There's also a sleek hard-plastic dust cover, such as is found on some PC keyboards—and a set of bass and treble controls. If you're into taping programs, the two-event timer will also switch certain models of recorders on and off. The Sony ICF-2010 and ICF-2001D have none of these features.

In some respects, the '500 also performs quite well. Its ultimate selectivity, for example, is the best of any portable we have measured, and even better than that of many tabletop models. And its choice of bandwidths is excellent—these are clearly better thought out than those of the Sony '2010 and '2001D. Too, the '500's aural quality in the regular AM or synchronous-detection modes, while hardly sterling, is slightly better than that of most high-tech radios.

That's the good news. The bad news is that radio enthusiasts will find it somewhat lacking in performance, especially as compared to Sony's '2010 and '2001D, in the very areas of most concern to them. Sensitivity to weak signals within the lower ranges—2 to 5 MHz—is mediocre. Spurious signals from local AM, FM and television stations sometimes intrude, causing unnecessary interference to desired signals. And distortion in the single sideband mode runs as high as 12%.

Ergonomic shortcomings include two-handed operation (volume control on left, tuning controls on right), stiff pushbuttons, the lack of dedicated memory-choice pushbuttons, and the presence of an essentially pointless AGC control knob that, if inadvertently switched, deadens the set.

The big news, of course, is the '500's synchronous detector with selectable sideband. In reality, what the industry tends to lump under the catchall rubric "synchronous detection" is not always the same thing from one design to another. There is a basic difference between the true synchronous detector used in Sony's '2010 and '2001D, and the quasi-synchronous, or synchrophase, detector apparently used by Grundig. Sony's synchronous detector works no better than does Grundig's when it comes to rejecting adjacent-channel interference. However, Sony's virtually eliminates selective-fading distortion; Grundig's doesn't, and the ears quickly pick up on the difference.

However, Grundig has designed the '500 to be easy to operate, and to that end the use of what behaves as a synchrophase detector has been a success. Whereas to operate Sony's version requires careful tuning and the pushing of a button, Grundig's functions simply by letting the set be detuned—without raising distortion as it would on an ordinary set. Operation just couldn't be any easier.

Another hallmark of the '500 is an inviting appearance. This radio is not only sleek—the "Movado watch" of world band radios, if you will—it is also unintimidating. Whereas Sony's '2010 and '2001D bristle with buttons and other controls, the '500 has far fewer to perform pretty much the same tasks the Sony does.

But there is a rub in all this. To call up a station in memory on the Sony, you push only one button. On the '500, you have to push up to three. It's not the pushing of buttons as such that is the problem here. Rather, it is that it's so much easier to remember, visually, what are in the Sony memories—36 little buttons lined up neatly, tic-tac-toe, in rows and columns—than it is to remember an abstract two-digit number that has to be entered in a multi-function keypad.

Withal, Grundig's Satellit 500 is a set that had to be. For too long, world band radios have looked and operated as if they were designed of, by and for radio engineers—certainly not for the public. In contrast, the '500 is, above all, designed for people.

This doesn't alter one essential fact: that for all the attention to ergonomics, appearance and high-tech circuitry, the '500—at least in early production—is deficient in two basic key variables, spurious signal rejection and, to some extent, sensitivity. For listeners located well away from local broadcasting stations and who do not tune the tropical frequencies below about 5.2 MHz, these shortcomings are pretty much beside the point. For them, the '500 makes a logical—even exciting—choice. But for those in proximity to local AM, FM and TV stations, or those who tune world band's nether frequencies, the '500's performance shortcomings could result in disappointment. If you are in doubt, buy on a money-back basis.

The Magnavox D2935 continues to be the best bargain among world band radios.

| Magnavox D2935 |
| Philips D2935 |

Prices: *Magnavox:* $179.99 in U.S.; *Philips:* $210–330 in Europe.

Advantages: Pleasant audio quality. Numerous helpful tuning features. Superior adjacent-channel selectivity. Superior rejection of certain spurious signals ("images"). Superior sensitivity to weak signals. Built-in dual-voltage AC power supply for use worldwide.

Disadvantages: Membrane keypad lacks "feel." Memory buttons more complicated than most to use and can be inadvertently deprogramed if wrong buttons pressed. A bit larger and heavier for travel than most mid-sized portables.

Overall: A simplified and more compact version of the Magnavox and Philips D2999, the D2935 is an exceptional performer within its price class. This is the best buy of any world band portable on the market—grab it while you can!

★ ★ ★ ★   *Editor's Choice*

| Sangean ATS-803A |
| Realistic DX-440 |
| Eska RX 33 |
| Matsui MR-4099 |
| Emerson ATS-803A |
| Siemens RK 651 |
| Quelle Universum |

Prices: *ATS-803A:* $249.95 in U.S., $150–330 in Europe; *DX-440:* $199.95 in U.S., $230–250 in Europe; *RX 33:* $260–280 in Europe; *MR-4099:* $130–170 in Europe; *Emerson:* About $335 in Canada; *RK 651:* $170–200; *Universum:* $180–200 in Europe.

Advantages: Numerous helpful tuning features. Two bandwidths allow for superior tradeoff between audio fidelity and adjacent-channel rejection. Superior rejection of certain spurious signals ("images"). Good sensitivity to weak signals. Superior reception of "utility" stations for price class (see "Eavesdropping on Disaster"). Some versions come standard with dual-voltage AC adaptor for worldwide use. FM stereo through headphones.

Disadvantages: None.

Overall: With balanced all-around performance, the various designations of the ATS-803A, an improved version of the earlier ATS-803, are second only to the Philips and Magnavox D2935 as best buys in their price class. On the "A" (improved) version, the "mono stereo" switch reads "wide narrow;" avoid any sample that reads otherwise, as its performance will be inferior.

The Sangean ATS-803A receives world band, ham and "utility" signals.

★ ★ ★

Sony WA-8800

Prices: $500–530 outside North America.

Advantages: Comes equipped with built-in stereo cassette recorder, FM stereo reception and stereo speakers. Separately displayed World Time clock/alarm. High sensitivity aids in reception of weak stations.

Disadvantages: Lacks digital frequency display. Slightly limited coverage of world band spectrum. Adjacent-channel rejection, although reasonable, not equal to that of certain other Sony models. Costly for world band performance class. Not available in North America.

Overall: If you must have a portable complete with built-in cassette recorder, this is the model to get. North Americans will find it at various electronic and airport shops abroad.

★ ★

Philips D2615

Prices: Under $100 in Europe.

Advantages: Relatively pleasant audio quality.

Disadvantages: Mediocre overall performance. Lacks any meaningful frequency display, making it an arduous hit-and-miss procedure to locate a desired station. Not available in North America.

Overall: A suboptimal choice, even at under $100.

Radio Shack's Realistic DX-360 is a disappointing performer at any price.

★

Realistic DX-360

Prices: $79.95 in U.S.

Advantages: Inexpensive. Fairly pleasant audio quality.

Disadvantages: Lacks any form of even remotely accurate frequency display, making it an arduous, hit-and-miss exercise to locate a desired station. Mediocre rejection of adjacent-channel signals. Mediocre rejection of certain spurious signals ("images"). Slightly limited coverage of world band spectrum. Minimally discounted.

Overall: The archetype "multiband shortwave radio" of twenty years ago. Its aural performance is bad enough, but the kicker with this radio and many other cheap multiband portables is that you have virtually no idea where you are tuning—and there are over 1,000 world band channels from which to choose. One can but wonder how many people have obtained a '360 from Radio Shack stores "to see what world band radio is like," only to be turned off for good by the '360's disappointing performance. Too, although it is cheap, it is no bargain. Inexpensive as it is, the Realistic DX-360 costs roughly the same, after everyday discounts, as do a number of competing models, such as the Magnavox or Philips D1875 and various Sangean models, that at least give you a good idea of where you are tuning.

Sony's entry into the gilt-edged world band radio market, the CRF-V21, comes complete with video display, radio fax facilities, and a thermal printer.

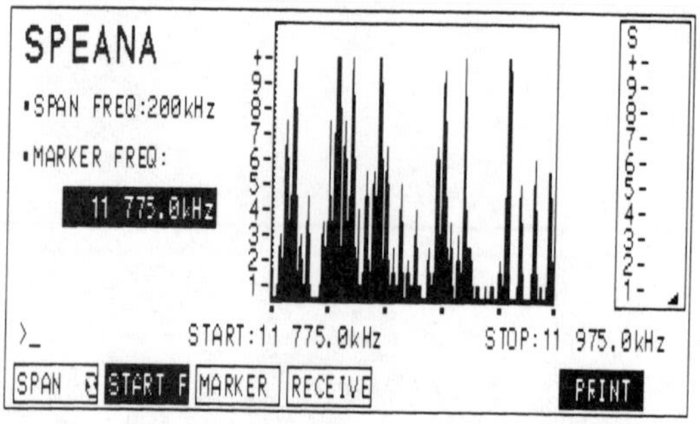

200 kHz of world band spectrum occupancy as displayed on the Sony CRF-V21's video screen.

★ ★ ★ ★ **New for 1990**

Sony CRF-V21

Prices: $6,500.00 in U.S.

Advantages: High-tech synchronous detection circuit with selectable sideband; this results in superior reduction of adjacent-channel interference and selective fading distortion with world band signals, as well as within the longwave and mediumwave AM broadcasting bands. Two bandwidths allow for superior tradeoff between audio fidelity and adjacent-channel rejection. Numerous helpful tuning features, including 350 memory channels. Keypad unusually straightforward to operate. Receives and processes off-the-air narrow-band FM, RTTY and fax signals. Covers longwave down to 9 kHz, as well as the satellite fax frequencies of 137.62 MHz, 141.12 MHz, 1.691 GHz and 1.6945 GHz. Liquid-crystal video display (LCD) for various functions, including frequency, station name (when memory call-up is used), separately displayed World Time, RTTY and fax. LCD also acts as a spectrum monitor. Built-in thermal printer provides LCD print-screen function and hard-copy fax with very high resolution (reportedly 850 dpi). World Time clock displays seconds numerically. Alarm/sleep/timer/scanner/activity-search facilities nominally can also be used to do hands-off spectrum occupancy surveys. Tunes and displays in precise 10 Hz increments. Outstanding tuning knob, except for tuning rate, has unsurpassed ergonomics. The best portable, by a small margin, for reception of utility and ham signals (see "Eavesdropping on Disaster"). Generally superior sensitivity to weak signals, plus blocking, AGC threshold, dynamic range, ultimate rejection, skirt selectivity, phase noise, image rejection, IF rejection and stability. Very low audio distortion in the AM and synchronous-detection modes. Comes standard with broadband active antenna; AN-P1200 satellite antenna available at extra cost. Worldwide 110/120/220/240V AC power supply and rechargeable NiCd battery pack. Except with U.S. version, comes with RS232-C port for computer interface. Night light.

Disadvantages: Expensive. Audio quality only average. Has only one tone control. Complex to operate and generally not user-friendly. Lack of a built-in telescopic antenna encumbers portable operation. Mediocre ergonomics. Wide bandwidth somewhat broad for world band reception. Video display lacks contrast and thus is very difficult to read. Somewhat heavy and large for truly portable applications. Tuning knob turn rates either too slow or too fast. Flip-over night light ineffective; also is easily mistaken for carrying handle, which can result in the light's being broken. Slow-sweep spectrum occupancy function of LCD does not operate in true real time. Two of three spectrum-occupancy "slice" widths too wide for use on shortwave, while the remaining (third) only barely narrow enough to be of use. AGC decay much too fast for proper use with single-sideband signals. Mediocre suppression of unwanted sideband for a premium receiving device. Mediocre front-end selectivity.

Overall: A fax-oriented receiver laden with features aplenty, as a world band receiver the CRF-V21 nonetheless doesn't so much as equal the performance of tabletop models costing around $1,000, and only slightly exceeds the performance level of some portables costing a tenth as much.

Comments on New Model: The Sony CRF-V21 is a world band receiver that attempts to be many things to many people by incorporating a number of disparate features. In addition to reception of world band frequencies, longwave down to a very low 9 kHz, and AM/FM broadcast channels, it offers the capability to receive radio fax, radio teletype (RTTY), narrow-band FM and satellite fax transmissions—and to print out these fax messages, along with other data, on a built-in high resolution thermal printer. A large liquid crystal video display (LCD) serves a variety of important functions—most notably that of a spectrum monitor—but is very difficult to read. Finally, the 'V21 is one of the few world band receivers available with synchronous detection coupled to selectable sideband.

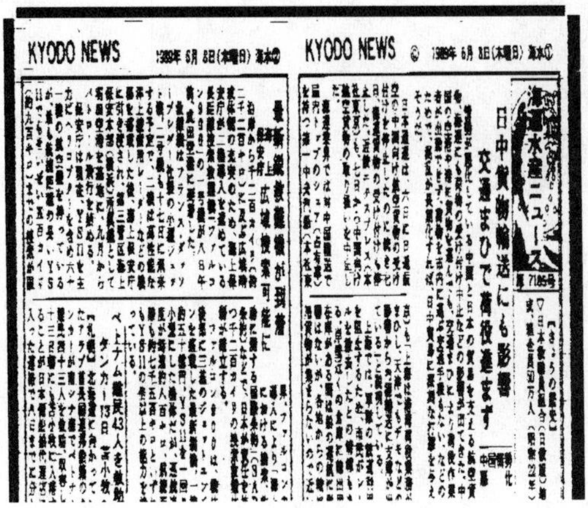
KYODO NEWS 1989年6月8日(木曜日)

KYODO NEWS 1989年6月8日(木曜日)

日中貨物輸送にも影響

ベトナム難民43人を救助

The Sony CRF-V21 produces fax output, including of Japanese news.

Despite this wealth of features, the 'V21's test results are not exceptional. Indeed, in some respects this model is substandard—its audio quality is barely average, for example. In addition, the poor ergonomics of the 'V21 sometimes make operating the set a frustrating experience.

Overall, the 'V21 falls well short of its potential. It offers a number of interesting and unique features, coupled to worthy but unexceptional overall world band performance. In addition, the ergonomics are disappointing, and the otherwise-commendable central display is hard to read—all at a price several times the cost of most competing world band "supersets."

The beefy Grundig Satellit 650 has top-notch audio quality.

★★★★ *Editor's Choice*

Grundig Satellit 650

Prices: $999.00 in U.S., $700–900 in Europe.

Advantages: Excellent audio quality. Two full bandwidths and a third pseudo-bandwidth allow for superior tradeoff between audio fidelity and adjacent-channel rejection. Superior rejection of spurious signals. High sensitivity to weak signals. Numerous helpful tuning features. World Time clock. Alarm/timer facilities. Superior FM reception. Large size and heft make it relatively well-suited for use as a home receiver. Built-in dual-voltage AC power supply for use worldwide.

Disadvantages: Too large and heavy for portable use except around the home, in the yard, and on automobile trips. Less likely than most models to be steeply discounted. Motorized preselector tuning results in above-average mechanical complexity. Construction quality below norm for price class.

Overall: A favorite for hour-after-hour listening—but less so for DXing tough catches—the massive '650 is one of the best-sounding world band radios available, although it lacks synchronous selectable sideband.

★★★★ *Editor's Choice*

Magnavox D2999
Philips D2999

Prices: *Magnavox:* $299.95 in U.S.; *Philips:* $375–550 in Europe.

Advantages: Unusually pleasant audio quality—even better than that of its D2935 sibling—with flexible tone controls. Numerous helpful tuning features. Two bandwidths allow for superior tradeoff between audio fidelity and adjacent-channel rejection. Superior rejection of certain spurious signals ("images"). Lays down horizontally, with speakers on both the top and front, and thus is one of the few portables tested that also serves as a true tabletop receiver for use at home. World Time clock. Alarm facility. Built-in dual-voltage AC power supply for use worldwide.

Disadvantages: Mediocre reception of "utility" stations for a full-sized portable. Substandard front-end selectivity for size, but not price, class.

Overall: A fine-sounding world band receiver, the D2999 combines many of the virtues of a portable with at least some of those of a tabletop model. However, in many other respects it is remarkably similar to its less-costly D2935 sibling. Even then, so long as it continues to be available, it's still a bargain.

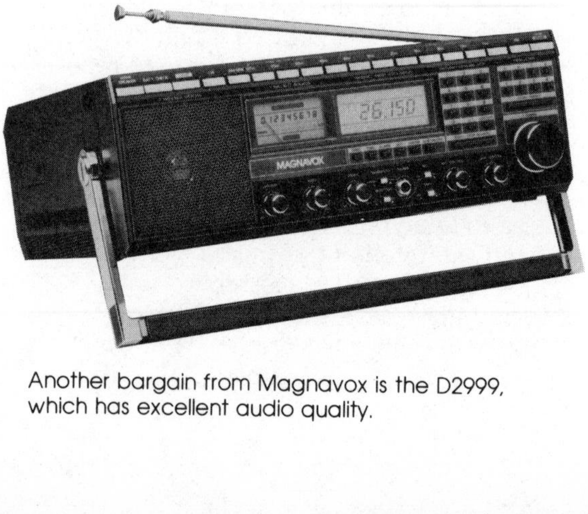

Another bargain from Magnavox is the D2999, which has excellent audio quality.

The Alconic Series 2959, which sells under numerous brand designations, is a jack-of-all-trades, master of none.

★ ★

Marc II NR-108F1 Pan Crusader

Prices: $300–550 worldwide.

Advantages: Unusually broad coverage of radio frequency spectrum. World Time clock. Sleep/timer facilities.

Disadvantages: Marginal overall performance within certain portions of the world band spectrum. Poor adjacent-channel rejection. Preselector tuning control adds greatly to complexity to operation. Not widely available.

Overall: Made in Japan, but the way it performs you'd think it was a product of Albania.

The Marc II NR-108F1, although somewhat costly, performs dismally.

★

Alconic Series 2959 Venturer Multiband Rhapsody Multiband

Prices: *Basic model:* $79.95–99.95; *With cassette player:* $129.95; *With cassette player, stereo audio and digital clock:* $159.00.

Advantages: Inexpensive. Covers VHF-TV and air/weather bands. Audio quality at least average. Genuine signal-strength meter, a rarity at this price. Built-in cassette player (two versions only). Stereo audio (one version only). Digital clock (one version only).

Disadvantages: World band coverage omits the 2, 3, 13, 15, 17, 21 and 26 MHz segments. Lacks any form of even remotely accurate frequency display, making it an arduous hit-and-miss exercise to locate a desired station. Mediocre overall performance.

Overall: For those who don't know any better. Sold widely under various names—or even no advertised name—but with identical appearance, by such mail order stores as Rand McNally, Haverhills, Adam York, SYNC, COMB, Blair Shoppe and Eddie Bauer, as well as by credit-card companies.

GOLDEN OLDIES

The following models have reportedly been discontinued, but may still be available new at some retail outlets. Prices are in the range of actual or estimated sale prices as of the time *Passport/90* went to press. Listed in order of overall rating.

★★★★ Panasonic RF-B600
★★★★ National B600

Under $400. Roughly comparable to the current Magnavox D2999 and Philips D2999, but the 'D2999 sounds better, while the 'B600 is better constructed and superior at handling single-sideband signals. A worthwhile buy when priced around $225.

★★★★ Grundig Satellit 400

Under $450. The predecessor to the Satellit 500, the 400 provides pleasant overall results. Nevertheless, it lacks many of the '500's high-tech features and ergonomic advantages, and in some respects—notably reception of single-sideband signals—is audibly inferior to the '500. A worthwhile buy when priced around $200.

★★★ Sony ICF-7600A
★★★ Sony ICF-7600AW

Under $150. Similar to the current Sony ICF-7601, but with lesser coverage of world band spectrum; notably, the 13 MHz segment is omitted. A worthwhile buy when priced around $85.

★★★ Sony ICF-4920
★★★ Sony ICF-5100 *Editor's Choice*

Under $150. Similar in all but styling to the current Sony ICF-SW20. A worthwhile buy when priced at less than the 'SW20.

★★ Grundig Yacht Boy 215

Under $150. A modest performer with a World Time clock/timer. Lacks coverage of important 13 MHz band. A worthwhile when priced around $90—mainly because of its clock/timer feature.

★★ Grundig Yacht Boy 210

Under $130. Identical to Grundig Yacht Boy 215, preceding, except that clock/timer facilities are omitted. A worthwhile buy when priced around $75.

★★ Magnavox D1835
★★ Philips D1835 *Editor's Choice*

Under $70. Essentially identical in performance, but not in styling, to current Magnavox D1835 and Philips D1835. A worthwhile buy when priced at less than the '1835.

★ Sangean ATS-801

Under $100. Essentially identical, except for battery operation, to the current Sangean ATS-802. Not worth buying at any price.

The Passport *equipment review team consists of Lawrence Magne, J. Robert Sherwood and Jock Elliott.*

COMPARATIVE RATINGS OF TABLETOP RECEIVERS

For most, a good portable is more than adequate to enjoy the offerings found on world band radio. For others, though, something more is needed.

Superior Tough-Signal Performance

That "more" is a tabletop receiver. These often excel at flushing out the really tough catches—faint signals and stations swamped by interference from competing signals. They also do unusually well with non-broadcasting—ham and "utility"—signals, many of which are in the single-sideband mode (see "Eavesdropping on Disaster" elsewhere in this edition).

Tabletop models can also be useful if you live in a part of the world, such as central and western North America, where signals tend to be weak and made choppy by high-latitude "flutter" fading—a common problem when world band signals have to traverse paths close to the polar region. If you place a string on a globe, then run it from where you live to where the signals are being transmitted from, you can get a feel for how much this high-latitude phenomenon might affect your listening quality.

Another plus of tabletop models is for listening during the day, when most signals are of relatively modest strength. A good tabletop won't guarantee reception of a faorite weak daytime station, but it will certainly help.

What tabletop receivers don't necessarily do is to deliver better audio quality. Like portables, tabletop models run the audio gamut from shrill to mellow.

For the most part, tabletop receivers are pricey, with the very best going for thousands of dollars. But this isn't always the case, as the new Lowe HF-225 suggests. Too, most tabletop models also require an outboard antenna—indeed, the quality of performance of a tabletop receiver will be determined in large part by the quality and proper placement of its antenna. A good outdoor wire antenna, such as the Eavesdropper or Alpha Delta Sloper, usually runs from $60 to $80. A short amplified antenna, suitable for use indoors and sometimes outdoors, sells for somewhat more.

What The Ratings Mean

Models that are new for 1990 are covered in this year's Buyer's Guide at length. Every model, regardless of its year of introduction, has been taken through the various testing "hurdles" we established and have perfected since 1977, when IBS first started evaluating world band equipment.

Each model is thoroughly tested in the laboratory, using criteria developed especially for the unique, strenuous requirements of world band reception. The set then undergoes "hands on" evaluation, which usually runs a number of weeks, before we commence preparing our detailed internal report, which forms the basis for our findings summarized in this "Buyer's Guide." Those models that we feel represent something special within their price and size classes are designated as *Editor's Choices*.

Our unabridged laboratory and hands-on test results are far too exhaustive to reproduce here, as they run quite a number of pages for each model. If you would like a copy of these detailed reports, they are now being made available as *Radio Database International White Papers*, details of which may be found elsewhere in this edition.

Receivers are listed in order of suitability for listening to difficult-to-hear world band radio broadcasts. Models that are unusually appropriate for hour-after-hour listening to world band programs are so indicated under "Advantages."

In this regard, keep in mind that if you listen mainly to weaker stations—or to speech, such as newscasts—audio quality will be of less importance than if you listen often to musical programs over strong, clear stations. Too, when shopping, remember that most tabletop models, unlike portables, are available only from electronics and world band specialty outlets.

For the U.S., "list" prices are quoted. Unless otherwise noted, in the U.S. discounts of up to 10% are not unusual, whereas in Canada prices tend to run slightly higher than U.S. list. As list prices are largely an American phenomenon, the observed *selling* price limits, expressed in dollars for the sake of comparison, are cited for the European Economic Community.

PROFESSIONAL MONITOR RECEIVERS

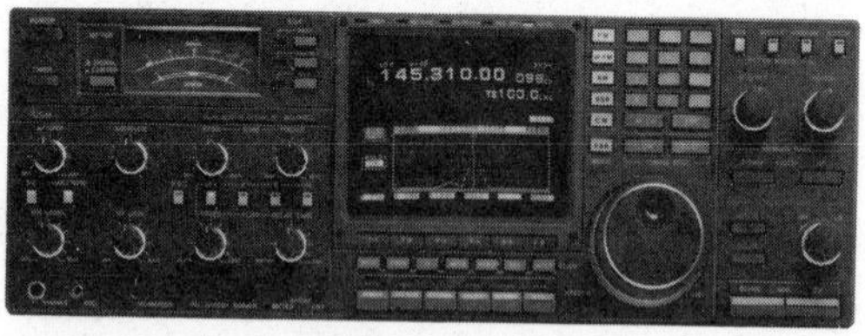

ICOM's new IC-R9000, with proper bandwidth filters, can provide unsurpassed tough-signal performance and superior audio quality.

★ ★ ★ ★ ★ **New for 1990** *Editor's Choice*

ICOM IC-R9000

Price: $5,459.00 in U.S., more in Europe.

Advantages: Unusually appropriate for listening to world band programs over extended periods. Sensitivity, IF rejection, image rejection, skirt selectivity, ultimate selectivity, front-end selectivity, blocking, phase noise, AGC threshold, notch depth and stability all either superb or excellent. Flexible, above-average audio for a tabletop model, especially when a suitable outboard speaker is used. Video display of radio spectrum occupancy. Generally superior quality of internal construction. Sophisticated scanner facilities. Broad coverage of radio spectrum. Exceptionally flexible operating controls include passband tuning (IF shift), variable notch filter, noise blanker, a thousand tunable programmable channel memories, and two shortwave antenna inputs. Wide variety of I/O ports for computer and other use. Remote control available. Very good ergonomics. Superb reception of "utility" and "ham" signals. World Time clock.

Disadvantages: Very expensive. Power supply runs hot (remediable, see story). Widths of two bandwidth filters too broad for reception of most world band radio signals (remediable, see story). Widths of two single-sideband bandwidths almost identical (remediable, see story). Some distortion when very powerful signals received. Construction quality of front-panel controls only average.

Overall: The ICOM IC-R9000, with at least one changed bandwidth filter and better cooling, is the best receiver we have ever tested. It is a well-thought-out, well-designed receiver that offers peak performance at around five times the price of most other world band supersets.

Comments on New Model: The new ICOM IC-R9000 receiver's most prominent characteristic is a TV-type (cathode ray tube) video display. Among other things, it provides operating feedback—frequency (in 0.01 kHz steps), mode and filter selection—plus memory and scan information.

The display also shows an amber pip for each signal that's on the air within the viewing range of the display. That range—or "slice"—is chosen by the listener, so you can see 50, 100 or 200 kHz of spectrum at a glance. Of course, all you see for each signal is a pip. The display doesn't tell you the names of the stations whose pips you're seeing, and the readout is more like a series of slightly delayed snapshots of the spectrum than it is a continuous real-time display. But it can help when you're dialing about, as the display shows even faint signals that you might otherwise tend to pass over when tuning solely by ear.

The '9000 covers a large chunk of the radio spectrum: longwave above 100 kHz, mediumwave, shortwave (including world band), VHF and UHF. The U.S. and European versions cover from 0.1-1998.8 MHz, while versions sold in other parts of the world have reduced coverage: Australia 2-87.5 and 108-1999.8 MHz; Germany 0.15-26.1, 28-29.7, 144-146 and 430-440 MHz; and France 0.1-87.5 and 108-1999.8 MHz.

This receiver has almost every feature you can imagine, with the exception of synchronous detection. There are two shortwave antenna inputs; three bandwidths for the AM mode and two for the single-sideband mode; passband tuning ("IF Shift"); a keypad; a large tuning knob; Megahertz up/down slewing controls for quick large-scale jumps in frequency; a highly adjustable automatic gain control; a superb tunable notch filter to eliminate even the most stubborn of heterodynes (whistles); three levels of attenuation; a World Time clock; a noise blanker that is adjustable for width and level; a true RF gain control; scan speed and delay time controls; video in and video out jacks; a voice scan control switch; frequency-readout alignment controls; a dimmer switch and brightness controls for the front panel displays; a fully programmable timer; a delayed-off (sleep) timer; a switch for sending a synthesized voice announcement of frequency to an external tape recorder; a series of multi-function switches for the video display; and, of course, the video display itself.

There are also no less than 1,000 channel memories, each of which is fully tunable. Each channel can store frequency, mode, filter choice, tuning rate, and up to eight alphanumeric characters in memory—to display station name, for example. In addition, there are interfaces for sophisticated remote and computer control.

In the AM mode, used for essentially all world band broadcasts, three bandwidth filters can be selected manually: wide, 11.3 kHz; medium, 7.8 kHz; and narrow, 2.6 kHz. In the single-sideband and most other modes, bandwidths are 2.8 kHz and 2.5 kHz. All have excellent-to-superb shape factors and superb ultimate rejection. But while the narrow AM bandwidth is well-chosen, the medium and wide are too broad for most world band listening purposes. As to the single-sideband bandwidths, one measures 2.8 kHz, while the other is 2.5 kHz—there's hardly any difference. Various ICOM dealers, including Electronic Equipment Bank and Universal Shortwave in the U.S., have indicated that they plan to offer substitute filters with more suitable bandwidths. EEB, for example, plans to offer $150 custom-made Collins mechanical filters with bandwidths of 4 kHz and 6 kHz not only for the '9000, but also for various other models. These filters, which are to have 10 or 11 elements instead of the usual 7 or 8, are being designed to produce unusually high skirt selectivity and ultimate rejection.

The '9000—especially its power supply—generates excessive heat, so various ICOM dealers are also offering thermostatically activated low-noise computer-type cooling fans to alleviate this. Our unit failed during testing, apparently because of excessive heat, so this sort of supplementary cooling is highly recommended.

The audio quality of the '9000, aside from "breakup" distortion with very powerful signals, is above average—especially when a good outboard speaker is used. However, the '9000 doesn't have synchronous detection. This means that sideband selection has to be done manually—an imperfect solution, but nonetheless a relatively easy procedure with this set. Further aiding listening pleasure is the IF shift, which can be adjusted to provide the best mix of tonal quality and interference rejection for the specific signal being heard. The '9000's audio is also enhanced by the inclusion of powerful separate bass and treble tone controls.

Overall, the '9000 exhibits superior ergonomics, mainly because of the control layout on the front panel. However, the keypad buttons are small and wobbly, and slide-on plastic knobs are used.

For this kind of money, one would expect that the '9000 would be nigh perfect. The bad news is that it isn't...even if it comes close. But what counts is the good news: that with professional-grade replacement filters and a cooling fan, ICOM's new superset would qualify as the best-performing receiver we have tested.

★★★★★ *Editor's Choice*

Japan Radio NRD-93

Price: $6,410.00 in U.S., $6,000 to $10,000 elsewhere.

Advantages: Unusually appropriate for listening to world band programs over extended periods. Superb all-around performance. Professional-quality construction with legendary durability to survive around-the-clock use in such punishing environments as the tropical high seas. Unusually easy to repair on-the-spot. Excellent ergonomics and unsurpassed "feel" of controls. Above-average audio for a tabletop model. Sophisticated optional scanner allows for a certain degree of automated listening. Superb reception of "utility" and ham signals.

Disadvantages: Very expensive, although U.S. price, as quoted by Japan Radio's New York office, is somewhat lower than in years past. Lacks certain advanced-technology tuning aids. Distribution limited to Japan Radio offices and a few specialty organizations, such as shipyards.

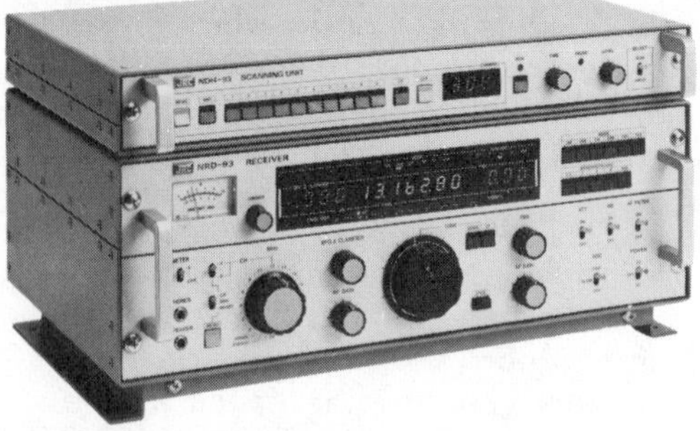

Japan Radio's NRD-93 is the toughest, best-constructed model tested.

Overall: The incomparable ruggedness and quality of construction set the Japan Radio NRD-93 apart from all other models tested. It is a lovely set to operate for bandscanning hour-after-hour, but its receiving performance is not appreciably different from that of less-costly tabletop models.

Comment: In 1988, lightning virtually destroyed *Passport's* South American monitoring facility, partially melting the cabinet of the main Japan Radio NRD-515 receiver. The receiver was pulled from the charred debris, plugged in, and worked—and continues to work—perfectly.

TUNING IN THE ARMED FORCES RADIO & TELEVISION SERVICE

The U.S. Armed Forces Radio and Television Service is difficult to tune in on shortwave, but it can be heard well—via satellite.

Operating around-the-clock, AFRTS radio operates from the new INMARSAT system on the frequency of 1536.950 MHz, with 1537.000 MHz as an alternative. All but a few remote parts of the world are covered by this system's three large footprints.

Anybody with a suitable receiver and antenna can receive AFRTS radio, with its around-the-clock news, sports wrapups, live baseball and football games, weather forecasts, commentaries—free from the usual ads. These programs originate with virtually all the U.S. radio networks—CBS, NBC, ABC, APR, NPR, Mutual, AP, USA Today, and so on.

The Pentagon recommends a $5,750 receiving configuration manufactured by Sea-Tel Incorporated of Martinez, California. However, there are other alternatives for world band listeners. In particular, the new ICOM IC-R9000, reported on in this Buyer's Guide, covers the AFRTS frequencies, along with all the world band frequencies. At even lower cost is ICOM's IC-R7000; however, this model doesn't receive world band radio.

Neither comes equipped with the necessary satellite antenna. However, these are available from specialized sources, including some world band firms, such as Electronic Equipment Bank, that also sell the necessary receivers.

TABLETOP RECEIVERS

★★★★★ *Editor's Choice*

Kenwood R-5000

Price: $1,049.95 in U.S.; $1,000-1,500 in Europe.

Advantages: Unusually appropriate for listening to world band programs over extended periods. Superb all-around performance. Unusually good audio for a tabletop, provided a suitable outboard speaker is used. Exceptionally flexible operating controls. Excellent reception of "utility" and ham signals.

Disadvantages: Ergonomics only fair. Replacement of standard, but mediocre, wide bandwidth filter with high-quality YK-88A-1 substitute adds to cost. Audio badly distorted at tape-recording output.

Overall: The Kenwood R-5000's combination of superior tough-signal performance and above-average audio quality makes it the optimum receiver in its price class for those who need a receiver for both quality program listening and DXing. In the United Kingdom, some samples may appear under the "Trio" brand name.

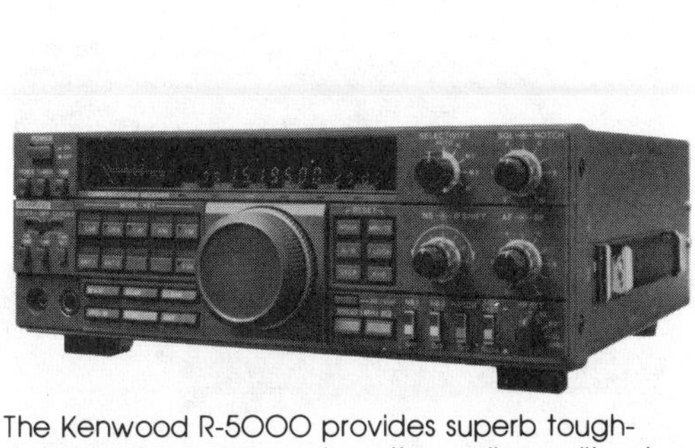

The Kenwood R-5000 provides superb tough-signal performance and worthy audio quality at a fair price.

The Japan Radio NRD-525 excels in receiving signals in diverse modes.

★★★★★ *Editor's Choice*

Japan Radio NRD-525

Price: $1,349.00 in U.S., $1,300–2,000 in Europe.

Advantages: Superb all-around performance. Highly flexible operating controls. Very good ergonomics. Quality of construction slightly above average. Computer-type modular plug-in circuit boards enhance ease of repair. Sophisticated scanner allows for a certain degree of automated listening. Excellent-to-superb reception of "utility" and ham signals.

Disadvantages: Audio quality only fair. Surface-mounted devices make replacement of discrete components very difficult. Relatively limited dealer network.

Overall: A superb performer that's well put together—although hardly like the NRD-93—but is somewhat lacking in fidelity. The prominent choice in its price class for listening to signals in diverse modes.

The 1990 ICOM IC-R71, still a superior DX receiver, is now minus one of its features found in past years.

★ ★ ★ ★ Altered for 1990

ICOM IC-R71

Price: $999.00 in U.S., $1,000–1,600 in Europe.

Advantages: Superb reception of weak, hard-to-hear signals. Flexible operating controls. Excellent reception of "utility" and ham signals.

Disadvantages: Mediocre audio quality. Substandard ergonomics. Operating system software erases, requiring reprogramming by ICOM service center, should backup battery die.

Overall: A favorite among serious world band DXers, but not equal to other tabletop models for quality-audio program listening.

Comments on Altered Model: The variable-bandwidth ("passband tuning") circuitry formerly found on the 'R71 was deleted from samples coming on the market as of March, 1989. The newer version's right-hand knob is not concentric and is simply labeled "NOTCH"—*not* "P.B.T-NOTCH."

A proposed solution, which appeared in *'73 Magazine*, to the 'R71's erasable software may be obtained for $10 and a self-addressed stamped envelope from Bob Roehrig, 314 S. Harrison St., Batavia IL 60510 USA.

★ ★ ★ ★ New for 1990 *Editor's Choice*

Lowe HF-225

Price: £344 plus power supply, accessories and VAT in United Kingdom; under $700—including keypad, power supply, shipping and tariff—if sent to the U.S.

Advantages: Unusually appropriate for listening to world band programs over extended periods. Straightforward to operate for a tabletop model. Generally excellent ergonomics. Best bandwidth flexibility of any model tested. One of the most ruggedly-built sets tested. Very good audio when suitable outboard speaker is used. Optional synchronous detection feature provides reduced distortion (see "Disadvantages"). Optional battery pack allows for field portable use. Operating manual unusually helpful. Attractively priced for performance offered.

Disadvantages: Some operating controls provide limited flexibility. Slightly less sensitive to weak signals than some tabletop models tested. Automatic-gain control recovery time somewhat slow. Optional synchronous detector circuit does not select one sideband over another, thus defeating one of its two main purposes. Two of four bandwidths supplied are too wide for most world band applications. Currently not distributed within North America.

Lowe's new HF-225 shows that good things can come in small packages.

Overall: A tough, easy-to-operate set with superior audio quality.

Comments on New Model: The Lowe HF-225 shows numerous refinements over its predecessor, the HF-125. In effect, it's had its "shakedown cruise," with the result that the various annoyances that could be traced to its digital circuits have now been eliminated.

However, the pluses of the '125 remain, right down to the well-written user's manual. Like the '125, the '225 has a small footprint—that is, it takes up very little room on your desk. This small size also allows it to second as a portable, if the right options—NiCd battery pack, active antenna and carrying case—are purchased.

But the '225 is, at heart, a tabletop, with tabletop-grade performance and generally excellent ergonomics—right down to the excellent flip-out elevation feet. To begin with, the '225 has remarkably few controls, and these have excellent "feel" and are well laid-out. There are only nine controls in all, as compared with the dozens found on some Japanese radios. There's also an analog signal-strength meter. Otherwise, the front panel is remarkably free from clutter.

The keypad, which is optional and highly recommended, is outboard—a plus, inasmuch as it lays down flat, like the keypad on a calculator or telephone. It also uses the familiar three-by-three-plus-zero format found on most telephones and some calculators.

Equally praiseworthy is how the keypad works. If you want to hear, say, the BBC on 5975 kHz, you just tap in 5-9-7-5, and there it is. Unless you're tuning below 3 MHz, there's no fooling around with "enter" keys, "kHz" keys, leading zeroes, decimals—or any of the time wasters found on other keypads. It is, hands down, the best keypad available on any set, regardless of price.

The '225 sounds very good, too—provided it is used in concert with an outboard speaker, as the one built into the set faces upwards and provides only plain-vanilla audio quality. Especially noteworthy is the '225's low distortion. Our lab measurements show that overall distortion—not just audio distortion, but all distortion from the antenna through to the speaker—is consistently less than one half of one percent. When you hook up a good speaker to this receiver—Lowe offers no less than the Wharfedale Diamond III speaker as an option—it sounds first-rate, although control over the aural frequency response is limited somewhat by the presence of only a single tone control.

There's another reason the '225 sounds so exceptional. It's the only tabletop model tested that can be equipped, albeit at extra cost, with a synchronous detector. Our tests show that this does indeed reduce distortion, but it doesn't allow for selectable sideband (however, you can choose sidebands reasonably well manually, thanks to the set's precise tuning increments). This is only half a loaf, but it's a good half-loaf, and it is more than you get with other tabletop models.

Another thing that helps this set sound so good is that it comes with no less than four voice bandwidths—2.3, 5.6, 8.8 and 11 kHz—from which to choose. Most receivers come with only two, so this is a real plus. And they work very well, with top-drawer skirt and ultimate selectivity. Of the four bandwidths, the widest is appropriate for listening to local AM stations, while at least two of the other three work nicely for the varying conditions found on shortwave. One could only wish that the 8.8 kHz bandwidth were somewhat narrower—more like the nominal 7 kHz it's supposed to be, according to the dial readout. Perhaps an alteration to bring this about could be accomplished by such specialty firms as Radio West in the U.S., or even Lowe itself.

Another advantage of the '225 is that it is built to almost professional standards of ruggedness. You just don't expect to find this level of construction quality on a model selling for anywhere near this price. Time is the only certain measure of a frequency-of-repair track record, but we would expect the '225 to hold up unusually well.

However, this receiver has a relatively limited lineup of features. For example, it doesn't have a notch filter, passband tuning or a scanner, and the frequency readout is only to the nearest kilohertz, even though the synthesizer tunes in exceptionally precise—if unusual—8 Hz increments. The paucity of controls can actually complicate things a bit, too, when you're switching modes and such. Too, when you turn the receiver off, then on again, the AM bandwidth goes to the default setting of 8.8 kHz (the display shows this as "7 kHz")—regardless of where you had it set originally.

Overall, the '225 performs very well, and sounds unusually good. Our various laboratory measurements show selectivity to be excellent or better, and nearly all other laboratory measurements of performance are of a comparable standard. The exceptions are noise-floor measurements of sensitivity, close-in dynamic range, AGC decay time and front-end selectivity.

Taken together, this means that the '225 is an excellent all-around performer, but not equal to the more-costly models of tabletop sets for DXing faint stations—especially if you live near local radio transmitters or use the radio with a high-gain outdoor antenna.

As of when we are going to press, the '225 was not yet available from dealers in North America. Thus, U.S. and Canadian buyers have been ordering the set directly from the manufacturer in England. However, a number of American firms reportedly are considering offering the set for under $700.

Models from Kenwood, ICOM and Japan Radio in the $1,000–5,500 range outclass the '225 for tough-signal DXing. But the bottom line is that the new Lowe HF-225 is the best program listener's radio—tabletop or portable—that can be found on the sunny side of $1,000.

★★★★

Yaesu FRG-8800

Price: $784.00 in U.S., $800–1,100 in Europe

Advantages: Flexible operating controls. Audio quality slightly above average for tabletop model. Fairly good ergonomics. World Time clock.

Disadvantages: Bandwidths somewhat broad for most world band receiving applications. Reception of "utility" and ham signals, although acceptable, is below average for tabletop model.

Overall: A proven, well-balanced performer in need of tighter selectivity.

The Yaesu FRG-8800 is an established mid-range performer.

Kenwood's R-2000 suffices for hearing major programs, but is less successful with more demanding applications.

★★★½

Kenwood R-2000

Price: $799.95 in U.S., $750–1,250 in Europe.

Advantages: Straightforward to operate, with good ergonomics. Audio quality slightly above average for tabletop model. World Time clock. Reception of "utility" and ham signals, although not outstanding, is superior within its price class.

Disadvantages: Performance materially compromised by "overloading" in many parts of the world, such as Europe and even Eastern North America, or when high-gain antennas are used. Bandwidths too broad for most world band applications.

Overall: Generally pleasurable for listening to most world band programs, but in need of tighter selectivity and better dynamic range for more demanding applications. Occasionally sold in the United Kingdom under "Trio" brand name.

★★½

Heathkit/Zenith SW-7800

Price: $299.95 in U.S.

Advantages: One of the lowest-priced tabletop models tested. Relatively visible availability in North America through Heath's vast catalog mailings. Helpful construction assistance from factory advisors.

Disadvantages: Mediocre performance for a tabletop model. Barely functional for reception of "utility" and ham signals. Available only in kit form, requiring dozens of hours to construct.

Overall: At this price, the SW-7800 is attractive vis-a-vis increasingly higher-priced Japanese alternatives. However, unless kits are your special passion, you may wish to consider, instead, one of the better portables.

Heathkit's SW-7800 is the only world band radio available in kit form.

Sharper Image's Tunemaster Classic Radio is an eyestopper. It's also the worst performing tabletop we have ever tested.

★ New for 1990

Tunemaster Classic Radio

Price: \$199.00 plus \$7.50 shipping in U.S.

Advantages: Eye-catching appearance; styled after a French art-deco radio originally built in the 1940s. Available in either of two colors. Also covers VHF from 110–137 and 144–164 MHz. Audio quality at least average. Inexpensive for a tabletop model.

Disadvantages: Lacks digital readout. Analog readout provides virtually no indication of what channel is being tuned. Portions of analog readout misaligned or mislabeled. Lacks synthesized tuning circuitry. Lacks channel memories. Lacks keypad tuning. String-and-pulley tuning arrangement has spongy response. Fine-tuning knob, with limited tuning range, located on back of set. Mediocre adjacent-channel selectivity. Poor rejection of certain spurious signals ("images"). Mediocre dynamic range results in significant overloading when connected to outdoor antenna (comes with no built-in antenna or attenuator). Relatively unstable, making for marginal reception of single-sideband signals.

Overall: What a dog!

Comments on New Model: With 63 stores throughout the U.S., five stores in Japan, one in Switzerland—and more opening nearly every month—The Sharper Image is a visible presence. In it, you can find all sorts of novel yuppy items from \$895 toy Ferrari cars to \$4,500 rebuilt Coca-Cola vending machines from the Fifties. It's the sort of place you spend money not because you have to, but because you have it and want to spend it on just about anything.

Nowadays, that "anything" includes a world band radio made exclusively for The Sharper Image by one of the Hong Kong original equipment manufacture (oem) firms. Called the Tunemaster Classic Radio, it covers the usual FM and mediumwave AM bands, plus the shortwave spectrum from 2–21.5 MHz and two VHF ranges.

Right off, it's obvious this is no everyday radio. Your eye falls on what almost looks like the grille, hood and fenders of an old car. There, in either white or razzleberry red—your choice—is today's reincarnation of a French art-deco radio from bygone days, juiced up a bit with the addition of some bright-metal trim and "serious electronics," to quote Sharper Image's catalog.

Indeed, it is an eyestopper. Unfortunately, when you hear it you may wish you had an earstopper. Those "serious electronics" are merely seriously deficient, being made in the spirit of a cheap multiband radio—which, *in mufti*, it is. Its adjacent-channel selectivity is mediocre, allowing stations to interfere with each other; its dime store single-conversion circuity lets through all manner of "image" signals that sound like a telegraph operator gone amok; and the set's dynamic range is so mediocre that in many parts of the world—Eastern North America, for example—it overloads at night when an outdoor antenna is connected. And it comes with no built-in antenna as an alternative, or any attenuator to help cope with the overloading.

This radio tunes with a knob, of course—and only a knob, albeit one aided by a limited-range fine-tuning control secreted on the back of the set. So there's no keypad, channel memories, slewing controls, scanner facilities—or any of the other useful tuning aids that can be found at the same price or less on various world band portables.

In fact, there's no digital frequency readout to tell you where the radio is tuned to, and the archaic needle-and-dial tuning scheme is so coarse that it is virtually impossible to divine what channel the set is on. You have to grope through the hundreds of world band channels to hunt and peck for the station you hope to hear. As for receiving single-sideband signals, forget it. This set is too drifty to provide acceptable reception in this specialized mode . . . unless, of course, you wish to keep retuning it periodically as it drifts off frequency.

However, if The Sharper Image's mid-1989 catalog is to be believed, there may be some unusual frequencies the Tunemaster can receive. "One customer called us to describe how it felt when he and his family tuned in an English-speaking Hong-Kong station, and heard about events in China *while they happened*. Order today, and explore the nations of the world by radio."

That is exceptional reception, indeed . . . considering there are no world band broadcasts in English originating from Hong Kong. It also points out how difficult it is to tell so much as what you're listening to with a receiver of this caliber.

The Passport *review team consists of Lawrence Magne, J. Robert Sherwood and Jock Elliott, with from-the-field feedback from Tony Jones.*

LINIPLEX WITHDRAWN FROM NORTH AMERICAN MARKET

In early 1989, the British Liniplex F2 advanced-fidelity receiver, reported on in the 1989 *Passport to World Band Radio*, was withdrawn from the North American market because of poor sales.

This receiver performs well, notably because its synchronous detector and selectable sideband circuitry outclass any others currently available. However, aside from this, the F2 lacks nearly all the features listeners have come to expect from modern world band receiving devices. It has, for example, only one bandwidth, and even with all options lacks numerous tuning aids.

We have not tested the F2, but have tested the similar preceding model, the F1. Based on those findings, it would appear that the F2, when used with its OSC-1 tuning synthesizer, would probably rank in performance in the four-star category.

As of press time, the Liniplex F2, including the OSC-1 synthesizer and VAT, was still available in the United Kingdom for around the equivalent of $2,600.

ADD-ON DEVICE ENRICHES FIDELITY

Sherwood SE-3 MK II

Let's face it: Listening to world band radio is not the same as tuning in to your favorite local AM or FM station.

By the time a typical world band signal reaches your ears, it will have traveled thousands of kilometers and bounced several times off energized layers in the atmosphere. Because this part of the atmosphere—the ionosphere—changes constantly, world band signals don't always bounce back to earth in a consistent manner. As a result, the station to which you are tuned will fade in and out in strength—sometimes many times each second. In addition, world band stations are twice as crowded on the radio dial as are local broadcasters, so sometimes while listening to one station you will hear interference from another alongside.

The quality of world band listening on most good radios is usually acceptable, even if hardly high fidelity. But there are times when you can't help but wonder, "Wouldn't it be great if all this fading and interference could be cut down?"

Enter *selectable sideband* with *synchronous detection*, known collectively among radio cognoscenti as ECSS-s (Exalted Carrier Selectable Sideband—synchronous). This pair of high-tech ideas helps reduce fading and adjacent channel interference.

To understand what these two concepts do, let's set the scene. A world band signal is really a kind of radio sandwich—a carrier wave in the middle, flanked by a lower and an upper sideband. The carrier functions solely as a vehicle for "delivering" the sidebands, each of which contains the actual voices, music and other information you're trying to hear. In fact, if you listen to a carrier all by itself—say, from a station that's about to come on the air—the most you will hear is some hiss and static.

So, why have a carrier at all? Indeed, why have two sidebands when each contains the same sounds?

The reason is that the carrier and "extra" sideband allow low cost radios to make the station coming out of the speaker sound intelligible.

However, on sophisticated radios that have selectable-sideband circuitry, you can slice off either of the two sidebands. You can also replace the station's carrier, which has been worn down by its long journey, with a fresh new carrier generated inside your radio. This can be done manually on many better receivers, but to tune it in properly requires a safecracker's touch, and it still won't sound fully lifelike. Synchronous detection does these same things, but easily and with perfect results.

Selectable sideband can help reduce interference by allowing you to choose which sideband you would like to hear. For example, if interference is coming from a station on the next channel up, you can chose the lower sideband. Your receiver will "clip off" the annoying inter-

Sherwood Engineering's SE-3 Mark II Enhances Listening Pleasure

ference by tuning in only the sideband that is farthest from the annoying channel. Conversely, if the interference is on the next channel down—smack next to the lower sideband—you can select the upper sideband.

Given the great potential of synchronous detection for making world band listening more pleasurable, here's a surprise: None of the world band tabletops includes this sophisticated mode of reception. True, the British-made Lowe HF-225 offers synchronous detection, but not it's tied into selectable sideband.

The American firm of Sherwood Engineering has come to the rescue by offering the SE-3 Mark II, a $399.00 enhanced-fidelity device that can be installed as an after-market accessory on some, but not all, tabletop world band receivers. Since the SE-3 plugs directly into a receiver's circuitry—the IF output—initial installation often requires the services of Sherwood Engineering or an experienced technician.

The strategy of the SE-3 is to take a receiver's IF output and replace virtually all the circuitry that normally follows that stage. This means that not only the detection, but also the audio is handled by the SE-3.

This makes good sense. Most tabletop receivers are engineered to be able to receive tough signals intelligibly. Fidelity is rarely an engineering priority.

To a large extent, the "tough-signal" sections of a receiver stop at the IF output—the "fidelity" portions tend to be concentrated in subsequent stages. By replacing all the post-IF stages with fresh circuitry designed specifically to enhance fidelity, the SE-3 allows the listener to have the best of both worlds: high tough-signal performance, plus enhanced fidelity. It's like an automobile that handles like a sports car, but rides like a luxury sedan.

To find out how well the SE-3 works, we evaluated it with a Japan Radio NRD-525—one of the best tabletop receivers we have ever tested. Bear in mind that the SE-3 may perform differently with different models of receivers, although tests we did earlier using the SE-3 with a Drake R-7 receiver produced nearly identical results.

The '525 is a true world band superset, but it cannot be purchased from the factory with synchronous detection. In addition, audio quality is not one of its strong points: The sound coming out of its speaker is, politely put, simply not as crisp and clean as it should be.

For our evaluation, we purposefully tuned in world band signals that suffer from fading and adjacent channel interference. We then switched back and forth between the '525 with and without the SE-3, which was connected to a Realistic Minimus 7 speaker.

The SE-3 makes listening to the '525 a vastly different experience: Distortion and other untoward effects of fading are reduced substantially—although a slight hissing sound can sometimes be heard in the background when the SE-3 is in use. This is partly the result of connecting an enhanced-fidelity device to a receiver that has traces of circuit noise in its pre-IF output stages.

In addition, the configuration's ability to select either the upper or lower sideband with varying degrees of offset from the carrier can result in the almost-total elimination of interfering signals. As an added bonus, with the SE-3 the '525's audio is quieter and cleaner.

On the minus side, the SE-3 complicates operation by adding to the number of controls and to the complexity of tuning. Too, although the instructions for operating the SE-3 are fairly straightforward and produce the desired results, they are written for the person with a fair amount of technical knowledge. The same is true of the labeling of the controls on the SE-3.

The SE-3 comes equipped with high- and low-cut audio filters designed to help the listener obtain optimum tonal quality. In practice, we've found that these make little difference. Other bells and whistles include a worthwhile 5 kHz audio notch filter, which reduces annoying heterodyne ("whistle") interference, and a synchrophase detector to use when bandscanning.

A synchrophase detector—this term was coined ten years ago by the R. L. Drake Company, although an engineer at Motorola who helped develop the concept suggests the term "quasi-synchronous" as an alternative—does the same thing as a synchronous detector, except that it doesn't truly replace the station's transmitted carrier. The plus is that you can tune up and down the band—"bandscan"—more successfully with it than you can with a true synchronous detector. The minus is that a synchrophase detector doesn't eliminate distortion brought about by fading.

Unfortunately, some chip and receiver manufacturers call synchrophase detection "synchronous detection," which misleads the consumer. However, the SE-3 not only uses the correct nomenclature, it is the only device we have tested—or know of, for that matter—that includes *both* a synchronous and a synchrophase detector.

Overall, the Japan Radio NRD-525 provides substantially more listening pleasure when it is equipped with the Sherwood SE-3 enhanced-fidelity accessory. The result is a world band superset that is exceptionally pleasant to listen to for long periods of time.

WORLDSCAN

WORLDWIDE BROADCASTS IN ENGLISH

Country-by-Country Guide to Best-Heard Stations

Dozens of countries, large and small, broadcast in English over world band radio. This "Worldwide Broadcasts" section provides you with the times and channels where you are most likely to hear them.

Times *and days of the week* are given in World Time (UTC), which is explained in the glossary at the back of the book. During the summer, some broadcasts are heard one hour earlier to compensate for savings, or summer, time. Programs that are heard summers only are preceded by a "J" (for June), whereas those heard winter only are preceded by a "D" for (December). Transmissions not preceded by a "J" or a "D" are heard year-around.

Frequencies in bold—say, **15260**—often come in best, as these are from relay transmitters located near the intended listening audience. If you are in North America or Europe, best reception is usually found at times given in bold— **2000-2030**, for example.

AFGHANISTAN

RADIO AFGHANISTAN (**Europe**)

6020, 11755, 15510 1900-1930

ALBANIA

RADIO TIRANA

7120 **1830-1900 (Europe)**
7205 **0630-0700 (Europe)**
9440 **0230-0300** & **0330-0400 (N America)**
9480 **1830-1900** & **2230-2300 (Europe)**
9500 **0230-0300 (N America), 0330-0400 (N America), 0630-0700 (Europe)**, 0800-0830 (SE Asia & Australia), 1400-1430 (SE Asia & Australia)
9760 **0230-0300, 0330-0400** & **2330-2400 (N America)**
11835 0800-0830 (S Asia & Australia)
11855 1130-1200 (S Asia & Australia)
11985 1400-1430 (SE Asia & Australia)
15185 1130-1200 (SE Asia & Australia)

ALGERIA

RTV ALGERIENNE

9535 **1900-2000 (Europe** & N Africa)
15215 1900-2000 (W Africa & S America)

ARGENTINA

RADIO ARGENTINA-RAE

9690 & 11710 **0200-0300** & **0400-0500 (Americas)**
15345 **1730-1830** & W/F-M **2200-2300 (Europe)**

AUSTRALIA

RADIO AUSTRALIA

5995 0830-1900 (Pacific)
6035 **1530-2030** (S Asia & **Europe**)
6060 1430-2030 (Pacific)
6080 1100-2000 (Pacific)
7205 **1530-2030** (S Asia & **Europe**)
7215 1100-1300 & 1500-2030 (Pacific)
9580 **0800-2030** (Pacific & **N America**)
9620 2000-2130 (E Asia & Pacific)
9655 M-Sa **0700-0800** & **0800-1030** (Pacific & **Europe**)
9710 1100-1230 (E Asia & Pacific)
11720 0830-0930 (Pacific)
11800 1100-1230 (E Asia)
11910 0400-0630 & Su 0630-0730 (Pacific)
15160 2100-0800 (Pacific)
15240 0000-0100 & 2200-2400 (Pacific)
15320 **2200-0600** (Pacific & **N America**)
15395 0100-0400 (SE Asia), **2100-0100** (Pacific & **N America**), 0500-0900 (SE Asia)
17795 **2100-0600** (Pacific & **N America**)
21525 Sa 0200-0430 & Sa/Su 0430-0730 (S Asia)

AUSTRIA

RADIO AUSTRIA INTERNATIONAL

5945 **1930-2000 (Europe)**
6015 0530-0600 (N America)
6155 **0400-0630, 0730-0800, 1130-1200, 1430-1500, 1630-1700** & **1930-2000 Europe**
9875 Su **0100-0200, 0130-0200**, Su/M **0400-0430** & **0430-0500 (Americas)**
13730 **0130-0200 (N America), 0730-0800 (Europe)**, 1130-1200 (E Asia), **1130-1200 (Europe)**, 1330-1400 (E Asia), **1330-1400 (Europe), 1430-1500 (Europe), 1630-1700 (Europe)**
15450 1030-1100 (Australia), 1130-1200 (E Asia), **1130-1200 (E North Am)**, 1330-1400 (E Asia)
17870 **1130-1200 (E North Am)**
21490 1030-1100 (Australia), **1430-1500 (W Europe** & W Africa), **1630-1700 (W Europe** & W Africa)

BANGLADESH

RADIO BANGLADESH **(Europe)**

7520 & 11510 **1815-1900**
15195 & 17714 **0800-0830, 1230-1300**

BELGIUM

BELGISCHE RADIO & TV

5910 **1830-1855 & 2200-2225 (Europe)**
9925 **0030-0055 (Americas)**, M-F **0900-0925 (Europe), 2200-2225 (Americas)**
11695 M-F 0700-0725 (Australia), M-F 0800-0825 (Australia), **1730-1755 (Europe), 1830-1855 (Europe)**
17555 M-Sa **1300-1355 (E North Am)**

BRAZIL

RADIO NACIONAL

11745 **0200-0250 (Americas)**
15265 **1800-1850 (Europe)**

BULGARIA

RADIO SOFIA

6070 **1930-2000 (Europe)**
7115 **0400-0500 (E North Am & Europe), 2130-2200 (Europe)**
9700 **0000-0100 (E North Am), 0730-0800 (Europe), 1930-2000 (Europe), 2130-2200 (Europe), 2230-2330 (Europe)**
11660 **1830-1900 (Europe), 2030-2100 (Europe), 2130-2230 (Europe), 2300-2400 (E North Am)**
11720 **0000-0100 (E North Am), 0730-0800 (Europe), 1930-2000 (Europe), 2230-2330 (Europe)**
11750 **2030-2100 (Europe)**
15290 **0300-0400 & 2030-2100 (E North Am)**
15330 **1830-1900, 2030-2100, 2130-2230 & 2300-2400 (Europe)**
17825 **0630-0700 (Europe)**

CANADA

CANADIAN BC CORP **(E North Am)**

6065 1200-1300, Sa/Su 1300-1400
6195 Su 0000-0300, Tu-Sa 0200-0300, M 0300-0310, M 0330-0610, Tu-Sa 0500-0610, Su 0400-0610
9625 Su 0000-0300, Tu-Sa 0200-0300, M 0300-0310, M 0330-0610, Tu-Sa 0500-0610, Su 0400-0610, Su 1200-1700, Sa 1200-1505, M-F 1200-1255, Sa 1700-1805, Su 1800-2400, M-F 2200-2225, M-F 2240-2330
11720 Su 1400-1700, Sa 1400-1505, Sa 1700-1805, Su 1800-2400, M-F 2200-2225, M-F 2240-2330

RADIO CANADA INTL

5960 Su/M **0130-0200, 2330-0130 & 2200-2230 (E North Am)**
5995 **1715-1730** & M-F **1930-2000 (Europe)**
6050 M-F **0615-0630** & M-F **0645-0700 (Europe)**
7155 M-F **0615-0630** & M-F **0645-0700 (Europe)**
7235 **1715-1730** & M-F **1930-2000 (Europe)**
7295 M-F **0515-0530** & M-F **0545-0600 (Europe)**
9555 **1545-1600** & M-F **1830-1900 (Europe)**
9625 M-F **1300-1400 (E North Am)**
9645 0300-0330 & Sa/Su 0330-0400 (Mideast)
9755 Su/M **0030-0100 (E North Am &** C America), Su/M **0130-0200 (E North Am** & C America), Tu-Sa 0200-0300 (C America & S America), **2330-0130 (E North Am** & C America), **2200-2230 (E North Am** & C America), **2300-2330 (E North Am** & C America)
11730 0300-0330 & Sa/Su 0330-0400 (Mideast)
11790 M-F 0400-0430 (Mideast)
11840 M-F 0615-0630 & M-F 0645-0700 (Mideast)
11855 M-F **1300-1400 (E North Am)**
11905 **2200-2230 (E North Am** & C America)
11935 **1545-1600 & 1615-1630 (Europe)**
11955 Su **1400-1700 (E North Am)**
13650 **1545-1600 & 1715-1730 (Europe)**
15225 M-F 0515-0530 & M-F 0545-0600 (Mideast)
15275 M-F 0400-0430 (Mideast)
15325 **1715-1730**, M-F **1930-2000 & 2100-2200 (Europe)**
15325 **1545-1600 (Europe)**
17820 M-F 1200-1400 (C & S America), Su 1400-1700 (C & S America), M-Sa **1545-1600 (Europe), 1715-1730 (Europe)**, 1800-1830 (Africa), Sa/Su 1830-1900 (Africa), M-F 1900-1930 (Africa), 2130-
17875 M-F **1930-2000 & 2100-2200 (Europe)**

CHINA (PR)

RADIO BEIJING

3985 **2200-2230 (Europe)**
6560 0830-0930 (E Asia)
6860 **2000-2200 (Europe)**
8425 0300-0500 (E Asia)
9665 **0000-0100 & 1100-1300 (Americas)**
9690 **0300-0400 (N America)**
9700 0830-1030 (Australia)
9710 **2000-2200 (Europe)**
9820 **2000-2200 (Europe)**
11500 **2000-2200 (Europe)**
11600 1200-1400 (Pacific)
11685 **0400-0500 (W North Am)**
11715 **0000-0100 & 0300-0400 (N America)**
11755 0830-1030 (Australia)
11840 **0400-0500 (N America)**
11855 **1300-1500 (W North Am)**
11980 **0400-0500 (W North Am)**
15440 0830-1030 (Australia)
15450 1200-1300 (Pacific)
15455 **0300-0400 (W North Am)**
17710 0830-1030 (Australia)
17855 **0000-0100, 0300-0400 & 1100-1300 (Americas)**

CHINA (TAIWAN)

VOICE OF FREE CHINA

5985 **0200-0300, 0300-0400 & 0700-0800 (N & C America)**
7445 0200-0400 (E Asia)
9680 **0200-0400 (W North Am)**
9765 0200-0400 (Australia)
9852 **2200-2300 (Europe)**
9955 **2200-2300 (Europe)**
11740 0200-0300 (C America)
11805 **2200-2300 (Europe)**
15345 0200-0400 (E Asia)
15345 **2200-2300 (Europe)**
15370 2200-2300 (Australia)
17612 **2200-2300 (Europe)**

COSTA RICA

ADVENTIST WORLD R (C America)
11870 1300-1400, 2200-2400

CUBA

RADIO HABANA
6165 **2200-2300 (W Europe** & Atlantic)
9525 **0600-0800 (W North Am)**
9655 **0000-0600 (N America)**
11725 2040-2140 (S America)
11795 **1830-2000 (Europe)**
11835 **0600-0800 (W North Am)**

CZECHOSLOVAKIA

RADIO PRAGUE
5930 **0100-0200 (Europe & Americas), 0300-0400 (Europe & Americas), 1800-1830 (Europe), 1900-2000 (Europe)**
6055 **0100-0200 (E North Am), 0300-0400 (E North Am), 1530-1630 (Europe), 2200-2230 (W Europe)**
7345 **0100-0200 (Americas), 0300-0400 (Americas), 1530-1630 (Europe), 1800-1830 (Europe), 1900-2000 (Europe)**
9540 **0100-0200 & 0300-0400 (E North Am)**
9740 **0100-0200 & 0300-0400 (Americas)**
11685 0730-0800, 0830-0900, Sa/Su 0900-0930 & (Australia)
11695 **0300-0400 (Americas)**
11990 **0100-0200 & 0300-0400 (Americas)**
13715 **0100-0200 & 0300-0400 (Americas)**
15540 **0100-0200 & 0300-0400 (Americas)**
17840 0730-0800, 0830-0900, Sa/Su 0900-0930 (Australia) .
21705 0730-0800, 0830-0900, Sa/Su 0900-0930 (Australia)

ECUADOR

HCJB-VO THE ANDES
6075 1200-1230 (E Asia)
6130 0700-1130 (Pacific)
6205 M-F **0645-0700 & 0700-0830 (Europe)**
6230 **0500-0700 (N America)**
9610 M-F **0645-0700 & 0700-0830 (Europe)**
9720 **0030-0430 & 0500-0700 (N America)**
9745 **0030-0300, 0500-0700** & 0700-1030 (Australia)
11740 **1130-1600 (E North Am)**
11775 **0030-0430 & 0500-0700 (N America)**
11910 **0030-0130 (Americas)**
11925 0700-1130 (Australia)
15115 **1200-1630 (Americas)**
15155 **0030-0430 (N America)**
15230 **0030-0130 (Americas)**
15270 **1900-2000 & 2130-2200 (Europe)**
17790 **1900-2000 & 2130-2200 (Europe)**
17890 **1200-1600 (N America)**

EGYPT

RADIO CAIRO
9475 **0200-0330 (N America)**
9675 **0200-0330 (N America)**
9900 **2115-2245 (Europe)**

FINLAND

RADIO FINLAND
6120 **0730-0755, 1930-1945 & 2200-2225 (Europe)**
9530 **1930-1945 (Europe)**
9550 **1830-1845 (Europe)**
9560 **0730-0755 (Europe)**
9635 **0330-0400 (N America)**
9670 2200-2225 (E Asia)
11755 **0330-0400 (Americas), 0730-0755 (Europe), 1930-1945 (Europe), 2200-2225 (Europe)**
11855 0930-0955 (E Asia)
11945 M-F **1200-1225 (E North Am)**, M-F **1300-1325 (E North Am), 1400-1425 (E North Am)**, Sa/Su **1425-1500 (E North Am)**, 2100-2125 (E Asia)
15185 **0230-0300 (Americas), 1830-1845 (Europe)**
15245 0930-0955 (E Asia)
15400 M-F **1200-1225**, M-F **1300-1325, 1400-1425**, Sa/Su **1425-1500 (E North Am)**
17795 0800-0825 (Australia), 0830-0855 (E Asia), 0900-0925 (Australia)
21550 0800-0825 (Australia), M-F **1100-1125 (N America)**, M-F **1200-1225 (N America), 1300-1325 (N America)**, Sa/Su **1325-1400 (N America)**

FRANCE

RADIO FRANCE INTERNATIONALE
6175 **1600-1700 (Europe** & N Africa)
9800 **0315-0345 (Americas)**
11670 0315-0345 (C America)
15360 1600-1700 (Mideast & Africa)
15365 **1245-1315 (E North Am** & C America)
17620 1600-1700 (Africa)
17695 1400-1430 (SE Asia)
17720 **1245-1315 (E North Am** & C America)
21635 **1245-1315 (E North Am)**
21770 1400-1430 (SE Asia)

GERMANY (DR)

RADIO BERLIN INTERNATIONAL
6080 **0045-0130 & 0200-0330 (E North Am)**

7185 Sa/Su **0845-0930 (Europe)**
7260 **1815-1900 (Europe)**
7295 **1645-1730 & 1815-1900 (W Europe)**
9620 **0245-0330 & 0400-0530 (N America)**
9730 **0330-0415 (E North Am)**, Sa/Su **0845-0930 (W Europe)**, **2200-2330 (E North Am)**
11785 **0245-0330 & 0400-0530 (N America)**
11890 **0045-0130**, **0200-0330** & **1000-1045 (N America)**
15125 **0145-0230 & 0300-0430 (N America)**
21465 Sa/Su 0845-0930 (E Asia)
21540 0845-0930 & 1000-1045 (E Asia & Australia)

GERMANY (FR)

DEUTSCHE WELLE
5960 **0500-0550 (N America)**
6040 **0100-0150 (N America)**
6085 **0300-0350 (N America)**
6085 **0100-0150 (E North Am)**
6120 **0500-0550 (N America)**
6130 **0300-0350 & 0500-0550 (N America)**
6145 **0100-0150 (N America)**
6160 0900-0950 (Australia)
9565 **0100-0150 (E North Am)**
9605 **0300-0350 (N America)**
9615 0200-0250 (E & S Asia)
9670 **0500-0550 (N America)**, 2100-2150 (Australia)
9700 **0300-0350 & 0500-0550 (N America)**
9735 **0100-0150 (N America)**
9765 2100-2150 (Australia)
11785 2100-2150 (Australia)
11810 **0300-0350 (E North Am)**
11835 0200-0250 (S & E Asia)
11845 **0500-0550 (N America)**
11865 **0100-0150 (N America)**
11945 0900-0950 (Australia)
15105 **0100-0150 (E North Am)**
15205 **0300-0350 (E North Am)**
15435 2100-2150 (Australia)
17765 0900-0950 (Australia)
17780 0900-0950 (Australia)
17875 0900-0950 (Australia)
21650 0900-0950 (Australia)
21680 0900-0950 (Australia)

GHANA

RADIO GHANA (W Africa)
6130 0645-0800, 1845-2000

GREECE

I FONI TIS HELLADAS
7430 **0135-0145 (N America)**, **0335-0345 (N America)**, **1920-1930 (Europe)**
9395 **0135-0145 (N America** & Pacific), **0335-0345 (N America** & Pacific), **1920-1930 (Europe)**
9420 **0135-0145 & 0335-0345 (N America)**
9425 **1920-1930 (Europe)**
9855 **1235-1245 (N America & Europe)**
9905 **1235-1245 (N America & Europe)**
11645 **0135-0145 (N America** & Pacific), 1035-1045 (E Asia), **1235-1245 (N America & Europe)**, **1535-1545 (N America & Europe)**
15630 0835-0845 (Australia), 1035-1050 (E Asia), **1235-1245 (N America & Europe)**, **1535-1545 (N America & Europe)**
17565 0835-0845 (Australia)

GUAM

ADVENTIST WORLD RADIO
11700 Sa/Su 0200-0300 (E Asia)
KTWR-TRANS WORLD RADIO
11805 0805-0930 (E Asia), 0930-1100 (Australia)

GUINEA

RTV GUINEENNE
7125 1845-1855 (W Africa)

HOLLAND

RADIO NEDERLAND
5955 **1130-1225 & 1430-1525 (Europe)**
6165 **0030-0125 & 0330-0425 (W North Am)**
9590 **0330-0425 (W North Am)**
9630 0730-0825 (Australia)
9675 1030-1125 (Australia)
9715 **1130-1225 (Europe)**
9715 0730-0825 (Australia)
9895 **2030-2125 (W Europe)**
15315 **0030-0125 (E North Am)**
17575 1130-1225 (E Asia)
21485 0830-0925 (E Asia)

HUNGARY

RADIO BUDAPEST
6110 Tu-Su **0030-0100 (E North Am)**, **0130-0200 (E North Am)**, W/Sa **0200-0230 (E North Am)**, Tu/W/F/Sa **0230-0245 (E North Am)**, **1930-2000 (Europe)**, **2100-2130 (Europe)**, Tu/F **2230-2300 (Europe)**
7220 Su **1045-1100**, Sa **1130-1145**, M/Th **1615-1630**, **1930-2000** & **2100-2130 (Europe)**
9520 Tu-Su **0030-0100**, **0130-0200**, W/Sa **0200-0230** & Tu/W/F/Sa **0230-0245 (E North Am)**
9585 Tu-Su **0030-0100 (E North Am)**, **0130-0200 (E North Am)**, W/Sa **0200-0230 (E North Am)**, Tu/W/F/Sa **0230-0245 (E North Am)**, Su **1045-1100 (Europe)**, Sa **1130-1145 (Europe)**, M/Th **1615-1630 (Europe)**, **1930-2000 (Europe)**, **2100-2130 (Europe)**
9835 Tu-Su **0030-0100 (E North Am)**, **0130-0200 (E North Am)**, W/Sa **0200-0230 (E North Am)**, Tu/W/F/Sa **0230-0245 (E North Am)**, Su **1045-1100 (Europe)**, Sa **1130-1145 (Europe)**, M/Th **1615-1630 (Europe)**, **1930-2000 (Europe)**, **2100-2130 (Europe)**

11910 Tu-Su **0030-0100 (E North Am), 0130-0200 (E North Am)**, W/Sa **0200-0230 (E North Am)**, Tu/W/F/Sa **0230-0245 (E North Am)**, Su **1045-1100 (Europe)**, Sa **1130-1145 (Europe)**, M-Th **1615-1630 (Europe), 1930-2000 (Europe), 2100-2130 (Europe)**
15160 Tu-Su **0030-0100 (E North Am), 0130-0200 (E North Am)**, W/Sa **0200-0230 (E North Am)**, Tu/W/F/Sa **0230-0245 (E North Am)**, Su **1045-1100 (Europe)**, Sa **1130-1145 (Europe)**, M/Th **1615-1630 (Europe), 1930-2000 (Europe), 2100-2130 (Europe)**
15220 Su **1045-1100**, Sa **1130-1145** & M-Th **1615-1630 (Europe)**

INDIA

ALL INDIA RADIO

7265 2000-2230 (Australia)
7412 **1845-1945, 2045-2230 (Europe)**
9550 0230-0250, 2045-2230 (Australia)
9910 **2045-2230 (Europe** & Australia), 2245-0115 (E Asia)
11620 **1845-1945 & 2045-2230 (Europe)**
11715 2045-2230 (Australia), 2245-0115 (E Asia)
11860 1000-1100 (Australia)
11925 1000-1100 (E Asia)
15155 1000-1100 (E Asia)
15335 1000-1100 (Australia)
17387 1000-1100 (E Asia)
17740 1000-1100 (E Asia)

INDONESIA

VOICE OF INDONESIA

11744 0100-0200, 0800-0900, 1500-1600 (Asia & Pacific)
11788 0100-0200 (Asia), 0800-0900 (Asia)

IRAN

VOICE OF THE ISLAMIC REPUBLIC

6080 **1930-2030 (Europe)**
9022 **1930-2030 (Europe)**

IRAQ

RADIO BAGHDAD

7295 **2100-2250 (Europe)**
9515 **0230-0425 (E North Am)**
9770 **2100-2255 (Europe)**
11880 **0230-0425 (N America)**
11945 **0130-0325 (N America)**
13660 **2000-2055 (Europe)**

ISRAEL

KOL ISRAEL

9385 **0000-0030, 0100-0125, 0200-0230 (E North Am)**
9435 **0000-0030 (W Europe & E North Am), 0100-0125 (W Europe & E North Am), 0200-0225 (W Europe & E North Am), 0500-0515 (Europe), 2000-2030 (W Europe & E North Am), 2230-2300 (W Europe & E North Am)**
9455 **0500-0515 (Europe)**
9855 **2000-2030 & 2230-2300 (Europe)**

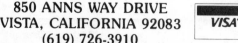

11585 **0500-0515, 1100-1130, 1700-1715 (Europe & E North Am)**
11605 **0000-0030, 0100-0125, 0200-0225, 2000-2030 & 2230-2300 (Europe & E North Am)**
12077 **0000-0030 (E North Am), 0100-0125 (E North Am), 0200-0225 (E North Am), 2130-2200 (Europe & E North Am), 2300-2330 (Europe)**
15615 **0000-0025, 0100-0125 & 2300-2330 (E North Am)**
15640 **0000-0025, 0100-0125, 0300-0315, 1900-1930, 2130-2155 & 2300-2330 (E North Am)**
15650 1100-1130 (Asia & Australia)
17575 **0400-0415, 1000-1030 & 2130-2155 (W Europe & E North Am)**
17590 **1000-1030 & 1900-1930 (W Europe & E North Am)**
17630 0400-0415 (Asia & Australia)
21760 **1000-1030 (W Europe & E North Am)**

ITALY

ADVENTIST WORLD R **(Europe)**
7257 **0730-0800, 1430-1500**
9670 Su **0900-1000**
INTL RADIO RELAY **(Europe)**
9865 Su **0830-1130**
RTV ITALIANA
5990 2200-2225 (E Asia)
6165 **0425-0440 (Europe**
7275 **0425-0440 & 1935-1955 (Europe)**
7290 **1930-1955 (Europe)**
9575 **0100-0120 (E North Am), 0425-0440 (Europe)**
9710 **1935-1955 (Europe)**, 2200-2225 (E Asia)
11800 **0100-0120 (E North Am), 1935-1955 (Europe)**, 2200-2225 (E Asia)
15330 2200-2225 (E Asia)

JAPAN

RADIO JAPAN/NHK
5960 **0100-0200 & 0300-0400 (E North Am)**
5990 **0500-0600, 1400-1600, 1700-1800 & 1900-1930 (W North Am)**
6025 2100-2200 (E Asia)
6120 **1100-1200 (N America)**
7140 1400-1600 (E Asia)
9695 1500-1600, 1700-1800 & 1900-2000 (E Asia)
11800 **2100-2130 & 2300-2400 (Europe)**
11815 2100-2200 & 2300-2400 (E Asia)
11840 0900-1000, 1100-1200 & 1400-1430 (E Asia)
11865 **1400-1600, 1700-1800 & 1900-1930** (Pacific & **N America)**
15325 **0700-0800 (Europe)**
17765 0300-0400, 0500-0600, 0700-0800 & 2300-2400 (E Asia)
17825 **0100-0130, 0300-0330 & 0400-0600 (W North Am)**
17835 0300-0400 (E Asia)
21500 **0700-0800 (Europe)**
21690 **0700-0800 (Europe)**
21695 **0700-0800 (Europe)**
21700 **1500-1600 (Europe)**

JORDAN

RADIO JORDAN **(Europe & E North Am)**
9560 **0500-2200**
13655 **0500-2200**

KOREA (DPR)

RADIO PYONGYANG
6576 **2000-2050 (Europe)**
9325 **1300-1350, 1500-1550 & 1700-1750 (Europe)**
9345 **1300-1350 & 2000-2050 (Europe)**
9540 0600-0650 & 0800-0850 (Asia)
9600 1200-1250 (C America)
11735 1100-1150 (C America), 1400-1450 (E Asia), 2300-2350 (C America)
11740 **1500-1550 & 1700-1750 (Europe)**
13650 2300-2350 (C America)
15160 0800-0850 (Asia)
15180 0800-0850 (Asia)
15340 0700-0750 (Asia)

KOREA (REPUBLIC)

RADIO KOREA
6060 **0600-0700 (E North Am)**
6480 **2030-2130 (Europe)**
7275 0045-0100, 0600-0700, 1115-1130, 1330-1345 & 1545-1600 (E Asia)
7550 **0800-0900 (Europe)**
9570 **0600-0700 (W North Am)**
9750 **1400-1500 (N America)**
11740 1115-1130 & 1330-1345 (E Asia)
13670 **0800-0900 & 0915-0930 (Europe)**
15575 **0045-0100 (E North Am), 0245-0300 (E North Am)**, 1100-1200 (Africa), **1400-1500 (E North Am), 1800-1900 (Europe), 2030-2130 (Europe), 2330-0030 (E North Am)**

KUWAIT

RADIO KUWAIT
11665 **1800-2100 (Europe & E North Am)**

LUXEMBOURG

RADIO LUXEMBOURG
6090 **0000-0300 (Europe)**

MALAYSIA

VOICE OF MALAYSIA
15295 0555-0825 (Australia)

MALTA

RADIO MEDITERRANEAN
6110 **2230-2330 (Europe)**
VOICE OF THE MEDITERRANEAN
9765 **0600-0700 (Europe)**
11925 **1400-1500 (Europe)**

MONACO

TRANS WORLD RADIO (**W Europe**)

7105 **0625-0800**
9480 **0800-0840**, Su **0840-1000**
9485 **0625-0840**, Su **0840-1000**

MONGOLIA

RADIO ULAN BATOR

9616 0910-0940, W/Th/Sa-M 1200-1230, 1200-1230 & 1445-1515 (E Asia)
9985 **1940-2010 (Europe)**
12015 0910-0940 & W/Th/Sa-M 1200-1230 (E Asia)
12050 **1940-2010 (Europe)**
15305 1445-1515 (E Asia)

NETHERLANDS ANTILLES

TRANS WORLD RADIO (**N America**)

9535 **0300-0430**, Su/M **0430-0530**
11815 **1100-1255**, Sa/Su **1255-1335**, Sa **1330-1400**
11930 **0300-0430**, Su/M **0430-0530**
15345 **1100-1255**, Sa/Su **1255-1335**, Sa **1330-1400**

NEW ZEALAND

RADIO NEW ZEALAND

6100 0900-1205 (Australia)
9850 0900-1115 (Australia)
11780 1730-2015 (Pacific)
15150 Sa 0045-0230, 0230-0600, Sa-Su 0600-0630, 0900-1115, 1730-2015 & 2245-0045 (Pacific)
17705 Sa 0045-0230, 0230-0600, Sa/Su 0600-0630 & 2245-0045 (Pacific)

NICARAGUA

LA VOZ DE NICARAGUA

6100 Tu-Su **0400-0600 (Americas)**

NIGERIA

VOICE OF NIGERIA (W Africa)

7255 0500-0600, 0800-1700, 1900-2030

NORTHERN MARIANA IS

KYOI-CHRISTIAN SCIENCE MONITOR

9455 2000-2200 (E Asia)
9530 0800-1200 & 1400-1600 (E Asia)
15250 1200-1400 (Australia)
15405 2200-0200 (E Asia)
17780 0200-0800 (E Asia)
17855 0800-1000 (Australia)

NORWAY

RADIO NORWAY INTERNATIONAL

6035 Su **1300-1330 (Europe)**
9590 Su **1300-1330** & Su **1900-1930 (Europe)**
9605 Su **2300-2330 (E North Am)**
15165 Su 0600-0630 (Pacific), Su **0800-0830 (W North Am** & Pacific)
15180 Su 1000-1030 (Australia)
15190 Su 1400-1430 (Australia), Su **2300-2330 (E North Am)**
15220 Su **1900-1930 (Europe)**
15265 Su **1600-1630 (N America)**
15310 Su **1600-1630** & Su **1700-1730 (N America)**
15325 Su **1200-1230 (N America)**
17780 Su **1600-1630** & Su **1700-1730 (N America)**
17840 Su 0900-0930 (E Asia & Australia)
21705 Su 1400-1430 (Australia)
21730 Su 0800-0830 (Australia)
25730 Su 1700-1730 & Su 2200-2230 (S America)

PAKISTAN

RADIO PAKISTAN

15605 1600-1630 (Mideast)
17660 0230-0245 (SE Asia), **1100-1120 (Europe)**

PHILIPPINES

RADIO VERITAS ASIA

9770 1500-1530 (Asia)
15330 0130-0155 (Asia)

POLAND

RADIO POLONIA (**Europe**)

6095 **1200-1225**
6135 **0630-0700, 1430-1455, 1600-1630, 1830-1855, 2230-2355**
7125 **2230-2355**
7270 **0630-0700, 2230-2355**
7285 **1200-1225, 1430-1455, 1830-1855**
9525 **1230-1300, 1630-1700, 1830-1855, 2000-2030**
9540 **1430-1455, 1600-1630**
9675 **0630-0700**
11815 **1200-1230, 1430-1455**
11840 **1230-1300, 1630-1700, 1830-1855, 2000-2030**
15120 **1230-1300, 1630-1700**

PORTUGAL

RADIO PORTUGAL INTERNATIONAL

9615 Sa/Su **0845-0900 (Europe)**
9680 Tu-Sa **0230-0300 (E North Am)**
9705 Tu-Sa **0230-0300 (N America)**
11740 M-F **2000-2030 (Europe)**

ROMANIA

RADIO BUCHAREST

5990 **0200-0300 (Americas), 0400-0430 (Americas), 1930-2030 (Europe), 2100-2130 (Europe)**
6155 **0200-0300 & 0400-0430 (Americas)**
7145 **1930-2030 & 2100-2130 (Europe)**
7195 **1500-1530, 1930-2030 & 2100-2130 (Europe)**
9510 **0200-0300 & 0400-0430 (Americas)**
9570 **0200-0300 & 0400-0430 (Americas)**
9690 **1300-1330, 1930-2030, 2100-2130 (Europe)**
9750 **1930-2030 & 2100-2130 (Europe)**

11810 0645-0715 (Australia), **1930-2030 (Europe)**
11830 **0200-0300** & **0400-0430 (Americas)**
11940 **0200-0300**, **0400-0430** & 0645-0715 (Australia)
15250 0645-0715 (Australia)
15335 0645-0715 (Asia & Australia)
15380 **0200-0300** & **0400-0430 (Americas)**
17720 0645-0715 (Australia), 1200-1230 (S Asia)
17805 0645-0715 (Australia)
17850 **1300-1400 (W Europe)**
21665 0645-0715 (Australia), **1300-1400 (W Europe)**

SOUTH AFRICA

RADIO RSA
6010 **0200-0300 (N America)**
9580 **0200-0300 (N America)**
9615 **0200-0300 (N America)**
11760 **0200-0300 (N America)**
15365 **1800-1900 (W Europe)**
17730 1300-1400 (Asia)
17795 **1800-1900 (W Europe)**
21590 **1100-1200 (Europe)**, 1200-1300 (Africa), 1300-1400 (Asia), **1400-1600 (Europe)**, **1800-1900 (W Europe)**
25790 1400-1600 (Africa & Mideast)
SOUTH AFRICAN BC (S Africa)
4810 M-F 1610-1655, 1930-0300
4880 0300-0520, 1630-2400

SPAIN

RADIO NACIONAL DE ESPANA
9630 **0000-0200** & **0500-0600 (N America)**
9765 **1900-2000** & **2100-2200 (Europe)**
11790 **1900-2000** & **2100-2200 (Europe)**
11880 **0000-0200 (E North Am)**
15110 **0000-0200** & **0500-0600 (E North Am)**
15280 **1900-2000** & **2100-2200 (Europe)**

SRI LANKA

SRI LANKA BROADCASTING CORP
11800 **1745-1815 (Europe)**

SURINAME

RADIO SURINAME INTERNATIONAL
17755 M-F **1735-1745 (Europe)**
17835 M-F **1735-1745 (Europe)**

SWEDEN

RADIO SWEDEN
6065 **1600-1630** & **1700-1730 (Europe)**
7265 **1700-1730 (Europe)**
9615 **1700-1730 (Europe)**
9655 **2100-2130 (Europe)**
9695 **0300-0330 (N America)**
11705 **0300-0330 (N America)**, **2100-2130 (W Europe)**
15190 1230-1300 (E Asia)
15345 **1530-1600 (E North Am)**
17800 0100-0130 (Australia)
17860 **1530-1600 (E North Am)**
17880 **1530-1600 (N America)**
21610 1230-1300 (E Asia & Australia), 1400-1430 (E Asia & Australia), **1530-1600 (E North Am)**

SWITZERLAND

SWISS RADIO INTERNATIONAL
3985 **0730-0800** & **1830-1900 (Europe)**
6135 **0200-0230** & **0400-0430 (N America)**
6165 **0730-0800**, **1300-1330** & **1830-1900 (Europe)**
6190 **2230-2300 (W Europe)**
9535 **0730-0800**, **1300-1330** & **1830-1900 (Europe)**
9560 0830-0900 & 1000-1030 (Australia)
9620 1330-1400 (E Asia)
9725 **0400-0430 (N America)**
9885 **0200-0230** & **0400-0430 (N America)**
11935 1100-1130 (E Asia)
12030 **1300-1330 (Europe)**
12035 **0200-0230** & **0400-0430 (N America)**
13635 1100-1130 (Australia)
13685 0830-0900 & 1000-1030 (Australia)
15570 1100-1130 (E Asia & Australia)
17670 0830-0900 & 1000-1030 (Australia)
17730 **0200-0230 (W North Am)**
17830 0830-0900, 1000-1030 & 1100-1130 (Australia)
21695 0830-0900 & 1000-1030 (Australia)

SYRIA

SYRIAN BROADCASTING SERVICE
9950 **2005-2105 (Europe)**, **2105-2205 (E North Am)**
12085 **2005-2105 (Europe)**, 2105-2205 (Australia)
15095 **2005-2105 (Europe)**
17710 **2005-2105 (Europe)**, 2105-2205 (Australia)

THAILAND

RADIO THAILAND (Asia)
9655 0500-0600, 1130-1230, 2300-0430
11905 0500-0600, 1130-1230, 2300-0430

TOGO

RADIO LOME (W Africa)
5047 1935-1945

TURKEY

TURKISH RTV CORPORATION
7250 **2300-2350 (Europe)**
9445 **0400-0450** & **2300-2350 (E North Am)**
9685 **2200-2250 (Europe)**
9825 **2000-2050** & **2100-2150 (Europe)**

UNITED ARAB EMIRATES

UAE RADIO
9555 **0330-0400 (E North Am)**
11730 0530-0600 (Australia)
11955 **0330-0400 (E North Am)**
15320 **1030-1100**, **1330-1400** & **1600-1645 (Europe)**

15435 0530-0600 (Australia), **1030-1100 (Europe)**, **1330-1400 (Europe)**, **1600-1640 (Europe)**
15555 **0330-0400 (E North Am)**
17775 0530-0600 (Australia), **1030-1100 (Europe)**, **1330-1400 (Europe)**
17830 0530-0600 (E Asia)
17890 **0330-0400 (E North Am)**
21605 **1030-1100**, **1330-1400** & **1600-1645 (Europe)**
21700 0530-0600 (Australia)

VOICE OF THE UAE
6170 **2200-2400 (E North Am)**
9595 **2200-2400 (E North Am)**
11965 **2200-2400 (E North Am)**
11985 **2200-2400 (E North Am)**
13605 **2200-2400 (E North Am)**

UNITED KINGDOM

BBC WORLD SERVICE
3955 **0400-0730**, **1615-1830** & **1830-2300 (Europe)**
5965 **1100-1130 (N America)**, 2000-2145 (E Asia), 2200-2215 (E Asia)
5975 **0730-0945**, **0945-1030**, Sa/Su **0900-1030** & **1030-1500 (Europe)**
6175 **2200-0430 (N America)**
6195 0900-1615 (Asia), 1100-1330 (C America), Sa/Su 1330-1345 (C America), 2100-0045 (Asia)
7145 2200-2300 (Asia)
7150 0600-0815 (C America & Australia), **0700-0915 (Europe)**
7180 0815-1000, 1245-1500, 1500-1615 & 2000-2145 (E Asia)
7185 **0300-0700 (Europe)**,
7275 1745-2030 (Australia)
7325 **0700-2300 (Europe)**, **2200-0330 (E North Am)**, 2200-0330 (C America)
9410 0100-2300 **(Europe)**
9515 **1100-1330**, Su **1330-1345**, Sa/Su **1500-1600** & **1600-1745 (N America)**
9570 1950-0045 (Australia)
9590 **0030-0230** & **2200-0030 (N America)**
9640 0545-0815 (C America)
9660 **0230-0330 (E North Am)**, **0700-0730 (Europe)**, Sa/Su **0730-0800 (Europe)**, Sa/Su **0800-0900 (Europe)**, **0900-1515 (Europe)**
9725 0930-1000 (Asia)
9740 1030-1515 (Asia & Australia)
9760 **0600-1615 (Europe** & N Africa), 0900-1030 (Africa), **1030-1615 (Europe** & W Africa)
9915 **0330-0430 (E North Am)**, **0730-0745 (Europe)**, **2200-0530 (W North Am)**, **2200-0330 (E North Am)**
11715 2000-2100 (E Asia)
11750 0900-1030 (E Asia & Australia), 1745-2200 (Australia)
11775 1100-1330 (C America), Su 1330-1345 (C America), Sa/Su **1500-1600 (N America)**, **1600-1745 (N America)**
11945 2200-0045 (E Asia)
11955 0600-0915 (Australia), 0930-1000 (E Asia), 2200-0030 (E Asia & Australia)
12095 **0200-0400 (Europe)**, **2200-0330 (E North Am)**, **0400-0730 (Europe)**, **0730-0915 (Europe)**, **0915-1700 (Europe)**, **1700-2000 (Europe)**, **2000-2300 (Europe)**, 0300-0500 (E Europe), **0500-0730 (Europe)**, **0730-0900 (Europe)**, **0900-2300 (Europe)**, 2200-0430 (C America)
15070 0400-0600 (E Europe), **0500-2115 (Europe)**, 2000-2300 (S America), 2115-2300 (Africa)
15140 Su 1900-2000 & 2000-2300 (Australia)
15260 Sa/Su **1500-1600**, **1600-1745** & 2000-0330 (**Americas.**
15280 Su 0100-0300, 0300-1000, 1145-1200 & 2200-2215 (E Asia)
15360 0000-0045 (E Asia), 0100-0200 (E Asia), 0600-1130 (E Asia & Australia)
17815 Su 0100-0300 & 0300-0945 (E Asia)
17830 0900-1030 (E Asia)
17875 0100-0200 (E Asia), 2215-0045 (E Asia)
21710 0700-1615 (Africa)
25750 1100-1745 (Africa)

USA

KNLS (E Asia)
7355 Tu-Su 1500-1600, 1800-1900
7365 0800-0900
9815 1600-1700
11650 1800-1900
11700 Tu-Su 1500-1600
11715 0800-0900
11930 1000-1100
12025 1600-1700

KUSW **(E North Am)**
6130 Su **1100-1400**
6135 Su **0700-1100**
6155 Tu-Su **0500-0600**, Su **0600-0700**
6175 Tu-Su **0500-0600**, Su **0600-0700**
9815 Tu-Su **0300-0500**
9850 Su **1100-1600**
11680 Tu-Su **0000-0300**
11695 Tu-Su **0100-0500**
15225 Su **1600-1800**, **1800-1900**
15580 Tu-Su **0000-0100**, M-Sa **2200-2400**
15650 M-Sa **1900-2200**

KVOH (C America)
13695 0100-0310
17775 M-Sa 0100-0235, Tu-Sa 0235-0300, Su 2000-2030, Sa/Su 2030-2100, 2100-0100

VOICE OF AMERICA
3980 **0430-0700**, **1600-1630** & **1700-1730 (Europe)**
5985 1000-1200 (Australia)
5995 **0000-0200** & Tu-Sa **0200-0230 (Americas)**
5995 **0400-0700 (Europe)**
6030 **1000-1200 (Americas)**
6040 **0400-0700** & **1700-2200 (Europe)**
6080 0600-0700 (W Africa)

6130 **0000-0200** (**Americas**)
6165 **1000-1200** (**Americas**)
7200 **0400-0700** (**Europe**)
7325 **0600-0700** (**Europe**)
9455 **0000-0200** (**Americas**)
9525 1900-2000 (E Asia & Australia)
9575 0300-0700 & M-F 0815-0845 (Africa)
9590 **1000-1200** (**Americas**)
9760 1100-1700 (Asia), **1700-2200** (**Europe**)
9775 **0000-0200** & Tu-Sa **0200-0230** (**Americas**)
9815 **0000-0200** & Tu-Sa **0200-0230** (**Americas**)
11580 **0000-0200** & Tu-Sa **0200-0230** (**Americas**)
11695 **0000-0100** (**Americas**)
11715 1200-1330 (Asia & Australia)
11720 1000-1200 (Asia & Australia)
11760 **1700-2200** (**Europe**)
11760 **1700-2200** (**Europe**)
11870 1900-2000 & 2100-2200 (Australia)
11965 1900-2000 & 2100-2200 (Australia)
15160 1400-1500 (E Asia)
15205 **1500-1900** & **1700-2200** (**Europe**)
15290 2200-0100 (E Asia)
17735 2100-2400 (Australia)
17820 2200-0100 (E Asia)

WCSN-CHRISTIAN SCIENCE MONITOR
7365 M-F **0600-0655** & **0700-0755** (**Europe**)
9465 Su-F **2000-2100**, **2100-2115**, M-Sa **2115-2155** (**Europe**)
9840 M-F **0600-0700** & **0700-0755** (**Europe**)
9850 0000-0100, M-F 0100-0115, Tu-F 0115-0155, 0200-0300 & M-F 0300-0355 (Africa)
9870 0400-0500 & M-F 0500-0555 (Africa)
15300 2200-2300, Su-F 2300-2315 & M-F 2315-2355 (Africa)
15610 Su-F **2000-2100**, **2100-2115** & M-Sa **2115-2155** (**Europe**)
21640 1600-1700, Su-F 1700-1715, M-F 1715-1755, 1800-1900, Su-F 1900-1915 & M-F 1915-1955 (Africa)
21780 **1400-1500** & M-F **1500-1555** (**Europe**)

WORLD HARVEST RADIO
5995 **1100-1300** (**E North Am**)
6100 **0600-0800** (**E North Am** & **W Europe**)
7355 **0800-1100** (**E North Am**)
7365 **0000-0600** (**E North Am**)
7405 **0200-0600** (**E North Am**)
9455 **1300-1600** (**E North Am**)
9465 **1100-1500** (**E North Am**)
9495 0100-0800 (S America)
9620 **0600-0800** (**E North Am** & **Europe**)
9770 **2100-2400** (**E North Am**)
11790 1100-1500 (C America)
13760 **1600-2100** (**E North Am** & **W Europe**), **2100-2400** (**E North Am** & **W Europe**)
15105 1400-1800 (C America)
17830 1800-2400 (C & S America)
21840 **1500-1700** (**E North Am** & **W Europe**)

WRNO WORLDWIDE (**E North Am**
6185 **0300-0600**, Su **0600-1200**
7355 **0000-0400**, **2300-2400**
9715 Su **1200-1430**
11965 **1430-1700**
13720 **2100-2400**
13760 **2100-2400**
15420 **1600-2100**

WSHB-CHRISTIAN SCIENCE MONITOR
6150 **1000-1100**, M-F **1100-1155**, **1200-1300**, M-F **1300-1355** & (**E North Am**)
7405 **0000-0100**, M-Sa **0100-0115** & Tu-Sa **0115-0155** (**E North Am**)
9455 **0200-0300** (**W North Am**), M-F **0300-0315** (**W North Am**), Tu-F **0315-0355** (**W North Am**), **0400-0500** (**W North Am**), M-F **0500-0515** (**W North Am**), Tu-F **0515-0555** (**W North Am**), **0600-0700** (**W North Am**), M-F **0700-0755** (**W North Am**), M-F 0800-0955 (S America), M-F 1000-1055 (S America), 1100-1155 (S America)
9465 **2200-2300**, Su-F **2300-2315** & M-F **2315-2355** (**E North Am**)
9495 **1000-1100**, M-F **1100-1155**, **1200-1300** & M-F **1305-1355** (**E North Am**)
11770 0800-0900 & M-F 0900-0955 (C America & Australia)
11930 M-F 1200-1300 & 1300-1355 (C America)
11980 M-F 0600-0700 & 0700-0755 (C America)
13760 M-Sa 0000-0100 (S America), 0100-0115 (S America), Tu-Su 0115-0155 (S America), M-F 0200-0300 (C America), 0300-0315 (C America), Tu-Su 0315-0355 (C America), M-F 0400-0500 (C America), 0500-0515 (C America), Tu-Su 0515-0555 (C America), **1400-1500** (**W North Am**), M-F **1500-1555** (**W North Am**)
15390 **2000-2100**, Su-F **2100-2115** & M-F **2115-2155** (**E North Am**)
15610 **2000-2100**, Su-F **2100-2115** & M-F **2115-2155** (**W North Am**)
17555 M-F 1400-1500 (C America), 1500-1555 (C America), Su-F 2000-2100 (S America), 2100-2115 (S America), M-Sa 2115-2155 (S America), Su-F 2200-2300 (S America), 2300-2315 (S America), M-Sa 2315-2355 (S America)
17855 0800-0900 & M-F 0900-0955 (C America & Australia)

WWCR
15690 **1300-0400** (**E North Am** & **Europe**)

WYFR-FAMILY RADIO
5950 **0500-0700**, **1000-1545** & **2300-0445** (**N America**)
6065 **0600-0800** (**W North Am**)
6175 **1300-1545** (**N America**)
7355 **0600-0745** (**Europe**), **1100-1245** (**W North Am**), **1900-2200** (**Europe**)

9455 **2000-2145 (Europe)**
9505 **0000-0445** & **2300-2400 (W North Am)**
9520 **0400-0445 (W North Am)**
9680 **0100-0200 (W North Am), 0600-0745 (Europe)**
9705 **1245-1445 (W North Am)**
9852 **0600-0745 (Europe)**
11580 **0500-0745 (Europe), 1100-1745 (W North Am), 1800-1900 (Europe), 2000-2345 (W North Am)**
11830 **1200-2245 (W North Am)**
13695 0500-0800 (W Africa), **1300-2245 (E North Am)**
13770 **1700-1745 (Europe)**
15215 **1200-2245 (W North Am)**
15345 **1600-1700 (Europe)**
15440 **1600-1700 (Europe)**
15566 0300-0345 (S America), 0500-0800 (W Africa & S Africa), **1900-2145 (Europe)**
17612 **1600-1700 (Europe)**, 1600-1700 (W Africa), 2000-2245 (W Africa)
17750 **2000-2200 (Europe)**
17845 1600-1700 & 2000-2245 (W Africa)
21525 1600-1700 & 2000-2245 (Africa)
21615 **1600-1700** & **1900-2200 (Europe)**
21735 **1600-1700 (Europe)**

USSR

RADIO KIEV
11780 **1800-1830 (Europe)**
11790 **2330-2400** & **0200-0230 (W North Am)**
15455 **0030-0100** & **0200-0230 (W North Am)**

RADIO MOSCOW
9450 **0500-1000** & **1100-1700 (Europe)**
9520 **0500-0700 (Europe)**
9530 **0300-0700** & **2300-0300 (E North Am** & **W Europe)**
9580 **0130-0400, 0530-0700** & **1800-2000 (W North Am)**
9600 **1600-2200 (W Europe)**
9610 **0300-0400 (E North Am), 0400-0500 (Europe), 2200-0300 (E North Am)**
9625 2100-2400 (E Asia & Australia)
9640 **0300-0700 (W Europe & E North Am)**
9645 1600-1800 (E Asia)
9655 **1300-1600 (W North Am)**
9705 1400-1800 (E Asia)
9720 **2200-0200 (N America)**
9765 **2200-0800 (E North Am)**
9865 **1600-1800 (Europe)**
9880 **0500-0700** & **2200-2300 (Europe)**
11690 2100-2400 (Australia)
11705 **0700-1630 (Europe)**
11750 **2100-0300 (N America)**
11770 **2200-0400 (E North Am)**
11790 **0400-0700 (W North Am)**
11830 **0630-1500 (Europe)**
11900 **0830-1600 (Europe)**
11950 **1600-2100 (Europe)**
12045 **2000-2200 (Europe)**
12050 **2100-0700** (Pacific & **W North Am)**
12060 **2200-0300 (E North Am)**
12070 **0300-0700 (Europe)**
12075 2100-2400 (Australia)
13605 0200-0700 (W North Am)
13790 **0800-1600 (Europe & E North Am)**
15125 **0500-0900** & **1000-1600 (Europe)**
15135 **1000-1400 (E North Am)**
15150 **1000-1530 (Europe)**
15175 **2100-2200 (W Europe)**
15260 **0430-1000 (Europe)**
15290 **2200-0300 (E North Am)**
15420 0000-1000 (Australia)
15425 0800-1100 (Asia)
15455 **0300-0600** & **2200-0200 (W North Am)**
15475 **1900-2100** & **2200-2400 (W Europe** & **E North Am)**
17645 0800-1400 (Asia)
17685 2300-1200 (Asia)
17860 2330-0700 (Australia)
25780 0500-1100 1130-1300 (E Africa)

RADIO TASHKENT (S Asia)
9540 1200-1230, 1330-1400
9600 1200-1230, 1330-1400
11785 1200-1230, 1330-1400
15455 1200-1230, 1330-1400
15460 1200-1230, 1330-1400

RADIO VILNIUS
13645 **2300-2330 (W North Am)**
11790 **2200-2230 (W North Am)**
15455 **2300-2330 (W North Am)**

RADIO YEREVAN
11790 **0350-0357 (W North Am)**
15455 **0250-0357 (W North Am)**

VATICAN STATE

VATICAN RADIO
6015 2205-2230 (Asia & Australia)
6150 **0050-0115** & **0310-0330 (N America)**
6185 **0600-0620 (Europe)**
6190 M-Sa **2000-2010** & **2050-2110 (W Europe** & N Africa)
7250 **1445-1500**, M-Sa **1600-1630**, M-Sa **2000-2010** & **2050-2110 (Europe)**
9605 **0050-0115 (N America)**
9615 2205-2230 (Asia)
9645 **0600-0620**, M-Sa **0700-0800**, M-Sa **1130-1200, 1445-1500**, M-Sa **1600-1630**, M-Sa **2000-2010** & **2050-2110 (Europe)**
11740 M-Sa **0700-0800**, M-Sa **1130-1200, 1445-1500** & M-Sa **1600-1630 (Europe** & N Africa)
11750 **0050-0115 (N America)**, 0200-0215 (S Asia), **0310-0330 (N America)**
11780 **0050-0115 (N America)**
11830 2205-2230 (Asia & Australia)
15120 2205-2230 (Asia & Australia)
15190 M-Sa 1200-1230 (Asia)
17865 M-Sa 1200-1230 (E Asia)
21515 M-Sa 1200-1230 (E Asia)

VIETNAM

VOICE OF VIETNAM (E Asia & **Americas)**
9840 **1330-1400, 1600-1630, 1800-1830, 1900-1930. 2030-2100**

15010 **1330-1400, 1600-1630, 1800-1830, 1900-1930, 2030-2100**

YUGOSLAVIA

RADIO LJUBLJANA

9620 M **2100-2130 (W Europe)**

RADIO YUGOSLAVIA

5980 **0100-0145 (W Europe & E North Am), 1930-2000 (W Europe), 2200-2245 (W Europe)**

7130 2200-2245 (E Asia & Australia)

7215 **0000-0045, 1830-1900 & 2100-2145 (Europe)**

9620 **0100-0145 (E North Am), 1730-1800 (Europe), 1930-2000 (Europe)**, 2200-2245 (E Asia & Australia)

9660 **0100-0145 (E North Am), 1830-1900 (Europe), 1930-2000 (Europe), 2200-2245 (Europe & E North Am)**

11735 **0000-0045 (E North Am), 1830-1900 (Europe)**

15105 **0000-0045 & 2100-2145 (W Europe & E North Am)**

15325 **1300-1330 (E North Am)**

15380 1300-1330 (E Asia & Australia)

17740 **1200-1230 (E North Am)**

21555 1200-1230 (E Asia & Australia)

25795 1200-1230 (Asia)

VOICES FROM HOME

For some, the offerings in English on world band radio are just icing on the cake. Their real interest is in listening to programs aimed at national compatriots. Voices from home.

"Home" may be a place of birth, or perhaps it's a favorite country you once visited or lived in. Vacationers and business travelers also turn to world band radio to keep in touch with the events that mean so much: politics, stocks, weather . . . how the local ball team is faring. For yet others, it is the perfect way to keep limber in a second tongue.

Following are frequencies for the most popular such stations. Those in bold usually come in best, as they are from relay transmitters close to the listening audience. For full details on times and target zones, please refer to The Blue Pages.

AUSTRIA -- German

RADIO AUSTRIA INTERNATIONAL

6015, 6155, 9870, 9875, 11780, 12010, 13730, 15410, 15450, 17870, 21490 kHz

CANADA -- French

CANADIAN BROADCASTING CORP

6065, 6195, 9625, 11720 kHz

RADIO CANADA INTERNATIONAL

5960, **5995**, **6030**, **6050**, 6120, 6140, **7155**, **7230**, **7235**, **7295**, 9535, **9555**, 9635, **9645**, 9650, **9740**, 9750, 9755, 9760, **11705**, **11730**, **11775**, **11790**, **11840**, 11855, 11880, **11915**, **11935**, 11940, 11945, 13650, 13660, 13670, 13680, 15140, 15150, **15160**, **15225**, 15235, 15260, **15275**, **15305**, **15315**, 15320, **15325**, 15425, 15440, 17795, **17820**, 17875, 21545, 21675 kHz

CHINA (PR) -- Standard Chinese

CENTRAL PEOPLES BROADCASTING

9020, 9064, 9080, 9170, 9380, 9390, 9455, 9755, 9775, 10260, 11000, 11040, 11100, 11330, 11505, 11610, 11630, 11740, 11925, 12120, 12200, 15030, 15500, 15550, 15590, 15710, 15880, 17605, 17700 kHz

RADIO BEIJING

9455, 9480, 9530, 9565, 9575, 9590, 9665, **9690**, 9700, **9745**, 9765, **9770**, 9945, 11445, 11650, **11685**, 11695, **11715**, **11790**, 11945, 11975, 12015, 12055, 15100, **15111**, **15130**, 15150, 15165, 15195, 15260, 15320, 15330, 15435, 15450, 15455, 17533, **17715**, 17855 kHz

CHINA (TAIWAN) -- Mandarin & Cantonese

VOICE OF FREE CHINA

5985, 6200, 7130, 7445, 9510, 9575, 9610, **9680**, 9765, 11745, 11825, 11860, **11885**, 11915, **15130**, **15215**, 15270, **15345**, 15370, **15440**, **17612**, 17720, **17805**, **17845** kHz

EGYPT -- Arabic

RADIO CAIRO

9455, 9475, 9620, 9700, 9755, 9770, 9805, 9850, 9900, 9940, 11665, 11785, 11880, 11905, 11980, 12050, 15175, 15210, 15220, 15285, 17720, 17745, 17770, 17800 kHz

FRANCE -- French

RADIO FRANCE INTERNATIONALE

3965, 5945, 5990, 6040, 6045, 6175, 7120, **7125**, **7135**, 7160, 7175, 7280, 9550, 9605, **9715**, 9745, **9790**, 9800, 9805, 11650, 11660, **11670**, 11695, 11700, 11705, 11790, 11800, 11845, **11895**, **11925**, 11930, 11965, 11995, 15135, 15155, 15180, 15190, 15195, **15215**, **15275**, **15285**, 15300, 15315, 15360, **15365**, 15425, **15435**, **15440**, 15460, 17620, 17695, **17705**, **17710**, **17720**, 17775, 17785, 17795, 17800, 17845, 17850, **17860**, **21520**, 21580, 21620, 21635, **21645**, 21685, 21730, 21770, 25820 kHz

GERMANY (DR) -- German

RADIO BERLIN INTERNATIONAL

5965, 6040, 6080, 6115, 6165, 7170, 7185, 7295, 9620, 9635, 9645, 9665, 9730, 11785,

11810, 11890, 11970, 13610, 13690, 13700, 15125, 15240, 17775, 17880, 21465, 21540 kHz
STIMME DER DDR
6115 kHz

GERMANY (FR) -- German
BAYERISCHER RUNDFUNK
6085 kHz
DEUTSCHE WELLE
3995, **6075**, 6085, 6100, 6145, 7130, 9545, **9605**, **9640**, 9650, **9690**, 9700, 9715, **9735**, 9760, **11765**, **11785**, **11795**, **11810**, 11950, **11965**, 13780, 15105, **15245**, **15250**, **15270**, 15275, **15410**, **15510**, 17560, **17715**, **17795**, **17810**, 17830, 17845, **17860**, 17875, **21560**, **21590**, 21600, 21630, **21640**, 21680, 25740 kHz
SENDER FREIES BERLIN-SFB
6190 kHz
RADIO IN THE AMERICAN SECTOR
6005 kHz
RADIO BREMEN
6190 kHz
SUDDEUTSCHER RUNDFUNK
6030 kHz
SUDWESTFUNK
7265 kHz

GREECE -- Greek
I FONI TIS HELLADAS
7430, 9395, 9420, 9425, 9855, 9905, 11595, 11615, 11645, 12045, 15630, 17565 kHz

IRAN -- Persian
VO THE ISLAMIC REPUBLIC
9022, 15084 kHz

IRAQ -- Arabic
RADIO BAGHDAD
9515, 9605, 9660, 9730, 11750, 11760, 11770, 11825, 11840, 11860, 11880, 11895, 11970, 12025, 13680, 15110, 15150, 15200, 15310, 15400, 15415, 15430, 17720, 17730, 17750, 17830 kHz

ISRAEL -- Hebrew
KOL ISRAEL -- Reshet He
9385, 9455, 9855, 11655, 11700, 12077, 13750, 15485, 15615, 15640, 15650, 17575, 17685, 21550, 21760 kHz
RASHUTH HASHIDUR -- Reshet Bet
9385, 9930, 11545, 11585, 11655, 13750, 15095, 15615, 17545, 17590 kHz

ITALY -- Italian
RTV ITALIANA -- External
9710, 15330, 17800, 21515, 21690 kHz
RTV ITALIANA -- Uno
6060, 9515 kHz
RTV ITALIANA -- Due
7175 kHz
RTV ITALIANA -- Tre
3995 kHz (irregular)

JAPAN -- Japanese
NHK -- Domestic Services
3970, 6005, 6130, 6175, 6190, 9535, 9550 kHz
RADIO JAPAN/NHK
5960, 5990, 6025, **6120**, **7125**, 7140, 9505, 9535, 9640, **9645**, **9675**, **9685**, 9695, 11705, **11730**, **11800**, 11815, 11840, 11850, 11865, 11870, 11875, 11935, 15140, 15195, 15230, 15270, 15300, **15325**, **15350**, **17755**, 17765, 17810, 17825, 17835, 17845, 21500, 21610, **21635**, **21640**, **21690**, **21695**, **21700** kHz
RADIO TANPA
3925, 3945, 6055, 6115, 9595, 9760 kHz

JORDAN -- Arabic
RADIO JORDAN
9530, 9835, 11810, 11820, 11920, 11940, 11955, 15435 kHz

KUWAIT -- Arabic
RADIO KUWAIT
9750, 9840, 9880, 11665, 11990, 15345, 15495, 15505, 17850, 17885, 17895, 21675 kHz

SAUDI ARABIA -- Arabic
BROADCASTING SERVICE OF KINGDOM
9570, 9705, 9720, 9740, 9870, 9885, 11730, 15060, 15140, 15170, 15435, 17740, 17895, 21505, 21510, 21670 kHz

SWEDEN -- Swedish
RADIO SWEDEN
6065, 7265, 9630, 9655, 9695, 11705, 11830, 15190, 15345, 15390, 17740, 17800, 17810, 17860, 17880, 21570, 21610, 21690 kHz
SVERIGES RIKSRADIO -- Programs 1 & 3
6065, 9615, 9630, 15345, 15390, 21610, 21690 kHz

SWITZERLAND
SWISS RADIO INTERNATIONAL
French 3985, 5965, 6135, 6165, 9535, 9560, **9620**, 9725, 9810, 9885, **11695**, 11935, 11955, 12030, **12035**, 13635, 13685, 15420, 15430, 15525, 15570, 17570, 17670, **17730**, 17830, 21550, 21630, 21695 kHz
German 3985, 5965, 6095, 6135, 6165, 9535, 9560, **9620**, 9725, 9810, 9885, **11695**, 11935, 11955, 12030, **12035**, 13635, 13685, 15420, 15430, 15525, 15570, 17570, 17670, **17730**, 17830, 21550, 21630, 21695 kHz

UNITED ARAB EMIRATES -- Arabic
UAE RADIO
9555, 11730, 11790, 11940, 11955, 15300, 15320, 15435, 15555, 17775, 17830, 17890, 21605, 21700 kHz
VOICE OF THE UAE
9595, 9695, 9780, 11815, 11965, 11985, 13605, 15135, 15395, 17645, 17705, 17820, 21515, 21735, 25670, 25900 kHz

WORLDSCAN: THE BLUE PAGES

Quick-Access Guide to World Band Frequencies

There are hundreds of channels of news and entertainment available on world band radio, with some channels being shared by many stations. With such an abundance from which to choose, it can take some doing to figure out what is actually on the air.

Ordinary listings of what's on world band radio are unwieldy because there is such a vast quantity of data. That's why *Passport to World Band Radio* includes these quick-access "Blue Pages." Now, everything—stations, times, languages, targets and more—can be found at a glance. If something is not clear, the glossary at the back of the book explains it. There is also a handy key to languages and symbols at the bottom of each set of Blue Pages.

For example, if you're in North America listening to the channel of 6175 kHz at 2300 World Time, you'll see that the BBC World Service is broadcast in English to this area at that time. The transmitter is located in Canada and operates at a power of 250 kW.

World Time Simplifies Listening

World Time (UTC)—a handy concept also known as GMT—is used to eliminate the potential complication of so many time zones throughout the world. It treats the entire planet as a single zone and is announced regularly on the hour by many world band stations.

For example, if you're in New York and it's 6:00 AM EST, you will hear the time announced as "11 hours UTC." A glance at your clock shows that this is five hours ahead of your local time. You can either keep this "add five hours" figure in your head or use a separate clock for World Time. A growing number of world band radios come with World Time clocks built in, and 24-hour UTC clocks are also widely available as accessories.

World Band Stations Heard Outside Intended Target

With several hundred stations on the air at the same time, many piled atop each other like so much cordwood, you can't begin to hear all—or even most—of them. Nevertheless, even stations not targeted to your part of the world may be audible. Tune around, using The Blue Pages as your "radio map," and you'll discover a wealth of stations that can be enjoyed even though they're beamed to completely different parts of our planet.

GUIDE TO BLUE PAGES FORMAT

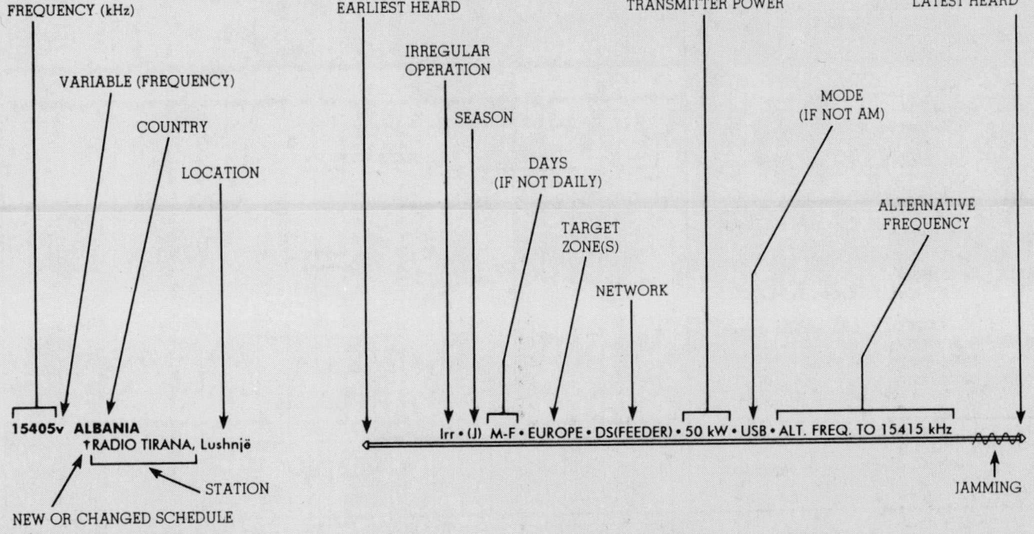

FREQUENCY	COUNTRY, STATION, LOCATION	TARGET • NETWORK • POWER (kW) — World Time 0–24
2310	**AUSTRALIA** †ABC/CAAMA RADIO, Alice Springs	DS-ENGLISH, ETC • 50 kW
	CHINA (PR) YUNNAN PEOPLES BS, Kunming	DS-3/CHINESE, ETC • 15 kW; Irr • DS-3 • 15 kW
2325	**AUSTRALIA** †ABC/CAAMA RADIO, Tennant Creek	DS-ENGLISH, ETC • 50 kW
	INDONESIA †MUSIC RADIO, Jakarta, Jawa	DS
2340	**CHINA (PR)** FUJIAN PEOPLES BS, Fuzhou	DS-1, TAIWAN SVC • 10 kW; Th/Sa-Tu • DS-1 • 10 kW
2350	**INDONESIA** †RRI, Yogyakarta, Jawa	DS • 1 kW
2360	**GUATEMALA** R MAYA DE BARILLAS, Huehuetenango	DS-SPANISH, ETC • 0.5 kW
2380	**BRAZIL** †RADIO EDUCADORA, Limeira	PORTUGUESE • DS • 0.25 kW
	FALKLAND ISLANDS †FALKLAND IS BC STN, Stanley	Alternative Frequency to 3958 kHz
2390	**GUATEMALA** LA VOZ DE ATITLAN, Santiago Atitlán	DS-SPANISH, ETC • 1 kW; Su • DS-SPANISH, ETC • 1 kW
	INDONESIA †RRI, Cirebon, Jawa	DS • 1 kW; Irr • DS • 1 kW
	MEXICO RADIO HUAYACOCOTLA, Huayacocotla	DS • 0.5 kW
2410	**BRAZIL** R TRANSAMAZONICA, Sen'r Guiomard	PORTUGUESE • DS • 1 kW
	PAPUA NEW GUINEA †RADIO ENGA, Wabag	DS-TEMP INACTIVE • 10 kW; Sa/Su • DS-TEMP INACTIVE • 10 kW
2415	**CHINA (PR)** WENZHOU PEOPLES BS, Wenzhou	DS
2420	**BRAZIL** RADIO SAO CARLOS, São Carlos	PORTUGUESE • DS • 0.5 kW
2432v	**INDONESIA** †RRI, Palembang,Sumatera	DS • 1 kW
2439.5	**INDONESIA** †RRI, Surakarta, Jawa	DS • 1 kW
2445	**CHINA (PR)** JIANGXI PEOPLES BS, Nanchang	DS-1 • 10 kW; W-M • DS-1 • 10 kW
2460	**BRAZIL** †PROGRESSO DO ACRE, Rio Branco	PORTUGUESE • DS • 1 kW
	CHINA (PR) YUNNAN PEOPLES BS, Kunming	DS-1 • 15 kW
2470	**BRAZIL** †RADIO CACIQUE, Sorocaba	Irr • PORTUGUESE • DS • 1 kW
2472v	**INDONESIA** †RRI, Purwokerto, Jawa	DS • 1 kW
2475	**CHINA (PR)** ZHEJIANG PBS, Hangzhou	DS-1 • 10 kW; W-M • DS-1 • 10 kW
2478	**INDONESIA** †RADIO PANCARAN, Jakarta, Jawa	DS
2485	**AUSTRALIA** †AUSTRALIAN BC CORP, Katherine	DS • 50 kW
2490	**BRAZIL** RADIO 8 SETEMBRO, Descalvado	PORTUGUESE • DS • 0.25 kW
	CHINA (PR) †VO THE STRAIT-PLA, Fuzhou	(D) • TAIWAN-1 • 10 kW
2495v	**MADAGASCAR** RADIO MADAGASIKARA, Antananarivo	Alternative Frequency to 5010v kHz
2500	**USA** WWV, Ft Collins,Colorado	WEATHER/WORLD TIME • 2.5 kW
	WWVH, Kekaha, Hawaii	WEATHER/WORLD TIME • 5 kW
2560	**CHINA (PR)** CENTRAL PEOPLES BS, Urümqi	(D) • DS-MINORITIES • 15 kW
	XINJIANG PBS, Urümqi	(D) • DS-UIGHUR • 15 kW; (D) Su • DS-UIGHUR • 15 kW
2581.6	**INDONESIA** RPD TENGAH SELATAN, Soë, Timur	DS • 0.3 kW
2582.4	**INDONESIA** †RPD TENGAH SELATAN, Soë, Timur	DS • 0.3 kW
2618	**INDONESIA** †RPD SAMBAS, Sambas, Kalimantan	DS • 0.25 kW
2675	**INDONESIA** †H B SOCIAL RADIO, Jakarta, Jawa	DS
2695	**INDONESIA** †RPD ENDE, Ende, Flores	DS • 0.5 kW
2727	**INDONESIA** †R ANGKASA JAYA, Lubuklinggau	DS
2850v	**KOREA (DPR)** KOREAN CENTRAL BS, Pyongyang	DS • 100 kW
2904.8	**INDONESIA** †RPD NGADA, Bajawa, N Tenggara	DS • 0.5 kW

0 Prime Time-Americas 6 Prime Time-E Asia 12 Prime Time-S Asia 18 Prime Time-Europe 24

SUMMER ONLY (J) WINTER ONLY (D) JAMMING / OR /\ EARLIEST HEARD ◁ LATEST HEARD ▷ NEW OR CHANGED FOR 1990 †

FREQUENCY	COUNTRY, STATION, LOCATION	TARGET • NETWORK • POWER (kW)
2962.7	INDONESIA †RPD MANGGARAI, Ruteng, Flores	DS • 0.3 kW
3143	INDONESIA †RPD BELITUNG, Tanjung Pandan, Sum	DS • 0.3 kW
3200	CHINA (PR) †VO THE STRAIT-PLA, Fuzhou	(D) • TAIWAN-2 • 10 kW
	SWAZILAND †TRANS WORLD RADIO, Manzini	(D) • S AFRICA • 25 kW; (J) • S AFRICA • 25 kW
3200.3	BOLIVIA †RADIO 9 DE ABRIL, Pulacayo	DS; Tu-Su • DS
3204.4	INDONESIA RRI, Bandung, Jawa	DS • 10 kW
3205	BRAZIL R RIBEIRAO PRETO, Ribeirão Prêto	PORTUGUESE • DS • 1 kW
	†R VALE RIO MADEIRA, Humaitá	PORTUGUESE • DS • 5 kW
	INDIA ALL INDIA RADIO, Lucknow	DS-B/ENGLISH, ETC • 10 kW
	PAPUA NEW GUINEA RADIO WEST SEPIK, Vanimo	DS • 10 kW
3210	CHINA (PR) GANNAN PEOPLES BS, Hezuo	Alternative Frequency to 5971v kHz
	PERU RADIO TRUJILLO, Trujillo	DS-SPANISH
3210v	MOZAMBIQUE †RADIO MOCAMBIQUE, Maputo	PORTUGUESE • DS • 100 kW
3214.8	INDONESIA †RRI, Manado, Sulawesi	DS • 10 kW
3215	SOUTH AFRICA SOUTH AFRICAN BC, Meyerton	ENGLISH & AFRIKAANS • DS-RADIO ORANJE • 100 kW
3216v	VENEZUELA ONDAS PANAMERICANA, El Vigía	Irr • DS • 1 kW
3220	CHINA (PR) CENTRAL PEOPLES BS	DS-1
	ECUADOR HCJB-VO THE ANDES, Quito	DS-SPANISH, QUECHUA • 10 kW
	PAPUA NEW GUINEA RADIO MOROBE, Lae	DS • 10 kW
3220v	KOREA (DPR) KANGWONG PS, Wonsan	DS
3222	TOGO RADIO KARA, Lama-Kara	DS-FRENCH, ETC • 10 kW
3222.8	INDONESIA †RRI, Mataram, Lombok	DS • 5 kW
3223	INDIA ALL INDIA RADIO, Simla	DS-ENGLISH, ETC • 2.5 kW
3225v	VENEZUELA RADIO OCCIDENTE, Tovar	DS • 1 kW
3229.3	PERU R SOL DE LOS ANDES, Juliaca	DS-SPANISH, ETC • 0.4 kW • ALT. FREQ. TO 3230.3 kHz; Irr • DS-SPANISH, ETC • 0.4 kW • ALT. FREQ. TO 3230.3 kHz
3230	LIBERIA †RADIO ELWA, Monrovia	DS • 10 kW; Sa-Tu/Th • DS • 10 kW
	NEPAL †RADIO NEPAL, Harriharpur	Alternative Frequency to 7165 kHz
3230.3	PERU R SOL DE LOS ANDES, Juliaca	Alternative Frequency to 3229.3 kHz
3231.8	INDONESIA †RRI, Bukittinggi, Sumat'a	DS • 10 kW
3232	MADAGASCAR R MADAGASIKARA, Antananarivo	DS-2
3235	BRAZIL RADIO CLUBE, Marilia	PORTUGUESE • DS • 0.5 kW
	INDIA ALL INDIA RADIO, Gauhati	DS-B/ENGLISH, ETC • 10 kW
	PAPUA NEW GUINEA R WEST NEW BRITAIN, Kimbe	DS • 2 kW
3240	GHANA GHANA BC CORP, Accra	Alternative Frequency to 4915 kHz
	SWAZILAND †TRANS WORLD RADIO, Manzini	S AFRICA • 25 kW; (J) • S AFRICA • 25 kW; (J) Sa/Su • S AFRICA • 25 kW
3240v	ECUADOR †R ANTENA LIBRE, Esmeraldas	DS • 1 kW
3241.4	INDONESIA †RRI, Ambon, Maluku	DS • 1 kW
3245	BRAZIL RADIO CLUBE, Varginha	PORTUGUESE • DS • 1 kW; M-Sa • PORTUGUESE • DS • 1 kW
	PAPUA NEW GUINEA RADIO GULF, Kerema	DS • 10 kW
3250	INDONESIA †RRI, Banjarmasin, Kali'n	DS • 10 kW
	KOREA (DPR) †RADIO PYONGYANG, Pyongyang	JAPANESE • E ASIA • 100 kW; E ASIA • 100 kW
	PERU RADIO QOLLYASUYO, Juliaca	Irr • DS • 1 kW

World Time 0–24: 0 Prime Time-Americas 6 Prime Time-E Asia 12 Prime Time-S Asia 18 Prime Time-Europe 24

ENGLISH ▬ ARABIC ▭ CHINESE ▭ FRENCH ═ GERMAN ▬ RUSSIAN ═ SPANISH ▬ OTHER —

FREQUENCY COUNTRY, STATION, LOCATION — TARGET • NETWORK • POWER (kW) — World Time

0 1 2 3 4 5 6 7 8 9 10 11 12 13 14 15 16 17 18 19 20 21 22 23 24

3250v HONDURAS
†RADIO LUZ Y VIDA, Santa Bárbara — DS • 0.8 kW; Su/M • DS • 0.8 kW; Tu-Sa • DS • 0.8 kW

3254v VENEZUELA
LA VOZ DE EL TIGRE, El Tigre — DS-"RADIO 980" • 1 kW; Irr • DS • 1 kW

3255 BRAZIL
R EDUCADORA CARIRI, Crato — PORTUGUESE • DS • 1 kW; Tu-Su • PORTUGUESE • DS • 1 kW

INDIA
†ALL INDIA RADIO, Shillong — DS

LIBERIA
LIBERIAN BC SYSTEM, Monrovia — DS-ENGLISH, ETC • 50 kW; M-F • DS-ENGLISH, ETC • 50 kW; M-Sa • DS-ENGLISH, ETC • 50 kW

UNITED KINGDOM
†BBC, Via Maseru, Lesotho — S AFRICA • 100 kW

3255v ECUADOR
LV DEL TRIUNFO, Sto Domingo Clrdos — Irr • DS • 1 kW

3259 JAPAN
†NHK, Fukuoka — Irr • JAPANESE • DS-1 (FEEDER) • 0.6 kW • USB

3260 CHINA (PR)
GUIZHOU PEOPLES BS, Guiyang — DS-1 • 10 kW

ECUADOR
LV DE RIO CARRIZAL, Calceta — DS • 3 kW

NIGER
†LA VOIX DU SAHEL, Niamey — DS-FRENCH, ETC • 4 kW; Sa • DS-FRENCH, ETC • 4 kW

PAPUA NEW GUINEA
RADIO MADANG, Madang — DS • 10 kW

PERU
LA VOZ DE OXAPAMPA, Oxapampa — DS • 2.5 kW; Irr • DS • 2.5 kW

3264.8 INDONESIA
†RRI, Bengkulu, Sumatera — DS • 10 kW

3265v INDONESIA
†RRI, Gorontalo, Sulawesi — DS • 10 kW

3268 INDIA
ALL INDIA RADIO, Kohima — DS-ENGLISH, ETC • 2 kW

3269.3 ECUADOR
ECOS DEL ORIENTE, Lago Agrio — DS

3270 NAMIBIA
†R SOUTHWEST AFRICA, Windhoek — ENGLISH, GERMAN & AFRIKAANS • DS • 100 kW; DS • 100 kW

3275 BRAZIL
†RADIO DIFUSORA, Cáceres — Alternative Frequency to 5055 kHz

PAPUA NEW GUINEA
†R SOUTH HIGHLANDS, Mendi — DS • 2 kW

VENEZUELA
RADIO MARA, Maracaibo — DS • 1 kW

3277 INDIA
RADIO KASHMIR, Srinagar — DS-B/ENGLISH, ETC • 7.5 kW

3277v INDONESIA
†RRI, Jakarta, Jawa — DS • 1 kW

3279.8 ECUADOR
LA VOZ DEL NAPO, Tena — DS-SPANISH, ETC • 2.5 kW; Su • DS-SPANISH, ETC • 2.5 kW

3280 BOLIVIA
†RADIO CHACO, Yacuiba — DS • 1 kW

CHINA (PR)
VOICE OF PUJIANG, Shanghai — E ASIA • CHINESE, ETC

3280v MOZAMBIQUE
†EP DE SOFALA, Beira — DS-2 • 100 kW

3280.2 PERU
RADIO HUARI, Ayacucho — DS-SPANISH, ETC • 1 kW

3285 BELIZE
RADIO BELIZE, Belmopan — DS-ENGLISH,SPANISH • 1 kW

3286v ECUADOR
RADIO RIO TARQUI, Cuenca — DS • 0.36 kW

3288v MADAGASCAR
R MADAGASIKARA, Antananarivo — M-Sa • DS • 100 kW; DS-FRENCH, ETC • 100 kW

3290 CHINA (PR)
CENTRAL PEOPLES BS — DS-2; W/F • DS-2

NAMIBIA
†R SOUTHWEST AFRICA, Windhoek — ENGLISH, GERMAN & AFRIKAANS • DS • 100 kW; DS • 100 kW; M-F • DS • 100 kW; Sa/Su • DS • 100 kW; ENGLISH & AFRIKAANS • DS • 100 kW

PAPUA NEW GUINEA
RADIO CENTRAL, Port Moresby — DS-ENGLISH, ETC • 10 kW

PERU
(con'd) RADIO TAYABAMBA, Tayabamba — DS • 1 kW

0 Prime Time-Americas 6 Prime Time-E Asia 12 Prime Time-S Asia 18 Prime Time-Europe 24

SUMMER ONLY (J) WINTER ONLY (D) JAMMING / OR /\ EARLIEST HEARD ◁ LATEST HEARD ▷ NEW OR CHANGED FOR 1990 †

FREQUENCY	COUNTRY, STATION, LOCATION	TARGET • NETWORK • POWER (kW)
3290 (con'd)	**TRISTAN DA CUNHA** TRISTAN BC SERVICE, Edinburgh	Su • DS • 0.04 kW; M-F • DS • 0.04 kW; M/W/F • DS • 0.04 kW
3295	**INDIA** ALL INDIA RADIO, Delhi	DS • 10 kW; S ASIA • URDU • 10 kW
3300	**BURUNDI** †LA VOIX DE LA REV, Bujumbura	M-F • DS • 25 kW; Sa/Su • DS • 25 kW; Su • DS • 25 kW; DS-FRENCH, ETC • 25 kW; M-F • DS-FRENCH, ETC • 25 kW; M-Sa • DS-FRENCH, ETC • 25 kW; Sa/Su • DS-FRENCH, ETC • 25 kW
	CHINA (PR) †VO THE STRAIT-PLA, Fuzhou	(D) • TAIWAN-1 • 10 kW
	GUATEMALA RADIO CULTURAL, Guatemala City	DS • 10 kW; M • DS • 10 kW; M-Sa • DS • 10 kW; Tu-Su • DS • 10 kW; Su • DS • 10 kW
3305	**INDIA** ALL INDIA RADIO, Ranchi	DS-ENGLISH, ETC • 2 kW
	PAPUA NEW GUINEA RADIO WESTERN, Daru	DS-ENGLISH, ETC • 10 kW
3305.7	**ZIMBABWE** ZIMBABWE BC CORP, Gweru	Irr • DS-ENGLISH, ETC • 10/100 kW; Irr • M-Sa • DS-ENGLISH, ETC • 10/100 kW
3306	**INDONESIA** RRI, Dili, Timur	DS • 10 kW
3306v	**INDONESIA** †RRI, Dili, Timur	DS • 10 kW
3310	**CHINA (PR)** JILIN PEOPLES BS, Changchun	DS • 10 kW; Su • DS • 10 kW
	PERU †RADIO BAGUA, Bagua	DS • 1 kW
3310.3	**BOLIVIA** †RADIO SAN MIGUEL, Riberalta	DS • 1 kW; Tu-Su • DS • 1 kW
3315	**INDIA** ALL INDIA RADIO, Bhopal	DS-ENGLISH, ETC • 10 kW
	PAPUA NEW GUINEA †RADIO MANUS, Lorengau	DS-ENGLISH, ETC • 2 kW
3315v	**ECUADOR** RADIO PASTAZA, Puyo	DS • 2.5 kW
3316	**SIERRA LEONE** †SIERRA LEONE BS, Goderich	DS-ENGLISH, ETC • 10 kW
3320	**KOREA (DPR)** †RADIO PYONGYANG, Pyongyang	E ASIA
	SOUTH AFRICA †SOUTH AFRICAN BC, Meyerton	ENGLISH & AFRIKAANS • DS-RADIO ORION • 100 kW; M-F • DS-MARKET PRICES • 100 kW; RADIO SUID-AFRIKA • 100 kW
3322.4	**ECUADOR** RADIO SANGAY, Macas	Irr • DS • 1 kW
3324.8	**GUATEMALA** R MAYA DE BARILLAS, Huehuetenango	DS-SPANISH, ETC • 1 kW
3325	**BRAZIL** RADIO LIBERAL, Belém	PORTUGUESE • DS • 5 kW
	RDIF UNIVERSITARIA, Guarulhos	PORTUGUESE • DS • 1 kW
	INDONESIA †RRI, Palangkaráya, Kali'n	DS • 10 kW
	PAPUA NEW GUINEA †R NORTH SOLOMONS, Kieta	DS-TEMP INACTIVE • 10 kW
3325v	**ECUADOR** ONDAS QUEVEDENAS, Quevedo	Irr • DS • 1.5 kW
3326	**NIGERIA** RADIO NIGERIA, Lagos	DS-1/ENGLISH, ETC • 50 kW
3329.6	**PERU** ONDAS DEL HUALLAGA, Huánuco	Alternative Frequency to 3330.4 kHz
3330	**RWANDA** R REP RWANDAISE, Kigali	DS-FRENCH, ETC • 5 kW; Su • DS-FRENCH, ETC • 5 kW
3330.4	**PERU** ONDAS DEL HUALLAGA, Huánuco	DS • 0.5 kW • ALT. FREQ. TO 3329.6 kHz; Su • DS • 0.5 kW • ALT. FREQ. TO 3329.6 kHz
3331v	**COMOROS** RADIO COMORO, Moroni	DS-FRENCH, ETC • 4 kW
3335	**BRAZIL** RADIO ALVORADA, Londrina	PORTUGUESE • DS • 5 kW; Tu-Su • PORTUGUESE • DS • 5 kW
	CHINA (TAIWAN) CENTRAL BC SYSTEM, T'ai-pei	PRC-5 • 10 kW
	PAPUA NEW GUINEA RADIO EAST SEPIK, Wewak	DS • 10 kW

World Time 0–24: 0 Prime Time-Americas 6 Prime Time-E Asia 12 Prime Time-S Asia 18 Prime Time-Europe 24

ENGLISH ▬ ARABIC ▭▭▭ CHINESE ▯▯▯ FRENCH ═ GERMAN ═ RUSSIAN ═ SPANISH ═ OTHER —

FREQUENCY	COUNTRY, STATION, LOCATION	TARGET • NETWORK • POWER (kW)
3338v	**MOZAMBIQUE** †RADIO MOCAMBIQUE, Maputo	DS • 10 kW
3339.5	**PERU** RADIO ALTURA, Cerro de Pasco	DS • 1 kW
3340.2	**BOLIVIA** RADIO VILOCO, Viloco	DS-SPANISH, ETC • 1 kW
		Irr • Su/M • DS-SPANISH, ETC • 1 kW
3345	**INDIA** RADIO KASHMIR, Jammu	DS-ENGLISH, ETC • 1 kW
	INDONESIA RRI, Ternate, Maluku	DS • 10 kW
	PAPUA NEW GUINEA †RADIO NORTHERN, Popondetta	DS-ENGLISH, ETC • 2 kW
3346	**ZAMBIA** †RADIO ZAMBIA-ZBS, Lusaka	DS • 50 kW
3346v	**ANGOLA** ER DO HUAMBO, Huambo	Irr • PORTUGUESE • DS • 10 kW
3349.8	**BOLIVIA** †RADIO 27 DICIEMBRE, Villa Montes	DS • 1 kW
		Tu-Su • DS • 1 kW
3350	**GHANA** GHANA BC CORP, Accra	Irr • DS-1/ENGLISH ETC • 10 kW
	KOREA (DPR) SOUTH PYONGYANG PS, Pyŏngsong	DS
3354v	**ANGOLA** RADIO NACIONAL, Luanda	PORTUGUESE • DS-A
3355	**INDIA** ALL INDIA RADIO, Kurseong	DS-ENGLISH, ETC • 10 kW
	INDONESIA †RRI, Sumenep, Jawa	DS • 1 kW
	NEW CALEDONIA RFO-N CALEDONIE, Nouméa	Irr • PACIFIC • DS-FRENCH, ETC • 20 kW
	PAPUA NEW GUINEA RADIO SIMBU, Kundiawa	DS • 10 kW
3356	**BOTSWANA** RADIO BOTSWANA, Gaborone	DS-ENGLISH, ETC • 50 kW
3360	**ECUADOR** RADIO FEDERACION, Sucúa	DS-SPANISH, SHUAR • 10 kW
	GUATEMALA LA VOZ DE NAHUALA, Nahualá	DS-SPANISH, ETC • 0.5/1 kW
		Su • DS-SPANISH, ETC • 0.5/1 kW
	PAPUA NEW GUINEA †RADIO MILNE BAY, Alotau	Alternative Frequency to 3365 kHz
3365	**BRAZIL** †RADIO CULTURA, Araraquara	PORTUGUESE • DS • 1 kW
	INDIA ALL INDIA RADIO, Delhi	DS-ENGLISH, ETC • 10 kW
	PAPUA NEW GUINEA †RADIO MILNE BAY, Alotau	DS-ENGLISH, ETC • 10 kW • ALT. FREQ. TO 3360 kHz
3366	**GHANA** GHANA BC CORP, Accra	DS-2 • 50 kW
3370	**GUATEMALA** RADIO TEZULUTLAN, Cobán	DS-SPANISH, ETC • 1/5 kW
3370v	**MADAGASCAR** R MADAGASIKARA, Antananarivo	Irr • DS
	MOZAMBIQUE EP DE SOFALA, Beira	PORTUGUESE • DS-1 • 10 kW
3370.5	**BOLIVIA** RADIO FLORIDA, Samaipata	DS • 1 kW
		Tu-Su • DS • 1 kW
		Su • DS • 1 kW
3375	**BRAZIL** R NACIONAL, S Gabriel Cachoeira	PORTUGUESE • DS • 5 kW
	RADIO EDUCADORA, Guajará Mirim	PORTUGUESE • DS • 5 kW
	†RADIO EQUATORIAL, Macapá	PORTUGUESE • DS • 1 kW
	INDIA ALL INDIA RADIO, Gauhati	DS-A/ENGLISH, ETC • 10 kW
	PAPUA NEW GUINEA R WESTERN HIGHLAND, Mount Hagen	DS • 10 kW
3375v	**ANGOLA** RADIO NACIONAL, Luanda	PORTUGUESE • DS-A • 10 kW
3376	**INDONESIA** †RRI, Medan, Sumatera	DS • 7.5 kW
3377.5	**JAPAN** †NHK, Osaka	Irr • JAPANESE • DS-2 (FEEDER) • 0.5 kW
3378	**AUSTRIA** SCHULUNGSSENDER, Vienna	M-F • DS-ARMY TRAINING • 10 kW
3380	**GUATEMALA** †RADIO CHORTIS, Jocotán	DS-SPANISH, CHORTI • 1 kW
		Tu-Su • DS • 1 kW
		M-Sa • DS-SPANISH, CHORTI • 1 kW
	MALAWI MALAWI BC CORP, Limbe	DS-ENGLISH, ETC • 100 kW
		(J) • DS-ENGLISH, ETC • 100 kW
3380.3	**BOLIVIA** RADIO CUMBRE, Tazna	Irr • DS • 0.5/1 kW
3381	**ECUADOR** RADIO IRIS, Esmeraldas	DS • 10 kW
		M-Sa • DS • 10 kW
3385 (con'd)	**BRAZIL** R EDUCACAO RURAL, Tefé	PORTUGUESE • DS • 1 kW

World Time 0–24: 0 Prime Time-Americas 6 Prime Time-E Asia 12 Prime Time-S Asia 18 Prime Time-Europe 24

SUMMER ONLY (J) WINTER ONLY (D) JAMMING / OR /\ EARLIEST HEARD ◁ LATEST HEARD ▷ NEW OR CHANGED FOR 1990 †

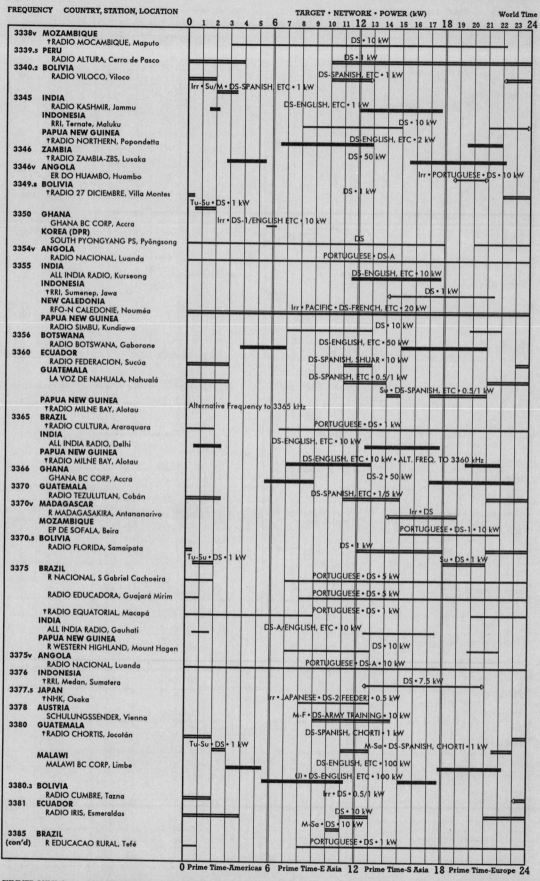

FREQUENCY	COUNTRY, STATION, LOCATION	TARGET • NETWORK • POWER (kW)
3385 (con'd)	**FRENCH GUIANA** RFO-GUYANE, Cayenne	DS • 4 kW
	INDONESIA RRI, Kupang, Timur	DS • 10 kW; Su • DS • 10 kW
	MALAYSIA RTM-SARAWAK, Miri	DS-IBAN • 10 kW
	PAPUA NEW GUINEA †R EAST NEW BRITAIN, Rabaul	DS • 10 kW
3390	**ZAIRE** RADIO CANDIP, Bunia	DS-SCOLAIRE • 1 kW
3390.3	**BOLIVIA** RADIO CAMARGO, Camargo	DS • 1 kW; Irr • DS • 1 kW
3394.8	**ECUADOR** †RADIO ZARACAY, Santo Domingo	DS • 5 kW
3395	**INDONESIA** †RRI, Tanjungkarang, Sum	DS • 10 kW
	PAPUA NEW GUINEA †EASTERN HIGHLANDS, Goroka	DS • 2 kW
3396v	**ZIMBABWE** ZIMBABWE BC CORP, Gweru	M-Sa • DS-R1 • 20/100 kW; DS-R1/R3 • 20/100 kW
3400	**ICELAND** RIKISUTVARPID, Reykjavik	(D) • ATLANTIC & EUROPE • DS • 10 kW • USB
3401v	**BRAZIL** RADIO 6 DE AGOSTO, Xapurí	PORTUGUESE • DS • 2 kW; Tu-Su • PORTUGUESE • DS • 2 kW
3450.2	**PERU** †RADIO OYON, Oyón	DS-SPANISH,QUECHUA • 1 kW; Tu-Su • DS • 1 kW
3460	**INDONESIA** †RPD ACEH TIMUR, Langsa, Sumatera	DS
3465.7	**PERU** †REINA DE LA SELVA, Chachapoyas	DS
3473v	**BOLIVIA** †RADIO PADILLA, Padilla	DS • 0.5 kW
3480	**CLANDESTINE (ASIA)** "VO NAT SALVATION", Haeju, N Korea	TO KOREA (REP) • 100 kW
3535	**CHINA (PR)** †VO THE STRAIT-PLA, Fuzhou	(D) • TAIWAN-1 • 10 kW
3543	**CLANDESTINE (M EAST)** †"VO KURD FIGHTERS", Eastern Iraq	MIDEAST
	†"VO THE CRUSADER", Eastern Iraq	PERSIAN • MIDEAST • MOJAHEDIN-E KHALQ
3569v	**BRAZIL** †RADIO 3 DE JULHO, Brasiléia	PORTUGUESE • DS • 1.5 kW
3607.5	**JAPAN** †NHK, Tokyo-Shobu	Irr • JAPANESE • DS-1 (FEEDER) • 0.9 kW • USB
3644.5	**INDONESIA** †RRI, Fak Fak, Irian Jaya	DS • 0.5 kW
3650v	**CLANDESTINE (C AMER)** †"LA VOZ POPULAR", Guatemala	Sa • GUATEMALA REBELS
3654	**INDONESIA** †RPD LUWU, Luwu, Sulawesi	DS
3665v	**PAKISTAN (AZAD K)** AZAD KASHMIR RADIO, Muzaffarabad	DS • 1 kW
3710v	**CHINA (PR)** JIANGXI PEOPLES BS, Nanchang	Irr • DS-1/3695-3725KHZV; Irr • W-M • DS-1/3695-3725KHZV
	CLANDESTINE (AFRICA) †"VO BROAD MASSES", Ethiopia	E AFRICA • PLF OF ERITREA
3725v	**CLANDESTINE (C AMER)** "R VENCEREMOS", Morazán, Salvador	FMLN/ANTI-SALVADOR • ALT. FREQ. TO 3765v kHz; M-Sa • FMLN/ANTI-SALVADOR • ALT. FREQ. TO 3765v kHz; Su • FMLN/ANTI-SALVADOR • ALT. FREQ. TO 3765v kHz
3765v	**CLANDESTINE (C AMER)** "R VENCEREMOS", Morazán, Salvador	Alternative Frequency to 3725v kHz
3775	**INDONESIA** †RPD SUMBAWA, Sumbawa Besar	DS • 0.075 kW
3778v	**IRAN** †VO THE ISLAMIC REP, Tehrān	PERSIAN • MIDEAST • DS • 100 kW
3800	**CLANDESTINE (ASIA)** †"VO AFGHANISTAN"	MIDEAST & S ASIA • ANTI-AFGHAN GOVT
3815	**CHINA (PR)** CENTRAL PEOPLES BS	TAIWAN-1
3840	**CLANDESTINE (ASIA)** †"VO AFGHANISTAN"	MIDEAST & S ASIA • ANTI-AFGHAN GOVT
3900	**CHINA (PR)** HULUNBEI'ER PBS, Hailar	DS-CHINESE
3904.8	**INDONESIA** †RRI, Banda Aceh, Sumat'a	DS • 10 kW
	†RRI, Merauke, Irian Jaya	DS • 1 kW
3905	**INDIA** ALL INDIA RADIO, Delhi	S ASIA • 100 kW; MIDEAST • 100 kW; Su • DS • 100 kW; DS-ENGLISH, ETC • 100 kW
	PAPUA NEW GUINEA RADIO NEW IRELAND, Kavieng	DS • 2 kW; DS • 4 kW

World Time 0–24: 0 Prime Time-Americas 6 Prime Time-E Asia 12 Prime Time-S Asia 18 Prime Time-Europe 24

ENGLISH ARABIC CHINESE FRENCH GERMAN RUSSIAN SPANISH OTHER

FREQUENCY	COUNTRY, STATION, LOCATION	TARGET • NETWORK • POWER (kW)
3905v	**CLANDESTINE (M EAST)** "VO THE CRUSADER", Eastern Iraq	MIDEAST • MOJAHEDIN-E KHALQ
3910	**CHINA (PR)** YUNNAN PEOPLES BS, Kunming	DS-LITERARY SVC
3912	**CLANDESTINE (ASIA)** †"VO THE PEOPLE", South Korea	Irr • E ASIA • TO NORTH KOREA
3915	**UNITED KINGDOM** †BBC, Via Singapore	SE ASIA • 100 kW (D) • SE ASIA • 100 kW
3920	**KOREA (DPR)** NORTH PYONGYANG PS, Sinuiju	DS
3925	**CANADA** †R CANADA INTL, Via Tokyo, Japan	Sa • JAPANESE • E ASIA & PACIFIC • 10/50 kW
	INDIA ALL INDIA RADIO, Delhi	DS-ENGLISH, ETC • 100 kW
	JAPAN †RADIO TANPA, Multiple Locations	JAPANESE • DS-1 • 10/50 kW Su-F • JAPANESE • DS-1 • 10/50 kW
	RADIO TANPA, Tokyo-Nagara	JAPANESE • DS-1 • 50 kW
3927.4	**SOUTH AFRICA** †CAPITAL RADIO, Umtata	DS • 20 kW
3930	**CLANDESTINE (M EAST)** "VO THE CRUSADER", Eastern Iraq	MIDEAST • MOJAHEDIN-E KHALQ
	KOREA (REPUBLIC) KOREAN BC SYSTEM, Suwon	KOREAN • DS-1 • 5 kW
3935v	**CLANDESTINE (M EAST)** †"VO THE MARTYRS", Near Iran	MIDEAST • ANTI-IRANIAN GOVT
3940	**CHINA (PR)** HUBEI PEOPLES BS, Wuhan	DS-1 M-Sa • DS-1
	HONG KONG RTV HONG KONG, Kowloon	Irr • E ASIA • SPECIAL EVENTS • 2 kW
3940v	**CLANDESTINE (AFRICA)** †"VO BROAD MASSES", Ethiopia	E AFRICA • PLF OF ERITREA
3945	**INDONESIA** †RRI, Denpasar, Bali	DS • 1/10 kW
	JAPAN †RADIO TANPA, Tokyo-Nagara	JAPANESE • DS-2 • 10 kW
	VANUATU †RADIO VANUATU, Vila, Efate Island	DS-ENGLISH,FR,ETC • 10 kW M-Sa • DS-ENGLISH,FR,ETC • 10 kW
3950	**CHINA (PR)** QINGHAI PEOPLES BS, Xining	DS-1/CHINESE • 10 kW
3955	**UNITED KINGDOM** †BBC, Daventry	EUROPE • 100 kW (D) • EUROPE • 100 kW
	†BBC, Multiple Locations	EUROPE • 100/250 kW (D) • EUROPE • 100/250 kW
	†BBC, Skelton, Cumbria	W EUROPE & N AFRICA • 250 kW
3955v	**PAKISTAN** PAKISTAN BC CORP, Rawalpindi	DS • 10 kW F • DS • 10 kW
3958	**FALKLAND ISLANDS** †FALKLAND IS BC STN, Stanley	DS-TEMP INACTIVE • 1/3.5 kW • USB • ALT. FREQ. TO 2380 kHz
3959.8	**INDONESIA** †RRI, Palu, Sulawesi	DS • 10 kW
3960	**CHINA (PR)** RADIO BEIJING, Beijing	JAPANESE • E ASIA • 10 kW
	XINJIANG PBS, Urümqi	(D) • DS-CHINESE • 50 kW
	KOREA (DPR) CHAGONG PROVINCIAL, Kanggye	DS
	MONGOLIA †RADIO ULAN BATOR, Dalandzadgad	DS-1 • 12 kW Tu/F • DS-1 • 12 kW W/Th/Sa-M • DS-1 • 12 kW
	USA †RFE-RL, Via Germany (FR)	WEST USSR • 20 kW
	USSR †RADIO MOSCOW, Via Mongolia	E ASIA • 12 kW
3965	**AFGHANISTAN** RADIO AFGHANISTAN, Via USSR	DS-1
	FRANCE †R FRANCE INTL, Issoudun-Allouis	EUROPE • 4 kW
3965v	**CLANDESTINE (M EAST)** "VO THE CRUSADER", Eastern Iraq	MIDEAST • MOJAHEDIN-E KHALQ
3970	**CAMEROON** CAMEROON RTV CORP, Buea	Irr • DS-FRENCH,ENG,ETC • 4 kW Irr • M-Sa • DS-FRENCH,ENG,ETC • 4 kW
	CHINA (PR) NEI MONGGOL PBS, Hohhot	DS-CHINESE Sa/Su • DS-CHINESE
	JAPAN †NHK, Nagoya	Irr • JAPANESE • DS-1(FEEDER) • 0.3 kW • USB
	†NHK, Sapporo	Irr • JAPANESE • DS-1(FEEDER) • 0.6 kW
(con'd)	**USA** †RFE-RL, Via Biblis, GFR	E EUROPE • 100 kW

World Time: 0 Prime Time-Americas 6 Prime Time-E Asia 12 Prime Time-S Asia 18 Prime Time-Europe 24

SUMMER ONLY (J) WINTER ONLY (D) JAMMING / OR /\ EARLIEST HEARD ◁ LATEST HEARD ▷ NEW OR CHANGED FOR 1990 †

FREQUENCY	COUNTRY, STATION, LOCATION	TARGET • NETWORK • POWER (kW) — World Time 0–24
3970 (con'd)	USA †RFE-RL, Via Biblis, GFR	M-Sa • E EUROPE • 100 kW
3975	UNITED KINGDOM †BBC, Skelton, Cumbria	(D) • EUROPE • 250 kW; (J) • EUROPE • 250 kW
3976v	INDONESIA †RRI, Surabaya, Jawa	DS • 10 kW
3980	KOREA (DPR) NORTH HAMGYONG PS, Ch'öngjin	DS
	USA †VOA, Via Ismaning, GFR	EUROPE • 100 kW; (D) • EUROPE • 100 kW; (J) • EUROPE • 100 kW
3980v	PAKISTAN PAKISTAN BC CORP, Islamabad	DS • 100 kW
	PERU RADIO EL PORVENIR, El Porvenir	Irr • DS • 0.5 kW
3985	CHINA (PR) RADIO BEIJING, Via Switzerland	EUROPE • 250 kW
	CLANDESTINE (ASIA) "ECHO OF HOPE", Seoul, South Korea	E ASIA • KOREANS IN JAPAN • 50 kW
	SWITZERLAND †SWISS RADIO INTL, Beromünster	EUROPE • 250 kW; PORTUGUESE • EUROPE • 250 kW; M-Sa • EUROPE • 250 kW; Su • EUROPE • 250 kW
	USA †RFE-RL, Via Biblis, GFR	WEST USSR • 100 kW
3985.8	INDONESIA †RRI, Manokwari, Irian Jaya	DS • 1 kW; Irr • DS • 1 kW
3990	CHINA (PR) CENTRAL PEOPLES BS, Urümqi	(D) • DS-MINORITIES • 50 kW
	VOICE OF PUJIANG, Shanghai	E ASIA • CHINESE, ETC
	XINJIANG PBS, Urümqi	(D) • DS-UIGHUR • 50 kW; (D) Su • DS-UIGHUR • 50 kW
	UNITED KINGDOM †BBC, Via Zyyi, Cyprus	(D) • E EUROPE & MIDEAST • 20 kW; (D) Su • E EUROPE & MIDEAST • 20 kW
	USA †RFE-RL, Via Biblis, GFR	E EUROPE & WEST USSR • 100 kW; M-Sa • E EUROPE • 100 kW
	VOA, Via M'rovia, Liberia	W AFRICA • 15 kW • LSB; W AFRICA • 50 kW; M-F • W AFRICA • 15 kW • LSB
3994v	ANGOLA ER DA HUILA, Lubango	Irr • PORTUGUESE • DS • 1 kW
3995	GERMANY (FR) †DEUTSCHE WELLE, Jülich	EUROPE • 100 kW; (D) • EUROPE • 100 kW
	ITALY RTV ITALIANA, Rome	ITALIAN • EUROPE • DS-3 • 50 kW
	USSR RADIO MOSCOW, Khabarovsk	(D) • DS-2 • 50 kW
	TUVIN RADIO, Kyzyl	DS • 15 kW
3995v	CLANDESTINE (M EAST) "VO THE CRUSADER", Eastern Iraq	MIDEAST • MOJAHEDIN-E KHALQ
3999	GREENLAND KALAALLIT NUNAATA, Nuuk	DS • 1 kW; Tu-Su • DS • 1 kW; M-Sa • DS • 1 kW
4000v	CAMEROON CAMEROON RTV CORP, Bafoussam	DS-FRENCH, ENG, ETC • 20 kW
4000.2	INDONESIA †RRI, Kendari, Sulawesi	DS • 5 kW
4002.7	INDONESIA †RRI, Padang, Sumatera	DS • 10 kW
4005v	CLANDESTINE (M EAST) †"VO IRANIAN REV'N", Afghanistan	MIDEAST • ANTI-IRANIAN GOVT; PERSIAN • MIDEAST • ANTI-IRANIAN GOVT
4008v	PERU †RADIO GRAU, Huancabamba	Alternative Frequency to 5277v kHz
4010	USSR KIRGHIZ RADIO, Frunze, Kirgiziya	DS-1 • 50 kW
	†RADIO MOSCOW	(D) • E ASIA
4010v	CLANDESTINE (M EAST) †"VO IRAN COMMUNIST, Afghanistan	F • PERSIAN • MIDEAST • ANTI-IRANIAN GOVT; PERSIAN • MIDEAST • ANTI-IRANIAN GOVT; Sa-Th • PERSIAN • MIDEAST • ANTI-IRANIAN GOVT
4011v	PERU †FRECUENCIA POPULAR, Rioja	DS • 0.6 kW; Tu-Su • DS • 0.6 kW; M-Sa • DS • 0.6 kW
4020	CHINA (PR) †RADIO BEIJING, Beijing	E ASIA • FEEDER • 10 kW

0 Prime Time-Americas 6 Prime Time-E Asia 12 Prime Time-S Asia 18 Prime Time-Europe 24

ENGLISH ARABIC CHINESE FRENCH GERMAN RUSSIAN SPANISH OTHER

FREQUENCY	COUNTRY, STATION, LOCATION	TARGET • NETWORK • POWER (kW)
4025	**USSR**	
	RADIO MOSCOW, Vladivostok	E ASIA
4030	**USSR**	
	†BASHKIR RADIO, Ufa	DS-RUSSIAN,BASHKIR • 50 kW
	CHUKOT RADIO, Anadyr'	DS • 15 kW
	RADIO MOSCOW	(D) • EUROPE • DANISH,SWEDISH,ETC
4030v	**CLANDESTINE (M EAST)**	
	"VO IRAQI PEOPLE"	MIDEAST • IRAQI COMMUNIST
4035	**CHINA (PR)**	
	CENTRAL PEOPLES BS, Lhasa	DS-MINORITIES • 50 kW
	†RADIO BEIJING, Lhasa	S ASIA • 50 kW
	XIZANG PEOPLES BS, Lhasa	DS-TIBETAN • 50 kW
4039.2	**PERU**	
	RADIO MARGINAL, Tocache	DS • 1 kW
4040	**USSR**	
	ARMENIAN RADIO, Yerevan	DS-1 • 15 kW
	RADIO MOSCOW, Vladivostok	DS-2 • 50 kW
4045	**USSR**	
	RADIO MOSCOW, Moscow	(D) • E EUROPE
		(D) • E EUROPE • WS
4050	**USSR**	
	KIRGHIZ RADIO, Frunze	DS-2 • 50 kW
	R TIKHIY OKEAN, Yuzhno-Sakhalinsk	MARINERS(FEEDER) • 15 kW • USB
		Sa • MARINERS(FEEDER) • 15 kW • USB
		Su-F • MARINERS(FEEDER) • 15 kW • USB
	SAKHALIN RADIO, Yuzhno-Sakhalinsk	DS(FEEDER) • 15 kW • USB
4060	**USSR**	
	RADIO MOSCOW, Ryazan'	(D) • E EUROPE • 100 kW
		(D) • E EUROPE • WS • 100 kW
4070v	**CLANDESTINE (M EAST)**	
	†"VO KURDISH PEOPLE, Middle East	MIDEAST • ANTI-IRAQI GOVT
		Irr • MIDEAST • ANTI-IRAQI GOVT
4080v	**USSR**	
	†RADIO MOSCOW, Via Mongolia	E ASIA • 50 kW
	†RADIO ULAN BATOR, Ulan Bator	DS-1 • 50 kW
		Tu/F • DS-1 • 50 kW
		W/Th/Sa-M • DS-1 • 50 kW
4100	**CHINA (PR)**	
	TIANJIN PEOPLES BS, Tianjin	Irr • DS • 0.5 kW
		DS • 0.5 kW
4100v	**CLANDESTINE (M EAST)**	
	†"VO IRANIAN KURDS"	MIDEAST • ANTI-IRANIAN GOVT
		PERSIAN • MIDEAST • ANTI-IRANIAN GOVT
4110v	**CLANDESTINE (M EAST)**	
	†"VO THE MARTYRS", Near Iran	Irr • MIDEAST • ANTI-IRANIAN GOVT
4117v	**BRAZIL**	
	RADIO DIFUSORA, Sena Madureira	PORTUGUESE • DS • 0.25 kW
		M-Sa • PORTUGUESE • DS • 0.25 kW
		Tu-Su • PORTUGUESE • DS • 0.25 kW
4119v	**CLANDESTINE (ASIA)**	
	"VO NAT SALVATION", Haeju, N Korea	TO KOREA (REP) • 100 kW
4130	**CHINA (PR)**	
	†RADIO BEIJING, Beijing	E ASIA • FEEDER • 10 kW
		(D) • E ASIA • FEEDER • 10 kW
	†VO THE STRAIT-PLA, Fuzhou	(J) • TAIWAN-1 • 10 kW
		TAIWAN-1 • 10 kW
	CLANDESTINE (ASIA)	
	†"DEM KAMPUCHEA", Beijing, China (PR)	PRO-KHMER ROUGE • 50 kW
	SPAIN	
	†R NACIONAL ESPANA, Via Beijing	(D) • E ASIA • FEEDER • 10 kW
4160v	**CLANDESTINE (ASIA)**	
	†"ECHO OF PUBLIC", Korea (DPR)	E ASIA • 50 kW
	CLANDESTINE (M EAST)	
	†"VO THE MARTYRS", Near Iran	MIDEAST • ANTI-IRANIAN GOVT
		PERSIAN • MIDEAST • ANTI-IRANIAN GOVT
	†"VO THE WORKER", Near Iran	PERSIAN • MIDEAST • ANTI-IRANIAN GOVT
4190	**CHINA (PR)**	
	CENTRAL PEOPLES BS	DS-MINORITIES
4194v	**PERU**	
	RADIO UCHIZA, Uchiza	DS
4200	**CHINA (PR)**	
	†RADIO BEIJING, Beijing	E ASIA • FEEDER • 10 kW
	CLANDESTINE (ASIA)	
	†"VO AFGHANISTAN"	MIDEAST & S ASIA • ANTI-AFGHAN GOVT
4220	**CHINA (PR)**	
	CENTRAL PEOPLES BS, Urümqi	DS-MINORITIES
	XINJIANG PBS, Urümqi	DS-MONGOLIAN
4238.3	**PERU**	
	†RADIO INCA, Baños del Inca	DS

World Time: 0 1 2 3 4 5 6 7 8 9 10 11 12 13 14 15 16 17 18 19 20 21 22 23 24

0 Prime Time-Americas 6 Prime Time-E Asia 12 Prime Time-S Asia 18 Prime Time-Europe 24

SUMMER ONLY (J) WINTER ONLY (D) JAMMING / OR ⋀ EARLIEST HEARD ◁ LATEST HEARD ▷ NEW OR CHANGED FOR 1990 †

FREQUENCY	COUNTRY, STATION, LOCATION	TARGET • NETWORK • POWER (kW)
4250	**CHINA (PR)**	
	CENTRAL PEOPLES BS	DS-2 • 50 kW
	CLANDESTINE (S AMER)	
	†"REV ARMED FORCES", Colombia	Su • S AMERICA • USB
4250v	**CLANDESTINE (M EAST)**	
	†"VO THE MARTYRS", Near Iran	Irr • MIDEAST • ANTI-IRANIAN GOVT
4258	**CLANDESTINE (M EAST)**	
	†"VO KURD FIGHTERS", Eastern Iraq	MIDEAST
	†"VO THE CRUSADER", Eastern Iraq	PERSIAN • MIDEAST • MOJAHEDIN-E KHALQ
4271	**ECUADOR**	
	RADIO GONZANAMA, Gonzanamá	DS
4299.4	**PERU**	
	†RADIO MODERNA, Celendín	DS • 0.25 kW
4320	**CLANDESTINE (M EAST)**	
	†"AL-QUDS RADIO", Syria	Irr • MIDEAST
4330	**CHINA (PR)**	
	CENTRAL PEOPLES BS, Urümqi	DS-MINORITIES • 50 kW
	†VO THE STRAIT-PLA, Fuzhou	(D) • TAIWAN-2 • 10 kW
	XINJIANG PBS, Urümqi	DS-KAZAKH • 50 kW
4395	**USSR**	
	RADIO MOSCOW, Yakutsk	DS-2/DS-3 • 100 kW
4421.4	**BOLIVIA**	
	RADIOEMISORA REYES, Reyes	DS • 0.35 kW
		Su • DS • 0.35 kW
4430	**PERU**	
	†FRECUENCIA LIDER, Bambamarca	DS • 0.85 kW
4437v	**LAOS**	
	CAPITAL RADIO, Vientiane	DS
		Sa • DS
4441v	**BOLIVIA**	
	RADIO SANTA ROSA, Santa Rosa	Irr • DS
4450	**CLANDESTINE (ASIA)**	
	"VO NAT SALVATION", Haeju, N Korea	TO KOREA (REP) • 100 kW
4460	**CHINA (PR)**	
	CENTRAL PEOPLES BS, Beijing	DS-1 • 10/15 kW
		Tu • DS-1 • 10/15 kW
4461.8	**PERU**	
	†RADIO NORANDINA, Celendín	DS
4465	**USA**	
	RFE-RL, Via Holzkirchen, GFR	W EUROPE • (FEEDER) • 10 kW • ISU
		W EUROPE • (FEEDER) • 10 kW • ISL
4472v	**BOLIVIA**	
	RADIO MOVIMA, Santa Ana	DS • 0.25 kW
		Irr • DS • 0.25 kW
4485	**PERU**	
	†LA VOZ DE CELENDIN, Celendin	DS
	USSR	
	KAMCHATKA RADIO, Petropavlovsk	DS • 50 kW
	R TIKHIY OKEAN, Petropavlovsk	PACIFIC • MARINERS • 50 kW
		Sa • PACIFIC • MARINERS • 50 kW
		Su-F • PACIFIC • MARINERS • 50 kW
4485v	**CLANDESTINE (M EAST)**	
	†"VO IRAN COMMUNIST, Afghanistan	F • PERSIAN • MIDEAST • ANTI-IRANIAN GOVT
		PERSIAN • MIDEAST • ANTI-IRANIAN GOVT
		Sa-Th • PERSIAN • MIDEAST • ANTI-IRANIAN GOVT
4495	**PERU**	
	†RADIO PAJATEN, Contumaza	DS
4500	**CHINA (PR)**	
	XINJIANG PBS, Urümqi	DS-CHINESE • 50 kW
4510	**USSR**	
	†UZBEK RADIO, Fergana	M-F • DS • 15 kW
4518v	**BOLIVIA**	
	†RADIO HORIZONTE, Riberalta	DS
		Tu-Su • DS
4520	**USSR**	
	KHANTY-MANSIYSK R, Khanty-Mansiysk	DS • 50 kW
	KORYASK RADIO, Palana	Sa/Su • DS • 15 kW
		Su • DS • 15 kW
		Irr • W/F • DS • 15 kW
4525	**CHINA (PR)**	
	CENTRAL PEOPLES BS, Dongsheng	DS-MINORITIES • 10 kW
	NEI MONGGOL PBS, Dongsheng	DS-MONGOLIAN • 10 kW
4557v	**CLANDESTINE (ASIA)**	
	"VO NAT SALVATION", Haeju, N Korea	TO KOREA (REP) • 100 kW
4565	**USA**	
	RFE-RL, Via Holzkirchen, GFR	W EUROPE • (FEEDER) • 10 kW • ISU
		W EUROPE • (FEEDER) • 10 kW • ISL
4588	**ARGENTINA**	
	†RADIO RIVADAVIA, Buenos Aires	Su • DS(FEEDER) • 2.5 kW • USB
		M-Sa • DS(FEEDER) • 2.5 kW • USB
		Tu-Su • DS(FEEDER) • 2.5 kW • USB
		Irr • Su • DS(FEEDER) • 2.5 kW • USB
4600	**BOLIVIA**	
	†R PERLA DEL ACRE, Cobija	DS
4606.7 (con'd)	**PERU**	
	RADIO AYAVIRI, Ayaviri	DS

World Time: 0 1 2 3 4 5 6 7 8 9 10 11 12 13 14 15 16 17 18 19 20 21 22 23 24

0 Prime Time-Americas 6 Prime Time-E Asia 12 Prime Time-S Asia 18 Prime Time-Europe 24

ENGLISH ARABIC CHINESE FRENCH GERMAN RUSSIAN SPANISH OTHER

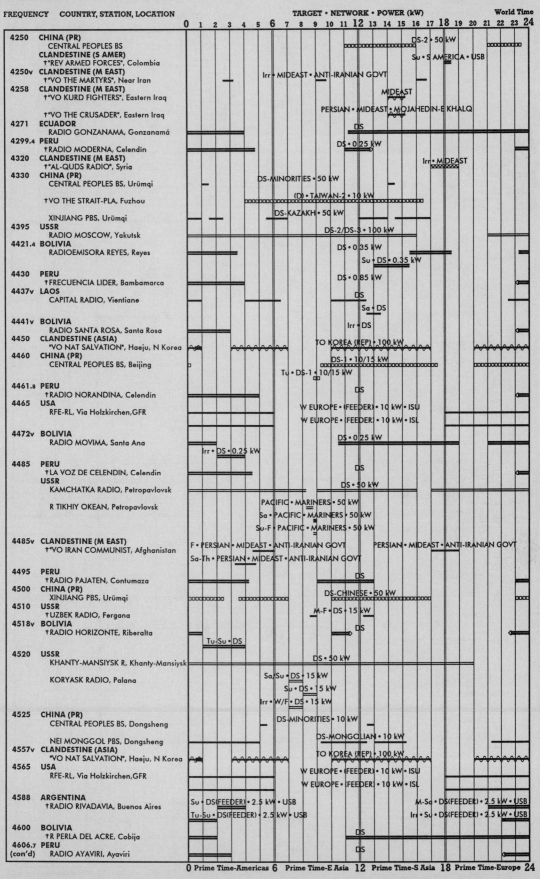

FREQUENCY	COUNTRY, STATION, LOCATION	TARGET • NETWORK • POWER (kW)
4606.7 (con'd)	**PERU** RADIO AYAVIRI, Ayaviri	Irr • DS
4607.3	**INDONESIA** †RRI, Serui, Irian Jaya	DS • 0.5 kW
4610	**USSR** †KAZAKH RADIO, Alma-Ata	Sa • DS-1 • 50 kW Sa-M • DS-1 • 50 kW Su-F • DS-1 • 50 kW Tu-F • DS-1 • 50 kW DS-1/RUSSIAN, ETC • 50 kW
	KHABAROVSK RADIO, Khabarovsk	DS • 50 kW
4620	**CHINA (PR)** RADIO BEIJING, Beijing	E ASIA • 10 kW
4635	**USSR** TADZHIK RADIO, Dushanbé	DS-1 • 50 kW
4646v	**ZAIRE** †RADIO BUKAVU, Bukavu	DS-FRENCH, ETC • 4 kW
4649	**BOLIVIA** †RADIO SANTA ANA, Santa Ana	DS • 1 kW Irr • DS • 1 kW
4660v	**VIETNAM** BINH TRI THIEN BS, Hué	Alternative Frequency to 4700v kHz
4665v	**CLANDESTINE (M EAST)** †"VO IRANIAN KURDS"	MIDEAST • ANTI-IRANIAN GOVT PERSIAN • MIDEAST • ANTI-IRANIAN GOVT
4680v	**ECUADOR** R NACIONAL ESPEJO, Quito	DS • 5 kW
4681v	**BOLIVIA** RADIO PAITITI, Guayaramerín	DS • 0.75 kW Tu-Su • DS • 0.75 kW
4700	**INDONESIA** RK INFORMASI PER'N, Surabaya, Jawa	DS • 2 kW
4700v	**BOLIVIA** †RADIO RIBERALTA, Riberalta	DS • 0.5 kW • ALT. FREQ. TO 4735v kHz Irr • DS • 0.5 kW • ALT. FREQ. TO 4735v kHz
	PERU RADIO WAIRA, Chota	DS • 1 kW
	VIETNAM BINH TRI THIEN BS, Hué	DS • ALT. FREQ. TO 4660v kHz
4705	**PERU** RADIO IMPERIO, Rioja	DS • 0.25 kW
4705v	**VIETNAM** GIA LAI-KON TUM BS, Pleiku	DS
4719	**INDONESIA** †RRI, Ujung Pandang	DS • 50 kW • ALT. FREQ. TO 4753v kHz
4720v	**BOLIVIA** †RADIO ABAROA, Riberalta	DS • 0.5 kW
4725v	**BURMA** BURMA BC SERVICE, Rangoon	DS-MINORITIES • 50 kW
4732v	**PERU** RADIO SAN JUAN, Caraz	Irr • DS
4735	**CHINA (PR)** CENTRAL PEOPLES BS, Urümqi	DS-MINORITIES • 50 kW
	XINJIANG PBS, Urümqi	DS-UIGHUR • 50 kW Su • DS-UIGHUR • 50 kW
4735v	**BOLIVIA** †RADIO RIBERALTA, Riberalta	Alternative Frequency to 4700v kHz
4739.7	**BOLIVIA** †RADIO MAMORE, Guayaramerín	DS • 0.5 kW Irr • DS • 0.5 kW
4740	**AFGHANISTAN** RADIO AFGHANISTAN, Via USSR	MIDEAST & S ASIA • DS-1 • 100 kW
4747.5	**BOLIVIA** LA VOZ DEL TROPICO, Villa Tunari	DS • 0.25 kW M-Sa • DS • 0.25 kW Su • DS • 0.25 kW
4750	**CAMEROON** CAMEROON RTV CORP, Bertoua	Irr • DS-FRENCH,ENG,ETC • 20 kW
	CHINA (PR) CENTRAL PEOPLES BS	DS-MINORITIES • 15 kW
	HULUNBEI'ER PBS	DS-MONGOLIAN • 15 kW
	XIZANG PEOPLES BS, Lhasa	DS-CHINESE • 50 kW
	MONGOLIA †RADIO ULAN BATOR, Olgiy	DS-1 • 12 kW Tu/F • DS-1 • 12 kW W/Th/Sa-M • DS-1 • 12 kW
	USSR †RADIO MOSCOW, Via Mongolia	E ASIA • 12 kW
4751v	**ZAIRE** LA VOIX DU ZAIRE, Lubumbashi	Irr • DS-FRENCH, ETC • 10 kW
4752v	**PERU** †RADIO HUANTA 2000, Huanta	DS • 1 kW Irr • DS • 1 kW

World Time: 0 Prime Time-Americas 6 Prime Time-E Asia 12 Prime Time-S Asia 18 Prime Time-Europe 24

SUMMER ONLY (J) WINTER ONLY (D) JAMMING / OR /\ EARLIEST HEARD ◁ LATEST HEARD ▷ NEW OR CHANGED FOR 1990 †

FREQUENCY	COUNTRY, STATION, LOCATION	TARGET • NETWORK • POWER (kW)
4753v	**INDONESIA** †RRI, Ujung Pandang	Alternative Frequency to 4719 kHz
4755	**BRAZIL** R EDUCACAO RURAL, Campo Grande	PORTUGUESE • DS • 10 kW; M-Sa • PORTUGUESE • DS • 10 kW; Tu-Su • PORTUGUESE • DS • 10 kW
	RADIO DO MARANHAO, São Luís	PORTUGUESE • DS-TEMP INACTIVE • 2 kW
	COLOMBIA CARACOL BOGOTA, Bogota	DS • 5 kW
	HONDURAS SANI RADIO, Puerto Lempira	DS-SPANISH, ETC • 10 kW
	INDIA †ALL INDIA RADIO, Delhi	(J) • S ASIA • 50 kW
4760	**AFGHANISTAN** †RADIO AFGHANISTAN, Via USSR	Alternative Frequency to 4940 kHz; (D) • EUROPE • ALT. FREQ. TO 9640 kHz
	CHINA (PR) YUNNAN PEOPLES BS, Kunming	DS-1 • 50 kW
	INDIA †ALL INDIA RADIO, Port Blair	DS • 50 kW
	LIBERIA RADIO ELWA, Monrovia	DS • 10 kW; F-Su • DS • 10 kW; M-Sa • DS • 10 kW; Sa/Su • DS • 10 kW
	SWAZILAND †TRANS WORLD RADIO, Manzini	S AFRICA • 25 kW; (D) • S AFRICA • 25 kW; (J) • S AFRICA • 25 kW; (D) Sa/Su • S AFRICA • 25 kW
4760.2	**ECUADOR** EMISORA ATALAYA, Guayaquil	DS • 5 kW; Irr • Sa/Su • DS • 5 kW; Tu-Su • DS • 5 kW
4764.8	**BOLIVIA** RADIO HUANAY, Huanay	DS • 1 kW
4765	**BRAZIL** RADIO NACIONAL, Cruzeiro do Sul	PORTUGUESE • DS • 10 kW; Tu-Su • PORTUGUESE • DS • 10 kW
	†RADIO RURAL, Santarém	PORTUGUESE • DS • 10 kW
	USSR RADIO MOSCOW, Via Havana, Cuba	C AMERICA • 10 kW
4770	**ANGOLA** ER LUNDA NORTE, Dundo-Luachimo	Irr • PORTUGUESE • DS • 0.5 kW
	NIGERIA RADIO NIGERIA, Kaduna	DS-2/ENGLISH, ETC • 50 kW
	VENEZUELA R MUNDIAL BOLIVAR, Ciudad Bolívar	Irr • DS • 1 kW
4770v	**VIETNAM** SON LA BC STATION, Son La	DS
4771v	**KOREA (DPR)** RADIO PYONGYANG, Pyongyang	Irr • E ASIA
4774.8	**INDONESIA** †RRI, Jakarta, Jawa	DS • 50 kW
4775	**AFGHANISTAN** RADIO KABUL, Kabul	DS • 100 kW
	BRAZIL †PORTAL DA AMAZONIA, Cuiabá	PORTUGUESE • DS • 1 kW
	†RADIO CONGONHAS, Congonhas	PORTUGUESE • DS • 1 kW
	CLANDESTINE (M EAST) †"R IRAN TOILERS", Via R Afghanistan	PERSIAN • MIDEAST • TUDEH COMMUNIST • 100 kW
	INDIA ALL INDIA RADIO, Gauhati	DS-B • 10 kW
	PERU RADIO TARMA, Tarma	DS • 1 kW
4775.3	**BOLIVIA** †RADIO LOS ANDES, Tarija	Tu-Su • DS • 3 kW; DS • 3 kW
4777	**GABON** †RTV GABONAISE, Libreville	DS • 100 kW; M-Sa • DS • 100 kW; Irr • DS • 100 kW
4780	**VENEZUELA** LV DE CARABOBO, Valencia	DS • 1 kW; M-Sa • DS • 1 kW
4780v	**DJIBOUTI (JIBUTI)** RTV DE DJIBOUTI, Djibouti	DS • 20 kW; F • DS • 20 kW; Irr • DS-RAMADAN • 20 kW; Sa-Th • DS • 20 kW
	PAKISTAN RADIO PAKISTAN, Islamabad	MIDEAST & S ASIA • 100 kW
4783v	**MALI** RTV MALIENNE, Bamako	M-Sa • DS-FRENCH, ETC • 18 kW; DS-FRENCH, ETC • 18 kW
4785 (con'd)	**BOLIVIA** RADIO BALLIVIAN, San Borja	DS • 0.5 kW

World Time 0–24: 0 Prime Time-Americas 6 Prime Time-E Asia 12 Prime Time-S Asia 18 Prime Time-Europe 24

ENGLISH ▬ ARABIC ▭ CHINESE ▫▫▫ FRENCH ═ GERMAN ═ RUSSIAN ═ SPANISH ═ OTHER —

FREQUENCY	COUNTRY, STATION, LOCATION	TARGET • NETWORK • POWER (kW)
4785 (con'd)	**BRAZIL**	
	†RADIO BRASIL, Campinas	PORTUGUESE • DS • 1 kW
	†RADIO CAIARI, Pôrto Velho	PORTUGUESE • DS • 1 kW
	RADIO RIBAMAR, São Luís	PORTUGUESE • DS • 5 kW
	CHINA (PR)	
	ZHEJIANG PBS, Qu Xian	DS-1 • 10 kW
		W-M • DS-1 • 10 kW
	COLOMBIA	
	ECOS DEL COMBEIMA, Ibagué	Irr • DS-SUPER • 5 kW
	TANZANIA	
	†RADIO TANZANIA, Dar es Salaam	DS • 50 kW
	USSR	
	AZERBAIJANI RADIO, Baku	DS-1/RUSSIAN,AZERI • 50 kW
4785.7	**PERU**	
	†RADIO COOPERATIVA, Satipo	DS • 1 kW
4789.6	**INDONESIA**	
	RRI, Fak Fak, Irian Jaya	DS • 1 kW
4789.7	**PERU**	
	†RADIO ATLANTIDA, Iquitos	DS • 1/3 kW
4790	**SWAZILAND**	
	†TRANS WORLD RADIO, Manzini	(D) • S AFRICA • 25 kW
4790v	**PAKISTAN (AZAD K)**	
	AZAD KASHMIR RADIO, Via Islamabad	DS • 100 kW
4795	**BRAZIL**	
	†RADIO AQUIDAUANA, Aquidauana	PORTUGUESE • DS • 2 kW
		M-Sa • PORTUGUESE • DS • 2 kW
		Tu-Su • PORTUGUESE • DS • 2 kW
	CAMEROON	
	CAMEROON RTV CORP, Douala	M-F • DS • 100 kW
		DS-FRENCH,ENG,ETC • 100 kW
	USSR	
	BURYAT RADIO, Ulan-Ude	DS • 50 kW
4795.5	**ECUADOR**	
	LV DE LOS CARAS, Bahía de Caráquez	DS • 5 kW
4796	**BOLIVIA**	
	†R NUEVA AMERICA, La Paz	DS • 10 kW
		Tu-Su • DS • 10 kW
		Irr • M-Sa • DS • 10 kW
		Su • DS • 10 kW
		DS-SPANISH, AYMARA • 10 kW
4798v	**VIETNAM**	
	NGHIA BIN BS, Nghia Binh	DS
		Irr • DS
4799.8	**DOMINICAN REPUBLIC**	
	†RADIO NORTE, Santiago	Irr • DS • 1 kW
	GUATEMALA	
	R BUENAS NUEVAS, San Sebastián	DS
4800	**CHINA (PR)**	
	CENTRAL PEOPLES BS	DS-2
		DS-MINORITIES
	XINJIANG PBS, Urümqi	(D) • DS-CHINESE • 50 kW
	INDIA	
	ALL INDIA RADIO, Hyderabad	DS-ENGLISH, ETC • 10 kW
	LESOTHO	
	RADIO LESOTHO, Maseru	DS-ENGLISH,SESOTHO • 100 kW
	USSR	
	YAKUT RADIO, Yakutsk	DS • 50 kW
4800v	**ECUADOR**	
	RADIO POPULAR, Cuenca	DS • 5 kW
		Irr • DS • 5 kW
4800.7	**PERU**	
	†RADIO ONDA AZUL, Puno	DS-SPANISH, ETC • 1.5 kW
4805	**BRAZIL**	
	†DIFUSORA AMAZONAS, Manaus	PORTUGUESE • DS • 5 kW
	†RADIO ITATIAIA, Belo Horizonte	PORTUGUESE • DS • 0.5 kW
4805.4	**INDONESIA**	
	†RRI, Kupang, Timor	DS • 0.3 kW
4810	**SOUTH AFRICA**	
	†SOUTH AFRICAN BC, Meyerton	ENGLISH & AFRIKAANS • DS-RADIO ORION • 100 kW
		M-F • DS-MARKET PRICES • 100 kW
		RADIO SUID-AFRIKA • 100 kW
	USSR	
	ARMENIAN RADIO, Yerevan	DS-1 • 50 kW
		DS-2 • 50 kW
	†RADIO MOSCOW	(D) • JAPANESE • E ASIA
4810v	**BOLIVIA**	
	RADIO LIBERTAD, Dist. Santa Fe	Irr • DS
		Irr • M-Sa • DS
4810.2	**PERU**	
	RADIO SAN MARTIN, Tarapoto	DS • 3 kW
		Irr • DS • 3 kW
		M-Sa • DS • 3 kW
4810.4	**ECUADOR**	
	LV DE GALAPAGOS, San Cristóbal	DS • 5 kW

World Time: 0 Prime Time-Americas 6 Prime Time-E Asia 12 Prime Time-S Asia 18 Prime Time-Europe 24

SUMMER ONLY (J) WINTER ONLY (D) JAMMING / OR ∧ EARLIEST HEARD ◁ LATEST HEARD ▷ NEW OR CHANGED FOR 1990 †

FREQUENCY	COUNTRY, STATION, LOCATION	TARGET • NETWORK • POWER (kW)
4815	BOLIVIA †RADIO NACIONAL, La Paz	Irr • DS-SPANISH, ETC • 1 kW
	BRAZIL †R NAC TABATINGA, Benjamim Constant	PORTUGUESE • DS • 10 kW
	†RADIO DIFUSORA, Londrina	PORTUGUESE • DS • 0.5 kW
	BURKINA FASO RTV BURKINA, Ouagadougou	DS-FRENCH, ETC • 50 kW
		M-F • DS-FRENCH, ETC • 50 kW
	CHINA (PR) †RADIO BEIJING, Togtoh	E ASIA & EAST USSR • RUSSIAN, MONGOLIAN • 10 kW
4815v	PAKISTAN PAKISTAN BC CORP, Karachi	(D) • DS-ENGLISH, ETC • 10 kW
4815.4	COLOMBIA RADIO GUATAPURI, Valledupar	Irr • DS • 1 kW
4819.7	ECUADOR RADIO PAZ Y BIEN, Ambato	DS-SPANISH, ETC • 1.5 kW
		Tu-Su • DS-SPANISH, ETC • 1.5 kW
4820	BOTSWANA †RADIO BOTSWANA, Gaborone	Alternative Frequency to 4830 kHz
	HONDURAS LA VOZ EVANGELICA, Tegucigalpa	DS • 5 kW
		M • DS • 5 kW
		Tu-Su • DS • 5 kW
	INDIA ALL INDIA RADIO, Calcutta	DS • 10 kW
	USSR KHANTY-MANSIYSK R, Khanty-Mansiysk	DS • 50 kW
4820v	VIETNAM HA TUYEN BS, Ha Tuyen	DS
4820.3	ANGOLA †ER DA HUILA, Lubango	Irr • PORTUGUESE • DS • 25 kW
4820.8	PERU †RADIO ATAHUALPA, Cajamarca	DS • 1 kW
4825	BRAZIL R CANCAO NOVA, Cachoeira Paulista	PORTUGUESE • DS • 10 kW
	RADIO EDUCADORA, Bragança	PORTUGUESE • DS • 5 kW
	GUATEMALA RADIO MAM, Cabricán	DS/SPANISH, ETC • 1 kW
	MAURITANIA ORT DE MAURITANIE, Nouakchott	Alternative Frequency to 4845 kHz
	USSR RADIO MOSCOW, Star'obel'sk	(D) • EUROPE • 100 kW
	RADIO MOSCOW, Vladivostok	(D) • JAPANESE • E ASIA • 100 kW
		(J) • E ASIA • CHINESE, KOREAN • 100 kW
	†TURKMEN RADIO, Ashkhabad	DS-1/RUSSIAN, ETC • 50 kW
4825v	PERU LV DE LA SELVA, Iquitos	DS • 10 kW
4826.2	PERU RADIO SICUANI, Sicuani	DS-SPANISH, ETC • 0.35 kW
		Tu-Su • DS • 0.35 kW
4830	BOLIVIA †RADIO GRIGOTA, Santa Cruz	Tu-Su • DS • 1 kW; DS • 1 kW
		Irr • Tu-Su • DS • 1 kW
	BOTSWANA †RADIO BOTSWANA, Gaborone	DS-ENGLISH, ETC • 50 kW • ALT. FREQ. TO 4820 kHz
	GABON †AFRIQUE NUMERO UN, Moyabi	Alternative Frequency to 9580 kHz
	THAILAND RADIO THAILAND, Pathum Thani	DS-1 • 10 kW
	VENEZUELA RADIO TACHIRA, San Cristóbal	DS • 10 kW
		Irr • Tu-Su • DS • 10 kW
4831	PERU RADIO HUANTA, Huanta	Alternative Frequency to 4890v kHz
4831v	MONGOLIA †RADIO ULAN BATOR, Altai	DS • 12 kW
		Tu/F • DS • 12 kW
		W/Th/Sa-M • DS • 12 kW
	USSR †RADIO MOSCOW, Via Mongolia	E ASIA • 12 kW
4832	COSTA RICA RADIO RELOJ, San José	Irr • DS • 3 kW
4835	AUSTRALIA †ABC/CAAMA RADIO, Alice Springs	DS-ENGLISH, ETC • 50 kW
	GUATEMALA RADIO TEZULUTLAN, Cobán	DS-SPANISH, ETC • 2.5/3 kW
	MALAYSIA RTM-SARAWAK, Kuching-Stapok	DS-MALAY, MELANEU • 10 kW
	PERU RADIO MARANON, Jaén	DS • 1 kW
4835v	MALI RTV MALIENNE, Bamako	Irr • M-Sa • DS-FRENCH, ETC • 18 kW; Irr • DS-FRENCH, ETC • 18 kW
	PAKISTAN PAKISTAN BC CORP, Islamabad	(D) • DS • 100 kW
4839v	ZAIRE †RADIO BUKAVU, Bukavu	Alternative Frequency to 4862v kHz

World Time 0–24: 0 Prime Time-Americas 6 Prime Time-E Asia 12 Prime Time-S Asia 18 Prime Time-Europe 24

ENGLISH ▬ ARABIC ▬ CHINESE ▬ FRENCH ▬ GERMAN ▬ RUSSIAN ▬ SPANISH ▬ OTHER ▬

World Time 0 1 2 3 4 5 6 7 8 9 10 11 12 13 14 15 16 17 18 19 20 21 22 23 24

FREQUENCY	COUNTRY, STATION, LOCATION	TARGET • NETWORK • POWER (kW)
4840	**CHINA (PR)** HEILONGJIANG PBS, Harbin	DS-CHINESE, KOREAN • 50 kW
	†VO THE STRAIT-PLA, Fuzhou	TAIWAN-1 • 10 kW
	ECUADOR †R INTEROCEANICA, Santa Rosa	DS • 1 kW
	INDIA ALL INDIA RADIO, Bombay	DS • 10 kW Sa • DS • 10 kW
	PERU RADIO ANDAHUAYLAS, Andahuaylas	DS-SPANISH,QUECHUA • 2 kW
	VENEZUELA RADIO VALERA, Valera	DS • 1 kW Tu-Su • DS • 1 kW
4844.4	**GUATEMALA** RADIO K'EKCHI, San Cristóbal V	DS-SPANISH, ETC • 1/5 kW M-Sa • DS-SPANISH, ETC • 1/5 kW Su • DS-SPANISH, ETC • 1/5 kW Tu-Su • DS-SPANISH, ETC • 1/5 kW
4845	**BRAZIL** †R METEOROLOGIA, Ibitinga	PORTUGUESE • DS • 1 kW
	†RADIO NACIONAL, Manaus	PORTUGUESE • DS • 250 kW
	INDONESIA †RRI, Ambon, Maluku	Irr • DS • 10 kW
	MALAYSIA †RADIO MALAYSIA, Kajang	DS-TAMIL • 50 kW Sa-Th • DS-TAMIL • 50 kW Sa/Su • DS-TAMIL • 50 kW Su • DS-TAMIL • 50 kW
	MAURITANIA ORT DE MAURITANIE, Nouakchott	DS-FRENCH,ARAB,ETC • 100 kW • ALT. FREQ. TO 4825 kHz F • DS-FRENCH,ARAB,ETC • 100 kW • ALT. FREQ. TO 4825 kHz Sa-Th • DS-FRENCH,ARAB,ETC • 100 kW • ALT. FREQ. TO 4825 kHz
4845v	**COLOMBIA** RADIO BUCARAMANGA, Bucaramanga	Irr • DS • 1 kW
4845.2	**BOLIVIA** †RADIO FIDES, La Paz	Su • DS • 5 kW DS • 5 kW Tu-Su • DS • 5 kW M-Sa • DS • 5 kW Irr • DS • 5 kW
4850	**CAMEROON** CAMEROON RTV CORP, Yaoundé	DS-ENGLISH, FRENCH • 100 kW
	CHINA (PR) CENTRAL PEOPLES BS	TAIWAN-2
	INDIA ALL INDIA RADIO, Kohima	DS • 2 kW
	MONGOLIA †RADIO ULAN BATOR, Ulan Bator	DS-1 • 100 kW DS-1 • 50 kW Tu/F • DS-1 • 50 kW W/Th/Sa-M • DS-1 • 50 kW
	USSR †RADIO MOSCOW, Via Ulan Bator	E ASIA • 50 kW
	†UZBEK RADIO, Tashkent	DS-2/RUSSIAN, ETC • 50 kW
	VENEZUELA RADIO CAPITAL, Caracas	DS • 1 kW Su/M • DS • 1 kW
4851v	**ECUADOR** RADIO LUZ Y VIDA, Loja	DS • 5 kW Irr • DS • 5 kW
4853	**YEMEN (PDR)** †"VO PALESTINE", Via Radio San'ā	Irr • PLO • 100 kW
	RADIO SAN'A, San'ā	Irr • DS • 100 kW Irr • F • DS • 100 kW
4855	**BOLIVIA** †RADIO CENTENARIO, Santa Cruz	Tu-Sa • DS • 1 kW DS • 1 kW Irr • Tu-Sa • DS • 1 kW M-F • DS • 1 kW
	BRAZIL R MUNDO MELHOR, Gov Valadares	PORTUGUESE • DS • 1 kW M-Sa • PORTUGUESE • DS • 1 kW
	†RADIO ARUANA, Barra do Garças	PORTUGUESE • DS • 1 kW
	PERU †RADIO PAMPAS, Pampas	DS
4855v	**MOZAMBIQUE** †RADIO MOCAMBIQUE, Maputo	PORTUGUESE • DS • 20 kW
4855.8	**INDONESIA** †RRI, Palembang,Sumatera	DS • 10 kW
4856.7	**BOLIVIA** †RADIO EL CONDOR, Uyuni	DS-SPANISH, ETC
4860	**INDIA** ALL INDIA RADIO, Delhi	Su • DS • 20 kW DS-FORCES PROGRAM • 20 kW DS-ENGLISH, ETC • 20 kW
(con'd)	**USSR** CHITA RADIO, Chita	DS • 15 kW

0 Prime Time-Americas 6 Prime Time-E Asia 12 Prime Time-S Asia 18 Prime Time-Europe 24

FREQUENCY	COUNTRY, STATION, LOCATION	TARGET • NETWORK • POWER (kW)
4860 (con'd)	**USSR** CHITA RADIO, Serpukhov	(D) • E EUROPE • 100 kW
4860v	**ANGOLA** †ER DO LUNDA SUL, Saurimo	PORTUGUESE • DS • 5 kW
	PERU R CHINCHAYCOCHA, Junín	Irr • DS • 0.5 kW
4862v	**ZAIRE** †RADIO BUKAVU, Bukavu	DS-FRENCH, ETC • 4 kW • ALT. FREQ. TO 4839v kHz Su • DS-FRENCH, ETC • 4 kW • ALT. FREQ. TO 4839v kHz
4864.5	**BOLIVIA** †RADIO 16 DE MARZO, Oruro	DS Irr • Tu-Su • DS M-Sa • DS
4865	**BRAZIL** †R VERDES FLORESTAS, Cruzeiro do Sul	PORTUGUESE • DS • 5 kW
	RADIO SOCIEDADE, Feira de Santana	PORTUGUESE • DS • 1 kW
	CHINA (PR) GANSU PEOPLES BS, Lanzhou	DS-1 • 50 kW
	COLOMBIA LV DEL CINARUCO, Arauca	DS-CARACOL • 1 kW Tu-Su • DS-CARACOL • 1 kW
	MONGOLIA †RADIO ULAN BATOR, Saynshand	DS-1 • 12 kW Tu/F • DS-1 • 12 kW W/Th/Sa-M • DS-1 • 12 kW
	USSR †RADIO MOSCOW, Via Mongolia	E ASIA • 12 kW
4865v	**MOZAMBIQUE** RADIO MOCAMBIQUE, Maputo	PORTUGUESE • DS • 20 kW
4870	**BENIN** †ORT DU BENIN, Cotonou	M-F • DS-FRENCH, ETC • 30 kW Irr • DS • 30 kW DS-FRENCH, ETC • 30 kW Sa/Su • DS-FRENCH, ETC • 30 kW
	ECUADOR RADIO RIO AMAZONAS, Macuma	DS-SPANISH, ETC • 5 kW Irr • DS-SPANISH, ETC • 5 kW Tu-Su • DS-SPANISH, ETC • 5 kW Irr • Tu-Su • DS-SPANISH, ETC • 5 kW
	PERU †RADIO COSMOS, Lircay	DS
	SRI LANKA SRI LANKA BC CORP, Colombo-Ekala	DS-SINHALA 2 • 10 kW
4870v	**MOZAMBIQUE** EP DA ZAMBEZIA, Quelimane	Irr • DS-PORTUGUESE, ETC • 0.25 kW
4871	**INDONESIA** †RRI, Wamena, Irian Jaya	DS • 0.5 kW
4874.6	**INDONESIA** †RRI, Sorong, Irian Jaya	DS • 10 kW
4875	**BRAZIL** †R JORNAL DO BRASIL, Rio de Janeiro	PORTUGUESE • DS • 10 kW
	†RADIO NACIONAL, Boa Vista	PORTUGUESE • DS • 10 kW
	CHINA (PR) VOICE OF JINLING, Nanjing	E ASIA • 50 kW
	USSR †GEORGIAN RADIO, Tbilisi	Irr • DS-2
4875.2	**COLOMBIA** RADIO SUPER, Medellín	DS-SUPER • 2 kW
4875.5	**BOLIVIA** †R LA CRUZ DEL SUR, La Paz	DS • 10 kW M-F • DS • 10 kW
4876v	**PERU** RADIO CENTRAL, Bella Vista	DS • 1 kW • ALT. FREQ. TO 4921v kHz
4878	**KAMPUCHEA (CAMBODIA)** VO THE PEOPLE, Phnom Penh	DS
4879v	**PAKISTAN** PAKISTAN BC CORP, Quetta	DS • 10 kW Th-Sa • DS • 10 kW
4880	**BRAZIL** †R DIFUSORA ACREANA, Rio Branco	PORTUGUESE • DS • 5 kW
	INDIA ALL INDIA RADIO, Lucknow	DS-B/ENGLISH, ETC • 10 kW
	SOUTH AFRICA †SOUTH AFRICAN BC, Meyerton	DS-RADIO FIVE • 100 kW
4880v	**BANGLADESH** †RADIO BANGLADESH, Dhaka	DS • 100 kW
4881.7	**PERU** †RADIO NUEVO MUNDO, Pucallpa	DS • 0.25/1 kW
4883	**CHINA (PR)** †RADIO BEIJING, Hohhot	(D) • E ASIA & EAST USSR • RUSSIAN, MONGOLIAN • 50 kW
4885	**ANGOLA** ER DO ZAIRE, M'banza Congo	PORTUGUESE • DS • 5 kW
	BRAZIL †R CLUBE DO PARA, Belém	PORTUGUESE • DS • 5 kW
	†RADIO CARAJA, Anápolis	PORTUGUESE • DS • 0.5 kW
	COLOMBIA ONDAS DEL META, Villavicencio	DS-SUPER • 5 kW
(con'd)	**KENYA** VOICE OF KENYA, Nairobi	DS-EASTERN • 10 kW

World Time 0–24

0 Prime Time-Americas 6 Prime Time-E Asia 12 Prime Time-S Asia 18 Prime Time-Europe 24

ENGLISH ▬ ARABIC ▭ CHINESE ▫▫▫ FRENCH ═ GERMAN ═ RUSSIAN ═ SPANISH ═ OTHER —

FREQUENCY	COUNTRY, STATION, LOCATION	TARGET • NETWORK • POWER (kW)
4885 (con'd)	KENYA VOICE OF KENYA, Nairobi	M-Sa • DS-EASTERN • 10 kW DS-NATIONAL • 100 kW Sa/Su • DS-NATIONAL • 100 kW
4885v	VIETNAM THAN HOA BS, Thanh Hoa	DS
4885.3	PERU RADIO HUANCAVELICA, Huancavelica	DS • 1 kW Irr • DS • 1 kW
4889.7	ECUADOR †CENTINELA DEL SUR, Loja	DS • 2 kW Tu-Su • DS • 2 kW M-Sa • DS • 2 kW
4890	FRANCE R FRANCE INTL, Via Moyabi, Gabon	C AFRICA • 250 kW
	PAPUA NEW GUINEA †NATIONAL BC OF PNG, Port Moresby	DS-ENGLISH, ETC • 2 kW
4890v	PERU RADIO HUANTA, Huanta	DS-SPANISH,QUECHUA • 0.5 kW • ALT. FREQ. TO 4831 kHz Irr • DS • 0.5 kW • ALT. FREQ. TO 4831 kHz
	SENEGAL ORT DU SENEGAL, Dakar	DS-FRENCH, ETC • 100 kW M-Sa • DS-FRENCH, ETC • 100 kW
4893v	MONGOLIA †RADIO ULAN BATOR, Murun	DS-1 • 12 kW Tu/F • DS-1 • 12 kW W/Th/Sa-M • DS-1 • 12 kW
	USSR †RADIO MOSCOW, Via Mongolia	E ASIA • 12 kW
4895	BRAZIL RADIO BARE, Manaus	PORTUGUESE • DS • 1 kW
	COLOMBIA LV DEL RIO ARAUCA, Arauca	DS-RCN • 10 kW M-Sa • DS-RCN • 10 kW
	INDIA †ALL INDIA RADIO, Kurseong	(D) • S ASIA & E ASIA • 20 kW DS-ENGLISH, ETC • 20 kW
	MALAYSIA RTM-SARAWAK, Kuching-Stapok	DS-IBAN • 10 kW
	PERU RADIO CHANCHAMAYO, La Merced	DS • 0.4 kW Tu-Su • DS • 0.4 kW Irr • Tu-Su • DS • 0.4 kW
	USSR TYUMEN RADIO, Tyumen	DS • 15 kW
4895v	VIETNAM VOICE OF VIETNAM, Hanoi	DS Su • DS
4900	CHINA (PR) †VO THE STRAIT-PLA, Fuzhou	Irr • (J) • TAIWAN-2 • 10/50 kW
4900v	ECUADOR RADIO LIBERTADOR, Saquisilí	Irr • DS • 1 kW
	GUINEA RTV GUINEENNE, Conakry	M-Sa • DS-FRENCH, ETC • 18 kW DS • 18 kW DS-FRENCH, ETC • 18 kW Sa/Su • DS-FRENCH, ETC • 18 kW
	INDONESIA †RRI, Surakarta, Jawa	DS • 0.5 kW
4901.5	BOLIVIA †R SAN IGNACIO, S Ignacio de Moxos	Irr • DS DS
4902	SRI LANKA SRI LANKA BC CORP, Colombo-Ekala	DS-SINHALA 1 • 10 kW
4902v	INDONESIA †RRI, Surakarta, Jawa	DS • 10 kW
4904.5	CHAD RADIODIF NATIONALE, N'Djamena	DS-FRENCH, ETC • 100 kW
4905	BRAZIL R RELOGIO FEDERAL, Rio de Janeiro	PORTUGUESE • DS • 5 kW Irr • PORTUGUESE • DS • 5 kW
	†RADIO ANHANGUERA, Araguaína	PORTUGUESE • DS • 1 kW
	CHINA (PR) CENTRAL PEOPLES BS, Beijing	DS-1 • 10 kW
4907v	CAMBODIA †VO THE PEOPLE, Phnom Penh	DS • 50 kW Su • DS • 50 kW
4908v	PERU RADIO COBRIZA 2000, Pacaycasa	Alternative Frequency to 4927v kHz
4910	AUSTRALIA †ABC/CAAMA RADIO, Tennant Creek	DS-ENGLISH, ETC • 50 kW
4910v	HONDURAS LV DE LA MOSQUITIA, Puerto Lempira	DS-SPANISH,MISKITO • 0.5 kW DS-SPANISH,ENGLISH • 0.5 kW
	ZAMBIA †RADIO ZAMBIA, Lusaka	DS-ENGLISH, ETC • 50 kW F/Sa • DS-ENGLISH, ETC • 50 kW

World Time: 0 Prime Time-Americas 6 Prime Time-E Asia 12 Prime Time-S Asia 18 Prime Time-Europe 24

SUMMER ONLY (J) WINTER ONLY (D) JAMMING / OR /\ EARLIEST HEARD ◁ LATEST HEARD ▷ NEW OR CHANGED FOR 1990 †

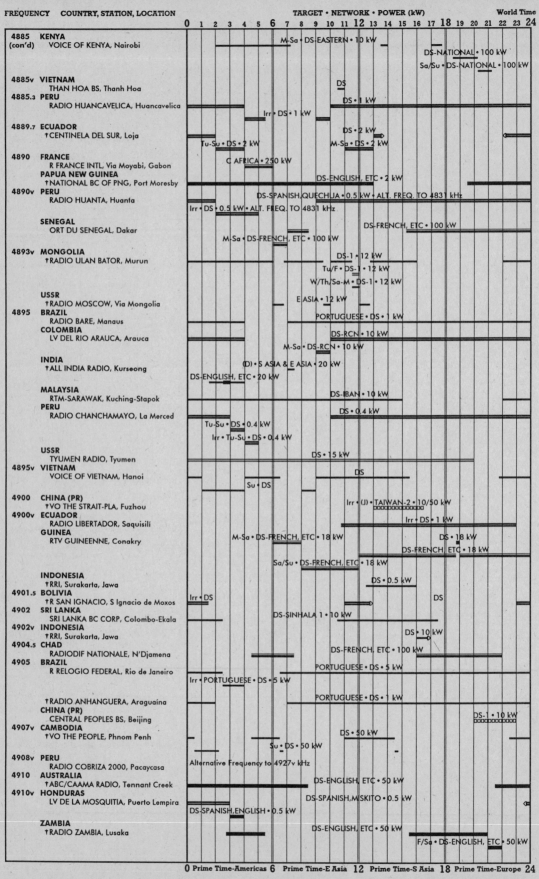

FREQUENCY	COUNTRY, STATION, LOCATION	TARGET • NETWORK • POWER (kW)
4910.6	**PERU** †RADIO LIBERTAD, Trujillo	DS • 1 kW
4910.8	**PERU** †RADIO TAWANTINSUYO, Cuzco	DS-SPANISH, ETC • 5 kW; Irr • DS • 5 kW
4911v	**ECUADOR** EM GRAN COLOMBIA, Quito	Irr • DS • 10 kW
4915	**BRAZIL** RADIO ANHANGUERA, Goiânia	PORTUGUESE • DS • 10 kW; Irr • PORTUGUESE • DS • 10 kW
	RADIO NACIONAL, Macapá	PORTUGUESE • DS • 10 kW
	CHINA (PR) GUANGXI PEOPLES BS, Nanning	DS-1/CHINESE, ETC • 10 kW
	GHANA GHANA BC CORP, Accra	DS-1/ENGLISH, ETC • 50 kW • ALT. FREQ. TO 3240 kHz; Sa/Su • DS-1/ENGLISH, ETC • 50 kW • ALT. FREQ. TO 3240 kHz
	KENYA VOICE OF KENYA, Nairobi	DS-CENTRAL • 100 kW; M-Sa • DS-CENTRAL • 100 kW
4915v	**COLOMBIA** ARMONIAS CAQUETA, Florencia	DS • 3 kW; Tu-Su • DS • 3 kW; M-Sa • DS • 3 kW
4920	**AUSTRALIA** †AUSTRALIAN BC CORP, Brisbane	DS • 10 kW
	ECUADOR †RADIO QUITO, Quito	DS • 5 kW; Tu-Su • DS • 5 kW; M-Sa • DS • 5 kW
	INDIA ALL INDIA RADIO, Madras	DS-A/ENGLISH, ETC • 10 kW
	USSR YAKUT RADIO, Yakutsk	DS • 50 kW
4921v	**PERU** RADIO CENTRAL, Bella Vista	Alternative Frequency to 4876v kHz
4922v	**PERU** ONDAS DEL TITICACA, Puno	DS-SPANISH, ETC • 1 kW; Tu-Su • DS • 1 kW
4925	**BRAZIL** RADIO DIFUSORA, Taubaté	PORTUGUESE • DS • 1 kW
	CHINA (PR) HEILONGJIANG PBS, Harbin	DS-CHINESE, KOREAN • 50 kW
	COLOMBIA †EM MERIDIANO 70, Arauca	DS • 2.5 kW
4925v	**MOZAMBIQUE** RADIO MOCAMBIQUE, Maputo	PORTUGUESE • DS • 7.5 kW
4925.6	**EQUATORIAL GUINEA** RADIO NACIONAL, Batá	DS-SPANISH, ETC • 100 kW • ALT. FREQ. TO 5004v kHz
4926v	**MOZAMBIQUE** †RADIO MOCAMBIQUE, Maputo	DS • 10 kW
4927	**INDONESIA** †RRI, Jambi, Sumatera	DS • 7.5 kW; Su • DS • 7.5 kW
4927v	**PERU** RADIO COBRIZA 2000, Pacaycasa	Irr • DS • ALT. FREQ. TO 4908v kHz
4930	**HAITI** RADIO STATION 4VEH, Cap Haïtien	Irr • 1.5 kW
	NAMIBIA R SOUTHWEST AFRICA, Windhoek	DS-1 • 100 kW
	USSR RADIO MOSCOW, Ashkabad	DS-2 • 50 kW
	RADIO MOSCOW, Tbilisi	DS-2 • 50 kW
4932v	**INDONESIA** †RRI, Surakarta, Jawa	DS • 10 kW
4934	**KENYA** VOICE OF KENYA, Nairobi	DS-GENERAL • 100 kW; M-Sa • DS-GENERAL • 100 kW; Sa/Su • DS-GENERAL • 100 kW
4935	**BOLIVIA** †RADIO CORDECH, Sucre	DS • 1 kW; M-Sa • DS • 1 kW
	BRAZIL †R JORNAL A CRITICA, Manaus	PORTUGUESE • DS • 5 kW • ALT. FREQ. TO 5055 kHz
	RADIO DIFUSORA, Jataí	PORTUGUESE • DS • 2.5 kW
4935v	**BRAZIL** RADIO CAPIXABA, Vitória	Irr • PORTUGUESE • DS • 1 kW
	PERU RADIO TROPICAL, Tarapoto	DS • 1 kW
4939.6	**VENEZUELA** †RADIO CONTINENTAL, Barinas	DS • 1 kW
4940	**AFGHANISTAN** †RADIO AFGHANISTAN, Via USSR	Irr • S ASIA • ALT. FREQ. TO 4760 kHz; S ASIA • ALT. FREQ. TO 4760 kHz; S ASIA • DS-1 • ALT. FREQ. TO 4760 kHz
	CHINA (PR) QINGHAI PEOPLES BS, Xining	DS-1/CHINESE • 10 kW
(con'd)	**INDIA** ALL INDIA RADIO, Gauhati	DS-A/ENGLISH, ETC • 10 kW

World Time: 0 Prime Time-Americas 6 Prime Time-E Asia 12 Prime Time-S Asia 18 Prime Time-Europe 24

ENGLISH ▬ ARABIC ▭ CHINESE ▫▫▫ FRENCH ═ GERMAN ▬ RUSSIAN ═ SPANISH ═ OTHER —

FREQUENCY	COUNTRY, STATION, LOCATION	TARGET • NETWORK • POWER (kW) World Time 0–24
4940 (con'd)	**IVORY COAST** RTV IVOIRIENNE, Abidjan	W AFRICA • DS • 100 kW
	MARSHALL ISLANDS †WSZO-R MARSHALLS, Majuro	Alternative Frequency to 6070 kHz
	SRI LANKA SRI LANKA BC CORP, Colombo-Ekala	DS-ENGLISH • 10 kW
	USSR UKRAINIAN RADIO, Kiev	DS-2 • 50 kW
4942v	**PERU** RADIO ABANCAY, Abancay	DS-SPANISH,QUECHUA • 1 kW
4945	**BOLIVIA** †RADIO ILLIMANI, La Paz	DS • 10 kW; Tu-Su • DS • 10 kW; M-Sa • DS • 10 kW
	BRAZIL RADIO DIFUSORA, Poços de Caldas	PORTUGUESE • DS • 1 kW; Tu-Su • PORTUGUESE • DS • 1 kW
	RADIO NACIONAL, Pôrto Velho	PORTUGUESE • DS • 50 kW; Tu-Sa • PORTUGUESE • DS • 50 kW
	VOZ SAO FRANCISCO, Petrolina	PORTUGUESE • DS • 2 kW
4945v	**URUGUAY** LA VOZ DE ARTIGAS, Artigas	Irr • FEEDER
4945.3	**COLOMBIA** CARACOL NEIVA, Neiva	DS-CARACOL • 2.5 kW
4950	**CHINA (PR)** CENTRAL PEOPLES BS, Abagnar Qi	DS-MINORITIES
	VOICE OF PUJIANG, Shanghai	E ASIA • CHINESE, ETC
	XILINGOL PBS, Abagnar Qi	DS-MONGOLIAN
	CLANDESTINE (AFRICA) †"PAZ E PROGRESSO", Pietersburg, S Af	PORTUGUESE • ANTI-ANGOLA, CUBA • 5 kW
	MALAYSIA †RTM-SARAWAK, Kuching-Stapok	DS • 10 kW
	PAKISTAN PAKISTAN BC CORP, Peshawar	DS • 10 kW; (D) • DS-ENGLISH, ETC • 10 kW
	RADIO PAKISTAN, Islamabad	(D) • MIDEAST • 100 kW
4950.2	**PERU** †R MADRE DE DIOS, Puerto Maldonado	DS • 5 kW
4953v	**ANGOLA** †RADIO NACIONAL, Luanda	PORTUGUESE • DS
4955	**BRAZIL** RADIO CLUBE, Rondonópolis	PORTUGUESE • DS • 2.5 kW; M-Sa • PORTUGUESE • DS • 2.5 kW
	RADIO CULTURA, Campos	PORTUGUESE • DS • 2.5 kW
4955v	**BRAZIL** RADIO MARAJOARA, Belém	PORTUGUESE • DS • 10 kW
	PERU R CULTURAL AMAUTA, Huanta	DS-SPANISH, ETC • 1 kW
4957.5	**USSR** †AZERBAIJANI RADIO, Baku	DS-2 • 50 kW
4960	**CHINA (PR)** RADIO BEIJING, Kunming	JAPANESE • E ASIA • 50 kW
	INDIA ALL INDIA RADIO, Delhi	DS • 10 kW
4960v	**ECUADOR** RADIO FEDERACION, Sucúa	DS-SPANISH, ETC • 5 kW; Tu-Su • DS-SPANISH, ETC • 5 kW; M-W • DS-SPANISH, ETC • 5 kW; Irr • Tu-Su • DS-SPANISH, ETC • 5 kW
	MADAGASCAR RADIO MADAGASIKARA, Antananarivo	Irr • DS; Irr • M-Sa • DS
4960.3	**PERU** RADIO LA MERCED, La Merced	Tu-Su • DS • 0.5 kW; DS • 0.5 kW; M-Sa • DS • 0.5 kW
4964.5	**BOLIVIA** †RADIO JUAN XXIII, San Ignacio Velasco	DS • 3 kW; M-Sa • DS • 3 kW; Su • DS • 3 kW
4965	**BRAZIL** RADIO ALVORADA, Parintins	PORTUGUESE • DS • 5 kW
	NAMIBIA †SW AFRICA BC CORP, Windhoek	DS • 100 kW; M-F • DS • 100 kW; Sa/Su • DS • 100 kW
	SOUTH AFRICA †RADIO RSA, Meyerton	S AFRICA • 250 kW
4965v	**BRAZIL** RADIO POTI, Natal	PORTUGUESE • DS • 1 kW
4966	**PERU** RADIO SAN MIGUEL, Cuzco	DS-SPANISH, ETC • 5 kW; Tu-Su • DS • 5 kW
4968	**SRI LANKA** SRI LANKA BC CORP, Colombo-Ekala	DS-TAMIL • 10 kW

0 Prime Time-Americas 6 Prime Time-E Asia 12 Prime Time-S Asia 18 Prime Time-Europe 24

SUMMER ONLY (J) WINTER ONLY (D) JAMMING / OR /\ EARLIEST HEARD ◁ LATEST HEARD ▷ NEW OR CHANGED FOR 1990 †

FREQUENCY	COUNTRY, STATION, LOCATION	TARGET • NETWORK • POWER (kW)
4969.8	**ANGOLA** ER DA CABINDA, Cabinda	Irr • PORTUGUESE • DS • 1 kW
4970	**CHINA (PR)** CENTRAL PEOPLES BS, Urümqi	DS-MINORITIES • 50 kW
	XINJIANG PBS, Urümqi	DS-KAZAKH • 50 kW
	MALAYSIA †RTM-KOTA KINABALU, Kota Kinabalu	DS-MALAY • 10 kW
	PERU †RADIO IMAGEN, Tarapoto	DS • 1 kW
		Su • DS • 1 kW
		Tu-Su • DS • 1 kW
4970v	**VENEZUELA** RADIO RUMBOS, Caracas	DS • 10 kW
		M-Sa • DS • 10 kW
		Tu-Su • DS • 10 kW
4971	**ECUADOR** RADIO TARQUI, Quito	Irr • DS • 3 kW
4975	**BOLIVIA** MARIA AUXILIADORA, Montero	DS • 1 kW
		M • DS • 1 kW
		M-Sa • DS • 1 kW
	BRAZIL †RADIO IGUATEMI, Osasco	PORTUGUESE • DS • 1 kW
	†RADIO TUPI, São Paulo	PORTUGUESE • DS • 1 kW
	CHINA (PR) FUJIAN PEOPLES BS, Jianyang	DS-1, TAIWAN SVC • 10 kW
		Th/Sa/Tu • DS-1 • 10 kW
	CLANDESTINE (AFRICA) †"AV DO GALO NEGRO", Jamba, Angola	S AFRICA • UNITA/PORT,ETC
		Irr • S AFRICA • UNITA/PORT,ETC
	PERU †RADIO DEL PACIFICO, Lima	DS • 4 kW
		Tu-Su • DS • 4 kW
	USSR RADIO DUSHANBE, Dushanbé	MIDEAST & S ASIA • DARI, PERSIAN • 50 kW
	RADIO MOSCOW, Dushanbé	MIDEAST & S ASIA • PASHTU,URDU,DARI • 50 kW
	†TADZHIK RADIO, Dushanbé	DS-2/RUSSIAN, ETC • 50 kW
4975v	**COLOMBIA** ONDAS ORTEGUAZA, Florencia	DS-TODELAR • 1 kW
		Irr • DS-TODELAR • 1 kW
4976	**BRAZIL** RADIO TIMBIRA, São Luís	PORTUGUESE • DS • 2.5 kW
	UGANDA RADIO UGANDA, Kampala	DS-ENGLISH, ETC • 50 kW
		M-F • DS-ENGLISH, ETC • 50 kW
		M-Sa • DS-ENGLISH, ETC • 50 kW
4977v	**ECUADOR** RADIO TARQUI, Quito	Irr • DS • 3 kW
4977.2	**PERU** †RADIO LA HORA, Cuzco	DS-SPANISH,QUECHUA • 1 kW
4980	**CHINA (PR)** CENTRAL PEOPLES BS, Urümqi	DS-MINORITIES • 50 kW
	XINJIANG PBS, Urümqi	DS-MONGOLIAN • 50 kW
	SWAZILAND SWAZI COMMERCIAL R, Sandlane	M-F • PORTUGUESE • S AFRICA • PARALELO 27 • 100 kW
		S AFRICA • 100 kW
		M-F • S AFRICA • 100 kW
		Sa/Su • PORTUGUESE • S AFRICA • PARALELO 27 • 100 kW
	VENEZUELA ECOS DEL TORBES, San Cristóbal	DS • 10 kW
		Su • DS • 10 kW
4980v	**PAKISTAN (AZAD K)** AZAD KASHMIR RADIO, Via Islamabad	DS • 100 kW
4980.6	**ECUADOR** ONDAS AZUAYAS, Cuenca	Irr • DS • 10 kW
4985	**BRAZIL** R BRASIL CENTRAL, Goiânia	PORTUGUESE • DS • 10 kW
4990	**CHINA (PR)** HUNAN PEOPLES BS, Changsha	DS-1 • 10 kW
		W/Th/Sa-M • DS-1 • 10 kW
	ECUADOR RADIO BAHA'I, Otavalo	DS • 1 kW
	INDIA †ALL INDIA RADIO, Madras	S ASIA • 100 kW
	NIGERIA RADIO NIGERIA, Lagos	DS-1/ENGLISH, ETC • 50 kW
	USSR ARMENIAN RADIO, Yerevan	DS-1 • 50 kW
	RADIO YEREVAN, Yerevan	MIDEAST • 50 kW
4990.6	**PERU** †RADIO ANCASH, Huáraz	DS • 5/10 kW
4991	**BOLIVIA** RADIO ANIMAS, Chocaya	Tu-Su • DS • 1 kW
		DS • 1 kW
		M-Sa • DS • 1 kW

World Time: 0 1 2 3 4 5 6 7 8 9 10 11 12 13 14 15 16 17 18 19 20 21 22 23 24

0 Prime Time-Americas 6 Prime Time-E Asia 12 Prime Time-S Asia 18 Prime Time-Europe 24

ENGLISH ▬ ARABIC ▭ CHINESE ▫▫▫ FRENCH ═ GERMAN ═ RUSSIAN ═ SPANISH ═ OTHER —

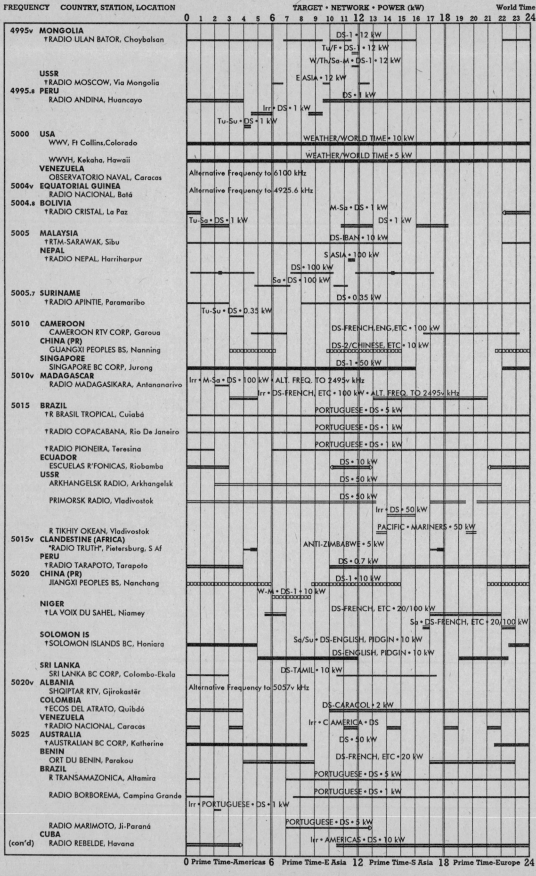

FREQUENCY	COUNTRY, STATION, LOCATION	TARGET • NETWORK • POWER (kW)
4995v	**MONGOLIA** †RADIO ULAN BATOR, Choybalsan	DS-1 • 12 kW; Tu/F • DS-1 • 12 kW; W/Th/Sa-M • DS-1 • 12 kW
	USSR †RADIO MOSCOW, Via Mongolia	E ASIA • 12 kW
4995.8	**PERU** RADIO ANDINA, Huancayo	DS • 1 kW; Irr • DS • 1 kW; Tu-Su • DS • 1 kW
5000	**USA** WWV, Ft Collins,Colorado	WEATHER/WORLD TIME • 10 kW
	WWVH, Kekaha, Hawaii	WEATHER/WORLD TIME • 5 kW
	VENEZUELA OBSERVATORIO NAVAL, Caracas	Alternative Frequency to 6100 kHz
5004v	**EQUATORIAL GUINEA** RADIO NACIONAL, Batá	Alternative Frequency to 4925.6 kHz
5004.8	**BOLIVIA** †RADIO CRISTAL, La Paz	M-Sa • DS • 1 kW; Tu-Sa • DS • 1 kW; DS • 1 kW
5005	**MALAYSIA** †RTM-SARAWAK, Sibu	DS-IBAN • 10 kW
	NEPAL †RADIO NEPAL, Harriharpur	S ASIA • 100 kW; DS • 100 kW; Sa • DS • 100 kW
5005.7	**SURINAME** †RADIO APINTIE, Paramaribo	DS • 0.35 kW; Tu-Su • DS • 0.35 kW
5010	**CAMEROON** CAMEROON RTV CORP, Garoua	DS-FRENCH,ENG,ETC • 100 kW
	CHINA (PR) GUANGXI PEOPLES BS, Nanning	DS-2/CHINESE, ETC • 10 kW
	SINGAPORE SINGAPORE BC CORP, Jurong	DS-1 • 50 kW
5010v	**MADAGASCAR** RADIO MADAGASIKARA, Antananarivo	Irr • M-Sa • DS • 100 kW • ALT. FREQ. TO 2495v kHz; Irr • DS-FRENCH, ETC • 100 kW • ALT. FREQ. TO 2495v kHz
5015	**BRAZIL** †R BRASIL TROPICAL, Cuiabá	PORTUGUESE • DS • 5 kW
	†RADIO COPACABANA, Rio De Janeiro	PORTUGUESE • DS • 1 kW
	†RADIO PIONEIRA, Teresina	PORTUGUESE • DS • 1 kW
	ECUADOR ESCUELAS R'FONICAS, Riobamba	DS • 10 kW
	USSR ARKHANGELSK RADIO, Arkhangelsk	DS • 50 kW
	PRIMORSK RADIO, Vladivostok	DS • 50 kW; Irr • DS • 50 kW
	R TIKHIY OKEAN, Vladivostok	PACIFIC • MARINERS • 50 kW
5015v	**CLANDESTINE (AFRICA)** "RADIO TRUTH", Pietersburg, S Af	ANTI-ZIMBABWE • 5 kW
	PERU †RADIO TARAPOTO, Tarapoto	DS • 0.7 kW
5020	**CHINA (PR)** JIANGXI PEOPLES BS, Nanchang	DS-1 • 10 kW; W-M • DS-1 • 10 kW
	NIGER †LA VOIX DU SAHEL, Niamey	DS-FRENCH, ETC • 20/100 kW; Sa • DS-FRENCH, ETC • 20/100 kW
	SOLOMON IS †SOLOMON ISLANDS BC, Honiara	Sa/Su • DS-ENGLISH, PIDGIN • 10 kW; DS-ENGLISH, PIDGIN • 10 kW
	SRI LANKA SRI LANKA BC CORP, Colombo-Ekala	DS-TAMIL • 10 kW
5020v	**ALBANIA** SHQIPTAR RTV, Gjirokastër	Alternative Frequency to 5057v kHz
	COLOMBIA †ECOS DEL ATRATO, Quibdó	DS-CARACOL • 2 kW
	VENEZUELA †RADIO NACIONAL, Caracas	Irr • C AMERICA • DS
5025	**AUSTRALIA** †AUSTRALIAN BC CORP, Katherine	DS • 50 kW
	BENIN ORT DU BENIN, Parakou	DS-FRENCH, ETC • 20 kW
	BRAZIL R TRANSAMAZONICA, Altamira	PORTUGUESE • DS • 5 kW
	RADIO BORBOREMA, Campina Grande	PORTUGUESE • DS • 1 kW; Irr • PORTUGUESE • DS • 1 kW
	RADIO MARIMOTO, Ji-Paraná	PORTUGUESE • DS • 5 kW
(con'd)	**CUBA** RADIO REBELDE, Havana	Irr • AMERICAS • DS • 10 kW

World Time 0–24: 0 Prime Time-Americas 6 Prime Time-E Asia 12 Prime Time-S Asia 18 Prime Time-Europe 24

SUMMER ONLY (J) WINTER ONLY (D) JAMMING / OR /\ EARLIEST HEARD ◁ LATEST HEARD ▷ NEW OR CHANGED FOR 1990 †

FREQUENCY	COUNTRY, STATION, LOCATION	TARGET • NETWORK • POWER (kW)
5025 (con'd)	**PERU** RADIO QUILLABAMBA, Quillabamba	DS-SPANISH, ETC • 5 kW; Tu-Su • DS • 5 kW; M-Sa • DS-SPANISH, ETC • 5 kW
	TONGA †TONGA BC COMMISS'N, Nuku'alofa	Alternative Frequency to 5030 kHz
5026	**UGANDA** RADIO UGANDA, Kampala	DS-ENGLISH,SWAHILI • 50/250 kW; M-F • DS-ENGLISH,SWAHILI • 50/250 kW; M-Sa • DS-ENGLISH,SWAHILI • 50/250 kW
5030	**CHINA (PR)** CENTRAL PEOPLES BS, Xi'an	DS-2 • 10 kW; DS-MINORITIES • 10 kW
	COSTA RICA †RADIO IMPACTO, San José	DS • 20 kW • ALT. FREQ. TO 5044 kHz; M-Sa • DS • 20 kW • ALT. FREQ. TO 5044 kHz
	ECUADOR †RADIO CATOLICA, Quito	DS • 9 kW • ALT. FREQ. TO 5055 kHz
	MALAYSIA RTM-SARAWAK, Kuching-Stapok	DS-BIDAYUTH • 10 kW
	TONGA †TONGA BC COMMISS'N, Nuku'alofa	M-Sa • DS-ENGLISH, TONGAN • 1 kW • ALT. FREQ. TO 5025 kHz; Tu-Su • DS-ENGLISH, TONGAN • 1 kW • ALT. FREQ. TO 5025 kHz
5030v	**PERU** †RADIO LOS ANDES, Huamachuco	DS • 1 kW
5034	**CENTRAL AFRICAN REP** RTV CENTRAFRICAINE, Bangui	DS-FRENCH, ETC • 100 kW
5035	**AUSTRIA** SCHULUNGSSENDER, Vienna	M-F • DS-ARMY TRAINING • 10 kW
	BRAZIL R EDUCACAO RURAL, Coarí	PORTUGUESE • DS • 1 kW
	RADIO APARECIDA, Aparecida	PORTUGUESE • DS • 2.5 kW
	KAMPUCHEA (CAMBODIA) VO THE PEOPLE, Phnom Penh	DS
	PERU RADIO MOYOBAMBA, Moyobamba	DS • 1 kW
	USSR KAZAKH RADIO, Alma-Ata	DS-2/RUSSIAN, ETC • 50 kW
	RADIO ALMA-ATA, Alma-Ata	ASIA • 50 kW
	RADIO TASHKENT, Alma-Ata	ASIA • 50 kW
5039.8	**PERU** RADIO LIBERTAD, Junín	DS • 1 kW; Irr • DS • 1 kW
5040	**CHINA (PR)** FUJIAN PEOPLES BS, Fuzhou	DS-1, TAIWAN SVC • 10 kW; Th/Sa-Tu • DS-1 • 10 kW
	ECUADOR †LA VOZ DEL UPANO, Macas	DS • 10 kW
	USSR GEORGIAN RADIO, Tbilisi	DS-1 • 50 kW
	VENEZUELA RADIO MATURIN, Maturín	Irr • DS • 10 kW
5040v	**ANGOLA** ER DE BENGUELA, Benguela	PORTUGUESE • DS • 1 kW
5044	**COSTA RICA** †RADIO IMPACTO, San José	Alternative Frequency to 5030 kHz
5045	**BRAZIL** R CULTURA DO PARA, Belém	PORTUGUESE • DS • 10 kW
	RADIO DIFUSORA, Presidente Prudente	PORTUGUESE • DS • 0.5 kW; Tu-Su • PORTUGUESE • DS • 0.5 kW
	PERU †RADIO RIOJA, Rioja	DS • 1 kW • ALT. FREQ. TO 5049.5 kHz
5045v	**PAKISTAN** PAKISTAN BC CORP, Islamabad	(J) • DS • 10 kW
5046v	**INDONESIA** †RRI, Yogyakarta, Jawa	DS • 20 kW
5047	**TOGO** †RADIO LOME, Lomé-Togblekope	DS • 100 kW; DS-FRENCH, ETC • 100 kW
5049.5	**PERU** †RADIO RIOJA, Rioja	Alternative Frequency to 5045 kHz
5049.8	**ECUADOR** R JESUS GRAN PODER, Quito	DS • 5 kW
5050	**CHINA (PR)** GUANGXI RADIO, Nanning	SE ASIA • 50 kW
	RADIO BEIJING, Nanning	SE ASIA • 50 kW
	COLOMBIA LA VOZ DE YOPAL, Yopal	DS-CARACOL • 1 kW; Irr • DS-CARACOL • 1 kW
	INDIA ALL INDIA RADIO, Aizawl	Sa • DS • 10 kW; DS-ENGLISH, ETC • 10 kW
(con'd)	**PERU** †RADIO MUNICIPAL, Cangallo	DS • 0.5 kW

World Time: 0 1 2 3 4 5 6 7 8 9 10 11 12 13 14 15 16 17 18 19 20 21 22 23 24

0 Prime Time-Americas 6 Prime Time-E Asia 12 Prime Time-S Asia 18 Prime Time-Europe 24

ENGLISH ARABIC CHINESE FRENCH GERMAN RUSSIAN SPANISH OTHER

FREQUENCY	COUNTRY, STATION, LOCATION	TARGET • NETWORK • POWER (kW)
5050 (con'd)	TANZANIA †RADIO TANZANIA, Dar es Salaam	DS-TEMP INACTIVE • 10 kW
5052	SINGAPORE SINGAPORE BC CORP, Jurong	DS-1 • 50 kW
5055	BRAZIL †R JORNAL A CRITICA, Manaus	Alternative Frequency to 4935 kHz
	†RADIO DIFUSORA, Cáceres	PORTUGUESE • DS • 1 kW • ALT. FREQ. TO 3275 kHz
		M-Sa • PORTUGUESE • DS • 1 kW • ALT. FREQ. TO 3275 kHz
	COSTA RICA †FARO DEL CARIBE, San José	DS • 5 kW
	ECUADOR †RADIO CATOLICA, Quito	Alternative Frequency to 5030 kHz
	FRENCH GUIANA †RFO-GUYANE, Cayenne	DS • 10 kW
	SWAZILAND †TRANS WORLD RADIO, Manzini	S AFRICA • 25 kW
		(J) • S AFRICA • 25 kW
		(D) • S AFRICA • 25 kW
		(D) Sa/Su • S AFRICA • 25 kW
5055.4	INDONESIA †RRI, Nabire, Irian Jaya	DS • 1 kW
5057v	ALBANIA SHQIPTAR RTV, Gjirokastër	DS • 50 kW • ALT. FREQ. TO 5020v kHz
5059	PERU †RADIO LIRCAY, Lircay	DS • 1 kW
5060	CHINA (PR) CENTRAL PEOPLES BS, Changji	DS-MINORITIES • 10 kW
	XINJIANG PBS, Changji	DS-MONGOLIAN • 10 kW
5060v	ECUADOR †R NAC PROGRESO, Loja	DS • 5 kW
5061v	ANGOLA ER DO HUAMBO, Huambo	DS • 1 kW
5066v	ZAIRE RADIO CANDIP, Bunia	DS-FRENCH, ETC • 1 kW
		Sa/Su • DS-FRENCH, ETC • 1 kW
		Su • DS-FRENCH, ETC • 1 kW
5068	COLOMBIA †LV DE LAS CANAS, Cali	Irr • DS
5075	CHINA (PR) CENTRAL PEOPLES BS, Urümqi	DS-2 • 50 kW
	COLOMBIA †CARACOL BOGOTA, Bogotá	Alternative Frequency to 5095 kHz
5081	PERU RADIO MUNDO, Cuzco	DS-SPANISH, ETC • 1 kW
5090	CHINA (PR) CENTRAL PEOPLES BS, Xi'an	TAIWAN-2 • 50 kW
5090v	PAKISTAN PAKISTAN BC CORP, Islamabad	DS • 100 kW
5095	COLOMBIA †CARACOL BOGOTA, Bogotá	DS • 50 kW • ALT. FREQ. TO 5075 kHz
5110v	CLANDESTINE (ASIA) †"NATIONALITIES STN, Burma	SE ASIA
5125	CHINA (PR) CENTRAL PEOPLES BS, Beijing	TAIWAN-1 • 10 kW
	USA RFE-RL, Via Holzkirchen,GFR	W EUROPE • (FEEDER) • 10 kW • ISU
		W EUROPE • (FEEDER) • 10 kW • ISL
5132v	PERU RADIO VISION, Juanjuí	DS • 0.1 kW
5145	CHINA (PR) RADIO BEIJING, Beijing	E ASIA & EAST USSR • RUSSIAN, MONGOLIAN • 120 kW
5159.6	BOLIVIA †RADIO GALAXIA, Guayaramerín	Tu-Su • DS • 0.1 kW
		DS • 0.1 kW
		M-Sa • DS • 0.1 kW
5163	CHINA (PR) CENTRAL PEOPLES BS, Xi'an	DS-2 • 50 kW
5175	CHINA (PR) HUNAN METEOROLOGY	Irr • E ASIA • WEATHER, MUSIC
5192v	ANGOLA EP DO MOXICO, Luena	Irr • PORTUGUESE • DS • 5 kW
5195	GERMANY (FR) DEUTSCHE WELLE, Elmshorn	Irr • W EUROPE • (FEEDER) • 10 kW • USB
5220	CHINA (PR) †RADIO BEIJING, Beijing	E ASIA • FEEDER • 10 kW
		(D) • E ASIA • FEEDER • 10 kW
		(J) • E ASIA • FEEDER • 10 kW
	SPAIN †R NACIONAL ESPANA, Via Beijing	(D) • E ASIA • FEEDER • 10 kW
5240	CHINA (PR) †VO THE STRAIT-PLA, Fuzhou	(D) • TAIWAN-1 • 10 kW
5250	CHINA (PR) †RADIO BEIJING, Beijing	(D) • E ASIA • FEEDER • 10 kW
	SPAIN †R NACIONAL ESPANA, Via Beijing	(D) • E ASIA • FEEDER • 10 kW
5256.4	INDONESIA †RRI, Sibolga, Sumatera	DS • 1 kW
5260	USSR KAZAKH RADIO, Alma-Ata	DS-2/RUSSIAN, ETC • 50 kW
5275	USA FAMILY RADIO, Via Taiwan	E ASIA • 250 kW

World Time 0 1 2 3 4 5 6 7 8 9 10 11 12 13 14 15 16 17 18 19 20 21 22 23 24

0 Prime Time-Americas 6 Prime Time-E Asia 12 Prime Time-S Asia 18 Prime Time-Europe 24

SUMMER ONLY (J) WINTER ONLY (D) JAMMING / OR /\ EARLIEST HEARD ◁ LATEST HEARD ▷ NEW OR CHANGED FOR 1990 †

FREQUENCY	COUNTRY, STATION, LOCATION	TARGET • NETWORK • POWER (kW)
5275.5	PERU †RADIO ONDA POPULAR, Bambamarca	DS • 0.25 kW; Irr • DS • 0.25 kW
5277v	PERU †RADIO GRAU, Huancabamba	DS • 0.5 kW • ALT. FREQ. TO 4008v kHz
5280	GERMANY (FR) DEUTSCHE WELLE, Elmshorn	Irr • E NORTH AM • (FEEDER) • 20 kW • LSB
5290	USSR KRASNOYARSK RADIO, Krasnoyarsk	DS • 100 kW
5290v	CHAD RADIODIF NATIONALE, Moundou	DS-FRENCH,ARAB,ETC • 2.5 kW
5295	USA RFE-RL, Via Holzkirchen,GFR	Irr • W EUROPE • (FEEDER) • 10 kW • ISU; W EUROPE • (FEEDER) • 10 kW • ISU; W EUROPE • (FEEDER) • 10 kW • ISL
5300	CLANDESTINE (ASIA) †"VO AFGHANISTAN"	MIDEAST & S ASIA • ANTI-AFGHAN GOVT
5320	CHINA (PR) CENTRAL PEOPLES BS, Beijing	DS-1 • 10/15 kW; W-M • DS-1 • 10/15 kW
5325	PERU †RADIO ACOBAMBA, Acobamba	DS
5405v	ANGOLA †EP DE NAMIBE, Moçâmedes	Irr • PORTUGUESE • DS • 5 kW
5408v	CLANDESTINE (ASIA) †"VO NATIONAL ARMY", Southern Laos	SE ASIA • KAMPUCHEAN REBELS
5420	CHINA (PR) CENTRAL PEOPLES BS, Beijing	DS-MINORITIES • 10 kW
5440	CHINA (PR) CENTRAL PEOPLES BS, Urümqi	DS-MINORITIES • 50 kW
	XINJIANG PBS, Urümqi	DS-KAZAKH • 50 kW
5505.2	BOLIVIA RADIO 2 DE FEBRERO, Rurrenabaque	Irr • DS • 0.5 kW; Irr • Tu-Su • DS • 0.5 kW; Irr • M-Sa • DS • 0.5 kW
5510	CHINA (PR) †VO THE STRAIT-PLA, Fuzhou	(J) • TAIWAN-1 • 10 kW
5510v	CLANDESTINE (M EAST) †"VO IRAQI KURDS", Middle East	MIDEAST • ANTI-IRAQI GOVT; Irr • MIDEAST • ANTI-IRAQI GOVT
5538.7	PERU FRECUENCIA MODULAR, Celendín	DS; Irr • DS
5567.2	COLOMBIA RADIO NUEVA VIDA, Cúcuta	DS • 0.2 kW; Irr • DS • 0.2 kW
5581.3	BOLIVIA †RADIO SAN JOSE, San José Chiquitos	Irr • DS • 0.5 kW; DS • 0.5 kW
5613v	VIETNAM HOANG LIEN SON BS, Hoang Lien Son	DS • ALT. FREQ. TO 5733v kHz
5618v	PERU †RADIO ILUCAN, Cutervo	DS • 0.2 kW; Su • DS • 0.2 kW
5656.7	PERU RADIO BAMBAMARCA, Bambamarca	DS • 0.1 kW
5661	PERU †LA VOZ DE CUTERVO, Cutervo	DS • 0.7 kW
5700	PERU FREC SAN IGNACIO, San Ignacio	DS • 0.1 kW; Irr • DS • 0.1 kW
5720	PERU †R SAN MIGUEL, S Miguel Pallaques	DS; Tu-Su • DS
5733v	VIETNAM HOANG LIEN SON BS, Hoang Lien Son	Alternative Frequency to 5613v kHz
5745	USA †VOA, Greenville, NC	C AMERICA • (FEEDER) • 40 kW • USB
5780	USSR TASS NEWS AGENCY, Moscow	M-F • DS • 15 kW
5800	CHINA (PR) CENTRAL PEOPLES BS, Urümqi	DS-MINORITIES • 50 kW
	XINJIANG PBS, Urümqi	DS-UIGHUR • 50 kW; Su • DS-UIGHUR • 50 kW
	PERU R NUEVO CAJAMARCA, N Cajamarca	DS • 0.25 kW; Irr • DS • 0.25 kW
5815	USSR RADIO MOSCOW, Moscow	Irr • (D) • DS-2(FEEDER) • 15 kW • LSB; Irr • (D) • DS-1(FEEDER) • 15 kW • LSB
5816	PERU †LV DEL ALTIPLANO, Puno	Irr • DS-SPANISH,QUECHUA • 1 kW
5825	CLANDESTINE (ASIA) †"VO AFGHANISTAN"	MIDEAST & S ASIA • ANTI-AFGHAN GOVT
5850	CHINA (PR) RADIO BEIJING, Beijing	E ASIA & EAST USSR • RUSSIAN, MONGOLIAN • 120 kW

World Time 0 1 2 3 4 5 6 7 8 9 10 11 12 13 14 15 16 17 18 19 20 21 22 23 24

0 Prime Time-Americas 6 Prime Time-E Asia 12 Prime Time-S Asia 18 Prime Time-Europe 24

ENGLISH ▬ ARABIC ▬ CHINESE ▭ FRENCH ═ GERMAN ▬ RUSSIAN ═ SPANISH ═ OTHER —

FREQUENCY	COUNTRY, STATION, LOCATION	TARGET • NETWORK • POWER (kW)
5860	**CHINA (PR)**	
	CENTRAL PEOPLES BS, Shijiazhuang	DS-1 • 50 kW
5871v	**KOREA (DPR)**	
	RADIO PYONGYANG, Pyongyang	Irr • E ASIA
5875	**SAUDI ARABIA**	
	BS OF THE KINGDOM, Ad Dir'iyah	MIDEAST • DS-GENERAL/DS-2 • 50 kW
	UNITED KINGDOM	
	†BBC, Skelton, Cumbria	EUROPE • 250 kW
5880	**CHINA (PR)**	
	CENTRAL PEOPLES BS, Beijing	DS-1 • 10 kW
5885v	**CLANDESTINE (ASIA)**	
	†"ECHO OF PUBLIC", Korea (DPR)	E ASIA • 50 kW
5889v	**CLANDESTINE (C AMER)**	
	†"RADIO LIBERACION", Costa Rica	C AMERICA • ANTI-SANDINISTA
5900	**ISRAEL**	
	KOL ISRAEL, Tel Aviv	MIDEAST • DS-D • 20 kW
	USSR	
	R TIKHIY OKEAN, Petropavlovsk-Kam	(D) • MARINERS • 100 kW
		(D) Sa • MARINERS • 100 kW
		(D) Su-F • MARINERS • 100 kW
	RADIO MOSCOW	(D) • DS-1
	RADIO MOSCOW, Kenga	DS-2 • 100 kW
		(D) • DS-1 • 100 kW
	RADIO MOSCOW, Petropavlovsk-Kam	(D) • DS-1 • 100 kW
		(J) • W NORTH AM • WS • 100 kW
	RADIO MOSCOW, Vologda	DS-3 • 100 kW
5900v	**CHINA (PR)**	
	SICHUAN PEOPLES BS, Chengdu	DS-2/CHINESE, ETC • 15 kW
5905	**USSR**	
	RADIO KIEV, Ryazan'	(D) • EUROPE • 100 kW
	RADIO MOSCOW	(D) • C AMERICA
		(D) • DS-1
	RADIO MOSCOW, Ryazan'	(D) • EUROPE • 100 kW
		(D) • EUROPE • WS, UK SERVICE • 100 kW
5905v	**PAKISTAN**	
	PAKISTAN BC CORP, Islamabad	(D) • DS • 10 kW
	PAKISTAN BC CORP, Karachi	(J) • DS-ENGLISH, ETC • 10 kW
	RADIO PAKISTAN, Islamabad	(D) • S ASIA • FEEDER • 10 kW
5910	**BELGIUM**	
	†BELGISCHE RADIO TV, Wavre	EUROPE • 100 kW • ALT. FREQ. TO 5915 kHz
		(D) M-F • EUROPE • 100 kW • ALT. FREQ. TO 5915 kHz
		M-Sa • EUROPE • 100 kW • ALT. FREQ. TO 5915 kHz
		Su • EUROPE • 100 kW • ALT. FREQ. TO 5915 kHz
	USSR	
	R TIKHIY OKEAN	(D) • PACIFIC • MARINERS
		(D) Sa • PACIFIC • MARINERS
		(D) Su-F • PACIFIC • MARINERS
	RADIO MOSCOW	(D) • EUROPE
	RADIO MOSCOW, Chita	DS-1 • 100 kW
	RADIO MOSCOW, Moscow	DS-1 • 50 kW
		DS-2 • 50 kW
5915	**BELGIUM**	
	BELGISCHE RADIO TV, Wavre	Alternative Frequency to 5910 kHz
	CHINA (PR)	
	CENTRAL PEOPLES BS, Beijing	DS-1 • 50 kW
	ISRAEL	
	†KOL ISRAEL, Tel Aviv	(D) • EUROPE & E NORTH AM • 300 kW
	USSR	
	RADIO ALMA-ATA, Alma-Ata	ASIA • 100 kW
	RADIO MOSCOW	(D) • C AMERICA • N AMERICAN
		(D) • C AMERICA
		(D) • C AMERICA • WS
	RADIO TASHKENT, Alma-Ata	ASIA • 100 kW
5920	**CHINA (PR)**	
	GUANGXI PEOPLES BS, Nanning	DS-3
	CLANDESTINE (ASIA)	
	†"VO AFGHANISTAN"	Irr • MIDEAST & S ASIA • ANTI-AFGHAN GOVT
	USSR	
	†RADIO MOSCOW	(D) • JAPANESE • E ASIA
	RADIO MOSCOW, Khabarovsk	(D) • DS-2 • 100 kW
		(D) • W NORTH AM • WS • 100 kW
	RADIO MOSCOW, Orcha	(D) • DS-3 • 100 kW
(con'd)	RADIO MOSCOW, Tula	(D) • ATLANTIC • MARINERS • 100 kW

World Time 0–24: 0 Prime Time-Americas 6 Prime Time-E Asia 12 Prime Time-S Asia 18 Prime Time-Europe 24

SUMMER ONLY (J) WINTER ONLY (D) JAMMING / OR /\ EARLIEST HEARD ◁ LATEST HEARD ▷ NEW OR CHANGED FOR 1990 †

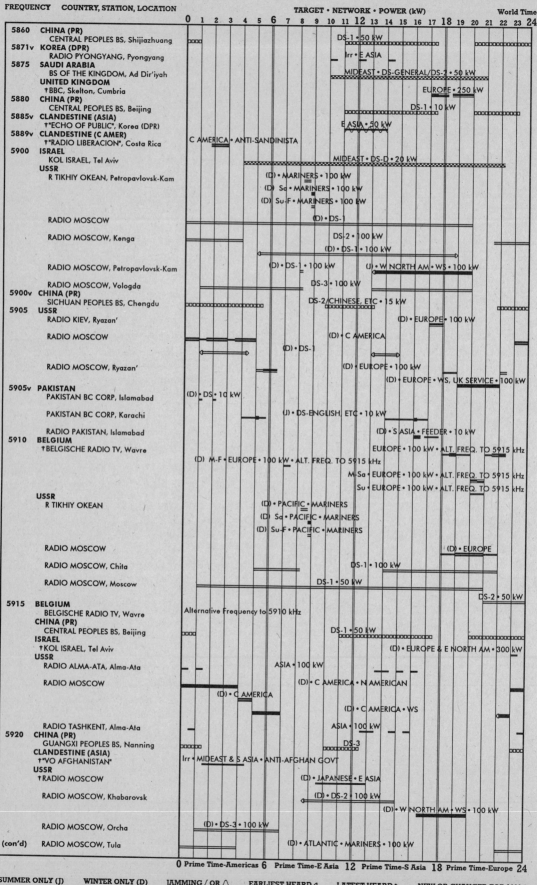

FREQUENCY	COUNTRY, STATION, LOCATION	TARGET • NETWORK • POWER (kW)
5920 (con'd)	**USSR** RADIO MOSCOW, Tula	(D) • N AFRICA • WS • 100 kW; EUROPE • 100 kW; EUROPE • WS • 100 kW
5920v	**VIETNAM** VOICE OF VIETNAM, Bac Ninh	Irr • DS • 5 kW; Irr • Su • DS • 5 kW
5925	**USSR** ESTONIAN RADIO, Tallinn	DS-1 • 50 kW; Su • DS-1 • 50 kW; Su • EUROPE • 50 kW; M-Sa • EUROPE • 50 kW; EUROPE • 50 kW
	RADIO TALLINN, Tallinn	
5929.3	**CLANDESTINE (C AMER)** †"15 DE SETIEMBRE", Honduras	Irr • C AMERICA • FDN/ANTI-SANDINIST
5930	**CZECHOSLOVAKIA** RADIO PRAGUE, Prague	EUROPE & AMERICAS • 120 kW; EUROPE • 120 kW
	USSR †MURMANSK RADIO, Murmansk	DS • 50 kW
	RADIO TBILISI, Tbilisi	Sa/Su • MIDEAST • 50 kW
5930v	**BOLIVIA** RADIO CENTINELA, Tupiza	Irr • DS
	PAKISTAN PAKISTAN BC CORP, Karachi	DS • 10 kW
5935	**CHINA (PR)** RADIO BEIJING, Lhasa	S ASIA • HINDI • 50 kW
	XIZANG PEOPLES BS, Lhasa	DS-CHINESE • 50 kW
	USSR LATVIAN RADIO, Riga	Tu-Th/Sa • W EUROPE & ATLANTIC • DS-1 • 50 kW; W • W EUROPE & ATLANTIC • DS-1 • 50 kW; Su • W EUROPE & ATLANTIC • DS-2 • 50 kW; DS-1 • 50 kW
	RADIO MOSCOW, Kenga	EUROPE & ATLANTIC • DS-2 • 50 kW
	RADIO MOSCOW, Riga	(D) • EUROPE & ATLANTIC • DS-2 • 50 kW; M/W/F • EUROPE & ATLANTIC • DS-2 • 50 kW; M-Sa • EUROPE & ATLANTIC • DS-2 • 50 kW; Irr • Su/M/F • EUROPE & ATLANTIC • DS-2 • 50 kW; Su/Tu/F • EUROPE & ATLANTIC • DS-2 • 50 kW; Th-Tu • EUROPE & ATLANTIC • DS-2 • 50 kW; M/W/Th/Sa • EUROPE & ATLANTIC • MARINERS • 50 kW; (D) • ATLANTIC • MARINERS • 50 kW
	RADIO MOSCOW, Tula	
	RADIO RIGA, Riga	Su • EUROPE & ATLANTIC • 50 kW; Tu-Th/Sa • EUROPE & ATLANTIC • 50 kW; Tu/Th/Sa/Su • EUROPE & ATLANTIC • 50 kW
5940	**USSR** MAGADAN RADIO, Magadan	DS • 50 kW
	RADIO MOSCOW	(D) • E NORTH AM • N AMERICAN
	RADIO MOSCOW, Petropavlovsk-Kam	(D) • JAPANESE • E ASIA • 100 kW
	RADIO MOSCOW, Serpuhkov	(J) • EUROPE • WS, GREEK, ETC • 120 kW
	RADIO MOSCOW, Syzran'	(D) • DS-2 • 100 kW
5945	**AUSTRIA** †RADIO AUSTRIA INTL, Vienna	EUROPE • 100 kW
	FRANCE †R FRANCE INTL, Issoudun-Allouis	E NORTH AM • 100 kW; (D) • E NORTH AM • 100 kW
	USSR RADIO MOSCOW	(J) • DS-2; (D) • EUROPE • WS, SWEDISH, ETC
	RADIO MOSCOW, Komsomol'sk'Amure	DS-1(FEEDER) • 15 kW • USB
	†RADIO TASHKENT, Frunze, Kirgiziya	S ASIA & MIDEAST • 100 kW; (D) • S ASIA & MIDEAST • 100 kW
5949v	**NICARAGUA** †LV DE NICARAGUA, Managua	Irr • DS
5950	**CHINA (PR)** CENTRAL PEOPLES BS, Lhasa	DS-MINORITIES • 50 kW
	HEILONGJIANG PBS, Harbin	DS-CHINESE, KOREAN • 50 kW
	XIZANG PEOPLES BS, Lhasa	DS-TIBETAN • 50 kW
	CHINA (TAIWAN) VO FREE CHINA, Via Okeechobee,USA	Alternative Frequency to 5985 kHz
	USA †WYFR-FAMILY RADIO, Okeechobee, Fl	E NORTH AM • 100 kW • ALT. FREQ. TO 5985 kHz; W NORTH AM • 100 kW • ALT. FREQ. TO 5985 kHz; E NORTH AM • 100 kW
	USSR R TIKHIY OKEAN, Petropavlovsk-Kam	E ASIA & PACIFIC • MARINERS • 100 kW; Sa • E ASIA & PACIFIC • MARINERS • 100 kW
(con'd)		

World Time: 0 Prime Time-Americas 6 Prime Time-E Asia 12 Prime Time-S Asia 18 Prime Time-Europe 24

ENGLISH ▬ ARABIC ▭ CHINESE ▫▫▫ FRENCH ═ GERMAN ▬ RUSSIAN ═ SPANISH ▬ OTHER —

FREQUENCY	COUNTRY, STATION, LOCATION	TARGET • NETWORK • POWER (kW)
5950 (con'd)	**USSR**	
	R TIKHIY OKEAN, Petropavlovsk-Kam	Su-F • E ASIA & PACIFIC • MARINERS • 100 kW
	RADIO MOSCOW, Leningrad	(D) • W EUROPE & ATLANTIC • 100 kW
	RADIO MOSCOW, Petropavlovsk-Kam	(D) • JAPANESE • E ASIA & PACIFIC • 100 kW
	RS SOV BELORUSSIA, Minsk	(D) • EUROPE • 100 kW
	YEMEN (REPUBLIC)	
	†"VO PALESTINE", Via Radio San'ā	PLO • 50 kW
	†RADIO SAN'A, San'ā	DS • 50 kW
		F • DS • 50 kW
		Irr • DS-RAMADAN • 50 kW
5950.3	**GUYANA**	
	†VOICE OF GUYANA, Georgetown	Irr • DS • 10 kW
5954v	**BOLIVIA**	
	†RADIO PIO DOCE, Llallagua-Siglo XX	DS-SPANISH, ETC • 1 kW
		M-Sa • DS-SPANISH, ETC • 1 kW
5954.2	**COSTA RICA**	
	RADIO CASINO, Limón	Irr • DS • 0.7 kW
		Irr • M • DS • 0.7 kW
		Irr • Tu-Su • DS • 0.7 kW
5954.8	**COLOMBIA**	
	LA VOZ CENTAUROS, Villavicencio	DS-CARACOL • 5 kW
5955	**BOTSWANA**	
	RADIO BOTSWANA, Gaborone	DS-ENGLISH, ETC • 50 kW
	BRAZIL	
	RADIO GAZETA, São Paulo	PORTUGUESE • DS • 7.5 kW
	CAMEROON	
	CAMEROON RTV CORP, Bafoussam	DS-FRENCH,ENG,ETC • 20 kW
		Sa/Su • DS-FRENCH,ENG,ETC • 20 kW
	GUATEMALA	
	RADIO CULTURAL, Guatemala City	Irr • DS • 0.25/10 kW
		Irr • M • DS • 0.25/10 kW
		Irr • Tu-Su • DS • 0.25/10 kW
		Irr • M-Sa • DS • 0.25/10 kW
		Irr • Su • DS • 0.25/10 kW
	HOLLAND	
	†RADIO NEDERLAND, Flevoland	EUROPE • 500 kW
		(D) • EUROPE • 500 kW
		Su • EUROPE • 500 kW
	TURKEY	
	†TURKISH RTV CORP, Ankara	(D) • TURKISH • E EUROPE • 250 kW
	USA	
	†RFE-RL, Via Germany	WEST USSR • 250 kW
	VOA, Via Kaválla, Greece	(D) • E EUROPE • 250 kW
	†VOA, Via Philippines	E ASIA • 250 kW
	USSR	
	†RADIO TASHKENT, Tashkent	(D) • MIDEAST • 100 kW
	YUGOSLAVIA	
	†RADIO YUGOSLAVIA, Bijeljina	E EUROPE • 250 kW
5955.3	**PERU**	
	RADIO HUANCAYO, Huancayo	DS • 0.5 kW
5960	**CANADA**	
	†R CANADA INTL, Sackville, NB	(J) • E NORTH AM & C AMERICA • 250 kW
		(D) • E NORTH AM & C AMERICA • 250 kW
		(D) Su/M • E NORTH AM & C AMERICA • 250 kW
		(J) Su/M • E NORTH AM & C AMERICA • 250 kW
		(D) Tu-Sa • E NORTH AM & C AMERICA • 250 kW
		(J) Tu-Sa • E NORTH AM & C AMERICA • 250 kW
	CHINA (PR)	
	YUNNAN PEOPLES BS, Kunming	DS-2/CHINESE, ETC • 50 kW
	GERMANY (FR)	
	DEUTSCHE WELLE, Multiple Locations	N AMERICA & C AMERICA • 100/500 kW
	INDIA	
	RADIO KASHMIR, Jammu	Su • DS-A • 1 kW
		DS-A/ENGLISH, ETC • 1 kW
	JAPAN	
	RADIO JAPAN/NHK, Via Sackville, Can	JAPANESE • E NORTH AM & C AMERICA • GENERAL • 250 kW
		(D) • E NORTH AM & C AMERICA • GENERAL • 250 kW
		(J) • E NORTH AM & C AMERICA • GENERAL • 250 kW
	MONGOLIA	
	RADIO ULAN BATOR, Ulan Bator	(D) • 50 kW
		(D) • DS-2 • 50 kW
	SOUTH AFRICA	
	†RADIO RSA, Meyerton	(J) • S AFRICA • 250 kW
	USSR	
	KAZAKH RADIO, Alma-Ata	DS-2/RUSSIAN, ETC • 50 kW
	RADIO MOSCOW, Sverdlovsk	E EUROPE • 250 kW
	†RADIO MOSCOW, Vladivostok	(D) • JAPANESE • E ASIA • 100 kW
		(D) • E ASIA • WS • 100 kW
5964.8 (con'd)	**BOLIVIA**	
	†RADIO NACIONAL, Huanuni	Tu-Su • DS • 2.5 kW
		DS • 2.5 kW

World Time: 0 Prime Time-Americas 6 Prime Time-E Asia 12 Prime Time-S Asia 18 Prime Time-Europe 24

SUMMER ONLY (J) WINTER ONLY (D) JAMMING / OR /\ EARLIEST HEARD ◁ LATEST HEARD ▷ NEW OR CHANGED FOR 1990 †

FREQUENCY	COUNTRY, STATION, LOCATION	TARGET • NETWORK • POWER (kW)
5964.8 (con'd)	**BOLIVIA** †RADIO NACIONAL, Huanuni	Irr • Tu-Su • DS • 2.5 kW; M-Sa • DS • 2.5 kW; Su • DS • 2.5 kW
5965	**BOTSWANA** RADIO BOTSWANA, Gaborone	DS-ENGLISH, ETC • 50 kW
	CANADA R CANADA INTL, Via United Kingdom	(D) • EUROPE & WEST USSR • 300 kW
	CUBA †RADIO HABANA, Havana	C AMERICA • 50 kW
	ECUADOR †LA VOZ DEL UPANO, Macas	DS • 10 kW
	GERMANY (DR) R BERLIN INTL, Nauen	W EUROPE • 50 kW
	MALAYSIA RADIO MALAYSIA, Kajang	DS-MALAY • 100 kW
	NIGERIA RADIO PLATEAU, Jos	DS-ENGLISH, ETC • 10 kW
	PAPUA NEW GUINEA R WESTERN HIGHLAND, Mount Hagen	M-F • DS-ENGLISH, ETC • 10 kW
	SWITZERLAND RED CROSS BC SVC, Schwarzenburg	Irr • M/Th • S AMERICA • 150 kW
	SWISS RADIO INTL, Schwarzenburg	S AMERICA • 150 kW
	UNITED KINGDOM †BBC, Daventry	(D) • WEST USSR • 300 kW
	†BBC, Rampisham	(J) • WEST USSR • 500 kW
	†BBC, Via Hong Kong	(D) • E ASIA • 250 kW; (D) • JAPANESE • E ASIA • 250 kW
	†BBC, Via Maṣīrah, Oman	S ASIA • 100 kW; (D) • MIDEAST & S ASIA • 100 kW
	†BBC, Via Sackville, Can	(D) • N AMERICA • 250 kW
	USA VOA, Via Rhodes, Greece	MIDEAST • 50 kW
	†VOA, Via Wertachtal, GFR	(D) • E EUROPE & MIDEAST • 500 kW; (J) • E EUROPE & MIDEAST • 500 kW
	†VOA, Via Woofferton, UK	E EUROPE & MIDEAST • 250 kW; (D) • E EUROPE & MIDEAST • 250 kW; (J) • E EUROPE & MIDEAST • 250 kW
	USSR RADIO MOSCOW, Armavir	(D) • DS-1 • 100 kW; DS-1 • 100 kW
5969v	**INDONESIA** †RRI, Banjarmasin, Kali'n	DS • 1 kW
5970	**BRAZIL** RADIO ITATIAIA, Belo Horizonte	PORTUGUESE • DS • 5 kW
	USA †RFE-RL, Via Germany	E EUROPE • 100 kW
	†RFE-RL, Via Portugal	M-Sa • E EUROPE • 250 kW; E EUROPE • 250 kW
	USSR KAZAKH RADIO, Alma-Ata	Sa • DS-1 • 100 kW; Sa-M • DS-1 • 100 kW; Su-F • DS-1 • 100 kW; Tu-F • DS-1 • 100 kW; DS-1/RUSSIAN, ETC • 100 kW
	RADIO MOSCOW, Komsomol'sk 'Amure	DS-2 • 50 kW
	YEMEN (PDR) "VO PALESTINE", Via PDR Yemen BC	MIDEAST • PLO • 100 kW
	PDR YEMEN BC SVC, Aden	MIDEAST • DS • 100 kW; F • MIDEAST • DS • 100 kW; Irr • MIDEAST • DS-RAMADAN • 100 kW
5971v	**CHINA (PR)** GANNAN PEOPLES BS, Hezuo	DS-CHINESE, TIBETAN • 15 kW • ALT. FREQ. TO 3210 kHz
5974v	**INDONESIA** †RRI, Pekanbaru, Sumatera	Irr • DS • 5 kW
5975	**CHINA (PR)** RADIO BEIJING, Beijing	KOREAN • E ASIA • 120 kW
	KOREA (REPUBLIC) †RADIO KOREA, Hwasung	KOREAN • E ASIA • 10 kW; JAPANESE • E ASIA • 10 kW; E ASIA • 10 kW
	UNITED KINGDOM †BBC, Daventry	EUROPE & N AFRICA • 300 kW
	†BBC, Multiple Locations	(J) Sa/Su • EUROPE & N AFRICA • 300/500 kW
	†BBC, Rampisham	W EUROPE & N AFRICA • 500 kW; (D) • W EUROPE & N AFRICA • 500 kW
	†BBC, Via Antigua	C AMERICA • 250 kW
(con'd)	†BBC, Via Maṣīrah, Oman	(D) • MIDEAST & S ASIA • 100 kW

World Time 0–24: 0 Prime Time-Americas 6 Prime Time-E Asia 12 Prime Time-S Asia 18 Prime Time-Europe 24

ENGLISH ARABIC CHINESE FRENCH GERMAN RUSSIAN SPANISH OTHER

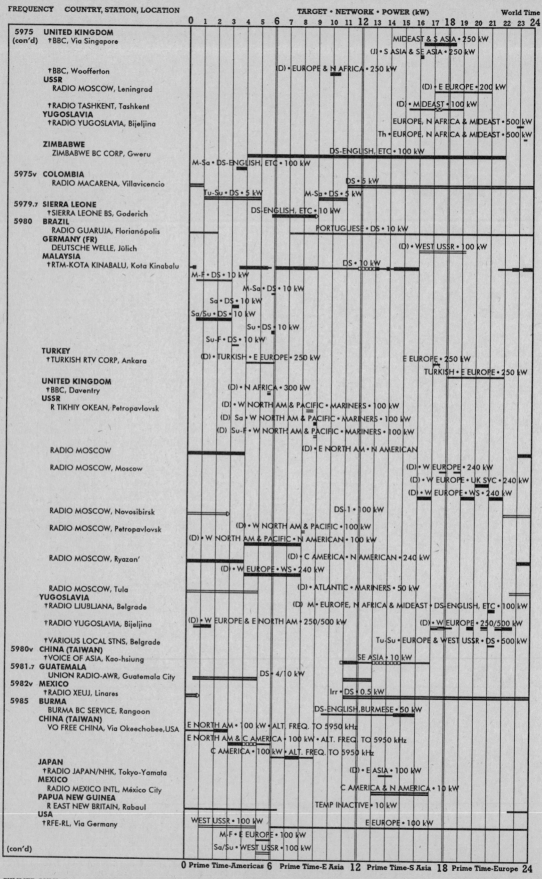

FREQUENCY	COUNTRY, STATION, LOCATION	TARGET • NETWORK • POWER (kW)
5975 (con'd)	**UNITED KINGDOM** †BBC, Via Singapore	MIDEAST & S ASIA • 250 kW
		(J) • S ASIA & SE ASIA • 250 kW
	†BBC, Woofferton	(D) • EUROPE & N AFRICA • 250 kW
	USSR RADIO MOSCOW, Leningrad	(D) • E EUROPE • 200 kW
	†RADIO TASHKENT, Tashkent	(D) • MIDEAST • 100 kW
	YUGOSLAVIA †RADIO YUGOSLAVIA, Bijeljina	EUROPE, N AFRICA & MIDEAST • 500 kW
		Th • EUROPE, N AFRICA & MIDEAST • 500 kW
	ZIMBABWE ZIMBABWE BC CORP, Gweru	DS-ENGLISH, ETC • 100 kW
		M-Sa • DS-ENGLISH, ETC • 100 kW
5975v	**COLOMBIA** RADIO MACARENA, Villavicencio	DS • 5 kW
		Tu-Su • DS • 5 kW
		M-Sa • DS • 5 kW
5979.7	**SIERRA LEONE** †SIERRA LEONE BS, Goderich	DS-ENGLISH, ETC • 10 kW
5980	**BRAZIL** RADIO GUARUJA, Florianópolis	PORTUGUESE • DS • 10 kW
	GERMANY (FR) DEUTSCHE WELLE, Jülich	(D) • WEST USSR • 100 kW
	MALAYSIA †RTM-KOTA KINABALU, Kota Kinabalu	DS • 10 kW
		M-F • DS • 10 kW
		M-Sa • DS • 10 kW
		Sa • DS • 10 kW
		Sa/Su • DS • 10 kW
		Su • DS • 10 kW
		Su-F • DS • 10 kW
	TURKEY †TURKISH RTV CORP, Ankara	(D) • TURKISH • E EUROPE • 250 kW
		E EUROPE • 250 kW
		TURKISH • E EUROPE • 250 kW
	UNITED KINGDOM †BBC, Daventry	(D) • N AFRICA • 300 kW
	USSR R TIKHIY OKEAN, Petropavlovsk	(D) • W NORTH AM & PACIFIC • MARINERS • 100 kW
		(D) Sa • W NORTH AM & PACIFIC • MARINERS • 100 kW
		(D) Su-F • W NORTH AM & PACIFIC • MARINERS • 100 kW
	RADIO MOSCOW	(D) • E NORTH AM • N AMERICAN
	RADIO MOSCOW, Moscow	(D) • W EUROPE • 240 kW
		(D) • W EUROPE • UK SVC • 240 kW
		(D) • W EUROPE • WS • 240 kW
	RADIO MOSCOW, Novosibirsk	DS-1 • 100 kW
	RADIO MOSCOW, Petropavlovsk	(D) • W NORTH AM & PACIFIC • 100 kW
		(D) • W NORTH AM & PACIFIC • N AMERICAN • 100 kW
	RADIO MOSCOW, Ryazan'	(D) • C AMERICA • N AMERICAN • 240 kW
		(D) • W EUROPE • WS • 240 kW
	RADIO MOSCOW, Tula	(D) • ATLANTIC • MARINERS • 50 kW
	YUGOSLAVIA †RADIO LJUBLJANA, Belgrade	(D) M • EUROPE, N AFRICA & MIDEAST • DS-ENGLISH, ETC • 100 kW
	†RADIO YUGOSLAVIA, Bijeljina	(D) • W EUROPE & E NORTH AM • 250/500 kW
		(D) • W EUROPE • 250/500 kW
	†VARIOUS LOCAL STNS, Belgrade	Tu-Su • EUROPE & WEST USSR • DS • 500 kW
5980v	**CHINA (TAIWAN)** †VOICE OF ASIA, Kao-hsiung	SE ASIA • 10 kW
5981.7	**GUATEMALA** UNION RADIO-AWR, Guatemala City	DS • 4/10 kW
5982v	**MEXICO** †RADIO XEUJ, Linares	Irr • DS • 0.5 kW
5985	**BURMA** BURMA BC SERVICE, Rangoon	DS-ENGLISH, BURMESE • 50 kW
	CHINA (TAIWAN) VO FREE CHINA, Via Okeechobee, USA	E NORTH AM • 100 kW • ALT. FREQ. TO 5950 kHz
		E NORTH AM & C AMERICA • 100 kW • ALT. FREQ. TO 5950 kHz
		C AMERICA • 100 kW • ALT. FREQ. TO 5950 kHz
	JAPAN †RADIO JAPAN/NHK, Tokyo-Yamata	(D) • E ASIA • 100 kW
	MEXICO RADIO MEXICO INTL, México City	C AMERICA & N AMERICA • 10 kW
	PAPUA NEW GUINEA R EAST NEW BRITAIN, Rabaul	TEMP INACTIVE • 10 kW
	USA †RFE-RL, Via Germany	WEST USSR • 100 kW
		E EUROPE • 100 kW
		M-F • E EUROPE • 100 kW
		Sa/Su • WEST USSR • 100 kW
(con'd)		

World Time 0–24: 0 Prime Time-Americas 6 Prime Time-E Asia 12 Prime Time-S Asia 18 Prime Time-Europe 24

SUMMER ONLY (J) WINTER ONLY (D) JAMMING / OR /\ EARLIEST HEARD ◁ LATEST HEARD ▷ NEW OR CHANGED FOR 1990 †

FREQUENCY	COUNTRY, STATION, LOCATION	TARGET • NETWORK • POWER (kW) — World Time 0–24
5985 (con'd)	**USA** VOA, Delano, California	PACIFIC & AUSTRALIA • 250 kW
	VOA, Via Kaválla, Greece	(D) • WEST USSR • 250 kW; (J) • WEST USSR • 250 kW
	†WYFR-FAMILY RADIO, Okeechobee, Fl	Alternative Frequency to 5950 kHz
5990	**ARGENTINA** RADIO NACIONAL, Viedma	DS • 1 kW
	BRAZIL RADIO MEC, Rio de Janeiro	PORTUGUESE • DS • 7.5 kW
	ETHIOPIA VOICE OF ETHIOPIA, Gedja	DS • 100 kW; M-Sa • DS • 100 kW; M-F • DS • 100 kW; Sa/Su • DS • 100 kW; Su • DS • 100 kW
	FRANCE R FRANCE INTL, Issoudun-Allouis	(D) • E EUROPE • 500 kW; (D) • W EUROPE & W AFRICA • 100 kW
	GERMANY (FR) DEUTSCHE WELLE, Jülich	(D) • WEST USSR • 100 kW
	HOLLAND †RADIO NEDERLAND, Flevoland	(D) • N AFRICA • 500 kW
	INDIA ALL INDIA RADIO, Bhopal	Su • DS • 10 kW; DS-ENGLISH, ETC • 10 kW
	ITALY †RTV ITALIANA, Rome	(D) • S AMERICA • 100 kW; EUROPE • 100 kW; (D) • N AFRICA • 100 kW; (D) • E ASIA • 100 kW; (D) • EUROPE • 100 kW; (D) • N AFRICA & W AFRICA • 100 kW
	JAPAN †RADIO JAPAN/NHK, Tokyo-Yamata	(D) • W NORTH AM • GENERAL • 300 kW; (D) • JAPANESE • W NORTH AM • GENERAL • 300 kW
	ROMANIA †RADIO BUCHAREST, Bucharest	AMERICAS • 250 kW; (D) • EUROPE • 250 kW; (D) • AMERICAS • 250 kW
	UNITED KINGDOM †BBC, Rampisham	(D) • WEST USSR • 500 kW
	†BBC, Via Zyyi, Cyprus	(D) • PERSIAN • MIDEAST & S ASIA • 250 kW; (D) • EUROPE & WEST USSR • 250 kW
	USSR RADIO MOSCOW, Nikolayevsk 'Amure	DS-2 • 50 kW
	RADIO MOSCOW, Tbilisi	(D) • DS-1 • 100 kW
5990v	**CHINA (PR)** HUBEI METEOROLOGY, Baokang	E ASIA • WEATHER • 15 kW
5995	**AUSTRALIA** †RADIO AUSTRALIA, Shepparton	PACIFIC • 100 kW
	BOLIVIA RADIO LOYOLA, Sucre	DS-SPANISH, QUECHUA • 0.5 kW
	CANADA †R CANADA INTL, Via United Kingdom	(D) • EUROPE • 300 kW; (J) • EUROPE • 300 kW; (D) M-F • EUROPE • 300 kW; (D) Sa/Su • EUROPE • 300 kW
	CHINA (PR) CENTRAL PEOPLES BS, Lhasa	DS-MINORITIES • 50 kW
	XIZANG PEOPLES BS, Lhasa	DS-TIBETAN • 50 kW
	CLANDESTINE (M EAST) "VO THE CRUSADER", Eastern Iraq	MIDEAST • MOJAHEDIN-E KHALQ
	FRANCE R FRANCE INTL, Issoudun-Allouis	(J) • W EUROPE & W AFRICA • 100 kW
	GERMANY (FR) †DEUTSCHE WELLE, Wertachtal	(D) • E EUROPE • 500 kW; (J) • E EUROPE • 500 kW
	GUAM †ADVENTIST WORLD R, Agat	(D) • E ASIA • 100 kW
	MALAWI MALAWI BC CORP, Limbe	DS-ENGLISH, ETC • 20/100 kW; (D) • DS-ENGLISH, ETC • 20/100 kW
	MALI RTV MALIENNE, Bamako	DS-FRENCH, ETC • 50 kW; M-Sa • DS-FRENCH, ETC • 50 kW
	POLAND †RADIO POLONIA, Warsaw	EUROPE • 8 kW
	UNITED KINGDOM †BBC, Rampisham	(D) • E AFRICA • 500 kW
	BBC, Skelton, Cumbria	EUROPE • 250 kW
	†BBC, Via Hong Kong	E ASIA • 250 kW; (D) • E ASIA • 250 kW; (J) • E ASIA • 250 kW
(con'd)	**USA** †VOA, Greenville, NC	C AMERICA & S AMERICA • 500 kW

0 Prime Time-Americas 6 Prime Time-E Asia 12 Prime Time-S Asia 18 Prime Time-Europe 24

ENGLISH ▬ ARABIC ⧗ CHINESE ▫▫▫ FRENCH ═ GERMAN ═ RUSSIAN ═ SPANISH ═ OTHER —

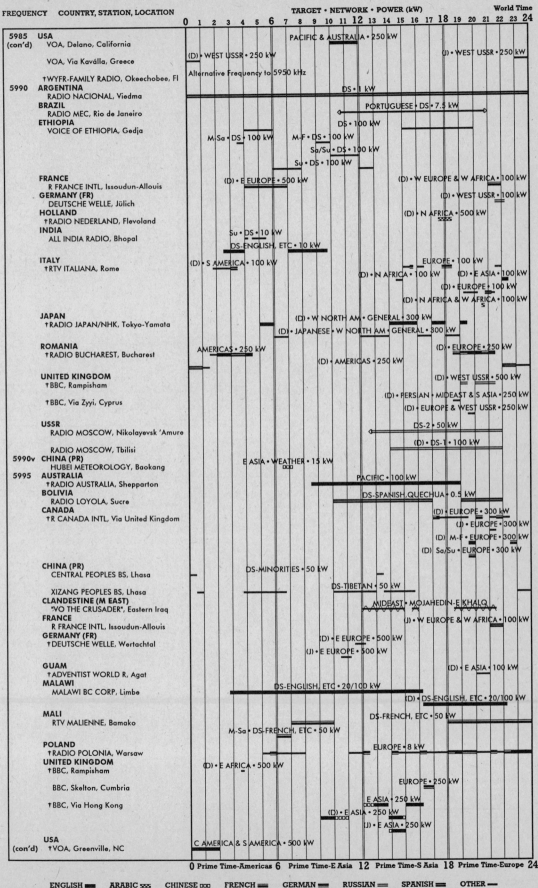

FREQUENCY	COUNTRY, STATION, LOCATION	TARGET • NETWORK • POWER (kW)
5995 (con'd)	**USA**	
	†VOA, Greenville, NC	Tu-Sa • C AMERICA & S AMERICA • 500 kW
	VOA, Via Tangier, Morocco	(D) • EUROPE • 100 kW
	†VOA, Via Wertachtal, GFR	(J) • E EUROPE & WEST USSR • 500 kW
	WORLD HARVEST R, Noblesville, Indiana	(D) • E NORTH AM • 100 kW
	USSR	
	†UZBEK RADIO, Tashkent	DS-1/RUSSIAN, ETC • 50 kW
5995.2	**PERU**	
	†RADIO MELODIA, Arequipa	DS • 5 kW
5995.3	**ECUADOR**	
	LA VOZ DEL UPANO, Macas	DS
6000	**BRAZIL**	
	†RADIO GUAIBA, Pôrto Alegre	PORTUGUESE • DS • 7.5 kW
	CHINA (PR)	
	†VO THE STRAIT-PLA, Fuzhou	TAIWAN-2 • 30 kW
		(J) • TAIWAN-2 • 30 kW
	GERMANY (FR)	
	†DEUTSCHE WELLE, Jülich	N AFRICA • 100 kW
	DEUTSCHE WELLE, Wertachtal	(D) • WEST USSR • 500 kW
	SINGAPORE	
	SINGAPORE BC CORP, Jurong	DS-3 • 50 kW
	UNITED KINGDOM	
	†BBC, Via Zyyi, Cyprus	(D) • MIDEAST • 100 kW
		(D) M-Sa • MIDEAST • 100 kW
	USSR	
	RADIO MOSCOW, Ul'yanovsk	(D) • DS-1 • 240 kW
		(D) • E EUROPE • 240 kW
	RADIO MOSCOW, Via Havana, Cuba	N AMERICA • N AMERICAN SVC, WS • 100 kW
		(D) • N AMERICA • WS • 100 kW
6005	**BOLIVIA**	
	†RADIO HORIZONTE, La Paz	DS • 4 kW
	CAMEROON	
	CAMEROON RTV CORP, Buea	Irr • DS-FRENCH, ENG, ETC • 4 kW
		Irr • Su • DS-FRENCH, ENG, ETC • 4 kW
	CANADA	
	CFCX-CFCF, Montréal, Québec	DS • 0.5 kW
	CHINA (PR)	
	GANSU PEOPLES BS, Lanzhou	DS-1 • 15 kW
	GERMANY (FR)	
	R AMERICAN SECTOR, Berlin	EUROPE • RIAS-1 • 100 kW
	IRAQ	
	†RADIO BAGHDAD, Balad-Salah el Deen	(D) • MIDEAST • 500 kW
	JAPAN	
	†NHK, Nagoya	Irr • JAPANESE • DS-1(FEEDER) • 0.3 kW • USB
	†NHK, Sapporo	Irr • JAPANESE • DS-1(FEEDER) • 0.6 kW
	PHILIPPINES	
	FAR EAST BC CO, Bocaue	(D) • E ASIA • 50 kW
	ROMANIA	
	RADIO BUCHAREST, Bucharest	(D) • WEST USSR • 250 kW
	SRI LANKA	
	SRI LANKA BC CORP, Colombo-Ekala	S ASIA • 10 kW
	UNITED KINGDOM	
	†BBC, Via Ascension	S AMERICA • 250 kW
		S AFRICA • 250 kW
		W AFRICA & S AFRICA • 125 kW
	†BBC, Via Seychelles	E AFRICA • 250 kW
	USSR	
	RADIO MOSCOW, Krasnodar	(D) • MIDEAST • 120 kW
	YUGOSLAVIA	
	†RADIO YUGOSLAVIA, Bijeljina	WEST USSR • 500 kW
		EUROPE • 250 kW
6005.5	**COSTA RICA**	
	†RADIO RELOJ, San José	Irr • DS • 3 kW
6006v	**CLANDESTINE (ASIA)**	
	"VO MALAYAN DEM'Y, Hengyang, China	SE ASIA • MALAY COMMUNIST • 10 kW
6008v	**MEXICO**	
	†RADIO MIL, México City	Irr • DS • 5 kW
6009	**CLANDESTINE (AFRICA)**	
	†"VO CHADIAN REV'N", Tripoli, Libya	C AFRICA • ANTI-CHAD • 500 kW
6010	**BRAZIL**	
	R INCONFIDENCIA, Belo Horizonte	PORTUGUESE • DS • 25 kW
	CANADA	
	R CANADA INTL, Via United Kingdom	(D) • E EUROPE & WEST USSR • 300 kW
	INDIA	
	ALL INDIA RADIO, Calcutta	DS • 10 kW
	PHILIPPINES	
	†RADIO VERITAS ASIA, Palauig	(D) • E ASIA • 250 kW
	SOUTH AFRICA	
	†RADIO RSA, Meyerton	(J) • N AMERICA • 500 kW
	UNITED KINGDOM	
	†BBC, Rampisham	(D) • EUROPE & WEST USSR • 500 kW
	†BBC, Skelton, Cumbria	(D) • EUROPE • 250 kW
(con'd)		(J) • EUROPE • 250 kW

World Time: 0 Prime Time-Americas 6 Prime Time-E Asia 12 Prime Time-S Asia 18 Prime Time-Europe 24

SUMMER ONLY (J) WINTER ONLY (D) JAMMING / OR /\ EARLIEST HEARD ◁ LATEST HEARD ▷ NEW OR CHANGED FOR 1990 †

FREQUENCY   COUNTRY, STATION, LOCATION

TARGET • NETWORK • POWER (kW)

World Time

0 1 2 3 4 5 6 7 8 9 10 11 12 13 14 15 16 17 18 19 20 21 22 23 24

Frequency	Country, Station, Location	Target • Network • Power
6010	UNITED KINGDOM	
(con'd)	†BBC, Via Maṣīrah, Oman	S ASIA • 100 kW
	USA	
	†VOA, Via Kaválla, Greece	(J) • S ASIA • 250 kW
	USSR	
	†LITHUANIAN RADIO, Kaunas	DS-1/RUSSIAN, ETC • 50 kW
	RADIO KIEV, Vinnitsa	(D) • EUROPE • 100 kW
	RADIO MOSCOW, Novosibirsk	DS-1 • 100 kW
	RADIO MOSCOW, Vinnitsa	(D) • EUROPE • 100 kW
	RS SOV BELORUSSIA, Vinnitsa	(D) • M/Tu/Th/F • EUROPE • 100 kW
		(D) • W/Sa/Su • EUROPE • 100 kW
6010v	VENEZUELA	
	RADIO LOS ANDES, Mérida	Irr • DS • 1 kW
6011v	PERU	
	RADIO AMERICA, Lima	DS • 2.5/5 kW
6012	ANTARCTICA	
	AFAN-US MILITARY, McMurdo Base	DS • 1 kW
6014.6	PARAGUAY	
	†EMISORAS PARAGUAY, Asunción	DS • 0.3 kW
6015	AUSTRIA	
	†RADIO AUSTRIA INTL, Via Sackville, Can	N AMERICA • 250 kW
	BOLIVIA	DS • 10 kW
	†RADIO EL MUNDO, Santa Cruz	Su • DS • 10 kW
		Tu-Su • DS • 10 kW M-Sa • DS • 10 kW
	CANADA	
	†R CANADA INTL, Via United Kingdom	(J) • EUROPE & WEST USSR • 300 kW
	CHINA (PR)	
	CENTRAL PEOPLES BS, Beijing	TAIWAN-1 • 50 kW
	GERMANY (FR)	
	†DEUTSCHE WELLE, Wertachtal	(D) • E EUROPE • 500 kW
		(J) • E EUROPE • 500 kW
	IVORY COAST	
	RTV IVOIRIENNE, Abidjan	W AFRICA • DS • 500 kW
	KOREA (REPUBLIC)	
	†KOREAN BC SYSTEM, Hwasung	KOREAN • E ASIA • EDUCATIONAL 1 • 100 kW
	UNITED KINGDOM	
	†BBC, Daventry	(J) • WEST USSR • 300 kW
	†BBC, Skelton, Cumbria	(J) • EUROPE • 250 kW
		(J) • Su • MIDEAST • 250 kW
	†BBC, Via Zyyi, Cyprus	(D) • MIDEAST • 100 kW
		(J) • MIDEAST • 100 kW
	USA	
	†RFE-RL, Via Germany	WEST USSR • 250 kW
	†VOA, Via Ismaning, GFR	(D) • WEST USSR • 100 kW
	†VOA, Via Kaválla, Greece	MIDEAST & S ASIA • 250 kW
		(D) • MIDEAST & S ASIA • 250 kW
		(D) • MIDEAST • 250 kW
	VOA, Via Philippines	SE ASIA • 50/250 kW
	†VOA, Via Wertachtal, GFR	(J) • MIDEAST • 500 kW
	USSR	
	RADIO MOSCOW, Minsk	DS-2 • 100 kW
	VATICAN STATE	
	†VATICAN RADIO, Sta Maria di Galeria	(D) • JAPANESE • ASIA & AUSTRALIA • 100 kW
		(D) • ASIA & AUSTRALIA • 100 kW
6015v	TANZANIA	
	VOICE OF TANZANIA, Dole, Zanzibar	DS-SWAHILI • 50 kW
6020	AFGHANISTAN	
	RADIO AFGHANISTAN, Via USSR	(D) • EUROPE • 100 kW • ALT. FREQ. TO 11830 kHz
	AUSTRALIA	
	RADIO AUSTRALIA, Brandon	PACIFIC • 10 kW
	BRAZIL	
	R EDUCADORA BAHIA, Salvador	PORTUGUESE • DS • 10 kW
	RADIO GAUCHA, Pôrto Alegre	PORTUGUESE • DS • 7.5 kW
	HOLLAND	
	†RADIO NEDERLAND, Flevoland	C AMERICA • 500 kW
		S AMERICA • 500 kW N AFRICA • 500 kW
		E NORTH AM • 500 kW EUROPE • 500 kW
		(D) • E NORTH AM • 500 kW
	RADIO NEDERLAND, Via Madagascar	S AFRICA • 300 kW
	†RADIO NEDERLAND, Via Neth Antilles	C AMERICA • 300 kW
		M-Sa • C AMERICA • 300 kW
	INDIA	
	ALL INDIA RADIO, Simla	DS • 2.5 kW
	MEXICO	
	†RADIO XEUW, Veracruz	Irr • DS • 0.25 kW
	PAPUA NEW GUINEA	
	R NORTH SOLOMONS, Kieta	Irr • M-F • DS-ENGLISH, ETC • 10 kW
	PERU	DS • 5 kW
(con'd)	RADIO VICTORIA, Lima	

0 Prime Time-Americas 6   Prime Time-E Asia 12   Prime Time-S Asia 18   Prime Time-Europe 24

ENGLISH ▬   ARABIC ⋙   CHINESE ▭▭▭   FRENCH ══   GERMAN ▭   RUSSIAN ═══   SPANISH ═   OTHER ─

FREQUENCY	COUNTRY, STATION, LOCATION	TARGET • NETWORK • POWER (kW)
6020 (con'd)	**SPAIN**	
	†R NACIONAL ESPANA, Noblejas	(D) • EUROPE • 350 kW
		(D) M-F • EUROPE • 350 kW
	USA	
	†VOA, Greenville, NC	W AFRICA • 250 kW
		(D) • EUROPE • 250 kW
		M-F • W AFRICA • 250 kW
	USSR	
	R TIKHIY OKEAN, Khabarovsk	(D) • E ASIA & PACIFIC • MARINERS • 50 kW
		(D) Sa • E ASIA & PACIFIC • MARINERS • 50 kW
		(D) Su-F • E ASIA & PACIFIC • MARINERS • 50 kW
	RADIO MOSCOW, Khabarovsk	(D) • E ASIA & PACIFIC • N AMERICAN • 50 kW
		JAPANESE • E ASIA & PACIFIC • 50 kW
		(D) • E ASIA & PACIFIC • 50 kW
		E ASIA & PACIFIC • WS • 50 kW
	UKRAINIAN RADIO, Kiev	DS • 100 kW
	ZIMBABWE	
	ZIMBABWE BC CORP, Gweru	DS-1 • 20/100 kW
6025	**BOLIVIA**	
	†RADIO ILLIMANI, La Paz	DS • 10 kW
		Tu-Su • DS • 10 kW
		M-Sa • DS • 10 kW
	CANADA	
	R CANADA INTL, Via Sines, Portugal	(D) • WEST USSR • 250 kW
	CHINA (PR)	
	†RADIO BEIJING, Kunming	SE ASIA • 50 kW
	DOMINICAN REPUBLIC	
	†RADIO AMANECER, Santo Domingo	DS • 1 kW
	GERMANY (FR)	
	†DEUTSCHE WELLE, Via Cyclops, Malta	EUROPE, N AFRICA & MIDEAST • 250 kW
	DEUTSCHE WELLE, Wertachtal	(D) • E EUROPE • 500 kW
	HUNGARY	
	RADIO KOSSUTH, Szekésfehérvár	EUROPE • DS • 100 kW
	JAPAN	
	†RADIO JAPAN/NHK, Tokyo-Yamata	(D) • JAPANESE • E ASIA • GENERAL • 300 kW
		(D) • E ASIA • GENERAL • 300 kW
	MALAYSIA	
	†RADIO MALAYSIA, Kajang	DS-CHINESE • 100 kW
		Sa-Th • DS-CHINESE • 100 kW
		Sa/Su • DS-CHINESE • 100 kW
	NIGERIA	
	FEDERAL RADIO CORP, Enugu	DS-ENGLISH, ETC • 10 kW
	PARAGUAY	
	†RADIO NACIONAL, Asunción	DS-SPANISH, GUARANI • 0.6/2 kW
	UNITED KINGDOM	
	†BBC, Rampisham	(D) • WEST USSR • 500 kW
	†BBC, Via Zyyi, Cyprus	(J) • WEST USSR • 100 kW
	USA	
	†VOA, Via Wertachtal, GFR	(J) • E EUROPE • 500 kW
6025v	**MOZAMBIQUE**	
	EP DE SOFALA, Beira	DS • 10 kW
6029.6	**CHILE**	
	RADIO SANTA MARIA, Coihaique	DS • 1 kW
6030	**CANADA**	
	CFVP-CFCN, Calgary, Alberta	DS • 0.1 kW
	R CANADA INTL, Via United Kingdom	(J) • EUROPE • 300 kW
	CYPRUS	
	CYPRUS BC CORP, Zyyi	(D) F-Su • EUROPE • 250 kW
	GERMANY (FR)	
	†SUDDEUTSCHER RFUNK, Mühlacker	EUROPE • DS-1 • 20 kW
	IRAN	
	†VO THE ISLAMIC REP, Tehrān	Alternative Frequency to 6080 kHz
	PHILIPPINES	
	FAR EAST BC CO, Bocaue	SE ASIA • 50 kW
	UNITED KINGDOM	
	†BBC, Daventry	(D) • MIDEAST • 300 kW
		(D) M-Sa • MIDEAST • 300 kW
	†BBC, Rampisham	(D) • W EUROPE • 500 kW
		(J) • W EUROPE • 250 kW
	†BBC, Via Maṣīrah, Oman	MIDEAST • 100 kW
	†BBC, Via Zyyi, Cyprus	(D) • EUROPE & WEST USSR • 100 kW
	USA	
	†VOA, Cincinnati, Ohio	C AMERICA • 175 kW
	†VOA, Greenville, NC	C AMERICA • 250 kW
	VOA, Via Philippines	E ASIA • 250 kW
	USSR	
	RADIO MOSCOW	(D) • DS-3
	RADIO MOSCOW, Moscow	DS-2 • 100 kW
	RADIO MOSCOW, Sverdlovsk	DS-2 • 100 kW

World Time: 0 Prime Time-Americas 6 Prime Time-E Asia 12 Prime Time-S Asia 18 Prime Time-Europe 24

SUMMER ONLY (J) WINTER ONLY (D) JAMMING / OR /\ EARLIEST HEARD ◁ LATEST HEARD ▷ NEW OR CHANGED FOR 1990 †

FREQUENCY	COUNTRY, STATION, LOCATION	TARGET • NETWORK • POWER (kW)
6030v	**BRAZIL** †RADIO GLOBO, Rio de Janeiro	PORTUGUESE • DS • 10 kW
6035	**AUSTRALIA** RADIO AUSTRALIA, Carnarvon	S ASIA & EUROPE • 250/300 kW; SE ASIA • 250 kW
	BELGIUM †BELGISCHE RADIO TV, Wavre	(D) • EUROPE • 100 kW; (J) • EUROPE • 100 kW; (D) M-F • EUROPE • 100 kW; (J) M-F • EUROPE • 100 kW; (D) Sa • EUROPE • 100 kW; (J) Sa/Su • EUROPE • 100 kW
	BHUTAN BHUTAN BC SERVICE, Thimbu	Su • DS • 5 kW; M-Sa • DS • 5 kW
	BULGARIA RADIO SOFIA, Sofia	EUROPE • 250 kW
	CANADA †R CANADA INTL, Via Sines, Portugal	(J) • WEST USSR • 250 kW
	CHINA (PR) RADIO BEIJING, Kunming	SE ASIA • VIETNAMESE • 50 kW
	YUNNAN PEOPLES BS, Kunming	DS-LITERARY SVC • 50 kW; SE ASIA • VIETNAMESE • 50 kW
	GERMANY (FR) †DEUTSCHE WELLE, Multiple Locations	(D) • S ASIA • 100/500 kW
	NORWAY †RADIO NORWAY INTL, Fredrikstad	(D) M-Sa • EUROPE • 350 kW; (D) Su • EUROPE • 350 kW
	SWITZERLAND SWISS RADIO INTL, Schwarzenburg	W EUROPE • 150 kW
	USA VOA, Via M'rovia, Liberia	W AFRICA • 250 kW
	USSR R TIKHIY OKEAN, Vladivostok	(D) • PACIFIC & N AMERICA • MARINERS • 100 kW; (D) Sa • PACIFIC & N AMERICA • MARINERS • 100 kW; (D) Su-F • PACIFIC & N AMERICA • MARINERS • 100 kW
	RADIO MOSCOW, Vladivostok	(D) • PACIFIC & N AMERICA • DS-1 • 100 kW; (D) • PACIFIC & N AMERICA • DS-2 • 100 kW
	VATICAN STATE †VATICAN RADIO, Sta Maria di Galeria	(D) • C AMERICA • 100 kW
6035v	**COLOMBIA** LV DEL GUAVIARE, San José Guaviare	DS • 5 kW
6040	**BRAZIL** R CLUBE PARANAENSE, Curitiba	PORTUGUESE • DS • 7.5 kW
	CHINA (TAIWAN) †CENTRAL BC SYSTEM, T'ai-pei	PRC-5 • 7.5 kW
	FRANCE R FRANCE INTL, Issoudun-Allouis	(J) • W EUROPE • 100 kW
	GERMANY (DR) R BERLIN INTL, Nauen	S AMERICA • 500 kW; W EUROPE • 50 kW; Sa/Su • W EUROPE • 50 kW
	GERMANY (FR) DEUTSCHE WELLE, Via Antigua	N AMERICA • 250 kW
	PAPUA NEW GUINEA RADIO MILNE BAY, Alotau	Irr • M-F • DS/ENGLISH, ETC • 10 kW
	USA †VOA, Greenville, NC	C AMERICA • 250/500 kW
	†VOA, Via Kaválla, Greece	(J) • WEST USSR • 250 kW
	†VOA, Via Wertachtal, GFR	(D) • E EUROPE & MIDEAST • 500 kW
	†VOA, Via Woofferton, UK	EUROPE • 250/300 kW; EUROPE & N AFRICA • 250 kW
	USSR RADIO MOSCOW	(D) • N AMERICAN
	RADIO MOSCOW, Ashkhabad	DS-1 • 50 kW
	YUGOSLAVIA †RADIO YUGOSLAVIA, Bijeljina	E EUROPE & MIDEAST • 250 kW
6045	**BULGARIA** RADIO SOFIA	(D) • C AMERICA
	CHINA (PR) NEI MONGGOL PBS, Hohhot	DS-CHINESE • 15 kW; Sa/Su • DS-CHINESE • 15 kW
	CLANDESTINE (AFRICA) "CUBANS IN AFRICA", Pietersburg, S Af	S AFRICA • TO CUBAN TROOPS
	FRANCE †R FRANCE INTL, Issoudun-Allouis	(D) • E EUROPE & WEST USSR • 100 kW; (D) • W EUROPE • 100 kW
	GERMANY (FR) DEUTSCHE WELLE, Multiple Locations	C AMERICA & S AMERICA • 100/500 kW
	INDIA ALL INDIA RADIO, Delhi	MIDEAST & S ASIA • 100 kW; DS • 100 kW

(con'd)

World Time: 0 Prime Time-Americas 6 Prime Time-E Asia 12 Prime Time-S Asia 18 Prime Time-Europe 24

ENGLISH ▬ ARABIC ⌧ CHINESE ▫▫▫ FRENCH ═ GERMAN ▬ RUSSIAN ═ SPANISH ═ OTHER —

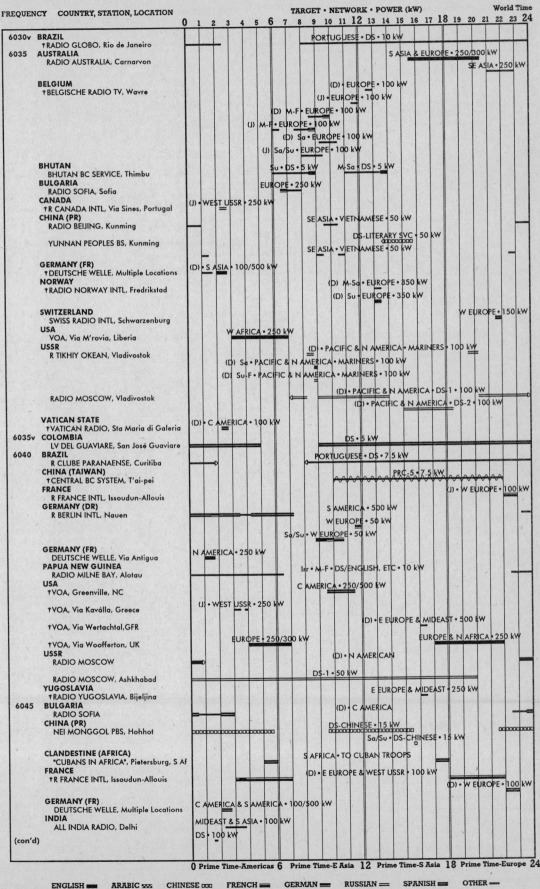

FREQUENCY | COUNTRY, STATION, LOCATION | TARGET • NETWORK • POWER (kW) | World Time 0 1 2 3 4 5 6 7 8 9 10 11 12 13 14 15 16 17 18 19 20 21 22 23 24

6045 (con'd) **KENYA**
VOICE OF KENYA, Koma Rock
- DS-GENERAL • 250 kW
- M-Sa • DS-GENERAL • 250 kW

MEXICO
†RADIO UNIVERSIDAD, San Luis Potosí
- Irr • DS • 0.25 kW

ROMANIA
RADIO BUCHAREST, Bucharest
- (D) • WEST USSR • 250 kW

SENEGAL
ORT DU SENEGAL, Tambacounda
- DS-FRENCH, ETC • 4 kW

UNITED KINGDOM
†BBC, Multiple Locations
- (D) • EUROPE & WEST USSR • 100/250 kW
- (D) Sa/Su • EUROPE & WEST USSR • 100/250 kW

†BBC, Skelton, Cumbria
- (J) • EUROPE • 250 kW

URUGUAY
RADIO SPORT, Montevideo
- DS • 1 kW

USSR
RADIO MOSCOW, Moscow
- (D) • E EUROPE • RUSSIAN, POLISH • 240 kW

RADIO MOSCOW, Via Havana, Cuba
- (D) • N AMERICA • 100 kW

ZIMBABWE
ZIMBABWE BC CORP, Gweru
- M-F • DS-EDUCATIONAL • 10 kW

6045v **PERU**
†RADIO SANTA ROSA, Lima
- DS • 3/10 kW
- Tu-Sa • DS • 3/10 kW

6045.6 **COLOMBIA**
RADIO MELODIA, Bogotá
- Irr • DS • 5 kW

6050 **BRAZIL**
RADIO GUARANI, Belo Horizonte
- PORTUGUESE • DS • 10 kW

CANADA
†R CANADA INTL, Via United Kingdom
- (D) M-F • EUROPE • 100 kW
- (J) M-F • EUROPE • 100 kW

ECUADOR
†HCJB-VO THE ANDES, Quito
- AMERICAS • DS-SPANISH, QUECHUA • 100 kW
- PACIFIC & AUSTRALIA • 100 kW

INDIA
ALL INDIA RADIO, Delhi
- DS-ENGLISH, ETC • 100 kW

ITALY
†RTV ITALIANA, Rome
- (D) • E EUROPE • 100 kW

MALAYSIA
†RTM-SARAWAK, Sibu
- DS-IBAN • 10 kW
- Irr • DS-IBAN • 10 kW

NIGERIA
FEDERAL RADIO CORP, Ibadan
- DS-ENGLISH, ETC • 50 kW

SRI LANKA
†SRI LANKA BC CORP, Colombo-Ekala
- S ASIA • 10 kW

TURKEY
†TURKISH RTV CORP, Ankara
- (D) • TURKISH • N AFRICA • 250 kW

UNITED KINGDOM
†BBC, Rampisham
- (D) • EUROPE • 500 kW

†BBC, Via Zyyi, Cyprus
- (D) • MIDEAST • 100 kW
- EUROPE • 100/250 kW
- (D) • WEST USSR • 100 kW
- (D) Sa • EUROPE • 100 kW
- (D) • EUROPE • 100 kW
- (D) • MIDEAST & WEST USSR • 100 kW
- (J) Sa • EUROPE • 100 kW
- (J) • EUROPE • 100/250 kW
- (J) • MIDEAST & WEST USSR • 250 kW
- (D) Sa/Su • EUROPE • 100 kW
- (D) M-F • EUROPE • 100 kW
- (J) Sa/Su • EUROPE • 100 kW
- (J) M-F • EUROPE • 250 kW
- (D) M-Sa • MIDEAST & WEST USSR • 100 kW
- (J) M-Sa • MIDEAST & WEST USSR • 250 kW

USA
†RFE-RL, Via Germany
- WEST USSR • 100 kW

USSR
†RADIO MOSCOW, Khabarovsk
- EAST USSR & W NORTH AM • 100 kW
- (D) • JAPANESE • EAST USSR & W NORTH AM • 100 kW
- (D) • EAST USSR & W NORTH AM • 100 kW
- (J) • EAST USSR & W NORTH AM • 100 kW

6055 **CANADA**
†R CANADA INTL, Via Tokyo, Japan
- Sa • JAPANESE • E ASIA & PACIFIC • 50 kW

CZECHOSLOVAKIA
RADIO PRAGUE, Piešťany-Velké K'y
- (D) • W EUROPE & E NORTH AM • ENG, FR, GERMAN, ETC • 250 kW
- (D) • E NORTH AM & C AMERICA • 250 kW
- W EUROPE • 250 kW

RADIO PRAGUE, Prague
- EUROPE • 400 kW
- Sa/Su • EUROPE • 400 kW
- EUROPE • ENG, FR, GERMAN, ETC • 400 kW

JAPAN
†RADIO TANPA, Tokyo-Nagara
- JAPANESE • DS-1 • 50 kW
- Su-F • JAPANESE • DS-1 • 50 kW

KUWAIT
RADIO KUWAIT, Jadādīyah
- Irr • MIDEAST • DS-RAMADAN • 250 kW
- MIDEAST • DS-MAIN PROGRAM • 250 kW

(con'd)

0 Prime Time-Americas 6 Prime Time-E Asia 12 Prime Time-S Asia 18 Prime Time-Europe 24

SUMMER ONLY (J) | WINTER ONLY (D) | JAMMING / OR /\ | EARLIEST HEARD ◁ | LATEST HEARD ▷ | NEW OR CHANGED FOR 1990 †

FREQUENCY	COUNTRY, STATION, LOCATION	TARGET • NETWORK • POWER (kW)
6055 (con'd)	**RWANDA** R REP RWANDAISE, Kigali	DS-FRENCH, ETC • 50 kW
		Su • DS-FRENCH, ETC • 50 kW
6055.3	**PERU** RADIO CONTINENTAL, Arequipa	DS • 2 kW
6058v	**CHINA (PR)** SICHUAN PEOPLES BS, Xichang	DS-1 • 50 kW
		W-M • DS-1 • 50 kW
6060	**ARGENTINA** †R ARGENTINA-RAE, Buenos Aires	S AMERICA • 50 kW
		Sa/Su • S AMERICA • 50 kW
		Tu/Th • S AMERICA • 50 kW
		W/F-M • S AMERICA • 50 kW
	†RADIO NACIONAL, Buenos Aires	S AMERICA • DS • 50 kW
		Sa/Su • S AMERICA • DS • 50 kW
	AUSTRALIA RADIO AUSTRALIA, Shepparton	PACIFIC & N AMERICA • 50 kW
		PACIFIC • 100 kW
	BRAZIL RADIO UNIVERSO, Curitiba	PORTUGUESE • DS • 10 kW
	CUBA †RADIO HABANA, Havana	C AMERICA • 50 kW
		Su • C AMERICA • 50 kW
	ITALY †RTV ITALIANA, Caltanissetta	ITALIAN • EUROPE, N AFRICA & MIDEAST • DS-1 • 50 kW
		M-Sa • EUROPE, N AFRICA & MIDEAST • DS-1 • 50 kW
		Su • EUROPE, N AFRICA & MIDEAST • DS-1 • 50 kW
	RTV ITALIANA, Rome	EUROPE, MIDEAST & N AFRICA • DS-ENG,FR,ITALIAN • 50 kW
	KOREA (REPUBLIC) †RADIO KOREA, In-Kimjae	E NORTH AM • 250 kW
		KOREAN • E NORTH AM • 250 kW
	MALAYSIA †RTM-SARAWAK, Miri	DS-IBAN • 10 kW
	NIGER †LA VOIX DU SAHEL, Niamey	DS-FRENCH, ETC • 4/20 kW
		Sa • DS-FRENCH, ETC • 4/20 kW
	PHILIPPINES †RADIO VERITAS ASIA, Palauig	(D) • E ASIA • 250 kW
	UNITED KINGDOM †BBC, Rampisham	(D) • WEST USSR • 500 kW
	†BBC, Via Maṣīrah, Oman	(D) • S ASIA • 100 kW
	†BBC, Via Zyyi, Cyprus	(D) • S ASIA • 250 kW
	USA VOA, Via Ismaning, GFR	(D) • WEST USSR • 100 kW
	VOA, Via Kaválla, Greece	(D) • MIDEAST & S ASIA • PERSIAN • 250 kW
	VOA, Via Wertachtal, GFR	E EUROPE • 500 kW
		(D) • E EUROPE • 500 kW
		(J) • E EUROPE • 500 kW
	VOA, Via Wooffertson, UK	E EUROPE & WEST USSR • 300 kW
		(D) • E EUROPE & WEST USSR • 300 kW
		(J) • E EUROPE & WEST USSR • 300 kW
	USSR RADIO MOSCOW, Chita	(D) • E ASIA • 250 kW
		(D) • JAPANESE • E ASIA • 250 kW
	ZAMBIA †RADIO ZAMBIA-ZBS, Lusaka	DS-ENGLISH, ETC • 10 kW
		F/Sa • DS-ENGLISH, ETC • 10 kW
6061v	**PERU** RADIO JSV, Huánuco	Tu-Sa • DS • 5 kW
		DS • 5 kW
		M-F • DS • 5 kW
6065	**CANADA** CANADIAN BC CORP, Sackville, NB	DS-NORTHERN • 100 kW
		M-F • DS-NORTHERN • 100 kW
		Sa/Su • DS-NORTHERN • 100 kW
	COLOMBIA RADIO SUPER, Bogotá	Irr • DS-SUPER • 5 kW
	INDIA ALL INDIA RADIO, Kohima	DS-ENGLISH, ETC • 2 kW
	PAKISTAN PAKISTAN BC CORP, Islamabad	S ASIA • 100 kW
	SOUTH AFRICA RADIO RSA, Meyerton	S AMERICA • 500 kW
	SWEDEN †RADIO SWEDEN, Hörby	EUROPE • 350 kW
		(J) M-F • SWEDISH • EUROPE • 350 kW
		(J) M-F • EUROPE • 350 kW
(con'd)		

World Time: 0 1 2 3 4 5 6 7 8 9 10 11 12 13 14 15 16 17 18 19 20 21 22 23 24

0 Prime Time-Americas 6 Prime Time-E Asia 12 Prime Time-S Asia 18 Prime Time-Europe 24

ENGLISH ▬ ARABIC ▭ CHINESE ▫▫▫ FRENCH ═ GERMAN ═ RUSSIAN ═ SPANISH ═ OTHER —

FREQUENCY	COUNTRY, STATION, LOCATION	TARGET • NETWORK • POWER (kW)
6065 (con'd)	SWEDEN	
	†RADIO SWEDEN, Hörby	(J) Sa/Su • EUROPE • 350 kW
	†RADIO SWEDEN, Karlsborg	EUROPE & W AFRICA • 350 kW
		SWEDISH • WEST USSR • 350 kW
		SWEDISH • EUROPE & W AFRICA • 350 kW
		(D) • EUROPE & W AFRICA • 350 kW
		(J) • EUROPE & W AFRICA • 350 kW
		M-F • SWEDISH • EUROPE • 350 kW
		M-F • EUROPE • 350 kW
		Sa/Su • EUROPE • 350 kW
	†SVERIGES RIKSRADIO, Hörby	(D) M-F • SWEDISH • EUROPE • DS-1 • 350 kW
		(J) M-F • SWEDISH • EUROPE • DS-1 • 350 kW
	†SVERIGES RIKSRADIO, Karlsborg	M-F • SWEDISH • EUROPE • DS-1 • 350 kW
		(D) • SWEDISH • EUROPE • DS-1 • 350 kW
		M-Sa • SWEDISH • EUROPE • DS-1 • 350 kW
		(J) • SWEDISH • EUROPE • DS-1 • 350 kW
		Su • SWEDISH • EUROPE • DS-1 • 350 kW
		SWEDISH • EUROPE • DS-1/DS-3 • 350 kW
		Sa/Su • SWEDISH • EUROPE • DS-1/DS-3 • 350 kW
	UNITED KINGDOM	
	†BBC, Various Locations	S ASIA • 100/250 kW
	†BBC, Via Singapore	SE ASIA • 250 kW
		(J) • S ASIA • 250 kW
		(D) M-F • S ASIA • 250 kW
		M-Sa • S ASIA • 250 kW
		Su • SE ASIA • 250 kW
	USA	
	WYFR-FAMILY RADIO, Okeechobee, Fl	C AMERICA • 50 kW
		W NORTH AM • 100 kW
	USSR	
	RADIO MOSCOW, Petropavlovsk-Kam	(J) • JAPANESE • WS, JAPANESE • 100 kW
		(J) • WS, JAPANESE • 100 kW
	RADIO YEREVAN, Armavir	MIDEAST • 100 kW
	RS SOV BELORUSSIA, Minsk	(D) • EUROPE • 100 kW
6070	BRAZIL	
	RADIO CAPITAL, Rio de Janeiro	Irr • PORTUGUESE • DS • 7.5 kW
	BULGARIA	
	†RADIO SOFIA, Sofia	(D) • EUROPE • 250 kW
	RADIO SOFIA, Stolnik	EUROPE, MIDEAST & N AFRICA • 150 kW
		M-Sa • EUROPE, MIDEAST & N AFRICA • 150 kW
		Su • EUROPE, MIDEAST & N AFRICA • 150 kW
	CANADA	
	CFRX-CFRB, Toronto, Ontario	DS • 1 kW
	CHINA (PR)	
	JILIN PEOPLES BS, Changchun	DS • 15 kW
		Su • DS • 15 kW
	INDONESIA	
	†RRI, Jayapura, Irian Jaya	DS • 20 kW
	LIBERIA	
	RADIO ELWA, Monrovia	W AFRICA • 50 kW
		Sa/Su • DS • 10 kW
	MARSHALL ISLANDS	
	†WSZO-R MARSHALLS, Majuro	Irr • PACIFIC • DS • 10 kW
		Irr • Su • PACIFIC • DS • 10 kW
		Irr • Su-F • PACIFIC • DS • 10 kW
		Irr • M-Sa • PACIFIC • DS-ENGLISH, ETC • 10 kW • ALT. FREQ. TO 4940 kHz
	SWAZILAND	
	†TRANS WORLD RADIO, Manzini	(D) • S AFRICA • 25 kW
	THAILAND	
	RADIO THAILAND, Pathum Thani	DS-1 • 10 kW
	UNITED KINGDOM	
	†BBC, Via Zyyi, Cyprus	(D) • WEST USSR • 100 kW
	USA	
	†RFE-RL, Via Germany	E EUROPE • 100 kW
	USSR	
	RADIO MOSCOW	(D) • E NORTH AM • N AMERICAN
	RADIO MOSCOW, Khabarovsk	(D) • W NORTH AM • N AMERICAN • 100 kW
	RADIO MOSCOW, Khar'kov	DS-2 • 100 kW
	RADIO MOSCOW, Novosibirsk	(D) • DS-1 • 100 kW
6070v	PAKISTAN	
	PAKISTAN BC CORP, Peshawar	(J) • DS-ENGLISH, ETC • 10 kW
	PAKISTAN BC CORP, Rawalpindi	(D) • DS-ENGLISH, ETC • 10 kW
6072v	COSTA RICA	
	RADIO RUMBO, Cartago	Irr • DS • 1 kW

World Time 0–24: 0 Prime Time-Americas 6 Prime Time-E Asia 12 Prime Time-S Asia 18 Prime Time-Europe 24

SUMMER ONLY (J) WINTER ONLY (D) JAMMING / OR /\ EARLIEST HEARD ◁ LATEST HEARD ▷ NEW OR CHANGED FOR 1990 †

FREQUENCY COUNTRY, STATION, LOCATION

6075 COLOMBIA
†CARACOL BOGOTA, Bogotá
ECUADOR
HCJB-VO THE ANDES, Quito
GERMANY (FR)
†DEUTSCHE WELLE, Multiple Locations
†DEUTSCHE WELLE, Via Montserrat
KENYA
VOICE OF KENYA, Koma Rock
SRI LANKA
SRI LANKA BC CORP, Colombo-Ekala
URUGUAY
†LA VOZ DE ARTIGAS, Artigas
USA
RADIO MARTI, Cincinnati, Ohio

6075v HONDURAS
†LA VOZ DEL JUNCO, Santa Barbara

6078.8 BOLIVIA
†RADIO SAN GABRIEL, La Paz

6080 ALBANIA
RADIO TIRANA, Lushnjë
AUSTRALIA
RADIO AUSTRALIA, Shepparton
BRAZIL
†RADIO ANHANGUERA
CANADA
CKFX-CKWX, Vancouver, BC
CHILE
RADIO PATAGONIA, Coihaique
CHINA (PR)
CENTRAL PEOPLES BS, Hailar
HULUNBEI'ER PBS, Hailar
†RADIO BEIJING, Via France
ECUADOR
HCJB-VO THE ANDES, Quito
GERMANY (DR)
R BERLIN INTL, Nauen
IRAN
†VO THE ISLAMIC REP, Tehrān
JAPAN
†RADIO JAPAN/NHK, Tokyo-Yamata
PAPUA NEW GUINEA
RADIO WESTERN, Daru
SEYCHELLES
FAR EAST BC ASS'N, North Pt, Mahé Is
UNITED KINGDOM
†BBC, Via Singapore
USA
VOA, Greenville, NC
VOA, Via Rhodes, Greece
VOA, Via Woofferton, UK
USSR
R TIKHIY OKEAN, Komsomol'sk 'Amure
RADIO MOSCOW, Komsomol'sk 'Amure
RADIO MOSCOW, Novosibirsk

6081v BOLIVIA
†R 21 DE DICIEMBRE, Catavi

6085 (con'd) AFGHANISTAN
†RADIO AFGHANISTAN, Kabul

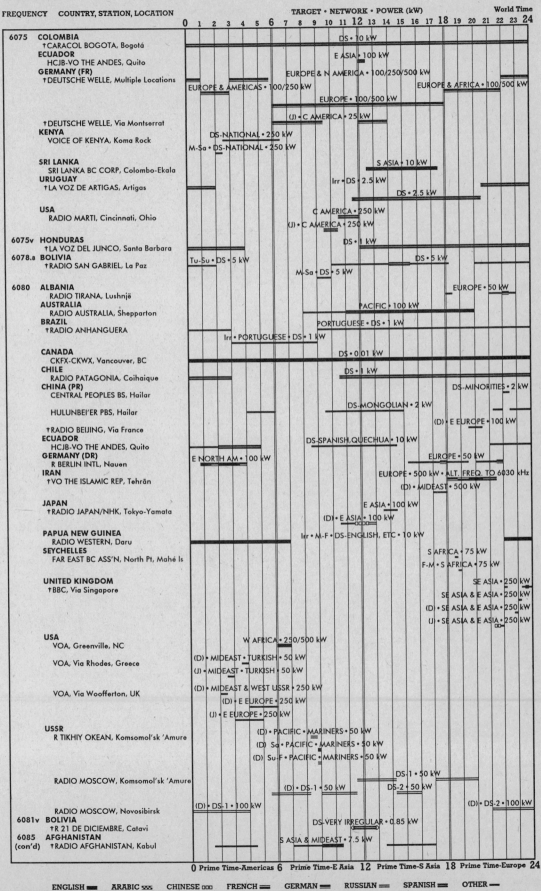

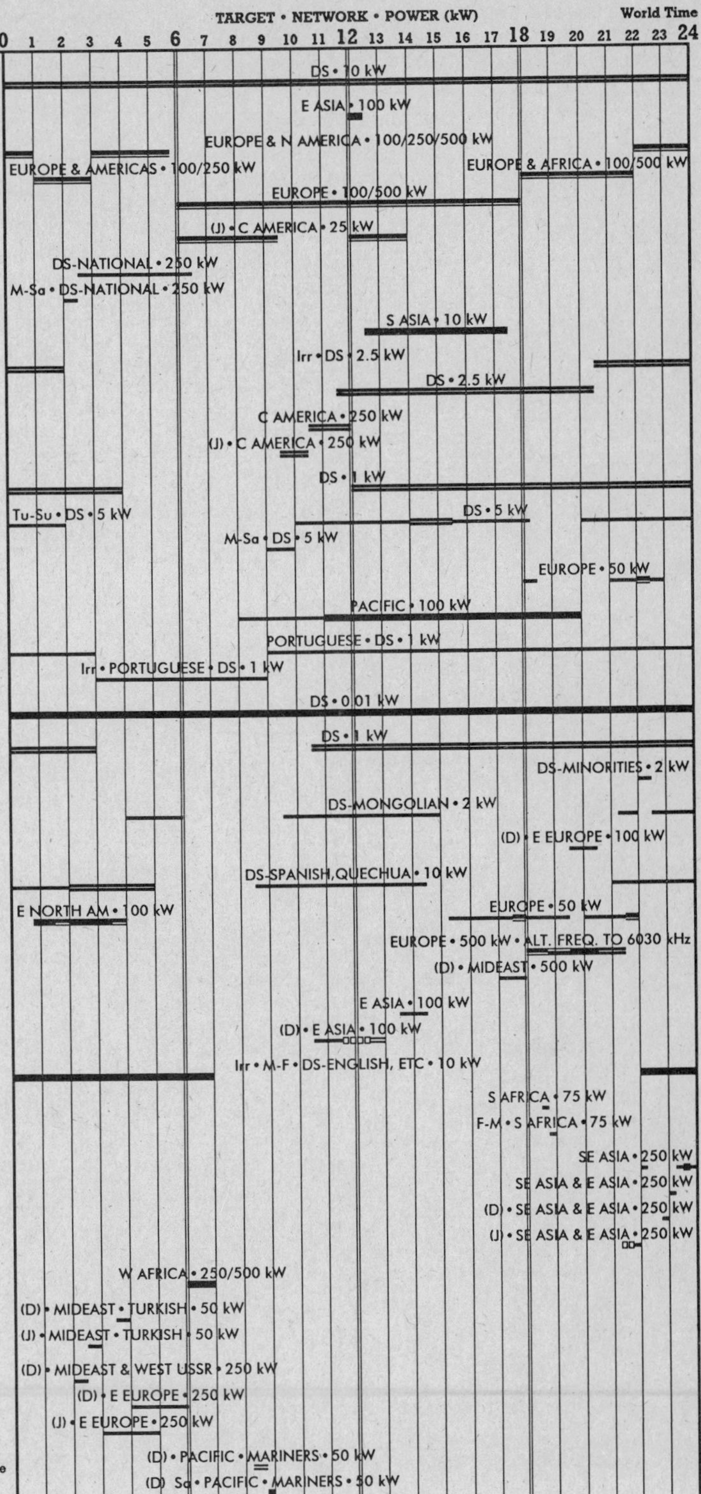

ENGLISH ▬ ARABIC ▭ CHINESE ▯▯▯ FRENCH ═ GERMAN ═ RUSSIAN ═ SPANISH ═ OTHER —

FREQUENCY	COUNTRY, STATION, LOCATION	TARGET • NETWORK • POWER (kW)
6085 (con'd)	**AFGHANISTAN** †RADIO AFGHANISTAN, Kabul	S ASIA & MIDEAST • DS-2 • 7.5 kW
	BULGARIA RADIO SOFIA, Stolnik	EUROPE, MIDEAST & N AFRICA • 150 kW
		M-Sa • EUROPE, MIDEAST & N AFRICA • 150 kW
		(D) • EUROPE, MIDEAST & N AFRICA • 150 kW
		Su • EUROPE, MIDEAST & N AFRICA • 150 kW
	GERMANY (FR) BAYERISCHER RFUNK, Ismaning	DS-1, ARD-NACHT • 100 kW
	†DEUTSCHE WELLE, Various Locations	N AMERICA • 250 kW
		(J) • N AMERICA • 250 kW
	†DEUTSCHE WELLE, Via Cyclops, Malta	(J) • E NORTH AM & C AMERICA • 250 kW
	OMAN RADIO OMAN, Sīb	MIDEAST & N AFRICA • DS • 100 kW
		(D) • MIDEAST & N AFRICA • DS • 100 kW
		Irr • MIDEAST & N AFRICA • DS-RAMADAN • 100 kW
	UNITED KINGDOM †BBC, Rampisham	(D) • WEST USSR • 500 kW
	†BBC, Via Zyyi, Cyprus	(D) • EUROPE • 100 kW
		(J) • EUROPE • 250 kW
		(J) • MIDEAST & WEST USSR • 250 kW
		(J) M-Sa • MIDEAST & WEST USSR • 250 kW
	USA VOA, Via Kaválla, Greece	(D) • USSR • 250 kW
	†WYFR-FAMILY RADIO, Okeechobee, Fl	C AMERICA • 50/100 kW
6087	**CHINA (TAIWAN)** CENTRAL BC SYSTEM, T'ai-pei	PRC-4 • 50 kW
6090	**ARGENTINA** RADIO BELGRANO, Buenos Aires	DS • 1 kW
	BRAZIL RADIO BANDEIRANTES, São Paulo	PORTUGUESE • DS • 10 kW
		Irr • PORTUGUESE • DS • 10 kW
	CAMBODIA †VO THE PEOPLE, Phnom Penh	DS • 50 kW
		Su • DS • 50 kW
	INDIA ALL INDIA RADIO, Delhi	SE ASIA • HINDI, TAMIL, ETC • 50 kW
	LIBERIA †LIBERIAN BC SYSTEM, Monrovia	DS-ENGLISH, ETC • 50 kW
		Th-Tu • DS-ENGLISH, ETC • 50 kW
	LUXEMBOURG RADIO LUXEMBOURG, Junglinster	EUROPE • 250/500 kW
		M-F • EUROPE • 250 kW
	USA VOA, Via Tangier, Morocco	(J) • N AFRICA • 100 kW
	VOA, Via Wertachtal, GFR	(J) • WEST USSR • 500 kW
	†VOA, Via Woofferton, UK	(D) • WEST USSR • 250 kW
		(D) • N AFRICA • 250 kW
	USSR IRKUTSK RADIO, Irkutsk	DS • 50 kW
	RADIO KIEV, Kiev	(D) • EUROPE • 100 kW
	RADIO MOSCOW, Orenburg	(D) • DS-1 • 100 kW
	RADIO MOSCOW, Simferopol	(D) • EUROPE • 240 kW
		(D) • EUROPE • WS • 240 kW
	RS SOV BELORUSSIA, Kiev	(D) M/Tu/Th/F • EUROPE • 100 kW
		(D) W/Sa/Su • EUROPE • 100 kW
6090v	**NIGERIA** RADIO NIGERIA, Kaduna	DS-1/ENGLISH, ETC • 250 kW
	PAKISTAN PAKISTAN BC CORP, Islamabad	DS-ENGLISH, ETC • 100 kW
6094.6	**BOLIVIA** †RADIO COSMOS, Cochabamba	DS • 1 kW
		M-Sa • DS • 1 kW
6095	**CHINA (PR)** CENTRAL PEOPLES BS, Nanchang	TAIWAN-2 • 50 kW
		Th-Tu • TAIWAN-2 • 50 kW
	POLAND †RADIO POLONIA, Warsaw	ATLANTIC & N AMERICA • 100 kW
		EUROPE • 100 kW
		EUROPE & N AFRICA • 100 kW
	SOMALIA RADIO MOGADISHU, Mogadishu	E AFRICA • 50 kW
	SWITZERLAND †RED CROSS BC SVC, Schwarzenburg	Irr • Tu/F • C AMERICA & S AMERICA • 150 kW
	†SWISS RADIO INTL, Schwarzenburg	C AMERICA & S AMERICA • 150 kW
(con'd)		M • C AMERICA & S AMERICA • 150 kW

World Time 0–24: 0 Prime Time-Americas 6 Prime Time-E Asia 12 Prime Time-S Asia 18 Prime Time-Europe 24

SUMMER ONLY (J) WINTER ONLY (D) JAMMING / OR ⋀ EARLIEST HEARD ◁ LATEST HEARD ▷ NEW OR CHANGED FOR 1990 †

FREQUENCY	COUNTRY, STATION, LOCATION	TARGET • NETWORK • POWER (kW)
6095 (con'd)	**SWITZERLAND** †SWISS RADIO INTL, Schwarzenburg	Tu-Su • C AMERICA & S AMERICA • 150 kW
	UNITED KINGDOM †BBC, Via Maşīrah, Oman	(J) • PERSIAN • MIDEAST & S ASIA • 100 kW
	USA †KNLS-NEW LIFE STN, Anchor Pt, Alaska	(D) • EAST USSR • 100 kW
	†RFE-RL, Via Germany	WEST USSR • 100 kW
	†RFE-RL, Via Portugal	WEST USSR • 50 kW
	†VOA, Delano, California	C AMERICA & S AMERICA • 250 kW
	VOA, Via Ismaning, GFR	(D) • WEST USSR • 100 kW
	†VOA, Via Kavália, Greece	(J) • E EUROPE • 250 kW
	†VOA, Via Rhodes, Greece	(J) • MIDEAST • 50 kW
	VOA, Via Tangier, Morocco	N AFRICA • 50/100 kW
	VOA, Via Woofferton, UK	(D) • E EUROPE • 300 kW
	USSR RADIO MOSCOW, Kalinin	(D) • DS-1 • 100 kW
	RADIO MOSCOW, Serpuhkov	(D) • DS • 100 kW
6095v	**ALBANIA** RADIO TIRANA, Krujë	Alternative Frequency to 6121v kHz
6100	**AFGHANISTAN** †RADIO KABUL, Kabul	DS • 100 kW
	ARGENTINA R PROV SANTA CRUZ, Rio Gallegos	Irr • DS • 0.5 kW
	CHINA (PR) XINJIANG PBS, Urümqi	DS-CHINESE • 50 kW
	CLANDESTINE (ASIA) †"VO AFGHANISTAN"	Irr • MIDEAST & S ASIA • ANTI-AFGHAN GOVT
	CLANDESTINE (M EAST) "VO THE CRUSADER", Via R Baghdad	MIDEAST • MOJAHEDIN-E KHALQ • 250 kW
	GERMANY (FR) DEUTSCHE WELLE, Multiple Locations	E NORTH AM & C AMERICA • 100/500 kW
	KENYA VOICE OF KENYA, Koma Rock	DS-GENERAL • 250 kW; Sa/Su • DS-GENERAL • 250 kW
	KOREA (DPR) KOREAN CENTRAL BS, Kanggye	DS • 100 kW
	MALAYSIA †RADIO MALAYSIA, Kajang	DS-VERNACULARS • 100 kW
	VOICE OF MALAYSIA, Kajang	SE ASIA • 100 kW
	NEW ZEALAND †RADIO NEW ZEALAND, Wellington	(J) • AUSTRALIA & SE ASIA • 7.5 kW
	NICARAGUA †LV DE NICARAGUA, Managua	Tu-Su • C AMERICA & N AMERICA • 50 kW; M-Sa • C AMERICA & N AMERICA • 50 kW
	USA VOA, Via Philippines	SE ASIA • 50 kW
	WORLD HARVEST R, Noblesville, Indiana	(D) • E NORTH AM & W EUROPE • 100 kW
	USSR †LITHUANIAN RADIO, Kaunas	DS-2 • 50 kW
	RADIO MOSCOW, Kaunas	EUROPE • DS-1 • 50 kW
	RADIO MOSCOW, Kenga	(D) • E ASIA • 100 kW
	RADIO VILNIUS, Kaunas	EUROPE • 50 kW
	VENEZUELA OBSERVATORIO NAVAL, Caracas	DS • 1 kW • ALT. FREQ. TO 5000 kHz
	YUGOSLAVIA †RADIO YUGOSLAVIA, Belgrade	EUROPE, N AFRICA & MIDEAST • 100 kW; F-W • EUROPE, N AFRICA & MIDEAST • 100 kW
6100.2	**CLANDESTINE (AFRICA)** †"RADIO SIBONEY", South Africa	S AFRICA • TO CUBAN TROOPS
6105	**BRAZIL** †R CANCAO NOVA, Cachoeira Paulista	PORTUGUESE • DS • 5 kW
	ROMANIA RADIO BUCHAREST, Bucharest	(D) • EUROPE • 250 kW
	UNITED KINGDOM †BBC, Via Zyyi, Cyprus	(D) • PERSIAN • MIDEAST & S ASIA • 250 kW; (D) • WEST USSR • 250 kW
	USA †RFE-RL, Via Germany	E EUROPE & WEST USSR • 20/100 kW; M-Sa • E EUROPE • 100 kW
	VOA, Via Kavália, Greece	(D) • WEST USSR • 250 kW
	†VOA, Via Woofferton, UK	(J) • WEST USSR • 250 kW
	WYFR-FAMILY RADIO, Okeechobee, Fl	S AMERICA • 100 kW
	USSR RADIO MOSCOW, Kalinin	DS-1 • 120 kW; (D) • DS-1 • 120 kW
	RADIO MOSCOW, L'vov	(D) • E NORTH AM & C AMERICA • 500 kW

World Time 0–24: 0 Prime Time-Americas 6 Prime Time-E Asia 12 Prime Time-S Asia 18 Prime Time-Europe 24

ENGLISH ▬ ARABIC ▭ CHINESE ▫▫▫ FRENCH ═ GERMAN ▬ RUSSIAN ═ SPANISH ▬ OTHER —

FREQUENCY	COUNTRY, STATION, LOCATION	TARGET • NETWORK • POWER (kW)
6105v	**BRAZIL** †RADIO CULTURA, Foz do Iguaçú	PORTUGUESE • DS • 5 kW; M-Sa • PORTUGUESE • DS • 5 kW; Irr • PORTUGUESE • DS • 5 kW
	COSTA RICA †RADIO UNIVERSIDAD, San José	Irr • DS • 2 kW
	MEXICO †RADIO XEQM, Mérida	Irr • DS • 0.25 kW
6105.5	**BOLIVIA** †RADIO PANAMERICANA, La Paz	Tu-Sa • DS • 10 kW; DS • 10 kW; M-Sa • DS • 10 kW
6110	**ECUADOR** HCJB-VO THE ANDES, Quito	S AMERICA • 100 kW
	HUNGARY RADIO BUDAPEST, Various Locations	E NORTH AM; EUROPE; M • S AMERICA; Sa • EUROPE; S AMERICA; M • E NORTH AM; Tu/F • EUROPE; Su-Tu/Th/F • E NORTH AM; W/Th/Sa-M • S AMERICA; Tu-Su • S AMERICA; Tu-Su • E NORTH AM; Tu/W/F/Sa • E NORTH AM; Tu/W/F/Sa • S AMERICA; W/Sa • E NORTH AM
	INDIA ALL INDIA RADIO, Aligarh	S ASIA & E ASIA • 250 kW
	RADIO KASHMIR, Srinagar	Su • DS-B • 7.5 kW; DS-B/ENGLISH, ETC • 7.5 kW
	MALTA R MEDITERRANEAN, Cyclops	EUROPE • 250 kW
	UNITED KINGDOM †BBC, Rampisham	(D) • W EUROPE & N AFRICA • 500 kW
	†BBC, Via Antigua	(D) • C AMERICA • 125 kW
	†BBC, Via Ascension	S AMERICA • 250 kW
	USA VOA, Via Philippines	S ASIA & SE ASIA • 250 kW; E ASIA • 250 kW
	USSR RADIO BAKU, Baku	MIDEAST • ARABIC, PERSIAN, ETC • 200 kW
	RADIO MOSCOW, Baku	MIDEAST • DS-2 • 200 kW
	RADIO MOSCOW, Novosibirsk	(D) • E ASIA • 100 kW
6112v	**MOZAMBIQUE** †RADIO MOCAMBIQUE, Maputo	PORTUGUESE • DS • 100 kW
6115	**CHINA (PR)** †VO THE STRAIT-PLA, Fuzhou	(J) • TAIWAN-1 • 10/50 kW
	GERMANY (DR) †R BERLIN INTL, Königswusterhausen	EUROPE • 50 kW
	STIMME DER DDR, Königswusterhausen	DS • 50 kW
	INDIA ALL INDIA RADIO, Delhi	MIDEAST • 100 kW
	ALL INDIA RADIO, Madras	DS-VIVIDH BHARATI • 100 kW
	JAPAN RADIO TANPA, Tokyo-Nagara	JAPANESE • DS-2 • 50 kW
	MEXICO †RADIO UNIVERSIDAD, Hermosillo	Irr • DS • 1 kW
	PERU †RADIO UNION, Lima	DS • 10 kW; M-Sa • DS • 10 kW; Su • DS • 10 kW
	USA †RFE-RL, Via Germany	E EUROPE • 100 kW
	†RFE-RL, Via Portugal	E EUROPE & WEST USSR • 250 kW; M-Sa • E EUROPE • 250 kW; Su • WEST USSR • 250 kW
	USSR R TIKHIY OKEAN, Khabarovsk	EAST USSR & PACIFIC • MARINERS • 50 kW
	RADIO MOSCOW, Khabarovsk	EAST USSR & PACIFIC • DS-1/MARINERS • 50 kW
	RADIO MOSCOW, Simferopol'	DS-2 • 100 kW
6115v	**CONGO** RTV CONGOLAISE, Brazzaville	Irr • DS-FRENCH, ETC • 50 kW; Irr • DS • 50 kW
6116	**COLOMBIA** †LA VOZ DEL LLANO, Villavicencio	DS • 2/10 kW
6120	**BRAZIL** RADIO GLOBO, São Paulo	PORTUGUESE • DS • 7.5 kW
	CANADA R CANADA INTL, Sackville, NB	Su/M • E NORTH AM • 250 kW
(con'd)	**FINLAND** †RADIO FINLAND, Pori	EUROPE • 100 kW

World Time: 0 Prime Time-Americas 6 Prime Time-E Asia 12 Prime Time-S Asia 18 Prime Time-Europe 24

SUMMER ONLY (J) WINTER ONLY (D) JAMMING / OR /\ EARLIEST HEARD ◁ LATEST HEARD ▷ NEW OR CHANGED FOR 1990 †

FREQUENCY	COUNTRY, STATION, LOCATION	TARGET • NETWORK • POWER (kW)
6120 (con'd)	**GERMANY (FR)** DEUTSCHE WELLE, Jülich	(D) • N AMERICA • 100 kW
	INDIA †ALL INDIA RADIO, Delhi	(D) • SE ASIA • 50 kW
	ALL INDIA RADIO, Hyderabad	Su • DS • 10 kW
		DS-ENGLISH, ETC • 10 kW
	JAPAN RADIO JAPAN/NHK, Via Sackville, Can	N AMERICA • GENERAL • 250 kW
		(D) • JAPANESE • N AMERICA • GENERAL • 250 kW
		(J) • JAPANESE • N AMERICA • GENERAL • 250 kW
	PHILIPPINES FAR EAST BC CO, Iba	(D) • USSR • 100 kW
	TURKEY †TURKISH RTV CORP, Ankara	(D) • WEST USSR • 250 kW
		(J) • WEST USSR • 250 kW
	UNITED KINGDOM †BBC, Via Zyyi, Cyprus	(D) • MIDEAST & E AFRICA • 250 kW
	USSR RADIO MOSCOW, Moscow	(D) • E EUROPE & W AFRICA • 250 kW
6120v	**LIBYA** †RADIO JAMAHIRIYA, Tripoli	EUROPE • 500 kW • ALT. FREQ. TO 15415v kHz
	NICARAGUA †RADIO ZINICA, Bluefields	Irr • DS • 2 kW
6121v	**ALBANIA** RADIO TIRANA, Krujë	S AMERICA • 100 kW • ALT. FREQ. TO 6095v kHz
6125	**AFGHANISTAN** †RADIO KABUL, Kabul	DS • 100 kW
	ALBANIA RADIO TIRANA, Lushnjë	EUROPE • GREEK • 50 kW
	CHINA (PR) CENTRAL PEOPLES BS, Shijiazhuang	DS-1 • 50 kW
	UNITED KINGDOM †BBC, Daventry	(J) • EUROPE & N AFRICA • 300 kW
		(J) • E EUROPE • 300 kW
		(J) Su • EUROPE & N AFRICA • 300 kW
		(J) Su • E EUROPE • 300 kW
	†BBC, Rampisham	(D) • E EUROPE • 500 kW
		(D) Su • E EUROPE • 500 kW
	†BBC, Skelton, Cumbria	(D) • EUROPE & N AFRICA • 250 kW
		(D) Su • EUROPE & N AFRICA • 250 kW
	†BBC, Various Locations	E EUROPE • 300/500 kW
	USA VOA, Cincinnati, Ohio	N AFRICA • 250 kW
	VOA, Via Wertachtal, GFR	(J) • WEST USSR • 500 kW
	†VOA, Via Woofferton, UK	N AFRICA • 250 kW
		(D) • WEST USSR • 250 kW
		(J) • E EUROPE & MIDEAST • 250 kW
	USSR RADIO MOSCOW, Ashkhabad	(D) • DS-1 • 100 kW
	RADIO MOSCOW, Ul'yanovsk	(D) • DS-1 • 100 kW
6127	**INDONESIA** †RRI, Nabire, Irian Jaya	DS • 0.5 kW
6130	**CANADA** CHNX-CHNS, Halifax, NS	DS • 0.5 kW
	ECUADOR †HCJB-VO THE ANDES, Quito	PACIFIC • 250 kW
		(D) • PACIFIC • 250 kW
	GERMANY (FR) †DEUTSCHE WELLE, Jülich	(D) • N AMERICA • 100 kW
		(J) • N AMERICA • 100 kW
	†DEUTSCHE WELLE, Wertachtal	(D) • WEST USSR • 500 kW
		(D) • E EUROPE • 500 kW
		(J) • E EUROPE • 500 kW
		(D) • W EUROPE • 500 kW
		(J) • W EUROPE • 500 kW
	GHANA RADIO GHANA, Accra	W AFRICA • 100 kW
	INDIA ALL INDIA RADIO, Gauhati	DS-B • 10 kW
		Su • DS-B • 10 kW
	JAPAN †NHK, Fukuoka	Irr • JAPANESE • DS-1(FEEDER) • 0.6 kW • USB
	PORTUGAL R PORTUGAL INTL, Lisbon-S Gabriel	M-F • EUROPE • 100 kW
	SOUTH AFRICA †RADIO RSA, Meyerton	S AFRICA • 250/500 kW
	USA KUSW, Salt Lake City, Utah	(D) Su • E NORTH AM • 100 kW
	VOA, Greenville, NC	C AMERICA & S AMERICA • 250 kW
(con'd)	†VOA, Via Philippines	(D) • E ASIA • 250 kW

World Time 0–24: 0 Prime Time-Americas 6 Prime Time-E Asia 12 Prime Time-S Asia 18 Prime Time-Europe 24

ENGLISH ▬ ARABIC ▭ CHINESE ▫▫▫ FRENCH ═ GERMAN ▬ RUSSIAN ═ SPANISH ═ OTHER —

FREQUENCY	COUNTRY, STATION, LOCATION	TARGET • NETWORK • POWER (kW)
6130 (con'd)	**USSR**	
	RADIO MOSCOW, Moscow	EUROPE • 240 kW
	RADIO MOSCOW, Novosibirsk	(D) • DS-2 • 100 kW
	RADIO MOSCOW, Star'obel'sk	(J) • EUROPE • 100 kW
	RADIO MOSCOW, Vladivostok	(D) • W NORTH AM • N AMERICAN, WS • 240 kW
6130v	**LAOS**	
	LAO NATIONAL RADIO, Vientiane	DS • 10 kW
	PAKISTAN	
	PAKISTAN BC CORP, Islamabad	(D) • DS • 100 kW
		DS-ENGLISH, ETC • 100 kW
	PAKISTAN BC CORP, Rawalpindi	Th-Sa • DS • 10 kW
		DS-ENGLISH, ETC • 10 kW
	VENEZUELA	
	R VALLES DEL TUY, Ocumare Del Tuy	Irr • DS/VERY IRR • 1 kW
6135	**BRAZIL**	
	RADIO APARECIDA, Aparecida	PORTUGUESE • DS • 7.5 kW
	CHILE	
	RADIO UNIVERSIDAD, Concepción	DS • 10 kW
	KOREA (REPUBLIC)	
	KOREAN BC SYSTEM, Suwon	KOREAN • E ASIA • EDUCATIONAL-2 • 100 kW
	RADIO KOREA, Suwon	KOREAN • E ASIA • 100 kW
		JAPANESE • E ASIA • 100 kW
		E ASIA • 100 kW
	MADAGASCAR	
	R MADAGASIKARA, Antananarivo	DS-FRENCH, ETC • 100 kW
	POLAND	
	†RADIO POLONIA, Warsaw	W AFRICA & ATLANTIC • 100 kW
		EUROPE • 100 kW
		W EUROPE & N AFRICA • 100 kW
		(D) • EUROPE • 100 kW
	SWITZERLAND	
	RED CROSS BC SVC, Schwarzenburg	Irr • Tu/F • N AMERICA & C AMERICA • 150 kW
	SWISS RADIO INTL, Schwarzenburg	N AMERICA & C AMERICA • 150 kW
		M • N AMERICA & C AMERICA • 150 kW
		Tu-Su • N AMERICA & C AMERICA • 150 kW
	UNITED KINGDOM	
	†BBC, Skelton, Cumbria	(J) • E EUROPE & WEST USSR • 250 kW
	USA	
	†KUSW, Salt Lake City,Utah	Su • E NORTH AM • 100 kW
	†RFE-RL, Via Germany	E EUROPE & WEST USSR • 100 kW
	†RFE-RL, Via Pals, Spain	WEST USSR • 250 kW
	USSR	
	†AZERBAIJANI RADIO, Baku	DS-2 • 100 kW
	†RADIO ALMA-ATA, Alma-Ata	(D) • E ASIA • 100 kW
	RADIO BAKU, Baku	MIDEAST • ARABIC,PERSIAN,ETC • 100 kW
	†RADIO TASHKENT, Alma-Ata	(D) • E ASIA • 100 kW
	YEMEN (REPUBLIC)	
	"VO PALESTINE", Via Radio San'ā	E AFRICA • PLO • 50 kW
	RADIO SAN'A, San'ā	E AFRICA • DS • 50 kW
		F • E AFRICA • DS • 50 kW
6135v	**BOLIVIA**	
	†RADIO SANTA CRUZ, Santa Cruz	DS-SPANISH, ETC • 10 kW
		Irr • DS • 10 kW
		M-Sa • DS-SPANISH, ETC • 10 kW
	SOCIETY ISLANDS	
	†RFO-TAHITI, Papeete	DS-FRENCH,TAHITIAN • 4 kW
6140	**AUSTRALIA**	
	AUSTRALIAN BC CORP, Perth	DS • 10 kW
	BURUNDI	
	†LA VOIX DE LA REV, Gitega	DS • 100 kW
		Su • DS • 100 kW
		Su • DS-FRENCH, ETC • 100 kW
		M-F • DS • 100 kW
		Sa/Su • DS • 100 kW
		DS-FRENCH, ETC • 100 kW
		M-F • DS-FRENCH, ETC • 100 kW
		M-Sa • DS-FRENCH, ETC • 100 kW
		Sa/Su • DS-FRENCH, ETC • 100 kW
	CANADA	
	†R CANADA INTL, Sackville, NB	(D) M-F • EUROPE • 250 kW
		(D) • EUROPE • 250 kW
		(J) M-F • EUROPE • 250 kW
	R CANADA INTL, Via United Kingdom	(D) • EUROPE & WEST USSR • 300 kW
	CHINA (PR)	
	RADIO BEIJING, Baoding	EAST USSR • 120 kW
	RADIO BEIJING, Kunming	SE ASIA • 50 kW
	COSTA RICA	
(con'd)	†RADIO IMPACTO, San José	Alternative Frequency to 6150 kHz

World Time: 0 Prime Time-Americas 6 Prime Time-E Asia 12 Prime Time-S Asia 18 Prime Time-Europe 24

SUMMER ONLY (J) WINTER ONLY (D) JAMMING / OR ⋀ EARLIEST HEARD ◁ LATEST HEARD ▷ NEW OR CHANGED FOR 1990 †

FREQUENCY	COUNTRY, STATION, LOCATION	TARGET • NETWORK • POWER (kW)
6140 (con'd)	CUBA †RADIO HABANA, Havana	(D) • N AMERICA • 50 kW
	GERMANY (FR) †DEUTSCHE WELLE, Wertachtal	E EUROPE & MIDEAST • 500 kW
	INDIA †ALL INDIA RADIO, Delhi	S ASIA • 100 kW
	ALL INDIA RADIO, Ranchi	DS • 10 kW
		Su • DS • 10 kW
	PAPUA NEW GUINEA RADIO EAST SEPIK, Wewak	Irr • M-F • DS-ENGLISH, ETC • 10 kW
	PERU RADIO HUAYLLAY, Huayllay	DS • 1 kW
		M-Sa • DS • 1 kW
	SOUTH AFRICA RADIO RSA, Meyerton	(J) • S AMERICA • 250 kW
	TURKEY †TURKISH RTV CORP, Ankara	(J) • TURKISH • E EUROPE • 250 kW
	UNITED KINGDOM †BBC, Rampisham	(D) • WEST USSR • 500 kW
		(D) • E EUROPE & MIDEAST • 500 kW
		(D) M-F • E EUROPE & MIDEAST • 500 kW
		(D) M-Sa • E EUROPE & MIDEAST • 500 kW
	URUGUAY RADIO MONTE CARLO, Montevideo	DS • 1.5 kW
	USA †RFE-RL, Via Pals, Spain	WEST USSR • 250 kW
	VOA, Via Kaválla, Greece	(D) • USSR • 250 kW
	VOA, Via Woofferton, UK	(D) • USSR • 250 kW
		(J) • USSR • 300 kW
	USSR RADIO MOSCOW, Voronej	DS-1 • 100 kW
	RADIO MOSCOW, Zhigulevsk	(D) • EUROPE • WS, SWEDISH, ETC • 100 kW
6140.7	BOLIVIA †R LUIS DE FUENTES, Tarija	Irr • DS • 1 kW
6145	ALGERIA "VO PALESTINE", Via RTV Algerienne	N AFRICA & MIDEAST • PLO • 50 kW
	RTV ALGERIENNE, Algiers	N AFRICA & MIDEAST • DS • 50 kW
	CLANDESTINE (M EAST) "VO THE CRUSADER", Via R Baghdad	MIDEAST • MOJAHEDIN-E KHALQ
	GERMANY (FR) †DEUTSCHE WELLE, Jülich	(D) • N AFRICA & MIDEAST • 100 kW
	†DEUTSCHE WELLE, Multiple Locations	C AMERICA & S AMERICA • 100/250/500 kW
		N AMERICA • 100/500 kW
	DEUTSCHE WELLE, Wertachtal	(D) • N AMERICA • 500 kW
	NIGERIA CROSS RIVER RADIO, Calabar	DS-ENGLISH, ETC • 10 kW
	PHILIPPINES FAR EAST BC CO, Bocaue	(D) • E ASIA • 50 kW
	USA VOA, Via Kaválla, Greece	(D) • S ASIA • 250 kW
	USSR RADIO MOSCOW, Moscow	(D) • C AMERICA • 100 kW
		(D) • EUROPE • 100 kW
		(D) • EUROPE • WS • 100 kW
	VATICAN STATE †VATICAN RADIO, Sta Maria di Galeria	(D) • S ASIA • 100 kW
6148v	THAILAND ROYAL PALACE STN, Bangkok	Irr • Tu-Sa • DS
6150	BRAZIL RADIO RECORD, São Paulo	Irr • PORTUGUESE • DS • 7.5 kW
		PORTUGUESE • DS • 7.5 kW
	CANADA †R CANADA INTL, Via Tokyo, Japan	(D) • E ASIA • 300 kW
		(J) • E ASIA • 300 kW
	†R CANADA INTL, Via Xi'an, China(PR)	(D) • JAPANESE • E ASIA • 120 kW
	CHINA (PR) HEILONGJIANG PBS, Qiqihar	DS-CHINESE, KOREAN • 50 kW
	CLANDESTINE (S AMER) †"REV ARMED FORCES", Colombia	Su • S AMERICA • USB
	COSTA RICA †RADIO IMPACTO, San José	DS • 20 kW • ALT. FREQ. TO 6140 kHz
		M-Sa • DS • 20 kW • ALT. FREQ. TO 6140 kHz
	DENMARK †DANMARKS RADIO, Copenhagen	(D) • E ASIA • 50 kW
	FRANCE R FRANCE INTL, Issoudun-Allouis	EUROPE • 500 kW
	KENYA VOICE OF KENYA, Koma Rock	DS-NATIONAL • 250 kW
		Sa/Su • DS-NATIONAL • 250 kW
(con'd)	PERU RADIO CONCORDIA, Arequipa	DS • 1 kW

World Time: 0 1 2 3 4 5 6 7 8 9 10 11 12 13 14 15 16 17 18 19 20 21 22 23 24

0 Prime Time-Americas 6 Prime Time-E Asia 12 Prime Time-S Asia 18 Prime Time-Europe 24

ENGLISH ▬ ARABIC ▭ CHINESE ▫▫▫ FRENCH ═ GERMAN ▬ RUSSIAN ═ SPANISH ═ OTHER —

FREQUENCY	COUNTRY, STATION, LOCATION	TARGET • NETWORK • POWER (kW)
6150 (con'd)	**ROMANIA** RADIO BUCHAREST, Bucharest	(D) • EUROPE • 250 kW
	UNITED KINGDOM †BBC, Rampisham	E EUROPE • 500 kW
		(J) • E EUROPE & WEST USSR • 500 kW
		M-F • E EUROPE • 500 kW
		M-Sa • E EUROPE • 500 kW
		Su • E EUROPE • 500 kW
	USA VOA, Via Kavála, Greece	(D) • MIDEAST & S ASIA • HINDI,PERSIAN,ETC • 250 kW
	VOA, Via Tangier,Morocco	N AFRICA • 100 kW
		(J) • WEST USSR • 100 kW
	†VOA, Via Woofferton, UK	(D) • WEST USSR • 300 kW
		(D) • E EUROPE • 300 kW
		(J) • E EUROPE • 300 kW
	†WSHB, Cypress Creek, SC	(D) • E NORTH AM • 500 kW
		(D) M-F • E NORTH AM • 500 kW
		(D) Sa/Su • E NORTH AM • 500 kW
	VATICAN STATE VATICAN RADIO, Sta Maria di Galeria	N AMERICA & C AMERICA • 500 kW
		N AMERICA • 100 kW
	YUGOSLAVIA †RADIO YUGOSLAVIA, Bijeljina	EUROPE • 250 kW
6150v	**CYPRUS** RADIO BAYRAK, Yeni Iskele	DS-2/6145-6165KHZV • 7.5 kW
		Th-Tu • DS-2/6145-6165KHZV • 7.5 kW
		W • DS-2/6145-6165KHZV • 7.5 kW
6150.2	**COLOMBIA** †CARACOL NEIVA, Neiva	DS-CARACOL
6154v	**ANGOLA** ER DE BENGUELA, Benguela	DS • 1 kW
6154.8	**PERU** RADIO PUCALLPA, Pucallpa	DS • 1 kW
		M-Sa • DS • 1 kW
6155	**AUSTRIA** †RADIO AUSTRIA INTL, Vienna	EUROPE • 300 kW
		M-Sa • EUROPE • 300 kW
		Su • EUROPE • 300 kW
	BOLIVIA †RADIO FIDES, La Paz	Su • DS • 10 kW
		DS • 10 kW
		Tu-Su • DS • 10 kW
		M-Sa • DS • 10 kW
		Irr • DS • 10 kW
	CHINA (PR) GANSU PEOPLES BS, Lanzhou	DS-1 • 15 kW
	INDIA †ALL INDIA RADIO, Delhi	S ASIA • URDU • 100 kW
		(D) • S ASIA • 100 kW
		DS-ENGLISH, ETC • 100 kW
	ROMANIA †RADIO BUCHAREST, Bucharest	(D) • AMERICAS • 250 kW
	SINGAPORE SINGAPORE BC CORP, Jurong	SE ASIA & PACIFIC • DS-MALAY • 50 kW
	TOGO RADIO KARA, Lama-Kara	DS-FRENCH, ETC • 10 kW
		Sa/Su • DS-FRENCH, ETC • 10 kW
	UNITED KINGDOM †BBC, Via Ascension	(D) • C AFRICA • 250 kW
		(D) • W AFRICA • 250 kW
	†BBC, Via Delano, USA	(D) • C AMERICA • 250 kW
	USA KUSW, Salt Lake City,Utah	(J) Su • E NORTH AM • 100 kW
		(J) Tu-Su • E NORTH AM • 100 kW
	USSR RADIO MOSCOW, Nikolayevsk 'Amure	DS-2 • 50 kW
6155.2	**BOLIVIA** RADIO FIDES, La Paz	Tu-Su • DS • 10 kW
	SWAZILAND SWAZI COMMERCIAL R, Sandlane	M-F • S AFRICA • PARALELO 27 • 10 kW
		S AFRICA • 10 kW
		M-F • S AFRICA • 10 kW
		Sa/Su • S AFRICA • PARALELO 27 • 10 kW
6160	**ALGERIA** "VO PALESTINE", Via RTV Algerienne	EUROPE & N AFRICA • PLO • 50 kW
	RTV ALGERIENNE, Ouled Fayet	EUROPE & N AFRICA • DS-1 • 50 kW
	BRAZIL †R NOVA ESPERANCA, Pôrto Alegre	PORTUGUESE • DS • 10 kW
	†RADIO RIO MAR, Manaus	PORTUGUESE • DS • 10 kW
		Sa • DS • 10 kW
		Su-F • DS • 10 kW
(con'd)	**BULGARIA** †RADIO SOFIA, Sofia	EUROPE & MIDEAST • 250 kW

World Time: 0 1 2 3 4 5 6 7 8 9 10 11 12 13 14 15 16 17 18 19 20 21 22 23 24

0 Prime Time-Americas 6 Prime Time-E Asia 12 Prime Time-S Asia 18 Prime Time-Europe 24

SUMMER ONLY (J) WINTER ONLY (D) JAMMING / OR /\ EARLIEST HEARD ◁ LATEST HEARD ▷ NEW OR CHANGED FOR 1990 †

FREQUENCY	COUNTRY, STATION, LOCATION	TARGET • NETWORK • POWER (kW)
6160 (con'd)	**CANADA**	
	CKZN-CBN, St John's, Nfld	DS • 0.3 kW
	CKZU-CBU, Vancouver, BC	DS • 0.5 kW
		M-Sa • DS • 0.5 kW
	GERMANY (FR)	
	DEUTSCHE WELLE, Via Antigua	AUSTRALIA & SE ASIA • 250 kW
	PHILIPPINES	
	RADIO VERITAS ASIA, Palauig	SE ASIA • 250 kW
		E ASIA • 250 kW
	USA	
	VOA, Via Kaválla, Greece	N AFRICA & W AFRICA • 250 kW
		(D) • WEST USSR • 250 kW
		(J) • WEST USSR • 250 kW
	†VOA, Via Wertachtal, GFR	(D) • WEST USSR • 500 kW
	†VOA, Via Woofferton, UK	(D) • E EUROPE & WEST USSR • 300 kW
		(J) • E EUROPE & WEST USSR • 300 kW
	USSR	
	RADIO MOSCOW, Kazan'	(D) • DS-2 • 100 kW
6160.3	**COLOMBIA**	
	RCN BOGOTA, Bogotá	Irr • DS-RCN • 10 kW
6160.4	**ARGENTINA**	
	†RADIO MALARGUE, Malargüé	DS • 0.3 kW
6165	**CHINA (PR)**	
	RADIO BEIJING, Kunming	SE ASIA • 50 kW
	RADIO BEIJING, Via Switzerland	EUROPE • 250 kW
	CUBA	
	RADIO HABANA, Via USSR	(D) • W EUROPE & ATLANTIC • 100 kW • ALT. FREQ. TO 7150 kHz
	GERMANY (DR)	
	†R BERLIN INTL, Königswusterhausen	(D) • C AMERICA • 100 kW
	HOLLAND	
	†RADIO NEDERLAND, Via Neth Antilles	E NORTH AM • 300 kW
		C AMERICA & S AMERICA • 300 kW
		W NORTH AM • 300 kW
		C AMERICA • 300 kW
	ITALY	
	†RTV ITALIANA, Rome	(D) • E EUROPE & WEST USSR • 100 kW
		(D) • EUROPE, N AFRICA & MIDEAST • 100 kW
	KOREA (REPUBLIC)	
	RADIO KOREA, In-Kimjae	JAPANESE • E ASIA • 100 kW
		E ASIA • 100 kW
	MEXICO	
	LV AMERICA LATINA, México City	Irr • DS • 0.5/10 kW
	SWITZERLAND	
	†SWISS RADIO INTL, Various Locations	EUROPE & N AFRICA • 250 kW
		M-Sa • EUROPE & N AFRICA • 250 kW
		Su • EUROPE & N AFRICA • 250 kW
	USA	
	†VOA, Greenville, NC	C AMERICA • 250 kW
	USSR	
	RADIO KIEV, Kiev	(D) • EUROPE • 100 kW
	RADIO MOSCOW, Vladivostok	(D) • E ASIA • 100 kW
	RS SOV BELORUSSIA, Kiev	(D) M/Tu/Th/F • EUROPE • 100 kW
		(D) W/Sa/Su • EUROPE • 100 kW
	ZAMBIA	
	†RADIO ZAMBIA-ZBS, Lusaka	DS-ENGLISH, ETC • 50 kW
		F/Sa • DS-ENGLISH, ETC • 50 kW
6170	**ALBANIA**	
	RADIO TIRANA, Lushnjë	EUROPE • FRENCH, ALBANIAN • 50/100 kW
	BRAZIL	
	RADIO CULTURA, São Paulo	PORTUGUESE • DS • 7.5 kW
	CHINA (PR)	
	†VO THE STRAIT-PLA, Fuzhou	(J) • TAIWAN-1 • 10/50 kW
	COLOMBIA	
	LA VOZ DE LA SELVA, Florencia	DS • 2 kW
	FRENCH GUIANA	
	RFO-GUYANE, Cayenne	DS • 4 kW
	GERMANY (FR)	
	†DEUTSCHE WELLE, Via Sri Lanka	S ASIA & SE ASIA • 250 kW
	DEUTSCHE WELLE, Wertachtal	(J) • E EUROPE • 500 kW
	INDIA	
	†ALL INDIA RADIO, Delhi	S ASIA • 50/100 kW
	UNITED ARAB EMIRATES	
	†VOICE OF THE UAE, Abu Dhabi	(D) • E NORTH AM • 500 kW
	USA	
	†RFE-RL, Via Germany	WEST USSR • 20/100 kW
	†RFE-RL, Via Portugal	WEST USSR • 50 kW
	USSR	
	RADIO MOSCOW, Armavir	DS-1 • 100 kW
6174 (con'd)	**PERU**	
	†RADIO TAWANTINSUYO, Cuzco	DS-SPANISH, QUECHUA • 5 kW

World Time: 0 Prime Time-Americas 6 Prime Time-E Asia 12 Prime Time-S Asia 18 Prime Time-Europe 24

ENGLISH ARABIC CHINESE FRENCH GERMAN RUSSIAN SPANISH OTHER

FREQUENCY	COUNTRY, STATION, LOCATION	TARGET • NETWORK • POWER (kW)
6174 (con'd)	**PERU** †RADIO TAWANTINSUYO, Cuzco	Irr • DS • 5 kW
6175	**CLANDESTINE (M EAST)** "VO THE CRUSADER", Via R Baghdad	MIDEAST • MOJAHEDIN-E KHALQ
	COSTA RICA †FARO DEL CARIBE, San José	DS • 2.5 kW
	FRANCE R FRANCE INTL, Issoudun-Allouis	EUROPE & N AFRICA • 100 kW
	JAPAN †NHK, Tokyo-Shobu	Irr • JAPANESE • DS-1(FEEDER) • 0.9 kW • USB
	MALAYSIA VOICE OF MALAYSIA, Kajang	SE ASIA • 50 kW
	PAKISTAN RADIO PAKISTAN, Islamabad	MIDEAST • 100 kW
	UNITED KINGDOM †BBC, Via Sackville, Can	N AMERICA • 250 kW
		(D) • N AMERICA • 250 kW
	USA KUSW, Salt Lake City,Utah	Su • E NORTH AM • 100 kW
		Tu-Su • E NORTH AM • 100 kW
	†WYFR-FAMILY RADIO, Okeechobee, Fl	S AMERICA • 100 kW
		C AMERICA • 100 kW
		(D) • N AMERICA • 100 kW
6176	**CHINA (PR)** SHAANXI PEOPLES BS, Xi'an	DS-1 • 15/50 kW
6179v	**ARGENTINA** RADIO NACIONAL, Mendoza	DS • 1 kW
6180	**BRAZIL** †R NAC DA AMAZONIA, Brasília	PORTUGUESE • DS • 250 kW
	CHINA (TAIWAN) CENTRAL BC SYSTEM, T'ai-pei	PRC-2 • 10/50 kW
	GUATEMALA LV DE GUATEMALA, Guatemala City	Irr • DS • 1 kW
	KOREA (DPR) RADIO PYONGYANG, Pyongyang	E ASIA & EAST USSR • 200 kW
	NETHERLANDS ANTILLES †TRANS WORLD RADIO, Bonaire	C AMERICA • 100 kW
	SENEGAL ORT DU SENEGAL, Ziguinchor	DS-FRENCH, ETC • 4 kW
	UNITED KINGDOM †BBC, Via Zyyi, Cyprus	EUROPE & WEST USSR • 100/250 kW
		(J) Sa/Su • E EUROPE & WEST USSR • 100 kW
		(D) • EUROPE & WEST USSR • 250 kW
		(J) • EUROPE & WEST USSR • 100 kW
		(D) • EUROPE • 250 kW
	USA †VOA, Via M'rovia, Liberia	W AFRICA & S AFRICA • 250 kW
		W AFRICA & C AFRICA • 250 kW
		M-F • W AFRICA & C AFRICA • 250 kW
	VOA, Via Woofferton, UK	WEST USSR • 250 kW
	USSR KAZAKH RADIO, Alma-Ata	Sa • DS-1 • 100 kW
		Sa-M • DS-1 • 100 kW
		Su-F • DS-1 • 100 kW
		Tu-F • DS-1 • 100 kW
		DS-1/RUSSIAN, ETC • 100 kW
	RADIO MOSCOW, Tula	(D) • MIDEAST • 100 kW
		(D) • N AFRICA & MIDEAST • 100 kW
	VENEZUELA RADIO TURISMO, Valera	DS • 1 kW
6185	**ALBANIA** RADIO TIRANA, Lushnjë	EUROPE • 50 kW
	BOLIVIA †BATALLON COLORADOS, La Paz	Irr • DS • 1/3 kW
	LIBYA RADIO JAMAHIRIYA, Tripoli	Irr • DS-RAMADAN • 100 kW
		DS • 100 kW
	MEXICO RADIO EDUCACION, México City	Irr • DS • 1 kW
	USA WRNO WORLDWIDE, New Orleans, La	E NORTH AM • 100 kW
		(J) • E NORTH AM • 100 kW
		Su • E NORTH AM • ENG, RUSSIAN, ETC • 100 kW
	USSR RS SOV BELORUSSIA, Ryazan'	EUROPE • 240 kW
	VATICAN STATE VATICAN RADIO, Sta Maria di Galeria	EUROPE • 100 kW
		EUROPE & WEST USSR • 100 kW
6188	**PERU** RADIO ORIENTE, Yurimaguas	DS • 1.5 kW
6190	**ALBANIA** RADIO TIRANA, Lushnjë	WEST USSR • 50 kW
	GERMANY (FR) FREIES BERLIN-SFB, Bremen	EUROPE • DS • 10 kW
		Sa • EUROPE • DS • 10 kW
(con'd)		

World Time: 0 Prime Time-Americas 6 Prime Time-E Asia 12 Prime Time-S Asia 18 Prime Time-Europe 24

SUMMER ONLY (J) WINTER ONLY (D) JAMMING / OR /\ EARLIEST HEARD ◁ LATEST HEARD ▷ NEW OR CHANGED FOR 1990 †

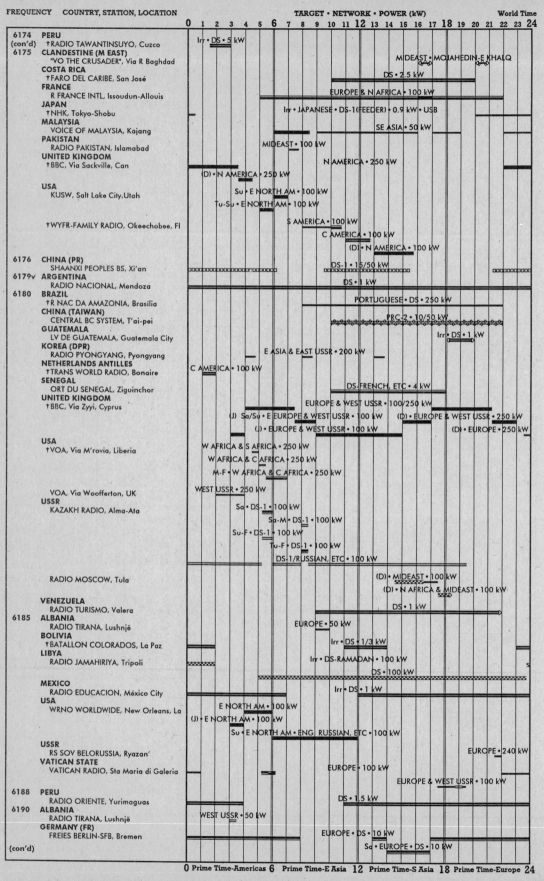

FREQUENCY	COUNTRY, STATION, LOCATION	TARGET • NETWORK • POWER (kW)
6190 (con'd)	**GERMANY (FR)** FREIES BERLIN-SFB, Bremen	Su-F • EUROPE • DS • 10 kW
	RADIO BREMEN, Bremen	Sa • EUROPE • DS • 10 kW
		Su-F • EUROPE • DS • 10 kW
	INDIA ALL INDIA RADIO, Delhi	DS • 10 kW
	JAPAN †NHK, Osaka	Irr • JAPANESE • DS-2(FEEDER) • 0.5 kW
	ROMANIA RADIO BUCHAREST, Bucharest	(D) • EUROPE • 250 kW
	SWITZERLAND SWISS RADIO INTL, Schwarzenburg	W EUROPE • 150 kW
	UNITED KINGDOM †BBC, Via Maseru, Lesotho	S AFRICA • 100 kW
		F-Su • S AFRICA • 100 kW
	USA VOA, Greenville, NC	C AMERICA & S AMERICA • 250 kW
	USSR R TIKHIY OKEAN, Nikolayevsk 'Amure	(D) • PACIFIC • MARINERS • 50 kW
		(D) Sa • PACIFIC • MARINERS • 50 kW
		(D) Su-F • PACIFIC • MARINERS • 50 kW
	RADIO MOSCOW, Frunze	MIDEAST • 100 kW
	RADIO MOSCOW, Nikolayevsk 'Amure	(D) • PACIFIC • DS-1 • 50 kW
	RADIO MOSCOW, Omsk	(D) • DS-2 • 100 kW
	VATICAN STATE VATICAN RADIO, Sta Maria di Galeria	EUROPE • 100 kW
		W EUROPE & N AFRICA • 100 kW
		Su • EUROPE • 100 kW
		M-Sa • ENGLISH, FRENCH & SPANISH • EUROPE • 100 kW
6191.7	**PERU** †RADIO CUZCO, Cuzco	DS-SPANISH, QUECHUA • 1 kW
6195	**CANADA** CANADIAN BC CORP, Sackville, NB	M • DS-NORTHERN • 100 kW
		M-F • DS-NORTHERN • 100 kW
		Su • DS-NORTHERN • 100 kW
		Tu-Sa • DS-NORTHERN • 100 kW
	CLANDESTINE (S AMER) †"REV ARMED FORCES", Colombia	Su • S AMERICA
	EGYPT RADIO CAIRO, Kafr Silîm-Abis	N AMERICA • 250 kW
	KOREA (DPR) RADIO PYONGYANG, Pyongyang	E ASIA • 100 kW
	NIGERIA RIMA RADIO, Sokoto	DS-ENGLISH, ETC • 10 kW
	UNITED KINGDOM †BBC, Daventry	WEST USSR • 300 kW
		(D) • WEST USSR • 300 kW
		(J) • WEST USSR • 300 kW
	†BBC, Multiple Locations	EUROPE, MIDEAST & N AFRICA • 250/300/500 kW
		(D) • EUROPE & N AFRICA • 250/300 kW
		(D) • EUROPE, MIDEAST & N AFRICA • 250/300/500 kW
		(J) • EUROPE, MIDEAST & N AFRICA • 250/300/500 kW
		(J) • MIDEAST & WEST USSR • 300/500 kW
	†BBC, Rampisham	(D) • EUROPE & WEST USSR • 500 kW
		(J) • E EUROPE & MIDEAST • 500 kW
	†BBC, Via Antigua	C AMERICA • 250 kW
		(D) M-F • S AMERICA • 250 kW
		Sa/Su • C AMERICA • 250 kW
	†BBC, Via Singapore	E ASIA & SE ASIA • 125 kW
		(J) • E ASIA & SE ASIA • 125 kW
	†BBC, Via Zyyi, Cyprus	(D) • EUROPE • 100 kW
		(D) Su • MIDEAST & WEST USSR • 250 kW
	USSR RADIO MOSCOW, Baku	DS-2 • 50 kW
6195v	**BANGLADESH** †RADIO BANGLADESH, Dhaka	DS • 100 kW
6200	**CHINA (TAIWAN)** †VO FREE CHINA, T'ai-pei	E ASIA • 50/100 kW
		JAPANESE • E ASIA • 50/100 kW
	USSR RADIO KIEV, Leningrad	(D) • E NORTH AM • 100 kW
	RADIO MOSCOW, Leningrad	(D) • E NORTH AM • MARINERS • 100 kW
	RADIO MOSCOW, Ul'yanovsk	(D) • DS-1 • 100 kW
(con'd)		(D) • EUROPE • WS, CZECH, ETC • 100 kW

World Time: 0 Prime Time-Americas 6 Prime Time-E Asia 12 Prime Time-S Asia 18 Prime Time-Europe 24

ENGLISH ARABIC CHINESE FRENCH GERMAN RUSSIAN SPANISH OTHER

FREQUENCY	COUNTRY, STATION, LOCATION	TARGET • NETWORK • POWER (kW) — World Time 0–24
6200 (con'd)	**USSR** RADIO MOSCOW, Ulan-Ude	(D) • DS-1 • 50 kW
		(D) • DS-2 • 50 kW
	RADIO VILNIUS, Leningrad	(D) • E NORTH AM • 100 kW
6205	**ECUADOR** HCJB-VO THE ANDES, Quito	(D) • EUROPE • 500 kW
		(D) M-F • EUROPE • 500 kW
		(D) Sa/Su • EUROPE • 500 kW
6206v	**PIRATE (EUROPE)** †"R ORANG UTAN", Holland	Irr • Su • W EUROPE • 0.1 kW
6210	**USA** FAMILY RADIO, Via Taiwan	E ASIA • 250 kW
6210v	**PAKISTAN** RADIO PAKISTAN, Islamabad	(D) • MIDEAST • 250 kW
		(D) • EUROPE • 250 kW
6214.4	**CLANDESTINE (C AMER)** †"15 DE SETIEMBRE", Honduras	Irr • C AMERICA • FDN/ANTI-SANDINIST
6215	**INTERNATIONAL WATERS** WORLD MISSION R, Via Radio Caroline	Irr • ENGLISH, GERMAN & SPANISH • EUROPE
6215.2	**LEBANON** VOICE OF HOPE, Marjayoûn	Alternative Frequency to 6280.2 kHz
6220	**IRAN** †VO THE ISLAMIC REP, Tehrān	(D) • PERSIAN • MIDEAST • 100/500 kW
6220v	**PAKISTAN** PAKISTAN BC CORP, Rawalpindi	(J) • DS-ENGLISH, ETC • 10 kW
6225	**PIRATE (EUROPE)** †"RADIO MARABU", Germany (FR)	Irr • Su • GERMAN & ENGLISH • W EUROPE
6226	**PIRATE (EUROPE)** †"RADIO VANESSA", Germany (FR)	Irr • Su • GERMAN & ENGLISH • W EUROPE
6229	**PIRATE (EUROPE)** †"JOLLY ROGER R", Ireland	Sa/Su • W EUROPE
6230	**CLANDESTINE (M EAST)** "R IRAN TOILERS", Afghanistan	PERSIAN • MIDEAST • TUDEH COMMUNIST
	ECUADOR †HCJB-VO THE ANDES, Quito	N AMERICA & C AMERICA • 100 kW
	EGYPT †RADIO CAIRO, Abu Za'bal	MIDEAST • 100 kW
	MONACO †TRANS WORLD RADIO, Monte Carlo	(D) • EUROPE • 500 kW
		(D) F-Su • E EUROPE • 500 kW
		(D) • EUROPE • 100 kW
		(D) M-Sa • EUROPE • 500 kW
		(D) Th-Su • E EUROPE • 500 kW
		(D) Su • EUROPE • 500 kW
	PIRATE (EUROPE) †"BRITAIN R INTL", Germany (FR)	Irr • Su • ENGLISH & GERMAN • W EUROPE • 0.05 kW
6235	**PAKISTAN** RADIO PAKISTAN, Islamabad	(D) • MIDEAST • 100 kW
6235v	**PIRATE (EUROPE)** "RADIO GEMINI", England	Irr • Su • W EUROPE • 0.15 kW
6240	**BANGLADESH** †RADIO BANGLADESH, Dhaka	S ASIA • 250 kW
	CLANDESTINE (N AMER) "VOICE OF TOMORROW, Virginia, USA	Irr • E NORTH AM • NEO-NAZI PARTY
	PIRATE (EUROPE) †"WEEKEND MUSIC R", Scotland	Irr • Su • W EUROPE • 0.1 kW • ALT. FREQ. TO 6295 kHz
6248	**VATICAN STATE** †VATICAN RADIO, Vatican City	EUROPE • 80 kW
		Su • EUROPE • 80 kW
		Th • EUROPE • 80 kW
		M-Sa • ENGLISH, FRENCH & SPANISH • EUROPE • 80 kW
		M-Sa • ENGLISH, FRENCH, SPANISH & ITALIAN • EUROPE • 80 kW
6249.6	**EQUATORIAL GUINEA** RADIO NACIONAL, Malabo	DS • 10 kW
6250v	**KOREA (DPR)** RADIO PYONGYANG, Pyongyang	E ASIA • 50/100 kW
6260	**CHINA (PR)** QINGHAI PEOPLES BS, Xining	DS-1/CHINESE • 10 kW
6266	**PIRATE (EUROPE)** †"RADIO ORION", England	Alternative Frequency to 6299 kHz
6271v	**PIRATE (EUROPE)** "RADIO WAVES INTL", France	Irr • Su • ENGLISH & FRENCH • W EUROPE • 0.015 kW
6273	**PIRATE (EUROPE)** †"TRIANGLE NIGHT FM, N Ireland	Irr • Sa/Su • W EUROPE • 0.2 kW
6280	**PIRATE (EUROPE)** "WESTSIDE R INTL", Ireland	Su • W EUROPE • 0.08 kW
6280.2	**LEBANON** VOICE OF HOPE, Marjayoûn	DS • 12 kW • ALT. FREQ. TO 6215.2 kHz
		M-F • DS • 12 kW
		DS • 12 kW
		Sa/Su • DS • 12 kW
		DS-RUSSIAN, ETC • 12 kW
6290	**CHINA (PR)** †RADIO BEIJING, Beijing	(D) • FEEDER
6295	**PAKISTAN** PAKISTAN BC CORP, Islamabad	(D) • MIDEAST • DS • 100 kW
	RADIO PAKISTAN, Islamabad	(D) • MIDEAST • 100 kW
	PIRATE (EUROPE) †"WEEKEND MUSIC R", Scotland	Alternative Frequency to 6240 kHz
6295v	**PIRATE (EUROPE)** "RADIO KRISTEL", England	Irr • Su • W EUROPE

0 Prime Time-Americas 6 Prime Time-E Asia 12 Prime Time-S Asia 18 Prime Time-Europe 24

SUMMER ONLY (J) WINTER ONLY (D) JAMMING / OR /\ EARLIEST HEARD ◁ LATEST HEARD ▷ NEW OR CHANGED FOR 1990 †

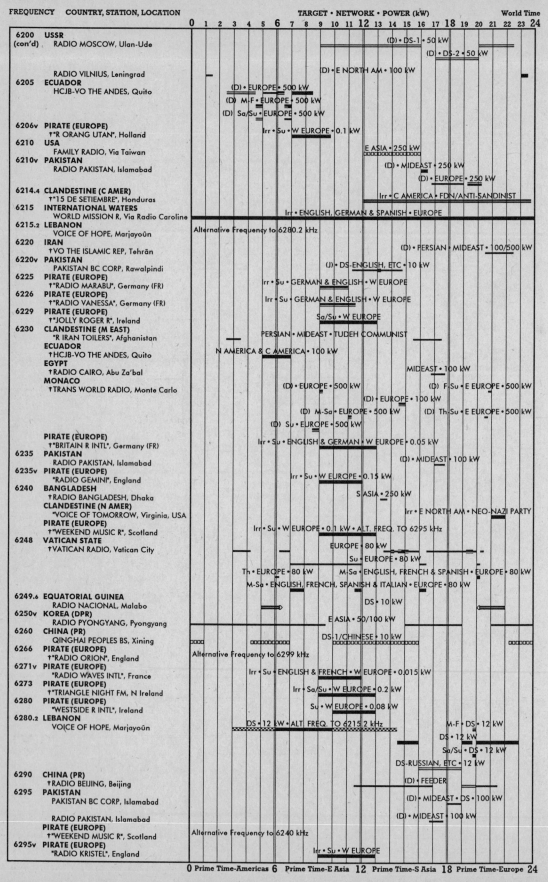

FREQUENCY	COUNTRY, STATION, LOCATION	TARGET • NETWORK • POWER (kW)
6297v	**PERU** †RADIO CHOTA, Chota	DS
6299	**PIRATE (EUROPE)** †"RADIO ORION", England	Sa/Su • W EUROPE • 0.018 kW • ALT. FREQ. TO 6266 kHz
6300	**USA** FAMILY RADIO, Via Taiwan	E ASIA • 250 kW
6304.5	**PERU** RADIO ACARI, Caraveli	DS
6305	**CLANDESTINE (C AMER)** "LA VOZ DEL CID", Guatemala?	C AMERICA • ANTI-CASTRO
6310	**PIRATE (EUROPE)** †"EAST COAST COMML", England	Alternative Frequency to 6815 kHz
6310v	**PIRATE (EUROPE)** †"RADIO BRIGITTE", Belgium	Alternative Frequency to 7490v kHz
6320v	**PIRATE (EUROPE)** †"RADIO STELLA", Scotland	Irr • Su • W EUROPE • 0.09 kW
6322v	**VIETNAM** SON LA BC STATION, Son La	DS
6323.6	**PERU** †ESTACION C, Moyobamba	Tu-Su • DS • 0.8 kW; DS • 0.8 kW; Irr • Tu-Su • DS • 0.8 kW
6325	**CLANDESTINE (ASIA)** †"VO THE KHMER", Kampuchea/Thailand	SE ASIA • PRO-REBEL STATION; Su • SE ASIA • PRO-REBEL STATION
6325.2	**TURKEY** †ISTANBUL POLICE R, Istanbul	TURKISH • DS • 1 kW
6340	**TURKEY** TURKISH POLICE R, Ankara	TURKISH • DS • 1 kW
6348	**CLANDESTINE (ASIA)** †"ECHO OF HOPE", Suwon, South Korea	E ASIA • KOREANS IN JAPAN • 50 kW
6390	**USSR** RADIO MOSCOW	(D) • DS-1(FEEDER) • ISL; (D) • DS-1(FEEDER) • ISU
6400	**CHINA (PR)** †VO THE STRAIT-PLA, Fuzhou	(D) • TAIWAN-1 • 10 kW
6400v	**KOREA (DPR)** RADIO PYONGYANG, Pyongyang	E ASIA • 50 kW
6430	**CHINA (PR)** †RADIO BEIJING, Beijing	(D) • FEEDER
	CLANDESTINE (M EAST) †"VO IRAN COMMUNIST, Afghanistan	F • PERSIAN • MIDEAST • ANTI-IRANIAN GOVT; PERSIAN • MIDEAST • ANTI-IRANIAN GOVT; Sa-Th • PERSIAN • MIDEAST • ANTI-IRANIAN GOVT
6435v	**CLANDESTINE (M EAST)** †"VO IRANIAN REV'N", Afghanistan	MIDEAST • ANTI-IRANIAN GOVT; PERSIAN • MIDEAST • ANTI-IRANIAN GOVT
6451v	**VIETNAM** VOICE OF VIETNAM, Hanoi	DS; Su • DS
6470	**CLANDESTINE (AFRICA)** †"RADIO SNM", Ethiopia	E AFRICA • ANTI-SOMALI GOVT
6480	**KOREA (REPUBLIC)** RADIO KOREA, In-Kimjae	EUROPE • 250 kW; KOREAN • EUROPE • 250 kW
6500	**CHINA (PR)** QINGHAI PEOPLES BS, Xining	DS-TIBETAN • 10 kW
6540	**KOREA (DPR)** RADIO PYONGYANG, Pyongyang	JAPANESE • E ASIA • 100 kW; MIDEAST & N AFRICA • 200 kW
6550v	**LEBANON** VOICE OF LEBANON, Beirut-Ashrafiyah	DS-PHALANGE • 8 kW
6555v	**CLANDESTINE (C AMER)** "R VENCEREMOS", Morazán, Salvador	C AMERICA • FMLN/ANTI-SALVADOR • ALT. FREQ. TO 6650v kHz; M-Sa • C AMERICA • FMLN/ANTI-SALVADOR • ALT. FREQ. TO 6650v kHz; Su • C AMERICA • FMLN/ANTI-SALVADOR • ALT. FREQ. TO 6650v kHz
6560	**CHINA (PR)** †RADIO BEIJING, Beijing	(J) • E ASIA • FEEDER
	KOREA (DPR) RADIO PYONGYANG, Pyongyang	JAPANESE • E ASIA • 100 kW
6570	**BURMA** BURMESE ARMY STN, Maymyo	DS
6571v	**PERU** †RADIO TACNA, Tacna	Irr • DS • 0.18 kW
6571.8	**ARGENTINA** †RADIO COLON, San Juan	Irr • DS(FEEDER) • USB
6575v	**VIETNAM** CAO BANG BS, Cao Bang	DS; Irr • DS
6576	**KOREA (DPR)** RADIO PYONGYANG, Pyongyang	C AMERICA • 400 kW; E ASIA & EAST USSR • 200 kW; WEST USSR & EUROPE • 200 kW
6590	**CHINA (PR)** †RADIO BEIJING, Beijing	FEEDER; (D) • FEEDER
6595	**KOREA (DPR)** RADIO PYONGYANG, Pyongyang	E ASIA • 100 kW
6600v	**CLANDESTINE (ASIA)** "VO THE PEOPLE", South Korea	E ASIA • TO NORTH KOREA

World Time: 0 Prime Time-Americas 6 Prime Time-E Asia 12 Prime Time-S Asia 18 Prime Time-Europe 24

ENGLISH ARABIC CHINESE FRENCH GERMAN RUSSIAN SPANISH OTHER

FREQUENCY	COUNTRY, STATION, LOCATION	TARGET • NETWORK • POWER (kW)
6615v	**VIETNAM** †BAC THAI BS, Bac Thai	DS
6641v	**VIETNAM** LAI CHAU BS, Lai Chau	DS
6647v	**LAOS** LAO NATIONAL RADIO, Paksé	DS • 1 kW
6650v	**CLANDESTINE (C AMER)** "R VENCEREMOS", Morazán, Salvador	Alternative Frequency to 6555v kHz
6667v	**CLANDESTINE (N AMER)** "LV DE ALPHA 66", Florida, USA	Irr • Tu/Th/Sa • C AMERICA • ANTI-CASTRO • 1 kW
6691.2	**PERU** †RADIO CUTERVO, Cutervo	DS • 1 kW Irr • DS • 1 kW Su • DS • 1 kW
6700v	**CLANDESTINE (ASIA)** "VO MALAYAN DEM'Y, Hengyang,China	SE ASIA • MALAY COMMUNIST • 10 kW
	CLANDESTINE (C AMER) †"FARABUNDO MARTI", El Salvador	M-Sa • C AMERICA • PRO-FPL REBELS Su • C AMERICA • PRO-FPL REBELS
6726.5	**PERU** †RADIO SATELITE, Santa Cruz	DS • 1 kW
6735v	**VIETNAM** HOANG LIEN SON BS, Hoang Lien Son	DS
6750	**CHINA (PR)** CENTRAL PEOPLES BS	DS-1
6760v	**CLANDESTINE (S AMER)** †"R PATRIA LIBRE", Colombia	AMERICAS • ELN REBELS
6765	**CHINA (PR)** †VO THE STRAIT-PLA, Fuzhou	(D) • TAIWAN-1 • 10 kW
6770	**USSR** TASS NEWS AGENCY, Moscow	M-F • DS • 15 kW
6790	**CHINA (PR)** CENTRAL PEOPLES BS, Beijing	TAIWAN-2 • 10 kW
6805	**USSR** RADIO MOSCOW	(D) • (FEEDER) • ISL (D) • (FEEDER) • ISU
6810	**CHINA (PR)** †RADIO BEIJING, Beijing	SE ASIA • 10 kW
6815	**PIRATE (EUROPE)** †"EAST COAST COMML", England	Irr • Su • W EUROPE • ALT. FREQ. TO 6310 kHz
	†"RADIO ORION", England	Irr • Sa/Su • W EUROPE • 0.018 kW
6815.3	**PERU** †RADIO UNIVERSO, Pandalle	M • DS • 0.04 kW Irr • M • DS • 0.04 kW Su • DS • 0.04 kW
6822.5	**USSR** RADIO MOSCOW, Serpukhov	(D) • DS-2(FEEDER) • 15 kW • USB
6825	**CHINA (PR)** †RADIO BEIJING, Beijing	E ASIA • FEEDER • 10 kW (D) • E ASIA • FEEDER • 10 kW (J) • E ASIA • FEEDER • 10 kW
6840	**CHINA (PR)** CENTRAL PEOPLES BS	DS-1 • 50 kW W-M • DS-1 • 50 kW
6860	**CHINA (PR)** †RADIO BEIJING, Kunming	(D) • S AMERICA • 120 kW
	†RADIO BEIJING, Xi'an	(D) • EUROPE • 120 kW
6873	**USA** VOA, Greenville, NC	N AFRICA • (FEEDER) • 40 kW • ISL (D) • N AFRICA • (FEEDER) • 40 kW • ISL (D) • N AFRICA • (FEEDER) • 40 kW • ISU (J) • N AFRICA • (FEEDER) • 40 kW • ISL (J) • N AFRICA • (FEEDER) • 40 kW • ISU
6890	**CHINA (PR)** CENTRAL PEOPLES BS, Beijing	DS-2 • 10 kW
	USSR RADIO MOSCOW, Moscow	(D) • MARINERS(FEEDER) • 15 kW • USB
6895.2	**PERU** †RADIO SENSACION, Huancabamba	DS Irr • DS
6900	**TURKEY** VO METEOROLOGY, Ankara	DS • 5 kW
6910	**USSR** RADIO MOSCOW, Moscow	Irr • (D) • DS-2(FEEDER) • 20 kW • USB
6911v	**IRELAND** †RADIO DUBLIN INTL, Dublin	Irr • Sa/Su • W EUROPE • 0.08 kW
6920	**CHINA (PR)** CENTRAL PEOPLES BS	DS-2 DS-MINORITIES
6933	**CHINA (PR)** †RADIO BEIJING, Xi'an	EUROPE & N AFRICA • 120 kW
6937	**CHINA (PR)** YUNNAN PEOPLES BS, Kunming	DS-3/CHINESE, ETC • 50 kW Irr • M-Sa • DS-3 • 50 kW
6955	**CHINA (PR)** †RADIO BEIJING, Beijing	E ASIA & SE ASIA • 120 kW (D) • MIDEAST • 120 kW MIDEAST • 120 kW
6957v	**CLANDESTINE (M EAST)** "VO IRAQI PEOPLE"	Irr • MIDEAST • IRAQI COMMUNIST • ALT. FREQ. TO 6995v kHz

World Time: 0 1 2 3 4 5 6 7 8 9 10 11 12 13 14 15 16 17 18 19 20 21 22 23 24

0 Prime Time-Americas 6 Prime Time-E Asia 12 Prime Time-S Asia 18 Prime Time-Europe 24

SUMMER ONLY (J) WINTER ONLY (D) JAMMING / OR /\ EARLIEST HEARD ◁ LATEST HEARD ▷ NEW OR CHANGED FOR 1990 †

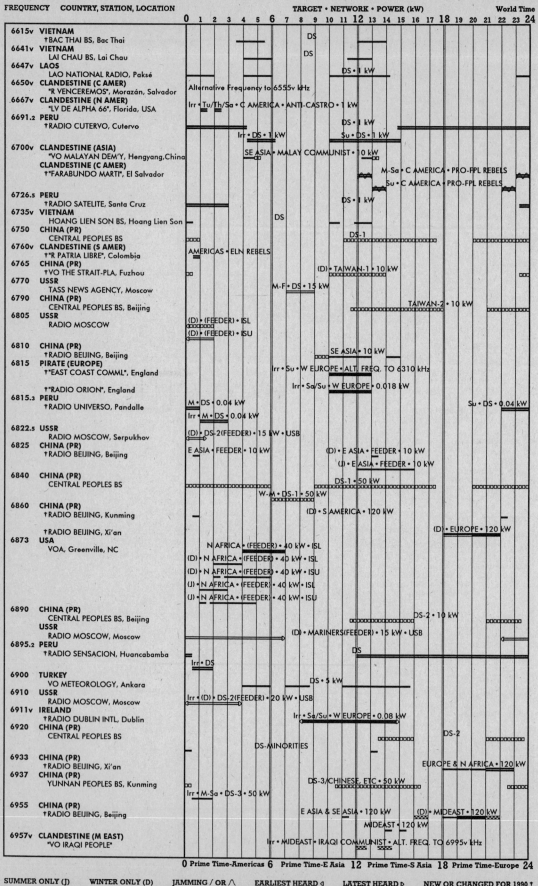

FREQUENCY	COUNTRY, STATION, LOCATION	TARGET • NETWORK • POWER (kW)
6974	**CHINA (PR)**	
	CENTRAL PEOPLES BS, Hohhot	DS-MINORITIES • 50 kW
	NEI MONGGOL PBS, Hohhot	DS-MONGOLIAN • 50 kW
6975	**GERMANY (FR)**	
	DEUTSCHE WELLE, Elmshorn	(D) • W EUROPE • (FEEDER) • 20 kW • USB
6995	**CHINA (PR)**	
	†RADIO BEIJING, Beijing	(D) • E ASIA • FEEDER • 10 kW
	†RADIO BEIJING, Kunming	SE ASIA • 120 kW
	†RADIO BEIJING, Xi'an	(D) • E AFRICA & S AFRICA • 120 kW
	CLANDESTINE (ASIA)	
	†"DEM KAMPUCHEA", Beijing, China (PR)	SE ASIA • PRO-KHMER ROUGE • 50 kW
	USA	
	RFE-RL, Via Holzkirchen,GFR	W EUROPE • (FEEDER) • 10 kW • ISL
		W EUROPE • (FEEDER) • 10 kW • ISU
6995v	**CLANDESTINE (M EAST)**	
	"VO IRAQI PEOPLE"	Alternative Frequency to 6957v kHz
7000v	**CLANDESTINE (C AMER)**	
	†"LA VOZ POPULAR", Guatemala	Sa • GUATEMALA REBELS
		F • GUATEMALA REBELS
7010	**PAKISTAN**	
	RADIO PAKISTAN, Islamabad	(D) • S ASIA • 100 kW
7020v	**CLANDESTINE (AFRICA)**	
	†"VO BROAD MASSES", Ethiopia	E AFRICA • PLF OF ERITREA
7075	**CLANDESTINE (M EAST)**	
	"RADIO IRAN", Abu Za'bal, Egypt	PERSIAN • MIDEAST • ANTI-IRANIAN GOVT • 100 kW
7080v	**BANGLADESH**	
	†RADIO BANGLADESH, Dhaka	DS
	CLANDESTINE (M EAST)	
	†"VO IRANIAN REV'N", Afghanistan	MIDEAST • ANTI-IRANIAN GOVT
		PERSIAN • MIDEAST • ANTI-IRANIAN GOVT
7095v	**PAKISTAN**	
	PAKISTAN BC CORP, Islamabad	(D) • DS • 10 kW
	RADIO PAKISTAN, Islamabad	(D) • S ASIA • 10 kW
7100	**ALBANIA**	
	RADIO TIRANA, Lushnjë	E EUROPE • 50 kW
	USSR	
	RADIO MOSCOW, Nikolayev	(D) • E NORTH AM • N AMERICAN • 500 kW
		(D) • EUROPE • WS • 500 kW
		(D) • E NORTH AM • 500 kW
	RADIO MOSCOW, Sverdlovsk	(D) • EUROPE • 100 kW
	RADIO MOSCOW, Tula	(D) • MIDEAST • 100 kW
	YAKUT RADIO, Yakutsk	DS • 50 kW
7105	**CHINA (TAIWAN)**	
	†CENTRAL BC SYSTEM, T'ai-pei	PRC-2 • 10/50 kW
	MONACO	
	†TRANS WORLD RADIO, Monte Carlo	(D) • W EUROPE • 100 kW
	ROMANIA	
	†RADIO BUCHAREST, Bucharest	EUROPE • 250 kW
		(D) • AFRICA • 250 kW
	UNITED KINGDOM	
	†BBC, Rampisham	(D) • E EUROPE & MIDEAST • 500 kW
		(D) Sa • E EUROPE & MIDEAST • 500 kW
		(D) Sa/Su • E EUROPE & MIDEAST • 500 kW
	†BBC, Via Ascension	C AFRICA • 250 kW
		(D) • W AFRICA & C AFRICA • 250 kW
		(J) • S AFRICA • 250 kW
	†BBC, Via Singapore	M-Sa • S ASIA & SE ASIA • 100 kW
	USA	
	†VOA, Via Kaválla, Greece	MIDEAST & S ASIA • 250 kW
		(J) • WEST USSR • 250 kW
		(J) • MIDEAST & S ASIA • 250 kW
	†VOA, Via Philippines	E ASIA • 250 kW
		(D) • SE ASIA • 250 kW
	VOA, Via Rhodes, Greece	(J) • MIDEAST • TURKISH • 50 kW
	VOA, Via Wertachtal,GFR	(D) • WEST USSR • 500 kW
	USSR	
	RADIO MOSCOW, Serpuhkov	DS-1 • 100 kW
	RADIO MOSCOW, Simferopol'	(D) • AMERICAS • 100 kW
7110	**ALBANIA**	
	RADIO TIRANA, Lushnjë	EUROPE • GREEK,ITALIAN,ETC • 50 kW
	CHINA (PR)	
	CENTRAL PEOPLES BS, Lhasa	DS-MINORITIES • 50 kW
	RADIO BEIJING, Lhasa	S ASIA • HINDI • 50 kW
	XIZANG PEOPLES BS, Lhasa	DS-TIBETAN • 50 kW
	ETHIOPIA	
	VOICE OF ETHIOPIA, Gedja	DS • 100 kW
		M-Sa • DS • 100 kW
		M-F • DS • 100 kW
(con'd)		

World Time: 0 1 2 3 4 5 6 7 8 9 10 11 12 13 14 15 16 17 18 19 20 21 22 23 24

0 Prime Time-Americas 6 Prime Time-E Asia 12 Prime Time-S Asia 18 Prime Time-Europe 24

ENGLISH ARABIC CHINESE FRENCH GERMAN RUSSIAN SPANISH OTHER

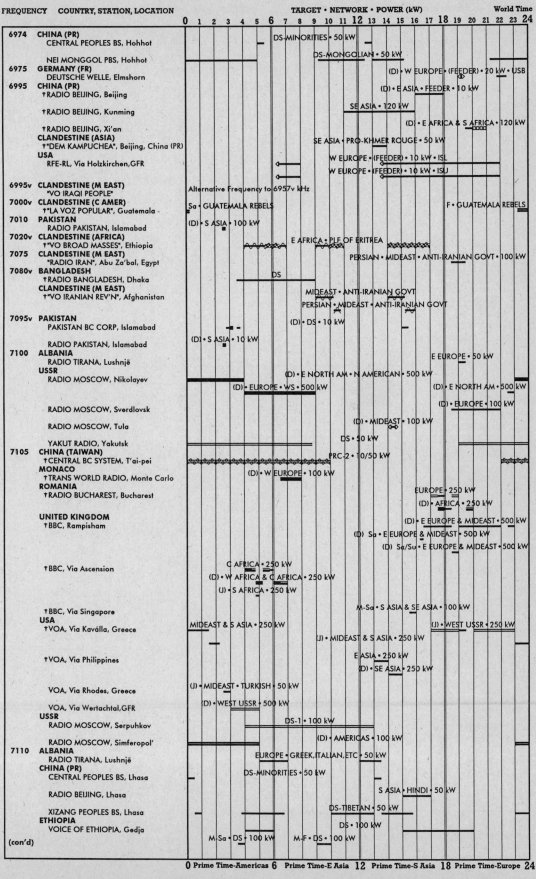

FREQUENCY	COUNTRY, STATION, LOCATION	TARGET • NETWORK • POWER (kW)
7110 (con'd)	ETHIOPIA VOICE OF ETHIOPIA, Gedja	Sa/Su • DS • 100 kW Su • DS • 100 kW
	HOLLAND †RADIO NEDERLAND, Flevoland	(D) • MIDEAST • 500 kW
	INDIA †ALL INDIA RADIO, Delhi	S ASIA • 20/50 kW DS-ENGLISH, ETC • 20 kW
	IRAN †VO THE ISLAMIC REP, Tehrān	(D) • EUROPE & MIDEAST • 500 kW • ALT. FREQ. TO 7285 kHz
	MALI RTV MALIENNE, Bamako	DS-FRENCH, ETC • 50 kW Su • DS-FRENCH, ETC • 50 kW
	SWEDEN IBRA RADIO, Via Cyclops, Malta	EUROPE • 250 kW
	TURKEY †TURKISH RTV CORP, Ankara	(D) • E EUROPE • 250 kW • ALT. FREQ. TO 7180 kHz (J) • E EUROPE • 250 kW • ALT. FREQ. TO 7180 kHz
	UGANDA RADIO UGANDA, Kampala	DS-ENGLISH,SWAHILI • 50 kW Sa/Su • DS-ENGLISH,SWAHILI • 50 kW Su • DS-ENGLISH,SWAHILI • 50 kW
	USSR RADIO MOSCOW, Omsk	(D) • DS-2 • 100 kW
7111v	LAOS LAO NATIONAL RADIO, Vientiane	SE ASIA • 25 kW
7113v	MOZAMBIQUE †RADIO MOCAMBIQUE, Maputo	DS • 25 kW
7115	BULGARIA †RADIO SOFIA, Plovdiv	EUROPE • 500 kW (D) • E NORTH AM & EUROPE • 500 kW (D) • EUROPE • 500 kW (D) Su • EUROPE • 500 kW
	THAILAND RADIO THAILAND, Pathum Thani	Irr • DS-1 • 10 kW
	USA †RFE-RL, Via Germany	E EUROPE • 100 kW
	†RFE-RL, Via Portugal	E EUROPE & WEST USSR • 50/250 kW M-F • E EUROPE • 250 kW Sa/Su • WEST USSR • 250 kW
	VOA, Via Sri Lanka	S ASIA • 10 kW
	USSR RADIO MOSCOW, Via Plovdiv,Bulgaria	(D) • E NORTH AM • N AMERICAN • 500 kW (D) • E NORTH AM & EUROPE • WS • 500 kW
7120	ALBANIA RADIO TIRANA, Lushnjë	EUROPE • 100 kW MIDEAST • ARABIC, PERSIAN • 100 kW
	AUSTRALIA †RADIO AUSTRALIA, Darwin	E ASIA & SE ASIA • 250 kW
	†RADIO AUSTRALIA, Multiple Locations	E ASIA & SE ASIA • 250/300 kW
	CHAD RADIODIF NATIONALE, N'Djamena	DS-FRENCH, ETC • 100 kW Sa/Su • DS-FRENCH, ETC • 100 kW
	CHINA (PR) †RADIO BEIJING, Hohhot	EAST USSR • 50 kW (J) • EAST USSR • RUSSIAN, MONGOLIAN • 50 kW
	†RADIO BEIJING, Via France	Alternative Frequency to 9845 kHz
	FRANCE R FRANCE INTL, Issoudun-Allouis	S ASIA & SE ASIA • 500 kW
	GERMANY (FR) DEUTSCHE WELLE, Jülich	(D) • WEST USSR • 100 kW
	†DEUTSCHE WELLE, Wertachtal	(J) • W EUROPE • 500 kW
	INDIA †ALL INDIA RADIO, Delhi	E ASIA • CHINESE, CANTONESE • 100 kW
	KUWAIT RADIO KUWAIT, Jadādīyah	MIDEAST & N AFRICA • DS-MAIN PROGRAM • 250 kW
	SOMALIA RADIO HARGEISA, Hargeisa	DS-SOMALI,ARABIC • 10 kW
	UNITED KINGDOM †BBC, Rampisham	(D) • WEST USSR • 500 kW
	†BBC, Skelton, Cumbria	(J) • EUROPE & WEST USSR • 100 kW
	USA †VOA, Via Philippines	S ASIA & SE ASIA • 50 kW E ASIA • 250 kW
	†VOA, Via Wertachtal, GFR	(J) • MIDEAST & WEST USSR • 500 kW
	†VOA, Via Woofferton, UK	(D) • WEST USSR • 250/300 kW
(con'd)	USSR RADIO MOSCOW, Novosibirsk	DS-2/TO NORTH POLE • 100 kW

World Time: 0 Prime Time-Americas 6 Prime Time-E Asia 12 Prime Time-S Asia 18 Prime Time-Europe 24

SUMMER ONLY (J) WINTER ONLY (D) JAMMING / OR /\ EARLIEST HEARD ◁ LATEST HEARD ▷ NEW OR CHANGED FOR 1990 †

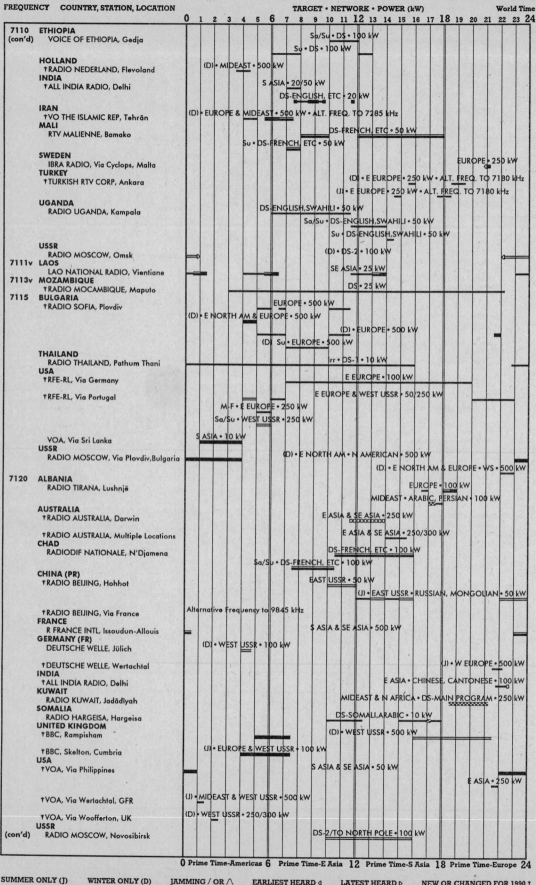

FREQUENCY	COUNTRY, STATION, LOCATION	TARGET • NETWORK • POWER (kW)
7120 (con'd)	**USSR** RADIO MOSCOW, Simferopol'	(J) • DS-1 • 100 kW
	RADIO MOSCOW, Tula	DS-3 • 50 kW
7125	**FRANCE** †R FRANCE INTL, Via Xi'an, China	(D) • S ASIA • 150 kW
	GERMANY (FR) †DEUTSCHE WELLE, Wertachtal	(D) • E EUROPE • 500 kW
	INDIA †ALL INDIA RADIO, Ranchi	DS • 10 kW
	ITALY †ADVENTIST WORLD R, Forlì	Alternative Frequency to 7257 kHz
	JAPAN †RADIO JAPAN/NHK, Via Moyabi, Gabon	(J) • S AFRICA • GENERAL • 500 kW; (J) • JAPANESE • S AFRICA • GENERAL • 500 kW
	POLAND †RADIO POLONIA, Warsaw	EUROPE • 100 kW; N AFRICA & W AFRICA • 100 kW; (D) • EUROPE • 100 kW; (D) • N AFRICA & E AFRICA • 100 kW; (D) • N AFRICA & W AFRICA • 100 kW
	UNITED KINGDOM †BBC, Via Maṣīrah, Oman	(D) • MIDEAST & S ASIA • 100 kW
	USA VOA, Via Kaválla, Greece	(D) • WEST USSR • 250 kW
	VOA, Via Sri Lanka	S ASIA • 10 kW
	†VOA, Via Woofferton, UK	(J) • E EUROPE & MIDEAST • 300 kW; (D) • E EUROPE & MIDEAST • TURKISH • 300 kW
	USSR †GEORGIAN RADIO	DS-1
	RADIO MOSCOW, Yerevan	(D) • DS-1 • 100 kW
	VATICAN STATE VATICAN RADIO, Sta Maria di Galeria	S ASIA • 500 kW
7125v	**GUINEA** RTV GUINEENNE, Conakry	M-Sa • DS-FRENCH, ETC • 100 kW; DS • 100 kW; DS-FRENCH, ETC • 100 kW; Sa/Su • DS-FRENCH, ETC • 100 kW
7130	**CHINA (TAIWAN)** VO FREE CHINA, T'ai-pei	SE ASIA • 50/100 kW; E ASIA • 50/100 kW; JAPANESE • E ASIA • 50/100 kW
	CLANDESTINE (M EAST) "VO THE CRUSADER", Via R Baghdad	MIDEAST • MOJAHEDIN-E KHALQ
	GERMANY (FR) †DEUTSCHE WELLE, Jülich	(D) • E EUROPE • 100 kW; (J) • E EUROPE • 100 kW
	DEUTSCHE WELLE, Wertachtal	W EUROPE & S AMERICA • 500 kW
	MALAYSIA †RTM-SARAWAK, Kuching-Stapok	DS-BIDAYUTH • 10 kW
	UNITED KINGDOM †BBC, Skelton, Cumbria	(D) • WEST USSR • 100 kW
	†BBC, Via Zyyi, Cyprus	(J) • E EUROPE • 250 kW
	USA VOA, Via Kaválla, Greece	E EUROPE • 250 kW; (J) • MIDEAST & S ASIA • 250 kW
	VOA, Via Woofferton, UK	(D) • E EUROPE • 250 kW
	USSR RADIO MOSCOW, Krasnodar	(D) • EUROPE • WS • 100 kW
	RADIO MOSCOW, Minsk	MIDEAST • 100 kW; (D) • MIDEAST • 100 kW; (D) • DS-3 • 100 kW; (D) • EUROPE • WS • 100 kW
	RADIO MOSCOW, Serpuhkov	DS-2 • 100 kW
	RADIO MOSCOW, Yerevan	S ASIA • MARINERS • 100 kW
	YUGOSLAVIA †RADIO YUGOSLAVIA, Belgrade	(D) • E ASIA & AUSTRALIA • 500 kW
7133	**UNIDENTIFIED**	
7135	**ALBANIA** RADIO TIRANA, Lushnjë	EUROPE • 100 kW
	AUSTRALIA RADIO AUSTRALIA, Shepparton	S ASIA & SE ASIA • 100 kW
	BULGARIA †RADIO SOFIA, Plovdiv	(D) • EUROPE • 500 kW • ALT. FREQ. TO 9655 kHz; (D) • EUROPE • 500 kW; (D) Su • EUROPE • 500 kW
	CANADA †R CANADA INTL, Via United Kingdom	(D) • EUROPE • 300 kW
	FRANCE †R FRANCE INTL, Issoudun-Allouis	N AFRICA & C AFRICA • 100/500 kW; (D) • N AFRICA & W AFRICA • 100/500 kW; (D) • E EUROPE & WEST USSR • 500 kW; (J) • E EUROPE & WEST USSR • 500 kW
(con'd)	R FRANCE INTL, Via Moyabi, Gabon	C AFRICA & E AFRICA • 250 kW

World Time: 0 1 2 3 4 5 6 7 8 9 10 11 12 13 14 15 16 17 18 19 20 21 22 23 24

0 Prime Time-Americas 6 Prime Time-E Asia 12 Prime Time-S Asia 18 Prime Time-Europe 24

ENGLISH ARABIC CHINESE FRENCH GERMAN RUSSIAN SPANISH OTHER

FREQUENCY	COUNTRY, STATION, LOCATION	TARGET • NETWORK • POWER (kW)
7135 (con'd)	**FRANCE**	
	R FRANCE INTL, Via Moyabi, Gabon	E AFRICA & C AFRICA • 250 kW
		C AFRICA • 250 kW
	GERMANY (FR)	
	DEUTSCHE WELLE, Jülich	(D) • W EUROPE • 100 kW
	ROMANIA	
	RADIO BUCHAREST, Bucharest	EUROPE • 250 kW
	UNITED KINGDOM	
	†BBC, Via Zyyi, Cyprus	MIDEAST & S ASIA • 250 kW
		PERSIAN • MIDEAST & S ASIA • 250 kW
		(D) • MIDEAST & S ASIA • 250 kW
	USA	
	VOA, Via M'rovia, Liberia	W AFRICA • 50 kW
	USSR	
	RADIO KIEV, L'vov	(D) • ATLANTIC & C AMERICA • 240 kW
	†RADIO MOSCOW, Komsomol'sk 'Amure	(D) • E ASIA • 500 kW
		E ASIA • 500 kW
		(D) • JAPANESE • E ASIA • 500 kW
	RADIO MOSCOW, L'vov	(D) • C AMERICA & W EUROPE • 240 kW
	RADIO MOSCOW, Moscow	(D) • W EUROPE & ATLANTIC • WS • 100 kW
	RADIO MOSCOW, Novosibirsk	DS-2 • 50 kW
	RADIO MOSCOW, Via Plovdiv, Bulgaria	(D) • C AMERICA • 500 kW
7140	**BELGIUM**	
	RT BELGE FRANCAISE, Wavre	(D) • EUROPE • 100 kW
		(D) Su • EUROPE • 100 kW
	CHINA (PR)	
	†RADIO BEIJING, Xi'an	WEST USSR • 120 kW
	GERMANY (FR)	
	†DEUTSCHE WELLE, Jülich	(J) • WEST USSR • 100 kW
	INDIA	
	ALL INDIA RADIO, Delhi	S ASIA • 100 kW
	ALL INDIA RADIO, Hyderabad	DS • 10 kW
		Su • DS • 10 kW
	ITALY	
	†RADIO ITALIA INTL, Spoleto	DS • 0.5 kW
	JAPAN	
	†RADIO JAPAN/NHK, Tokyo-Yamata	(D) • JAPANESE • E ASIA • GENERAL • 300 kW
		(D) • E ASIA • GENERAL • 300 kW
	KENYA	
	VOICE OF KENYA, Nairobi	DS-NATIONAL • 100 kW
	UNITED KINGDOM	
	†BBC, Rampisham	(D) M-Sa • E EUROPE & MIDEAST • 500 kW
		(D) • E EUROPE & MIDEAST • GREEK, TURKISH • 500 kW
	†BBC, Via Maşirah, Oman	(J) • MIDEAST • 100 kW
	†BBC, Via Zyyi, Cyprus	(D) • E AFRICA • 250 kW
		(D) • MIDEAST & E AFRICA • 20/250 kW
	USA	
	†VOA, Via Woofferton, UK	(J) • E EUROPE & WEST USSR • 300 kW
	USSR	
	RADIO MOSCOW, Armavir	(D) • W AFRICA & ATLANTIC • MARINERS, ARABIC • 100 kW
	RADIO MOSCOW, Kazan'	(J) • E EUROPE • POLISH • 100 kW
	YUGOSLAVIA	
	†RADIO YUGOSLAVIA, Bijeljina	EUROPE & N AFRICA • 250 kW
7145	**ALGERIA**	
	"VO PALESTINE", Via RTV Algerienne	N AFRICA & MIDEAST • PLO • 100 kW
	RTV ALGERIENNE, Bouchaoui	N AFRICA & MIDEAST • DS-1 • 100 kW
	CLANDESTINE (AFRICA)	
	†"AV DO GALO NEGRO", Jamba, Angola	S AFRICA • UNITA/PORT,ETC
	FRANCE	
	R FRANCE INTL, Issoudun-Allouis	EUROPE • 500 kW
	GERMANY (FR)	
	DEUTSCHE WELLE, Jülich	(D) • WEST USSR • 100 kW
	INDIA	
	†ALL INDIA RADIO, Delhi	S ASIA • 100 kW
	MALAYSIA	
	†RTM-SARAWAK, Kuching-Stapok	DS-MALAY • 10 kW
	NIGERIA	
	KWARA STATE BC, Ilorin	DS-ENGLISH, ETC • 10 kW
	POLAND	
	†RADIO POLONIA, Warsaw	EUROPE • 100 kW
		W EUROPE & W AFRICA • 100 kW
	ROMANIA	
	†RADIO BUCHAREST, Bucharest	(D) • EUROPE • 250 kW
	UNITED KINGDOM	
	†BBC, Via Singapore	(D) • SE ASIA • 100 kW
		(D) • E ASIA & SE ASIA • 100 kW
	USA	
	†RFE-RL, Via Germany	WEST USSR • 100 kW
(con'd)	†RFE-RL, Via Pals, Spain	WEST USSR • 250 kW

World Time: 0 1 2 3 4 5 6 7 8 9 10 11 12 13 14 15 16 17 18 19 20 21 22 23 24

0 Prime Time-Americas 6 Prime Time-E Asia 12 Prime Time-S Asia 18 Prime Time-Europe 24

SUMMER ONLY (J) WINTER ONLY (D) JAMMING / OR /\ EARLIEST HEARD ◁ LATEST HEARD ▷ NEW OR CHANGED FOR 1990 †

FREQUENCY	COUNTRY, STATION, LOCATION	TARGET • NETWORK • POWER (kW)
7145 (con'd)	**USA** †RFE-RL, Via Portugal	E EUROPE • 250 kW
	USSR RADIO MOSCOW, Tula	(D) • DS-1 • 100 kW
7149v	**SOUTH AFRICA** CAPITAL RADIO, Umtata	DS • 20 kW
7150	**BULGARIA** †RADIO SOFIA, Plovdiv	(D) • MIDEAST • 500 kW
	CAMEROON CAMEROON RTV CORP, Douala	DS-ENGLISH, FRENCH • 100 kW
	CHINA (TAIWAN) †CENTRAL BC SYSTEM, T'ai-pei	PRC-1 • 100 kW
	CUBA RADIO HABANA, Via USSR	Alternative Frequency to 6165 kHz
	GERMANY (FR) †DEUTSCHE WELLE, Jülich	C AFRICA & S AFRICA • 100 kW
	†DEUTSCHE WELLE, Wertachtal	(D) • E EUROPE • 500 kW (J) • E EUROPE • 500 kW
	SAUDI ARABIA BS OF THE KINGDOM, Riyadh	EUROPE • DS-GENERAL • 350 kW
	UNITED KINGDOM †BBC, Daventry	(D) • EUROPE & N AFRICA • 300 kW
	†BBC, Rampisham	C AMERICA & AUSTRALIA • 500 kW (D) • E EUROPE & MIDEAST • 500 kW (J) • E EUROPE & MIDEAST • 100 kW (J) Sa/Su • E EUROPE & MIDEAST • 100 kW (J) Su • E EUROPE & MIDEAST • 100 kW
	BBC, Various Locations	W EUROPE & N AFRICA • 250/500 kW
	USSR RADIO KIEV, L'vov	(D) • W EUROPE & E NORTH AM • 500 kW
	RADIO MOSCOW, L'vov	(D) • E NORTH AM • N AMERICAN • 500 kW (D) • EUROPE • WS/UK SERVICE • 500 kW
	ZAIRE RADIO CANDIP, Bunia	DS-FRENCH, ETC • 1 kW Sa/Su • DS-FRENCH, ETC • 1 kW Su • DS-FRENCH, ETC • 1 kW
7155	**ALBANIA** RADIO TIRANA, Lushnjë	EUROPE • GREEK, ETC • 50 kW
	CANADA R CANADA INTL, Via United Kingdom	(D) M-F • EUROPE • 100 kW
	NIGER †LA VOIX DU SAHEL, Niamey	DS-FRENCH,ETC • 4/20 kW Sa • DS-FRENCH ETC • 4/20 kW
	UNITED KINGDOM BBC, Daventry	(D) • E EUROPE • 250 kW (D) Su • E EUROPE • 250 kW
	USA †RFE-RL, Via Pals, Spain	WEST USSR • 250 kW
	USSR RADIO MOSCOW, Zhigulevsk	(J) • USSR • 100 kW (J) • EUROPE • ITALIAN, RUSSIAN • 240 kW
7155v	**ANGOLA** †ER DO LOBITO, Lobito	DS • 1 kW
7160	**FRANCE** R FRANCE INTL, Multiple Locations	AFRICA • 100/250/500 kW
	INDIA ALL INDIA RADIO, Aligarh	DS-ENGLISH, ETC • 250 kW
	†ALL INDIA RADIO, Madras	DS • 10 kW Sa/Su • DS • 10 kW Su • DS • 10 kW S ASIA • TAMIL • 10 kW
	MALAYSIA †RTM-SARAWAK, Kuching-Stapok	DS • 10 kW
	MONACO †TRANS WORLD RADIO, Monte Carlo	(J) • EUROPE • 500 kW (D) M-Sa • EUROPE • 500 kW (J) Su • EUROPE • 500 kW
	TURKEY †TURKISH RTV CORP, Ankara	(D) • MIDEAST • 250 kW
	UNITED KINGDOM †BBC, Via Maşīrah, Oman	(J) • MIDEAST • 100 kW PERSIAN • MIDEAST • ENGLISH, PERSIAN • 100 kW MIDEAST • ENGLISH, PERSIAN • 100 kW
	†BBC, Via Singapore	SE ASIA • 250 kW (D) • E ASIA & SE ASIA • 250 kW (J) • E ASIA & SE ASIA • 250 kW
	†BBC, Via Zyyi, Cyprus	(D) • E AFRICA & MIDEAST • 250 kW
	USSR RADIO MOSCOW, Kazan'	(J) • EUROPE • 240 kW
(con'd)	†RADIO MOSCOW, Khabarovsk	(D) • JAPANESE • E ASIA • 100 kW

World Time 0–24: 0 Prime Time-Americas 6 Prime Time-E Asia 12 Prime Time-S Asia 18 Prime Time-Europe 24

ENGLISH ▬ ARABIC ▭ CHINESE ▫▫▫ FRENCH ═ GERMAN ═ RUSSIAN ═ SPANISH ═ OTHER —

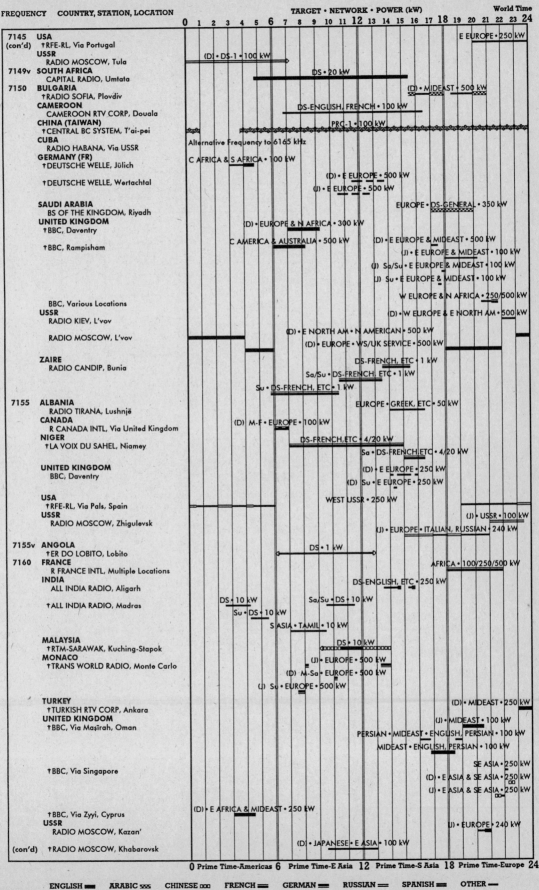

FREQUENCY	COUNTRY, STATION, LOCATION	TARGET • NETWORK • POWER (kW)
7160 (con'd)	USSR	
	RADIO MOSCOW, L'vov	W AFRICA • 240 kW
	RADIO MOSCOW, Omsk	(J) • DS-1 • 100 kW
	RADIO MOSCOW, Tula	W AFRICA & S AMERICA • 240 kW
7165	ALBANIA	
	RADIO TIRANA, Krujë	WEST USSR • 100 kW
		EUROPE • 100 kW
	RADIO TIRANA, Lushnjë	MIDEAST • 100 kW
		WEST USSR • 100 kW
		EUROPE • 100 kW
		EUROPE • 50 kW
	BELGIUM	
	†RT BELGE FRANCAISE, Wavre	(D) • EUROPE • 100 kW
		(D) Su • EUROPE • 100 kW
	CAMEROON	
	CAMEROON RTV CORP, Bertoua	Irr • DS-FRENCH,ENG,ETC • 20 kW
	CANADA	
	†R CANADA INTL, Via United Kingdom	(J) • EUROPE • 300 kW
	CHINA (PR)	
	RADIO BEIJING, Beijing	S ASIA • HINDI • 120 kW
	ETHIOPIA	
	VOICE OF ETHIOPIA, Gedja	E AFRICA • 100 kW
	NEPAL	
	†RADIO NEPAL, Harriharpur	S ASIA • 100 kW • ALT. FREQ. TO 3230 kHz
		DS • 100 kW • ALT. FREQ. TO 3230 kHz
		Sa • DS • 100 kW • ALT. FREQ. TO 3230 kHz
	SINGAPORE	
	SINGAPORE BC CORP, Jurong	DS-4 • 10 kW
	TANZANIA	
	RADIO TANZANIA, Dar es Salaam	E AFRICA & S AFRICA • 10 kW
		Sa/Su • E AFRICA & S AFRICA • 10 kW
	UNITED KINGDOM	
	†BBC, Skelton, Cumbria	EUROPE • 100/250 kW
	USA	
	†RFE-RL, Via Germany	E EUROPE • 100 kW
	†RFE-RL, Via Portugal	E EUROPE & WEST USSR • 250 kW
		M-Sa • E EUROPE • 250 kW
		Su • WEST USSR • 250 kW
	USSR	
	RADIO KIEV, Kiev	(D) • E NORTH AM • 500 kW
	RADIO MOSCOW, Kiev	(D) • E NORTH AM • MARINERS • 500 kW
		(D) • EUROPE & E NORTH AM • WS • 500 kW
	RADIO MOSCOW, Serpuhkov	DS-1 • 50 kW
	RADIO VILNIUS, Kiev	(D) • E NORTH AM • 500 kW
	YUGOSLAVIA	
	†RADIO YUGOSLAVIA, Bijeljina	WEST USSR • 500 kW
7165v	LAOS	
	LAO NATIONAL RADIO, Luang Prabang	DS • 1 kW
7170	ALBANIA	
	RADIO TIRANA, Lushnjë	EUROPE • GREEK, ITALIAN, ETC • 50 kW
	CHINA (PR)	
	XIZANG PEOPLES BS, Lhasa	DS-CHINESE • 50 kW
	GERMANY (DR)	
	†R BERLIN INTL, Königswusterhausen	EUROPE • 50 kW
	PAKISTAN	
	PAKISTAN BC CORP, Quetta	DS-ENGLISH, ETC • 10 kW
		F • DS-ENGLISH, ETC • 10 kW
		Th-Sa • DS-ENGLISH, ETC • 10 kW
	UNITED KINGDOM	
	†BBC, Rampisham	(D) • WEST USSR • 500 kW
	†BBC, Skelton, Cumbria	(J) • WEST USSR • 250 kW
	USA	
	VOA, Via Ismaning, GFR	(D) • WEST USSR • 100 kW
	VOA, Via Kaválla, Greece	(D) • WEST USSR • 250 kW
	VOA, Via Woofferton, UK	N AFRICA • 300 kW
		(J) • N AFRICA • 300 kW
	USSR	
	RADIO KIEV, L'vov	(D) • EUROPE • 100 kW
	RADIO MOSCOW, Komsomol'sk 'Amure	(D) • PACIFIC • 100 kW
	RADIO MOSCOW, Krasnoyarsk	(D) • E ASIA • 500 kW
	RS SOV BELORUSSIA, L'vov	(D) M/Tu/Th/F • EUROPE • 100 kW
		(D) W/Sa/Su • EUROPE • 100 kW
7170v (con'd)	NEW CALEDONIA	
	†RFO-N CALEDONIE, Nouméa	PACIFIC • DS-FRENCH, ETC • 20 kW

World Time 0–24: 0 Prime Time-Americas 6 Prime Time-E Asia 12 Prime Time-S Asia 18 Prime Time-Europe 24

SUMMER ONLY (J) WINTER ONLY (D) JAMMING / OR /\ EARLIEST HEARD ◁ LATEST HEARD ▷ NEW OR CHANGED FOR 1990 †

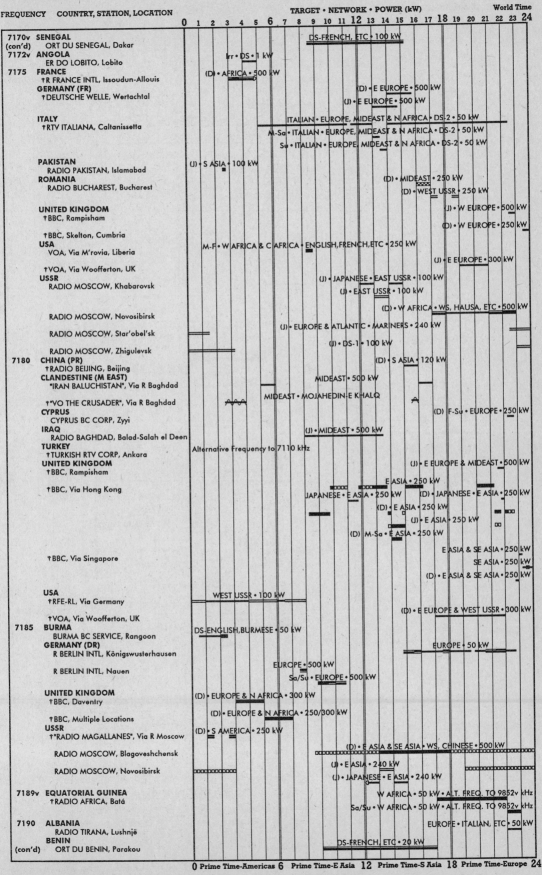

FREQUENCY	COUNTRY, STATION, LOCATION	TARGET • NETWORK • POWER (kW)
7170v (con'd)	**SENEGAL** ORT DU SENEGAL, Dakar	DS-FRENCH, ETC • 100 kW
7172v	**ANGOLA** ER DO LOBITO, Lobito	Irr • DS • 1 kW
7175	**FRANCE** †R FRANCE INTL, Issoudun-Allouis	(D) • AFRICA • 500 kW
	GERMANY (FR) †DEUTSCHE WELLE, Wertachtal	(D) • E EUROPE • 500 kW (J) • E EUROPE • 500 kW
	ITALY †RTV ITALIANA, Caltanissetta	ITALIAN • EUROPE, MIDEAST & N AFRICA • DS-2 • 50 kW M-Sa • ITALIAN • EUROPE, MIDEAST & N AFRICA • DS-2 • 50 kW Su • ITALIAN • EUROPE, MIDEAST & N AFRICA • DS-2 • 50 kW
	PAKISTAN RADIO PAKISTAN, Islamabad	(J) • S ASIA • 100 kW
	ROMANIA RADIO BUCHAREST, Bucharest	(D) • MIDEAST • 250 kW (D) • WEST USSR • 250 kW
	UNITED KINGDOM †BBC, Rampisham	(J) • W EUROPE • 500 kW (D) • W EUROPE • 250 kW
	†BBC, Skelton, Cumbria	
	USA VOA, Via M'rovia, Liberia	M-F • W AFRICA & C AFRICA • ENGLISH,FRENCH,ETC • 250 kW
	†VOA, Via Woofferton, UK	(J) • E EUROPE • 300 kW
	USSR RADIO MOSCOW, Khabarovsk	(J) • JAPANESE • EAST USSR • 100 kW (J) • EAST USSR • 100 kW
	RADIO MOSCOW, Novosibirsk	(D) • W AFRICA • WS, HAUSA, ETC • 500 kW
	RADIO MOSCOW, Star'obel'sk	(J) • EUROPE & ATLANTIC • MARINERS • 240 kW
	RADIO MOSCOW, Zhigulevsk	(J) • DS-1 • 100 kW
7180	**CHINA (PR)** †RADIO BEIJING, Beijing	(D) • S ASIA • 120 kW
	CLANDESTINE (M EAST) "IRAN BALUCHISTAN", Via R Baghdad	MIDEAST • 500 kW
	†"VO THE CRUSADER", Via R Baghdad	MIDEAST • MOJAHEDIN-E KHALQ
	CYPRUS CYPRUS BC CORP, Zyyi	(D) F-Su • EUROPE • 250 kW
	IRAQ RADIO BAGHDAD, Balad-Salah el Deen	(J) • MIDEAST • 500 kW
	TURKEY †TURKISH RTV CORP, Ankara	Alternative Frequency to 7110 kHz
	UNITED KINGDOM †BBC, Rampisham	(J) • E EUROPE & MIDEAST • 500 kW
	†BBC, Via Hong Kong	E ASIA • 250 kW JAPANESE • E ASIA • 250 kW (D) • JAPANESE • E ASIA • 250 kW (D) • E ASIA • 250 kW (J) • E ASIA • 250 kW (D) M-Sa • E ASIA • 250 kW
	†BBC, Via Singapore	E ASIA & SE ASIA • 250 kW SE ASIA • 250 kW (D) • E ASIA & SE ASIA • 250 kW
	USA †RFE-RL, Via Germany	WEST USSR • 100 kW
	†VOA, Via Woofferton, UK	(D) • E EUROPE & WEST USSR • 300 kW
7185	**BURMA** BURMA BC SERVICE, Rangoon	DS-ENGLISH,BURMESE • 50 kW
	GERMANY (DR) R BERLIN INTL, Königswusterhausen	EUROPE • 50 kW
	R BERLIN INTL, Nauen	EUROPE • 500 kW Sa/Su • EUROPE • 500 kW
	UNITED KINGDOM †BBC, Daventry	(D) • EUROPE & N AFRICA • 300 kW
	†BBC, Multiple Locations	(D) • EUROPE & N AFRICA • 250/300 kW
	USSR †"RADIO MAGALLANES", Via R Moscow	(D) • S AMERICA • 250 kW
	RADIO MOSCOW, Blagoveshchensk	(D) • E ASIA & SE ASIA • WS, CHINESE • 500 kW
	RADIO MOSCOW, Novosibirsk	(J) • E ASIA • 240 kW (J) • JAPANESE • E ASIA • 240 kW
7189v	**EQUATORIAL GUINEA** †RADIO AFRICA, Batá	W AFRICA • 50 kW • ALT. FREQ. TO 9852v kHz Sa/Su • W AFRICA • 50 kW • ALT. FREQ. TO 9852v kHz
7190	**ALBANIA** RADIO TIRANA, Lushnjë	EUROPE • ITALIAN, ETC • 50 kW
(con'd)	**BENIN** ORT DU BENIN, Parakou	DS-FRENCH, ETC • 20 kW

World Time: 0–24

0 Prime Time-Americas 6 Prime Time-E Asia 12 Prime Time-S Asia 18 Prime Time-Europe 24

ENGLISH ARABIC CHINESE FRENCH GERMAN RUSSIAN SPANISH OTHER

FREQUENCY	COUNTRY, STATION, LOCATION	TARGET • NETWORK • POWER (kW)
7190 (con'd)	**CHINA (PR)**	
	RADIO BEIJING, Kunming	SE ASIA • 50 kW
	INDIA	
	†ALL INDIA RADIO, Shillong	DS
	PHILIPPINES	
	RADIO VERITAS ASIA, Palauig	JAPANESE • E ASIA • 250 kW; E ASIA • 250 kW
	SAUDI ARABIA	
	BS OF THE KINGDOM, Riyadh	PERSIAN • MIDEAST • 350 kW
	SRI LANKA	
	SRI LANKA BC CORP, Colombo-Ekala	Su • S ASIA • HINDI • 10 kW; S ASIA • HINDI, TAMIL, ETC • 10 kW
	USA	
	†RFE-RL, Via Germany	E EUROPE & WEST USSR • 100 kW
	†RFE-RL, Via Portugal	E EUROPE & WEST USSR • 250 kW; M-Sa • E EUROPE • 250 kW; Su • WEST USSR • 250 kW
	VOA, Via Tangier, Morocco	(D) • WEST USSR • 100 kW
	YEMEN (PDR)	
	"VO PALESTINE", Via PDR Yemen BC	MIDEAST • PLO • 100 kW
	PDR YEMEN BC SVC, Aden	MIDEAST • DS • 100 kW; F • MIDEAST • DS • 100 kW; Irr • MIDEAST • DS-RAMADAN • 100 kW
7195	**CHINA (PR)**	
	CENTRAL PEOPLES BS, Urümqi	(J) • DS-MINORITIES • 15 kW
	XINJIANG PBS, Urümqi	(J) • DS-UIGHUR • 15 kW; (J) Su • DS-UIGHUR • 15 kW
	ROMANIA	
	†RADIO BUCHAREST, Bucharest	(D) • MIDEAST • 250 kW; (D) • EUROPE • 250 kW; (D) • MIDEAST & EUROPE • 250 kW
	UGANDA	
	RADIO UGANDA, Kampala	DS-ENGLISH, ETC • 20 kW; Sa/Su • DS-ENGLISH, ETC • 20 kW; Su • DS-ENGLISH, ETC • 20 kW
	USA	
	VOA, Via M'rovia, Liberia	W AFRICA & C AFRICA • 50 kW
	USSR	
	RADIO KIEV, Tula	(D) • EUROPE • 240 kW
	RADIO MOSCOW, Komsomol'sk 'Amure	(J) • E ASIA & SE ASIA • 100 kW
	RADIO MOSCOW, Tula	(D) • EUROPE & E NORTH AM • WS, SPANISH • 100 kW
7200	**GABON**	
	†AFRIQUE NUMERO UN, Moyabi	C AFRICA • 250 kW
	KOREA (DPR)	
	RADIO PYONGYANG, Pyongyang	E ASIA & EAST USSR • 200 kW; E ASIA & SE ASIA • 200 kW; (D) • E ASIA & EAST USSR • 200 kW; (D) • E ASIA & SE ASIA • 200 kW
	SWAZILAND	
	†TRANS WORLD RADIO, Manzini	S AFRICA • 25 kW; (J) • S AFRICA • 25 kW
	USA	
	†RFE-RL, Via Germany	WEST USSR • 100 kW
	†RFE-RL, Via Portugal	E EUROPE • 250 kW
	†VOA, Via Philippines	(J) • E ASIA • 100 kW
	†VOA, Via Woofferton, UK	EUROPE & MIDEAST • 250 kW
	USSR	
	RADIO MOSCOW, Vladivostok	(D) • DS-2 • 50 kW; DS-2 • 50 kW
	RADIO MOSCOW, Zhigulevsk	DS-1 • 100 kW; (D) • DS-1 • 100 kW
	YAKUT RADIO, Yakutsk	DS • 50 kW
	YUGOSLAVIA	
	RADIO BEOGRAD, Belgrade	EUROPE, N AFRICA & MIDEAST • DS-1 • 100 kW; Su • DS-1 • 100 kW
7200v	**AFGHANISTAN**	
	RADIO AFGHANISTAN, Kabul	MIDEAST • 50 kW; DS-1 • 50 kW
	SOMALIA	
	RADIO MOGADISHU, Mogadishu	F • DS • 100 kW; Sa-Th • DS • 100 kW; DS-SOMALI, ARABIC • 100 kW
7205	**ALBANIA**	
	RADIO TIRANA, Lushnjë	WEST USSR • 100 kW; EUROPE • 100 kW; MIDEAST • 100 kW
(con'd)		

World Time: 0 Prime Time-Americas 6 Prime Time-E Asia 12 Prime Time-S Asia 18 Prime Time-Europe 24

SUMMER ONLY (J) WINTER ONLY (D) JAMMING / OR /\ EARLIEST HEARD ◁ LATEST HEARD ▷ NEW OR CHANGED FOR 1990 †

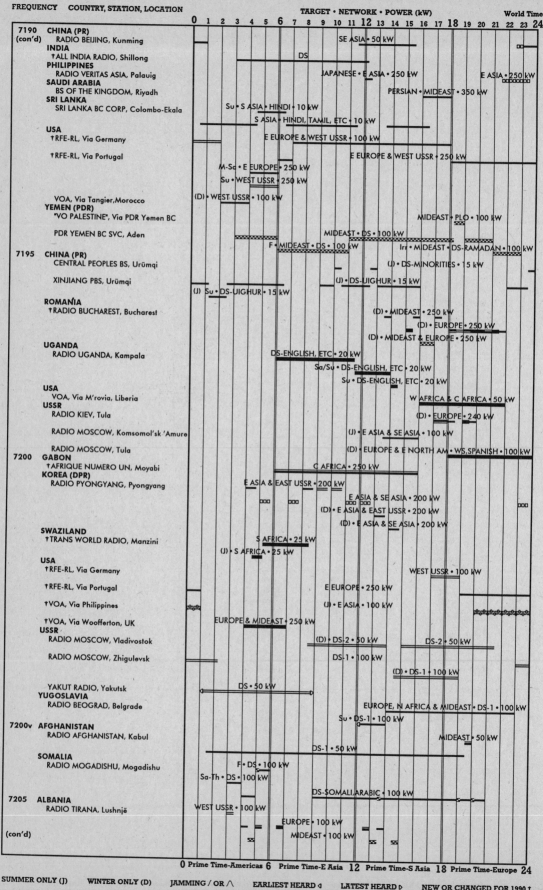

FREQUENCY	COUNTRY, STATION, LOCATION	TARGET • NETWORK • POWER (kW)
7205 (con'd)	**AUSTRALIA** †RADIO AUSTRALIA, Carnarvon	SE ASIA • 300 kW; S ASIA & EUROPE • 300 kW
	†RADIO AUSTRALIA, Shepparton	SE ASIA • 100 kW; (D) • SE ASIA • 100 kW; (J) • SE ASIA • 100 kW
	CAMEROON CAMEROON RTV CORP, Yaoundé	Irr • DS-FRENCH,ENG,ETC • 30 kW; Irr • Su • DS-FRENCH,ENG,ETC • 30 kW
	CYPRUS CYPRUS BC CORP, Zyyi	(J) F-Su • EUROPE • 250 kW
	CZECHOSLOVAKIA RADIO PRAGUE, Prague	W AFRICA • 120 kW
	INDIA ALL INDIA RADIO, Madras	S ASIA • TAMIL • 100 kW
	USA †VOA, Via Kavála, Greece	S ASIA • 250 kW; (J) • MIDEAST • 250 kW; (D) • S ASIA • 250 kW
	†VOA, Via Rhodes, Greece	(D) • MIDEAST • TURKISH, ARABIC • 50 kW
	USSR RADIO MOSCOW, Armavir	EUROPE & ATLANTIC • MARINERS • 100 kW
	RADIO MOSCOW, Kiev	(D) • ATLANTIC & C AMERICA • 100 kW
	RADIO MOSCOW, Krasnoyarsk	(D) • S ASIA • 500 kW
7205v	**ZAIRE** †LA VOIX DU ZAIRE, Lubumbashi	DS-FRENCH,ETC • 10 kW; Sa/Su • DS-FRENCH,ETC • 10 kW; Su • DS-FRENCH,ETC • 10 kW
7210	**HOLLAND** †RADIO NEDERLAND, Flevoland	(D) • MIDEAST • 500 kW
	INDIA †ALL INDIA RADIO, Calcutta	DS • 10 kW
	ALL INDIA RADIO, Delhi	DS • 50 kW
	JAPAN †RADIO JAPAN/NHK, Tokyo-Yamata	E ASIA & EAST USSR • 100 kW; (J) • E ASIA & EAST USSR • 100 kW
	SAUDI ARABIA BS OF THE KINGDOM, Riyadh	MIDEAST • 350 kW; EUROPE • DS-GENERAL • 350 kW
	SWAZILAND †TRANS WORLD RADIO, Manzini	(D) • S AFRICA • 25 kW
	SWITZERLAND RED CROSS BC SVC, Schwarzenburg	Irr • M • EUROPE & N AFRICA • 1ST OR LAST MONDAY • 150 kW; Irr • Su • EUROPE & N AFRICA • 1ST OR LAST SUNDAY • 150 kW
	UNITED KINGDOM †BBC, Daventry	(D) • E EUROPE & WEST USSR • 300 kW
	†BBC, Rampisham	(D) • E EUROPE & MIDEAST • 500 kW; (J) • W EUROPE • 500 kW; (D) M-F • E EUROPE & MIDEAST • 500 kW; (D) M-Sa • E EUROPE & MIDEAST • 500 kW
	†BBC, Skelton, Cumbria	(J) • EUROPE • 250 kW; E EUROPE • 250 kW; (D) • E EUROPE • 250 kW; (J) • E EUROPE • 250 kW; (D) • E EUROPE • 250 kW
	†BBC, Via Zyyi, Cyprus	(D) • WEST USSR • 250 kW
	USA †VOA, Via Philippines	(D) • E ASIA • 100 kW
	VOA, Via Woofferton, UK	(D) • E EUROPE & WEST USSR • 250 kW
	USSR BELORUSSIAN RADIO, Minsk	DS-1 • 15 kW • ALT. FREQ. TO 12005 kHz
	KHABAROVSK RADIO, Khabarovsk	DS-1 • 50 kW
	R TIKHIY OKEAN, Khabarovsk	EAST USSR & PACIFIC • MARINERS • 50 kW; Sa • EAST USSR & PACIFIC • MARINERS • 50 kW; Su-F • EAST USSR & PACIFIC • MARINERS • 50 kW
	RADIO MOSCOW, Moscow	DS-1 • 100 kW; DS-2 • 100 kW
7210v	**CHINA (PR)** YUNNAN PEOPLES BS, Kunming	DS-1 • 50 kW
	SENEGAL ORT DU SENEGAL, Dakar	W AFRICA • 100 kW; Sa/Su • W AFRICA • 100 kW
7215	**AUSTRALIA** RADIO AUSTRALIA, Shepparton	PACIFIC • 100 kW
(con'd)	**CHINA (PR)** †VOICE OF JINLING, Nanjing	E ASIA • 50 kW

World Time: 0 Prime Time-Americas 6 Prime Time-E Asia 12 Prime Time-S Asia 18 Prime Time-Europe 24

ENGLISH ▬ ARABIC ▭ CHINESE ▫▫▫ FRENCH ═ GERMAN ▬ RUSSIAN ═ SPANISH ═ OTHER —

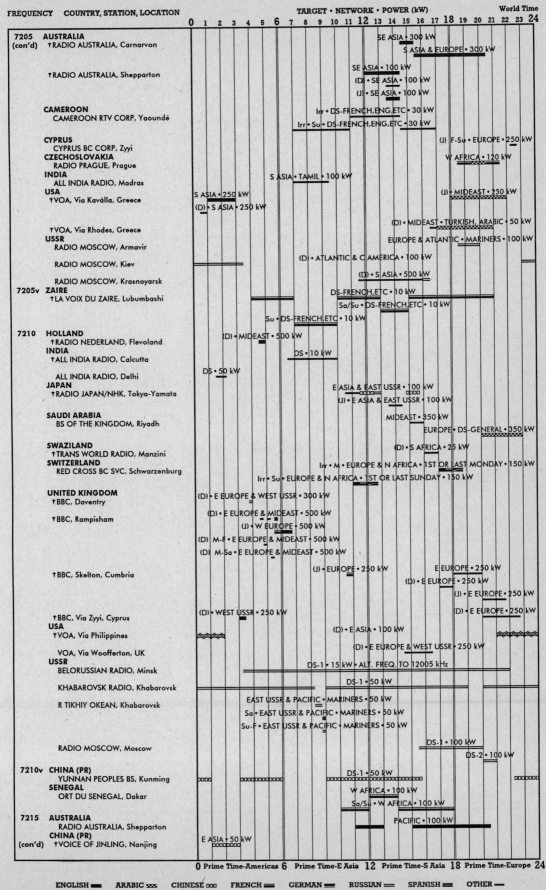

FREQUENCY	COUNTRY, STATION, LOCATION	TARGET • NETWORK • POWER (kW)
7215 (con'd)	**CLANDESTINE (M EAST)**	
	"VO THE CRUSADER", Via R Baghdad	MIDEAST • MOJAHEDIN-E KHALQ
	INDIA	
	ALL INDIA RADIO, Delhi	SE ASIA • 100 kW
	IRAN	
	†VO THE ISLAMIC REP, Tehrān	Irr • MIDEAST • RAMADAN • 500 kW
		MIDEAST • 100 kW
		MIDEAST • 500 kW
		USSR • 500 kW
	IVORY COAST	
	RTV IVOIRIENNE, Abidjan	W AFRICA • DS • 20 kW
	USA	
	†RFE-RL, Via Germany	WEST USSR • 100 kW
	USSR	
	RADIO MOSCOW, Via Plovdiv, Bulgaria	(D) • E NORTH AM • N AMERICAN • 250 kW
	YUGOSLAVIA	
	†RADIO YUGOSLAVIA, Bijeljina	(J) • EUROPE • 250 kW
7215v	**ANGOLA**	
	RADIO NACIONAL, Luanda	DS • 10 kW
7220	**CENTRAL AFRICAN REP**	
	RTV CENTRAFRICAINE, Bangui	DS-FRENCH, ETC • 20/50/100 kW
	CLANDESTINE (M EAST)	
	"RADIO IRAN", Via R Baghdad	MIDEAST • ANTI-IRANIAN GOVT • 500 kW
	"VO THE CRUSADER", Via R Baghdad	MIDEAST • MOJAHEDIN-E KHALQ
	HUNGARY	
	RADIO BUDAPEST, Various Locations	Sa • EUROPE
		EUROPE
		M/Th • EUROPE
		Su • EUROPE
	USA	
	†RFE-RL, Via Germany	WEST USSR • 100 kW
	†VOA, Via Woofferton, UK	(D) • E EUROPE • 300 kW • ALT. FREQ. TO 7295 kHz
	USSR	
	RADIO MOSCOW, Chita	E ASIA & SE ASIA • 500 kW
	YUGOSLAVIA	
	†RADIO YUGOSLAVIA, Bijeljina	EUROPE & N AFRICA • 250 kW
		F-W • EUROPE & N AFRICA • 250 kW
7220v	**ZAMBIA**	
	RADIO ZAMBIA-ZBS, Lusaka	DS-ENGLISH, ETC • 50 kW
7225	**CHINA (PR)**	
	SICHUAN PEOPLES BS, Chengdu	DS-1 • 15 kW
		W-M • DS-1 • 15 kW
	GERMANY (FR)	
	†DEUTSCHE WELLE, Via Cyclops, Malta	(D) • MIDEAST • 250 kW
	†DEUTSCHE WELLE, Via Kigali, Rwanda	C AFRICA & S AFRICA • 250 kW
	†DEUTSCHE WELLE, Via Sri Lanka	S ASIA • 250 kW
	INDIA	
	ALL INDIA RADIO, Aligarh	S ASIA • 250 kW
	ROMANIA	
	RADIO BUCHAREST, Bucharest	(D) • W EUROPE • 250 kW
	SAUDI ARABIA	
	BS OF THE KINGDOM, Riyadh	MIDEAST • DS-GENERAL • 350 kW
	USA	
	VOA, Via Philippines	SE ASIA • 250 kW
7225v	**PAKISTAN**	
	RADIO PAKISTAN, Islamabad	(J) • MIDEAST • 100 kW
7230	**BURKINA FASO**	
	RTV BURKINA, Ouagadougou	DS-FRENCH, ETC • 50 kW
		Th/Sa/Su • DS-FRENCH, ETC • 50 kW
	CANADA	
	R CANADA INTL, Via Sines, Portugal	(J) • E EUROPE & WEST USSR • 300 kW
	†R CANADA INTL, Via United Kingdom	EUROPE • 300 kW
		(D) • EUROPE • 300 kW
		(D) M-F • EUROPE • 300 kW
		(J) M-F • EUROPE • 300 kW
	INDIA	
	†ALL INDIA RADIO, Kurseong	(J) • S ASIA • 20 kW
		(J) • DS • 20 kW
	INDONESIA	
	†RRI, Fak Fak, Irian Jaya	DS • 0.5 kW
	IRAN	
	†VO THE ISLAMIC REP, Tehrān	Irr • MIDEAST & N AFRICA • RAMADAN • 100 kW
		(D) • MIDEAST & S ASIA • 100 kW
		(D) • MIDEAST & N AFRICA • 100 kW
	KOREA (DPR)	
	RADIO PYONGYANG, Pyongyang	E ASIA & EAST USSR • 200 kW
		E ASIA & S ASIA • 100 kW
	SOUTH AFRICA	
	†SOUTH AFRICAN BC, Meyerton	RADIO SUID-AFRIKA • 100 kW
	UNITED KINGDOM	
	†BBC, Daventry	(J) • E EUROPE & WEST USSR • 300 kW
	†BBC, Multiple Locations	(D) • E EUROPE & WEST USSR • 250/300 kW
(con'd)	†BBC, Rampisham	(D) Su • E EUROPE • 500 kW

World Time: 0 1 2 3 4 5 6 7 8 9 10 11 12 13 14 15 16 17 18 19 20 21 22 23 24

0 Prime Time-Americas 6 Prime Time-E Asia 12 Prime Time-S Asia 18 Prime Time-Europe 24

SUMMER ONLY (J) WINTER ONLY (D) JAMMING / OR /\ EARLIEST HEARD ◁ LATEST HEARD ▷ NEW OR CHANGED FOR 1990 †

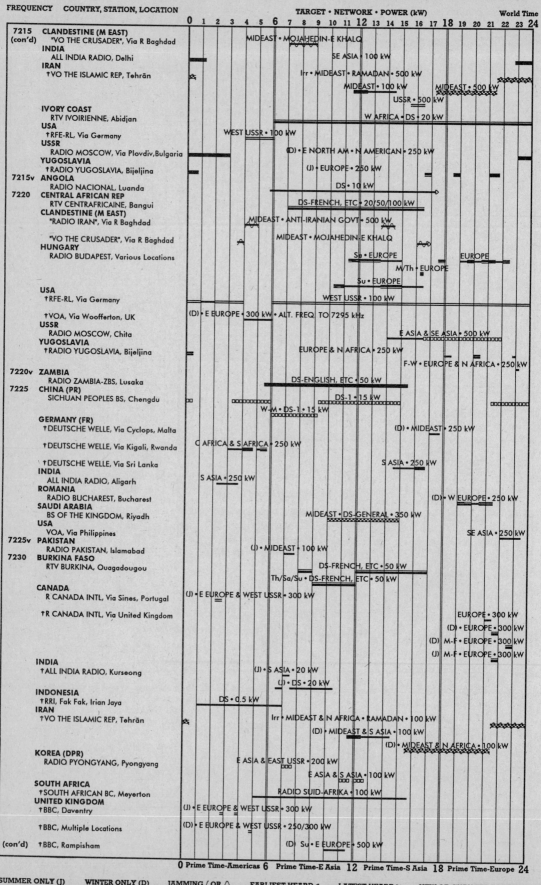

FREQUENCY	COUNTRY, STATION, LOCATION	TARGET • NETWORK • POWER (kW)
7230 (con'd)	**UNITED KINGDOM** †BBC, Skelton, Cumbria	(D) • EUROPE • 250 kW
	†BBC, Via Zyyi, Cyprus	(D) • EUROPE & WEST USSR • 250 kW
	USSR RADIO MOSCOW, Kiev	(D) • EUROPE & W AFRICA • MARINERS • 240 kW EUROPE • 240 kW (J) • EUROPE • 240 kW (D) • EUROPE • 240 kW
	RADIO MOSCOW, Krasnoyarsk	(D) • DS-2 • 100 kW
7235	**ALBANIA** RADIO TIRANA, Krujë	EUROPE • 50 kW
	CANADA R CANADA INTL, Via United Kingdom	EUROPE & WEST USSR • 300 kW (D) • EUROPE & WEST USSR • 300 kW M-F • EUROPE & WEST USSR • 300 kW Sa/Su • EUROPE & WEST USSR • 300 kW
	CHINA (PR) CENTRAL PEOPLES BS, Shijiazhuang	DS-2 • 50 kW
	GERMANY (FR) DEUTSCHE WELLE, Jülich	(J) • W EUROPE • 100 kW
	†DEUTSCHE WELLE, Multiple Locations	(D) • W EUROPE • 100/500 kW (J) • W EUROPE • 100/500 kW
	DEUTSCHE WELLE, Various Locations	MIDEAST • 250/500 kW
	†DEUTSCHE WELLE, Wertachtal	(D) • MIDEAST • 500 kW SE ASIA • 500 kW (D) • WEST USSR • 500 kW
	IRAQ †RADIO BAGHDAD, Balad-Salah el Deen	(D) • MIDEAST • 500 kW
	ITALY †RTV ITALIANA, Rome	(D) • N AFRICA & MIDEAST • 100 kW N AFRICA • 100 kW E EUROPE & MIDEAST • 100 kW E EUROPE & WEST USSR • 100 kW AUSTRALIA • 100 kW (J) • E EUROPE & WEST USSR • 100 kW (J) • E EUROPE • 100 kW
	PAKISTAN RADIO PAKISTAN, Islamabad	(D) • EUROPE • 250 kW
	UNITED KINGDOM †BBC, Via Zyyi, Cyprus	(D) • MIDEAST & S ASIA • 250 kW
	ZAMBIA RADIO ZAMBIA-ZBS, Lusaka	DS • 50 kW
7240	**CAMEROON** CAMEROON RTV CORP, Garoua	DS-FRENCH,ENG,ETC • 100 kW
	INDIA ALL INDIA RADIO, Bombay	DS • 10 kW Su • DS • 50 kW
	KENYA VOICE OF KENYA, Nairobi	DS-EASTERN • 10 kW Su • DS-EASTERN • 10 kW
	UNITED KINGDOM †BBC, Via Maşīrah, Oman	S ASIA • 100 kW
	BBC, Via Singapore	S ASIA • 100 kW
	USA VOA, Via Wertachtal,GFR	(J) • WEST USSR • 500 kW
	USSR †"RADIO MAGALLANES", Via R Moscow	(D) • S AMERICA • 500 kW
	RADIO MOSCOW, Khabarovsk	(D) • 100 kW
	RADIO MOSCOW, Tula	(D) • S AMERICA • 240 kW (D) • EUROPE • 240 kW
	YUGOSLAVIA †RADIO LJUBLJANA, Bijeljina	M • MIDEAST & E AFRICA • DS-ENGLISH, ETC • 250 kW
	†RADIO YUGOSLAVIA, Bijeljina	(D) • W EUROPE • 250 kW
	†RADIO ZAGREB, Bijeljina	Th • MIDEAST & E AFRICA • DS-MARINERS • 250 kW
	†VARIOUS LOCAL STNS, Belgrade	(D) Sa/Su • EUROPE, N AFRICA & MIDEAST • DS • 100 kW
	†VARIOUS LOCAL STNS, Bijeljina	Tu-Su • MIDEAST • DS • 250 kW
7242v	**MOZAMBIQUE** †RADIO MOCAMBIQUE, Maputo	PORTUGUESE • DS • 100 kW
7245	**ANGOLA** RADIO NACIONAL, Luanda	S AFRICA • 100 kW
	GERMANY (FR) †DEUTSCHE WELLE, Via Cyclops, Malta	(J) • MIDEAST • 250 kW
	LIBYA †RADIO JAMAHIRIYA, Tripoli	AFRICA • 500 kW • ALT. FREQ. TO 15450 kHz
	MAURITANIA ORT DE MAURITANIE, Nouakchott	DS-FRENCH,ARAB,ETC • 100 kW • ALT. FREQ. TO 9610 kHz F • DS-FRENCH,ARAB,ETC • 100 kW • ALT. FREQ. TO 9610 kHz
(con'd)		

World Time: 0 1 2 3 4 5 6 7 8 9 10 11 12 13 14 15 16 17 18 19 20 21 22 23 24

0 Prime Time-Americas 6 Prime Time-E Asia 12 Prime Time-S Asia 18 Prime Time-Europe 24

ENGLISH — ARABIC — CHINESE — FRENCH — GERMAN — RUSSIAN — SPANISH — OTHER —

FREQUENCY	COUNTRY, STATION, LOCATION	TARGET • NETWORK • POWER (kW)
7245 (con'd)	**USA**	
	†RFE-RL, Via Germany	WEST USSR • 100 kW
	†RFE-RL, Via Pals, Spain	WEST USSR • 250 kW
	†RFE-RL, Via Portugal	E EUROPE & WEST USSR • 250 kW
		M-Sa • E EUROPE • 250 kW
		Su • WEST USSR • 250 kW
	†VOA, Via Ismaning, GFR	(D) • WEST USSR • 100 kW
	†VOA, Via Wertachtal,GFR	(J) • WEST USSR • 500 kW
	USSR	
	R TIKHIY OKEAN, Khabarovsk	E ASIA & PACIFIC • MARINERS • 240 kW
	RADIO MOSCOW, Khabarovsk	240 kW
7246	**ALGERIA**	
	RTV ALGERIENNE, Ouled Fayet	Sa-Th • EUROPE & N AFRICA • DS-1 • 50 kW
		Sa-W • EUROPE & N AFRICA • DS-1 • 50 kW
		EUROPE & N AFRICA • DS-2/KABYL • 50 kW
		F • EUROPE & N AFRICA • DS-2/KABYL • 50 kW
		Th/F • EUROPE & N AFRICA • DS-2/KABYL • 50 kW
7250	**CHINA (TAIWAN)**	
	†CENTRAL BC SYSTEM, T'ai-pei	PRC-1 • 100 kW
	INDIA	
	ALL INDIA RADIO, Lucknow	DS-B • 10 kW
		Su • DS-B • 10 kW
	IRAQ	
	†RADIO BAGHDAD, Balad-Salah el Deen	(D) • MIDEAST • 500 kW
	SAUDI ARABIA	
	BS OF THE KINGDOM, Jiddah	C AFRICA • DS-HOLY KORAN • 50 kW
	SINGAPORE	
	SINGAPORE BC CORP, Jurong	DS-MALAY • 50 kW
	TURKEY	
	†TURKISH RTV CORP, Ankara	(D) • TURKISH • EUROPE • 250 kW
		(D) • EUROPE • 250 kW
	USSR	
	RADIO MOSCOW, Kazan'	EUROPE • 100 kW
	RADIO MOSCOW, Serpuhkov	(D) • C AMERICA • 100 kW
		(D) • DS-1 • 100 kW
	RADIO MOSCOW, Tula	EUROPE • 100 kW
	VATICAN STATE	
	†VATICAN RADIO, Sta Maria di Galeria	E EUROPE & WEST USSR • 100 kW
		W EUROPE & N AFRICA • 100 kW
		EUROPE • 100 kW
		Su • EUROPE • 100 kW
		Th • EUROPE • 100 kW
		M-Sa • ENGLISH, FRENCH & SPANISH • EUROPE • 100 kW
		M-Sa • ENGLISH, FRENCH, SPANISH & ITALIAN • EUROPE • 100 kW
	YUGOSLAVIA	
	†RADIO YUGOSLAVIA, Bijeljina	MIDEAST & N AFRICA • 500 kW
7255	**BOTSWANA**	
	RADIO BOTSWANA, Gaborone	DS-ENGLISH, ETC • 50 kW
	BULGARIA	
	†RADIO SOFIA, Stolnik	EUROPE, MIDEAST & N AFRICA • 150 kW
		(D) • EUROPE, MIDEAST & N AFRICA • 150 kW
		M-Sa • EUROPE, MIDEAST & N AFRICA • 150 kW
		(D) Su • EUROPE, MIDEAST & N AFRICA • 150 kW
	GERMANY (FR)	
	†DEUTSCHE WELLE, Wertachtal	(J) • E EUROPE • 500 kW
	INDIA	
	ALL INDIA RADIO, Aligarh	S ASIA & E ASIA • 250 kW
	NIGERIA	
	VOICE OF NIGERIA, Ikorodu	W AFRICA • 50 kW
	UNITED KINGDOM	
	BBC, Rampisham	(D) • E EUROPE & WEST USSR • 500 kW
		(J) • E EUROPE & MIDEAST • 100 kW
		(D) Su • E EUROPE & WEST USSR • 500 kW
	BBC, Skelton, Cumbria	(D) • E EUROPE • 250 kW
		(D) Su • E EUROPE • 250 kW
	USA	
	†RFE-RL, Via Germany	WEST USSR • 100/250 kW
	†RFE-RL, Via Pals, Spain	WEST USSR • 250 kW
	VOA, Via Kavála, Greece	(J) • N AFRICA • 250 kW
	USSR	
	†RADIO ALMA-ATA, Alma-Ata	(J) • E ASIA • 100 kW
	RADIO MOSCOW, Minsk	(D) • DS-3 • 100 kW
	†RADIO TASHKENT, Alma-Ata	(J) • E ASIA • 100 kW
7257	**ITALY**	
	†ADVENTIST WORLD R, Forli	EUROPE • 1.3 kW • ALT. FREQ. TO 7125 kHz
		EUROPE • 1.5 kW
		EUROPE • 1.3 kW
(con'd)		M-W • EUROPE • 1.3 kW • ALT. FREQ. TO 7125 kHz

World Time: 0 1 2 3 4 5 6 7 8 9 10 11 12 13 14 15 16 17 18 19 20 21 22 23 24

0 Prime Time-Americas 6 Prime Time-E Asia 12 Prime Time-S Asia 18 Prime Time-Europe 24

SUMMER ONLY (J) WINTER ONLY (D) JAMMING / OR ∧ EARLIEST HEARD ◃ LATEST HEARD ▹ NEW OR CHANGED FOR 1990 †

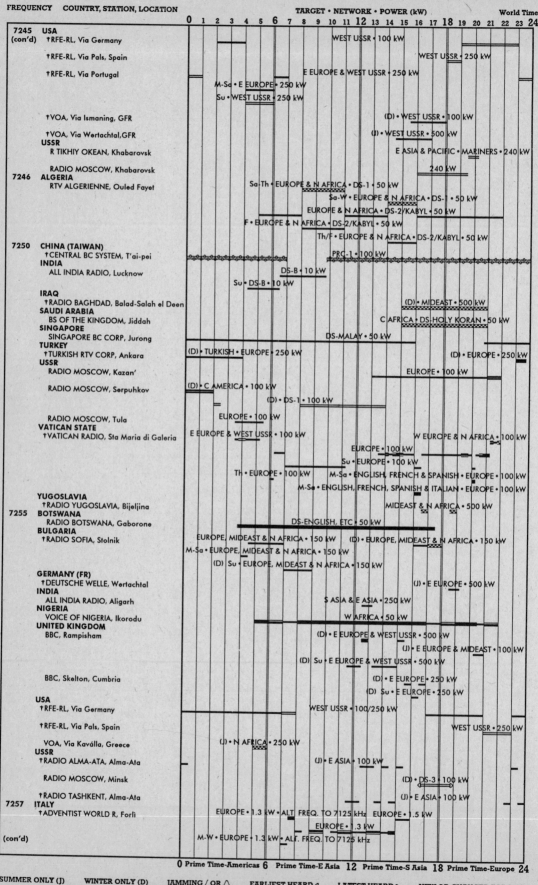

FREQUENCY | COUNTRY, STATION, LOCATION | TARGET • NETWORK • POWER (kW) | World Time 0–24

7257 (con'd) ITALY
†ADVENTIST WORLD R, Forlì
- M-W • EUROPE • 1.3 kW
- Su/M • EUROPE • 1.3 kW
- Th-Su • EUROPE • 1.3 kW • ALT. FREQ. TO 7125 kHz
- Th-Su • EUROPE • 1.3 kW
- Tu-Sa • EUROPE • 1.3 kW

7259.8 VANUATU
RADIO VANUATU, Vila, Efate Island
- DS-ENGLISH,FR,ETC • 10 kW

7260 CANADA
†R CANADA INTL, Via United Kingdom
- (D) • EUROPE & WEST USSR • 300 kW
- (J) • EUROPE & WEST USSR • 300 kW

CHINA (PR)
†RADIO BEIJING, Baoding
- (D) • S ASIA • 120 kW
- (D) • S ASIA & E AFRICA • 120 kW

GERMANY (DR)
R BERLIN INTL, Nauen
- EUROPE • 500 kW

INDIA
ALL INDIA RADIO, Bombay
- DS • 100 kW

UNITED KINGDOM
†BBC, Rampisham
- (D) • WEST USSR • 500 kW
- (D) • E EUROPE • 500 kW
- (J) • WEST USSR • 500 kW
- (J) • E EUROPE • 500 kW
- (D) M-F • E EUROPE • 500 kW
- (J) M-F • E EUROPE • 500 kW
- M-Sa • E EUROPE • 500 kW
- (D) M-Sa • E EUROPE • 500 kW
- (J) M-Sa • E EUROPE • 500 kW
- (D) Su • E EUROPE • 500 kW
- (J) Su • E EUROPE • 500 kW

†BBC, Via Zyyi, Cyprus
- (D) • WEST USSR • 250 kW

USA
VOA, Via Philippines
- (J) • SE ASIA • 250 kW

USSR
R TIKHIY OKEAN, Novosibirsk
- (D) • E ASIA & PACIFIC • MARINERS • 100 kW

R TIKHIY OKEAN, Petropavlovsk-Kam
- (D) • E ASIA & W NORTH AM • MARINERS • 100 kW
- (D) Sa • E ASIA & W NORTH AM • MARINERS • 100 kW
- (D) Su-F • E ASIA & W NORTH AM • MARINERS • 100 kW

†RADIO MOSCOW
- (D) • DS
- (D) • JAPANESE • E ASIA

RADIO MOSCOW, Novosibirsk
- (D) • E ASIA & PACIFIC • 100 kW

RADIO MOSCOW, Petropavlovsk-Kam
- (D) • E ASIA & W NORTH AM • 100 kW
- (D) • JAPANESE • E ASIA & W NORTH AM • 100 kW
- (D) • E ASIA & W NORTH AM • N AMERICAN • 100 kW

RADIO MOSCOW, Vinnitsa
- (D) • ATLANTIC • MARINERS • 100 kW

7260v COMOROS
RADIO COMORO, Moroni
- DS • 4 kW

7262v MONGOLIA
†RADIO ULAN BATOR, Ulan Bator
- DS • 25 kW
- Tu/F • DS • 25 kW
- W/Th/Sa-M • DS • 25 kW

USSR
†RADIO MOSCOW, Via Mongolia
- 25 kW

7265 ALBANIA
RADIO TIRANA, Krujë
- EUROPE • 50 kW

GERMANY (FR)
DEUTSCHE WELLE, Via Cyclops, Malta
- (D) • MIDEAST • 250 kW
- (J) • N AFRICA • 250 kW

SUDWESTFUNK, Rohrdorf
- EUROPE • DS-3, ARD-NACHT • 20 kW

INDIA
†ALL INDIA RADIO, Delhi
- SE ASIA • 100 kW
- AUSTRALIA • 100 kW
- MIDEAST & N AFRICA • PERSIAN, ARABIC • 100 kW

SWEDEN
†RADIO SWEDEN, Hörby
- EUROPE • 350 kW
- (D) • EUROPE • 350 kW
- (J) • SWEDISH • EUROPE • 350 kW
- (J) • EUROPE • 350 kW

TOGO
†RADIO LOME, Lomé-Togblekope
- DS • 100 kW
- DS-FRENCH, ETC • 100 kW

USA
VOA, Via Kaválla, Greece
- (D) • USSR • 250 kW

(con'd) †VOA, Via M'rovia, Liberia
- W AFRICA & S AFRICA • 250 kW

0 Prime Time-Americas 6 Prime Time-E Asia 12 Prime Time-S Asia 18 Prime Time-Europe 24

ENGLISH ▬ ARABIC ▭ CHINESE ▫ FRENCH ═ GERMAN ▬ RUSSIAN ═ SPANISH ═ OTHER —

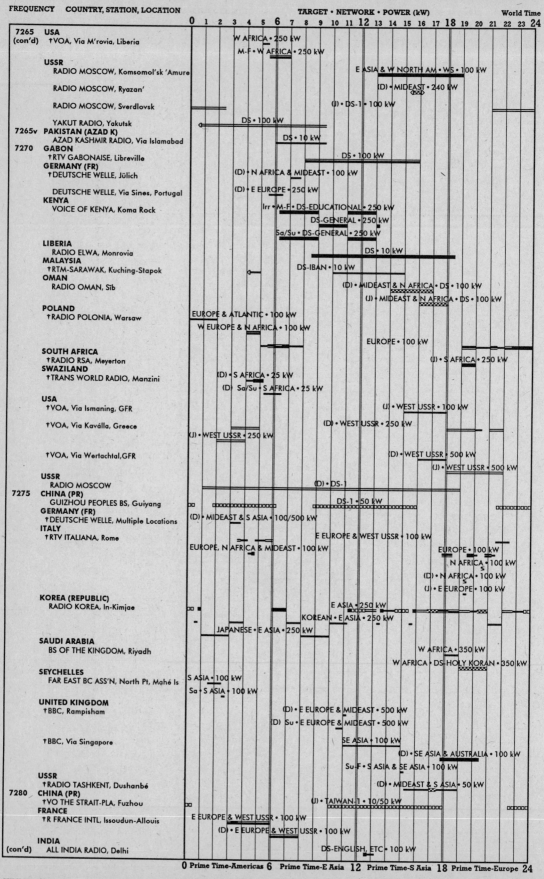

FREQUENCY	COUNTRY, STATION, LOCATION	TARGET • NETWORK • POWER (kW)
7265 (con'd)	**USA** †VOA, Via M'rovia, Liberia	W AFRICA • 250 kW; M-F • W AFRICA • 250 kW
	USSR RADIO MOSCOW, Komsomol'sk 'Amure	E ASIA & W NORTH AM • WS • 100 kW
	RADIO MOSCOW, Ryazan'	(D) • MIDEAST • 240 kW
	RADIO MOSCOW, Sverdlovsk	(J) • DS-1 • 100 kW
	YAKUT RADIO, Yakutsk	DS • 100 kW
7265v	**PAKISTAN (AZAD K)** AZAD KASHMIR RADIO, Via Islamabad	DS • 10 kW
7270	**GABON** †RTV GABONAISE, Libreville	DS • 100 kW
	GERMANY (FR) †DEUTSCHE WELLE, Jülich	(D) • N AFRICA & MIDEAST • 100 kW
	DEUTSCHE WELLE, Via Sines, Portugal	(D) • E EUROPE • 250 kW
	KENYA VOICE OF KENYA, Koma Rock	Irr • M-F • DS-EDUCATIONAL • 250 kW; DS-GENERAL • 250 kW; Sa/Su • DS-GENERAL • 250 kW
	LIBERIA RADIO ELWA, Monrovia	DS • 10 kW
	MALAYSIA †RTM-SARAWAK, Kuching-Stapok	DS-IBAN • 10 kW
	OMAN RADIO OMAN, Sib	(D) • MIDEAST & N AFRICA • DS • 100 kW; (J) • MIDEAST & N AFRICA • DS • 100 kW
	POLAND †RADIO POLONIA, Warsaw	EUROPE & ATLANTIC • 100 kW; W EUROPE & N AFRICA • 100 kW; EUROPE • 100 kW
	SOUTH AFRICA †RADIO RSA, Meyerton	(J) • S AFRICA • 250 kW
	SWAZILAND †TRANS WORLD RADIO, Manzini	(D) • S AFRICA • 25 kW; (D) Sa/Su • S AFRICA • 25 kW
	USA †VOA, Via Ismaning, GFR	(J) • WEST USSR • 100 kW
	†VOA, Via Kavála, Greece	(D) • WEST USSR • 250 kW; (J) • WEST USSR • 250 kW
	†VOA, Via Wertachtal, GFR	(D) • WEST USSR • 500 kW; (J) • WEST USSR • 500 kW
	USSR RADIO MOSCOW	(D) • DS-1
7275	**CHINA (PR)** GUIZHOU PEOPLES BS, Guiyang	DS-1 • 50 kW
	GERMANY (FR) †DEUTSCHE WELLE, Multiple Locations	(D) • MIDEAST & S ASIA • 100/500 kW
	ITALY †RTV ITALIANA, Rome	E EUROPE & WEST USSR • 100 kW; EUROPE, N AFRICA & MIDEAST • 100 kW; EUROPE • 100 kW; N AFRICA • 100 kW; (D) • N AFRICA • 100 kW; (J) • E EUROPE • 100 kW
	KOREA (REPUBLIC) RADIO KOREA, In-Kimjae	E ASIA • 250 kW; KOREAN • E ASIA • 250 kW; JAPANESE • E ASIA • 250 kW
	SAUDI ARABIA BS OF THE KINGDOM, Riyadh	W AFRICA • 350 kW; W AFRICA • DS-HOLY KORAN • 350 kW
	SEYCHELLES FAR EAST BC ASS'N, North Pt, Mahé Is	S ASIA • 100 kW; Sa • S ASIA • 100 kW
	UNITED KINGDOM †BBC, Rampisham	(D) • E EUROPE & MIDEAST • 500 kW; (D) Su • E EUROPE & MIDEAST • 500 kW
	†BBC, Via Singapore	SE ASIA • 100 kW; (D) • SE ASIA & AUSTRALIA • 100 kW; Su-F • S ASIA & SE ASIA • 100 kW
	USSR †RADIO TASHKENT, Dushanbé	(D) • MIDEAST & S ASIA • 50 kW
7280	**CHINA (PR)** †VO THE STRAIT-PLA, Fuzhou	(J) • TAIWAN-1 • 10/50 kW
	FRANCE †R FRANCE INTL, Issoudun-Allouis	E EUROPE & WEST USSR • 100 kW; (D) • E EUROPE & WEST USSR • 100 kW
(con'd)	**INDIA** ALL INDIA RADIO, Delhi	DS-ENGLISH, ETC • 100 kW

World Time: 0 Prime Time-Americas 6 Prime Time-E Asia 12 Prime Time-S Asia 18 Prime Time-Europe 24

SUMMER ONLY (J) WINTER ONLY (D) JAMMING / OR ⋀ EARLIEST HEARD ◁ LATEST HEARD ▷ NEW OR CHANGED FOR 1990 †

FREQUENCY	COUNTRY, STATION, LOCATION	TARGET • NETWORK • POWER (kW)
7280 (con'd)	**INDIA** ALL INDIA RADIO, Gauhati	DS • 10 kW; Su • DS • 10 kW
	IRAQ †RADIO BAGHDAD, Balad-Salah el Deen	(D) • S ASIA • 500 kW; (D) • W EUROPE • 500 kW
	JAPAN †RADIO JAPAN/NHK, Tokyo-Yamata	(D) • SE ASIA • GENERAL • 100 kW
	SAUDI ARABIA BS OF THE KINGDOM, Jiddah	MIDEAST & E AFRICA • DS-GENERAL • 50 kW
	UNITED ARAB EMIRATES †VOICE OF THE UAE, Abu Dhabi	(D) • MIDEAST & N AFRICA • 500 kW
	USA VOA, Via Kaválla, Greece	(D) • WEST USSR • 250 kW; (J) • S ASIA • 250 kW; (J) • WEST USSR • 250 kW; MIDEAST • PERSIAN, ETC • 250 kW
	VOA, Via M'rovia, Liberia	W AFRICA & C AFRICA • 250 kW
	USSR RADIO MOSCOW, Dushanbé	(D) • EUROPE • 500 kW
	RADIO MOSCOW, Kenga	(D) • E ASIA • 50 kW
	RADIO MOSCOW, Komsomol'sk 'Amure	E ASIA & AUSTRALIA • 240 kW; (D) • E ASIA & AUSTRALIA • 240 kW; (J) • JAPANESE • E ASIA & AUSTRALIA • 240 kW
	RADIO MOSCOW, Moscow	(D) • DS-1 • 200 kW
7285	**CANADA** R CANADA INTL, Via Sines, Portugal	(D) • EUROPE & WEST USSR • 250 kW
	CHINA (TAIWAN) †VOICE OF ASIA, Kao-hsiung	SE ASIA • 100 kW
	GERMANY (FR) †DEUTSCHE WELLE, Jülich	(J) • WEST USSR • 100 kW
	DEUTSCHE WELLE, Via Sines, Portugal	(D) • E EUROPE • 250 kW
	†DEUTSCHE WELLE, Wertachtal	S ASIA • 500 kW; (D) • WEST USSR • 500 kW
	HOLLAND †RADIO NEDERLAND, Via Madagascar	SE ASIA • 300 kW
	IRAN †VO THE ISLAMIC REP, Tehrān	Alternative Frequency to 7110 kHz
	NIGERIA RADIO NIGERIA, Lagos	DS-1/ENGLISH, ETC • 50 kW
	POLAND †RADIO POLONIA, Warsaw	EUROPE & N AFRICA • 100 kW; (D) • EUROPE • 100 kW; EUROPE • 100 kW; (D) • EUROPE & N AFRICA • 100 kW
	SOUTH AFRICA SOUTH AFRICAN BC, Meyerton	ENGLISH & AFRIKAANS • DS-RADIO ORANJE • 100 kW
	SWAZILAND †TRANS WORLD RADIO, Manzini	(J) • E AFRICA • 100 kW; S AFRICA • 25 kW
	UNITED KINGDOM †BBC, Skelton, Cumbria	(D) • EUROPE • 250 kW
	USA †VOA, Via Philippines	E ASIA • 100 kW
	USSR RADIO MOSCOW, Chita	(D) • SE ASIA • 500 kW
	RADIO MOSCOW, Moscow	(D) • DS-2 • 240 kW
7285v	**MALI** RTV MALIENNE, Bamako	DS-FRENCH, ETC • 50 kW; M-Sa • DS-FRENCH, ETC • 50 kW
7290	**HOLLAND** RADIO NEDERLAND, Flevoland	(J) • MIDEAST • 500 kW
	RADIO NEDERLAND, Via Madagascar	(J) • AUSTRALIA • 300 kW
	HONG KONG †RTV HONG KONG	SE ASIA • VIETNAMESE • 12 kW
	ITALY †RTV ITALIANA, Rome	EUROPE • 100 kW; (D) • EUROPE • 100 kW; (D) Su • EUROPE • 100 kW
	MONACO †TRANS WORLD RADIO, Monte Carlo	(D) • E EUROPE • 100 kW; (J) • E EUROPE • 100 kW; (J) Su • E EUROPE • 100 kW
	PIRATE (EUROPE) †"RADIO PACMAN", Holland	Irr • Su • W EUROPE • ENGLISH, DUTCH • 0.01 kW
	USA VOA, Via Kaválla, Greece	(D) • S ASIA • 250 kW
	USSR RADIO MOSCOW, Moscow	ATLANTIC • MARINERS • 240 kW
	RADIO MOSCOW, Vladivostok	(J) • W NORTH AM & PACIFIC • WS • 240 kW
7290v (con'd)	**PAKISTAN** PAKISTAN BC CORP, Islamabad	DS • 100 kW; DS-ENGLISH, ETC • 100 kW

World Time 0–24: 0 Prime Time-Americas 6 Prime Time-E Asia 12 Prime Time-S Asia 18 Prime Time-Europe 24

ENGLISH ▬ ARABIC ▩ CHINESE ▫▫▫ FRENCH ═ GERMAN ▬ RUSSIAN ═ SPANISH ▬ OTHER —

FREQUENCY | COUNTRY, STATION, LOCATION | TARGET • NETWORK • POWER (kW) | World Time 0–24

7290v (con'd) PAKISTAN
- PAKISTAN BC CORP, Islamabad — (J) • DS • 10 kW; (J) • DS • 100 kW
- RADIO PAKISTAN, Islamabad — (J) • S ASIA • FEEDER • 10 kW

7295 CANADA
- R CANADA INTL, Via United Kingdom — (J) M-F • EUROPE • 100 kW

CHINA (PR)
- †RADIO BEIJING, Baoding — (D) • JAPANESE • E ASIA • 120 kW; JAPANESE • E ASIA • 120 kW; (D) • E AFRICA & S AFRICA • 120 kW

GERMANY (DR)
- R BERLIN INTL, Nauen — W EUROPE • 100 kW; EUROPE & N AFRICA • 100 kW

GHANA
- GHANA BC CORP, Accra — DS-2 • 50 kW; Sa/Su • DS-2 • 50 kW; M-F • DS-EDUCATIONAL • 50 kW

HOLLAND
- RADIO NEDERLAND, Flevoland — (D) • EUROPE • 500 kW

INDIA
- ALL INDIA RADIO, Aizawl — DS • 50 kW

IRAQ
- RADIO BAGHDAD, Balad-Salah el Deen — (D) • EUROPE • 500 kW

ITALY
- †RADIO EUROPE — Sa-M • EUROPE • 0.04 kW

MALAYSIA
- †RADIO MALAYSIA, Kajang — DS • 100 kW; F-Su • DS • 100 kW; M-Th • DS • 100 kW; Irr • M-Th • DS • 100 kW; Sa/Su • DS • 100 kW

SOUTH AFRICA
- †RADIO RSA, Meyerton — (J) Sa/Su • S AFRICA • 250 kW; S AFRICA • 250 kW; (D) • S AFRICA • 250 kW; (J) • S AFRICA • 250 kW

USA
- †R FREE AFGHANISTAN, Via Germany — WEST USSR & S ASIA • 100 kW
- †RFE-RL, Via Germany — WEST USSR • 100 kW
- VOA, Via Kavália, Greece — (D) • MIDEAST & S ASIA • 250 kW
- †VOA, Via Woofferton, UK — Alternative Frequency to 7220 kHz; (J) • E EUROPE • 300 kW

USSR
- RADIO MOSCOW, Krasnoyarsk — (D) • SE ASIA • 500 kW; (D) • SE ASIA • WS • 500 kW
- RADIO MOSCOW, Moscow — (J) • DS-1 • 240 kW

ZAIRE
- LA VOIX DU ZAIRE, Mbuji-Mayi — DS • 10 kW; Irr • DS • 10 kW; Irr • Sa/Su • DS • 10 kW; Irr • Su • DS • 10 kW

7300 ALBANIA
- RADIO TIRANA, Lushnjë — N AMERICA & C AMERICA • 100 kW; WEST USSR • 100 kW; EUROPE • 100 kW; EUROPE • 50 kW; MIDEAST • PERSIAN, TURKISH • 100 kW

USSR
- †AZERBAIJANI RADIO, Baku — DS-2
- RADIO MOSCOW — (D) • C AMERICA
- RADIO YEREVAN, Yerevan — (D) • EUROPE • 100 kW; (D) M-Sa • EUROPE • 100 kW; (D) Su • EUROPE • 100 kW

7305 USSR
- RADIO MOSCOW, Krasnodar — DS-2 • 100 kW
- RADIO MOSCOW, Novosibirsk — (D) • DS-1 • 100 kW
- RADIO MOSCOW, Star'obel'sk — DS-2 • 100 kW; MIDEAST • 100 kW; MIDEAST • WS • 100 kW

7310 ALBANIA
- RADIO TIRANA, Lushnjë — EUROPE • 50 kW

TUNISIA
- RTV TUNISIENNE, Sfax — Irr • DS-RAMADAN • 100 kW; (D) • DS • 100 kW

USSR
- RADIO MOSCOW, Khabarovsk — (D) • DS-2 • 100 kW
- (con'd) RADIO MOSCOW, Moscow — (D) • E NORTH AM • N AMERICAN • 100 kW

0 Prime Time-Americas 6 Prime Time-E Asia 12 Prime Time-S Asia 18 Prime Time-Europe 24

SUMMER ONLY (J) WINTER ONLY (D) JAMMING / OR ⋀ EARLIEST HEARD ◁ LATEST HEARD ▷ NEW OR CHANGED FOR 1990 †

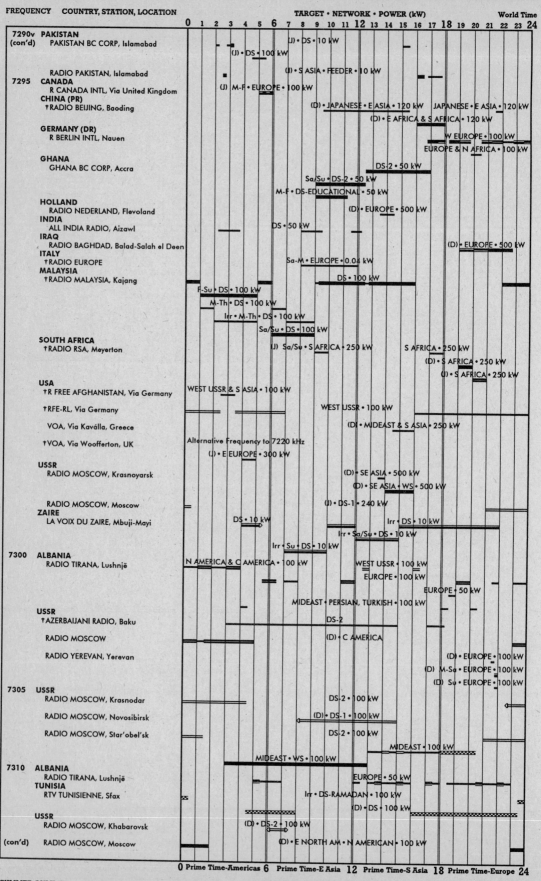

FREQUENCY	COUNTRY, STATION, LOCATION	TARGET • NETWORK • POWER (kW)
7310 (con'd)	**USSR** RADIO MOSCOW, Moscow	EUROPE & ATLANTIC • 100 kW; (D) • EUROPE & ATLANTIC • 100 kW; (D) • E NORTH AM • 100 kW; (D) • EUROPE & ATLANTIC • WS • 100 kW
	RADIO MOSCOW, Nikolayevsk 'Amure	DS-2 • 100 kW
7315	**CHINA (PR)** †RADIO BEIJING, Xi'an	(D) • AFRICA • 240 kW
	MONACO †TRANS WORLD RADIO, Monte Carlo	(D) • E EUROPE • 100 kW
	USSR RADIO MOSCOW	(D) • MARINERS
	RADIO MOSCOW, Irkutsk	(J) • E ASIA • WS • 500 kW; (D) • E ASIA • 500 kW; (D) • S ASIA • WS • 500 kW
	RADIO MOSCOW, Kalinin	(J) • DS-1 • 100 kW
7320	**UNITED KINGDOM** BBC, Rampisham	W EUROPE & N AFRICA • 500 kW
	USSR MAGADAN RADIO, Yakutsk	DS • 100 kW
	RADIO MOSCOW, Krasnodar	(D) • E NORTH AM • N AMERICAN • 500 kW
	RADIO MOSCOW, Minsk	(J) • E NORTH AM & C AMERICA • MARINERS • 100 kW; (J) • EUROPE • WS • 100 kW; (J) • EUROPE • 100 kW
7320v	**CLANDESTINE (ASIA)** †"VIET RESISTANCE R	SE ASIA • ANTI-VIETNAM GOVT
7325	**UNITED KINGDOM** †BBC, Daventry	(J) • C AMERICA • 300 kW; (J) • EUROPE & N AFRICA • 300 kW; (D) • E NORTH AM & C AMERICA • 300/500 kW
	†BBC, Multiple Locations	EUROPE & N AFRICA • 100/250/300 kW
	†BBC, Rampisham	(J) • E EUROPE & MIDEAST • 500 kW; (J) M-F • E EUROPE & MIDEAST • 500 kW; (J) M-Sa • E EUROPE & MIDEAST • 500 kW
	USA †VOA, Via Woofferton, UK	EUROPE • 300 kW
	USSR RADIO MOSCOW, Novosibirsk	DS-1 • 50 kW; (J) • DS-2 • 50 kW
	†RADIO TASHKENT, Frunze, Kirgiziya	(J) • S ASIA • 100 kW; (J) • MIDEAST • 100 kW
7330	**USSR** †"RADIO MAGALLANES", Via R Moscow	(D) • C AMERICA & S AMERICA • 240 kW
	RADIO KIEV, Kiev	(J) • ATLANTIC • 100 kW; (J) • EUROPE • 100 kW
	RADIO MOSCOW	(D) • W AFRICA & S AMERICA
	RADIO MOSCOW, Chita	E ASIA • 100 kW; (D) • S ASIA & MIDEAST • 100 kW
	RADIO MOSCOW, Khabarovsk	(D) • E ASIA • 240 kW
	†RADIO MOSCOW, Kiev	(J) • EUROPE & ATLANTIC • WS, MARINERS, GERMAN • 100 kW; (D) • C AMERICA & S AMERICA • 240 kW
	RS SOV BELORUSSIA, Kiev	(J) M/Tu/Th/F • EUROPE • 100 kW; (J) W/Sa/Su • EUROPE • 100 kW
7335	**CHINA (PR)** CENTRAL PEOPLES BS, Xi'an	DS-1 • 50 kW
	†RADIO BEIJING, Xi'an	(D) • E AFRICA & S AFRICA • 150 kW
	USSR R TIKHIY OKEAN, Khabarovsk	MARINERS • 100 kW
	RADIO MOSCOW, Khabarovsk	DS-1 • 100 kW; DS-2 • 100 kW
	RADIO MOSCOW, Simferopol'	(D) • N AMERICA & C AMERICA • N AMERICAN • 500 kW; (D) • N AMERICA & C AMERICA • 500 kW; (D) • EUROPE • UK SVC • 500 kW; (D) • N AMERICA & C AMERICA • WS • 500 kW; (D) • EUROPE • WS • 500 kW
	†RADIO TASHKENT, Tashkent	MIDEAST • 100 kW
7340	**CHINA (PR)** †RADIO BEIJING, Beijing	(D) • E EUROPE & WEST USSR • 500 kW
	USSR RADIO MOSCOW, Irkutsk	(D) • JAPANESE • E ASIA • 500 kW; (D) • S ASIA • 500 kW
(con'd)		

World Time 0–24: 0 Prime Time-Americas 6 Prime Time-E Asia 12 Prime Time-S Asia 18 Prime Time-Europe 24

ENGLISH ▬ ARABIC ▭ CHINESE ▫▫▫ FRENCH ═ GERMAN ═ RUSSIAN ═ SPANISH ═ OTHER —

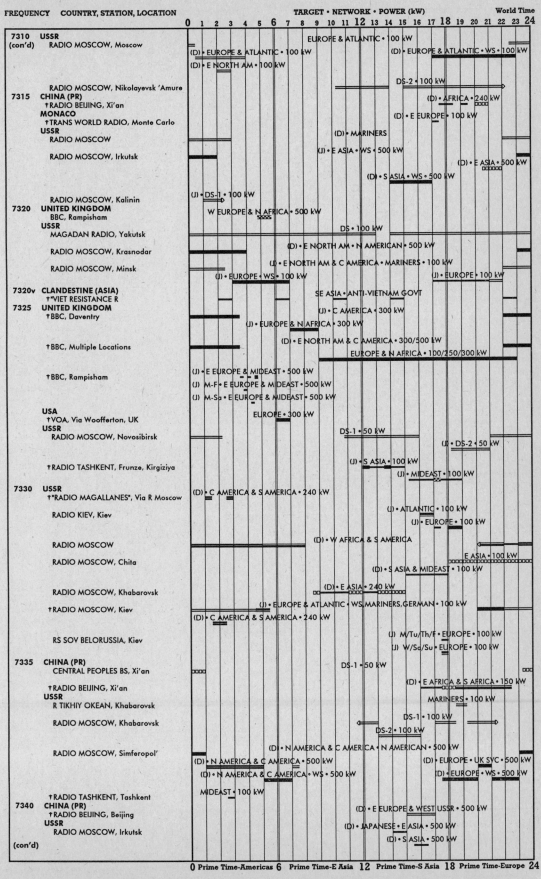

FREQUENCY	COUNTRY, STATION, LOCATION	TARGET • NETWORK • POWER (kW)
7340 (con'd)	**USSR**	
	RADIO MOSCOW, Irkutsk	(D) • E ASIA • 500 kW
	RADIO MOSCOW, Kalinin	(D) • EUROPE • 100 kW
	RADIO MOSCOW, Krasnoyarsk	(J) • DS-2 • 100 kW
	RADIO MOSCOW, Leningrad	(D) • DS-1 • 100 kW
	RADIO MOSCOW, Yerevan	(D) • ATLANTIC • 120 kW
	TASS NEWS AGENCY, Tula	M-F • DS • 50 kW
7345	**CZECHOSLOVAKIA**	
	RADIO PRAGUE, Prague	AMERICAS • 120 kW
		EUROPE • 120 kW
		M-F • EUROPE • 120 kW
		Sa/Su • EUROPE • 120 kW
		EUROPE • ENG,FR,GERMAN,ETC • 120 kW
	USSR	
	RADIO MOSCOW, Komsomol'sk 'Amure	DS-1 • 50 kW
	RADIO MOSCOW, Ul'yanovsk	(D) • DS-1 • 100 kW
	YAKUT RADIO, Yakutsk	DS • 100 kW
7350	**CHINA (PR)**	
	RADIO BEIJING, Kunming	SE ASIA • 50 kW
	†RADIO BEIJING, Xi'an	(D) • EUROPE & N AFRICA • 120 kW
	CLANDESTINE (ASIA)	
	"DEM KAMPUCHEA", Kunming, China	SE ASIA • PRO-KHMER ROUGE • 50 kW
	MONACO	
	†TRANS WORLD RADIO, Monte Carlo	(D) • E EUROPE • 500 kW
		(D) • E EUROPE & WEST USSR • 100 kW
		(D) F-Su • E EUROPE • 500 kW
		(D) M-F • E EUROPE • 500 kW
		(D) Tu/Th-Su • E EUROPE • 100 kW
	USSR	
	RADIO MOSCOW	(D) • DS-1
	RADIO MOSCOW, Irkutsk	(D) • WS
	RADIO MOSCOW, Moscow	(J) • EUROPE • POLISH,SPANISH,ETC • 100 kW
		(D) • EUROPE • GREEK, ETC • 100 kW
7355	**MONACO**	
	†TRANS WORLD RADIO, Monte Carlo	(J) F-Su • E EUROPE • 500 kW
		(J) Th-Su • E EUROPE • 500 kW
	SYRIA	
	SYRIAN BC SERVICE, Adhra	MIDEAST • VOICE OF IRAQ • 500 kW
	USA	
	†KNLS-NEW LIFE STN, Anchor Pt, Alaska	JAPANESE • E ASIA • 100 kW
		(D) • EAST USSR • 100 kW
		(J) • EAST USSR • 100 kW
		(D) • E ASIA • 100 kW
		(D) M • E ASIA • 100 kW
		(D) Tu-Su • E ASIA • 100 kW
	WORLD HARVEST R, Noblesville,Indiana	E NORTH AM & C AMERICA • 100 kW
	WRNO WORLDWIDE, New Orleans, La	E NORTH AM • 100 kW
		Irr • E NORTH AM • 100 kW
		(D) • E NORTH AM • 100 kW
	†WYFR-FAMILY RADIO, Okeechobee, Fl	EUROPE • 100 kW
		(D) • W NORTH AM • 100 kW
		(D) • EUROPE • 100 kW
		EUROPE & N AFRICA • 100 kW
	USSR	
	RADIO MOSCOW	(D) • DS
	RADIO MOSCOW, Novosibirsk	DS-1 • 100 kW
		(D) • S ASIA • 100 kW
	RADIO MOSCOW, Tula	MIDEAST • 100 kW
7360	**CHINA (PR)**	
	†RADIO BEIJING, Xi'an	SE ASIA • 120 kW
		(D) • EUROPE & WEST USSR • 120 kW
	USSR	
	RADIO MOSCOW, Krasnodar	(D) • C AMERICA • 500 kW
		EUROPE • 500 kW
7360v	**ITALY**	
	†EURO CHRISTIAN R	EUROPE • 0.8 kW
7365	**GUAM**	
	†ADVENTIST WORLD R, Agat	(D) • E ASIA • 100 kW
	NORTHERN MARIANA IS	
	KFBS-FAR EAST BC, Saipan Island	(D) • USSR • RUSSIAN, ETC • 100 kW
	USA	
	KGEI-VO FRIENDSHIP, Redwood City,Ca	(D) • USSR • 250 kW
(con'd)	†KNLS-NEW LIFE STN, Anchor Pt, Alaska	(D) • E ASIA • 100 kW

World Time: 0 Prime Time-Americas 6 Prime Time-E Asia 12 Prime Time-S Asia 18 Prime Time-Europe 24

SUMMER ONLY (J) WINTER ONLY (D) JAMMING / OR ∧ EARLIEST HEARD ◁ LATEST HEARD ▷ NEW OR CHANGED FOR 1990 †

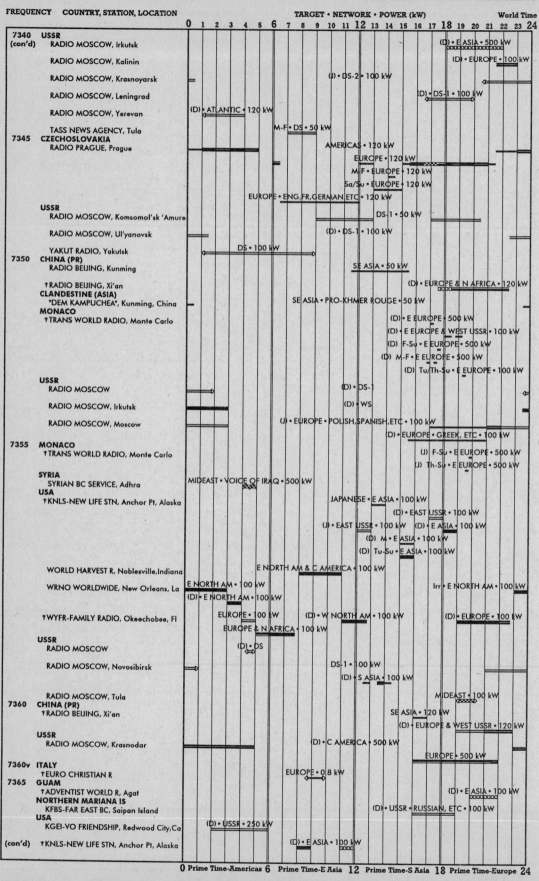

FREQUENCY	COUNTRY, STATION, LOCATION	TARGET • NETWORK • POWER (kW)
7365 (con'd)	**USA**	
	†KNLS-NEW LIFE STN, Anchor Pt, Alaska	(D) • JAPANESE • E ASIA • 100 kW
	†WCSN, Scotts Corners, Me	(D) • EUROPE • 500 kW
		(D) M-F • EUROPE • 500 kW
		(D) Sa/Su • EUROPE • 500 kW
	†WORLD HARVEST R, Noblesville, Indiana	E NORTH AM • 100 kW
		(J) • E NORTH AM • 100 kW
7365v	**PAKISTAN**	
	RADIO PAKISTAN, Islamabad	(D) • EUROPE & N AFRICA • 250 kW
	RADIO PAKISTAN, Karachi	(D) • MIDEAST • 50 kW
	VATICAN STATE	
	VATICAN RADIO, Vatican City	EUROPE • 80 kW
7370	**USSR**	
	R TIKHIY OKEAN, Khabarovsk	EAST USSR & PACIFIC • MARINERS • 100 kW
		Sa • EAST USSR & PACIFIC • MARINERS • 100 kW
		Su-F • EAST USSR & PACIFIC • MARINERS • 100 kW
	RADIO MOSCOW	(D) • AMERICAS
	RADIO MOSCOW, Khabarovsk	DS-1 • 100 kW
		(J) • DS-1 • 100 kW
	RADIO MOSCOW, Moscow	DS-1 • 100 kW
		(D) • EUROPE • 100 kW
7375	**CHINA (PR)**	
	RADIO BEIJING, Xi'an	E EUROPE & WEST USSR • 120 kW
7375v	**COSTA RICA**	
	†RADIO FOR PEACE, Ciudad Colón	M-F • C AMERICA & E NORTH AM • 2/5 kW
	PIRATE (EUROPE)	
	†"RADIO WAVES INTL", France	Irr • Su • ENGLISH & FRENCH • W EUROPE • 0.015 kW • ALT. FREQ. TO 7440v kHz
7380	**CLANDESTINE (C AMER)**	
	"LA VOZ DEL CID", Guatemala City	Irr • C AMERICA • ANTI-CASTRO
	USSR	
	RADIO MOSCOW, Irkutsk	(D) • E ASIA • 500 kW
	RADIO MOSCOW, Moscow	ATLANTIC • MARINERS • 240 kW
	RADIO MOSCOW, Sverdlovsk	(D) • E EUROPE • 100 kW
7384v	**LAOS**	
	LAO NATIONAL RADIO, Savannakhet	DS • 3 kW
		Sa/Su • DS • 3 kW
7385	**CHINA (PR)**	
	†RADIO BEIJING, Xi'an	EUROPE • 120 kW
	XINJIANG PBS, Urümqi	(J) • DS-CHINESE • 50 kW
7385v	**PAKISTAN**	
	PAKISTAN BC CORP, Islamabad	(J) • DS • 100 kW
	RADIO PAKISTAN, Islamabad	(D) • MIDEAST • 100 kW
7390	**USSR**	
	RADIO MOSCOW	(J) • E ASIA • CHINESE, MONGOLIAN
		(J) • DS-1
	RADIO MOSCOW, Khar'kov	C AMERICA & S AMERICA
		(D) • EUROPE
		(J) • EUROPE • WS, CZECH, HUNGARIAN
7400	**USA**	
	†WSHB, Cypress Creek, SC	Alternative Frequency to 7405 kHz
	USSR	
	†RADIO KIEV, Kiev	E NORTH AM
	†RADIO MOSCOW, Kiev	E NORTH AM
	RADIO MOSCOW, Moscow	(D) • DS-1 • 100 kW
		(J) • E EUROPE • 120 kW
	RADIO MOSCOW, Volgograd	(J) • DS-2 • 50 kW
	†RADIO VILNIUS, Kiev	E NORTH AM
7405	**USA**	
	†KNLS-NEW LIFE STN, Anchor Pt, Alaska	(D) • EAST USSR • 100 kW
	†WORLD HARVEST R, Noblesville, Indiana	(D) • E NORTH AM • 100 kW
	†WSHB, Cypress Creek, SC	E NORTH AM • 500 kW • ALT. FREQ. TO 7400 kHz
		M-Sa • E NORTH AM • 500 kW • ALT. FREQ. TO 7400 kHz
		Su • E NORTH AM • 500 kW • ALT. FREQ. TO 7400 kHz
		Su/M • E NORTH AM • 500 kW • ALT. FREQ. TO 7400 kHz
		Tu-Sa • E NORTH AM • 500 kW • ALT. FREQ. TO 7400 kHz
7410	**CLANDESTINE (N AMER)**	
	"VOICE OF TOMORROW, Virginia, USA	Irr • E NORTH AM • NEO-NAZI PARTY
	USSR	
	RADIO MOSCOW	(D) • DS-2(FEEDER) • USB
	RADIO MOSCOW, Vladivostok	(D) • DS-2(FEEDER) • 15 kW • USB
7412	**INDIA**	
	†ALL INDIA RADIO, Delhi	MIDEAST • 100 kW
		EUROPE • 100 kW
(con'd)		

World Time: 0 Prime Time-Americas 6 Prime Time-E Asia 12 Prime Time-S Asia 18 Prime Time-Europe 24

ENGLISH ▬ ARABIC ✕✕✕ CHINESE ▫▫▫ FRENCH ═ GERMAN ▬ RUSSIAN ═ SPANISH ═ OTHER —

FREQUENCY	COUNTRY, STATION, LOCATION	TARGET • NETWORK • POWER (kW)
7412 (con'd)	INDIA †ALL INDIA RADIO, Delhi	DS-ENGLISH, ETC • 100 kW
7420	CHINA (PR) †RADIO BEIJING, Beijing	(D) • S AMERICA • 240 kW (D) • WEST USSR & EUROPE • 240 kW
	USSR RADIO MOSCOW, Irkutsk	(D) • DS-1 • 50 kW
	RADIO MOSCOW, Khar'kov	(J) • E EUROPE • 100 kW
	RADIO MOSCOW, Minsk	(D) • EUROPE • 100 kW
	RADIO MOSCOW, Moscow	DS-1 • 100 kW (D) • DS-1 • 100 kW
	RADIO MOSCOW, Serpuhkov	(D) • DS-1 • 50 kW
	TASS NEWS AGENCY, Ul'yanovsk	M-F • DS • 100 kW
7420v	CLANDESTINE (M EAST) †"VO IRANIAN KURDS"	MIDEAST • ANTI-IRANIAN GOVT PERSIAN • MIDEAST • ANTI-IRANIAN GOVT
7425v	CLANDESTINE (S AMER) †"REV ARMED FORCES", Colombia	Su • S AMERICA • USB
7430	GREECE FONI TIS HELLADAS, Athens	GREEK • N AMERICA • 100 kW N AMERICA • 100 kW E EUROPE • 100 kW GREEK • EUROPE • 100 kW EUROPE • 100 kW GREEK • AUSTRALIA • 100 kW EUROPE • FRENCH, GERMAN • 100 kW (D) • GREEK • MIDEAST • GREEK, ARABIC • 100 kW (D) • MIDEAST • GREEK, ARABIC • 100 kW (D) • GREEK • USSR • GREEK, RUSSIAN • 100 kW (D) • USSR • GREEK, RUSSIAN • 100 kW
	FONI TIS HELLADAS, Kaválla	GREEK • MIDEAST • 250 kW (D) • GREEK • MIDEAST • 250 kW
7434v	VIETNAM VOICE OF VIETNAM	SE ASIA (D) • E ASIA
7440	CHINA (PR) CENTRAL PEOPLES BS	DS-1
	USSR †"RADIO MAGALLANES", Via R Moscow	(D) • S AMERICA • 250 kW
	RADIO MOSCOW, Kalinin	DS-3 • 50 kW
	†RADIO MOSCOW, Moscow	(J) • EUROPE & ATLANTIC • POLISH,MARINERS,WS • 250 kW (D) • W EUROPE & W AFRICA • 250 kW (D) • W AFRICA & S AMERICA • 250 kW
7440v	PIRATE (EUROPE) †"RADIO WAVES INTL", France	Alternative Frequency to 7375v kHz
7443	UNITED NATIONS UNITED NATIONS R, Via Switzerland	Tu-F • WEST USSR • 15 kW • USB • ALT. FREQ. TO 14500 kHz
7445	CHINA (TAIWAN) VO FREE CHINA, T'ai-pei	E ASIA • 50 kW
	†VOICE OF ASIA, Kao-hsiung	SE ASIA • 100 kW
7450	SPAIN †R NACIONAL ESPANA, Arganda	EUROPE • 100 kW (D) • EUROPE • 100 kW
7455	SYRIA SYRIAN BC SERVICE, Adhra	Alternative Frequency to 9950 kHz
7460	CLANDESTINE (M EAST) †"AL-QUDS RADIO", Syria	Irr • MIDEAST
	ISRAEL †KOL ISRAEL, Tel Aviv	(D) • WEST USSR • 300 kW
7462	USSR †RADIO MOSCOW	(D) • (FEEDER) • USB
7470	CHINA (PR) †RADIO BEIJING, Xi'an	WEST USSR & E EUROPE • 500 kW EUROPE & N AFRICA • 500 kW
7475	TUNISIA RTV TUNISIENNE, Sfax	Irr • DS-RAMADAN • 100 kW (D) • DS • 100 kW
7478	USA VOA, Via M'rovia, Liberia	W AFRICA • (FEEDER) • 40 kW • ISL
7480	CHINA (PR) RADIO BEIJING, Beijing	JAPANESE • E ASIA • 100 kW
7485v	CLANDESTINE (AFRICA) "VO BROAD MASSES", Ethiopia	E AFRICA • PLF OF ERITREA
7490	GERMANY (FR) †DEUTSCHE WELLE, Elmshorn	W EUROPE • (FEEDER) • 20 kW • LSB
7490v	PIRATE (EUROPE) †"RADIO BRIGITTE", Belgium	Irr • Su • W EUROPE • ENGLISH, DUTCH • ALT. FREQ. TO 6310v kHz
7493 (con'd)	USSR †R TIKHIY OKEAN, Birobidzhan	MARINERS(FEEDER) • 15 kW • LSB

World Time: 0 Prime Time-Americas 6 Prime Time-E Asia 12 Prime Time-S Asia 18 Prime Time-Europe 24

SUMMER ONLY (J) WINTER ONLY (D) JAMMING / OR ∧ EARLIEST HEARD ◁ LATEST HEARD ▷ NEW OR CHANGED FOR 1990 †

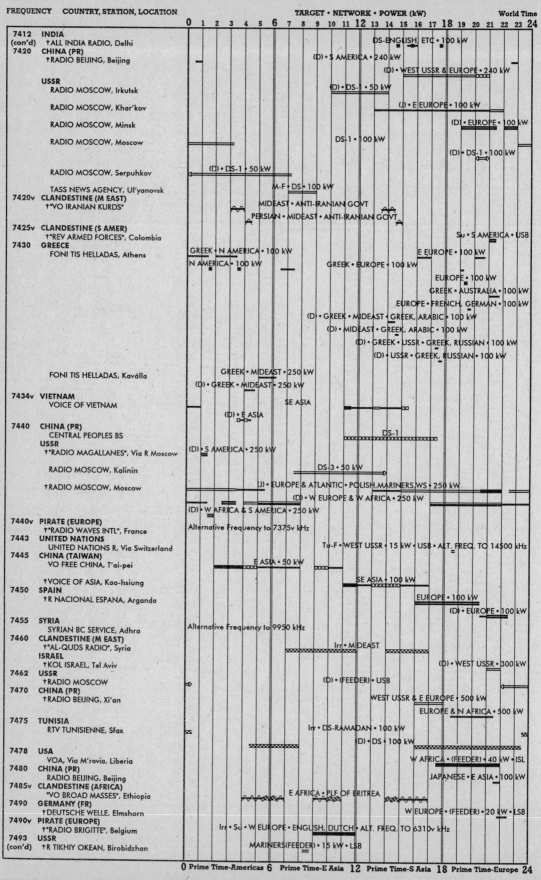

FREQUENCY	COUNTRY, STATION, LOCATION	TARGET • NETWORK • POWER (kW)
7493 (con'd)	USSR †R TIKHIY OKEAN, Birobidzhan	Sa • MARINERS(FEEDER) • 15 kW • LSB
		Su-F • MARINERS(FEEDER) • 15 kW • LSB
	†RADIO MOSCOW, Birobidzhan	DS-1(FEEDER) • 15 kW • LSB
7504	CHINA (PR) CENTRAL PEOPLES BS, Xi'an	DS-1 • 120 kW
		W-M • DS-1 • 120 kW
7516	CHINA (PR) CENTRAL PEOPLES BS, Beijing	DS-1 • 50 kW
7520	BANGLADESH †RADIO BANGLADESH, Dhaka	MIDEAST • 250 kW
		EUROPE • 250 kW
	USA †WWCR, Nashville, Tennessee	Alternative Frequency to 15690 kHz
7525	CHINA (PR) CENTRAL PEOPLES BS	DS-1
7550	KOREA (REPUBLIC) RADIO KOREA, In-Kimjae	EUROPE • 250 kW
		MIDEAST & AFRICA • 250 kW
		KOREAN • MIDEAST & AFRICA • 250 kW
7565	USSR KAZAKH TELEGRAPH, Alma-Ata	M/W/F • DS-NEWSCAST • 15 kW
7580	KOREA (DPR) RADIO PYONGYANG, Pyongyang	JAPANESE • E ASIA • 100 kW
7590	CHINA (PR) †RADIO BEIJING, Kunming	SE ASIA • 120 kW
		SE ASIA & S ASIA • 120 kW
7615	USSR RADIO MOSCOW, Moscow	Irr • (FEEDER) • 20 kW • LSB
7620	CHINA (PR) CENTRAL PEOPLES BS	TAIWAN-1
7651	USA †VOA, Greenville, NC	EUROPE & MIDEAST • (FEEDER) • 40 kW • ISL
		(D) • EUROPE & MIDEAST • (FEEDER) • 40 kW • ISU
		(J) • EUROPE & MIDEAST • (FEEDER) • 40 kW • ISU
7660	CHINA (PR) CENTRAL PEOPLES BS	DS-MINORITIES
	†RADIO BEIJING, Xi'an	WEST USSR & EUROPE • 120 kW
7670	BULGARIA BULGARIAN RADIO, Stolnik	DS-1 • 15 kW
7680	USSR †RADIO MOSCOW	(D) • (FEEDER) • USB
7695	USSR †RADIO MOSCOW	(D) • (FEEDER) • USB
7700	CHINA (PR) RADIO BEIJING, Kunming	E EUROPE • 50 kW
7725	USA VOA, Via Ismaning, GFR	(D) • E EUROPE & MIDEAST • (FEEDER) • 40 kW • USB
7768.5	USA †VOA, Greenville, NC	N AFRICA • 40 kW • LSB
7770	CHINA (PR) CENTRAL PEOPLES BS, Kunming	DS-2 • 50 kW
		Th/Sa-M • DS-2 • 50 kW
	ITALY †R CALABRIA INTL, Gioiosa Iónica	EUROPE • 0.2 kW
7780	CHINA (PR) †RADIO BEIJING, Kunming	(D) • EUROPE • 50 kW
7800	CHINA (PR) †RADIO BEIJING, Kunming	(D) • EUROPE & N AFRICA • 50 kW
7820	CHINA (PR) †RADIO BEIJING, Beijing	USSR • 120 kW
		(D) • S AMERICA • 120 kW
		(D) • E EUROPE & WEST USSR • 120 kW
		(J) • E EUROPE • 120 kW
7830	CLANDESTINE (AFRICA) †"VO TIGRE REVOL'N", Ethiopia	E AFRICA • TIGRE PLF
7850	CHINA (PR) HUNAN METEOROLOGY	E ASIA • WEATHER, MUSIC • ALT. FREQ. TO 7950 kHz
7890v	CLANDESTINE (AFRICA) †"VO TIGRE REVOL'N", Ethiopia	E AFRICA • TIGRE PLF
7925	USSR RADIO MOSCOW, Moscow	Irr • DS-3(FEEDER) • 20 kW • ISL
		Irr • DS-1(FEEDER) • 20 kW • ISU
7933	ICELAND RIKISUTVARPID, Reykjavik	ATLANTIC & EUROPE • DS-1 • 10 kW • USB
7935	CHINA (PR) CENTRAL PEOPLES BS, Beijing	DS-1 • 15 kW
7950	CHINA (PR) HUNAN METEOROLOGY	Alternative Frequency to 7850 kHz
8001	CHINA (PR) XINJIANG MET'OLOGY	E ASIA • CHINESE, KAZAKH
8003	PERU RADIO CHINCHIYAQUI, San Pablo	DS
8005	USSR RADIO MOSCOW, Moscow	Irr • DS-1(FEEDER) • 20 kW • ISU
		Irr • DS-2(FEEDER) • 20 kW • ISU
		Irr • (J) • DS-3(FEEDER) • 20 kW • ISL
		Irr • (D) • DS-2(FEEDER) • 20 kW • ISU
(con'd)		Irr • DS-3(FEEDER) • 20 kW • ISL

World Time 0–24: 0 Prime Time-Americas 6 Prime Time-E Asia 12 Prime Time-S Asia 18 Prime Time-Europe 24

ENGLISH ▬ ARABIC ▬ CHINESE ▫▫▫ FRENCH ═ GERMAN ▬ RUSSIAN ═ SPANISH ═ OTHER —

FREQUENCY	COUNTRY, STATION, LOCATION	TARGET • NETWORK • POWER (kW)
8005 (con'd)	**USSR** RADIO MOSCOW, Moscow	Irr • (D) • DS-3(FEEDER) • 20 kW • ISL
8007	**CHINA (PR)** CENTRAL PEOPLES BS, Xi'an	DS-MINORITIES • 50 kW; DS-2 • 50 kW
8064v	**PERU** PARAISO LOS ANDES, Moyobamba	DS
8260	**CHINA (PR)** †RADIO BEIJING, Beijing	E ASIA • FEEDER • 10 kW; (D) • E ASIA • FEEDER • 10 kW
8345	**CHINA (PR)** †RADIO BEIJING, Beijing	(J) • E ASIA • FEEDER • 10 kW
	CLANDESTINE (ASIA) "DEM KAMPUCHEA", China (PR)	SE ASIA • PRO-KHMER ROUGE; (D) • SE ASIA • PRO-KHMER ROUGE
8425	**CHINA (PR)** †RADIO BEIJING, Beijing	E ASIA • FEEDER • 100 kW; (D) • E ASIA • FEEDER • 100 kW
8450	**CHINA (PR)** †RADIO BEIJING, Beijing	E ASIA • FEEDER • 100 kW; (J) • E ASIA • FEEDER • 100 kW
8515	**PERU** RADIO AMISTAD, Soritor	DS • 0.2 kW
8566	**CHINA (PR)** CENTRAL PEOPLES BS	DS-MINORITIES
8660	**CHINA (PR)** †RADIO BEIJING, Beijing	E ASIA • FEEDER • 10 kW
8930v	**PERU** RADIO CONTINENTE, Juanjuí	DS • 0.15 kW; Irr • DS • 0.15 kW; M-Sa • DS • 0.15 kW
9010.5	**ISRAEL** KOL ISRAEL, Tel Aviv	(D) • PERSIAN • MIDEAST • 300 kW; (D) • WEST USSR & E EUROPE • 300 kW; (D) • HEBREW • WEST USSR & E EUROPE • 300 kW; (D) • AFRICA & S AMERICA • 300 kW
9020	**CHINA (PR)** CENTRAL PEOPLES BS	DS-2; Th/Sa-M • DS-2
9022	**IRAN** †VO THE ISLAMIC REP, Tehrān	PERSIAN • EUROPE, N AFRICA & C AMERICA • 500 kW; EUROPE, N AFRICA & C AMERICA • 500 kW; EUROPE & WEST USSR • 500 kW
9045	**CLANDESTINE (M EAST)** †"IRAN FREEDOM FLAG, Egypt	PERSIAN • MIDEAST • ANTI-IRANIAN GOVT • 100 kW; (D) • PERSIAN • MIDEAST • ANTI-IRANIAN GOVT • 100 kW
9064	**CHINA (PR)** CENTRAL PEOPLES BS, Kunming	DS-1 • 15 kW; W-M • DS-1 • 15 kW
9080	**CHINA (PR)** CENTRAL PEOPLES BS, Kunming	DS-1 • 50 kW
9090	**USSR** KAZAKH TELEGRAPH, Alma-Ata	M/W/F • DS-NEWSCAST • 15 kW
9105	**USSR** †RADIO MOSCOW	(D) • (FEEDER) • USB
9115	**ARGENTINA** †RADIO RIVADAVIA, Buenos Aires	Sa/Su • DS(FEEDER) • 10 kW • USB; Irr • Su • DS(FEEDER) • 10 kW • USB; Su • DS(FEEDER) • 10 kW • USB
9145	**USSR** †RADIO MOSCOW	(J) • (FEEDER) • USB
9150	**USSR** RADIO MOSCOW, Moscow	(J) • DS-1(FEEDER) • 20 kW • ISL; (J) • DS-1(FEEDER) • 20 kW • ISU
9170	**CHINA (PR)** CENTRAL PEOPLES BS, Beijing	TAIWAN-2 • 10 kW
9180	**USSR** †RADIO MOSCOW	(J) • (FEEDER) • USB
9200	**USSR** RADIO MOSCOW, Khabarovsk	(J) • DS-2(FEEDER) • 15 kW • LSB
9220	**KOREA (DPR)** RADIO PYONGYANG, Pyongyang	MIDEAST & AFRICA • 200 kW
9239.3	**USA** AFRTS-US MILITARY, Via Barford, UK	Irr • ATLANTIC • DS-ABC/CBS/NBC/NPR(FEEDER) • 4 kW • USB
9242.3	**USA** AFRTS-US MILITARY, Via Barford, UK	Irr • ATLANTIC • DS-ABC/CBS/NBC/NPR(FEEDER) • 4 kW • LSB
9244.3	**USA** AFRTS-US MILITARY, Via Barford, UK	Irr • ATLANTIC • DS-ABC/CBS/NBC/NPR(FEEDER) • 4 kW • LSB
9250	**USSR** †RADIO MOSCOW	(J) • (FEEDER) • USB
9270.3	**CLANDESTINE (ASIA)** †"OCTOBER STORM"	Irr • F-Su • E ASIA • ANTI-CHINESE GOVT
9280	**USA** FAMILY RADIO, Via Taiwan	E ASIA • 250 kW
9311	**CLANDESTINE (AFRICA)** †"VO TIGRE REVOL'N", Ethiopia	E AFRICA • TIGRE PLF
9320	**USSR** †RADIO MOSCOW	(D) • (FEEDER) • USB
9325	**KOREA (DPR)** RADIO PYONGYANG, Pyongyang	EUROPE & WEST USSR • 200 kW

World Time: 0 Prime Time-Americas 6 Prime Time-E Asia 12 Prime Time-S Asia 18 Prime Time-Europe 24

SUMMER ONLY (J) WINTER ONLY (D) JAMMING / OR /\ EARLIEST HEARD ◁ LATEST HEARD ▷ NEW OR CHANGED FOR 1990 †

FREQUENCY	COUNTRY, STATION, LOCATION	TARGET • NETWORK • POWER (kW)
9334.3	**USA** AFRTS-US MILITARY, Via Barford, UK	Irr • ATLANTIC • DS-ABC/CBS/NBC/NPR(FEEDER) • 4 kW • LSB
9343	**CLANDESTINE (AFRICA)** †"VO TIGRE REVOL'N", Ethiopia	E AFRICA • TIGRE PLF
9345	**KOREA (DPR)** RADIO PYONGYANG, Pyongyang	USSR & EUROPE • 200 kW
9350	**USA** †VOA, Delano, California	SE ASIA • (FEEDER) • 50 kW • ISU
		SE ASIA • (FEEDER) • 50 kW • ISL
9360	**SPAIN** R NACIONAL ESPANA, Noblejas	C AMERICA & S AMERICA • 350 kW
9365	**CHINA (PR)** †RADIO BEIJING, Xi'an	S AMERICA • 120 kW
		(J) • EUROPE & WEST USSR • 120 kW
9375	**ALBANIA** RADIO TIRANA, Lushnjë	EUROPE • 50 kW
9380	**CHINA (PR)** CENTRAL PEOPLES BS, Beijing	TAIWAN-1 • 15 kW
9385	**ISRAEL** †KOL ISRAEL, Tel Aviv	(D) • E NORTH AM • 300 kW
		(D) • HEBREW • E NORTH AM • 300 kW
		(D) • C AMERICA & S AMERICA • 300 kW
		(D) • E EUROPE & WEST USSR • 300 kW
		(D) • HEBREW • EUROPE & E NORTH AM • DS-B • 100 kW
	†RASHUTH HASHIDUR, Tel Aviv	(D) Su-F • HEBREW • EUROPE & E NORTH AM • DS-B • 50 kW
9390	**CHINA (PR)** CENTRAL PEOPLES BS	DS-2
9395	**GREECE** FONI TIS HELLADAS, Athens	GREEK • MIDEAST • 100 kW
		GREEK • EUROPE • 100 kW
		(D) • GREEK • MIDEAST • 100 kW
		EUROPE • 100 kW
		GREEK • AUSTRALIA • 100 kW
		GREEK • S AMERICA • 100 kW
		S AMERICA • 100 kW
		EUROPE • FRENCH, GERMAN • 100 kW
	FONI TIS HELLADAS, Kavâlla	GREEK • N AMERICA & PACIFIC • 250 kW
		(J) • EUROPE • 250 kW
		N AMERICA & PACIFIC • 250 kW
		(D) • GREEK • N AMERICA & PACIFIC • 250 kW
		(D) • N AMERICA & PACIFIC • 250 kW
9400	**CLANDESTINE (M EAST)** "RADIO IRAN", Abu Za'bal, Egypt	PERSIAN • MIDEAST • ANTI-IRANIAN GOVT • 100 kW
9410	**UNITED KINGDOM** †BBC, Multiple Locations	EUROPE & MIDEAST • 100/250 kW
		EUROPE, MIDEAST & N AFRICA • 250/300/500 kW
		EUROPE, MIDEAST & W AFRICA • 100/250 kW
	†BBC, Rampisham	WEST USSR • 500 kW
		E EUROPE & MIDEAST • 500 kW
	†BBC, Skelton, Cumbria	WEST USSR • 100 kW
9420	**GREECE** FONI TIS HELLADAS, Athens	GREEK • N AMERICA • 100 kW
		N AMERICA • 100 kW
9425	**GREECE** FONI TIS HELLADAS, Athens	GREEK • MIDEAST • 100 kW
		GREEK • EUROPE • 100 kW
		EUROPE • 100 kW
		GREEK • AUSTRALIA • 100 kW
		EUROPE • FRENCH, GERMAN • 100 kW
	FONI TIS HELLADAS, Kavâlla	GREEK • E EUROPE • 250 kW
		GREEK • MIDEAST • 250 kW
		EUROPE • 250 kW
		MIDEAST • 250 kW
		E EUROPE • 250 kW
		GREEK • AUSTRALIA • 250 kW
		(D) • GREEK • C AMERICA & S AMERICA • 250 kW
		(D) • C AMERICA & S AMERICA • 250 kW
		GREEK • USSR • GREEK, RUSSIAN • 250 kW
		USSR • GREEK, RUSSIAN • 250 kW
	RS MAKEDONIAS, Thessaloniki	(J) • GREEK • EUROPE • DS • 35 kW
9430	**ALBANIA** RADIO TIRANA, Lushnjë	EUROPE • 100 kW
9435	**CLANDESTINE (AFRICA)** †"VO ETHIOPIA UNITY, Sudan	Irr • E AFRICA • ALT. FREQ. TO 9550 kHz
	†"VO OROMO LIBER'N", Sudan	Irr • E AFRICA • ALT. FREQ. TO 9550 kHz
	ISRAEL †KOL ISRAEL, Tel Aviv	(D) • W EUROPE & E NORTH AM • 300 kW
		(D) • S AMERICA • 300 kW
		(D) • WEST USSR & E EUROPE • 300 kW

(con'd)

World Time: 0 Prime Time-Americas 6 Prime Time-E Asia 12 Prime Time-S Asia 18 Prime Time-Europe 24

ENGLISH ▬ ARABIC ▭ CHINESE ▫▫▫ FRENCH ═ GERMAN ▬ RUSSIAN ═ SPANISH ▬ OTHER —

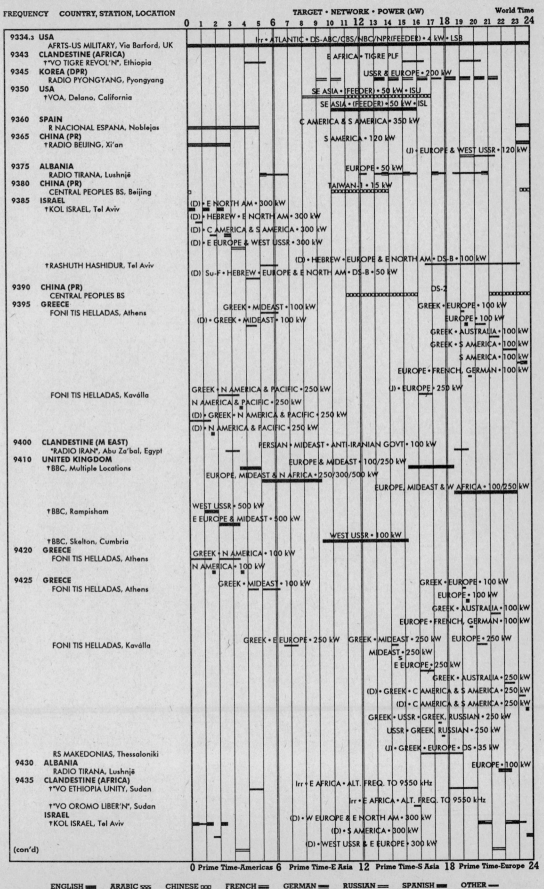

FREQUENCY	COUNTRY, STATION, LOCATION	TARGET • NETWORK • POWER (kW)
9435 (con'd)	**ISRAEL** †KOL ISRAEL, Tel Aviv	(D) • EUROPE, N AFRICA & C AMERICA • 300 kW
	MONACO †TRANS WORLD RADIO, Monte Carlo	(D) • MIDEAST & WEST USSR • 500 kW
		(J) • E EUROPE • 100 kW
		(J) Tu/Th-Su • E EUROPE & WEST USSR • 100 kW
	SUDAN †NATIONAL RTV CORP, Omdurman	Irr • DS-GENERAL
9440	**ALBANIA** †RADIO TIRANA, Lushnjë	Alternative Frequency to 9760 kHz
	CHINA (PR) †RADIO BEIJING, Beijing	MIDEAST & N AFRICA • 120 kW
	RADIO BEIJING, Xi'an	SE ASIA • 120 kW
	CLANDESTINE (ASIA) "DEM KAMPUCHEA", Xi'an, China (PR)	SE ASIA • PRO-KHMER ROUGE • 120 kW
9445	**TURKEY** †TURKISH RTV CORP, Ankara	Alternative Frequency to 9460 kHz
		TURKISH • E NORTH AM • 500 kW
		E NORTH AM • 500 kW
9450	**USSR** R TIKHIY OKEAN	(D) • E ASIA • MARINERS
	RADIO MOSCOW	(D) • E ASIA • CHINESE, MONGOLIAN
	RADIO MOSCOW, Moscow	W AFRICA & ATLANTIC • WS, MARINERS • 240 kW
		(D) • W AFRICA • AFRICAN SCE, WS, ETC • 240 kW
		(J) • E EUROPE • GREEK, ETC • 240 kW
		(D) • EUROPE • WS • 240 kW
		(D) • EUROPE • WS, GERMAN • 240 kW
	RADIO MOSCOW, Novosibirsk	(D) • E ASIA • 250 kW
		DS-1 • 50 kW
	RADIO MOSCOW, Yerevan	W AFRICA • 120 kW
		W AFRICA • AFRICAN • 120 kW
		W AFRICA • WS • 120 kW
9455	**CHINA (PR)** CENTRAL PEOPLES BS, Kunming	TAIWAN-1 • 50 kW
	†RADIO BEIJING, Kunming	(D) • S ASIA & S AFRICA • 50 kW
	CHINA (TAIWAN) VO FREE CHINA, Via Okeechobee, USA	(D) • EUROPE • 100 kW
	EGYPT RADIO CAIRO, Kafr Silîm-Abis	Irr • MIDEAST, EUROPE & N AFRICA • DS-GENERAL • 250 kW
		MIDEAST, EUROPE & N AFRICA • DS-GENERAL • 250 kW
	ISRAEL †KOL ISRAEL, Tel Aviv	(D) • EUROPE • 250 kW
		(D) • HEBREW • EUROPE • 250 kW
	NORTHERN MARIANA IS †KYOI, Saipan Island	E ASIA • 100 kW
	PAKISTAN RADIO PAKISTAN, Islamabad	(J) • MIDEAST • 100 kW
	USA VOA, Greenville, NC	C AMERICA & S AMERICA • 500 kW
		(D) • C AMERICA & S AMERICA • 500 kW
		(J) • C AMERICA & S AMERICA • 500 kW
	†WORLD HARVEST R, Noblesville, Indiana	(D) • E NORTH AM • 100 kW
	†WSHB, Cypress Creek, SC	W NORTH AM • 500 kW
		S AMERICA • 500 kW
		M-F • W NORTH AM • 500 kW
		M-F • S AMERICA • 500 kW
		Sa-M • W NORTH AM • 500 kW
		Sa/Su • W NORTH AM • 500 kW
		Sa/Su • S AMERICA • 500 kW
		Tu-F • W NORTH AM • 500 kW
	†WYFR-FAMILY RADIO, Okeechobee, Fl	(D) • EUROPE • 100 kW
9460	**TURKEY** †TURKISH RTV CORP, Ankara	TURKISH • EUROPE • 500 kW • ALT. FREQ. TO 9445 kHz
		TURKISH • EUROPE • 500 kW
9460v	**PAKISTAN** RADIO PAKISTAN, Islamabad	(D) • BANGLA • S ASIA • 100 kW
9465	**NORTHERN MARIANA IS** KFBS-FAR EAST BC, Saipan Island	(D) • USSR • 100 kW
		USSR • 100 kW
		(J) • USSR • 100 kW
		(J) F • USSR • 100 kW
		M-Sa • USSR • 100 kW
		(J) Sa-Th • USSR • 100 kW
		Su • USSR • 100 kW
		(J) Su-W • USSR • 100 kW
		(J) Th-Sa • USSR • 100 kW
(con'd)		

World Time: 0 1 2 3 4 5 6 7 8 9 10 11 12 13 14 15 16 17 18 19 20 21 22 23 24

0 Prime Time-Americas 6 Prime Time-E Asia 12 Prime Time-S Asia 18 Prime Time-Europe 24

SUMMER ONLY (J) WINTER ONLY (D) JAMMING / OR /\ EARLIEST HEARD ◁ LATEST HEARD ▷ NEW OR CHANGED FOR 1990 †

FREQUENCY	COUNTRY, STATION, LOCATION	TARGET • NETWORK • POWER (kW)
9465 (con'd)	**NORTHERN MARIANA IS**	
	KFBS-FAR EAST BC, Saipan Island	(J) • USSR • RUSSIAN, ETC • 100 kW
	†KYOI, Saipan Island	SE ASIA • 100 kW
	USA	
	†VOA, Delano, California	C AMERICA & S AMERICA • 250 kW
	†WCSN, Scotts Corners. Me	(D) • EUROPE • 500 kW
		(D) M-Sa • EUROPE • 500 kW
		(D) Sa • EUROPE • 500 kW
		(D) Su-F • EUROPE • 500 kW
		(D) Su • EUROPE • 500 kW
	†WMLK-ASBY OF YAWEH, Bethel, Pa	M-Sa • EUROPE & MIDEAST • 50 kW
		Su-F • EUROPE & MIDEAST • 50 kW
	†WORLD HARVEST R, Noblesville,Indiana	(J) • E NORTH AM • 100 kW
	†WSHB, Cypress Creek, SC	E NORTH AM • 500 kW
		M-F • E NORTH AM • 500 kW
		Sa • E NORTH AM • 500 kW
		Sa/Su • E NORTH AM • 500 kW
		Su-F • E NORTH AM • 500 kW
9465v	**PAKISTAN**	
	RADIO PAKISTAN, Karachi	MIDEAST • 50 kW
9470	**USSR**	
	†"RADIO MAGALLANES", Via R Moscow	(D) • S AMERICA • 100 kW
	RADIO MOSCOW	DS-1(FEEDER) • USB
	RADIO MOSCOW, Irkutsk	(D) • E ASIA
	RADIO MOSCOW, Minsk	DS-2
		(J) • DS-2
	RADIO MOSCOW, Ul'yanovsk	S AMERICA • 100 kW
		(D) • S AMERICA • 100 kW
		(J) • E EUROPE • 100 kW
		(J) • S AMERICA • 100 kW
		(D) • W AFRICA • AFRICAN SCE • 100 kW
	RADIO YEREVAN, Ul'yanovsk	S AMERICA • ARMENIAN,SPANISH • 100 kW
9475	**EGYPT**	
	†RADIO CAIRO, Kafr Silîm-Abis	N AMERICA & C AMERICA • 250 kW
		EUROPE • DS-GENERAL • 250 kW • ALT. FREQ. TO 9670 kHz
	PAKISTAN	
	PAKISTAN BC CORP, Islamabad	(J) • MIDEAST • DS • 100 kW
9475v	**PAKISTAN**	
	RADIO PAKISTAN, Karachi	MIDEAST • 50 kW
9480	**CHINA (PR)**	
	RADIO BEIJING, Beijing	SE ASIA & E ASIA • 120 kW
	†RADIO BEIJING, Xi'an	MIDEAST • 120 kW
		(D) • MIDEAST • 120 kW
	MONACO	
	†TRANS WORLD RADIO, Monte Carlo	(D) • W EUROPE • 100 kW
		(D) Su • W EUROPE • 100 kW
	USSR	
	RADIO MOSCOW	(D)
	RADIO MOSCOW, Novosibirsk	E ASIA • 250 kW
		(D) • E ASIA • 250 kW
		E ASIA • DS-2 • 250 kW
	RADIO MOSCOW, Yerevan	MIDEAST & E AFRICA • 120 kW
		(D) • N AFRICA • 120 kW
	RADIO YEREVAN, Yerevan	(D) • S AMERICA • ARMENIAN, SPANISH • 120 kW
9480v	**ALBANIA**	
	RADIO TIRANA	MIDEAST • ARABIC, TURKISH • 100 kW
	RADIO TIRANA, Krujë	C AFRICA & S AFRICA • 50/100 kW
		S AFRICA • 100 kW
		EUROPE • 100 kW
		WEST USSR • 100 kW
	RADIO TIRANA, Lushnjë	EUROPE • 100 kW
		C AFRICA & S AFRICA • 100 kW
		WEST USSR • 100 kW
9485	**MONACO**	
	†TRANS WORLD RADIO, Monte Carlo	(J) • W EUROPE • 100 kW
		(J) • WEST USSR • 100 kW
		(J) M • WEST USSR • 100 kW
		(J) Su • W EUROPE • 100 kW
		(J) Tu/W/F/Su • WEST USSR • 100 kW
9486	**PERU**	
	RADIO TACNA, Tacna	DS • 0.2 kW • ALT. FREQ. TO 9505v kHz
		M-Sa • DS • 0.2 kW • ALT. FREQ. TO 9505v kHz
		Tu-Su • DS • 0.2 kW • ALT. FREQ. TO 9505v kHz

World Time: 0 Prime Time-Americas 6 Prime Time-E Asia 12 Prime Time-S Asia 18 Prime Time-Europe 24

ENGLISH ARABIC CHINESE FRENCH GERMAN RUSSIAN SPANISH OTHER

FREQUENCY | COUNTRY, STATION, LOCATION | TARGET • NETWORK • POWER (kW) | World Time

0 1 2 3 4 5 6 7 8 9 10 11 12 13 14 15 16 17 18 19 20 21 22 23 24

9490 **CHINA (PR)**
- RADIO BEIJING, Lhasa — S ASIA • 50 kW
- XIZANG PEOPLES BS, Lhasa — DS-CHINESE • 50 kW

USSR
- RADIO MOSCOW, Nikolayev — S AMERICA • 500 kW; (J) • W AFRICA • 500 kW; (D) • W AFRICA • 500 kW; (D) • S AMERICA • 500 kW
- RADIO MOSCOW, Ul'yanovsk — DS-1/DS-2/POLAR • 240 kW

9495 **MONACO**
- †TRANS WORLD RADIO, Monte Carlo — (D) • E EUROPE • 100 kW; (D) • WEST USSR • 500 kW; (J) • E EUROPE • 100 kW; (D) • WEST USSR • 100 kW; (J) F-Su • E EUROPE • 500 kW; (J) • E EUROPE • 500 kW; (J) Sa/Su • E EUROPE • 500 kW; (J) • WEST USSR • 500 kW; (J) M-F • E EUROPE • 500 kW; (D) M • W EUROPE • 100 kW; (J) M • W EUROPE • 100 kW; (D) Sa/Su • E EUROPE • 500 kW; (D) Tu/Sa/Su • E EUROPE • 100 kW; (D) Sa/Su • WEST USSR • 500 kW; (J) Tu/Sa/Su • E EUROPE • 100 kW; (J) Sa/Su • WEST USSR • 500 kW; (D) Su • E EUROPE • 100 kW; (D) Su/Tu • W EUROPE • 100 kW; (J) Su/Tu • W EUROPE • 100 kW

NORTHERN MARIANA IS
- KFBS-FAR EAST BC, Saipan Island — E ASIA • 100 kW

USA
- †WORLD HARVEST R, Noblesville, Indiana — S AMERICA • 100 kW
- †WSHB, Cypress Creek, SC — (J) • E NORTH AM • 500 kW; (J) M-F • E NORTH AM • 500 kW; (J) Sa/Su • E NORTH AM • 500 kW

9495v **PAKISTAN**
- RADIO PAKISTAN, Karachi — HINDI • S ASIA • 50 kW

9500 **ALBANIA**
- RADIO TIRANA, Lushnjë — S AMERICA • 100 kW; WEST USSR • 100 kW; EUROPE • 100 kW; (J) • N AMERICA • 100 kW; C AMERICA • 100 kW; EUROPE • 50 kW; SE ASIA & AUSTRALIA • ENGLISH, INDONESIAN • 100 kW; MIDEAST • PERSIAN, TURKISH • 100 kW

CLANDESTINE (AFRICA)
- "VO LIBYAN PEOPLE", Southern Chad — N AFRICA • ANTI-QUADDAFI

USSR
- MAGADAN RADIO, Chita — DS-1 • 50 kW
- RADIO MOSCOW — DS-1
- RADIO MOSCOW, Armavir — MIDEAST & E AFRICA • 100 kW

VENEZUELA
- †RADIO NACIONAL, Caracas — Alternative Frequency to 11694 kHz

9505 **AUSTRALIA**
- RADIO AUSTRALIA, Carnarvon — SE ASIA • 300 kW
- RADIO AUSTRALIA, Darwin — SE ASIA • 250 kW

BRAZIL
- RADIO RECORD, São Paulo — Irr • PORTUGUESE • DS • 7.5 kW; PORTUGUESE • DS • 7.5 kW

CHINA (PR)
- †VO THE STRAIT-PLA, Fuzhou — (J) • TAIWAN-2 • 15 kW

CZECHOSLOVAKIA
- RADIO PRAGUE, Pieštány-Velké K'y — W EUROPE • 120 kW; Sa/Su • W EUROPE • 120 kW; W EUROPE • ENG, FR, GERMAN, ETC • 120 kW

GERMANY (FR)
- DEUTSCHE WELLE, Via Cyclops, Malta — (D) • E ASIA • 250 kW

HOLLAND
- RADIO NEDERLAND, Via Madagascar — SE ASIA & AUSTRALIA • 300 kW
- †RADIO NEDERLAND, Via Neth Antilles — Alternative Frequency to 9675 kHz

JAPAN
- †RADIO JAPAN/NHK, Tokyo-Yamata — (D) • JAPANESE • PACIFIC & W NORTH AM • GENERAL • 100 kW; (D) • PACIFIC & W NORTH AM • GENERAL • 100 kW

KOREA (DPR)
- RADIO PYONGYANG, Pyongyang — JAPANESE • E ASIA • 100 kW

PHILIPPINES
- RADIO VERITAS ASIA, Malolos — SE ASIA • 100 kW

USA
- †RFE-RL, Via Germany — WEST USSR • 100/250 kW
- (con'd) †RFE-RL, Via Pals, Spain — WEST USSR • 250 kW

0 Prime Time-Americas 6 Prime Time-E Asia 12 Prime Time-S Asia 18 Prime Time-Europe 24

SUMMER ONLY (J) | WINTER ONLY (D) | JAMMING / OR /\ | EARLIEST HEARD ◁ | LATEST HEARD ▷ | NEW OR CHANGED FOR 1990 †

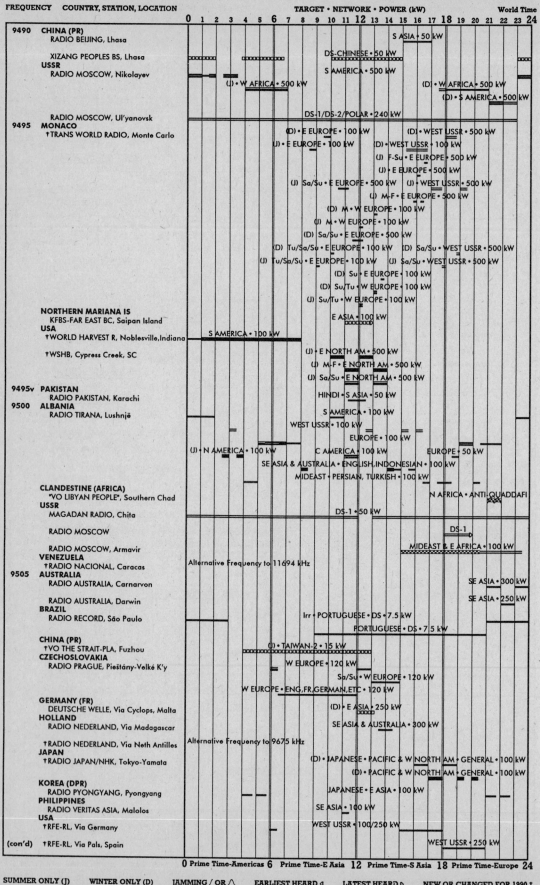

FREQUENCY	COUNTRY, STATION, LOCATION	TARGET • NETWORK • POWER (kW)
9505 (con'd)	**USA** †RFE-RL, Via Portugal	WEST USSR • 250 kW
	†WYFR-FAMILY RADIO, Okeechobee, Fl	W NORTH AM • 100 kW; (J) • S AMERICA • 100 kW; (D) • W NORTH AM • 100 kW
	USSR KAZAKH RADIO, Alma-Ata	DS-2/RUSSIAN, ETC • 50 kW
	YUGOSLAVIA RADIO BEOGRAD, Belgrade	EUROPE • DS-1 • 100 kW; Su • EUROPE • DS-1 • 100 kW
	ZAMBIA †RADIO ZAMBIA-ZBS, Lusaka	S AFRICA • 50 kW; F/Sa • S AFRICA • 50 kW
9505v	**PERU** RADIO TACNA, Tacna	Alternative Frequency to 9486 kHz
9509	**ALGERIA** †RTV ALGERIENNE, Ouled Fayet	Alternative Frequency to 9535 kHz
9510	**CHINA (TAIWAN)** VO FREE CHINA, T'ai-pei	EUROPE
	ROMANIA †RADIO BUCHAREST, Bucharest	AMERICAS • 250 kW; EUROPE • 250 kW; (D) • S ASIA • 250 kW; (D) • EUROPE • 250 kW
	SEYCHELLES FAR EAST BC ASS'N, North Pt, Mahé Is	E AFRICA • 100 kW
	UNITED KINGDOM BBC, Via Antigua	C AMERICA • 250 kW
	USSR RADIO MOSCOW, Vladivostok	(D) • E ASIA • 100 kW; (J) • E ASIA • 100 kW
9510v	**PERU** RADIO AMERICA, Lima	Irr • DS • 5/10 kW
9515	**BRAZIL** †R NOVAS DE PAZ, Curitiba	PORTUGUESE • DS • 10 kW
	BURKINA FASO RTV BURKINA, Ouagadougou	Irr • DS-FRENCH, ETC • 4/50 kW; Irr • Th/Sa/Su • DS-FRENCH, ETC • 4/50 kW
	CUBA RADIO HABANA, Via USSR	(D) • MIDEAST & E AFRICA • 200 kW
	GERMANY (FR) †DEUTSCHE WELLE, Via Cyclops, Malta	MIDEAST • 250 kW
	IRAQ †RADIO BAGHDAD, Balad-Salah el Deen	(D) • E NORTH AM & C AMERICA • 500 kW; (D) • MIDEAST • 500 kW
	ITALY †RTV ITALIANA, Caltanissetta	ITALIAN • EUROPE, N AFRICA & MIDEAST • DS-1 • 50 kW; M-Sa • EUROPE, N AFRICA & MIDEAST • DS-1 • 50 kW; Su • EUROPE, N AFRICA & MIDEAST • DS-1 • 50 kW
	KOREA (REPUBLIC) †RADIO KOREA, In-Kimjae	KOREAN • 250 kW; 250 kW; MIDEAST & AFRICA • 250 kW
	MEXICO LV AMERICA LATINA, México City	Irr • DS • 0.5 kW
	NETHERLANDS ANTILLES †TRANS WORLD RADIO, Bonaire	S AMERICA • 50/100 kW
	UNITED KINGDOM †BBC, Via Delano, USA	(D) • C AMERICA • 250 kW
	†BBC, Via Maseru, Lesotho	Alternative Frequency to 11940 kHz
	†BBC, Via Sackville, Can	N AMERICA • 250 kW; (D) • N AMERICA • 250 kW; (D) Sa/Su • N AMERICA • 250 kW; Su • N AMERICA • 250 kW
	BBC, Via Zyyi, Cyprus	E AFRICA • 100 kW
	USA †VOA, Via Philippines	E ASIA • 50 kW
	USSR RADIO MOSCOW, Kazan'	(J) • MIDEAST & E AFRICA • 240 kW
	RADIO MOSCOW, Leningrad	(D) • N AFRICA & MIDEAST • 240 kW
	RADIO MOSCOW, Yerevan	(J) • E AFRICA • 100 kW
9519v	**PERU** RADIO LA CRONICA, Lima	Irr • DS • 5 kW
9520	**HUNGARY** RADIO BUDAPEST, Various Locations	E NORTH AM • 100/250 kW; S AMERICA • 100/250 kW; M • S AMERICA • 100/250 kW; Tu/F • S AMERICA • 100/250 kW; M • E NORTH AM • 100/250 kW; W/Th/Sa-M • S AMERICA • 100/250 kW; Su-Tu/Th/F • E NORTH AM • 100/250 kW; Tu-Su • S AMERICA • 100/250 kW; Tu-Su • E NORTH AM • 100/250 kW; Tu/W/F/Sa • E NORTH AM • 100/250 kW; Tu/W/F/Sa • S AMERICA • 100/250 kW
(con'd)		

World Time: 0 Prime Time-Americas 6 Prime Time-E Asia 12 Prime Time-S Asia 18 Prime Time-Europe 24

ENGLISH ARABIC CHINESE FRENCH GERMAN RUSSIAN SPANISH OTHER

FREQUENCY   COUNTRY, STATION, LOCATION   TARGET • NETWORK • POWER (kW)   World Time

	0 1 2 3 4 5 6 7 8 9 10 11 12 13 14 15 16 17 18 19 20 21 22 23 24

9520 HUNGARY
(con'd)   RADIO BUDAPEST, Various Locations — W/Sa • E NORTH AM • 100/250 kW
USA
   †RFE-RL, Via Germany — WEST USSR • 100 kW

   †WYFR-FAMILY RADIO, Okeechobee, Fl — (J) • W NORTH AM • 100 kW
USSR
   RADIO MOSCOW, Irkutsk — (J) • E ASIA • 240 kW

   RADIO MOSCOW, Krasnodar — (D) • C AMERICA • 500 kW
      (D) • C AMERICA & EUROPE • WS • 500 kW

   RADIO MOSCOW, Moscow — ATLANTIC • 240 kW

   RADIO MOSCOW, Vladivostok — JAPANESE • E ASIA • 250 kW
9525 CUBA
   †RADIO HABANA, Havana — (D) • W NORTH AM • 500 kW
      (D) Su • W NORTH AM • 500 kW

INDIA
   ALL INDIA RADIO, Aizawl — (D) • SE ASIA • 250 kW

   ALL INDIA RADIO, Madras — DS-VIVIDH BHARATI • 100 kW
INDONESIA
   †RRI, Jakarta, Jawa — Irr • DS
JAPAN
   †RADIO JAPAN/NHK, Tokyo-Yamata — (D) • S AMERICA • 100 kW
POLAND
   †RADIO POLONIA, Warsaw — EUROPE, ATLANTIC & N AMERICA • 100 kW
      EUROPE & W AFRICA • 100 kW
      EUROPE & N AFRICA • 100 kW

SEYCHELLES
   FAR EAST BC ASS'N, North Pt, Mahé Is — S AFRICA • 75 kW
USA
   RADIO MARTI, Cincinnati, Ohio — C AMERICA • 250 kW
      (D) • C AMERICA • 250 kW

   †VOA, Cincinnati, Ohio — M-F • C AMERICA & S AMERICA • 250 kW

   †VOA, Delano, California — C AMERICA • 250 kW
      Sa/Su • C AMERICA • 250 kW

   VOA, Via M'rovia, Liberia — W AFRICA & C AFRICA • 250 kW
      M-F • W AFRICA & C AFRICA • 250 kW

   †VOA, Via Philippines — E ASIA & AUSTRALIA • 50/100 kW
      (D) • E ASIA & AUSTRALIA • 50 kW

9525v MOZAMBIQUE
   †RADIO MOCAMBIQUE, Maputo — Irr • DS • 25 kW
9530 CHINA (PR)
   RADIO BEIJING, Baoding — (D) • SE ASIA • 120 kW

   †RADIO BEIJING, Xi'an — (D) • SE ASIA • 150 kW
FINLAND
   †RADIO FINLAND, Pori — (D) • EUROPE & W AFRICA • 500 kW
JORDAN
   †RADIO JORDAN, Qasr el Kharana — MIDEAST & S ASIA • DS • 500 kW
NORTHERN MARIANA IS
   †KYOI, Saipan Island — (D) • E ASIA • 100 kW
ROMANIA
   †RADIO BUCHAREST, Bucharest — (D) • AFRICA • 250 kW
UNITED KINGDOM
   †BBC, Woofferton — (D) • EUROPE • 250 kW
USA
   VOA, Greenville, NC — W AFRICA • 500 kW

   VOA, Via Kaválla, Greece — (J) • MIDEAST & S ASIA • 250 kW   (J) • WEST USSR • 250 kW

   †VOA, Via Tangier, Morocco — (D) • MIDEAST • 100 kW
      (D) • E EUROPE • 35 kW
      (J) • MIDEAST • 100 kW
      (J) • WEST USSR • 100 kW

   †VOA, Via Wertachtal, GFR — N AFRICA & W AFRICA • 500 kW
      (J) • N AFRICA & W AFRICA • 500 kW

   VOA, Via Woofferton, UK — (D) • WEST USSR • 300 kW
USSR
   RADIO MOSCOW, Irkutsk — (J) • 50 kW

   RADIO MOSCOW, Moscow — (J) • E NORTH AM & W EUROPE • N AMERICAN • 500 kW
      (J) • E NORTH AM & W EUROPE • WS • 500 kW   (J) • AFRICA • AFRICAN • 240 kW
      (J) • AFRICA • WS • 240 kW

   RADIO MOSCOW, Tula — (J) • DS-2 • 100 kW
9535 ALGERIA
   †RTV ALGERIENNE, Ouled Fayet — EUROPE & N AFRICA • DS-3 • 50 kW • ALT. FREQ. TO 9509 kHz
(con'd) — EUROPE & N AFRICA • 50 kW • ALT. FREQ. TO 9509 kHz

0 Prime Time-Americas 6   Prime Time-E Asia 12   Prime Time-S Asia 18   Prime Time-Europe 24

SUMMER ONLY (J)   WINTER ONLY (D)   JAMMING / OR ∧   EARLIEST HEARD ◁   LATEST HEARD ▷   NEW OR CHANGED FOR 1990 †

FREQUENCY   COUNTRY, STATION, LOCATION   TARGET • NETWORK • POWER (kW)   World Time

0 1 2 3 4 5 6 7 8 9 10 11 12 13 14 15 16 17 18 19 20 21 22 23 24

Frequency	Country, Station, Location	Target • Network • Power
9535 (con'd)	ANGOLA RADIO NACIONAL, Luanda	S AFRICA • 100 kW
	CANADA ↑R CANADA INTL, Sackville, NB	Su/M • C AMERICA & S AMERICA • 250 kW (D) • C AMERICA & S AMERICA • 250 kW
		(D) Su/M • C AMERICA & S AMERICA • 250 kW (D) M-F • C AMERICA & S AMERICA • 250 kW
		Tu-Sa • C AMERICA & S AMERICA • 250 kW (D) Sa/Su • C AMERICA & S AMERICA • 250 kW
		(D) Tu/Sa • C AMERICA & S AMERICA • 250 kW
	↑R CANADA INTL, Via Xi'an, China(PR)	JAPANESE • E ASIA • 120 kW
	INDIA ALL INDIA RADIO, Aligarh	SE ASIA • 250 kW
	JAPAN ↑NHK, Fukuoka	Irr • JAPANESE • DS-1(FEEDER) • 0.6 kW • USB
	↑NHK, Osaka	Irr • JAPANESE • DS-2(FEEDER) • 0.5 kW
	↑NHK, Sapporo	Irr • JAPANESE • DS-1(FEEDER) • 0.6 kW
	↑RADIO JAPAN/NHK, Tokyo-Yamata	S ASIA & E AFRICA • 300 kW
		(D) • MIDEAST & N AFRICA • 300 kW
		(D) • EUROPE • 300 kW
		(J) • S ASIA • GENERAL • 300 kW
		(J) • JAPANESE • S ASIA • GENERAL • 300 kW
	NETHERLANDS ANTILLES TRANS WORLD RADIO, Bonaire	N AMERICA • 50 kW
		Su/M • N AMERICA • 50 kW
		Tu-Sa • C AMERICA • 50 kW
	SWITZERLAND ↑SWISS RADIO INTL, Lenk	EUROPE & N AFRICA • 250 kW
		M-Sa • EUROPE & N AFRICA • 250 kW
		Su • EUROPE & N AFRICA • 250 kW
9540	BRAZIL ↑R EDUCADORA BAHIA, Salvador	PORTUGUESE • DS • 10 kW
	CZECHOSLOVAKIA RADIO PRAGUE, Pieštány-Velké K'y	S AMERICA • 120 kW
		E NORTH AM & C AMERICA • 120 kW
	HOLLAND ↑RADIO NEDERLAND, Via Madagascar	(D) • W AFRICA & C AFRICA • 300 kW
	KOREA (DPR) RADIO PYONGYANG, Pyongyang	SE ASIA • 200 kW
		E ASIA & S ASIA • 100 kW
	PHILIPPINES RADIO VERITAS ASIA, Malolos	SE ASIA • 100 kW
		E ASIA • 100 kW
	POLAND ↑RADIO POLONIA, Warsaw	EUROPE • 100 kW
	SWAZILAND ↑TRANS WORLD RADIO, Manzini	(D) • E AFRICA • 25/100 kW
	UNITED KINGDOM ↑BBC, Via Ascension	(J) • C AFRICA • 250 kW
		(J) • S AFRICA • 250 kW
	USA ↑R FREE AFGHANISTAN, Via Germany	WEST USSR & S ASIA • 100 kW
	↑RFE-RL, Via Germany	WEST USSR • 100 kW
	↑RFE-RL, Via Pals, Spain	WEST USSR • 250 kW
	↑RFE-RL, Via Portugal	WEST USSR • 250 kW
	↑VOA, Via Kaválla, Greece	(J) • MIDEAST & S ASIA • 250 kW
	VOA, Via M'rovia, Liberia	W AFRICA & C AFRICA • 250 kW
	USSR RADIO MOSCOW, Moscow	DS-1 • 100 kW
		(J) • DS-1 • 100 kW
	RADIO MOSCOW, Petropavlovsk-Kam	(J) • JAPANESE • E ASIA • 200 kW
	↑RADIO TASHKENT, Tashkent	MIDEAST • 100 kW
		(D) • S ASIA • 100 kW
9540.5	VENEZUELA ↑RADIO NACIONAL, Caracas	C AMERICA & S AMERICA • 50 kW
9545	CLANDESTINE (M EAST) "IRAN BALUCHISTAN", Via R Baghdad	MIDEAST • MOJAHEDIN-E KHALQ • 500 kW
	GERMANY (FR) ↑DEUTSCHE WELLE, Jülich	E EUROPE & MIDEAST • 100 kW (J) • EUROPE • 100 kW
	↑DEUTSCHE WELLE, Multiple Locations	C AMERICA & S AMERICA • 250/500 kW
		EUROPE • 100/500 kW
	DEUTSCHE WELLE, Via Brasília, Brazil	S AMERICA & C AMERICA • 250 kW
	↑DEUTSCHE WELLE, Via Montserrat	(J) • C AMERICA • 25 kW
(con'd)	↑DEUTSCHE WELLE, Wertachtal	(D) • MIDEAST • 500 kW

0 Prime Time-Americas 6   Prime Time-E Asia 12   Prime Time-S Asia 18   Prime Time-Europe 24

FREQUENCY	COUNTRY, STATION, LOCATION	TARGET • NETWORK • POWER (kW)
9545 (con'd)	**INDIA** ALL INDIA RADIO, Aligarh	DS-ENGLISH, ETC • 250 kW
	SOLOMON IS SOLOMON ISLANDS BC, Honiara	Irr • Su-F • DS-ENGLISH, PIDGIN • 10 kW
		Sa • DS-ENGLISH, PIDGIN • 10 kW
		DS-ENGLISH, PIDGIN • 10 kW
	USA †VOA, Via Philippines	E ASIA • 250 kW
		S ASIA • 100 kW
	USSR BELORUSSIAN RADIO, Minsk	DS-2 • 15 kW
	RADIO MOSCOW, Khabarovsk	(J) • DS-2 • 50 kW
9545v	**PAKISTAN** PAKISTAN BC CORP, Islamabad	(J) • DS • 10 kW
		DS • 10 kW
		(D) • DS • 10 kW
9550	**BRAZIL** †R NOVA ESPERANCA, Pôrto Alegre	PORTUGUESE • DS • 5 kW
	CLANDESTINE (AFRICA) "RADIO SPLA", Ethiopia	N AFRICA • ANTI-SUDANESE GOVT • 100 kW
	†"VO ETHIOPIA UNITY, Sudan	Alternative Frequency to 9435 kHz
	†"VO OROMO LIBER'N", Sudan	Alternative Frequency to 9435 kHz
	CUBA †RADIO HABANA, Havana	(D) • S AMERICA • 50 kW
		Su • C AMERICA • 50 kW
		(D) • C AMERICA • 50 kW
		(J) • S AMERICA • 100 kW
	FINLAND †RADIO FINLAND, Pori	(J) • EUROPE & W AFRICA • 500 kW
	FRANCE †R FRANCE INTL, Issoudun-Allouis	(D) • E EUROPE & MIDEAST • 100 kW
	INDIA †ALL INDIA RADIO, Aligarh	S ASIA & E ASIA • 250 kW
		AUSTRALIA • 250 kW
		(J) • MIDEAST & S ASIA • 250 kW
		DS-ENGLISH, ETC • 250 kW
	JAPAN †NHK, Tokyo-Shobu	Irr • JAPANESE • DS-1(FEEDER) • 0.9 kW • USB
	LIBERIA RADIO ELWA, Monrovia	W AFRICA • 50 kW
	PHILIPPINES RADIO VERITAS ASIA, Malolos	SE ASIA • 100 kW
	SWAZILAND †TRANS WORLD RADIO, Manzini	S AFRICA & C AFRICA • 100 kW
		Sa/Su • S AFRICA & C AFRICA • 100 kW
	USA VOA, Cincinnati, Ohio	N AFRICA & W AFRICA • 250 kW
	†WYFR-FAMILY RADIO, Okeechobee, Fl	(J) • S AMERICA • 100 kW
	USSR RADIO MOSCOW, Moscow	(J) • ATLANTIC • MARINERS • 240 kW
		(D) • S ASIA & SE ASIA • 120 kW
9552v	**INDONESIA** †RRI, Ujung Pandang	DS • 10 kW
9555	**CANADA** †R CANADA INTL, Via United Kingdom	(D) • EUROPE • 300 kW
		(J) • EUROPE • 300 kW
		(J) M-F • EUROPE • 300 kW
		(J) Sa/Su • EUROPE • 300 kW
	KOREA (DPR) RADIO PYONGYANG, Pyongyang	SE ASIA • 200 kW
		E ASIA & S ASIA • 100 kW
	MEXICO †LA HORA EXACTA, México City	Irr • DS • 1 kW
	SOUTH AFRICA SOUTH AFRICAN BC, Meyerton	RADIO SUID-AFRIKA • 100 kW
	UNITED ARAB EMIRATES †UAE RADIO, Dubai	E NORTH AM & C AMERICA • 300 kW
	USA †R FREE AFGHANISTAN, Via Portugal	WEST USSR & S ASIA • 250 kW
	†RFE-RL, Via Portugal	E EUROPE & WEST USSR • 250 kW
	†WYFR-FAMILY RADIO, Okeechobee, Fl	(D) • C AMERICA • 100 kW
		(D) • S AMERICA • 100 kW
		(J) • S AMERICA • 100 kW
	USSR RADIO MOSCOW, Tula	DS-2 • 100 kW
9560	**CHINA (PR)** XINJIANG PBS, Urümqi	(J) • DS-CHINESE • 50 kW
	ETHIOPIA VOICE OF ETHIOPIA, Gedja	E AFRICA • 100 kW
	FINLAND RADIO FINLAND, Pori	EUROPE & W AFRICA • 500 kW
(con'd)	**GERMANY (DR)** †R BERLIN INTL, Nauen	W EUROPE • 500 kW

World Time: 0 Prime Time-Americas 6 Prime Time-E Asia 12 Prime Time-S Asia 18 Prime Time-Europe 24

SUMMER ONLY (J) WINTER ONLY (D) JAMMING / OR /\ EARLIEST HEARD ◃ LATEST HEARD ▹ NEW OR CHANGED FOR 1990 †

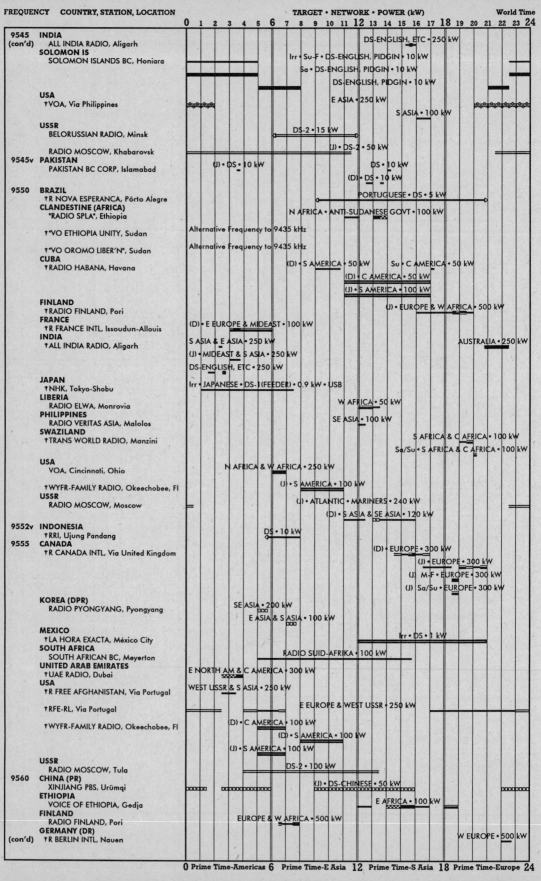

FREQUENCY	COUNTRY, STATION, LOCATION	TARGET • NETWORK • POWER (kW)
9560 (con'd)	**JORDAN** †RADIO JORDAN, Qasr el Kharana	EUROPE & E NORTH AM • 500 kW
		(D) • EUROPE & E NORTH AM • 500 kW
	NORWAY †RADIO NORWAY INTL, Sveio	N AMERICA • 500 kW
	PHILIPPINES RADIO VERITAS ASIA, Palauig	SE ASIA • VIETNAMESE, ETC • 250 kW
	SAUDI ARABIA BS OF THE KINGDOM, Riyadh	PERSIAN • MIDEAST • 350 kW
	SWITZERLAND †RED CROSS BC SVC, Schwarzenburg	Irr • M/Th • AUSTRALIA • 150 kW
	†SWISS RADIO INTL, Schwarzenburg	AUSTRALIA • 150 kW
		M-Sa • AUSTRALIA • 150 kW
		Su • AUSTRALIA • 150 kW
	UNITED KINGDOM †BBC, Via Zyyi, Cyprus	EUROPE • 250 kW
	USSR RADIO KIEV, L'vov	(J) • EUROPE • 100 kW
	RADIO MOSCOW, Serpukhov	(J) • W AFRICA & ATLANTIC • MARINERS • 240 kW
	RS SOV BELORUSSIA, L'vov	(J) M/Tu/Th/F • EUROPE • 100 kW
		(J) W/Sa/Su • EUROPE • 100 kW
9565	**CHINA (PR)** RADIO BEIJING, Xi'an	S ASIA & E AFRICA • 150 kW
	GERMANY (FR) †DEUTSCHE WELLE, Via Cyclops, Malta	(J) • E NORTH AM & C AMERICA • 250 kW
	†DEUTSCHE WELLE, Via Kigali, Rwanda	(J) • C AFRICA & S AFRICA • 250 kW
	†DEUTSCHE WELLE, Via Montserrat	(J) • C AMERICA • 25 kW
		(J) • C AMERICA • 50 kW
	INDIA †ALL INDIA RADIO, Aligarh	(J) • SE ASIA • 250 kW
	UNITED KINGDOM †BBC, Skelton, Cumbria	(J) • EUROPE • 250 kW
	USA †RFE-RL, Via Germany	WEST USSR • 100 kW
	†RFE-RL, Via Pals, Spain	WEST USSR • 250 kW
	†RFE-RL, Via Portugal	WEST USSR • 250 kW
	†VOA, Greenville, NC	N AFRICA • 500 kW
		M-F • N AFRICA • 500 kW
	VOA, Via Kavália, Greece	(J) • WEST USSR • 250 kW
	VOA, Via Rhodes, Greece	(J) • MIDEAST • TURKISH • 50 kW
	VOA, Via Woofferton, UK	(J) • WEST USSR • 300 kW
		(D) • MIDEAST & WEST USSR • 250 kW
		(J) • EUROPE • GREEK • 300 kW
	VOICE OF THE OAS, Cincinnati, Ohio	C AMERICA & S AMERICA • 175/250 kW
	USSR RADIO MOSCOW, Irkutsk	(J) • E ASIA • JAPANESE, KOREAN • 240 kW
		(J) • JAPANESE • E ASIA • JAPANESE, KOREAN • 240 kW
9565v	**BRAZIL** RADIO UNIVERSO, Curitiba	PORTUGUESE • DS • 7.5 kW
9570	**CHINA (PR)** †RADIO BEIJING, Xi'an	(D) • S AMERICA • 300 kW
		E AFRICA & S AFRICA • 300 kW
	KOREA (REPUBLIC) RADIO KOREA, In-Kimjae	W NORTH AM & C AMERICA • 250 kW
		KOREAN • W NORTH AM & C AMERICA • 250 kW
		KOREAN • S AMERICA • 250 kW
		S AMERICA • 250 kW
		SE ASIA • 250 kW
		KOREAN • SE ASIA • 250 kW
	ROMANIA †RADIO BUCHAREST, Bucharest	AMERICAS • 250 kW
		(D) • AFRICA • 250 kW
		(D) • AMERICAS • 250 kW
		(J) Su • ATLANTIC • MARINERS • 250 kW
		(D) • EUROPE • 250 kW
	SAUDI ARABIA BS OF THE KINGDOM, Jiddah	MIDEAST & E AFRICA • DS-2 • 50 kW
	UNITED KINGDOM BBC, Via Singapore	SE ASIA & AUSTRALIA • 250 kW
9575	**CHINA (PR)** †RADIO BEIJING, Xi'an	(D) • AUSTRALIA • CHINESE, CANTONESE • 150 kW
	CHINA (TAIWAN) VO FREE CHINA, T'ai-pei	SE ASIA
	INDIA †ALL INDIA RADIO, Aligarh	(J) • E ASIA • 250 kW
(con'd)	**IRAN** †VO THE ISLAMIC REP, Tehrān	(J) • MIDEAST • 500 kW

World Time: 0 Prime Time-Americas 6 Prime Time-E Asia 12 Prime Time-S Asia 18 Prime Time-Europe 24

ENGLISH ▬ ARABIC ▩ CHINESE ▢▢▢ FRENCH ═ GERMAN ▬ RUSSIAN ═ SPANISH ▬ OTHER —

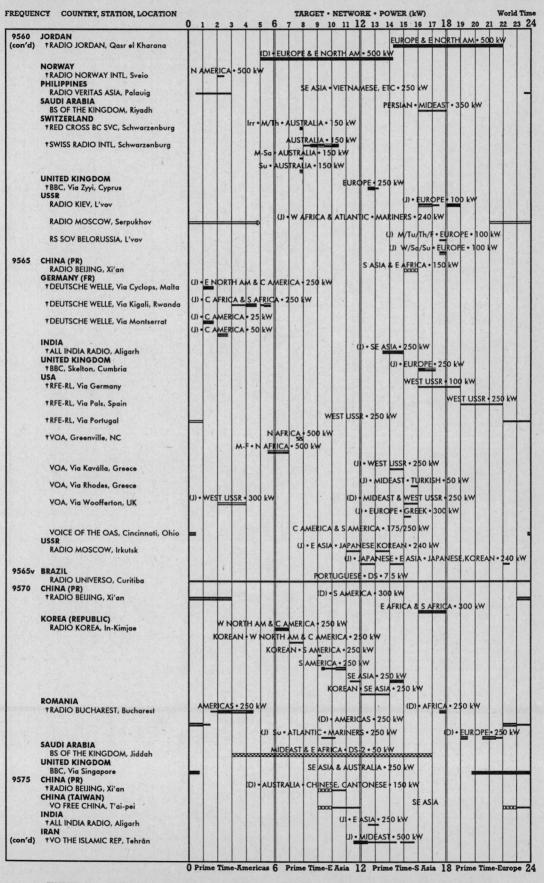

FREQUENCY	COUNTRY, STATION, LOCATION	TARGET • NETWORK • POWER (kW)
9575 (con'd)	**ITALY** †RTV ITALIANA, Rome	E NORTH AM • 100 kW
		S AMERICA • 100 kW
		EUROPE • 100 kW
		E EUROPE & WEST USSR • 100 kW
		(J) • EUROPE, MIDEAST & N AFRICA • 100 kW
		MIDEAST • 100 kW
		(J) • E EUROPE & WEST USSR • 100 kW
		(J) • EUROPE • 100 kW
	MOROCCO RADIO MEDI UN, Nador	Irr • EUROPE & N AFRICA • ARABIC,FR/RAMADAN • 250 kW
		EUROPE & N AFRICA • ARABIC, FRENCH • 250 kW
	NORTHERN MARIANA IS KFBS-FAR EAST BC, Saipan Island	E ASIA • 100 kW
	PORTUGAL RADIO RENASCENCA, Muge	Su • EUROPE • 100 kW
	UNITED KINGDOM †BBC, Daventry	(J) • EUROPE & WEST USSR • 300 kW
	USA †VOA, Cincinnati, Ohio	N AFRICA • 250 kW
		(J) • N AFRICA • 250 kW
	†VOA, Greenville, NC	(D) • N AFRICA • 250 kW
		M-F • W AFRICA • ENGLISH,FRENCH,ETC • 500 kW
	VOA, Via Philippines	E AFRICA • 250 kW
	VOA, Via Wertachtal,GFR	(D) • WEST USSR • 500 kW
	USSR RADIO MOSCOW, Irkutsk	(J) • DS-1 • 50 kW
	RADIO MOSCOW, Serpukhov	(J) • MIDEAST • WS • 240 kW
		(D) • MIDEAST & E AFRICA • WS,PORT,SWAHILI • 240 kW
9580	**AUSTRALIA** †RADIO AUSTRALIA, Shepparton	PACIFIC & N AMERICA • 100 kW
	CLANDESTINE (M EAST) "VO THE CRUSADER", Via R Baghdad	MIDEAST • MOJAHEDIN-E KHALQ
	GABON †AFRIQUE NUMERO UN, Moyabi	C AFRICA • 250 kW • ALT. FREQ. TO 4830 kHz
	JAPAN †RADIO JAPAN/NHK, Tokyo-Yamata	E ASIA • 100 kW
		(J) • E ASIA • 100 kW
	SOUTH AFRICA †RADIO RSA, Meyerton	S AMERICA • 250/500 kW
		N AMERICA • 500 kW
		(J) • S AFRICA • 250 kW
		(J) • S AMERICA • 250 kW
	UNITED KINGDOM BBC, Skelton, Cumbria	(J) • W EUROPE & W AFRICA • 250 kW
	†BBC, Via Ascension	(D) • C AFRICA • 250 kW
	†BBC, Via Maşirah, Oman	S ASIA • 100 kW
	†BBC, Via Singapore	SE ASIA • 100 kW
		SE ASIA & E ASIA • 100 kW
		(D) • SE ASIA & E ASIA • 100 kW
	†BBC, Via Zyyi, Cyprus	EUROPE & WEST USSR • 100 kW
		(D) • WEST USSR • 100 kW
		(J) • WEST USSR • 100 kW
		(J) • EUROPE & WEST USSR • 100 kW
	USA VOA, Via Rhodes, Greece	(D) • MIDEAST • TURKISH • 50 kW
	VOA, Via Woofferton, UK	N AFRICA • 250 kW
	USSR R TIKHIY OKEAN, Blagoveshchensk	(J) • W NORTH AM • MARINERS • 240 kW
		(J) Sa • W NORTH AM • MARINERS • 240 kW
		(J) Su-F • W NORTH AM • MARINERS • 240 kW
	RADIO MOSCOW, Blagoveshchensk	(D) • W NORTH AM • N AMERICAN • 240 kW
		(J) • W NORTH AM • WS • 240 kW
		(J) • W NORTH AM • N AMERICAN • 240 kW
	RADIO MOSCOW, Kazan'	(J) • EUROPE • POLISH • 200 kW
9585	**BRAZIL** RADIO EXCELSIOR, São Paulo	Irr • PORTUGUESE • DS • 10 kW
		PORTUGUESE • DS • 10 kW
	ECUADOR †HCJB-VO THE ANDES, Quito	(J) • EUROPE & WEST USSR • 500 kW
		(J) M-F • EUROPE & WEST USSR • 500 kW
		(J) Sa/Su • EUROPE & WEST USSR • 500 kW
	HUNGARY RADIO BUDAPEST, Various Locations	S AMERICA • 20/100 kW
		E NORTH AM • 20/100 kW
		EUROPE • 20/100 kW
		M • S AMERICA • 20/100 kW
		M/Th • EUROPE • 20/100 kW
		M • E NORTH AM • 20/100 kW
(con'd)		Sa • EUROPE • 20/100 kW

World Time: 0 Prime Time-Americas 6 Prime Time-E Asia 12 Prime Time-S Asia 18 Prime Time-Europe 24

SUMMER ONLY (J) WINTER ONLY (D) JAMMING / OR ∧ EARLIEST HEARD ◁ LATEST HEARD ▷ NEW OR CHANGED FOR 1990 †

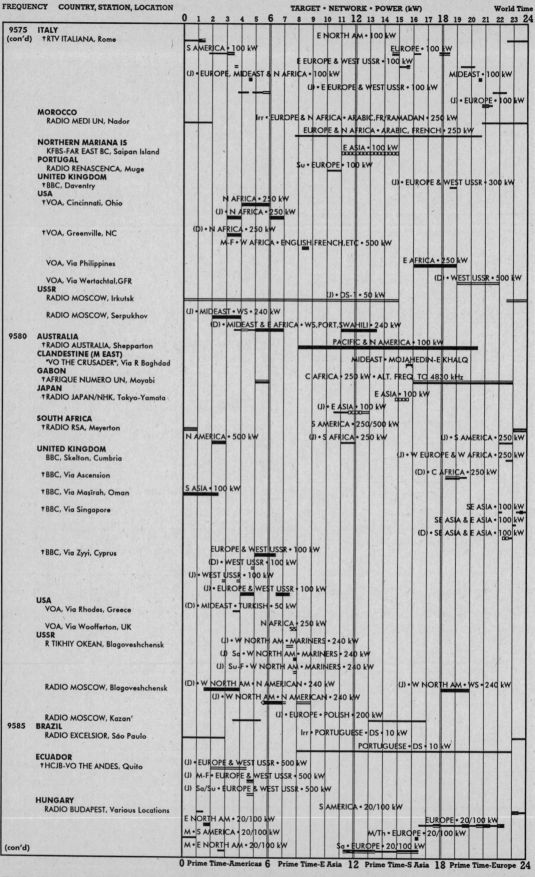

FREQUENCY	COUNTRY, STATION, LOCATION	TARGET • NETWORK • POWER (kW)
9585 (con'd)	**HUNGARY** RADIO BUDAPEST, Various Locations	Su-Tu/Th/F • E NORTH AM • 20/100 kW
		Su • EUROPE • 20/100 kW
		Tu-Su • S AMERICA • 20/100 kW
		Tu/F • S AMERICA • 20/100 kW
		Tu-Su • E NORTH AM • 20/100 kW
		W/Th/Sa-M • S AMERICA • 20/100 kW
		Tu/W/F/Sa • E NORTH AM • 20/100 kW
		Tu/W/F/Sa • S AMERICA • 20/100 kW
		W/Sa • E NORTH AM • 20/100 kW
	ITALY RTV ITALIANA, Rome	AUSTRALIA • 100 kW
	SOUTH AFRICA †RADIO RSA, Meyerton	(D) Sa/Su • S AFRICA • 250 kW
		(D) • S AFRICA • 250 kW
		(J) • E AFRICA & S AFRICA • 250 kW
		(J) • S AFRICA & W AFRICA • 500 kW
	USA †VOA, Via Kaválla, Greece	(J) • MIDEAST • 250 kW
		(J) • WEST USSR • 250 kW
	†VOA, Via Wertachtal, GFR	(J) • E EUROPE & WEST USSR • 500 kW
	VOA, Via Woofferton, UK	(D) • WEST USSR • 250 kW
		(J) • E EUROPE & WEST USSR • 250/300 kW
	USSR RADIO MOSCOW, Kenga	(J) • E ASIA • 500 kW
9585.6	**QATAR** QATAR BC SERVICE, Doha	EUROPE • DS • 250 kW
9590	**CHINA (PR)** †RADIO BEIJING, Xi'an	(D) • E ASIA • 150 kW
	CUBA RADIO HABANA, Via USSR	(J) • W AFRICA • 120 kW
	GUAM †KTWR-TRANS WORLD R, Merizo	E ASIA • 100 kW
	HOLLAND †RADIO NEDERLAND, Flevoland	C AMERICA & S AMERICA • 300 kW
	†RADIO NEDERLAND, Via Madagascar	SE ASIA • 300 kW
	†RADIO NEDERLAND, Via Neth Antilles	W NORTH AM • 300 kW
		C AMERICA & W NORTH AM • 300 kW
	NORWAY †RADIO NORWAY INTL, Fredrikstad	EUROPE & N AFRICA • 350 kW
		(D) M-Sa • EUROPE • 350 kW
		M-Sa • EUROPE • 350 kW
		Su • EUROPE • 350 kW
		(D) Su • EUROPE • 350 kW
	ROMANIA †RADIO BUCHAREST, Bucharest	(D) • MIDEAST • 250 kW
		Su • W EUROPE & ATLANTIC • MARINERS • 250 kW
	UNITED KINGDOM †BBC, Skelton, Cumbria	(D) • W EUROPE & W AFRICA • 250 kW
	BBC, Via Cincinnati, USA	E NORTH AM, C AMERICA & S AMERICA • 250 kW
	†BBC, Via Sackville, Can	N AMERICA • 250 kW
		(J) • N AMERICA • 250 kW
	†BBC, Via Zyyi, Cyprus	PERSIAN • MIDEAST • 100 kW
		(D) • MIDEAST • 100 kW
	USA RADIO MARTI, Cincinnati, Ohio	C AMERICA • 250 kW
	VOA, Greenville, NC	C AMERICA • 250 kW
9595	**BULGARIA** †RADIO SOFIA, Plovdiv	(D) • MIDEAST • 500 kW
	†RADIO SOFIA, Sofia	(D) • C AMERICA • 250 kW
	CANADA †R CANADA INTL, Via Tokyo, Japan	Sa • JAPANESE • E ASIA & PACIFIC • 50 kW
	CHINA (PR) CENTRAL PEOPLES BS, Urümqi	(J) • DS-MINORITIES • 50 kW
	XINJIANG PBS, Urümqi	(J) • DS-UIGHUR • 50 kW
		(J) Su • DS-UIGHUR • 50 kW
	CLANDESTINE (M EAST) "VO THE CRUSADER", Via R Baghdad	MIDEAST • MOJAHEDIN-E KHALQ
	DENMARK DANMARKS RADIO, Copenhagen	(D) • S AMERICA • 50 kW
	ETHIOPIA "RADIO FREEDOM", Via Vo Ethiopia	S AFRICA • ANC/ENGLISH, ETC • 100 kW
	"VOICE OF NAMIBIA", Via Vo Ethiopia	S AFRICA • SWAPO/ENGLISH, ETC • 100 kW
	JAPAN †RADIO TANPA, Tokyo-Nagara	JAPANESE • DS-1 • 50 kW
		Su-F • JAPANESE • DS-1 • 50 kW
	PHILIPPINES RADIO VERITAS ASIA, Palauig	SE ASIA • 250 kW
	UNITED ARAB EMIRATES †VOICE OF THE UAE, Abu Dhabi	E NORTH AM • 500 kW
(con'd)	**UNITED KINGDOM** †BBC, Via Seychelles	E AFRICA • 250 kW

World Time: 0 Prime Time-Americas 6 Prime Time-E Asia 12 Prime Time-S Asia 18 Prime Time-Europe 24

ENGLISH ARABIC CHINESE FRENCH GERMAN RUSSIAN SPANISH OTHER

FREQUENCY	COUNTRY, STATION, LOCATION	TARGET • NETWORK • POWER (kW)
9595 (con'd)	**UNITED KINGDOM**	
	†BBC, Via Seychelles	S AFRICA • 250 kW
		(J) • E AFRICA • 250 kW
		(J) • S AFRICA • 250 kW
	URUGUAY	
	†RADIO MONTE CARLO, Montevideo	DS • 1.5 kW
	USA	
	†RFE-RL, Via Germany	E EUROPE • 100 kW
		Sa/Su • E EUROPE • 100 kW
		Su • E EUROPE • 100 kW
	†RFE-RL, Via Portugal	E EUROPE • 250 kW
		M-Sa • E EUROPE • 250 kW
		Su • WEST USSR • 250 kW
	USSR	
	RADIO MOSCOW, Novosibirsk	E ASIA • 100 kW
		(J) • E ASIA • CHINESE, MONGOLIAN • 100 kW
9599.7	**BRAZIL**	
	†RADIO MEC, Rio de Janeiro	PORTUGUESE • DS • 7.5 kW
9600	**ALBANIA**	
	RADIO TIRANA, Lushnjë	SE ASIA • INDONESIAN • 100 kW
	CZECHOSLOVAKIA	
	RADIO PRAGUE, Prague	AFRICA • 120 kW
	GERMANY (FR)	
	†DEUTSCHE WELLE, Via Cyclops, Malta	(D) • MIDEAST • 250 kW
	KOREA (DPR)	
	RADIO PYONGYANG, Pyongyang	EAST USSR • 100 kW
		C AMERICA • 400 kW
		SE ASIA • 200 kW
	LIBYA	
	RADIO JAMAHIRIYA, Benghazi	MIDEAST • DS • 100 kW
	PORTUGAL	
	R PORTUGAL INTL, Lisbon-S Gabriel	S AMERICA • 100 kW
		Su/M • S AMERICA • 100 kW
		Tu-Sa • S AMERICA • 100 kW
	RADIO RENASCENCA, Muge	S AMERICA • 100 kW
	SWAZILAND	
	†TRANS WORLD RADIO, Manzini	(D) • E AFRICA • 25 kW
	UNITED KINGDOM	
	†BBC, Daventry	(D) • EUROPE & N AFRICA • 300 kW
	†BBC, Rampisham	(D) • WEST USSR • 500 kW
	†BBC, Skelton, Cumbria	(J) • EUROPE • 250 kW
	†BBC, Via Ascension	S AFRICA • 250 kW
		W AFRICA • 250 kW
		(J) • S AFRICA • 250 kW
	†BBC, Via Maşīrah, Oman	S ASIA • 100 kW
	†BBC, Via Seychelles	(D) • S AFRICA • 250 kW
	†BBC, Via Singapore	SE ASIA & S ASIA • 100 kW
	†BBC, Via Zyyi, Cyprus	(J) • E AFRICA • 100 kW
	USSR	
	MAGADAN RADIO, Blagoveshchensk	DS • 50 kW
	RADIO MOSCOW, Moscow	(J) • W EUROPE • 240 kW
	RADIO MOSCOW, Via Havana, Cuba	(J) • N AMERICA • 100 kW
	†RADIO TASHKENT, Tashkent	S ASIA • 100 kW
9600v	**MEXICO**	
	†RADIO UNIVERSIDAD, México City	Irr • DS • 0.25/1 kW
9605	**CHINA (PR)**	
	RADIO BEIJING, Kunming	SE ASIA • 50 kW
	CZECHOSLOVAKIA	
	RADIO PRAGUE, Prague	N AFRICA & E AFRICA • 120 kW
		M-F • N AFRICA & E AFRICA • 120 kW
	FRANCE	
	†R FRANCE INTL, Issoudun-Allouis	(D) • E EUROPE & WEST USSR • 100 kW
		(J) • E EUROPE & WEST USSR • 100 kW
	GERMANY (FR)	
	†DEUTSCHE WELLE, Jülich	(D) • N AMERICA • 100 kW
		SE ASIA • 100 kW
	DEUTSCHE WELLE, Via Antigua	(J) • N AMERICA & C AMERICA • 250 kW
	DEUTSCHE WELLE, Via Sackville, Can	N AMERICA • 250 kW
	†DEUTSCHE WELLE, Wertachtal	(D) • E EUROPE • 500 kW
		(D) • WEST USSR • 500 kW
		(J) • WEST USSR • 500 kW
	IRAQ	
(con'd)	†RADIO BAGHDAD, Balad-Salah el Deen	(D) • N AFRICA & C AFRICA • 500 kW

World Time: 0 1 2 3 4 5 6 7 8 9 10 11 12 13 14 15 16 17 18 19 20 21 22 23 24

0 Prime Time-Americas 6 Prime Time-E Asia 12 Prime Time-S Asia 18 Prime Time-Europe 24

SUMMER ONLY (J) WINTER ONLY (D) JAMMING / OR /\ EARLIEST HEARD ◁ LATEST HEARD ▷ NEW OR CHANGED FOR 1990 †

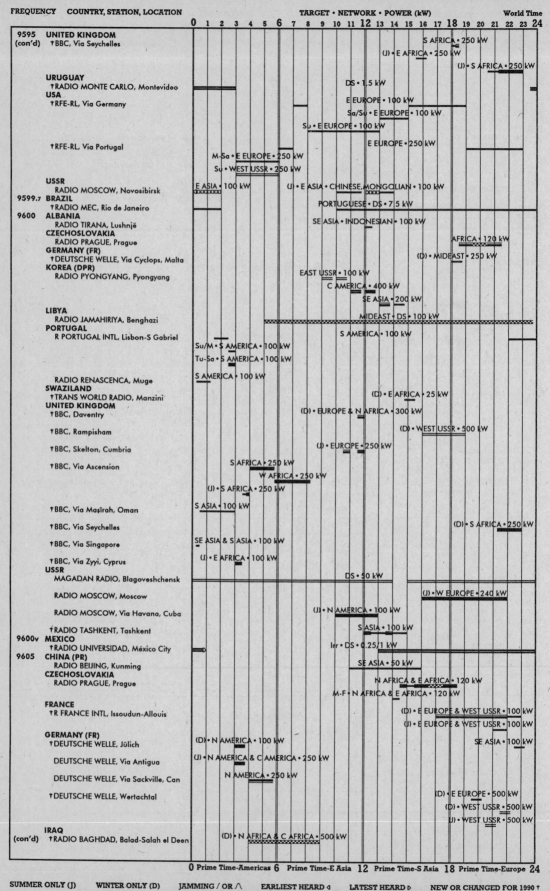

FREQUENCY	COUNTRY, STATION, LOCATION	TARGET • NETWORK • POWER (kW) — World Time 0–24
9605 (con'd)	**ITALY**	
	†ADVENTIST WORLD R, Via Portugal	Sa/Su • E EUROPE & WEST USSR • 250 kW
		Su • E EUROPE & WEST USSR • 250 kW
		Su • N AFRICA • 250 kW
	NORWAY	
	†RADIO NORWAY INTL, Sveio	(D) M-Sa • E NORTH AM • 500 kW
		(D) Su • E NORTH AM • 500 kW
	PHILIPPINES	
	RADIO VERITAS ASIA, Malolos	E ASIA • 100 kW
	UNITED KINGDOM	
	†BBC, Via Singapore	S ASIA • 250 kW
	USA	
	VOA, Via M'rovia, Liberia	W AFRICA • 15/250 kW
	†VOA, Via Tangier, Morocco	(J) • E EUROPE • 35/100 kW
	†WYFR-FAMILY RADIO, Okeechobee, Fl	S AMERICA • 100 kW
		(D) • C AMERICA • 100 kW
	USSR	
	RADIO MOSCOW, Serpukhov	(J) • DS-1 • 50 kW
		DS-1 • 50 kW
	VATICAN STATE	
	†VATICAN RADIO, Sta Maria di Galeria	N AMERICA • 100 kW
9610	**AUSTRALIA**	
	AUSTRALIAN BC CORP, Perth	DS • 10 kW
	CHINA (TAIWAN)	
	†CHINA BC CORP, T'ai-pei	E ASIA • DS
	VO FREE CHINA, T'ai-pei	AUSTRALIA
	CUBA	
	RADIO HABANA, Via USSR	(D) • W AFRICA • 100 kW
	ECUADOR	
	†HCJB-VO THE ANDES, Quito	(J) • EUROPE • 500 kW
		(J) M-F • EUROPE • 500 kW
		(J) Sa/Su • EUROPE • 500 kW
	INDIA	
	ALL INDIA RADIO, Aligarh	S ASIA • 250 kW
	ALL INDIA RADIO, Delhi	Su • DS • 100 kW
		DS-ENGLISH, ETC • 100 kW
	IRAN	
	†VO THE ISLAMIC REP, Tehrān	(D) • PERSIAN • MIDEAST & N AFRICA • 500 kW
	JAPAN	
	†RADIO JAPAN/NHK, Tokyo-Yamata	(D) • EUROPE • 300 kW
	MAURITANIA	
	ORT DE MAURITANIE, Nouakchott	Alternative Frequency to 7245 kHz
	SEYCHELLES	
	FAR EAST BC ASS'N, North Pt, Mahé Is	E AFRICA • 25 kW
		F-M • E AFRICA • 25 kW
		Sa/Su • E AFRICA • 25 kW
	SWAZILAND	
	†TRANS WORLD RADIO, Manzini	(J) • E AFRICA • 25 kW
	UNITED KINGDOM	
	†BBC, Rampisham	E EUROPE & MIDEAST • 500 kW
		Su • E EUROPE & MIDEAST • 500 kW
	†BBC, Via Antigua	(D) • S AMERICA • 250 kW
		(D) M-F • S AMERICA • 250 kW
		(D) Sa/Su • S AMERICA • 250 kW
	†BBC, Via Ascension	(J) • C AFRICA • 250 kW
	†BBC, Via Zyyi, Cyprus	(D) • E AFRICA • 250 kW
	USA	
	VOA, Via Philippines	SE ASIA • 50/250 kW
		(D) • SE ASIA • 250 kW
	USSR	
	RADIO MOSCOW, Alma-Ata	(D) • C AMERICA & S AMERICA • 500 kW
		(D) • EUROPE • 500 kW
		(D) • EUROPE • WS • 500 kW
	RADIO MOSCOW, Sverdlovsk	(J) • EUROPE • 100 kW
	RADIO MOSCOW, Tula	(J) • E NORTH AM & C AMERICA • N AMERICAN • 240 kW
		(J) • E NORTH AM & C AMERICA • 240 kW
		(J) • E NORTH AM & C AMERICA • WS • 240 kW
9614.5	**INDONESIA**	
	†RRI, Samarinda, Kalimantan	DS • 50 kW
9615	**BRAZIL**	
	RADIO CULTURA, São Paulo	PORTUGUESE • DS • 7.5 kW
	CANADA	
	R CANADA INTL, Via Sines, Portugal	(D) • WEST USSR • 250 kW
	GERMANY (FR)	
	†DEUTSCHE WELLE, Various Locations	MIDEAST & S ASIA • 250 kW
(con'd)	†DEUTSCHE WELLE, Via Cyclops, Malta	MIDEAST • 250 kW

0 Prime Time-Americas 6 Prime Time-E Asia 12 Prime Time-S Asia 18 Prime Time-Europe 24

ENGLISH ARABIC CHINESE FRENCH GERMAN RUSSIAN SPANISH OTHER

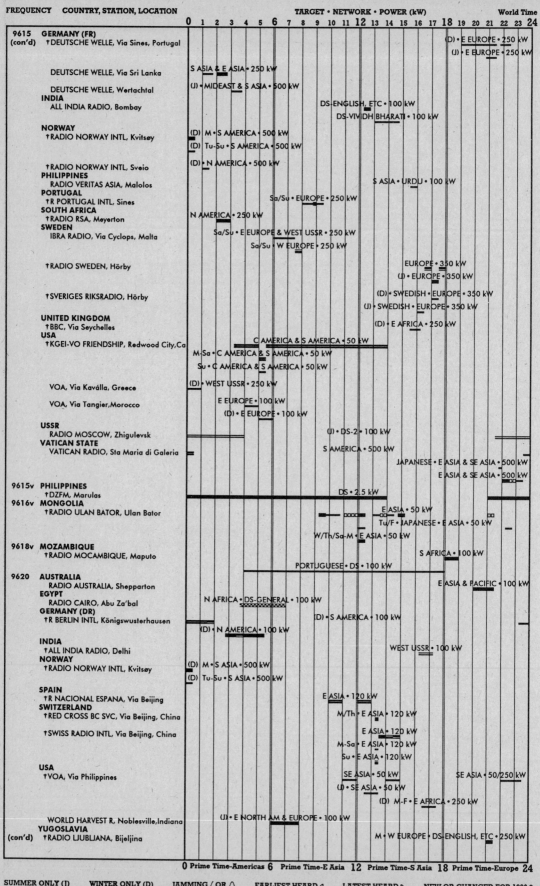

FREQUENCY	COUNTRY, STATION, LOCATION	TARGET • NETWORK • POWER (kW)
9615 (con'd)	**GERMANY (FR)** †DEUTSCHE WELLE, Via Sines, Portugal	(D) • E EUROPE • 250 kW
		(J) • E EUROPE • 250 kW
	DEUTSCHE WELLE, Via Sri Lanka	S ASIA & E ASIA • 250 kW
	DEUTSCHE WELLE, Wertachtal	(J) • MIDEAST & S ASIA • 500 kW
	INDIA ALL INDIA RADIO, Bombay	DS-ENGLISH, ETC • 100 kW
		DS-VIVIDH BHARATI • 100 kW
	NORWAY †RADIO NORWAY INTL, Kvitsøy	(D) M • S AMERICA • 500 kW
		(D) Tu-Su • S AMERICA • 500 kW
	†RADIO NORWAY INTL, Sveio	(D) • N AMERICA • 500 kW
	PHILIPPINES RADIO VERITAS ASIA, Malolos	S ASIA • URDU • 100 kW
	PORTUGAL †R PORTUGAL INTL, Sines	Sa/Su • EUROPE • 250 kW
	SOUTH AFRICA †RADIO RSA, Meyerton	N AMERICA • 250 kW
	SWEDEN IBRA RADIO, Via Cyclops, Malta	Sa/Su • E EUROPE & WEST USSR • 250 kW
		Sa/Su • W EUROPE • 250 kW
	†RADIO SWEDEN, Hörby	EUROPE • 350 kW
		(J) • EUROPE • 350 kW
	†SVERIGES RIKSRADIO, Hörby	(D) • SWEDISH • EUROPE • 350 kW
		(J) • SWEDISH • EUROPE • 350 kW
	UNITED KINGDOM †BBC, Via Seychelles	(D) • E AFRICA • 250 kW
	USA †KGEI-VO FRIENDSHIP, Redwood City,Ca	C AMERICA & S AMERICA • 50 kW
		M-Sa • C AMERICA & S AMERICA • 50 kW
		Su • C AMERICA & S AMERICA • 50 kW
	VOA, Via Kavála, Greece	(D) • WEST USSR • 250 kW
	VOA, Via Tangier,Morocco	E EUROPE • 100 kW
		(D) • E EUROPE • 100 kW
	USSR RADIO MOSCOW, Zhigulevsk	(J) • DS-2 • 100 kW
	VATICAN STATE VATICAN RADIO, Sta Maria di Galeria	S AMERICA • 500 kW
		JAPANESE • E ASIA & SE ASIA • 500 kW
		E ASIA & SE ASIA • 500 kW
9615v	**PHILIPPINES** †DZFM, Marulas	DS • 2.5 kW
9616v	**MONGOLIA** †RADIO ULAN BATOR, Ulan Bator	E ASIA • 50 kW
		Tu/F • JAPANESE • E ASIA • 50 kW
		W/Th/Sa-M • E ASIA • 50 kW
9618v	**MOZAMBIQUE** †RADIO MOCAMBIQUE, Maputo	S AFRICA • 100 kW
		PORTUGUESE • DS • 100 kW
9620	**AUSTRALIA** RADIO AUSTRALIA, Shepparton	E ASIA & PACIFIC • 100 kW
	EGYPT RADIO CAIRO, Abu Za'bal	N AFRICA • DS-GENERAL • 100 kW
	GERMANY (DR) †R BERLIN INTL, Königswusterhausen	(D) • S AMERICA • 100 kW
		(D) • N AMERICA • 100 kW
	INDIA †ALL INDIA RADIO, Delhi	WEST USSR • 100 kW
	NORWAY †RADIO NORWAY INTL, Kvitsøy	(D) M • S ASIA • 500 kW
		(D) Tu-Su • S ASIA • 500 kW
	SPAIN †R NACIONAL ESPANA, Via Beijing	E ASIA • 120 kW
	SWITZERLAND †RED CROSS BC SVC, Via Beijing, China	M/Th • E ASIA • 120 kW
	†SWISS RADIO INTL, Via Beijing, China	E ASIA • 120 kW
		M-Sa • E ASIA • 120 kW
		Su • E ASIA • 120 kW
	USA †VOA, Via Philippines	SE ASIA • 50 kW
		SE ASIA • 50/250 kW
		(J) • SE ASIA • 50 kW
		(D) M-F • E AFRICA • 250 kW
	WORLD HARVEST R, Noblesville,Indiana	(J) • E NORTH AM & EUROPE • 100 kW
(con'd)	**YUGOSLAVIA** †RADIO LJUBLJANA, Bijeljina	M • W EUROPE • DS-ENGLISH, ETC • 250 kW

World Time: 0 Prime Time-Americas 6 Prime Time-E Asia 12 Prime Time-S Asia 18 Prime Time-Europe 24

SUMMER ONLY (J) WINTER ONLY (D) JAMMING / OR /\ EARLIEST HEARD ◁ LATEST HEARD ▷ NEW OR CHANGED FOR 1990 †

FREQUENCY	COUNTRY, STATION, LOCATION	TARGET • NETWORK • POWER (kW)
9620 (con'd)	**YUGOSLAVIA**	
	†RADIO YUGOSLAVIA, Bijeljina	W AFRICA & S AMERICA • 250/500 kW
		(D) • E NORTH AM • 500 kW
		WEST USSR • 500 kW
		N AFRICA • 250 kW
		EUROPE • 250 kW
		E EUROPE & MIDEAST • 250 kW
		E ASIA & AUSTRALIA • 500 kW
		(D) • EUROPE • 250 kW
		(J) • E EUROPE & MIDEAST • 250 kW
	RADIO ZAGREB, Belgrade	Th • ATLANTIC & E NORTH AM • DS-MARINERS • 100 kW
	†VARIOUS LOCAL STNS, Bijeljina	Sa/Su • EUROPE, MIDEAST & N AFRICA • DS • 500 kW
		Tu-Su • W EUROPE • DS • 250 kW
9625	**CANADA**	
	CANADIAN BC CORP, Sackville, NB	M • DS-NORTHERN • 100 kW
		M-F • DS-NORTHERN • 100 kW
		Tu-Sa • DS-NORTHERN • 100 kW
		Sa • DS-NORTHERN • 100 kW
		Su • DS-NORTHERN • 100 kW
	R CANADA INTL, Sackville, NB	M-F • E NORTH AM • 250 kW
	CHINA (PR)	
	RADIO BEIJING, Kunming	E AFRICA & S AFRICA • 120 kW
		(J) • S ASIA • 120 kW
	GABON	
	ADVENTIST WORLD R, Moyabi	W AFRICA • VIA AFRIQUE NR UN • 500 kW
	GERMANY (FR)	
	DEUTSCHE WELLE, Via Cyclops, Malta	MIDEAST • 250 kW
	†DEUTSCHE WELLE, Wertachtal	(D) • E EUROPE • 500 kW
		(J) • E EUROPE • 500 kW
	ROMANIA	
	†RADIO BUCHAREST, Bucharest	EUROPE • 250 kW
		(D) • MIDEAST • 250 kW
	UNITED KINGDOM	
	†BBC, Via Zyyi, Cyprus	MIDEAST & E AFRICA • 20/100 kW
		(J) • MIDEAST & E AFRICA • 20 kW
	USA	
	†RFE-RL, Via Germany	WEST USSR • 100 kW
	†RFE-RL, Via Pals, Spain	WEST USSR • 250 kW
	†RFE-RL, Via Portugal	WEST USSR • 250 kW
	†WYFR-FAMILY RADIO, Okeechobee, Fl	(J) • S AMERICA • 100 kW
	USSR	
	RADIO MOSCOW, Chita	(D) • E ASIA • 500 kW
		(D) • E ASIA & AUSTRALIA • WS • 500 kW
	VATICAN STATE	
	VATICAN RADIO, Sta Maria di Galeria	AFRICA • 500 kW
		Su • AFRICA • 500 kW
		M-Sa • ENGLISH, FRENCH & SPANISH • AFRICA • 500 kW
9630	**BRAZIL**	
	RADIO APARECIDA, Aparecida	PORTUGUESE • DS • 10 kW
	CHINA (TAIWAN)	
	CENTRAL BC SYSTEM, T'ai-pei	E ASIA • PRC-4
	HOLLAND	
	†RADIO NEDERLAND, Via Neth Antilles	AUSTRALIA • 300 kW
	INDIA	
	ALL INDIA RADIO, Aligarh	Su • DS • 250 kW
		DS-ENGLISH, ETC • 250 kW
	ALL INDIA RADIO, Delhi	(J) • S ASIA • 100 kW
		DS-ENGLISH, ETC • 50 kW
	ITALY	
	†RTV ITALIANA, Rome	(D) • S AMERICA • 100 kW
	PORTUGAL	
	R PORTUGAL INTL, Sines	M-F • EUROPE • 250 kW
	SPAIN	
	†R NACIONAL ESPANA, Noblejas	E NORTH AM & C AMERICA • 350 kW
		N AMERICA & C AMERICA • 350 kW
	SWEDEN	
	†RADIO SWEDEN, Karlsborg	SWEDISH • EUROPE & W AFRICA • 350 kW
		EUROPE & W AFRICA • 350 kW
	†SVERIGES RIKSRADIO, Karlsborg	(D) • SWEDISH • EUROPE & W AFRICA • DS-1 • 350 kW
		(J) • SWEDISH • EUROPE & W AFRICA • DS-1 • 350 kW
	UNITED KINGDOM	
	†BBC, Via Seychelles	E AFRICA • 250 kW
		(D) • S AFRICA • 250 kW
	USA	
	VOA, Via Philippines	SE ASIA • 50/250 kW
	USSR	
	RADIO MOSCOW, Kazan'	(J) • DS-1 • 100 kW
	RADIO MOSCOW, Serpukhov	(D) • W AFRICA • 100 kW
		(J) • EUROPE & W AFRICA • 240 kW

World Time: 0 1 2 3 4 5 6 7 8 9 10 11 12 13 14 15 16 17 18 19 20 21 22 23 24

0 Prime Time-Americas 6 Prime Time-E Asia 12 Prime Time-S Asia 18 Prime Time-Europe 24

ENGLISH ▬ ARABIC ▬ CHINESE ▬ FRENCH ▬ GERMAN ▬ RUSSIAN ▬ SPANISH ▬ OTHER —

FREQUENCY | COUNTRY, STATION, LOCATION | TARGET • NETWORK • POWER (kW) | World Time 0–24

9635 **AFGHANISTAN**
†RADIO AFGHANISTAN, Kabul
- MIDEAST & N AFRICA • 100 kW
- (D) • MIDEAST & N AFRICA • 100 kW

CANADA
R CANADA INTL, Sackville, NB
- (D) M-F • E NORTH AM • 250 kW
- (J) M-F • E NORTH AM • 250 kW

FINLAND
†RADIO FINLAND, Pori
- (D) • N AMERICA • 500 kW
- (D) • N AFRICA & MIDEAST • 500 kW

GERMANY (DR)
†R BERLIN INTL, Nauen
- N AFRICA & W AFRICA • 500 kW

MALI
RTV MALIENNE, Bamako
- Irr • DS-FRENCH, ETC • 50 kW
- Irr • Su • DS-FRENCH, ETC • 50 kW

PORTUGAL
R PORTUGAL INTL, Lisbon-S Gabriel
- C AMERICA & S AMERICA • 100 kW
- Su/M • C AMERICA & S AMERICA • 100 kW

SINGAPORE
SINGAPORE BC CORP, Jurong
- DS-3 • 50 kW

UNITED KINGDOM
†BBC, Daventry
- (J) • WEST USSR • 300 kW
- (D) • EUROPE & N AFRICA • 300 kW

†BBC, Rampisham
- (D) Su • MIDEAST • 500 kW
- (D) • E EUROPE • 500 kW
- (J) • E EUROPE • 500 kW

†BBC, Skelton, Cumbria
- (D) • E EUROPE • 250 kW
- (J) • E EUROPE • 250 kW

†BBC, Various Locations
- (D) Su • E EUROPE • 250/500 kW
- (J) Su • E EUROPE • 250/500 kW

†BBC, Via Zyyi, Cyprus
- WEST USSR • 100 kW
- (D) • WEST USSR • 100 kW
- (D) • EUROPE • 100 kW
- (J) • WEST USSR • 100 kW

USA
†VOA, Via Kaválla, Greece
- S ASIA & MIDEAST • 250 kW
- (J) • S ASIA & MIDEAST • 250 kW
- (D) • S ASIA & MIDEAST • URDU, PERSIAN, ETC • 250 kW

USSR
R TIKHIY OKEAN, Vladivostok
- PACIFIC & W NORTH AM • MARINERS • 50 kW
- Sa • PACIFIC & W NORTH AM • MARINERS • 50 kW
- Su-F • PACIFIC & W NORTH AM • MARINERS • 50 kW

RADIO MOSCOW, Vladivostok
- W NORTH AM • N AMERICAN • 50 kW
- W NORTH AM • 50 kW
- W NORTH AM • WS • 50 kW

9638v **MOZAMBIQUE**
EP DE SOFALA, Beira
- DS-2 • 100 kW

9640 **AFGHANISTAN**
RADIO AFGHANISTAN, Via USSR
- Alternative Frequency to 4760 kHz

ALGERIA
"VO FREE SAHARA", Via RTV Algerienne
- W AFRICA & S AMERICA • POLISARIO FRONT • 50 kW

RTV ALGERIENNE, Bouchaoui
- W AFRICA & S AMERICA • 50 kW
- W AFRICA & S AMERICA • DS-3 • 50 kW

FINLAND
†RADIO FINLAND, Pori
- (D) • E EUROPE & WEST USSR • 250 kW

GERMANY (FR)
DEUTSCHE WELLE, Jülich
- E EUROPE & MIDEAST • 100 kW

DEUTSCHE WELLE, Multiple Locations
- (D) • MIDEAST • 100/500 kW

†DEUTSCHE WELLE, Via Sri Lanka
- (J) • AUSTRALIA • 250 kW

JAPAN
†RADIO JAPAN/NHK, Tokyo-Yamata
- (D) • JAPANESE • AUSTRALIA • GENERAL • 100 kW
- (D) • AUSTRALIA • GENERAL • 100 kW

KOREA (DPR)
RADIO PYONGYANG, Pyongyang
- MIDEAST & AFRICA • 200 kW

KOREA (REPUBLIC)
RADIO KOREA, In-Kimjae
- SE ASIA • 250 kW
- S AMERICA • 250 kW
- KOREAN • S AMERICA • 250 kW

PHILIPPINES
RADIO VERITAS ASIA, Malolos
- SE ASIA • 100 kW

ROMANIA
†RADIO BUCHAREST, Bucharest
- (D) • AFRICA • 250 kW
- (D) • W AFRICA • 250 kW

SWAZILAND
†TRANS WORLD RADIO, Manzini
- (D) • E AFRICA • 100 kW

UNITED KINGDOM
†BBC, Via Antigua
- C AMERICA • 125 kW

USA
VOA, Greenville, NC
- M-F • C AMERICA • FEED • 250 kW

USSR
†"RADIO MAGALLANES", Via R Moscow
- (D) • S AMERICA • 500 kW
- (D) Su-Tu/Th/F • S AMERICA • 500 kW

(con'd)

0 Prime Time-Americas 6 Prime Time-E Asia 12 Prime Time-S Asia 18 Prime Time-Europe 24

SUMMER ONLY (J) WINTER ONLY (D) JAMMING / OR /\ EARLIEST HEARD ◁ LATEST HEARD ▷ NEW OR CHANGED FOR 1990 †

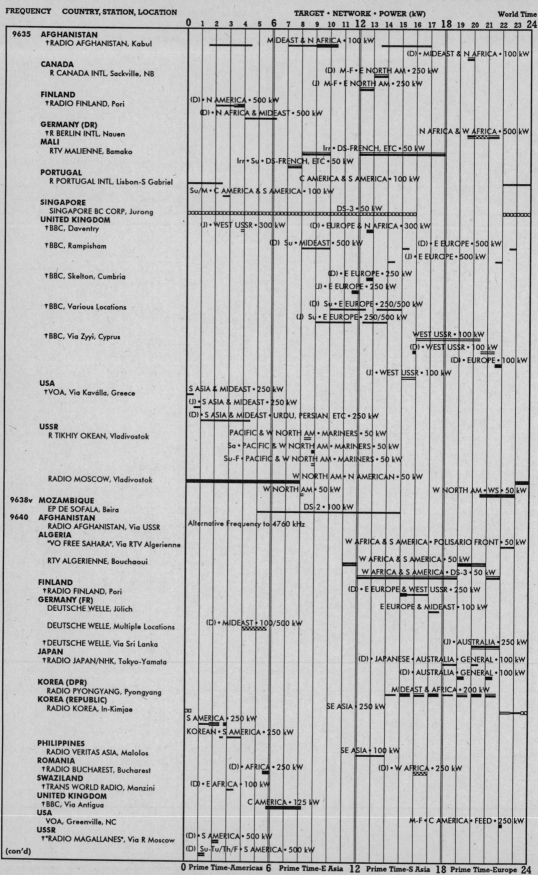

FREQUENCY | COUNTRY, STATION, LOCATION | TARGET • NETWORK • POWER (kW) | World Time 0–24

9640 (con'd) USSR

- RADIO KIEV, L'vov — (J) • E NORTH AM & C AMERICA • 500 kW
- RADIO MOSCOW, Armavir — (D) • S AMERICA • 500 kW
- RADIO MOSCOW, L'vov — (J) • E NORTH AM & C AMERICA • MARINERS • 500 kW; (J) • W EUROPE & E NORTH AM • WS • 500 kW
- RADIO MOSCOW, Moscow — (J) • EUROPE • 240 kW
- †RADIO MOSCOW, Star'obel'sk — (D) W/Sa • S AMERICA • 500 kW
- RADIO VILNIUS, L'vov — (J) • E NORTH AM & C AMERICA • 500 kW

VENEZUELA

- †ECOS DEL TORBES, San Cristóbal — DS • 10 kW; Su • DS • 10 kW

9645 AUSTRALIA

- †RADIO AUSTRALIA, Darwin — SE ASIA • 250 kW

BRAZIL

- RADIO BANDEIRANTES, São Paulo — PORTUGUESE • DS • 7.5 kW; Irr • PORTUGUESE • DS • 7.5 kW

CANADA

- †R CANADA INTL, Via Vienna, Austria — (D) • MIDEAST • 300 kW; (D) M-F • MIDEAST • 300 kW; (D) Sa/Su • MIDEAST • 300 kW

COSTA RICA

- †FARO DEL CARIBE, San José — DS • 0.5 kW

GERMANY (DR)

- †R BERLIN INTL, Königswusterhausen — S AMERICA • 100 kW; W AFRICA • 100 kW; EUROPE & N AFRICA • 100 kW

JAPAN

- †RADIO JAPAN/NHK, Via Moyabi, Gabon — (D) • S AFRICA • GENERAL • 500 kW; (D) • JAPANESE • S AFRICA • GENERAL • 500 kW

PHILIPPINES

- RADIO VERITAS ASIA, Palauig — JAPANESE • E ASIA • 100 kW

USA

- VOA, Via Sri Lanka — E ASIA • 35 kW
- VOA, Via Tangier, Morocco — (D) • E EUROPE • 100 kW

USSR

- BELORUSSIAN RADIO, Minsk — DS-1 • 50 kW
- RADIO MOSCOW, Chita — (J) • E ASIA • 500 kW; (J) • E ASIA • WS • 500 kW

VATICAN STATE

- VATICAN RADIO, Sta Maria di Galeria — C AMERICA • 100 kW; EUROPE & N AFRICA • 100 kW; EUROPE • 100 kW; Su • EUROPE • 100 kW; Su • EUROPE & N AFRICA • 100 kW; M-Sa • ENGLISH, FRENCH & SPANISH • EUROPE • 100 kW; M-Sa • ENGLISH, FRENCH, SPANISH & ITALIAN • EUROPE • 100 kW; M-Sa • ENGLISH, FRENCH, SPANISH & ITALIAN • EUROPE & N AFRICA • 100 kW

9645v PAKISTAN

- PAKISTAN BC CORP, Islamabad — (J) • DS • 10 kW
- RADIO PAKISTAN, Islamabad — (D) • S ASIA • FEEDER • 10 kW

9650 CANADA

- †R CANADA INTL, Sackville, NB — (D) M-F • E NORTH AM • 250 kW; (J) M-F • E NORTH AM • 250 kW
- R CANADA INTL, Via Sines, Portugal — (J) • WEST USSR • 250 kW
- †R CANADA INTL, Via Tokyo, Japan — (D) • EAST USSR • 300 kW; (J) • EAST USSR • 300 kW

CYPRUS

- †CYPRUS BC CORP, Zyyi — (J) F-Su • EUROPE • 250 kW

GERMANY (FR)

- †DEUTSCHE WELLE, Jülich — (J) • WEST USSR • 100 kW
- DEUTSCHE WELLE, Via Cyclops, Malta — (J) • MIDEAST • 250 kW
- †DEUTSCHE WELLE, Via Kigali, Rwanda — C AFRICA & S AFRICA • 250 kW
- †DEUTSCHE WELLE, Via Sines, Portugal — (D) • E EUROPE • 250 kW; (J) • E EUROPE • 250 kW
- †DEUTSCHE WELLE, Wertachtal — (D) • WEST USSR • 500 kW; (J) • WEST USSR • 500 kW; (D) • MIDEAST • 500 kW

INDIA

- †ALL INDIA RADIO, Delhi — E ASIA • CHINESE, CANTONESE • 100 kW

KOREA (DPR)

- RADIO PYONGYANG, Pyongyang — JAPANESE • E ASIA • 100 kW

MONACO

- †TRANS WORLD RADIO, Monte Carlo — (D) • EUROPE • 100 kW; (J) • EUROPE • 100 kW

(con'd)

0 Prime Time-Americas 6 Prime Time-E Asia 12 Prime Time-S Asia 18 Prime Time-Europe 24

ENGLISH — ARABIC — CHINESE — FRENCH — GERMAN — RUSSIAN — SPANISH — OTHER

FREQUENCY	COUNTRY, STATION, LOCATION	TARGET • NETWORK • POWER (kW)
9650 (con'd)	**NORWAY**	
	†RADIO NORWAY INTL, Sveio	(D) • W NORTH AM • 500 kW
	PHILIPPINES	
	RADIO VERITAS ASIA, Malolos	E ASIA • KOREAN • 100 kW
	SPAIN	
	R NACIONAL ESPANA, Noblejas	AUSTRALIA • 350 kW
	SWAZILAND	
	†TRANS WORLD RADIO, Manzini	(J) • E AFRICA • 25/100 kW
	UNITED KINGDOM	
	†BBC, Rampisham	(J) • WEST USSR • 500 kW
	†BBC, Via Zyyi, Cyprus	(D) • WEST USSR • 100 kW
	USA	
	†RFE-RL, Via Portugal	WEST USSR • 250 kW
	VOA, Via Tangier,Morocco	(D) • E EUROPE • 100 kW
	†VOA, Via Woofferton, UK	(J) • E EUROPE • 250 kW
	USSR	
	†"RADIO MAGALLANES", Via R Moscow	(D) • S AMERICA • 500 kW
	†P & PROGRESS, Frunze, Kirgiziya	(D) • S AMERICA • 500 kW
	†RADIO MOSCOW, Frunze	(D) • S AMERICA • 500 kW
		(D) • W AFRICA • 500 kW
	†RADIO MOSCOW, Frunze, Kirgiziya	(D) • S AMERICA • 500 kW
	RADIO MOSCOW, Moscow	(J) • S ASIA & SE ASIA • WS • 250 kW
	RADIO MOSCOW, Zhigulevsk	(J) • E EUROPE • 100 kW
	VATICAN STATE	
	VATICAN RADIO, Sta Maria di Galeria	S ASIA • 100 kW
9655	**AUSTRALIA**	
	†RADIO AUSTRALIA, Shepparton	PACIFIC & EUROPE • 100 kW
		M-Sa • PACIFIC & EUROPE • 100 kW
	BULGARIA	
	†RADIO SOFIA, Plovdiv	Alternative Frequency to 7135 kHz
	CUBA	
	†RADIO HABANA, Havana	(D) • N AMERICA • 250 kW
	ECUADOR	
	†HCJB-VO THE ANDES, Quito	EUROPE • 100 kW
	NORWAY	
	†RADIO NORWAY INTL, Kvitsøy	EUROPE • 500 kW
	†RADIO NORWAY INTL, Sveio	(D) • MIDEAST • 500 kW
	PERU	
	RADIO NORPERUANA, Chachapoyas	DS • 1 kW
	PHILIPPINES	
	FAR EAST BC CO, Bocaue	(J) • SE ASIA • 50 kW
	SWEDEN	
	†RADIO SWEDEN, Hörby	SWEDISH • EUROPE • 350 kW
		EUROPE • 350 kW
		(J) • WEST USSR • 350 kW
	USSR	
	RADIO MOSCOW, Kazan'	(D) • MIDEAST & S ASIA • 100 kW
	RADIO MOSCOW, Komsomol'sk 'Amure	(J) • W NORTH AM • WS • 240 kW
		(D) • E ASIA • 100 kW
	RADIO MOSCOW, Orcha	(J) • E NORTH AM & C AMERICA • MARINERS • 100 kW
9655v	**THAILAND**	
	RADIO THAILAND, Pathum Thani	ASIA • 10/50/100 kW
		JAPANESE • ASIA • 10/50/100 kW
		Sa/Su • ASIA • 10/50/100 kW
9660	**AUSTRALIA**	
	AUSTRALIAN BC CORP, Brisbane	DS • 10 kW
	IRAQ	
	†RADIO BAGHDAD, Balad-Salah el Deen	(D) • MIDEAST • 500 kW
	SEYCHELLES	
	FAR EAST BC ASS'N, North Pt, Mahé Is	S ASIA • 25 kW
		Su • S ASIA • 25 kW
	UNITED KINGDOM	
	BBC, Via Cincinnati, USA	E NORTH AM, C AMERICA & S AMERICA • 250 kW
	†BBC, Via Zyyi, Cyprus	EUROPE • 100 kW
		(D) • EUROPE • 100 kW
		Sa/Su • EUROPE • 100 kW
		(D) Sa/Su • EUROPE • 100 kW
	USA	
	†RFE-RL, Via Germany	WEST USSR • 250 kW
	†RFE-RL, Via Pals, Spain	WEST USSR • 250 kW
	†RFE-RL, Via Portugal	WEST USSR • 250 kW
	†VOA, Via Philippines	E ASIA • 250 kW
	VOA, Via Wertachtal,GFR	(J) • WEST USSR • 500 kW
(con'd)	†VOA, Via Woofferton, UK	(D) • E EUROPE & WEST USSR • 300 kW

World Time: 0 Prime Time-Americas 6 Prime Time-E Asia 12 Prime Time-S Asia 18 Prime Time-Europe 24

FREQUENCY	COUNTRY, STATION, LOCATION	TARGET • NETWORK • POWER (kW)
9660 (con'd)	**VENEZUELA** RADIO RUMBOS, Caracas	DS • 10 kW; M-Sa • DS • 10 kW; Tu-Su • DS • 10 kW
	YUGOSLAVIA †RADIO YUGOSLAVIA, Bijeljina	(D) • E NORTH AM • 500 kW; (D) • EUROPE • 250 kW; (D) • EUROPE & E NORTH AM • 500 kW; (J) • EUROPE • 250 kW
9665	**CHINA (PR)** †RADIO BEIJING, Shijiazhuang	(D) • E NORTH AM, C AMERICA & S AMERICA • 500 kW
	GERMANY (DR) R BERLIN INTL, Königswusterhausen	E AFRICA & S AFRICA • 100 kW
	R BERLIN INTL, Nauen	N AFRICA & W AFRICA • 100 kW
	INDIA †ALL INDIA RADIO, Aligarh	WEST USSR • 250 kW
	ROMANIA RADIO BUCHAREST, Bucharest	Su • ATLANTIC • MARINERS • 250 kW
	SWEDEN IBRA RADIO, Via Sines, Portugal	E EUROPE & WEST USSR • RUSSIAN, ETC • 250 kW
	TURKEY †TURKISH RTV CORP, Ankara	(J) • MIDEAST • 500 kW; (J) • MIDEAST • 250 kW
	USSR RADIO MOSCOW, Dushanbé	(J) • S AMERICA • 500 kW; (D) • S AMERICA • 500 kW; (J) Su-Tu • S AMERICA • 500 kW; (J) W-Sa • S AMERICA • 500 kW
	RADIO MOSCOW, Voronezh, RSFSR	(D) • MIDEAST & E AFRICA • ARABIC, PERSIAN, ETC • 240 kW
9665v	**BRAZIL** †RADIO MARUMBI, Florianópolis	PORTUGUESE • DS • 10 kW
	KOREA (DPR) KOREAN CENTRAL BS, Pyongyang	DS • 100/200 kW
9670	**CHINA (PR)** †RADIO BEIJING, Kunming	S ASIA • 50 kW; S AFRICA • 50 kW; (D) • C AFRICA • 50 kW
	ECUADOR HCJB-VO THE ANDES, Quito	S AMERICA • 100 kW
	EGYPT †RADIO CAIRO, Kafr Silîm-Abis	Alternative Frequency to 9475 kHz
	FINLAND †RADIO FINLAND, Pori	(J) • E EUROPE • 250 kW; (D) • E ASIA • 500 kW
	GERMANY (FR) †DEUTSCHE WELLE, Via Antigua	(D) • N AMERICA • 250 kW
	†DEUTSCHE WELLE, Via Sri Lanka	SE ASIA & AUSTRALIA • 250 kW
	IRAN †VO THE ISLAMIC REP, Tehrān	(D) • S ASIA • 100 kW
	ITALY †ADVENTIST WORLD R, Via Portugal	Su • E EUROPE & WEST USSR • 250 kW; Su • W EUROPE • 250 kW
	PHILIPPINES FAR EAST BC CO, Bocaue	SE ASIA & S ASIA • 50 kW; (D) • SE ASIA • 50 kW; (D) • S ASIA • 50 kW
	SWAZILAND †TRANS WORLD RADIO, Manzini	(J) • S AFRICA • 25 kW; (J) Sa/Su • S AFRICA • 25 kW
	SWEDEN IBRA RADIO, Via Sines, Portugal	E EUROPE & WEST USSR • 250 kW
	TURKEY †TURKISH RTV CORP, Ankara	(D) • WEST USSR • 500 kW
	UNITED KINGDOM BBC, Skelton, Cumbria	(D) • W EUROPE & W AFRICA • 250 kW
	†BBC, Via Singapore	(J) • S ASIA • 250 kW
	†BBC, Via Zyyi, Cyprus	(J) • MIDEAST • 100 kW; (D) • PERSIAN • MIDEAST & S ASIA • PERSIAN • 250 kW
	USA †VOA, Greenville, NC	C AMERICA & S AMERICA • 500 kW; (D) • C AMERICA • 500 kW; (J) • C AMERICA • 500 kW
	†VOA, Via Kavála, Greece	(D) • MIDEAST & S ASIA • 250 kW; (D) • WEST USSR • 250 kW; (J) • WEST USSR • 250 kW
	†VOA, Via Philippines	(D) • E AFRICA • 250 kW
	VOA, Via Rhodes, Greece	(D) • WEST USSR • 50 kW
	VOA, Via Tangier, Morocco	(D) • E EUROPE • 100 kW
	USSR RADIO MOSCOW, Irkutsk	DS-2 • 50 kW
	RADIO MOSCOW, Ivano-Frankovsk	(J) • E NORTH AM & C AMERICA • 240 kW
	RADIO MOSCOW, Kiev	DS-1 • 100 kW

World Time 0–24: 0 Prime Time-Americas 6 Prime Time-E Asia 12 Prime Time-S Asia 18 Prime Time-Europe 24

ENGLISH ARABIC CHINESE FRENCH GERMAN RUSSIAN SPANISH OTHER

FREQUENCY	COUNTRY, STATION, LOCATION	TARGET • NETWORK • POWER (kW)
9675	**BRAZIL** †R CANCAO NOVA, Cachoeira Paulista	PORTUGUESE • DS • 10 kW
	EGYPT RADIO CAIRO, Kafr Silîm-Abis	N AMERICA • 250 kW
	HOLLAND †RADIO NEDERLAND, Via Neth Antilles	AUSTRALIA • 300 kW • ALT. FREQ. TO 9505 kHz
	ICELAND RIKISUTVARPID, Reykjavik	(D) • ATLANTIC & EUROPE • DS-1 • 10 kW • USB
	INDIA †ALL INDIA RADIO, Delhi	DS-ENGLISH, ETC • 100 kW
		S ASIA • URDU • 100 kW
	JAPAN †RADIO JAPAN/NHK, Via French Guiana	(J) • S AMERICA • 500 kW
		JAPANESE • S AMERICA • GENERAL • 500 kW
	PERU †RADIO DEL PACIFICO, Lima	DS • 4 kW
		M-Sa • DS • 4 kW
	POLAND †RADIO POLONIA, Warsaw	(J) • EUROPE • 100 kW
	SOUTH AFRICA †RADIO RSA, Meyerton	(J) • AFRICA • 500 kW
	TUNISIA †RTV TUNISIENNE, Sfax	(D) • MIDEAST • DS • 100 kW
	USSR †LITHUANIAN RADIO	DS-1/RUSSIAN, ETC
	RADIO MOSCOW	(D)
	RADIO MOSCOW, Tashkent	S AMERICA • 500 kW
9680	**CHINA (TAIWAN)** VO FREE CHINA, Via Okeechobee,USA	W NORTH AM • 100 kW
	GERMANY (FR) †DEUTSCHE WELLE, Wertachtal	E EUROPE • 500 kW
		(D) • E EUROPE • 500 kW
		(J) • E EUROPE • 500 kW
	INDONESIA †RRI, Jakarta, Jawa	DS • 50/100 kW
	PHILIPPINES RADIO VERITAS ASIA, Malolos	E ASIA • KOREAN • 100 kW
	PORTUGAL R PORTUGAL INTL, Lisbon-S Gabriel	E NORTH AM • 100 kW
		Su/M • E NORTH AM • 100 kW
		Tu-Sa • E NORTH AM • 100 kW
	RADIO RENASCENCA, Muge	EUROPE • 100 kW
		Sa/Su • EUROPE • 100 kW
	SWITZERLAND SWISS RADIO INTL, Schwarzenburg	W EUROPE • 150 kW
	TURKEY †TURKISH RTV CORP, Ankara	(D) • TURKISH • SE ASIA • 500 kW
		(D) • SE ASIA • 500 kW
	UNITED KINGDOM †BBC, Via Singapore	SE ASIA • 100 kW
	USA †RFE-RL, Via Germany	WEST USSR • 100 kW
	†VOA, Via Kavála, Greece	(J) • MIDEAST & S ASIA • 250 kW
		MIDEAST & S ASIA • HINDI,PERSIAN,ETC • 250 kW
	†WYFR-FAMILY RADIO, Okeechobee, Fl	W NORTH AM • 100 kW
		EUROPE • 100 kW
9680v	**MEXICO** †RADIO XEQQ, México City	Irr • DS • 0.5 kW
9684v	**TANZANIA** RADIO TANZANIA, Dar es Salaam	S AFRICA • 50 kW
		DS • 50 kW
9685	**BRAZIL** †RADIO GAZETA, São Paulo	Irr • PORTUGUESE • DS • 7.5 kW
	IRAN †VO THE ISLAMIC REP, Tehrān	(D) • MIDEAST • 500 kW
		(D) • PERSIAN • MIDEAST • 500 kW
	JAPAN RADIO JAPAN/NHK, Via French Guiana	JAPANESE • S AMERICA • GENERAL • 500 kW
	ROMANIA RADIO BUCHAREST, Bucharest	(D) • AFRICA • 250 kW
	SWEDEN †IBRA RADIO, Via Sines, Portugal	MIDEAST • 250 kW
	TURKEY TURKISH RTV CORP, Ankara	(J) • TURKISH • EUROPE • 250 kW
		(J) • EUROPE • 250 kW
	USSR R TIKHIY OKEAN, Irkutsk	(J) • E ASIA & SE ASIA • MARINERS • 500 kW
	RADIO MOSCOW, Irkutsk	(D) • E ASIA & SE ASIA • 500 kW
		(J) • SE ASIA • 500 kW
		(J) • E ASIA & SE ASIA • 500 kW

World Time: 0 Prime Time-Americas 6 Prime Time-E Asia 12 Prime Time-S Asia 18 Prime Time-Europe 24

SUMMER ONLY (J) WINTER ONLY (D) JAMMING / OR /\ EARLIEST HEARD ◁ LATEST HEARD ▷ NEW OR CHANGED FOR 1990 †

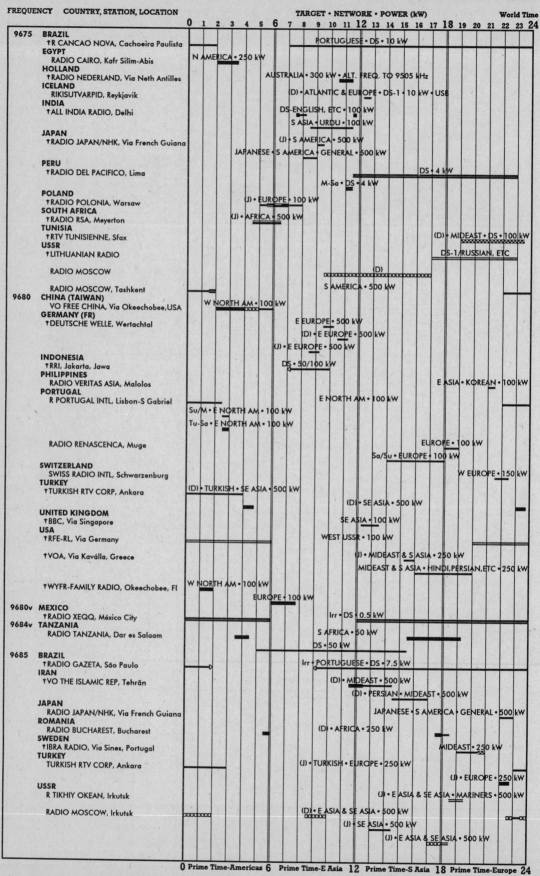

FREQUENCY	COUNTRY, STATION, LOCATION	TARGET • NETWORK • POWER (kW)
9688.8	**MADAGASCAR** R MADAGASIKARA, Antananarivo	DS-FRENCH, ETC • 10 kW
9690	**ARGENTINA** †R ARGENTINA-RAE, Buenos Aires	(D) • AMERICAS • 100 kW
	CHINA (PR) †RADIO BEIJING, Kunming	W EUROPE • 120 kW
	†RADIO BEIJING, Via Noblejas, Spain	N AMERICA & C AMERICA • 350 kW
	CHINA (TAIWAN) CENTRAL BC SYSTEM, T'ai-pei	E ASIA • PRC-5 • 10 kW
	GERMANY (FR) DEUTSCHE WELLE, Jülich	(D) • WEST USSR • 100 kW (J) • WEST USSR • 100 kW (J) • C AMERICA & AUSTRALIA • 250 kW
	†DEUTSCHE WELLE, Multiple Locations	(D) • MIDEAST & S ASIA • 100/500 kW (J) • MIDEAST & N AFRICA • 100/500 kW
	†DEUTSCHE WELLE, Via Antigua	C AMERICA & AUSTRALIA • 250 kW
	DEUTSCHE WELLE, Via Cyclops, Malta	(J) • MIDEAST • 250 kW
	†DEUTSCHE WELLE, Wertachtal	S ASIA & SE ASIA • 500 kW
	ROMANIA †RADIO BUCHAREST, Bucharest	EUROPE • 250 kW MIDEAST • 250 kW (D) • EUROPE • 250 kW (D) • MIDEAST & S ASIA • 250 kW (D) • MIDEAST • 250 kW (J) • WEST USSR • 250 kW WEST USSR • 250 kW
	USA VOA, Via Kavála, Greece	E AFRICA • 250 kW (D) • USSR • 250 kW (D) • WEST USSR • 250 kW
	VOA, Via Woofferton, UK	
	USSR RADIO MOSCOW, Tula	(J) • DS-1 • 100 kW
9695	**BRAZIL** †RADIO RIO MAR, Manaus	PORTUGUESE • DS • 7.5 kW Sa • DS • 7.5 kW Su-F • DS • 7.5 kW
	CAMBODIA VO THE PEOPLE, Phnom Penh	SE ASIA
	JAPAN †RADIO JAPAN/NHK, Tokyo-Yamata	(J) • E ASIA • GENERAL • 300 kW (J) • JAPANESE • E ASIA • GENERAL • 300 kW
	SWEDEN †RADIO SWEDEN, Hörby	S AMERICA • 350 kW SWEDISH • S AMERICA • 350 kW N AMERICA • 350 kW SWEDISH • N AMERICA • 350 kW
	UNITED ARAB EMIRATES VOICE OF THE UAE, Abu Dhabi	S ASIA • 120 kW
	USA †RFE-RL, Via Germany	E EUROPE • 100 kW
	†RFE-RL, Via Portugal	E EUROPE • 50/250 kW M-F • E EUROPE • 250 kW Sa/Su • WEST USSR • 250 kW
	VOA, Via Rhodes, Greece	MIDEAST • 50 kW
9700	**BULGARIA** †RADIO SOFIA, Sofia	(D) • E NORTH AM & C AMERICA • 250 kW (D) • EUROPE • 250 kW
	RADIO SOFIA, Stolnik	EUROPE, N AFRICA & MIDEAST • 150 kW Su • EUROPE, N AFRICA & MIDEAST • 150 kW
	CHINA (PR) †RADIO BEIJING, Xi'an	(D) • AUSTRALIA • 150 kW (D) • EUROPE & N AFRICA • 150 kW (D) • MIDEAST & S ASIA • 150 kW
	CLANDESTINE (AFRICA) †"AV DO GALO NEGRO", Jamba, Angola	S AFRICA • UNITA/PORT,ETC
	EGYPT RADIO CAIRO, Abu Za'bal	N AFRICA & W EUROPE • DS-VO THE ARABS • 100 kW
	GERMANY (FR) †DEUTSCHE WELLE, Multiple Locations	C AMERICA & S AMERICA • 100/500 kW C AMERICA & S AMERICA • 250/500 kW (D) • N AMERICA & C AMERICA • 250/500 kW
	†DEUTSCHE WELLE, Wertachtal	N AMERICA • 500 kW
	PHILIPPINES RADIO VERITAS ASIA, Malolos	S ASIA & SE ASIA • CHINESE,TAMIL,ETC • 100 kW
	USA VOA, Greenville, NC	W AFRICA • 500 kW
(con'd)		

World Time: 0 Prime Time-Americas 6 Prime Time-E Asia 12 Prime Time-S Asia 18 Prime Time-Europe 24

ENGLISH ▬ ARABIC ▦ CHINESE ▫▫▫ FRENCH ═ GERMAN ▬ RUSSIAN ═ SPANISH ▬ OTHER —

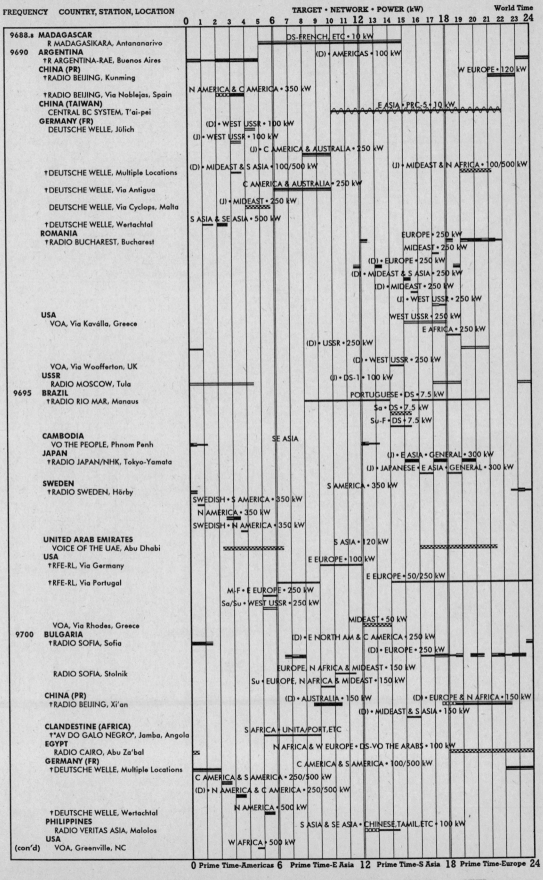

FREQUENCY	COUNTRY, STATION, LOCATION	TARGET • NETWORK • POWER (kW)
9700 (con'd)	USA	
	VOA, Via Kaválla, Greece	(D) • N AFRICA & W AFRICA • 250 kW
		MIDEAST & S ASIA • 250 kW
		(D) • MIDEAST • PERSIAN • 250 kW
	USSR	
	RADIO MOSCOW, Komsomol'sk 'Amure	(J) • DS-2 • 100 kW
	RADIO MOSCOW, Serpukhov	(J) • DS-2 • 100 kW
9705	BRAZIL	
	RADIO NACIONAL, Rio de Janeiro	PORTUGUESE • DS • 10 kW
	INDIA	
	†ALL INDIA RADIO, Delhi	(J) • S ASIA • 100 kW
	MEXICO	
	RADIO MEXICO INTL, México City	C AMERICA • 10 kW
	NIGER	
	†LA VOIX DU SAHEL, Niamey	DS-FRENCH, ETC • 100 kW
		Sa • DS-FRENCH, ETC • 100 kW
	PORTUGAL	
	R PORTUGAL INTL, Lisbon-S Gabriel	N AMERICA • 100 kW
		Su/M • N AMERICA • 100 kW
		Tu-Sa • N AMERICA • 100 kW
	SAUDI ARABIA	
	BS OF THE KINGDOM, Jiddah	EUROPE • 50 kW
		EUROPE • DS-GENERAL • 50 kW
	USA	
	†RFE-RL, Via Germany	E EUROPE • 100 kW
	†RFE-RL, Via Portugal	E EUROPE • 250 kW
		M-Sa • E EUROPE • 250 kW
		Su • WEST USSR • 250 kW
	VOA, Via Kaválla, Greece	MIDEAST & S ASIA • 250 kW
	†WYFR-FAMILY RADIO, Okeechobee, Fl	C AMERICA • 50 kW
		(D) • W NORTH AM • 100 kW
	USSR	
	RADIO MOSCOW, Vladivostok	(J) • E ASIA • WS • 500 kW
	VATICAN STATE	
	VATICAN RADIO, Sta Maria di Galeria	C AMERICA • 100 kW
9710	AUSTRALIA	
	†RADIO AUSTRALIA, Shepparton	PACIFIC • 50 kW
		E ASIA & PACIFIC • 100 kW
		JAPANESE • E ASIA & PACIFIC • 100 kW
		E ASIA & PACIFIC • ENGLISH, ETC • 100 kW
	CHINA (PR)	
	GANSU PEOPLES BS, Tian Shui	DS-1 • 15 kW
	†RADIO BEIJING, Xi'an	(D) • EUROPE • 120 kW
	ITALY	
	†RTV ITALIANA, Rome	C AMERICA • 100 kW
		E EUROPE & WEST USSR • 100 kW
		(D) • S ASIA & SE ASIA • 100 kW
		E EUROPE & MIDEAST • 100 kW
		E ASIA • 100 kW
		(D) • E AFRICA • 100 kW
		N AFRICA & W AFRICA • 100 kW
		(D) • MIDEAST • 100 kW
		N AFRICA • 100 kW
		(J) • N AFRICA • 100 kW
		AUSTRALIA • 100 kW
		(J) • E EUROPE & WEST USSR • 100 kW
		(J) • N AFRICA & E AFRICA • 100 kW
		(J) • EUROPE • 100 kW
		(J) Su • EUROPE • 100 kW
	PHILIPPINES	
	FAR EAST BC CO, Bocaue	SE ASIA • 50 kW
	USSR	
	†LITHUANIAN RADIO, Kaunas	DS-1/RUSSIAN, ETC • 100 kW
	RADIO KIEV, Kiev	(J) • EUROPE • 100 kW
	RADIO MOSCOW, Kenga	(J) • DS-1 • 100 kW
	RADIO MOSCOW, Kiev	(D) • S AMERICA • 500 kW
		(D) • N AFRICA & W AFRICA • 500 kW
		(J) • EUROPE • 100 kW
		(D) • N AFRICA & W AFRICA • AFRICAN • 500 kW
		(D) • N AFRICA & W AFRICA • WS • 500 kW
	RADIO MOSCOW, Via Havana, Cuba	(J) • N AMERICA • 100 kW
	RS SOV BELORUSSIA, Kiev	(J) M/Tu/Th/F • EUROPE • 100 kW
		(J) W/Sa/Su • EUROPE • 100 kW
9715	CANADA	
	R CANADA INTL, Via United Kingdom	E EUROPE • 300 kW
	ECUADOR	
	HCJB-VO THE ANDES, Quito	JAPANESE • E ASIA • 100 kW
(con'd)	FRANCE	
	†R FRANCE INTL, Issoudun-Allouis	S AMERICA • 500 kW

World Time: 0 1 2 3 4 5 6 7 8 9 10 11 12 13 14 15 16 17 18 19 20 21 22 23 24

0 Prime Time-Americas 6 Prime Time-E Asia 12 Prime Time-S Asia 18 Prime Time-Europe 24

SUMMER ONLY (J) WINTER ONLY (D) JAMMING / OR /\ EARLIEST HEARD ◁ LATEST HEARD ▷ NEW OR CHANGED FOR 1990 †

FREQUENCY	COUNTRY, STATION, LOCATION	TARGET • NETWORK • POWER (kW)
9715 (con'd)	**FRANCE** †R FRANCE INTL, Via French Guiana	S AMERICA • 500 kW
	GERMANY (FR) †DEUTSCHE WELLE, Wertachtal	E EUROPE & WEST USSR • 500 kW
		(D) • WEST USSR • 500 kW
		(D) • E EUROPE • 500 kW
		(J) • WEST USSR • 500 kW
		(J) • E ASIA • 500 kW
		(J) • E EUROPE • 500 kW
	HOLLAND RADIO NEDERLAND, Flevoland	EUROPE • 500 kW
		Su • EUROPE • 500 kW
	†RADIO NEDERLAND, Via Neth Antilles	W NORTH AM • 300 kW
		AUSTRALIA • 300 kW
	UNITED KINGDOM †BBC, Via Zyyi, Cyprus	(J) • E EUROPE • 250 kW
	USA VOA, Via Philippines	(J) • SE ASIA • 250 kW
	VOA, Via Rhodes, Greece	MIDEAST • 50 kW
		(J) • MIDEAST • 50 kW
	WRNO WORLDWIDE, New Orleans, La	Su • E NORTH AM • ENGLISH, ETC • 100 kW
	†WYFR-FAMILY RADIO, Okeechobee, Fl	C AMERICA • 50 kW
	USSR RADIO MOSCOW, Irkutsk	(D) • S ASIA • URDU, HINDI • 100 kW
	RADIO MOSCOW, Kingisepp	(J) • DS-1 • 200 kW
	RADIO TASHKENT, Tashkent	(J) • S ASIA • 50 kW
9716v	**BOLIVIA** †RADIO LA PLATA, Sucre	DS • 2 kW
		Irr • DS-SOCCER • 2 kW
9720	**ANGOLA** RADIO NACIONAL, Luanda	S AFRICA • 100 kW
	AUSTRALIA RADIO AUSTRALIA, Various Locations	E ASIA & SE ASIA • 250/300 kW
	CUBA RADIO HABANA, Via USSR	W EUROPE & N AFRICA • 120 kW
	DENMARK †DANMARKS RADIO, Copenhagen	E NORTH AM • 50 kW
	ECUADOR †HCJB-VO THE ANDES, Quito	(D) • N AMERICA & C AMERICA • 100 kW
		(D) • JAPANESE • N AMERICA & C AMERICA • 100 kW
	IRAN †VO THE ISLAMIC REP, Tehrān	(D) • PERSIAN • W NORTH AM • 100 kW
		(D) • W NORTH AM • 100 kW
	SAUDI ARABIA BS OF THE KINGDOM, Ad Dir'iyah	MIDEAST & E AFRICA • DS-GENERAL • 50 kW
	BS OF THE KINGDOM, Jiddah	WEST USSR • 50 kW
		WEST USSR • DS-GENERAL • 50 kW
	SRI LANKA SRI LANKA BC CORP, Colombo-Ekala	S ASIA • 100 kW
	USSR RADIO MOSCOW	(J) • DS-1
	RADIO MOSCOW, Moscow	(D) • W EUROPE & W AFRICA • 120 kW
	RADIO MOSCOW, Ryazan'	(J) • EUROPE • ITALIAN, ETC • 240 kW
	RADIO MOSCOW, Vinnitsa	(J) • N AMERICA • N AMERICAN • 240 kW
9725	**BRAZIL** R CLUBE PARANAENSE, Curitiba	Irr • PORTUGUESE • DS • 7.5 kW
		PORTUGUESE • DS • 7.5 kW
	CHINA (PR) RADIO BEIJING, Hohhot	EAST USSR • 50 kW
	SWITZERLAND RED CROSS BC SVC, Sottens	Irr • Tu/F • C AMERICA • 500 kW
		Irr • Tu/F • N AMERICA & C AMERICA • 500 kW
	SWISS RADIO INTL, Sottens	C AMERICA • 500 kW
		N AMERICA & C AMERICA • 500 kW
		M • C AMERICA • 500 kW
		M • N AMERICA & C AMERICA • 500 kW
		Tu-Su • C AMERICA • 500 kW
		Tu-Su • N AMERICA & C AMERICA • 500 kW
	UNITED KINGDOM BBC, Via Singapore	SE ASIA & E ASIA • 100/250 kW
		SE ASIA & AUSTRALIA • 100 kW
	USA †RFE-RL, Via Germany	E EUROPE & WEST USSR • 100/250 kW
(con'd)	†RFE-RL, Via Pals, Spain	WEST USSR • 250 kW

World Time 0–24: 0 Prime Time-Americas 6 Prime Time-E Asia 12 Prime Time-S Asia 18 Prime Time-Europe 24

ENGLISH ARABIC CHINESE FRENCH GERMAN RUSSIAN SPANISH OTHER

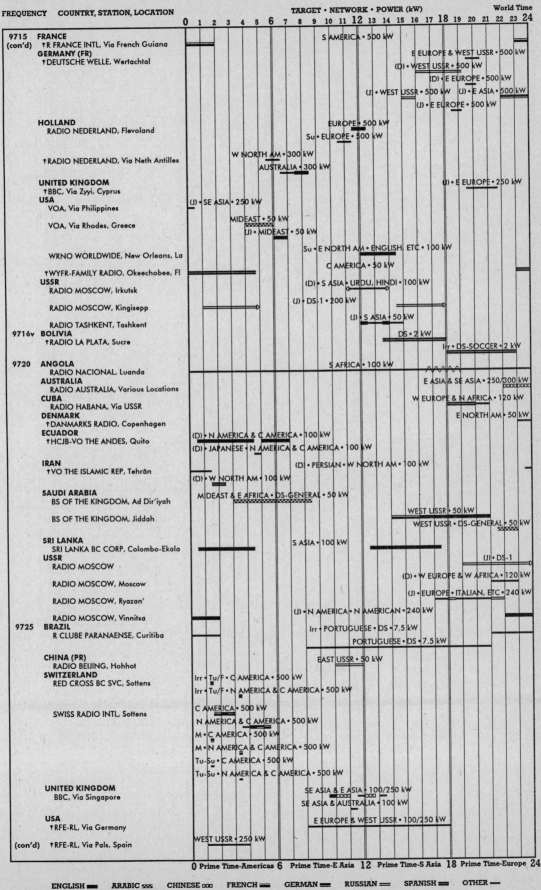

FREQUENCY	COUNTRY, STATION, LOCATION	TARGET • NETWORK • POWER (kW)
9725 (con'd)	**USA** †RFE-RL, Via Portugal	E EUROPE • 250 kW; M-Sa • E EUROPE • 250 kW; Su • WEST USSR • 250 kW
	VOA, Via Philippines	E ASIA • 250 kW
9730	**BURMA** BURMA BC SERVICE, Rangoon	DS-ENGLISH,BURMESE • 50 kW
	GERMANY (DR) †R BERLIN INTL, Königswusterhausen	W EUROPE • 50 kW; Sa/Su • W EUROPE • 100 kW
	†R BERLIN INTL, Nauen	E NORTH AM & C AMERICA • 100/500 kW
	IRAQ †RADIO BAGHDAD, Balad-Salah el Deen	(D) • N AFRICA • 500 kW
	PHILIPPINES RADIO VERITAS ASIA, Palauig	JAPANESE • E ASIA • 250 kW
	SAUDI ARABIA BS OF THE KINGDOM, Riyadh	MIDEAST & WEST USSR • 350 kW
	SEYCHELLES FAR EAST BC ASS'N, North Pt, Mahé Is	S ASIA • 25 kW
	SWAZILAND †TRANS WORLD RADIO, Manzini	(D) • S AFRICA • 25 kW
	UNITED KINGDOM †BBC, Via Singapore	(D) • S ASIA • 100/250 kW; (J) • SE ASIA & E ASIA • 100 kW
	USSR RADIO MOSCOW	(J) • EUROPE
	RADIO MOSCOW, Dushanbé	(D) • N AFRICA & MIDEAST • 500 kW
	RADIO MOSCOW, Irkutsk	(D) • SE ASIA • 500 kW
	TASS NEWS AGENCY, Ul'yanovsk	M-F • DS • 100 kW
	VIETNAM VOICE OF VIETNAM, Hanoi	SE ASIA • 15 kW
9735	**GERMANY (FR)** †DEUTSCHE WELLE, Multiple Locations	N AMERICA & C AMERICA • 250/500 kW
	†DEUTSCHE WELLE, Via Antigua	(J) • S AMERICA • 250 kW
	†DEUTSCHE WELLE, Via Kigali, Rwanda	C AFRICA & S AFRICA • 250 kW
	DEUTSCHE WELLE, Wertachtal	AUSTRALIA & C AMERICA • 500 kW
	OMAN †RADIO OMAN, Sib	(D) • MIDEAST & N AFRICA • DS • 100 kW; (J) • MIDEAST & N AFRICA • DS • 100 kW
	RADIO OMAN, Thamarīt	(D) • MIDEAST & N AFRICA • DS • 100 kW
	PARAGUAY †RADIO NACIONAL, Asunción	S AMERICA, C AMERICA & E NORTH AM • DS-SPANISH,GUARANI • 40/100 kW
	UNITED KINGDOM †BBC, Via Zyyi, Cyprus	(J) • EUROPE • 250 kW
	USA †VOA, Via Wertachtal,GFR	(D) • E EUROPE & WEST USSR • 500 kW
	†VOA, Via Woofferton, UK	(D) • E EUROPE & MIDEAST • 250 kW
	USSR RADIO MOSCOW, Armavir	(J) • W AFRICA & ATLANTIC • 100 kW; (J) • EUROPE • 100 kW
	RADIO MOSCOW, Irkutsk	(J) • E ASIA & SE ASIA • 500 kW
	RADIO MOSCOW, Novosibirsk	(J) • E ASIA • 200 kW
9740	**BULGARIA** RADIO SOFIA, Sofia	(D) • MIDEAST & E AFRICA • 250 kW
	CANADA R CANADA INTL, Via United Kingdom	(D) M-F • AFRICA • 300 kW
	CZECHOSLOVAKIA RADIO PRAGUE, Pieštány-Velké K'y	AMERICAS • ENG,FR, GERMAN,ETC • 120 kW; AMERICAS • 120 kW
	EGYPT RADIO CAIRO, Kafr Silîm-Abis	C AMERICA • 250 kW
	PHILIPPINES RADIO VERITAS ASIA, Malolos	E ASIA • 100 kW
	PORTUGAL †R PORTUGAL INTL, Lisbon-S Gabriel	Sa/Su • EUROPE • 100 kW
	SAUDI ARABIA BS OF THE KINGDOM, Riyadh	N AFRICA • DS-HOLY KORAN • 350 kW
	UNITED KINGDOM †BBC, Via Singapore	S ASIA & SE ASIA • 125/250 kW; ASIA & AUSTRALIA • 100/125 kW; (D) • SE ASIA • 250 kW
	†BBC, Via Zyyi, Cyprus	Su • MIDEAST & WEST USSR • 250 kW
	USA †VOA, Via Kavála, Greece	(D) • MIDEAST & S ASIA • 250 kW; (J) • WEST USSR • 250 kW; (D) • WEST USSR • 250 kW; (J) • MIDEAST & S ASIA • PERSIAN • 250 kW
(con'd)		

World Time 0–24: 0 Prime Time-Americas 6 Prime Time-E Asia 12 Prime Time-S Asia 18 Prime Time-Europe 24

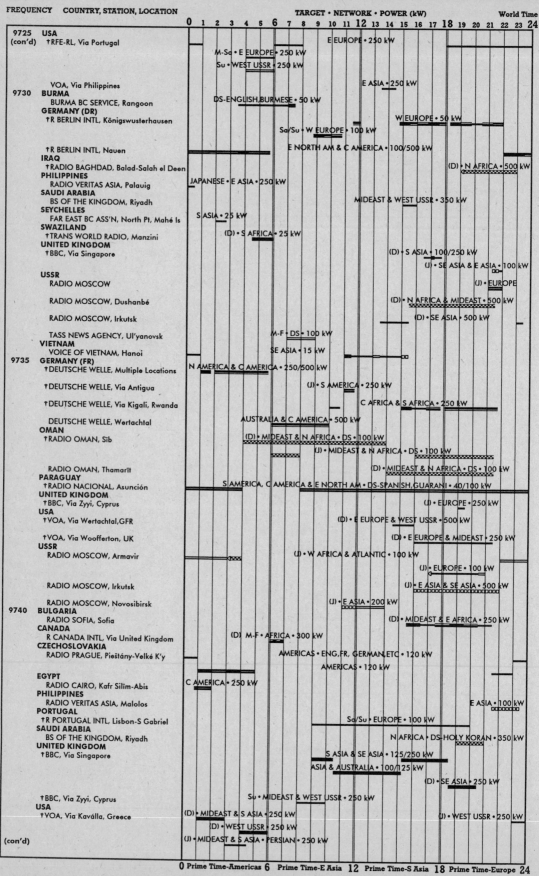

FREQUENCY	COUNTRY, STATION, LOCATION	TARGET • NETWORK • POWER (kW)
9740 (con'd)	**USSR** RADIO MOSCOW, Moscow	(J) • DS-1 • 240 kW
		(J) • EUROPE • 240 kW
9745	**ECUADOR** HCJB-VO THE ANDES, Quito	S AMERICA • 50 kW
		AUSTRALIA • 100 kW
		(J) • C AMERICA & N AMERICA • 100 kW
	FRANCE †R FRANCE INTL, Issoudun-Allouis	E EUROPE • 100 kW
	IRAN †VO THE ISLAMIC REP, Tehrān	(J) • EUROPE & MIDEAST • 500 kW
	SPAIN †R NACIONAL ESPANA, Noblejas	(D) • C AMERICA & S AMERICA • 350 kW
	SWAZILAND †TRANS WORLD RADIO, Manzini	(J) • S AFRICA • 25 kW
	USA VOA, Via Kavála, Greece	(J) • MIDEAST • 250 kW
	USSR RADIO MOSCOW, Moscow	(D) • W AFRICA • 240 kW
		(J) • C AMERICA • 240 kW
		(D) • S ASIA • 240 kW
		(D) • W AFRICA • AFRICAN • 240 kW
		(D) • W AFRICA • WS • 240 kW
9745v	**CHINA (PR)** †RADIO BEIJING, Via Bamako, Mali	(D) • E EUROPE • 50 kW
		(D) • C AFRICA & E AFRICA • 50 kW
9750	**CANADA** R CANADA INTL, Sackville, NB	(J) M-F • EUROPE • 250 kW
	GERMANY (FR) †DEUTSCHE WELLE, Wertachtal	MIDEAST • 500 kW
		(D) • N AFRICA • 500 kW
	INDIA ALL INDIA RADIO, Madras	DS-VIVIDH BHARATI • 100 kW
		Su • DS-VIVIDH BHARATI • 100 kW
	KOREA (REPUBLIC) RADIO KOREA, In-Kimjae	KOREAN • N AMERICA & C AMERICA • 250 kW
		N AMERICA & C AMERICA • 250 kW
	KUWAIT RADIO KUWAIT, Jadādīyah	PERSIAN • MIDEAST • 250 kW
		MIDEAST • DS-MAIN PROGRAM • 250 kW
	MALAYSIA VOICE OF MALAYSIA, Kajang	SE ASIA • 100 kW
	ROMANIA †RADIO BUCHAREST, Bucharest	(J) • EUROPE • 250 kW
	UNITED KINGDOM †BBC, Daventry	(J) • EUROPE, N AFRICA & MIDEAST • 300 kW
		(J) • E EUROPE & WEST USSR • 300 kW
	†BBC, Skelton, Cumbria	(D) • EUROPE & MIDEAST • 250 kW
		(D) Su • EUROPE & MIDEAST • 250 kW
	†BBC, Various Locations	E EUROPE & MIDEAST • 300/500 kW
		EUROPE & MIDEAST • 250/300/500 kW
		M-F • E EUROPE & MIDEAST • 300/500 kW
		M-Sa • E EUROPE & MIDEAST • 300/500 kW
	†BBC, Via Maṣīrah, Oman	WEST USSR • 100 kW
		(D) • MIDEAST & S ASIA • 100 kW
	†BBC, Via Zyyi, Cyprus	(J) • EUROPE & WEST USSR • 100 kW
	USA †RFE-RL, Via Germany	WEST USSR • 100 kW
	VOA, Via M'rovia, Liberia	M-F • W AFRICA • ENGLISH,FRENCH,ETC • 50 kW
	USSR RADIO MOSCOW, L'vov	(D) • WS • 500 kW
	RADIO MOSCOW, Tashkent	(J) • MIDEAST • 100 kW
		(J) • MIDEAST • WS • 100 kW
9750v	**ALBANIA** RADIO TIRANA, Krujë	S AMERICA • 100 kW
	SOCIETY ISLANDS †RFO-TAHITI, Papeete	DS-FRENCH,TAHITIAN • 4 kW
	VENEZUELA RADIO OCCIDENTE, Tovar	DS • 1 kW
9750.2	**CHILE** †RADIO MINERIA, Santiago	DS • 5 kW
		Irr • Sa/Su • DS • 5 kW
9755	**CANADA** †R CANADA INTL, Sackville, NB	(J) • E NORTH AM & C AMERICA • 250 kW
		(D) • E NORTH AM & C AMERICA • 250 kW
		E NORTH AM & C AMERICA • 250 kW
		(D) Su/M • E NORTH AM & C AMERICA • 250 kW
		(D) M-F • E NORTH AM & C AMERICA • 250 kW
		(J) Su/M • E NORTH AM & C AMERICA • 250 kW
		(D) Sa/Su • E NORTH AM & C AMERICA • 250 kW
		(D) Tu-Sa • E NORTH AM & C AMERICA • 250 kW
(con'd)		

World Time: 0 1 2 3 4 5 6 7 8 9 10 11 12 13 14 15 16 17 18 19 20 21 22 23 24

0 Prime Time-Americas 6 Prime Time-E Asia 12 Prime Time-S Asia 18 Prime Time-Europe 24

ENGLISH ARABIC CHINESE FRENCH GERMAN RUSSIAN SPANISH OTHER

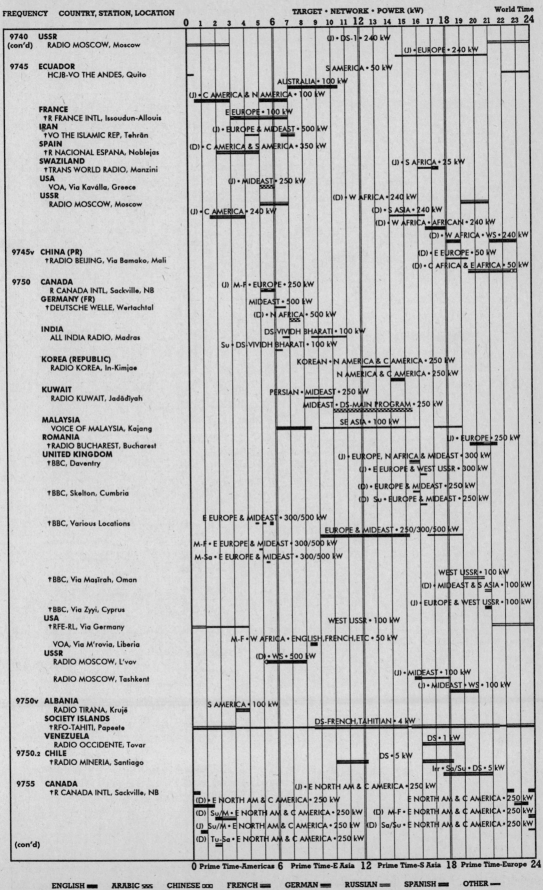

FREQUENCY	COUNTRY, STATION, LOCATION	TARGET • NETWORK • POWER (kW)
9755 (con'd)	**CANADA** †R CANADA INTL, Sackville, NB	(D) Tu-Sa • C AMERICA & S AMERICA • 250 kW
		(J) Tu-Sa • E NORTH AM & C AMERICA • 250 kW
	CHINA (PR) CENTRAL PEOPLES BS, Baoji	DS-2 • 50 kW
	CUBA RADIO HABANA, Havana	(D) • S AMERICA • 50 kW
	INDIA †ALL INDIA RADIO, Delhi	W AFRICA • 100 kW
	USA †VOA, Via Philippines	E ASIA • 250 kW
	VATICAN STATE VATICAN RADIO, Sta Maria di Galeria	WEST USSR • 500 kW
		EUROPE & WEST USSR • 100 kW
		EUROPE • 100 kW
		Su • EUROPE • 100 kW
		Th • EUROPE • 100 kW
9755v	**EGYPT** RADIO CAIRO, Cairo-Mokattam	EUROPE, N AFRICA & MIDEAST • DS-KORAN • 100 kW
		F • EUROPE, N AFRICA & MIDEAST • DS-KORAN • 100 kW
	PERU RADIO SIDERAL, Pucallpa	DS • 1.25 kW
9760	**ALBANIA** †RADIO TIRANA, Lushnjë	N AMERICA • 100 kW
		S AMERICA • 100 kW
		N AMERICA • 100 kW • ALT. FREQ. TO 9440 kHz
		(D) • N AMERICA • 100 kW
	AUSTRALIA †RADIO AUSTRALIA, Shepparton	JAPANESE • E ASIA • 100 kW
	BRAZIL RADIO NACIONAL, Brasília	AFRICA • 250 kW
	CANADA R CANADA INTL, Sackville, NB	(D) M-F • EUROPE • 250 kW
		(D) • EUROPE • 250 kW
	CUBA RADIO HABANA, Via USSR	(D) • MIDEAST & E AFRICA • 200 kW
	GERMANY (FR) †DEUTSCHE WELLE, Multiple Locations	(D) • S ASIA • 100/500 kW
	JAPAN RADIO TANPA, Tokyo-Nagara	JAPANESE • DS-2 • 50 kW
	UNITED KINGDOM †BBC, Daventry	(J) • EUROPE & N AFRICA • 300 kW
	†BBC, Rampisham	WEST USSR • 500 kW
	†BBC, Skelton, Cumbria	(D) • EUROPE & W AFRICA • 250 kW
	†BBC, Via Zyyi, Cyprus	M-F • E EUROPE • 250 kW
		M-Sa • E EUROPE • 250 kW
	†BBC, Woofferton	(D) • AFRICA • 250 kW
	USA †VOA, Via Kavála, Greece	(D) • N AFRICA • 250 kW
	VOA, Via Philippines	ASIA • 250 kW
	†VOA, Via Tangier,Morocco	(D) • WEST USSR • 35 kW
	VOA, Via Woofferton, UK	(J) • WEST USSR • 300 kW
		(J) • EUROPE & MIDEAST • 250 kW
	USSR RADIO MOSCOW, Ivano-Frankovsk	ATLANTIC • MARINERS • 100 kW
		(D) • W EUROPE & W AFRICA • 100 kW
		(D) • W EUROPE & W AFRICA • WS • 100 kW
	RADIO MOSCOW, Kenga	(J) • DS-1 • 100 kW
9765	**CHINA (PR)** †RADIO BEIJING, Beijing	(J) • WEST USSR & E EUROPE • 500 kW
	CHINA (TAIWAN) VO FREE CHINA, T'ai-pei	AUSTRALIA
		MIDEAST & N AFRICA • 100 kW
	ECUADOR HCJB-VO THE ANDES, Quito	S AMERICA • 100 kW
	GERMANY (FR) DEUTSCHE WELLE, Multiple Locations	SE ASIA & AUSTRALIA • 100/500 kW
	†DEUTSCHE WELLE, Wertachtal	C AFRICA & S AFRICA • 500 kW
	MALTA †VO MEDITERRANEAN, Cyclops	EUROPE, N AFRICA & MIDEAST • 250 kW
	SPAIN †R NACIONAL ESPANA, Arganda	(D) • EUROPE • 100 kW
	†R NACIONAL ESPANA, Noblejas	(J) • EUROPE • 350 kW
	UNITED KINGDOM BBC, Via Delano, USA	(D) • C AMERICA & S AMERICA • 250 kW
	USSR RADIO MOSCOW, L'vov	(J) • E NORTH AM & C AMERICA • N AMERICAN SVC, WS • 500 kW
9770	**AUSTRALIA** RADIO AUSTRALIA, Carnarvon	S ASIA & SE ASIA • 250 kW
(con'd)	RADIO AUSTRALIA, Darwin	SE ASIA • 250 kW

World Time 0–24: 0 Prime Time-Americas 6 Prime Time-E Asia 12 Prime Time-S Asia 18 Prime Time-Europe 24

SUMMER ONLY (J) WINTER ONLY (D) JAMMING / OR /\ EARLIEST HEARD ◁ LATEST HEARD ▷ NEW OR CHANGED FOR 1990 †

FREQUENCY	COUNTRY, STATION, LOCATION	TARGET • NETWORK • POWER (kW)
9770 (con'd)	**AUSTRALIA** RADIO AUSTRALIA, Shepparton	SE ASIA • 100 kW
	CUBA RADIO HABANA, Havana	(D) • S AMERICA • 500 kW; (J) • S AMERICA • 50 kW
	RADIO HABANA, Via USSR	(D) • N AFRICA & W AFRICA • 240 kW
	EGYPT RADIO CAIRO, Kafr Silîm-Abis	N AFRICA & MIDEAST • DS-NILE VALLEY • 250 kW; N AFRICA & MIDEAST • DS-VO THE ARABS • 250 kW
	GERMANY (FR) †DEUTSCHE WELLE, Jülich	(D) • E EUROPE • 100 kW; (J) • E EUROPE • 100 kW
	HOLLAND †RADIO NEDERLAND, Via Neth Antilles	M-Sa • AUSTRALIA • 300 kW
	IRAQ †RADIO BAGHDAD, Balad-Salah el Deen	(D) • EUROPE • 500 kW
	PHILIPPINES RADIO VERITAS ASIA, Malolos	S ASIA & SE ASIA • ENGLISH, BENGALI • 100 kW
	SEYCHELLES FAR EAST BC ASS'N, North Pt, Mahé Is	S AFRICA • 100 kW; E AFRICA • 75 kW
	UNITED KINGDOM †BBC, Rampisham	E EUROPE & MIDEAST • 500 kW; Sa/Su • E EUROPE & MIDEAST • 500 kW
	†BBC, Various Locations	E EUROPE & MIDEAST • 300/500 kW; Sa • E EUROPE & MIDEAST • 300/500 kW
	USA †VOA, Via Kaválla, Greece	(J) • N AFRICA & W AFRICA • 250 kW
	VOA, Via Philippines	S ASIA & SE ASIA • 250 kW
	WORLD HARVEST R, Noblesville, Indiana	(D) • E NORTH AM • 100 kW
9770v	**CHINA (PR)** †RADIO BEIJING, Via Bamako, Mali	(D) • N AMERICA • 50 kW
9775	**CHINA (PR)** CENTRAL PEOPLES BS, Baoji	DS-2 • 50 kW; DS-MINORITIES • 50 kW
	HOLLAND †RADIO NEDERLAND, Flevoland	(D) • EUROPE & N AFRICA • 500 kW
	†RADIO NEDERLAND, Via Neth Antilles	C AMERICA • 300 kW
	USA †VOA, Greenville, NC	C AMERICA & S AMERICA • 250 kW; Tu-Sa • C AMERICA & S AMERICA • 250 kW
	VOA, Via M'rovia, Liberia	(D) • S AMERICA • 250 kW; (J) • S AMERICA • 250 kW
	USSR †RADIO MOSCOW	EUROPE
	RADIO MOSCOW, Michurinsk	(J) • DS-1 • 100 kW
	†RADIO MOSCOW, Tula	E AFRICA • 100 kW; (D) • E AFRICA • 100 kW; (D) • DS-1 • 100 kW; (D) • E AFRICA • AFRICAN • 100 kW; (J) • DS-1 • 100 kW; (D) • E AFRICA • WS • 100 kW
9775v	**BANGLADESH** RADIO BANGLADESH, Dhaka	S ASIA • 250 kW
9778v	**DOMINICAN REPUBLIC** RADIO SANTIAGO, Santiago	Irr • DS • 1 kW
9779.4	**YEMEN (REPUBLIC)** "VO PALESTINE", Via Radio San'ā	PLO • 50 kW
	†RADIO SAN'A, San'ā	DS • 50 kW; F • DS • 50 kW; Irr • DS-RAMADAN • 50 kW
9780	**CHINA (PR)** QINGHAI PEOPLES BS, Xining	DS-1/CHINESE • 10 kW
	UNITED ARAB EMIRATES †VOICE OF THE UAE, Abu Dhabi	EUROPE • 500 kW
	USSR KAZAKH RADIO, Alma-Ata	Sa • DS-1 • 50 kW; Sa-M • DS-1 • 50 kW; Su-F • DS-1 • 50 kW; Tu-F • DS-1 • 50 kW; DS-1/RUSSIAN, ETC • 50 kW
	RADIO MOSCOW, Chita	(J) • DS-2 • 100 kW
	RADIO MOSCOW, Kazan'	EUROPE • 100 kW; EUROPE • WS • 100 kW
	RADIO MOSCOW, Nikolayevsk 'Amure	(D) • AUSTRALIA • WS • 200 kW; (D) • E ASIA • 100 kW

World Time: 0 Prime Time-Americas 6 Prime Time-E Asia 12 Prime Time-S Asia 18 Prime Time-Europe 24

ENGLISH ▬ ARABIC ▩ CHINESE ▭▭▭ FRENCH ═ GERMAN ▬ RUSSIAN ═ SPANISH ═ OTHER —

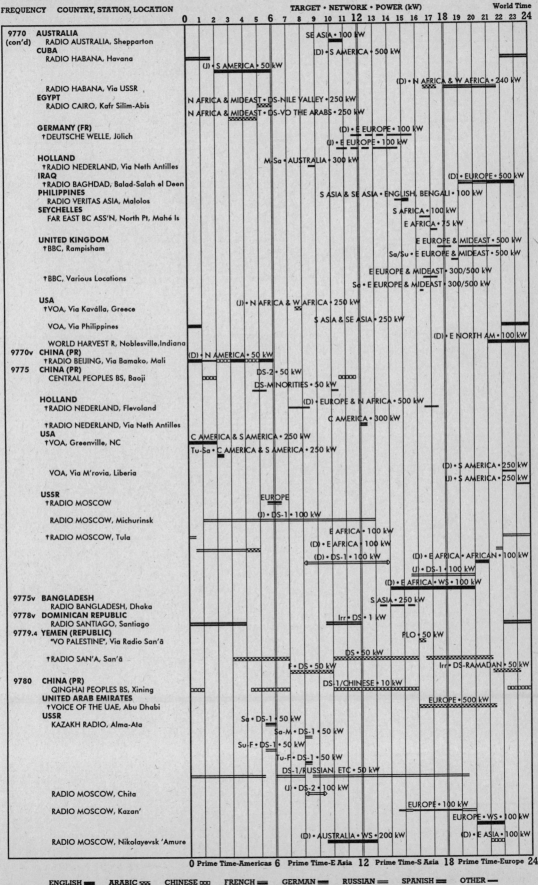

FREQUENCY	COUNTRY, STATION, LOCATION	TARGET • NETWORK • POWER (kW)
9785	**CHINA (PR)** †RADIO BEIJING, Xi'an	(D) • MIDEAST • 120 kW
	CHINA (TAIWAN) VO FREE CHINA, T'ai-pei	EUROPE
	GUAM †KTWR-TRANS WORLD R, Merizo	JAPANESE • E ASIA • 100 kW
	USA †KNLS-NEW LIFE STN, Anchor Pt, Alaska	(D) • USSR • 100 kW; (D) • E ASIA • 100 kW; (D) • EAST USSR • 100 kW
	USSR RADIO MOSCOW	(J) • E ASIA
	RADIO MOSCOW, Vinnitsa	(D) • N AFRICA & W AFRICA • WS • 100 kW; EUROPE • 100 kW
	†RADIO TASHKENT, Tashkent	(D) • MIDEAST • 100 kW
9790	**FRANCE** R FRANCE INTL, Issoudun-Allouis	E NORTH AM & C AMERICA • 100/500 kW; (D) • N AFRICA • 100 kW; (D) • E NORTH AM & C AMERICA • 100/500 kW
	†R FRANCE INTL, Multiple Locations	AFRICA • 100/250/500 kW
	†R FRANCE INTL, Via French Guiana	(D) • C AMERICA • 500 kW
	R FRANCE INTL, Via Moyabi, Gabon	C AFRICA • 500 kW
	USSR RADIO MOSCOW, Tallinn	(D) • DS-1 • 100 kW
	†RADIO TASHKENT, Tashkent	(J) • MIDEAST & S ASIA • 50 kW
9795	**MONACO** †TRANS WORLD RADIO, Monte Carlo	EUROPE • 100 kW; M-Sa • EUROPE • 100 kW; Su • EUROPE • 100 kW
	USSR BELORUSSIAN RADIO, Minsk	DS-1 • 50 kW
	R TIKHIY OKEAN, Komsomol'sk 'Amure	(D) • PACIFIC • MARINERS • 100 kW; (D) Sa • PACIFIC • MARINERS • 100 kW; (D) Su-F • PACIFIC • MARINERS • 100 kW
	RADIO MOSCOW	(J) • WS
	RADIO MOSCOW, Komsomol'sk 'Amure	(D) • W NORTH AM • 100 kW; (J) • E ASIA & PACIFIC • 100 kW; (J) • JAPANESE • E ASIA & PACIFIC • 100 kW; (D) • W NORTH AM • N AMERICAN • 100 kW; (J) • E ASIA & PACIFIC • WS • 100 kW
	RADIO MOSCOW, Tbilisi	S AMERICA & C AMERICA • 500 kW; (D) • S AMERICA & C AMERICA • 500 kW; (J) M/W/Th/Sa • S AMERICA & C AMERICA • 500 kW; (J) • S AMERICA & C AMERICA • 500 kW; (J) Tu/F/Su • S AMERICA & C AMERICA • 500 kW
	RADIO YEREVAN, Tbilisi	(D) • W EUROPE, S AMERICA & C AMERICA • 500 kW
9795v	**PAKISTAN** RADIO PAKISTAN, Islamabad	(D) • MIDEAST • 250 kW
9800	**FRANCE** †R FRANCE INTL, Multiple Locations	AMERICAS • 100/500 kW; (D) • AMERICAS • 100/500 kW
	PHILIPPINES FAR EAST BC CO, Iba	E ASIA • 100 kW
	USSR RADIO KIEV, Kiev	(J) • E NORTH AM & C AMERICA • 100 kW
	RADIO MOSCOW, Kazan'	(J) • EUROPE • 100 kW
	RADIO MOSCOW, Kiev	(J) • DS-2 • 100 kW
	RADIO MOSCOW, Moscow	DS-1 • 50 kW
9805	**EGYPT** RADIO CAIRO, Abu Za'bal	DS-GENERAL • 100 kW
	FRANCE †R FRANCE INTL, Issoudun-Allouis	S ASIA & SE ASIA • 500 kW; E EUROPE & WEST USSR • 100/500 kW; (J) • E EUROPE & WEST USSR • 100/500 kW
9810	**SWITZERLAND** †RED CROSS BC SVC, Schwarzenburg	Irr • M/Th • S AMERICA • 150 kW
	†SWISS RADIO INTL, Schwarzenburg	S AMERICA • 150 kW
	USSR R TIKHIY OKEAN, Khabarovsk	(J) • PACIFIC • MARINERS • 100 kW; (J) Sa • PACIFIC • MARINERS • 100 kW; (J) Su-F • PACIFIC • MARINERS • 100 kW
	RADIO MOSCOW, Khabarovsk	DS-1 • 100 kW; E ASIA • 100 kW
	RADIO MOSCOW, Moscow	W AFRICA & S AMERICA • MARINERS • 100 kW; (J) • W AFRICA & S AMERICA • 100 kW
(con'd)		

World Time: 0 Prime Time-Americas 6 Prime Time-E Asia 12 Prime Time-S Asia 18 Prime Time-Europe 24

SUMMER ONLY (J) WINTER ONLY (D) JAMMING / OR /\ EARLIEST HEARD ◁ LATEST HEARD ▷ NEW OR CHANGED FOR 1990 †

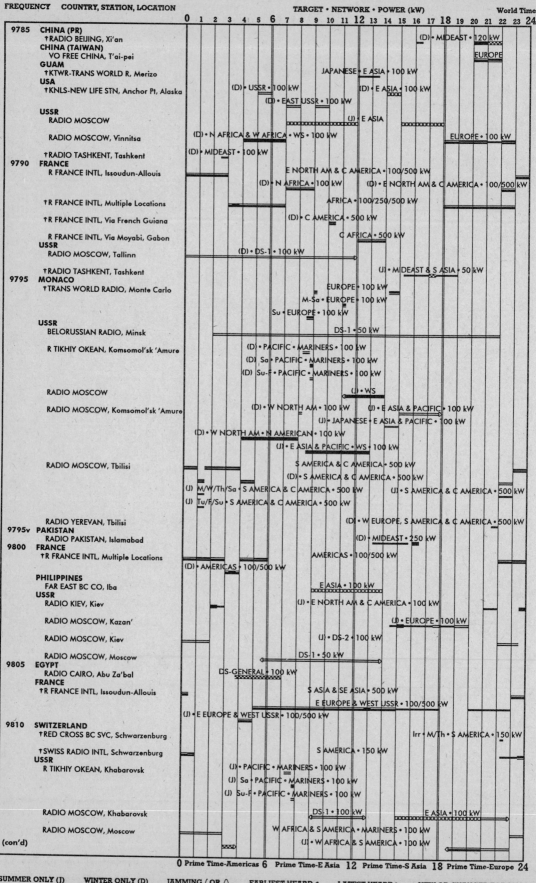

FREQUENCY	COUNTRY, STATION, LOCATION	TARGET • NETWORK • POWER (kW)
9810 (con'd)	**USSR** RADIO MOSCOW, Moscow	(D) • W AFRICA • WS, HAUSA, ETC • 100 kW
9815	**USA** †KNLS-NEW LIFE STN, Anchor Pt, Alaska	(D) • E ASIA • 100 kW
	KUSW, Salt Lake City, Utah	(D) Tu-Su • E NORTH AM • 100 kW
	†VOA, Delano, California	C AMERICA & S AMERICA • 250 kW
		Tu-Sa • C AMERICA & S AMERICA • 250 kW
9820	**CHINA (PR)** †RADIO BEIJING, Xi'an	(J) • EUROPE • 120 kW
	GUAM †KTWR-TRANS WORLD R, Merizo	E ASIA • 100 kW
		(D) • E ASIA • 100 kW
	USSR RADIO MOSCOW, Irkutsk	DS-1 • 100 kW
	RADIO MOSCOW, Kalinin	(J) • EUROPE • 100 kW
9825	**TURKEY** †TURKISH RTV CORP, Ankara	(D) • EUROPE • 250 kW
		(J) • EUROPE • 250 kW
	UNITED KINGDOM †BBC, Daventry	S AMERICA • 300 kW
		(D) • E EUROPE & MIDEAST • 300 kW
		(J) • W EUROPE & W AFRICA • 100 kW
		(J) • EUROPE & N AFRICA • 300 kW
		M-F • S AMERICA • 300 kW
		(D) M-Sa • E EUROPE & MIDEAST • 300 kW
		Sa/Su • S AMERICA • 300 kW
	†BBC, Multiple Locations	C AMERICA & S AMERICA • 300/500 kW
		W EUROPE & N AFRICA • 250/500 kW
	†BBC, Rampisham	(D) • E EUROPE & MIDEAST • 500 kW
		(J) • E EUROPE & MIDEAST • 500 kW
		(J) M-Sa • E EUROPE & MIDEAST • 500 kW
		(D) • E EUROPE • 500 kW
		(J) • W EUROPE • 500 kW
		(D) M-Sa • E EUROPE • 500 kW
		(D) Su • E EUROPE • 500 kW
	†BBC, Skelton, Cumbria	(D) • W AFRICA • 250 kW
		(D) • EUROPE, MIDEAST & W AFRICA • 100/250 kW
		(J) • EUROPE • 100 kW
		(J) Su • EUROPE • 100 kW
9830	**NORTHERN MARIANA IS** KFBS-FAR EAST BC, Saipan Island	E ASIA • 100 kW
		(J) F • USSR • 100 kW
		(J) • USSR • 100 kW
		(J) Sa-Th • USSR • 100 kW
		(J) Su-W • USSR • 100 kW
		(J) Th-Sa • USSR • 100 kW
		(J) • USSR • RUSSIAN, ETC • 100 kW
	PHILIPPINES FAR EAST BC CO, Bocaue	(D) • E ASIA • 50 kW
	†FAR EAST BC CO, Iba	(D) • E ASIA • 100 kW
		(J) • E ASIA • 100 kW
	USSR RADIO MOSCOW, Krasnodar	(D) • AFRICA • 100 kW
9835	**HUNGARY** RADIO BUDAPEST, Various Locations	E NORTH AM
		M • S AMERICA
		M • E NORTH AM
		Su-Tu/Th/F • E NORTH AM
		Tu-Su • S AMERICA
		Tu-Su • E NORTH AM
		Tu/W/F/Sa • E NORTH AM
		Tu/W/F/Sa • S AMERICA
		W/Sa • E NORTH AM
		Sa • EUROPE
		Su • EUROPE
		EUROPE
		M/Th • EUROPE
		S AMERICA
		Tu/F • S AMERICA
		W/Th/Sa-M • S AMERICA
	JORDAN †RADIO JORDAN, Qasr el Kharana	MIDEAST • DS • 500 kW
9840	**HOLLAND** RADIO NEDERLAND, Flevoland	N AFRICA • 500 kW
		N AFRICA & W AFRICA • 500 kW
	KUWAIT RADIO KUWAIT, Jadādīyah	Irr • DS-RAMADAN • 500 kW
		DS-MAIN PROGRAM • 500 kW
	NORTHERN MARIANA IS KFBS-FAR EAST BC, Saipan Island	(D) • SE ASIA • 100 kW
(con'd)	**USA** VOA, Greenville, NC	C AMERICA • 500 kW

World Time: 0 Prime Time-Americas 6 Prime Time-E Asia 12 Prime Time-S Asia 18 Prime Time-Europe 24

ENGLISH ▬ ARABIC ▭ CHINESE ▫▫▫ FRENCH ═ GERMAN ═ RUSSIAN ═ SPANISH ═ OTHER —

FREQUENCY	COUNTRY, STATION, LOCATION	TARGET • NETWORK • POWER (kW)
9840 (con'd)	**USA** †WCSN, Scotts Corners, Me	(J) • EUROPE • 500 kW
		(J) M-F • EUROPE • 500 kW
		(J) Sa/Su • EUROPE • 500 kW
	VIETNAM VOICE OF VIETNAM, Hanoi	SE ASIA • 30 kW
		(J) • E ASIA • 30 kW
		E ASIA & AMERICAS • 30 kW
		JAPANESE • E ASIA & AMERICAS • 30 kW
9845	**CHINA (PR)** †RADIO BEIJING, Via France	E EUROPE • 100 kW
		E EUROPE • 100 kW • ALT. FREQ. TO 7120 kHz
	CHINA (TAIWAN) VO FREE CHINA, T'ai-pei	SE ASIA
	PHILIPPINES FAR EAST BC CO, Iba	(J) • USSR • 100 kW
9850	**EGYPT** RADIO CAIRO, Kafr Silîm-Abis	N AFRICA & W EUROPE • DS-GENERAL • 250 kW
	NEW ZEALAND †RADIO NEW ZEALAND, Wellington	AUSTRALIA & SE ASIA • 7.5 kW
	USA KUSW, Salt Lake City,Utah	Su • E NORTH AM • 100 kW
		(J) Su • E NORTH AM • 100 kW
	†WCSN, Scotts Corners, Me	W AFRICA & S AFRICA • 500 kW
		E AFRICA • 500 kW
		M-F • W AFRICA & S AFRICA • 500 kW
		M-F • E AFRICA • 500 kW
		Sa-M • W AFRICA & S AFRICA • 500 kW
		Sa/Su • W AFRICA & S AFRICA • 500 kW
		Sa/Su • E AFRICA • 500 kW
		Tu-F • W AFRICA & S AFRICA • 500 kW
	USSR RADIO MOSCOW	(J)
	TASS NEWS AGENCY, Moscow	M-F • DS • 120 kW
9852v	**EQUATORIAL GUINEA** †RADIO AFRICA, Batá	Alternative Frequency to 7189v kHz
9852.5	**CHINA (TAIWAN)** †VO FREE CHINA, Via Okeechobee,USA	(D) • EUROPE • 100 kW
	USA WYFR-FAMILY RADIO, Okeechobee, Fl	EUROPE • 100 kW
9855	**GREECE** FONI TIS HELLADAS, Athens	(D) • GREEK • ATLANTIC • 100 kW
		(D) • MIDEAST • 100 kW
		(D) • N AFRICA • 100 kW
		(D) • GREEK • N AMERICA & EUROPE • 100 kW
		(D) • N AMERICA & EUROPE • 100 kW
	HOLLAND †RADIO NEDERLAND, Flevoland	Alternative Frequency to 9895 kHz
	ISRAEL KOL ISRAEL, Tel Aviv	(D) • WEST USSR & E EUROPE • 300 kW
		(D) Sa/Su • WEST USSR • 300 kW
		(D) • EUROPE • 300 kW
		(D) • HEBREW • WEST USSR & E EUROPE • 300 kW
		(D) • EUROPE, N AFRICA & C AMERICA • 300 kW
	USSR †RADIO MOSCOW	(D) • JAPANESE • E ASIA
9860	**BELGIUM** †BELGISCHE RADIO TV, Wavre	M-Sa • AFRICA • 250 kW
	CHINA (PR) †RADIO BEIJING, Kunming	(D) • USSR • 120 kW
	RADIO BEIJING, Xi'an	(D) • S AMERICA • 120 kW
	HOLLAND †RADIO NEDERLAND, Flevoland	Alternative Frequency to 9895 kHz
		MIDEAST • 500 kW
		(D) • MIDEAST • 500 kW
		(J) • N AFRICA • 500 kW
9860v	**PAKISTAN** RADIO PAKISTAN, Islamabad	MIDEAST • 250 kW
9865	**AFGHANISTAN** †RADIO AFGHANISTAN, Via USSR	(D) • MIDEAST
	ITALY †INTL RADIO RELAY, Milan	Su • EUROPE • 4 kW
	USSR RADIO MOSCOW	(D) • ATLANTIC • MARINERS
		(D) • DS-1
	RADIO MOSCOW, Alma-Ata	(J) • EUROPE & ATLANTIC
		(J) • EUROPE & ATLANTIC • WS
	RADIO MOSCOW, Komsomol'sk 'Amure	(J) • JAPANESE • E ASIA • 200 kW
(con'd)		(J) • E ASIA • WS • 200 kW

World Time: 0 1 2 3 4 5 6 7 8 9 10 11 12 13 14 15 16 17 18 19 20 21 22 23 24

0 Prime Time-Americas 6 Prime Time-E Asia 12 Prime Time-S Asia 18 Prime Time-Europe 24

SUMMER ONLY (J) WINTER ONLY (D) JAMMING / OR /\ EARLIEST HEARD ◁ LATEST HEARD ▷ NEW OR CHANGED FOR 1990 †

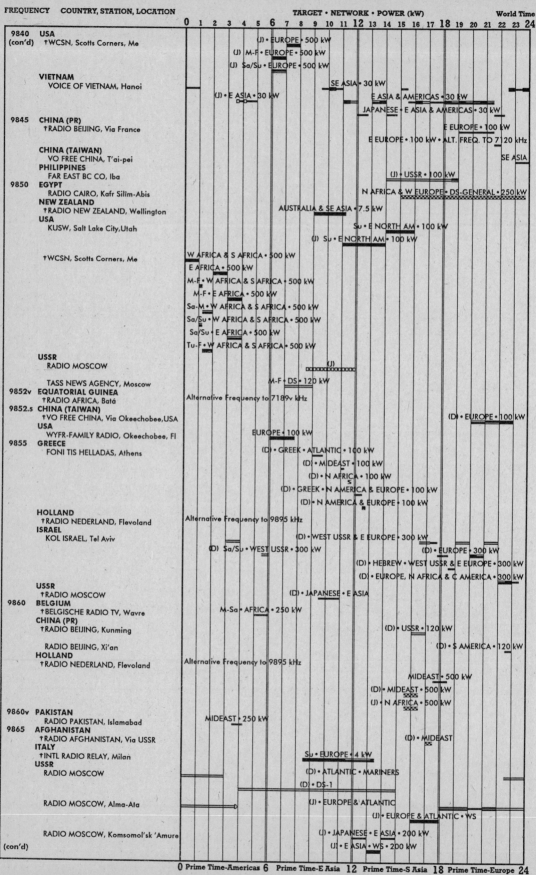

FREQUENCY COUNTRY, STATION, LOCATION — TARGET • NETWORK • POWER (kW) — World Time 0–24

9865 (con'd) **USSR**
RADIO MOSCOW, Krasnodar
(D) • N AFRICA & W AFRICA • AFRICAN • 250 kW
(D) • N AFRICA & W AFRICA • WS • 250 kW

RADIO MOSCOW, Ul'yanovsk
(D) • DS-1 • 100 kW

9870 AUSTRIA
†RADIO AUSTRIA INTL, Vienna
S AMERICA • 100/300 kW
C AMERICA • 300 kW
W EUROPE & W AFRICA • 100 kW
W EUROPE & W AFRICA • 100/500 kW
S AMERICA • 500 kW

KOREA (REPUBLIC)
RADIO KOREA, In-Kimjae
KOREAN • MIDEAST & AFRICA • 250 kW
MIDEAST & AFRICA • 250 kW

SAUDI ARABIA
BS OF THE KINGDOM, Riyadh
EUROPE • DS-GENERAL • 350 kW

USA
†KNLS-NEW LIFE STN, Anchor Pt, Alaska
(J) • E ASIA • 100 kW

†WCSN, Scotts Corners, Me
W AFRICA & S AFRICA • 500 kW
M-F • W AFRICA & S AFRICA • 500 kW
Sa/Su • W AFRICA & S AFRICA • 500 kW

9875 AUSTRIA
†RADIO AUSTRIA INTL, Vienna
N AMERICA & C AMERICA • 500 kW
(J) • AMERICAS
(J) M-Sa • AMERICAS
(J) Su • AMERICAS
(J) Su/M • AMERICAS
(J) Tu-Sa • AMERICAS

SPAIN
†R NACIONAL ESPANA, Noblejas
(D) • EUROPE • 350 kW
(J) • EUROPE • 350 kW
(D) M-F • EUROPE • 350 kW
(J) M-F • EUROPE • 350 kW

9880 CHINA (PR)
RADIO BEIJING, Beijing
SE ASIA • 120 kW

KUWAIT
RADIO KUWAIT, Jadādīyah
N AFRICA • DS-MAIN PROGRAM • 500 kW

USSR
RADIO MOSCOW, Kiev
(J) • EUROPE, C AMERICA & S AMERICA
(J) • EUROPE, C AMERICA & S AMERICA • N AMERICAN
(J) • EUROPE, C AMERICA & S AMERICA • WS

9885 SAUDI ARABIA
BS OF THE KINGDOM, Riyadh
EUROPE • DS-GENERAL • 350 kW

SWITZERLAND
RED CROSS BC SVC, Schwarzenburg
Irr • Tu/F • E NORTH AM & C AMERICA • 150 kW
Irr • Tu/F • N AMERICA • 150 kW
Irr • M/Th • AFRICA • ENGLISH, FRENCH • 250 kW

RED CROSS BC SVC, Sottens
Irr • M/Th • S AMERICA • 500 kW

SWISS RADIO INTL, Schwarzenburg
E NORTH AM & C AMERICA • 150 kW
N AMERICA • 150 kW
M • E NORTH AM & C AMERICA • 150 kW
M • N AMERICA • 150 kW
Tu-Su • E NORTH AM & C AMERICA • 150 kW
Tu-Su • N AMERICA • 150 kW
AFRICA • 150/250 kW
M-Sa • AFRICA • 250 kW
Su • AFRICA • 250 kW

SWISS RADIO INTL, Sottens
S AMERICA • 500 kW

9890 USSR
RADIO MOSCOW
ATLANTIC • MARINERS
(D) • ATLANTIC • MARINERS

9895 AFGHANISTAN
†RADIO AFGHANISTAN, Via USSR
(D) • MIDEAST

GUAM
†KTWR-TRANS WORLD R, Merizo
EAST USSR • 100 kW

HOLLAND
†RADIO NEDERLAND, Flevoland
C AMERICA & S AMERICA • 500 kW
S AMERICA • 500 kW
EUROPE • 500 kW
E NORTH AM • 500 kW
W EUROPE • 500 kW • ALT. FREQ. TO 9855 kHz
MIDEAST • 500 kW • ALT. FREQ. TO 9855 kHz
E NORTH AM • 500 kW • ALT. FREQ. TO 9855 kHz
W EUROPE & W AFRICA • 500 kW
(D) • MIDEAST • 500 kW
W EUROPE & W AFRICA • 500 kW • ALT. FREQ. TO 9860 kHz
(D) • EUROPE • 500 kW

USSR
†RADIO MOSCOW
(J) • DS-1
(D) • JAPANESE • E ASIA

RADIO MOSCOW, Petropavlovsk-Kam
(D) • JAPANESE • E ASIA • 100 kW

RADIO YEREVAN, Yerevan
(J) • EUROPE • 100 kW
(J) M-Sa • EUROPE • 100 kW

(con'd)

0 Prime Time-Americas 6 Prime Time-E Asia 12 Prime Time-S Asia 18 Prime Time-Europe 24

ENGLISH — ARABIC — CHINESE — FRENCH — GERMAN — RUSSIAN — SPANISH — OTHER

FREQUENCY	COUNTRY, STATION, LOCATION	TARGET • NETWORK • POWER (kW)
9895 (con'd)	**USSR** RADIO YEREVAN, Yerevan	(J) Su • EUROPE • 100 kW
9900	**CHINA (PR)** †RADIO BEIJING, Xi'an	S ASIA & E AFRICA • 120 kW
		E AFRICA & S AFRICA • 120 kW
	EGYPT †RADIO CAIRO, Kafr Silîm-Abis	N AMERICA • 250 kW
		EUROPE • 250 kW • ALT. FREQ. TO 9950 kHz
		EUROPE • 250 kW
9905	**GREECE** FONI TIS HELLADAS, Athens	GREEK • MIDEAST • 100 kW
		(J) • GREEK • MIDEAST • 100 kW
		(J) • GREEK • ATLANTIC • 100 kW
		(J) • MIDEAST • 100 kW
		(J) • N AFRICA • 100 kW
		(J) • GREEK • N AMERICA & EUROPE • 100 kW
		(J) • N AMERICA & EUROPE • 100 kW
	FONI TIS HELLADAS, Kaválla	(J) • GREEK • AFRICA • 250 kW
9910	**INDIA** †ALL INDIA RADIO, Delhi	E ASIA • 100 kW
		EUROPE • 100 kW
		EUROPE & AUSTRALIA • 100 kW
		MIDEAST • PERSIAN, ARABIC • 100 kW
9915	**UNITED KINGDOM** †BBC, Daventry	E EUROPE & WEST USSR • 100 kW
		(D) • E EUROPE & WEST USSR • 100 kW
	BBC, Multiple Locations	E NORTH AM, C AMERICA & S AMERICA • 300/500 kW
		E NORTH AM & C AMERICA • 300/500 kW
	†BBC, Rampisham	Tu/F • ATLANTIC & S AMERICA • FALKLANDS SVC • 500 kW
	†BBC, Skelton, Cumbria	(D) • EUROPE & W AFRICA • 250 kW
		(J) • EUROPE & W AFRICA • 250 kW
		(D) • E EUROPE & MIDEAST • TURKISH • 250 kW
	†BBC, Woofferton	(J) • W NORTH AM • 300 kW
9920	**CHINA (PR)** CENTRAL PEOPLES BS	DS-MINORITIES
	RADIO BEIJING, Kunming	S ASIA • 50 kW
	CLANDESTINE (ASIA) "DEM KAMPUCHEA", Kunming, China	(D) • SE ASIA • PRO-KHMER ROUGE • 50 kW
9925	**BELGIUM** †BELGISCHE RADIO TV, Wavre	AMERICAS • 100/250 kW
		(D) M-F • EUROPE • 100/250 kW
		(J) M-F • EUROPE • 100/250 kW
	†RT BELGE FRANCAISE, Wavre	(D) • AFRICA • 100/250 kW
		(J) • AFRICA • 100/250 kW
		(J) Su • EUROPE • 100 kW
		(J) • EUROPE • 100 kW
		(D) M-F • AFRICA • 100/250 kW
		(D) W/Sa/Su • AFRICA • 100/250 kW
		(J) M-F • AFRICA • 100/250 kW
		(D) M-Sa • AFRICA • 100/250 kW
		(J) M-Sa • AFRICA • 100/250 kW
		(J) Sa/Su • EUROPE • 100 kW
	ISRAEL KOL ISRAEL, Tel Aviv	Alternative Frequency to 9930 kHz
	RASHUTH HASHIDUR, Tel Aviv	Alternative Frequency to 9930 kHz
9930	**ISRAEL** KOL ISRAEL, Tel Aviv	(D) • PERSIAN • MIDEAST • 20 kW • ALT. FREQ. TO 9925 kHz
		(D) • WEST USSR & E EUROPE • 20 kW • ALT. FREQ. TO 9925 kHz
		(D) • EUROPE • 20 kW • ALT. FREQ. TO 9925 kHz
	RASHUTH HASHIDUR, Tel Aviv	(D) • HEBREW • WEST USSR & E EUROPE • DS-B • 20 kW • ALT. FREQ. TO 9925 kHz
		(D) • HEBREW • EUROPE • DS-B • 20 kW • ALT. FREQ. TO 9925 kHz
		(D) Su-F • HEBREW • WEST USSR & E EUROPE • DS-B • 20 kW • ALT. FREQ. TO 9925 kHz
9935	**GREECE** RS MAKEDONIAS, Thessaloniki	GREEK • MIDEAST • DS • 35 kW
		Su • GREEK • EUROPE • DS • 35 kW
9940	**EGYPT** †RADIO CAIRO, Kafr Silîm-Abis	AUSTRALIA • 250 kW
9940v	**CLANDESTINE (C AMER)** "LA VOZ DEL CID", Guatemala?	C AMERICA • ANTI-CASTRO
9945	**CHINA (PR)** †RADIO BEIJING, Beijing	E EUROPE • 120 kW
		(J) • E EUROPE & WEST USSR • 120 kW
	†RADIO BEIJING, Xi'an	E NORTH AM, C AMERICA & S AMERICA • 120 kW
		SE ASIA • 120 kW

World Time: 0 Prime Time-Americas 6 Prime Time-E Asia 12 Prime Time-S Asia 18 Prime Time-Europe 24

SUMMER ONLY (J) WINTER ONLY (D) JAMMING / OR /\ EARLIEST HEARD ◁ LATEST HEARD ▷ NEW OR CHANGED FOR 1990 †

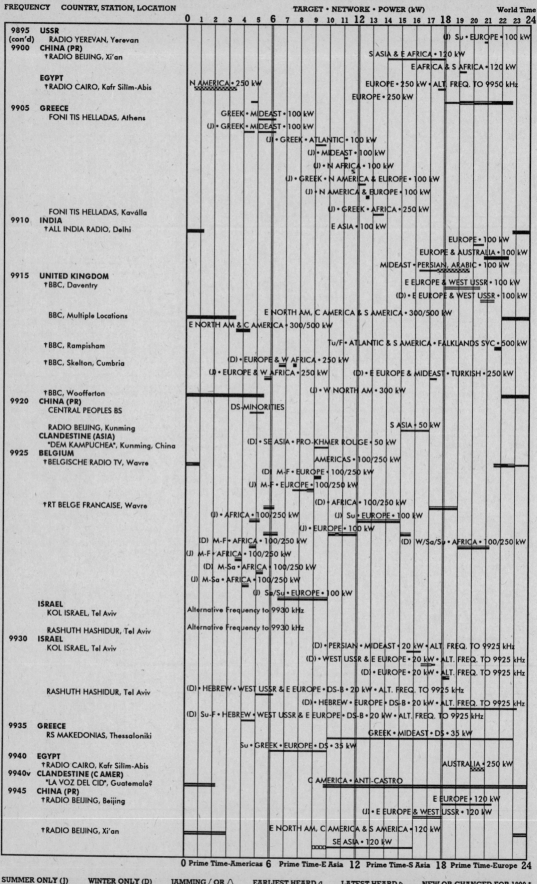

FREQUENCY	COUNTRY, STATION, LOCATION	TARGET • NETWORK • POWER (kW)
9950	EGYPT †RADIO CAIRO, Kafr Silîm-Abis	Alternative Frequency to 9900 kHz
	INDIA ALL INDIA RADIO, Delhi	DS-ENGLISH, ETC • 100 kW
	SYRIA †SYRIAN BC SERVICE, Adhra	USSR • 500 kW • ALT. FREQ. TO 7455 kHz
		(D) • C AMERICA & S AMERICA • 500 kW
		(D) • EUROPE • 500 kW
		(D) • E NORTH AM • 500 kW
		MIDEAST & N AFRICA • DS • 500 kW
9955	CHINA (TAIWAN) †VO FREE CHINA, T'ai-pei	SE ASIA
		MIDEAST & N AFRICA
		EUROPE
		EUROPE • 250 kW
	USA †FAMILY RADIO, Via Taiwan	USSR • 250 kW
9965	CHINA (PR) †RADIO BEIJING, Beijing	EUROPE, MIDEAST & N AFRICA • 120 kW
		(D) • WEST USSR • 120 kW
	CLANDESTINE (C AMER) †"RADIO CAIMAN", Guatemala City	C AMERICA • ANTI-CASTRO
9977	KOREA (DPR) RADIO PYONGYANG, Pyongyang	SE ASIA • 200 kW
		AFRICA • 200 kW
9978	ICELAND RIKISUTVARPID, Reykjavik	ATLANTIC & E NORTH AM • DS-1 • 10 kW • USB
9985	CHINA (PR) †RADIO BEIJING	E EUROPE
		(D) • E EUROPE & WEST USSR
	MONGOLIA †RADIO ULAN BATOR, Ulan Bator	EUROPE • 250 kW
		M/Tu/Th/F • AFRICA • 250 kW
9986	ICELAND RIKISUTVARPID, Reykjavik	(D) • ATLANTIC & EUROPE • DS • 10 kW • USB
10000	USA WWV, Ft Collins, Colorado	WEATHER/WORLD TIME • 10 kW
	WWVH, Kekaha, Hawaii	WEATHER/WORLD TIME • 10 kW
10010	CHINA (PR) †CENTRAL PEOPLES BS	(J) • DS-1
10010v	VIETNAM VOICE OF VIETNAM, Hanoi	E ASIA • 30 kW
10015v	CLANDESTINE (AFRICA) †"VO BROAD MASSES", Ethiopia	Irr • E AFRICA • PLF OF ERITREA
10060v	VIETNAM VOICE OF VIETNAM, Hanoi	DS • 30 kW
		Su • DS • 30 kW
10235	USA VOA, Greenville, NC	N AFRICA • (FEEDER) • 40 kW • USB
		(D) • N AFRICA • (FEEDER) • 40 kW • USB
		(J) • N AFRICA • (FEEDER) • 40 kW • USB
		M-F • N AFRICA • (FEEDER) • 40 kW • USB
		Th • W AFRICA • (FEEDER) • 40 kW • LSB
		M-F • W AFRICA • FRENCH, ENGLISH, ETC(FEEDER) • 40 kW • LSB
10260	CHINA (PR) CENTRAL PEOPLES BS, Beijing	DS-2 • 15 kW
		DS-MINORITIES • 15 kW
10275	USSR RADIO MOSCOW, Sverdlovsk	(J) • DS-1 (FEEDER) • 20 kW • LSB
10330	INDIA ALL INDIA RADIO, Delhi	S ASIA • 50 kW
		DS • 100 kW
10380	USA VOA, Greenville, NC	EUROPE & MIDEAST • (FEEDER) • 40 kW • LSB
10420	USA RFE-RL, Via Holzkirchen, GFR	W EUROPE • (FEEDER) • 10 kW • ISL
		W EUROPE • (FEEDER) • 10 kW • ISU
10454	USA †VOA, Greenville, NC	(D) • EUROPE & MIDEAST • (FEEDER) • 50 kW • ISL
		(D) • EUROPE & MIDEAST • (FEEDER) • 50 kW • ISU
		(J) • EUROPE & MIDEAST • (FEEDER) • 50 kW • ISL
		(J) • EUROPE & MIDEAST • (FEEDER) • 50 kW • ISU
10510v	ALBANIA RADIO TIRANA, Krujë	E ASIA • 100 kW
10670	USSR RADIO MOSCOW, Moscow	(J) • MARINERS(FEEDER) • 15 kW • USB
10855	USSR RADIO MOSCOW, Sverdlovsk	(J) • DS-2(FEEDER) • 15 kW • USB
10869	USA †VOA, Cincinnati, Ohio	W AFRICA • (FEEDER) • 50 kW • ISL
		(J) • W AFRICA • (FEEDER) • 50 kW • LSB
		W AFRICA • (FEEDER) • 50 kW • ISU
		M-F • W AFRICA • (FEEDER) • 50 kW • ISU
		Th • W AFRICA • (FEEDER) • 50 kW • ISU
(con'd)		

World Time: 0 1 2 3 4 5 6 7 8 9 10 11 12 13 14 15 16 17 18 19 20 21 22 23 24

0 Prime Time-Americas 6 Prime Time-E Asia 12 Prime Time-S Asia 18 Prime Time-Europe 24

ENGLISH — ARABIC — CHINESE — FRENCH — GERMAN — RUSSIAN — SPANISH — OTHER —

FREQUENCY	COUNTRY, STATION, LOCATION	TARGET • NETWORK • POWER (kW) — World Time 0–24
10869 (con'd)	USA †VOA, Cincinnati, Ohio	M-F • W AFRICA • ENGLISH,FRENCH,ETC(FEEDER) • 50 kW • ISU
10870	CLANDESTINE (M EAST) "R IRAN TOILERS", Afghanistan	PERSIAN • MIDEAST • TUDEH COMMUNIST
10922	GERMANY (FR) DEUTSCHE WELLE, Elmshorn	W EUROPE • (FEEDER) • 20 kW • USB
10945v	CHINA (PR) HUNAN METEOROLOGY	E ASIA • WEATHER, MUSIC
11000	CHINA (PR) CENTRAL PEOPLES BS	TAIWAN-2
		Th-Tu • TAIWAN-2
11020	USSR †RADIO MOSCOW	(D) • (FEEDER) • USB
11040	CHINA (PR) CENTRAL PEOPLES BS	DS-2
		Th/Sa-Tu • DS-2
11090	USA †VOA, Delano, California	SE ASIA • (FEEDER) • 50 kW • ISL
		SE ASIA • (FEEDER) • 50 kW • ISU
		M-F • SE ASIA • (FEEDER) • 50 kW • ISU
11100	CHINA (PR) CENTRAL PEOPLES BS, Beijing	TAIWAN-1 • 120 kW
11150	USA VOA, Greenville, NC	(J) • C AMERICA • (FEEDER) • 50 kW • USB
11330	CHINA (PR) CENTRAL PEOPLES BS	DS-1
		W-M • DS-1
11335	KOREA (DPR) RADIO PYONGYANG, Pyongyang	MIDEAST & AFRICA • 200 kW
11375	CHINA (PR) CENTRAL PEOPLES BS	DS-MINORITIES
11445	CHINA (PR) †RADIO BEIJING, Kunming	S AMERICA • 240 kW
		SE ASIA • 50 kW
		S ASIA • 120 kW
		(J) • S ASIA • 120 kW
		(J) • C AFRICA & E AFRICA • 120 kW
	†RADIO BEIJING, Xi'an	(J) • SE ASIA • 120 kW
11455	CHINA (PR) †RADIO BEIJING, Beijing	(J) • E ASIA • FEEDER • 15 kW
11490	CLANDESTINE (ASIA) †"VOICE OF UNITY", Abu Za'bal, Egypt	(D) • MIDEAST & S ASIA • PRO-AFGHAN REBELS • 100 kW
11500	CHINA (PR) †RADIO BEIJING, Beijing	(D) • WEST USSR • 120 kW
	†RADIO BEIJING, Kunming	(J) • S AMERICA • 120 kW
	†RADIO BEIJING, Xi'an	(J) • EUROPE • 120 kW
11505	CHINA (PR) CENTRAL PEOPLES BS, Beijing	DS-2 • 50/100 kW
		Th/Sa-Tu • DS-2 • 50/100 kW
11510	USSR RADIO MOSCOW, Moscow	(D) • DS-1(FEEDER) • 20 kW • ISL
		(D) • DS-1(FEEDER) • 20 kW • ISU
11510v	BANGLADESH †RADIO BANGLADESH, Dhaka	MIDEAST • 250 kW
		EUROPE • 250 kW
11515	CHINA (PR) †RADIO BEIJING, Beijing	WEST USSR • 120 kW
		JAPANESE • E ASIA • 120 kW
		E ASIA & SE ASIA • 120 kW
		(J) • MIDEAST & N AFRICA • 120 kW
11545	ISRAEL †RASHUTH HASHIDUR, Tel Aviv	(J) • HEBREW • W EUROPE & E NORTH AM • DS-B • 50 kW
		(J) Su-F • HEBREW • W EUROPE & E NORTH AM • DS-B • 50 kW
11550	TUNISIA †RTV TUNISIENNE, Sfax	DS • 100 kW
		(J) • DS • 100 kW
	USA †FAMILY RADIO, Via Taiwan	S ASIA • ENGLISH, HINDI • 250 kW
		E ASIA • 250 kW
11560	EGYPT †RADIO CAIRO, Kafr Silîm-Abis	MIDEAST • 250 kW
11570v	PAKISTAN PAKISTAN BC CORP, Islamabad	(J) • DS • 10 kW
	RADIO PAKISTAN, Islamabad	(D) • SE ASIA • 250 kW
		(J) • S ASIA • FEEDER • 10 kW
		(J) • EUROPE • 250 kW
		(J) • EUROPE & N AFRICA • 250 kW
	RADIO PAKISTAN, Karachi	(D) • S ASIA • 50 kW
11575	CHINA (PR) †RADIO BEIJING, Xi'an	MIDEAST & S ASIA • 120 kW
		(J) • MIDEAST • 120 kW
		(J) • E AFRICA & S AFRICA • 120 kW
11580 (con'd)	USA †VOA, Greenville, NC	C AMERICA & S AMERICA • 250 kW
		Tu-Sa • C AMERICA & S AMERICA • 250 kW

0 Prime Time-Americas 6 Prime Time-E Asia 12 Prime Time-S Asia 18 Prime Time-Europe 24

SUMMER ONLY (J) WINTER ONLY (D) JAMMING / OR /\ EARLIEST HEARD ◁ LATEST HEARD ▷ NEW OR CHANGED FOR 1990 †

FREQUENCY	COUNTRY, STATION, LOCATION	TARGET • NETWORK • POWER (kW)
11580 (con'd)	USA †WYFR-FAMILY RADIO, Okeechobee, Fl	EUROPE • 100 kW
		(D) • EUROPE • 100 kW
		(J) • EUROPE • 100 kW
		(J) • W NORTH AM • 100 kW
11585v	ISRAEL †KOL ISRAEL, Tel Aviv	(D) • EUROPE & E NORTH AM • 20/100 kW
		(J) • EUROPE & E NORTH AM • 100 kW
		(D) Sa/Su • EUROPE • 100 kW
	†RASHUTH HASHIDUR, Tel Aviv	HEBREW • EUROPE • DS-B • 20/100 kW
		(D) • HEBREW • EUROPE • DS-B • 20/100 kW
		(J) • HEBREW • EUROPE • DS-B • 100 kW
11595	GREECE FONI TIS HELLADAS, Kavália	(J) • GREEK • MIDEAST • 250 kW
		(J) • GREEK • C AMERICA & S AMERICA • 250 kW
		(J) • C AMERICA & S AMERICA • 250 kW
	RS MAKEDONIAS, Thessaloniki	GREEK • EUROPE • DS • 35 kW
		Su • GREEK • EUROPE • DS • 35 kW
		(J) • GREEK • EUROPE • DS • 35 kW
11600	CHINA (PR) †RADIO BEIJING, Kunming	PACIFIC • 120 kW
		(D) • S ASIA • 120 kW
		(J) • S ASIA • 120 kW
		(J) • S ASIA & E AFRICA • 120 kW
11605	ISRAEL †KOL ISRAEL, Tel Aviv	EUROPE, E NORTH AM & C AMERICA • 300 kW
		S AMERICA • 300 kW
		EUROPE • 300 kW
		(D) • S AMERICA • 300 kW
		WEST USSR • 300 kW
		(D) • MIDEAST • 300 kW
		(D) • WEST USSR • 300 kW
		(D) • EUROPE, N AFRICA & C AMERICA • 300 kW
11610	CHINA (PR) CENTRAL PEOPLES BS	DS-1
		W-M • DS-1
11615	CLANDESTINE (M EAST) †"IRAN FREEDOM FLAG, Egypt	PERSIAN • MIDEAST • ANTI-IRANIAN GOVT • 100 kW
	GREECE FONI TIS HELLADAS, Athens	GREEK • AFRICA • 100 kW
		GREEK • MIDEAST & WEST USSR • 100 kW
	PAKISTAN RADIO PAKISTAN, Islamabad	MIDEAST • 250 kW
		(J) • MIDEAST • 250 kW
		(J) • MIDEAST • 100 kW
11620	INDIA †ALL INDIA RADIO, Aligarh	MIDEAST • 250 kW
		EUROPE • 250 kW
	†ALL INDIA RADIO, Delhi	S ASIA • 100 kW
		DS-ENGLISH, ETC • 50 kW
11625	PAKISTAN RADIO PAKISTAN, Islamabad	(D) • E AFRICA • 100 kW
	SYRIA †SYRIAN BC SERVICE, Adhra	MIDEAST • 500 kW
		USSR • 500 kW
11630	CHINA (PR) CENTRAL PEOPLES BS, Beijing	DS-MINORITIES • 15 kW
		DS-2 • 15 kW
	USSR "RADIO MAGALLANES", Via R Moscow	(J) • S AMERICA • 240 kW
	RADIO MOSCOW, Moscow	(J) • W AFRICA & S AMERICA • 240 kW
	RADIO MOSCOW, Serpukhov	DS-1 • 50 kW
11632v	PAKISTAN RADIO PAKISTAN, Islamabad	(J) • EUROPE • 250 kW
11635	CLANDESTINE (C AMER) "LA VOZ DEL CID", Guatemala City	C AMERICA • ANTI-CASTRO
11635v	PAKISTAN RADIO PAKISTAN, Islamabad	(D) • MIDEAST • 100 kW
11640v	PAKISTAN RADIO PAKISTAN, Karachi	HINDI • S ASIA • 50 kW
11645	GREECE FONI TIS HELLADAS, Athens	GREEK • ATLANTIC • 100 kW
		GREEK • S AMERICA • 100 kW
		GREEK • E ASIA • 100 kW
		S AMERICA • 100 kW
		E ASIA • 100 kW
		USSR • GREEK, RUSSIAN • 100 kW
		MIDEAST • 100 kW
		N AFRICA • 100 kW
		(D) • GREEK • USSR • 100 kW
		(J) • GREEK • MIDEAST • 100 kW
		(J) • MIDEAST • 100 kW
		GREEK • USSR • GREEK, RUSSIAN • 100 kW
(con'd)		

World Time 0–24: 0 Prime Time-Americas 6 Prime Time-E Asia 12 Prime Time-S Asia 18 Prime Time-Europe 24

ENGLISH ARABIC CHINESE FRENCH GERMAN RUSSIAN SPANISH OTHER

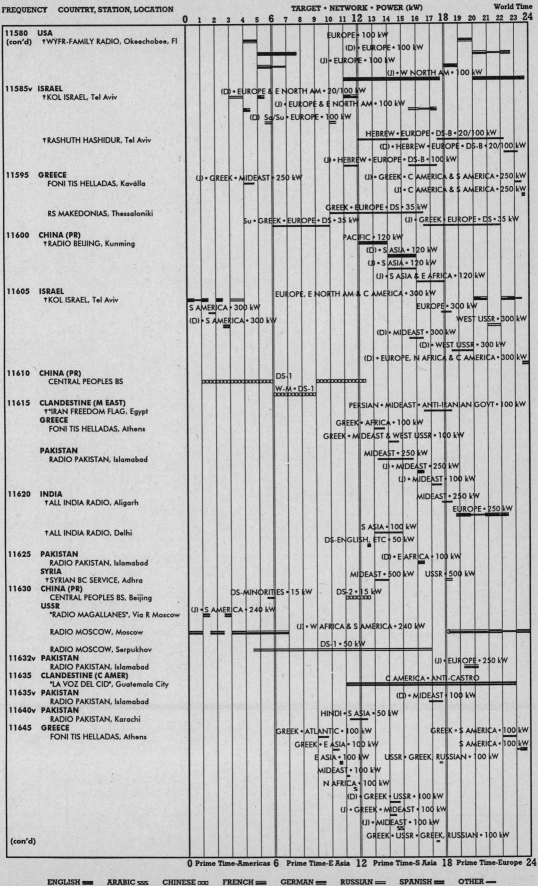

FREQUENCY	COUNTRY, STATION, LOCATION	TARGET • NETWORK • POWER (kW)
11645 (con'd)	**GREECE**	
	FONI TIS HELLADAS, Kaválla	GREEK • N AMERICA & EUROPE • 250 kW
		(J) • N AMERICA & PACIFIC • 250 kW
		N AMERICA & EUROPE • 250 kW
		(J) • GREEK • N AMERICA & PACIFIC • 250 kW
		(J) • GREEK • AFRICA • 250 kW
		(J) • GREEK • AFRICA • 100 kW
		(J) • AFRICA • 250 kW
11650	**CHINA (PR)**	
	†RADIO BEIJING, Beijing	(J) • AUSTRALIA • 100 kW
	RADIO BEIJING, Kunming	SE ASIA • 50 kW
	†RADIO BEIJING, Xi'an	(J) • S AMERICA • 120 kW
		(J) • WEST USSR & N AFRICA • 120 kW
	FRANCE	
	R FRANCE INTL, Issoudun-Allouis	M • ANTARCTICA • 100 kW • ALT. FREQ. TO 11660 kHz
	GUAM	
	†KTWR-TRANS WORLD R, Merizo	S ASIA • 100 kW
		(J) • E ASIA • 100 kW
	NORTHERN MARIANA IS	
	KFBS-FAR EAST BC, Saipan Island	EAST USSR • 100 kW
	PHILIPPINES	
	†FAR EAST BC CO, Iba	(J) • E ASIA • 100 kW
	USA	
	†KNLS-NEW LIFE STN, Anchor Pt, Alaska	(J) • E ASIA • 100 kW
11655	**ISRAEL**	
	†KOL ISRAEL, Tel Aviv	(J) Sa/Su • E EUROPE & WEST USSR • 300 kW
		(D) • WEST USSR • 45 kW • USB
		(D) • HEBREW • WEST USSR • 45 kW • USB
		(J) • E EUROPE & WEST USSR • 300 kW
	†RASHUTH HASHIDUR, Tel Aviv	(J) • HEBREW • E EUROPE & WEST USSR • DS-B • 300 kW
	USSR	
	RADIO MOSCOW, Alma-Ata	DS-2 • 50 kW
11660	**BELGIUM**	
	†RT BELGE FRANCAISE, Wavre	(D) • EUROPE • 100 kW
		(D) • AFRICA • 250 kW
		(J) • EUROPE • 100 kW
		(D) W/Sa/Su • AFRICA • 250 kW
		(D) M-F • EUROPE • 100 kW
		(J) M-F • EUROPE • 100 kW
		(D) M-Sa • EUROPE • 100 kW
		(J) M-Sa • EUROPE • 100 kW
	BULGARIA	
	†BULGARIAN RADIO, Sofia	(J) • EUROPE & N AFRICA • DS-1 • 250 kW
	†RADIO SOFIA, Sofia	(J) • E NORTH AM & C AMERICA • 250 kW
		(J) • EUROPE • 250 kW
	CHINA (PR)	
	†RADIO BEIJING, Kunming	SE ASIA • 50 kW
	FRANCE	
	R FRANCE INTL, Issoudun-Allouis	S ASIA & SE ASIA • 500 kW
		Alternative Frequency to 11650 kHz
	HOLLAND	
	†RADIO NEDERLAND, Flevoland	(D) • C AMERICA • 500 kW
		S AMERICA • 500 kW
		(J) • EUROPE • 500 kW
		(J) • E NORTH AM • 500 kW
	†RADIO NEDERLAND, Via Neth Antilles	C AMERICA • 300 kW
	MONACO	
	†TRANS WORLD RADIO, Monte Carlo	(D) • WEST USSR • 100 kW
		(J) • WEST USSR • 100 kW
		(J) • WEST USSR • 500 kW
		(D) Tu/W/F-Su • WEST USSR • 100 kW
	USSR	
	RADIO MOSCOW, Taldom	S ASIA & SE ASIA • 500 kW
11665	**EGYPT**	
	RADIO CAIRO, Abu Za'bal	C AFRICA & S AFRICA • DS-VO THE ARABS • 100 kW
		MIDEAST • DS-GENERAL • 100 kW
	GUAM	
	†KTWR-TRANS WORLD R, Merizo	E ASIA • 100 kW
		(D) • E ASIA • 100 kW
		(J) • E ASIA • 100 kW
	KUWAIT	
	RADIO KUWAIT, Jadādīyah	DS-MAIN PROGRAM
		EUROPE & E NORTH AM • 250 kW
11670	**FRANCE**	
	†R FRANCE INTL, Issoudun-Allouis	E EUROPE & WEST USSR • 500 kW
		E NORTH AM & C AMERICA • 100/500 kW
		(D) • E EUROPE • 500 kW
		(D) • E EUROPE & WEST USSR • 500 kW
		(J) • E EUROPE & WEST USSR • 500 kW
	†R FRANCE INTL, Multiple Locations	E NORTH AM, C AMERICA & S AMERICA • 100/500 kW
		C AMERICA • 100/500 kW
	†R FRANCE INTL, Via French Guiana	S AMERICA • 500 kW
		C AMERICA • 500 kW
(con'd)		(J) • C AMERICA • 500 kW

World Time: 0 Prime Time-Americas 6 Prime Time-E Asia 12 Prime Time-S Asia 18 Prime Time-Europe 24

SUMMER ONLY (J) WINTER ONLY (D) JAMMING / OR /\ EARLIEST HEARD ◁ LATEST HEARD ▷ NEW OR CHANGED FOR 1990 †

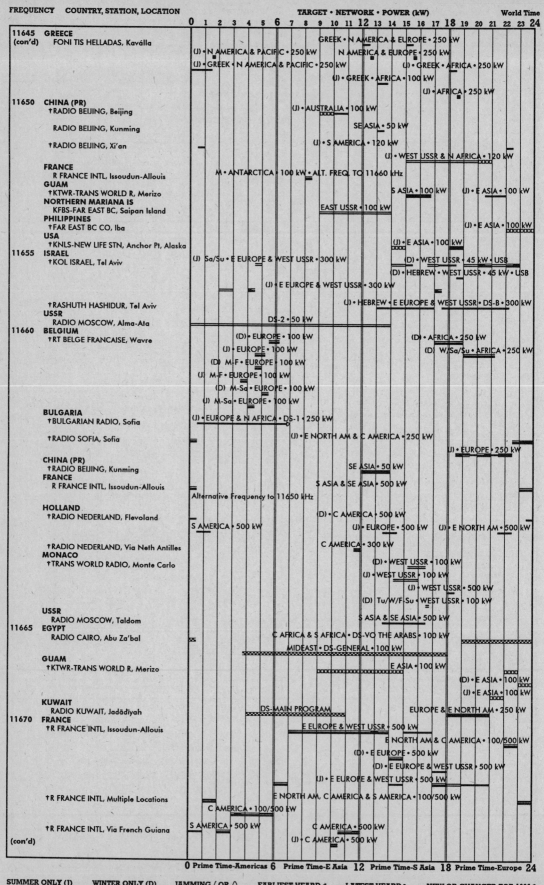

FREQUENCY	COUNTRY, STATION, LOCATION	TARGET • NETWORK • POWER (kW)
11670 (con'd)	**USSR** RADIO MOSCOW	(J) • E EUROPE
11672v	**PAKISTAN** RADIO PAKISTAN, Karachi	(J) • S ASIA • 50 kW
11675	**CHINA (PR)** †RADIO BEIJING, Xi'an	(J) • S ASIA • 120 kW
	USSR RADIO MOSCOW	(J) • EUROPE
		(D) • S ASIA • HINDI, URDU
	RADIO MOSCOW, Vladivostok	(J) • E ASIA & SE ASIA • CHI,CANTONESE,ETC • 100 kW
		(D) • ASIA • WS • 100 kW
11680	**UNITED KINGDOM** †BBC, Daventry	C AMERICA • 100 kW
	†BBC, Rampisham	(D) • W EUROPE & N AFRICA • 500 kW
		(J) • EUROPE & N AFRICA • 500 kW
		Su • E EUROPE • 500 kW
		(D) Su • WEST USSR • 500 kW
		(J) Su • E EUROPE • 500 kW
	†BBC, Skelton, Cumbria	(J) • EUROPE & N AFRICA • 250 kW
		(J) • W EUROPE & W AFRICA • 250 kW
	†BBC, Various Locations	EUROPE & N AFRICA • 300/500 kW
	USA †KGEI-VO FRIENDSHIP, Redwood City,Ca	(J) • WEST USSR • 250 kW
	KUSW, Salt Lake City,Utah	(D) Tu-Su • E NORTH AM • 100 kW
	VOA, Greenville, NC	(D) • S AMERICA • 500 kW
		(J) • S AMERICA • 250 kW
	USSR RADIO MOSCOW, Ul'yanovsk	DS-1 • 100 kW
11680v	**KOREA (DPR)** KOREAN CENTRAL BS, Pyongyang	DS • 100/200 kW
11685	**CHINA (PR)** †RADIO BEIJING, Kunming	(J) • SE ASIA • 120 kW
		S ASIA & SE ASIA • 120 kW
		(D) • S ASIA • 120 kW
		(D) • S ASIA & E AFRICA • 120 kW
	†RADIO BEIJING, Via French Guiana	W NORTH AM • 500 kW • ALT. FREQ. TO 11695 kHz
	CZECHOSLOVAKIA RADIO PRAGUE, Piešťany-Velké K'y	AUSTRALIA • 120 kW
		Sa/Su • AUSTRALIA • 120 kW
	RADIO PRAGUE, Prague	W AFRICA & S AMERICA • 120 kW
		MIDEAST & S ASIA • 120 kW
		M-F • MIDEAST & S ASIA • 120 kW
	SAUDI ARABIA BS OF THE KINGDOM, Riyadh	MIDEAST • 350 kW
11690	**USSR** R TIKHIY OKEAN, Khabarovsk	(J) • PACIFIC • MARINERS • 100 kW
	RADIO MOSCOW	(J) • AUSTRALIA • WS
	RADIO MOSCOW, Khabarovsk	(J) • PACIFIC • 100 kW
	RADIO MOSCOW, L'vov	(J) • EUROPE & N AFRICA • FRENCH,ITALIAN,ETC • 200 kW
	RADIO MOSCOW, Leningrad	(D) • DS-3 • 100 kW
11694	**VENEZUELA** †RADIO NACIONAL, Caracas	C AMERICA & S AMERICA • 50 kW • ALT. FREQ. TO 9500 kHz
11695	**BELGIUM** †BELGISCHE RADIO TV, Wavre	(J) M-F • EUROPE • 100/250 kW
		(D) • EUROPE • 100/250 kW
		(J) Sa/Su • EUROPE • 100/250 kW
		(J) • EUROPE • 100/250 kW
		(D) M-F • EUROPE • 100/250 kW
		(D) M-F • AUSTRALIA • 100/250 kW
		(J) M-F • AUSTRALIA • 100/250 kW
		Sa/Su • EUROPE • 100/250 kW
		(D) Sa/Su • EUROPE • 100/250 kW
		Su • EUROPE • 100/250 kW
		(D) Su • EUROPE • 100/250 kW
		(J) Su • EUROPE • 100/250 kW
	CHINA (PR) †RADIO BEIJING, Kunming	(D) • N AMERICA & C AMERICA • 240 kW
		(J) • S ASIA • 120 kW
		(J) • S ASIA & E AFRICA • 120 kW
	†RADIO BEIJING, Via French Guiana	Alternative Frequency to 11685 kHz
(con'd)	**CZECHOSLOVAKIA** †RADIO PRAGUE, Prague	(J) • AMERICAS • 250 kW

World Time 0–24: 0 Prime Time-Americas 6 Prime Time-E Asia 12 Prime Time-S Asia 18 Prime Time-Europe 24

ENGLISH ▬ ARABIC ▭ CHINESE ▫▫▫ FRENCH ═ GERMAN ▬ RUSSIAN ═ SPANISH ═ OTHER —

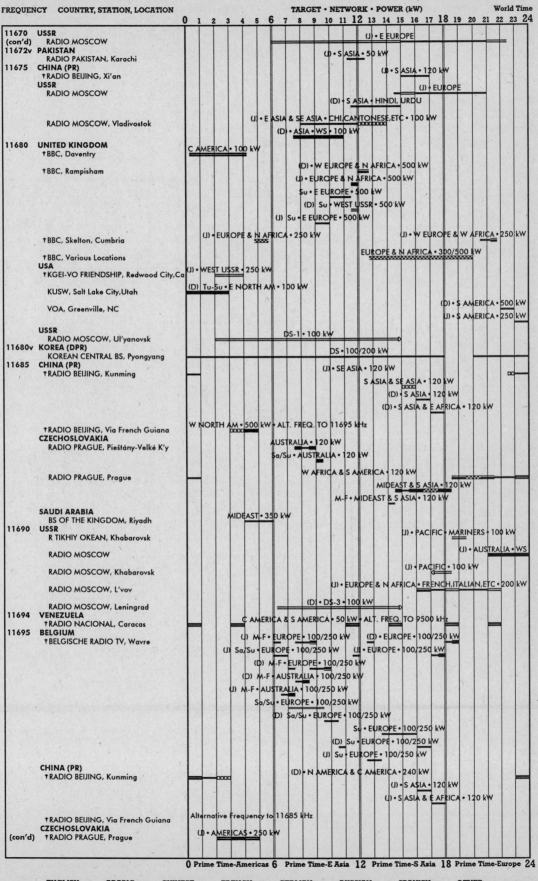

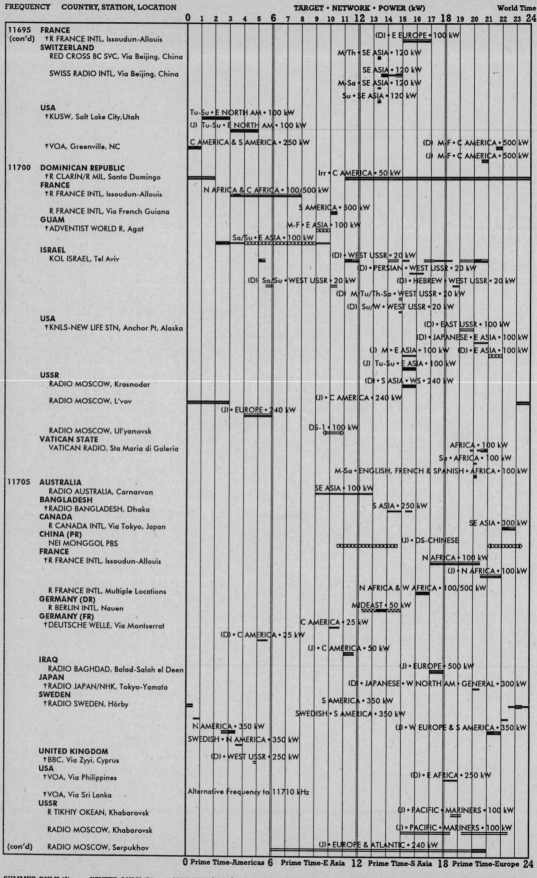

FREQUENCY	COUNTRY, STATION, LOCATION	TARGET • NETWORK • POWER (kW) — World Time 0–24
11695 (con'd)	**FRANCE**	
	†R FRANCE INTL, Issoudun-Allouis	(D) • E EUROPE • 100 kW
	SWITZERLAND	
	RED CROSS BC SVC, Via Beijing, China	M/Th • SE ASIA • 120 kW
	SWISS RADIO INTL, Via Beijing, China	SE ASIA • 120 kW
		M-Sa • SE ASIA • 120 kW
		Su • SE ASIA • 120 kW
	USA	
	†KUSW, Salt Lake City, Utah	Tu-Su • E NORTH AM • 100 kW
		(J) Tu-Su • E NORTH AM • 100 kW
	†VOA, Greenville, NC	C AMERICA & S AMERICA • 250 kW
		(D) M-F • C AMERICA • 500 kW
		(J) M-F • C AMERICA • 500 kW
11700	**DOMINICAN REPUBLIC**	
	†R CLARIN/R MIL, Santo Domingo	Irr • C AMERICA • 50 kW
	FRANCE	
	†R FRANCE INTL, Issoudun-Allouis	N AFRICA & C AFRICA • 100/500 kW
	R FRANCE INTL, Via French Guiana	S AMERICA • 500 kW
	GUAM	
	†ADVENTIST WORLD R, Agat	M-F • E ASIA • 100 kW
		Sa/Su • E ASIA • 100 kW
	ISRAEL	
	KOL ISRAEL, Tel Aviv	(D) • WEST USSR • 20 kW
		(D) • PERSIAN • WEST USSR • 20 kW
		(D) Sa/Su • WEST USSR • 20 kW
		(D) • HEBREW • WEST USSR • 20 kW
		(D) M/Tu/Th-Sa • WEST USSR • 20 kW
		(D) Su/W • WEST USSR • 20 kW
	USA	
	†KNLS-NEW LIFE STN, Anchor Pt, Alaska	(D) • EAST USSR • 100 kW
		(D) • JAPANESE • E ASIA • 100 kW
		(J) M • E ASIA • 100 kW
		(D) • E ASIA • 100 kW
		(J) Tu-Su • E ASIA • 100 kW
	USSR	
	RADIO MOSCOW, Krasnodar	(D) • S ASIA • WS • 240 kW
	RADIO MOSCOW, L'vov	(J) • C AMERICA • 240 kW
		(J) • EUROPE • 240 kW
	RADIO MOSCOW, Ul'yanovsk	DS-1 • 100 kW
	VATICAN STATE	
	VATICAN RADIO, Sta Maria di Galeria	AFRICA • 100 kW
		Su • AFRICA • 100 kW
		M-Sa • ENGLISH, FRENCH & SPANISH • AFRICA • 100 kW
11705	**AUSTRALIA**	
	RADIO AUSTRALIA, Carnarvon	SE ASIA • 100 kW
	BANGLADESH	
	†RADIO BANGLADESH, Dhaka	S ASIA • 250 kW
	CANADA	
	R CANADA INTL, Via Tokyo, Japan	SE ASIA • 300 kW
	CHINA (PR)	
	NEI MONGGOL PBS	(J) • DS-CHINESE
	FRANCE	
	†R FRANCE INTL, Issoudun-Allouis	N AFRICA • 100 kW
		(J) • N AFRICA • 100 kW
	R FRANCE INTL, Multiple Locations	N AFRICA & W AFRICA • 100/500 kW
	GERMANY (DR)	
	R BERLIN INTL, Nauen	MIDEAST • 50 kW
	GERMANY (FR)	
	†DEUTSCHE WELLE, Via Montserrat	C AMERICA • 25 kW
		(D) • C AMERICA • 25 kW
		(J) • C AMERICA • 50 kW
	IRAQ	
	RADIO BAGHDAD, Balad-Salah el Deen	(J) • EUROPE • 500 kW
	JAPAN	
	†RADIO JAPAN/NHK, Tokyo-Yamata	(D) • JAPANESE • W NORTH AM • GENERAL • 300 kW
	SWEDEN	
	†RADIO SWEDEN, Hörby	S AMERICA • 350 kW
		SWEDISH • S AMERICA • 350 kW
		N AMERICA • 350 kW
		(J) • W EUROPE & S AMERICA • 350 kW
		SWEDISH • N AMERICA • 350 kW
	UNITED KINGDOM	
	†BBC, Via Zyyi, Cyprus	(D) • WEST USSR • 250 kW
	USA	
	†VOA, Via Philippines	(D) • E AFRICA • 250 kW
	†VOA, Via Sri Lanka	Alternative Frequency to 11710 kHz
	USSR	
	R TIKHIY OKEAN, Khabarovsk	(J) • PACIFIC • MARINERS • 100 kW
	RADIO MOSCOW, Khabarovsk	(J) • PACIFIC • MARINERS • 100 kW
(con'd)	RADIO MOSCOW, Serpukhov	(J) • EUROPE & ATLANTIC • 240 kW

0 Prime Time-Americas 6 Prime Time-E Asia 12 Prime Time-S Asia 18 Prime Time-Europe 24

SUMMER ONLY (J) WINTER ONLY (D) JAMMING / OR /\ EARLIEST HEARD ◁ LATEST HEARD ▷ NEW OR CHANGED FOR 1990 †

FREQUENCY	COUNTRY, STATION, LOCATION	TARGET • NETWORK • POWER (kW)
11705 (con'd)	**USSR** RADIO MOSCOW, Serpukhov	(D) • EUROPE • WS • 240 kW
11710	**ARGENTINA** †R ARGENTINA-RAE, Buenos Aires	(J) • AMERICAS • 100 kW
		JAPANESE • E ASIA • 100 kW
		S AMERICA • 100 kW
	BULGARIA †RADIO SOFIA, Sofia	S AMERICA • 250 kW
	CLANDESTINE (AFRICA) "RADIO SPLA", Bantu Liben, Ethi'a	N AFRICA • ANTI-SUDANESE GOVT • 100 kW
	GUAM †KTWR-TRANS WORLD R, Merizo	E ASIA • 100 kW
	UNITED KINGDOM †BBC, Via Zyyi, Cyprus	(J) • E EUROPE & N AFRICA • 100 kW
	USA VOA, Via M'rovia, Liberia	M-F • W AFRICA • ENGLISH, FRENCH, ETC • 250 kW
	†VOA, Via Sri Lanka	S ASIA • 35 kW • ALT. FREQ. TO 11705 kHz
	VOA, Via Tangier, Morocco	(D) • E EUROPE • 100 kW
		(J) • E EUROPE • 100 kW
	†VOA, Via Woofferton, UK	WEST USSR • 250 kW
		(J) • WEST USSR • 250 kW
	USSR RADIO MOSCOW, Armavir	(J) • MIDEAST & S ASIA • 500 kW
		(J) • MIDEAST & S ASIA • WS • 500 kW
	RADIO MOSCOW, Moscow	(J) • DS-1 • 100 kW
		(D) • N AFRICA & MIDEAST • WS • 240 kW
	RADIO MOSCOW, Petropavlovsk-Kam	(J) • W NORTH AM • N AMERICAN • 100 kW
		(J) • W NORTH AM • WS • 100 kW
	RADIO MOSCOW, Via Havana, Cuba	(J) • N AMERICA • 100 kW
11715	**CHINA (PR)** †RADIO BEIJING, Via Bamako, Mali	N AMERICA • 100 kW
		C AFRICA & E AFRICA • 50 kW
		(D) • N AMERICA • 100 kW
	EGYPT RADIO CAIRO, Kafr Silîm-Abis	S AMERICA • 250 kW
	FINLAND †RADIO FINLAND, Pori	MIDEAST • 500 kW
	HOLLAND †RADIO NEDERLAND, Via Neth Antilles	S AMERICA • 300 kW
	INDIA †ALL INDIA RADIO, Aligarh	E ASIA • 250 kW
		AUSTRALIA • 250 kW
	IRAN †VO THE ISLAMIC REP, Tehrān	(J) • S ASIA • 100 kW
	TURKEY †TURKISH RTV CORP, Ankara	(D) • WEST USSR • 500 kW
	UNITED KINGDOM †BBC, Via Singapore	(J) • E ASIA • 250 kW
	†BBC, Woofferton	(J) Su • E EUROPE & MIDEAST • TURKISH • 250 kW
	USA †KNLS-NEW LIFE STN, Anchor Pt, Alaska	(J) • E ASIA • 100 kW
	VOA, Via M'rovia, Liberia	W AFRICA & S AFRICA • 250 kW
	†VOA, Via Philippines	ASIA & AUSTRALIA • 50/250 kW
		SE ASIA • 50/250 kW
	USSR RADIO MOSCOW, Komsomol'sk 'Amure	(J) • E ASIA • 240 kW
	VATICAN STATE VATICAN RADIO, Sta Maria di Galeria	EUROPE • 100 kW
		EUROPE & WEST USSR • 100 kW
		Su • E EUROPE & WEST USSR • 500 kW
		Th • EUROPE • 100 kW
11715v	**ALGERIA** "VO PALESTINE", Via RTV Algerienne	EUROPE • 50 kW
	RTV ALGERIENNE, Bouchaoui	EUROPE • DS • 50 kW
11720	**AUSTRALIA** †RADIO AUSTRALIA, Shepparton	PACIFIC • 100 kW
	BULGARIA †RADIO SOFIA, Sofia	AFRICA • 250 kW
		(D) • EUROPE • 250 kW
		EUROPE • 250 kW
		(D) • E NORTH AM & C AMERICA • 250 kW
	†RADIO SOFIA, Stolnik	EUROPE, N AFRICA & MIDEAST • 150 kW
		Su • EUROPE, N AFRICA & MIDEAST • 150 kW
	CANADA CANADIAN BC CORP, Sackville, NB	M-F • DS-NORTHERN • 100 kW
		Sa • DS-NORTHERN • 100 kW
		Su • DS-NORTHERN • 100 kW
(con'd)	**UNITED KINGDOM** †BBC, Daventry	(J) • N AFRICA & W AFRICA • 300 kW

World Time: 0 Prime Time-Americas 6 Prime Time-E Asia 12 Prime Time-S Asia 18 Prime Time-Europe 24

ENGLISH ▬ ARABIC ▨ CHINESE ▭ FRENCH ═ GERMAN ▬ RUSSIAN ═ SPANISH ▬ OTHER —

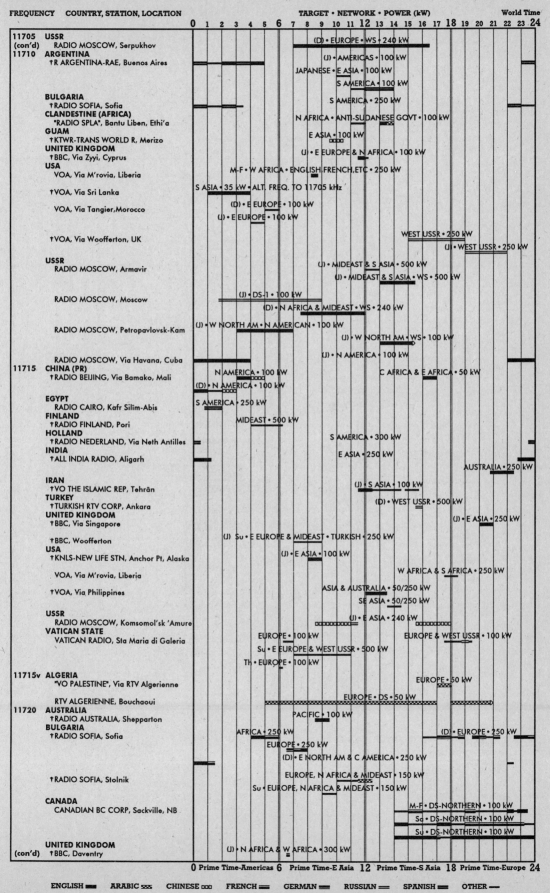

FREQUENCY	COUNTRY, STATION, LOCATION	TARGET • NETWORK • POWER (kW)
11720 (con'd)	**UNITED KINGDOM** †BBC, Via Zyyi, Cyprus	(J) • MIDEAST & S ASIA • 250 kW
		(D) • MIDEAST • 250 kW
		(D) • N AFRICA • 250 kW
		(J) • PERSIAN • MIDEAST & S ASIA • 250 kW
	USA †VOA, Via Philippines	ASIA & AUSTRALIA • 50/250 kW
	USSR RADIO MOSCOW, Tula	S ASIA • 240 kW
	†RADIO MOSCOW, Via Havana, Cuba	(J) • AMERICAS • 100 kW
	RADIO MOSCOW, Yerevan	DS-2 • 100 kW
	RADIO VILNIUS, L'vov	(J) • E NORTH AM & C AMERICA • 500 kW
11725	**CHINA (TAIWAN)** †CHINA BC CORP, T'ai-pei	E ASIA • DS
	CUBA RADIO HABANA, Havana	(J) • S AMERICA • 100 kW
		(D) • S AMERICA • 100 kW
		S AMERICA • 50/100 kW
		S AMERICA • 100 kW
	KOREA (REPUBLIC) RADIO KOREA, In-Kimjae	S AMERICA • 250 kW
	USA †RFE-RL, Via Portugal	E EUROPE & WEST USSR • 250 kW
		M-Sa • E EUROPE • 250 kW
		Su • WEST USSR • 250 kW
	VOA, Via Philippines	E ASIA • 250 kW
	†WYFR-FAMILY RADIO, Okeechobee, Fl	C AMERICA • 100 kW
	USSR RADIO MOSCOW, Kazan'	(D) • MIDEAST & E AFRICA • 100 kW
11730	**AUSTRALIA** RADIO AUSTRALIA, Darwin	E ASIA & SE ASIA • 250 kW
	CANADA R CANADA INTL, Sackville, NB	C AMERICA • 250 kW
	†R CANADA INTL, Via Vienna, Austria	(J) • MIDEAST • 300 kW
		(J) M-F • MIDEAST • 300 kW
		(J) Sa/Su • MIDEAST • 300 kW
	HOLLAND †RADIO NEDERLAND, Flevoland	C AMERICA • 500 kW • ALT. FREQ. TO 11950 kHz
	INDIA †ALL INDIA RADIO, Aligarh	(D) • SE ASIA • 250 kW
		DS-ENGLISH, ETC • 250 kW
	†ALL INDIA RADIO, Delhi	(J) • S ASIA • 100 kW
		DS-ENGLISH, ETC • 100 kW
		(D) • DS-ENGLISH, ETC • 100 kW
	JAPAN †RADIO JAPAN/NHK, Via French Guiana	(D) • JAPANESE • C AMERICA • GENERAL • 500 kW
	SAUDI ARABIA BS OF THE KINGDOM, Riyadh	MIDEAST & WEST USSR • DS-HOLY KORAN • 350 kW
	SPAIN R NACIONAL ESPANA, Noblejas	AUSTRALIA • 350 kW
	TURKEY TURKISH RTV CORP, Ankara	(D) • MIDEAST • 250 kW
	UNITED ARAB EMIRATES †UAE RADIO, Dubai	AUSTRALIA • 300 kW
	UNITED KINGDOM †BBC, Via Zyyi, Cyprus	(J) • MIDEAST & E AFRICA • 250 kW
	USSR R TIKHIY OKEAN, Khabarovsk	(J) • PACIFIC • MARINERS • 100 kW
		(J) Sa • PACIFIC • MARINERS • 100 kW
		(J) Su-F • PACIFIC • MARINERS • 100 kW
	RADIO MOSCOW, Chita	(J) • JAPANESE • E ASIA • 240 kW
		(J) • S ASIA • WS • 240 kW
	RADIO MOSCOW, Khabarovsk	(J) • E ASIA • 100 kW
		(J) • JAPANESE • E ASIA • 100 kW
11731	**ICELAND** RIKISUTVARPID, Reykjavik	ATLANTIC & E NORTH AM • DS-1 • 10 kW • USB
11734v	**TANZANIA** VOICE OF TANZANIA, Dole, Zanzibar	DS-SWAHILI • 50 kW
11735	**BULGARIA** RADIO SOFIA, Plovdiv	(D) • EUROPE • 500 kW
	†RADIO SOFIA, Sofia	AFRICA • 250 kW
	GUAM KTWR-TRANS WORLD R, Merizo	EAST USSR • 100 kW
	HOLLAND †RADIO NEDERLAND, Via Madagascar	Alternative Frequency to 15150 kHz
	KOREA (DPR) RADIO PYONGYANG, Kujang-dong	C AMERICA • 400 kW
(con'd)		E ASIA & S ASIA • 100 kW

World Time: 0 Prime Time-Americas 6 Prime Time-E Asia 12 Prime Time-S Asia 18 Prime Time-Europe 24

SUMMER ONLY (J) WINTER ONLY (D) JAMMING / OR ∧ EARLIEST HEARD ◁ LATEST HEARD ▷ NEW OR CHANGED FOR 1990 †

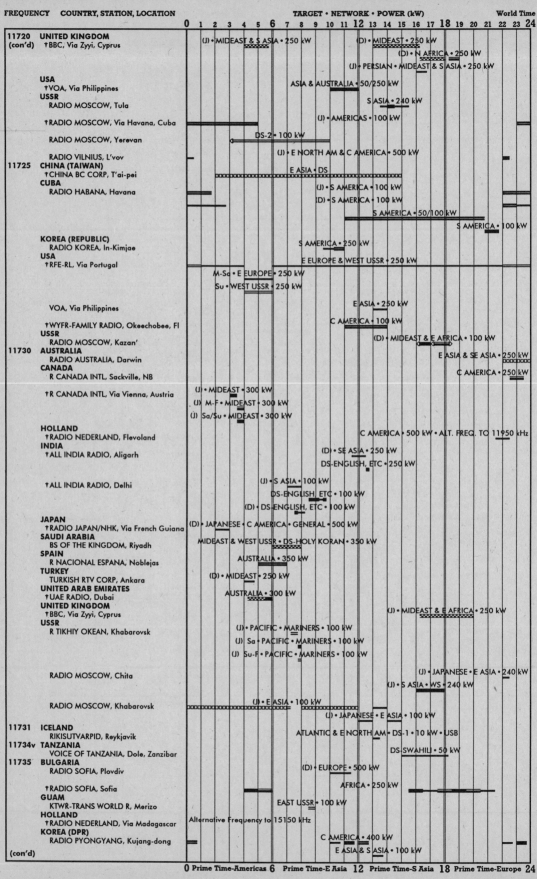

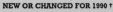

FREQUENCY	COUNTRY, STATION, LOCATION	TARGET • NETWORK • POWER (kW)
11735 (con'd)	**KOREA (DPR)** RADIO PYONGYANG, Pyongyang	C AMERICA • 400 kW
		SE ASIA • 200 kW
		E ASIA • 100 kW
	URUGUAY †RADIO ORIENTAL, Montevideo	Irr • DS • 1.5 kW
		DS • 1.5 kW
	USA KGEI-VO FRIENDSHIP, Redwood City,Ca	(J) • WEST USSR • 250 kW
	USSR RADIO MOSCOW, Serpukhov	(J) • E EUROPE & W AFRICA • 240 kW
	YUGOSLAVIA RADIO YUGOSLAVIA, Belgrade	(J) • USSR • 100 kW
		(J) • N AFRICA & W AFRICA • 100 kW
	†RADIO YUGOSLAVIA, Bijeljina	(D) • S ASIA & SE ASIA • 500 kW
		(D) • WEST USSR • 500 kW
		(J) • E NORTH AM • 500 kW
		(J) • EUROPE • 250 kW
	†VARIOUS LOCAL STNS, Belgrade	(D) Sa/Su • W EUROPE & E NORTH AM • DS • 100 kW
11740	**CHINA (PR)** CENTRAL PEOPLES BS, Beijing	DS-2 • 50 kW
	CHINA (TAIWAN) VO FREE CHINA, Via Okeechobee,USA	C AMERICA • 100 kW
	ECUADOR HCJB-VO THE ANDES, Quito	C AMERICA & E NORTH AM • 100 kW
	GERMANY (FR) †DEUTSCHE WELLE, Via Sri Lanka	SE ASIA • 250 kW
	HOLLAND †RADIO NEDERLAND, Flevoland	(D) • N AFRICA & W AFRICA • 500 kW
		(D) • W AFRICA • 500 kW
	†RADIO NEDERLAND, Via Madagascar	(J) • W AFRICA & C AFRICA • 300 kW
	ICELAND RIKISUTVARPID, Reykjavik	ATLANTIC & E NORTH AM • DS-1 • 10 kW • USB
	KOREA (DPR) RADIO PYONGYANG, Kujang-dong	WEST USSR & EUROPE • 200 kW
	KOREA (REPUBLIC) RADIO KOREA, In-Kimjae	KOREAN • E ASIA • 100 kW
		E ASIA • 100 kW
	PORTUGAL †R PORTUGAL INTL, Lisbon-S Gabriel	EUROPE • 100 kW
		M-F • EUROPE • 100 kW
		Sa/Su • EUROPE • 100 kW
	ROMANIA †RADIO BUCHAREST, Bucharest	(D) • S ASIA & SE ASIA • 250 kW
		(D) • MIDEAST • 250 kW
	SWAZILAND †TRANS WORLD RADIO, Manzini	E AFRICA • 100 kW
		(D) • E AFRICA • 100 kW
		(D) • S AFRICA • 25 kW
	UNITED KINGDOM †BBC, Skelton, Cumbria	(J) • EUROPE • 250 kW
	†BBC, Via Maşīrah, Oman	MIDEAST & S ASIA • 100 kW
		S ASIA & SE ASIA • 100 kW
		MIDEAST • 100 kW
		(D) • E AFRICA • 100 kW
		(J) • MIDEAST • 100 kW
	†BBC, Via Zyyi, Cyprus	(D) • MIDEAST & E AFRICA • 250 kW
	USA VOA, Delano, California	C AMERICA & S AMERICA • 250 kW
	VOA, Greenville, NC	(D) M-F • C AMERICA & S AMERICA • 250 kW
	†VOA, Via Kaválla, Greece	MIDEAST • 250 kW
		E AFRICA • 250 kW
		(D) • WEST USSR • 250 kW
	VOA, Via Rhodes, Greece	(J) • MIDEAST • TURKISH • 50 kW
	†VOA, Via Woofferton, UK	(J) • WEST USSR • 250 kW
	USSR RADIO MOSCOW, Novosibirsk	DS-1 • 50 kW
	RADIO MOSCOW, Tashkent	(D) • S ASIA • 100 kW
	VATICAN STATE †VATICAN RADIO, Sta Maria di Galeria	EUROPE • 100 kW
		EUROPE & N AFRICA • 100 kW
		Su • EUROPE • 100 kW
		Su • EUROPE & N AFRICA • 100 kW
		M-Sa • ENGLISH, FRENCH, SPANISH & ITALIAN • EUROPE • 100 kW
		M-Sa • ENGLISH, FRENCH, SPANISH & ITALIAN • EUROPE & N AFRICA • 100 kW

World Time: 0 Prime Time-Americas 6 Prime Time-E Asia 12 Prime Time-S Asia 18 Prime Time-Europe 24

ENGLISH ARABIC CHINESE FRENCH GERMAN RUSSIAN SPANISH OTHER

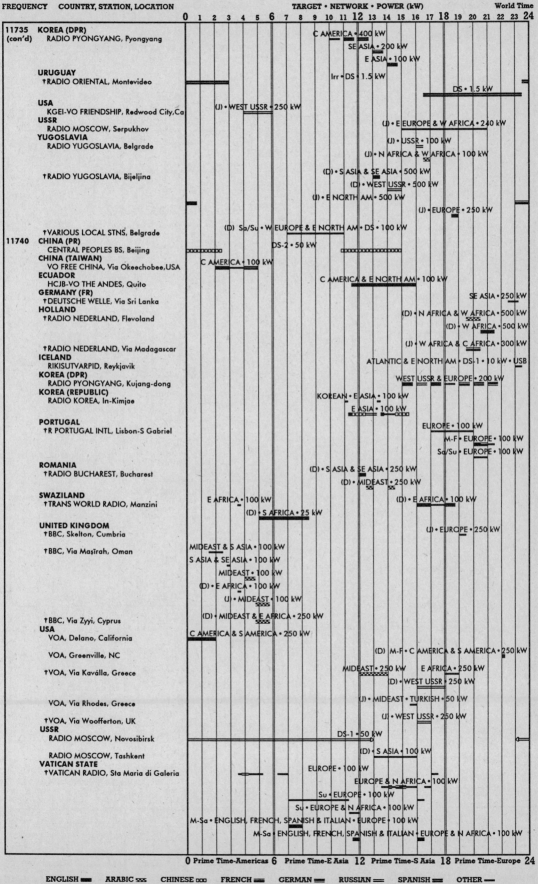

FREQUENCY — COUNTRY, STATION, LOCATION — TARGET • NETWORK • POWER (kW) — World Time 0 1 2 3 4 5 6 7 8 9 10 11 12 13 14 15 16 17 18 19 20 21 22 23 24

11744v INDONESIA
†VOICE OF INDONESIA, Jakarta — ASIA & PACIFIC • 100 kW • ALT. FREQ. TO 15150v kHz; JAPANESE • ASIA & PACIFIC • 100 kW • ALT. FREQ. TO 15150v kHz

11745 BRAZIL
RADIO NACIONAL, Brasília — AMERICAS • 250 kW

CHINA (PR)
†RADIO BEIJING, Beijing — (J) • WEST USSR • 120 kW; (J) • S AMERICA • 120 kW

CHINA (TAIWAN)
VO FREE CHINA, T'ai-pei — SE ASIA; E ASIA; JAPANESE • E ASIA

GERMANY (FR)
†DEUTSCHE WELLE, Via Cyclops, Malta — (D) • N AFRICA • 250 kW

ICELAND
RIKISUTVARPID, Reykjavik — (J) • ATLANTIC & EUROPE • DS-1 • 10 kW • USB

INDIA
ALL INDIA RADIO, Aligarh — SE ASIA • 250 kW

OMAN
RADIO OMAN, Sib — (J) • MIDEAST • DS • 100 kW

SOUTH AFRICA
†RADIO RSA, Meyerton — (D) • S AMERICA • 250 kW

USSR
RADIO MOSCOW, Minsk — W AFRICA • WS • 240 kW; (J) • W AFRICA • 240 kW
RADIO MOSCOW, Vinnitsa — (D) • W EUROPE & W AFRICA • 100 kW

11750 BULGARIA
RADIO SOFIA, Plovdiv — (J) • EUROPE • 500 kW

IRAQ
†RADIO BAGHDAD, Balad-Salah el Deen — (D) • EUROPE & N AFRICA • 500 kW

NORWAY
†RADIO NORWAY INTL, Kvitsøy — Alternative Frequency to 11760 kHz

UNITED KINGDOM
†BBC, Via Seychelles — E AFRICA • 250 kW; (D) • E AFRICA • 250 kW; (J) • E AFRICA • 250 kW
†BBC, Via Singapore — S ASIA & SE ASIA • 250 kW; SE ASIA & AUSTRALIA • 100/125/250 kW; (D) • E ASIA & AUSTRALIA • 125 kW; (D) • SE ASIA & AUSTRALIA • 250 kW; (J) • S ASIA & SE ASIA • 100/250 kW

USA
†RFE-RL, Via Portugal — WEST USSR • 250 kW
VOA, Via Tangier, Morocco — (D) • E EUROPE • 100 kW

USSR
RADIO MOSCOW, Kazan' — DS-1 • 100 kW
RADIO MOSCOW, Via Plovdiv, Bulgaria — (J) • N AMERICA • WS/N AMERICAN SCE • 500 kW

VATICAN STATE
†VATICAN RADIO, Sta Maria di Galeria — S AMERICA • 100 kW; N AMERICA • 100 kW; S ASIA • 100 kW; C AMERICA & S AMERICA • 100 kW

11755 AFGHANISTAN
RADIO AFGHANISTAN, Via USSR — (J) • EUROPE

CHINA (PR)
†RADIO BEIJING, Beijing — WEST USSR • 120 kW; AUSTRALIA • 240 kW

FINLAND
†RADIO FINLAND, Pori — AMERICAS • 500 kW; EUROPE & W AFRICA • 250/500 kW

PHILIPPINES
RADIO VERITAS ASIA, Palauig — SE ASIA • 250 kW

SWAZILAND
†TRANS WORLD RADIO, Manzini — (J) • S AFRICA • 25 kW

USSR
RADIO MOSCOW, Leningrad — MIDEAST • 240 kW
RADIO MOSCOW, Tbilisi — (J) • MIDEAST & S ASIA • MARINERS • 240 kW
RADIO MOSCOW, Tula — (J) • E AFRICA • 100 kW; (J) • E AFRICA • WS • 100 kW
RADIO MOSCOW, Vladivostok — (J) • W NORTH AM • WS • 100 kW

11760 CUBA
RADIO HABANA, Havana — (D) • C AMERICA • 100 kW; AMERICAS • 100 kW

ECUADOR
†HCJB-VO THE ANDES, Quito — JAPANESE • E ASIA • 100 kW

IRAQ
†RADIO BAGHDAD, Babylon — (D) • EUROPE & N AFRICA • 500 kW

NORWAY
†RADIO NORWAY INTL, Kvitsøy — (D) • MIDEAST & E AFRICA • 500 kW • ALT. FREQ. TO 11750 kHz
†RADIO NORWAY INTL, Sveio — (J) • W NORTH AM • 500 kW

SEYCHELLES
(con'd) FAR EAST BC ASS'N, North Pt, Mahé Is — E AFRICA & C AFRICA • 100 kW

0 Prime Time-Americas 6 Prime Time-E Asia 12 Prime Time-S Asia 18 Prime Time-Europe 24

SUMMER ONLY (J) — WINTER ONLY (D) — JAMMING / OR ⋀ — EARLIEST HEARD ◃ — LATEST HEARD ▹ — NEW OR CHANGED FOR 1990 †

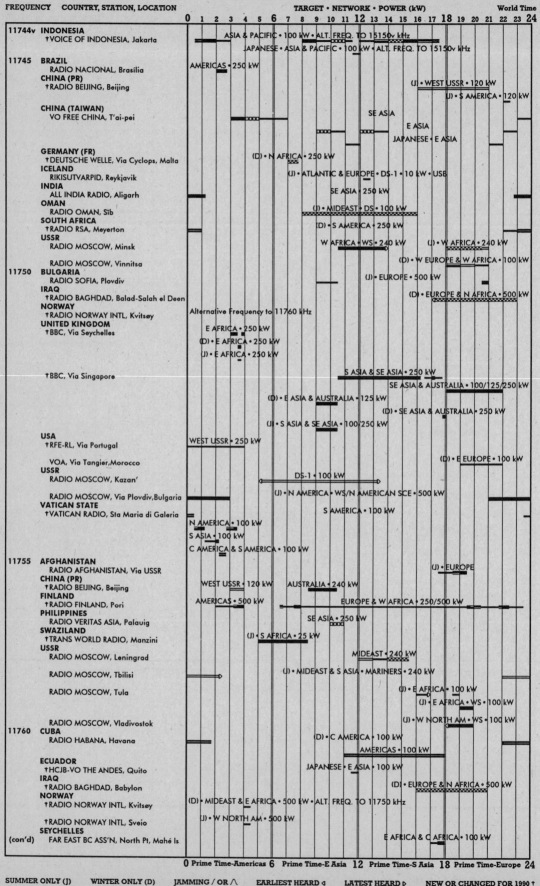

FREQUENCY	COUNTRY, STATION, LOCATION	TARGET • NETWORK • POWER (kW)
11760 (con'd)	**SEYCHELLES** FAR EAST BC ASS'N, North Pt, Mahé Is	Sa/Su • E AFRICA & C AFRICA • 100 kW
	SOUTH AFRICA †RADIO RSA, Meyerton	(D) • N AMERICA • 500 kW
	UNITED KINGDOM †BBC, Via Antigua	(J) • S AMERICA • 250 kW (J) M-F • S AMERICA • 250 kW (J) Sa/Su • S AMERICA • 250 kW
	†BBC, Via Maṣīrah, Oman	MIDEAST • 100 kW
	USA VOA, Greenville, NC	(D) • EUROPE • 250 kW
	VOA, Via Kaválla, Greece	(D) • WEST USSR • 250 kW
	VOA, Via M'rovia, Liberia	M-F • W AFRICA & C AFRICA • 250 kW
	VOA, Via Philippines	SE ASIA • 250 kW
	VOA, Via Rhodes, Greece	(D) • MIDEAST • TURKISH • 50 kW
	VOA, Via Woofferton, UK	(J) • WEST USSR • 250 kW (J) • EUROPE & MIDEAST • 250 kW (J) • EUROPE • 250 kW
	USSR RADIO MOSCOW, Khar'kov	DS-1 • 100 kW
	VATICAN STATE VATICAN RADIO, Sta Maria di Galeria	N AFRICA & W AFRICA • 100 kW
11760v	**COOK ISLANDS** †RADIO COOK ISLANDS, Rarotonga Is	DS-ENGLISH, MAORI • 0.5 kW M • DS • 0.5 kW Tu-Su • DS • 0.5 kW M-Sa • DS • 0.5 kW Su • DS • 0.5 kW
11765	**AUSTRALIA** †RADIO AUSTRALIA, Carnarvon	E ASIA & SE ASIA • 300 kW
	BULGARIA BULGARIAN RADIO, Sofia	EUROPE & N AFRICA • DS-1 • 250 kW
	RADIO SOFIA, Sofia	(D) • W AFRICA • 250 kW
	CHINA (PR) †RADIO BEIJING	(J) • EUROPE & WEST USSR
	GERMANY (FR) †DEUTSCHE WELLE, Jülich	W AFRICA • 100 kW
	†DEUTSCHE WELLE, Via Sri Lanka	(D) • SE ASIA & AUSTRALIA • 250 kW
	†DEUTSCHE WELLE, Wertachtal	C AFRICA & S AFRICA • 500 kW
	USSR RADIO MOSCOW, Alma-Ata	(J) • SE ASIA • VIETNAMESE, ETC • 100 kW
	RADIO MOSCOW, Irkutsk	(D) • E ASIA • 100 kW
	RADIO MOSCOW, Kenga	(J) • MIDEAST & E AFRICA • WS, ARABIC • 500 kW
11770	**IRAQ** †RADIO BAGHDAD, Balad-Salah el Deen	(J) • EUROPE • 500 kW
	USA †RFE-RL, Via Germany	WEST USSR • 250 kW
	†RFE-RL, Via Portugal	E EUROPE • 250 kW
	†WSHB, Cypress Creek, SC	(D) • C AMERICA & AUSTRALIA • 500 kW (D) M-F • C AMERICA & AUSTRALIA • 500 kW (D) Sa/Su • C AMERICA & AUSTRALIA • 500 kW
	†WYFR-FAMILY RADIO, Okeechobee, Fl	(J) • S AMERICA • 100 kW
	USSR RADIO MOSCOW, Kiev	E NORTH AM • N AMERICAN • 500 kW E NORTH AM • WS • 500 kW
	YEMEN (PDR) "VO PALESTINE", Via PDR Yemen BC	Irr • MIDEAST • PLO • 100 kW
	PDR YEMEN BC SVC, Aden	Irr • MIDEAST • DS • 100 kW Irr • F • MIDEAST • DS • 100 kW
11770v	**INDONESIA** †RRI, Jakarta, Jawa	Irr • DS • 250 kW
11775	**CANADA** R CANADA INTL, Via United Kingdom	(J) M-F • AFRICA • 100 kW
	CHINA (TAIWAN) CENTRAL BC SYSTEM, T'ai-pei	PRC-2 • 50/100 kW
	ECUADOR †HCJB-VO THE ANDES, Quito	C AMERICA & N AMERICA • 100 kW JAPANESE • C AMERICA & N AMERICA • 100 kW
	ROMANIA †RADIO BUCHAREST, Bucharest	MIDEAST & S ASIA • 250 kW (D) • AFRICA • 250 kW Su • ATLANTIC & N AFRICA • MARINERS • 250 kW
	SPAIN †R NACIONAL ESPANA, Noblejas	(D) • C AMERICA & S AMERICA • 350 kW
(con'd)	**TURKEY** TURKISH RTV CORP, Ankara	(J) • TURKISH • N AFRICA • 250 kW

World Time 0–24: 0 Prime Time-Americas 6 Prime Time-E Asia 12 Prime Time-S Asia 18 Prime Time-Europe 24

ENGLISH ▬ ARABIC ▨ CHINESE ▭ FRENCH ═ GERMAN ▬ RUSSIAN ═ SPANISH ▬ OTHER —

FREQUENCY	COUNTRY, STATION, LOCATION	TARGET • NETWORK • POWER (kW)
11775 (con'd)	**UNITED KINGDOM** BBC, Via Antigua	C AMERICA • 125 kW
		Su • C AMERICA • 125 kW
	†BBC, Via Sackville, Can	(J) • N AMERICA • 250 kW
		Sa/Su • N AMERICA • 250 kW
	USA †VOA, Via Philippines	SE ASIA • 50/250 kW
	†VOA, Via Woofferton, UK	(D) • N AFRICA • 250 kW
	USSR RADIO MOSCOW, Alma-Ata	(J) • SE ASIA • CANTONESE,VIET,ETC • 500 kW
		(J) • SE ASIA • WS • 500 kW
	RADIO MOSCOW, Armavir	(J) • E AFRICA • 240 kW
	RADIO MOSCOW, Chita	(D) • E ASIA & SE ASIA • 500 kW
	RADIO MOSCOW, Irkutsk	(D) • E ASIA & SE ASIA • CHI,INDONESIAN • 500 kW
11780	**AUSTRIA** †RADIO AUSTRIA INTL, Vienna	S ASIA & SE ASIA • 500 kW
		S AMERICA • 100/300 kW
		C AMERICA & S AMERICA • 100/300 kW
	BRAZIL †R NAC DA AMAZONIA, Brasilia	PORTUGUESE • DS • 250 kW
	CHINA (PR) †RADIO BEIJING, Kunming	SE ASIA • 50 kW
	CLANDESTINE (ASIA) †"DEM KAMPUCHEA", Kunming, China	SE ASIA • PRO-KHMER ROUGE • 50 kW
	IRAN †VO THE ISLAMIC REP, Tehrān	(J) • MIDEAST & N AFRICA • 500 kW
	KOREA (DPR) RADIO PYONGYANG, Kujang-dong	JAPANESE • E ASIA • 200 kW
	NEW ZEALAND †RADIO NEW ZEALAND, Wellington	Alternative Frequency to 15150 kHz
		PACIFIC • 7.5 kW • ALT. FREQ. TO 12045 kHz
	UNITED KINGDOM †BBC, Daventry	(J) • E EUROPE & MIDEAST • 300 kW
	†BBC, Rampisham	(D) • E EUROPE & MIDEAST • 500 kW
		(D) • WEST USSR • 500 kW
		(J) • E EUROPE & MIDEAST • 500 kW
		(J) Su • E EUROPE & MIDEAST • 500 kW
		(J) Sa/Su • E EUROPE & MIDEAST • 500 kW
		(D) Su • E EUROPE & MIDEAST • 500 kW
		(J) Su • E EUROPE & MIDEAST • 500 kW
	†BBC, Skelton, Cumbria	(D) • EUROPE & W AFRICA • 250 kW
		(J) • EUROPE & W AFRICA • 250 kW
	†BBC, Woofferton	(D) • N AFRICA & W AFRICA • 250 kW
	USA VOA, Via Kavála, Greece	MIDEAST & S ASIA • 250 kW
	VOA, Via Tangier,Morocco	(D) • E EUROPE • 35 kW
	USSR RADIO KIEV, L'vov	(J) • EUROPE • 240 kW
	RADIO MOSCOW, Simferopol'	DS-2 • 100 kW
	RS SOV BELORUSSIA, L'vov	(J) M/Tu/Th/F • EUROPE • 240 kW
		(J) W/Sa/Su • EUROPE • 240 kW
	VATICAN STATE †VATICAN RADIO, Sta Maria di Galeria	N AMERICA • 100 kW
11785	**BRAZIL** †RADIO GUAIBA, Pôrto Alegre	PORTUGUESE • DS • 7.5 kW
	EGYPT RADIO CAIRO, Abu Za'bal	N AFRICA & W EUROPE • DS-GENERAL • 100 kW
	RADIO CAIRO, Kafr Silîm-Abis	N AFRICA & W EUROPE • DS-GENERAL • 250 kW
	GERMANY (DR) †R BERLIN INTL, Nauen	S AMERICA • 500 kW
		N AMERICA • 500 kW
	GERMANY (FR) †DEUTSCHE WELLE, Via Kigali, Rwanda	(J) • C AFRICA & S AFRICA • 250 kW
	†DEUTSCHE WELLE, Via Sri Lanka	E AFRICA & S AFRICA • 250 kW
		SE ASIA & AUSTRALIA • 250 kW
		(J) • E ASIA • 250 kW
	UNITED KINGDOM †BBC, Via Zyyi, Cyprus	(D) • N AFRICA • 250 kW
	USA †VOA, Via Wertachtal, GFR	(J) • MIDEAST • 500 kW
	USSR RADIO MOSCOW, Ryazan'	(J) • EUROPE & W AFRICA • 240 kW
(con'd)	RADIO MOSCOW, Tashkent	SE ASIA & S ASIA • 100 kW

World Time: 0 Prime Time-Americas 6 Prime Time-E Asia 12 Prime Time-S Asia 18 Prime Time-Europe 24

SUMMER ONLY (J) WINTER ONLY (D) JAMMING / OR /\ EARLIEST HEARD ◁ LATEST HEARD ▷ NEW OR CHANGED FOR 1990 †

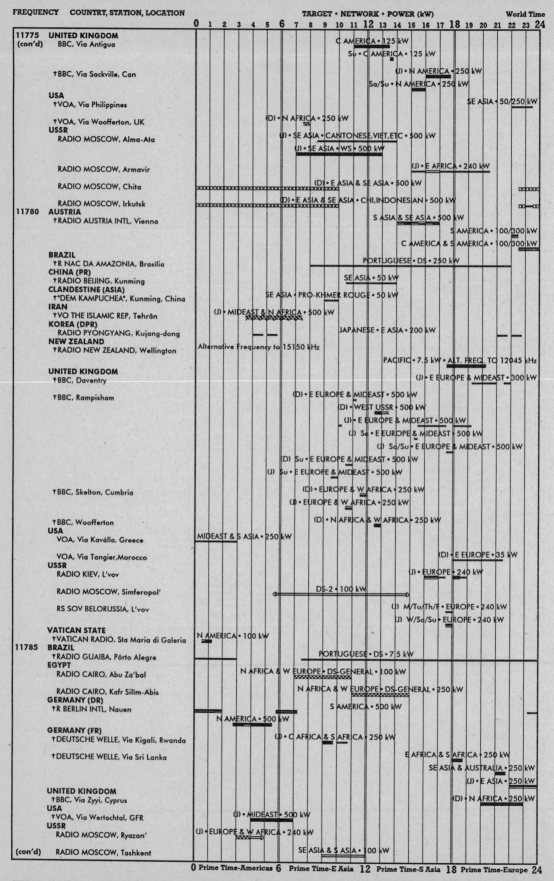

FREQUENCY	COUNTRY, STATION, LOCATION	TARGET • NETWORK • POWER (kW)
11785 (con'd)	USSR RADIO MOSCOW, Zhigulevsk	(J) • E EUROPE • GREEK, ETC • 100 kW
	RADIO TASHKENT, Tashkent	S ASIA • 100 kW
11785v	EGYPT RADIO CAIRO, Cairo-Mokattam	MIDEAST & N AFRICA • DS-VO THE ARABS • 50 kW
		MIDEAST & N AFRICA • DS-NILE VALLEY • 50 kW
11788v	INDONESIA †VOICE OF INDONESIA, Jakarta, Jawa	ASIA • 100/250 kW
		JAPANESE • ASIA • 100/250 kW
11790	CANADA †R CANADA INTL, Via Vienna, Austria	(D) • MIDEAST • 300 kW
		(D) M-F • MIDEAST • 300 kW
		(D) Sa/Su • MIDEAST • 300 kW
	CHINA (PR) †RADIO BEIJING, Via Bamako, Mali	C AFRICA & E AFRICA • 50 kW
		E EUROPE • 50 kW
		(D) • C AFRICA & E AFRICA • 100 kW
		(D) • C AFRICA & E AFRICA • 50 kW
		(D) • E NORTH AM & C AMERICA • 50 kW
	FRANCE †R FRANCE INTL, Issoudun-Allouis	(J) • E EUROPE & WEST USSR • 100 kW
	IRAN †VO THE ISLAMIC REP, Tehrān	S ASIA • 500 kW
	ROMANIA †RADIO BUCHAREST, Bucharest	(D) • W EUROPE • 250 kW
		(D) • EUROPE • 250 kW
		(D) • AFRICA • 250 kW
		(J) • EUROPE • 250 kW
	SEYCHELLES FAR EAST BC ASS'N, North Pt, Mahé Is	Su-W • S ASIA • 100 kW
		S ASIA • 100 kW
		F-M • E AFRICA • 100 kW
		Sa/Su • E AFRICA • 100 kW
	SPAIN †R NACIONAL ESPANA, Arganda	EUROPE • 100 kW
		(D) • EUROPE • 100 kW
		(J) • EUROPE • 100 kW
	UNITED ARAB EMIRATES †UAE RADIO, Dubai	EUROPE • 300 kW
	UNITED KINGDOM †BBC, Rampisham	(D) • EUROPE & WEST USSR • 500 kW
		(J) • EUROPE & WEST USSR • 250 kW
	†BBC, Skelton, Cumbria	(J) • WEST USSR • 250 kW
	†BBC, Via Zyyi, Cyprus	(D) • E EUROPE • 100 kW
	USA VOA, Via Tangier, Morocco	C AMERICA • 100 kW
	†WORLD HARVEST R, Noblesville, Indiana	(D) • C AMERICA • 100 kW
	USSR †RADIO KIEV, Blagoveshchensk	(J) • W NORTH AM • 240 kW
	†RADIO MOSCOW, Blagoveshchensk	(J) • W NORTH AM • 240 kW
		(D) • W NORTH AM • N AMERICAN • 240 kW
	RADIO MOSCOW, Ryazan'	(J) • W EUROPE & ATLANTIC • MARINERS • 240 kW
	†RADIO VILNIUS, Blagoveshchensk	(J) • W NORTH AM • 240 kW
	†RADIO YEREVAN, Blagoveshchensk	(J) • W NORTH AM • 240 kW
11795	CANADA †R CANADA INTL, Via Xi'an, China(PR)	(J) • JAPANESE • E ASIA • 120 kW
	CUBA RADIO HABANA, Havana	S AMERICA • 250 kW
		(J) • EUROPE • 250 kW
	ECUADOR HCJB-VO THE ANDES, Quito	S AMERICA • 100 kW
	GERMANY (FR) †DEUTSCHE WELLE, Jülich	(J) • S ASIA • 100 kW
		AUSTRALIA • 100 kW
		AFRICA • 100 kW
		(D) • S ASIA • 100 kW
		(D) • MIDEAST & S ASIA • 100 kW
		(J) • E EUROPE • 100 kW
		(J) • S AMERICA • 100 kW
	†DEUTSCHE WELLE, Via Antigua	C AMERICA & S AMERICA • 125/250 kW
	†DEUTSCHE WELLE, Via Cyclops, Malta	(D) • S ASIA • 250 kW
		(J) • E NORTH AM & C AMERICA • 250 kW
	†DEUTSCHE WELLE, Via Sines, Portugal	(J) • E EUROPE • 250 kW
	USSR RADIO MOSCOW, Tbilisi	DS-2 • 100 kW

World Time: 0 1 2 3 4 5 6 7 8 9 10 11 12 13 14 15 16 17 18 19 20 21 22 23 24

0 Prime Time-Americas 6 Prime Time-E Asia 12 Prime Time-S Asia 18 Prime Time-Europe 24

ENGLISH ARABIC CHINESE FRENCH GERMAN RUSSIAN SPANISH OTHER

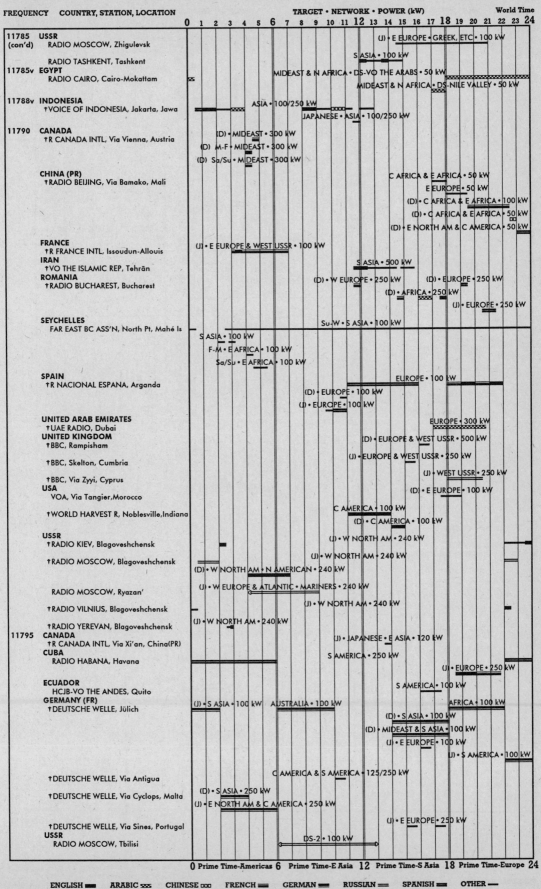

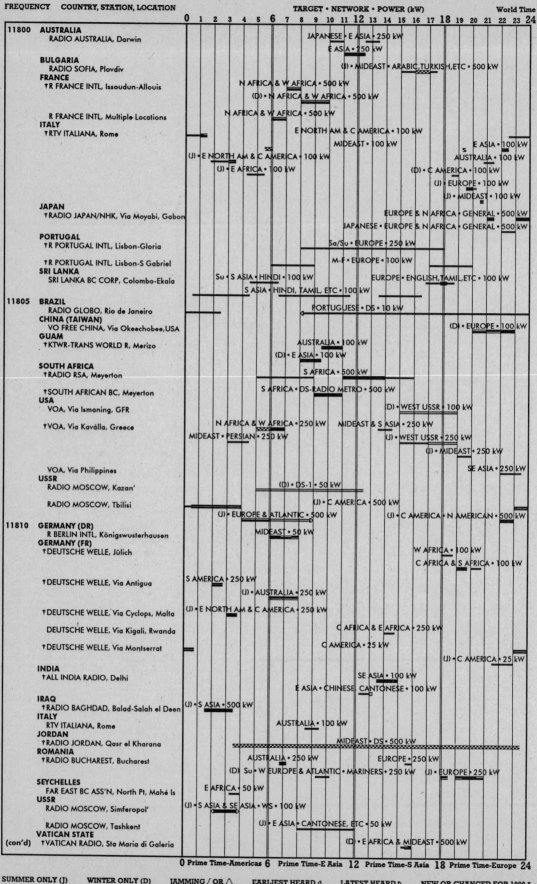

FREQUENCY	COUNTRY, STATION, LOCATION	TARGET • NETWORK • POWER (kW)
11800	**AUSTRALIA**	
	RADIO AUSTRALIA, Darwin	JAPANESE • E ASIA • 250 kW
		E ASIA • 250 kW
	BULGARIA	
	RADIO SOFIA, Plovdiv	(J) • MIDEAST • ARABIC,TURKISH,ETC • 500 kW
	FRANCE	
	†R FRANCE INTL, Issoudun-Allouis	N AFRICA & W AFRICA • 500 kW
		(D) • N AFRICA & W AFRICA • 500 kW
	R FRANCE INTL, Multiple Locations	N AFRICA & W AFRICA • 500 kW
	ITALY	
	†RTV ITALIANA, Rome	E NORTH AM & C AMERICA • 100 kW
		MIDEAST • 100 kW
		E ASIA • 100 kW
		(J) • E NORTH AM & C AMERICA • 100 kW
		AUSTRALIA • 100 kW
		(J) • E AFRICA • 100 kW
		(D) • C AMERICA • 100 kW
		(J) • EUROPE • 100 kW
		(J) • MIDEAST • 100 kW
	JAPAN	
	†RADIO JAPAN/NHK, Via Moyabi, Gabon	EUROPE & N AFRICA • GENERAL • 500 kW
		JAPANESE • EUROPE & N AFRICA • GENERAL • 500 kW
	PORTUGAL	
	†R PORTUGAL INTL, Lisbon-Gloria	Sa/Su • EUROPE • 250 kW
	†R PORTUGAL INTL, Lisbon-S Gabriel	M-F • EUROPE • 100 kW
	SRI LANKA	
	SRI LANKA BC CORP, Colombo-Ekala	Su • S ASIA • HINDI • 100 kW
		EUROPE • ENGLISH,TAMIL,ETC • 100 kW
		S ASIA • HINDI, TAMIL, ETC • 100 kW
11805	**BRAZIL**	
	RADIO GLOBO, Rio de Janeiro	PORTUGUESE • DS • 10 kW
	CHINA (TAIWAN)	
	VO FREE CHINA, Via Okeechobee,USA	(D) • EUROPE • 100 kW
	GUAM	
	†KTWR-TRANS WORLD R, Merizo	AUSTRALIA • 100 kW
		(D) • E ASIA • 100 kW
	SOUTH AFRICA	
	†RADIO RSA, Meyerton	S AFRICA • 500 kW
	†SOUTH AFRICAN BC, Meyerton	S AFRICA • DS-RADIO METRO • 500 kW
	USA	
	VOA, Via Ismaning, GFR	(D) • WEST USSR • 100 kW
	†VOA, Via Kaválla, Greece	N AFRICA & W AFRICA • 250 kW
		MIDEAST & S ASIA • 250 kW
		MIDEAST • PERSIAN • 250 kW
		(J) • WEST USSR • 250 kW
		(J) • MIDEAST • 250 kW
	VOA, Via Philippines	SE ASIA • 250 kW
	USSR	
	RADIO MOSCOW, Kazan'	(D) • DS-1 • 50 kW
	RADIO MOSCOW, Tbilisi	(J) • C AMERICA • 500 kW
		(J) • EUROPE & ATLANTIC • 500 kW
		(J) • C AMERICA • N AMERICAN • 500 kW
11810	**GERMANY (DR)**	
	R BERLIN INTL, Königswusterhausen	MIDEAST • 50 kW
	GERMANY (FR)	
	†DEUTSCHE WELLE, Jülich	W AFRICA • 100 kW
		C AFRICA & S AFRICA • 100 kW
	†DEUTSCHE WELLE, Via Antigua	S AMERICA • 250 kW
		(J) • AUSTRALIA • 250 kW
	†DEUTSCHE WELLE, Via Cyclops, Malta	(J) • E NORTH AM & C AMERICA • 250 kW
	DEUTSCHE WELLE, Via Kigali, Rwanda	C AFRICA & E AFRICA • 250 kW
	†DEUTSCHE WELLE, Via Montserrat	C AMERICA • 25 kW
		(J) • C AMERICA • 25 kW
	INDIA	
	†ALL INDIA RADIO, Delhi	SE ASIA • 100 kW
		E ASIA • CHINESE, CANTONESE • 100 kW
	IRAQ	
	†RADIO BAGHDAD, Balad-Salah el Deen	(J) • S ASIA • 500 kW
	ITALY	
	RTV ITALIANA, Rome	AUSTRALIA • 100 kW
	JORDAN	
	†RADIO JORDAN, Qasr el Kharana	MIDEAST • DS • 500 kW
	ROMANIA	
	†RADIO BUCHAREST, Bucharest	AUSTRALIA • 250 kW
		EUROPE • 250 kW
		(D) Su • W EUROPE & ATLANTIC • MARINERS • 250 kW
		(J) • EUROPE • 250 kW
	SEYCHELLES	
	FAR EAST BC ASS'N, North Pt, Mahé Is	E AFRICA • 50 kW
	USSR	
	RADIO MOSCOW, Simferopol'	(J) • S ASIA & SE ASIA • WS • 100 kW
	RADIO MOSCOW, Tashkent	(J) • E ASIA • CANTONESE, ETC • 50 kW
	VATICAN STATE	
(con'd)	†VATICAN RADIO, Sta Maria di Galeria	(D) • E AFRICA & MIDEAST • 500 kW

World Time: 0 Prime Time-Americas 6 Prime Time-E Asia 12 Prime Time-S Asia 18 Prime Time-Europe 24

SUMMER ONLY (J) WINTER ONLY (D) JAMMING / OR /\ EARLIEST HEARD ◁ LATEST HEARD ▷ NEW OR CHANGED FOR 1990 †

FREQUENCY	COUNTRY, STATION, LOCATION	TARGET • NETWORK • POWER (kW)
11810 (con'd)	**VATICAN STATE** †VATICAN RADIO, Sta Maria di Galeria	(D) • E AFRICA & MIDEAST • 100 kW (J) • E AFRICA & MIDEAST • 100 kW
11815	**BRAZIL** R BRASIL CENTRAL, Goiânia	PORTUGUESE • DS • 7.5 kW
	JAPAN †RADIO JAPAN/NHK, Tokyo-Yamata	JAPANESE • SE ASIA • GENERAL • 300 kW SE ASIA • GENERAL • 300 kW (D) • JAPANESE • E ASIA • GENERAL • 300 kW (J) • SE ASIA • GENERAL • 300 kW (D) • E ASIA • GENERAL • 300 kW (J) • JAPANESE • SE ASIA • GENERAL • 300 kW (J) • E ASIA • GENERAL • 300 kW (J) • JAPANESE • E ASIA • GENERAL • 300 kW
	NETHERLANDS ANTILLES †TRANS WORLD RADIO, Bonaire	E NORTH AM • 50 kW Sa • E NORTH AM • 50 kW Sa/Su • E NORTH AM • 50 kW
	POLAND †RADIO POLONIA, Warsaw	ATLANTIC & E NORTH AM • 100 kW (J) • EUROPE & N AFRICA • 100 kW W AFRICA & ATLANTIC • 100 kW (J) • W EUROPE & W AFRICA • 100 kW (J) • EUROPE • 100 kW
	SPAIN †R NACIONAL ESPANA, Noblejas	(D) • S AMERICA • 350 kW
	UNITED ARAB EMIRATES †VOICE OF THE UAE, Abu Dhabi	MIDEAST • 500 kW
	USA †RFE-RL, Via Germany	E EUROPE & WEST USSR • 100 kW Su • E EUROPE • 100 kW
	†RFE-RL, Via Portugal	E EUROPE • 250 kW M-Sa • E EUROPE • 250 kW Su • WEST USSR • 250 kW
	USSR R TIKHIY OKEAN, Khabarovsk	(J) • PACIFIC • MARINERS • 100 kW (J) Sa • PACIFIC • MARINERS • 100 kW (J) Su-F • PACIFIC • MARINERS • 100 kW
	RADIO MOSCOW, Khabarovsk	(J) • DS-1 • 100 kW
	RADIO MOSCOW, Sverdlovsk	(J) • DS-1 • 100 kW
11820	**AFGHANISTAN** †RADIO AFGHANISTAN, Via USSR	MIDEAST & S ASIA
	JORDAN †RADIO JORDAN, Qasr el Kharana	N AFRICA & C AMERICA • DS • 500 kW
	PHILIPPINES RADIO VERITAS ASIA, Malolos	SE ASIA & S ASIA • INDO,SINHALA,TAMIL • 100 kW E ASIA • 100 kW
	PORTUGAL †R PORTUGAL INTL, Lisbon-S Gabriel	E AFRICA & S AFRICA • 100 kW M-F • E AFRICA & S AFRICA • 100 kW Sa/Su • E AFRICA & S AFRICA • 100 kW
	QATAR †QATAR BC SERVICE, Doha-Al Khaisah	EUROPE • 250 kW
	UNITED KINGDOM †BBC, Via Ascension	S AFRICA • 250 kW (D) • S AMERICA • 250 kW (J) • S AMERICA • 250 kW (J) • S AFRICA • 250 kW (J) • C AFRICA • 250 kW (D) M-F • S AMERICA • 250 kW (J) M-F • S AMERICA • 250 kW (D) Sa/Su • S AMERICA • 250 kW (J) Sa/Su • S AMERICA • 250 kW
	BBC, Via Delano, USA	(J) • C AMERICA & S AMERICA • 250 kW
	USA KNLS-NEW LIFE STN, Anchor Pt, Alaska	(J) • E ASIA • 100 kW
	USSR RADIO MOSCOW, Frunze, Kirgiziya	(D) • SE ASIA • 500 kW (J) • S ASIA • 50 kW (D) • SE ASIA • WS • 500 kW
	RADIO MOSCOW, Voronezh	(J) • EUROPE • UK SVC • 100 kW (J) • EUROPE • WS • 100 kW
11820v	**MOZAMBIQUE** †RADIO MOCAMBIQUE, Maputo	Irr • S AFRICA • 120 kW PORTUGUESE • DS • 120 kW
11820.6	**QATAR** QATAR BC SERVICE, Doha	EUROPE • DS • 250 kW
11825 (con'd)	**CHINA (TAIWAN)** VO FREE CHINA, T'ai-pei	SE ASIA

World Time: 0 1 2 3 4 5 6 7 8 9 10 11 12 13 14 15 16 17 18 19 20 21 22 23 24

0 Prime Time-Americas 6 Prime Time-E Asia 12 Prime Time-S Asia 18 Prime Time-Europe 24

ENGLISH ARABIC CHINESE FRENCH GERMAN RUSSIAN SPANISH OTHER

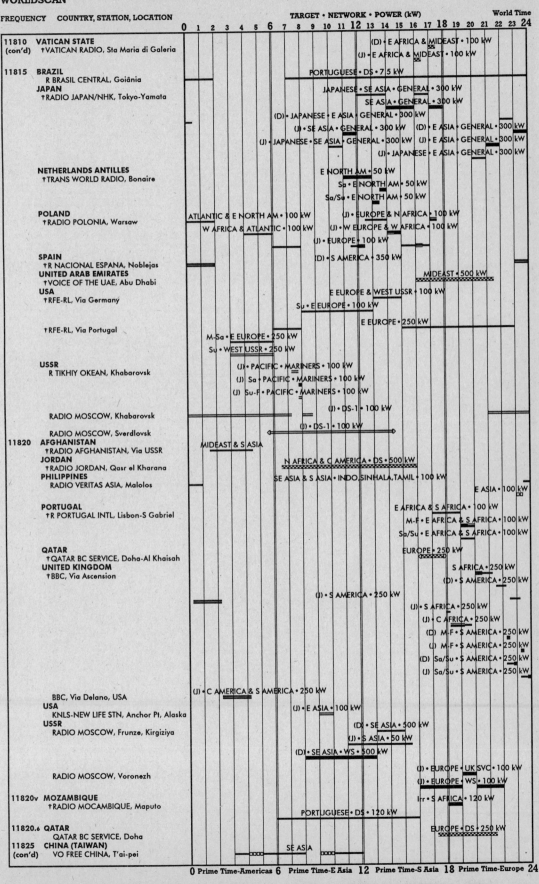

FREQUENCY	COUNTRY, STATION, LOCATION	TARGET • NETWORK • POWER (kW)
11825 (con'd)	**CLANDESTINE (AFRICA)**	
	†"VO LIBYAN PEOPLE", Southern Chad	N AFRICA • ANTI-QUADDAFI
	IRAQ	
	†RADIO BAGHDAD, Balad-Salah el Deen	(D) • E AFRICA • 500 kW
	SAUDI ARABIA	
	BS OF THE KINGDOM, Riyadh	S ASIA • BENGALI, URDU • 350 kW
	UNITED KINGDOM	
	†BBC, Via Zyyi, Cyprus	(D) • EUROPE • 100 kW
	USA	
	†RFE-RL, Via Germany	WEST USSR • 100 kW
	†RFE-RL, Via Portugal	E EUROPE & WEST USSR • 50/250 kW
	USSR	
	RADIO MOSCOW, Kenga	DS-1 • 100 kW
11825v	**SOCIETY ISLANDS**	
	†RFO-TAHITI, Papeete	PACIFIC • DS-FRENCH,TAHITIAN • 20 kW
11830	**AFGHANISTAN**	
	RADIO AFGHANISTAN, Via USSR	Alternative Frequency to 6020 kHz
	BRAZIL	
	†RADIO ANHANGUERA, Goiânia	PORTUGUESE • DS • 1 kW
	CLANDESTINE (AFRICA)	
	†"AV DO GALO NEGRO", Jamba, Angola	S AFRICA • UNITA/PORT,ETC
	GUAM	
	†KTWR-TRANS WORLD R, Merizo	E ASIA • 100 kW
	INDIA	
	ALL INDIA RADIO, Bombay	DS • 100 kW
	ALL INDIA RADIO, Delhi	Su • DS • 100 kW E AFRICA & S AFRICA • 100 kW DS-ENGLISH, ETC • 100 kW
	KOREA (DPR)	
	RADIO PYONGYANG, Kujang-dong	E ASIA & S ASIA • 100 kW SE ASIA • 200 kW SE ASIA • 100 kW
	LIBERIA	
	RADIO ELWA, Monrovia	F-Su • W AFRICA & C AFRICA • ENGLISH, ETC • 50 kW W AFRICA & C AFRICA • 50 kW Su • W AFRICA & C AFRICA • ENGLISH,FRENCH,ETC • 50 kW
	ROMANIA	
	†RADIO BUCHAREST, Bucharest	AMERICAS • 250 kW (J) • MIDEAST • 250 kW
	SWEDEN	
	†RADIO SWEDEN, Hörby	(J) • SWEDISH • E NORTH AM • 350 kW
	USA	
	VOICE OF THE OAS, Cincinnati, Ohio	C AMERICA & S AMERICA • 175/250 kW
	†WYFR-FAMILY RADIO, Okeechobee, Fl	(D) • S AMERICA • 100 kW W NORTH AM • 100 kW (D) • W NORTH AM • 100 kW (J) • S AMERICA • 100 kW (J) • C AMERICA • 100 kW
	USSR	
	RADIO MOSCOW, Moscow	(J) • EUROPE • WS • 240 kW
	VATICAN STATE	
	VATICAN RADIO, Sta Maria di Galeria	JAPANESE • ASIA & AUSTRALIA • 100 kW ASIA & AUSTRALIA • 100 kW
11835	**ALBANIA**	
	RADIO TIRANA, Lushnjë	C AFRICA & S AFRICA • 100 kW S ASIA & AUSTRALIA • 100 kW
	CUBA	
	†RADIO HABANA, Havana	(J) • W NORTH AM • 100 kW
	ECUADOR	
	†HCJB-VO THE ANDES, Quito	EUROPE & WEST USSR • 100 kW
	GERMANY (FR)	
	†DEUTSCHE WELLE, Via Sri Lanka	S ASIA & E ASIA • 250 kW (J) • S ASIA & E ASIA • 250 kW
	JAPAN	
	†RADIO JAPAN/NHK, Tokyo-Yamata	(J) • MIDEAST & N AFRICA • 300 kW (J) • EUROPE • 300 kW
	SRI LANKA	
	SRI LANKA BC CORP, Colombo-Ekala	SE ASIA & AUSTRALIA • 35 kW M • JAPANESE • SE ASIA & AUSTRALIA • 35 kW M/Tu/Th/F • SE ASIA & AUSTRALIA • 35 kW Sa • JAPANESE • SE ASIA & AUSTRALIA • 35 kW Su/W • SE ASIA & AUSTRALIA • 35 kW Tu-Su • SE ASIA & AUSTRALIA • 35 kW
	UNITED KINGDOM	
	†BBC, Via Maşīrah, Oman	(D) M-Sa • E EUROPE & MIDEAST • 100 kW (D) • E EUROPE & MIDEAST • GREEK, TURKISH • 100 kW
	†BBC, Via Zyyi, Cyprus	(J) • WEST USSR • 100 kW (D) Su • WEST USSR • 250 kW (J) Su • WEST USSR • 250 kW
	USA	
	VOA, Via Kavála, Greece	(D) • WEST USSR • 250 kW MIDEAST & S ASIA • HINDI,PERSIAN,ETC • 250 kW
	VOA, Via M'rovia, Liberia	C AFRICA & E AFRICA • 250 kW M-F • C AFRICA & E AFRICA • 250 kW
(con'd)		

World Time: 0 1 2 3 4 5 6 7 8 9 10 11 12 13 14 15 16 17 18 19 20 21 22 23 24

0 Prime Time-Americas 6 Prime Time-E Asia 12 Prime Time-S Asia 18 Prime Time-Europe 24

SUMMER ONLY (J) WINTER ONLY (D) JAMMING / OR /\ EARLIEST HEARD ◁ LATEST HEARD ▷ NEW OR CHANGED FOR 1990 †

FREQUENCY	COUNTRY, STATION, LOCATION	TARGET • NETWORK • POWER (kW)
11835 (con'd)	USA †VOA, Via Philippines	SE ASIA • 50 kW
	†VOA, Via Woofferton, UK	(D) • WEST USSR • 250 kW
		(J) • WEST USSR • 250 kW
	USSR RADIO MOSCOW, Armavir	(J) • S ASIA • 100 kW
	RADIO MOSCOW, Tashkent	(J) • S ASIA & SE ASIA • 500 kW
	YUGOSLAVIA †RADIO YUGOSLAVIA, Bijeljina	W AFRICA & S AMERICA • 500 kW
		N AFRICA • 500 kW
11835v	MOZAMBIQUE RADIO MOCAMBIQUE, Maputo	Irr • S AMERICA • 120 kW
11840	CANADA †R CANADA INTL, Via United Kingdom	(D) M-F • MIDEAST • 300 kW
	CHINA (PR) †RADIO BEIJING, Via Sackville, Can	(J) • N AMERICA • 250 kW
	GUAM †KTWR-TRANS WORLD R, Merizo	JAPANESE • E ASIA • 100 kW
	IRAQ †RADIO BAGHDAD, Balad-Salah el Deen	(D) • 500 kW
	JAPAN †RADIO JAPAN/NHK, Tokyo-Yamata	SE ASIA • 100 kW
		(J) • E ASIA • 100 kW
		E ASIA • GENERAL • 300 kW
		JAPANESE • E ASIA • GENERAL • 300 kW
		(D) • JAPANESE • E ASIA • GENERAL • 300 kW
		(J) • E ASIA • GENERAL • 300 kW
		(J) • JAPANESE • E ASIA • GENERAL • 300 kW
		(J) • JAPANESE • E ASIA • GENERAL • 100 kW
	OMAN RADIO OMAN, Sib	(J) • MIDEAST • DS • 100 kW
	POLAND †RADIO POLONIA, Warsaw	EUROPE & ATLANTIC • 100 kW
		W EUROPE & W AFRICA • 100 kW
		EUROPE & N AFRICA • 100 kW
	PORTUGAL †R PORTUGAL INTL, Lisbon-S Gabriel	S AMERICA • 100 kW
		M-F • W AFRICA • 100 kW
		Su/M • S AMERICA • 100 kW
		Tu-Sa • S AMERICA • 100 kW
	ROMANIA †RADIO BUCHAREST, Bucharest	(D) • AFRICA • 250 kW
	UNITED KINGDOM †BBC, Via Zyyi, Cyprus	(J) • E AFRICA • 250 kW
	USA VOA, Via Philippines	SE ASIA • 250 kW
	VOA, Via Wertachtal,GFR	N AFRICA • 500 kW
	USSR RADIO MOSCOW, Kenga	(J) • DS-1 • 50 kW
	RADIO MOSCOW, Via Havana, Cuba	N AMERICA • 100 kW
	RADIO MOSCOW, Vinnitsa	DS-2 • 100 kW
11845	CANADA R CANADA INTL, Sackville, NB	C AMERICA & S AMERICA • 250 kW
		Su/M • C AMERICA & S AMERICA • 250 kW
		Tu-Sa • C AMERICA & S AMERICA • 250 kW
		Tu-Sa • S AMERICA • 250 kW
	DENMARK †DANMARKS RADIO, Copenhagen	(D) • EUROPE & W AFRICA • 50 kW
		(D) • C AMERICA & S AMERICA • 50 kW
		(D) M-F • EUROPE & W AFRICA • DS • 50 kW
	FINLAND †RADIO FINLAND, Pori	Alternative Frequency to 11945 kHz
	FRANCE †R FRANCE INTL, Issoudun-Allouis	N AFRICA & W AFRICA • 100 kW
		W EUROPE & N AFRICA • 100 kW
	GERMANY (FR) †DEUTSCHE WELLE	(J) • N AMERICA & C AMERICA
	NORWAY †RADIO NORWAY INTL, Sveio	Alternative Frequency to 11850 kHz
		(J) M • S AMERICA • 500 kW
		(J) Tu-Su • S AMERICA • 500 kW
	UNITED KINGDOM †BBC, Various Locations	WEST USSR • 20/250/500 kW
	†BBC, Via Brasília	(D) • S AMERICA • 250 kW
	†BBC, Via Zyyi, Cyprus	(J) • E AFRICA • 250 kW
		(D) • WEST USSR • 20 kW
		(J) • WEST USSR • 250 kW
	USA †VOA, Via Kaválla, Greece	(D) • MIDEAST & S ASIA • 250 kW
(con'd)	USSR RADIO MOSCOW, Kazan'	(J) • S ASIA & SE ASIA • URDU, HINDI, ETC • 100 kW

World Time 0–24: 0 Prime Time-Americas 6 Prime Time-E Asia 12 Prime Time-S Asia 18 Prime Time-Europe 24

ENGLISH ARABIC CHINESE FRENCH GERMAN RUSSIAN SPANISH OTHER

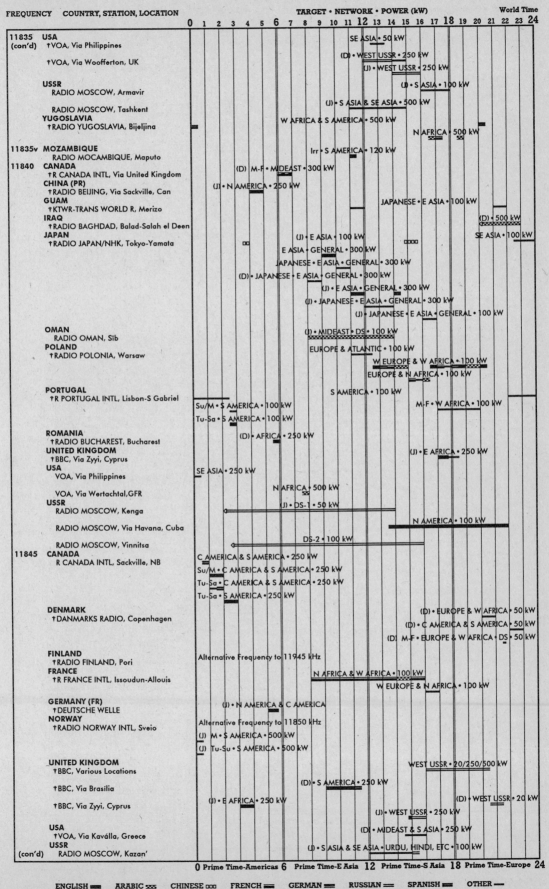

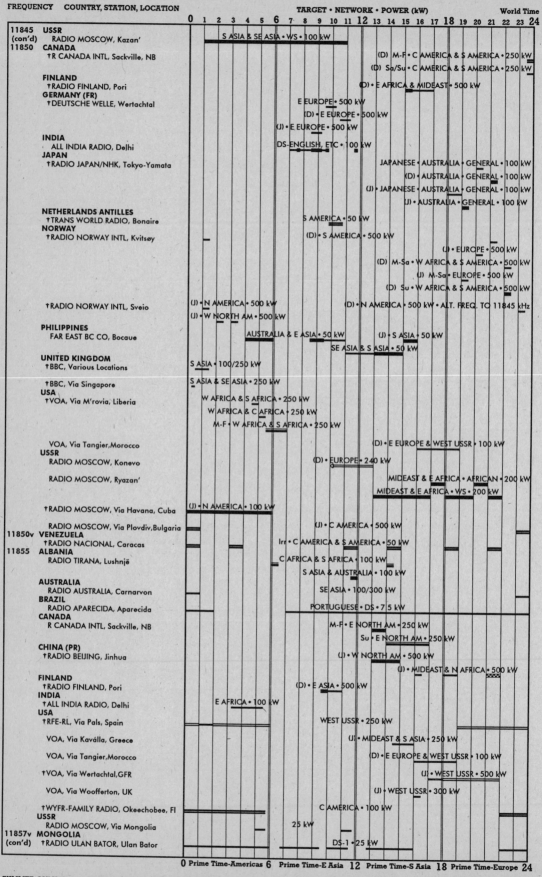

FREQUENCY	COUNTRY, STATION, LOCATION	TARGET • NETWORK • POWER (kW)
11845 (con'd)	**USSR** RADIO MOSCOW, Kazan'	S ASIA & SE ASIA • WS • 100 kW
11850	**CANADA** †R CANADA INTL, Sackville, NB	(D) M-F • C AMERICA & S AMERICA • 250 kW
		(D) Sa/Su • C AMERICA & S AMERICA • 250 kW
	FINLAND †RADIO FINLAND, Pori	(D) • E AFRICA & MIDEAST • 500 kW
	GERMANY (FR) †DEUTSCHE WELLE, Wertachtal	E EUROPE • 500 kW
		(D) • E EUROPE • 500 kW
		(J) • E EUROPE • 500 kW
	INDIA ALL INDIA RADIO, Delhi	DS-ENGLISH, ETC • 100 kW
	JAPAN †RADIO JAPAN/NHK, Tokyo-Yamata	JAPANESE • AUSTRALIA • GENERAL • 100 kW
		(D) • AUSTRALIA • GENERAL • 100 kW
		(J) • JAPANESE • AUSTRALIA • GENERAL • 100 kW
		(J) • AUSTRALIA • GENERAL • 100 kW
	NETHERLANDS ANTILLES †TRANS WORLD RADIO, Bonaire	S AMERICA • 50 kW
	NORWAY †RADIO NORWAY INTL, Kvitsøy	(D) • S AMERICA • 500 kW
		(J) • EUROPE • 500 kW
		(D) M-Sa • W AFRICA & S AMERICA • 500 kW
		(J) M-Sa • EUROPE • 500 kW
		(D) Su • W AFRICA & S AMERICA • 500 kW
	†RADIO NORWAY INTL, Sveio	(J) • N AMERICA • 500 kW
		(D) • N AMERICA • 500 kW • ALT. FREQ. TO 11845 kHz
		(J) • W NORTH AM • 500 kW
	PHILIPPINES FAR EAST BC CO, Bocaue	AUSTRALIA & E ASIA • 50 kW
		(J) • S ASIA • 50 kW
		SE ASIA & S ASIA • 50 kW
	UNITED KINGDOM †BBC, Various Locations	S ASIA • 100/250 kW
	†BBC, Via Singapore	S ASIA & SE ASIA • 250 kW
	USA †VOA, Via M'rovia, Liberia	W AFRICA & S AFRICA • 250 kW
		W AFRICA & C AFRICA • 250 kW
		M-F • W AFRICA & S AFRICA • 250 kW
	VOA, Via Tangier, Morocco	(D) • E EUROPE & WEST USSR • 100 kW
	USSR RADIO MOSCOW, Konevo	(D) • EUROPE • 240 kW
	RADIO MOSCOW, Ryazan'	MIDEAST & E AFRICA • AFRICAN • 200 kW
		MIDEAST & E AFRICA • WS • 200 kW
	†RADIO MOSCOW, Via Havana, Cuba	(J) • N AMERICA • 100 kW
	RADIO MOSCOW, Via Plovdiv, Bulgaria	(J) • C AMERICA • 500 kW
11850v	**VENEZUELA** †RADIO NACIONAL, Caracas	Irr • C AMERICA & S AMERICA • 50 kW
11855	**ALBANIA** RADIO TIRANA, Lushnjë	C AFRICA & S AFRICA • 100 kW
		S ASIA & AUSTRALIA • 100 kW
	AUSTRALIA RADIO AUSTRALIA, Carnarvon	SE ASIA • 100/300 kW
	BRAZIL RADIO APARECIDA, Aparecida	PORTUGUESE • DS • 7.5 kW
	CANADA R CANADA INTL, Sackville, NB	M-F • E NORTH AM • 250 kW
		Su • E NORTH AM • 250 kW
	CHINA (PR) †RADIO BEIJING, Jinhua	(J) • W NORTH AM • 500 kW
		(J) • MIDEAST & N AFRICA • 500 kW
	FINLAND †RADIO FINLAND, Pori	(D) • E ASIA • 500 kW
	INDIA †ALL INDIA RADIO, Delhi	E AFRICA • 100 kW
	USA †RFE-RL, Via Pals, Spain	WEST USSR • 250 kW
	VOA, Via Kaválla, Greece	(J) • MIDEAST & S ASIA • 250 kW
	VOA, Via Tangier, Morocco	(D) • E EUROPE & WEST USSR • 100 kW
	†VOA, Via Wertachtal, GFR	(J) • WEST USSR • 500 kW
	VOA, Via Woofferton, UK	(J) • WEST USSR • 300 kW
	†WYFR-FAMILY RADIO, Okeechobee, Fl	C AMERICA • 100 kW
	USSR RADIO MOSCOW, Via Mongolia	25 kW
11857v (con'd)	**MONGOLIA** †RADIO ULAN BATOR, Ulan Bator	DS-1 • 25 kW

World Time: 0 Prime Time-Americas 6 Prime Time-E Asia 12 Prime Time-S Asia 18 Prime Time-Europe 24

SUMMER ONLY (J) WINTER ONLY (D) JAMMING / OR /\ EARLIEST HEARD ◁ LATEST HEARD ▷ NEW OR CHANGED FOR 1990 †

FREQUENCY | COUNTRY, STATION, LOCATION | TARGET • NETWORK • POWER (kW) | World Time 0 1 2 3 4 5 6 7 8 9 10 11 12 13 14 15 16 17 18 19 20 21 22 23 24

11857v (con'd) MONGOLIA
†RADIO ULAN BATOR, Ulan Bator
Tu/F • DS-1 • 25 kW
W/Th/Sa/M • DS-1 • 25 kW

USSR
†RADIO MOSCOW, Via Mongolia
25 kW

11860 BULGARIA
†RADIO SOFIA, Sofia
EUROPE • 250 kW
(D) • S AMERICA • 250 kW
Su • EUROPE • 250 kW

CHINA (TAIWAN)
VO FREE CHINA, T'ai-pei
SE ASIA
MIDEAST & N AFRICA

INDIA
ALL INDIA RADIO, Aligarh
AUSTRALIA • 250 kW
W AFRICA • 250 kW

IRAQ
†RADIO BAGHDAD, Balad-Salah el Deen
(D) • MIDEAST • 500 kW

SEYCHELLES
FAR EAST BC ASS'N, North Pt, Mahé Is
E AFRICA & S AFRICA • 50 kW
E AFRICA • 25 kW
Sa/Su • E AFRICA • 25 kW

UNITED KINGDOM
†BBC, Via Ascension
C AFRICA • 250 kW
(J) • S AFRICA • 250 kW
M-Sa • C AFRICA • 250 kW

†BBC, Via Seychelles
E AFRICA & S AFRICA • 250 kW
E AFRICA • 250 kW

USA
KNLS-NEW LIFE STN, Anchor Pt, Alaska
(J) • EAST USSR • 100 kW

USSR
†"RADIO MAGALLANES", Via R Moscow
(J) • S AMERICA • 500 kW

R TIKHIY OKEAN, Krasnoyarsk
(J) • E ASIA & PACIFIC • MARINERS • 100 kW

RADIO KIEV, Khabarovsk
(D) • W NORTH AM • 100 kW

RADIO MOSCOW, Gor'kiy
(D) • S ASIA • TAMIL,SINHALA,ETC • 240 kW
(J) • MIDEAST & S ASIA • WS, ARABIC • 240 kW

RADIO MOSCOW, Khabarovsk
(D) • W NORTH AM • MARINERS • 100 kW

RADIO MOSCOW, Krasnoyarsk
(J) • E ASIA • 100 kW

RADIO VILNIUS, Khabarovsk
(D) • W NORTH AM • 100 kW

RADIO YEREVAN, Khabarovsk
(D) • W NORTH AM • 100 kW

11865 CHINA (PR)
CENTRAL PEOPLES BS
(J) • DS-MINORITIES

GERMANY (FR)
†DEUTSCHE WELLE, Jülich
S AMERICA • 100 kW
MIDEAST • 100 kW
(D) • WEST USSR • 100 kW
(J) • MIDEAST • 100 kW

†DEUTSCHE WELLE, Multiple Locations
N AMERICA & C AMERICA • 100/250 kW
C AMERICA & S AMERICA • 100/250 kW

†DEUTSCHE WELLE, Via Cyclops, Malta
(D) • E ASIA • 250 kW

†DEUTSCHE WELLE, Via Sines, Portugal
E EUROPE • 250 kW
(D) • E EUROPE • 250 kW

†DEUTSCHE WELLE, Wertachtal
(D) • MIDEAST & S ASIA • 500 kW
(J) • WEST USSR • 500 kW

JAPAN
†RADIO JAPAN/NHK, Tokyo-Yamata
(J) • JAPANESE • PACIFIC & N AMERICA • GENERAL • 300 kW
(J) • PACIFIC & N AMERICA • GENERAL • 300 kW

PHILIPPINES
FAR EAST BC CO, Bocaue
SE ASIA • 50 kW

SEYCHELLES
FAR EAST BC ASS'N, North Pt, Mahé Is
S ASIA • 25/50/100 kW

UNITED KINGDOM
†BBC, Via Antigua
(J) M-F • S AMERICA • 250 kW

†BBC, Via Zyyi, Cyprus
(D) M-F • E EUROPE • 100 kW
(D) M-Sa • E EUROPE • 100 kW

USA
†VOA, Via Woofferton, UK
E EUROPE & WEST USSR • 250/300 kW
(D) • E EUROPE & WEST USSR • 250 kW

USSR
RADIO MOSCOW, Novosibirsk
(J) • DS-2 • 100 kW

11870 ALBANIA
RADIO TIRANA, Lushnjë
S AMERICA • 100 kW
MIDEAST • TURKISH • 100 kW

BULGARIA
†RADIO SOFIA, Plovdiv
(D) • MIDEAST • 500 kW
(J) • MIDEAST • ARABIC,TURKISH,ETC • 500 kW

(con'd)

0 Prime Time-Americas 6 Prime Time-E Asia 12 Prime Time-S Asia 18 Prime Time-Europe 24

ENGLISH ARABIC CHINESE FRENCH GERMAN RUSSIAN SPANISH OTHER

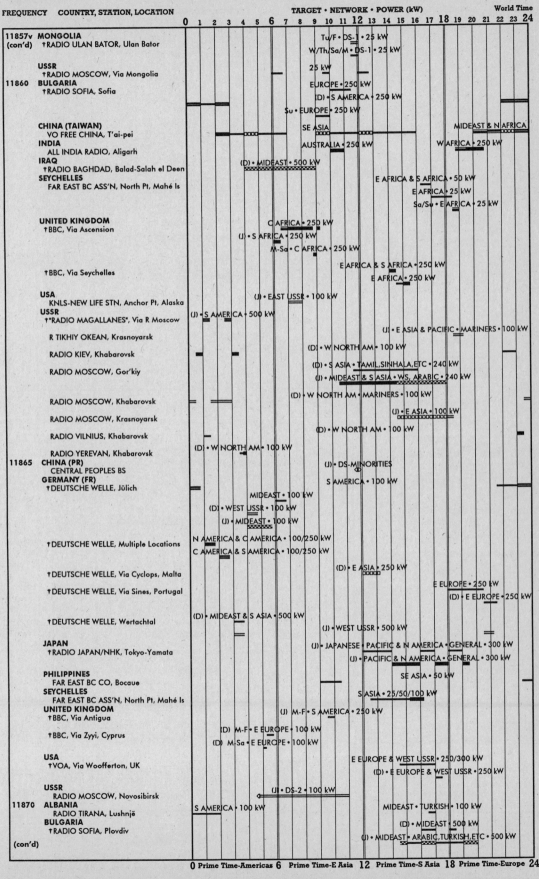

FREQUENCY	COUNTRY, STATION, LOCATION	TARGET • NETWORK • POWER (kW)
11870 (con'd)	**BULGARIA** RADIO SOFIA, Sofia	(J) • C AMERICA & S AMERICA • 250 kW
	CLANDESTINE (ASIA) "DEM KAMPUCHEA", Kunming, China	SE ASIA • PRO-KHMER ROUGE • 50 kW
	COSTA RICA †ADVENTIST WORLD R, Alajuela	C AMERICA • 40 kW
	INDIA ALL INDIA RADIO, Delhi	E ASIA • 100 kW
		Su • DS • 100 kW
		DS-ENGLISH, ETC • 100 kW
	JAPAN †RADIO JAPAN/NHK, Tokyo-Yamata	(D) • JAPANESE • W NORTH AM • 100 kW
		(D) • W NORTH AM • 100 kW
		(D) • JAPANESE • W NORTH AM • GENERAL • 100 kW
		(D) • W NORTH AM • GENERAL • 100 kW
	LAOS LAO NATIONAL RADIO, Via USSR	(D) • EUROPE • 240 kW
	MONGOLIA †RADIO ULAN BATOR, Ulan Bator	M/Tu/Th/F • AFRICA • 250 kW
	SEYCHELLES FAR EAST BC ASS'N, North Pt, Mahé Is	MIDEAST • 100 kW
	USA †VOA, Via Philippines	AUSTRALIA • 50/250 kW
		(J) • AUSTRALIA • 50/250 kW
	USSR RADIO MOSCOW, Khabarovsk	(J) • E ASIA & SE ASIA • CHI, CANTONESE, ETC • 240 kW
11875	**CUBA** RADIO HABANA, Havana	(J) • S AMERICA • 250 kW
	EGYPT RADIO CAIRO, Kafr Silîm-Abis	S AFRICA • 250 kW
	JAPAN †RADIO JAPAN/NHK, Tokyo-Yamata	SE ASIA • 100 kW
		(J) • S AMERICA • 100 kW
		(D) • JAPANESE • S AMERICA • GENERAL • 300 kW
	TURKEY †TURKISH RTV CORP, Ankara	EUROPE • 250 kW
	USA †RFE-RL, Via Germany	WEST USSR • 100 kW
	†VOA, Via Kavála, Greece	M-F • N AFRICA • 250 kW
	†VOA, Via Woofferton, UK	(J) • N AFRICA • 300 kW
11880	**CANADA** R CANADA INTL, Sackville, NB	AFRICA • 250 kW
	EGYPT RADIO CAIRO, Kafr Silîm-Abis	EUROPE • DS-NILE VALLEY • 250 kW
		EUROPE • DS-VO THE ARABS • 250 kW
	INDIA †ALL INDIA RADIO, Delhi	SE ASIA • 100 kW
	IRAQ †RADIO BAGHDAD, Balad-Salah el Deen	(D) • N AMERICA • 500 kW
		(D) • S AMERICA • 500 kW
	SOUTH AFRICA †SOUTH AFRICAN BC, Meyerton	DS-RADIO FIVE • 100 kW
	SPAIN †R NACIONAL ESPANA, Noblejas	(D) • E NORTH AM & C AMERICA • 350 kW
	USA †VOA, Greenville, NC	(J) • M-F • C AMERICA • 250 kW
	†VOA, Via Philippines	SE ASIA • 50 kW
	USSR RADIO MOSCOW, Moscow	(J) • EUROPE • 240 kW
		(J) • S ASIA • TAMIL, ETC • 240 kW
	ZAMBIA †RADIO ZAMBIA-ZBS, Lusaka	Su • S AFRICA • 50 kW
11885	**CHINA (TAIWAN)** VO FREE CHINA, Via Okeechobee, USA	(D) • S AMERICA • 100 kW
	JAPAN †RADIO JAPAN/NHK, Tokyo-Yamata	(D) • AUSTRALIA • 100 kW
	MALAYSIA †VOICE OF MALAYSIA, Kajang	E ASIA • 500 kW
	NETHERLANDS ANTILLES †TRANS WORLD RADIO, Bonaire	S AMERICA • 100 kW
	USA †R FREE AFGHANISTAN, Via Germany	WEST USSR & S ASIA • 250 kW
	†RFE-RL, Via Germany	WEST USSR • 250 kW
	†RFE-RL, Via Pals, Spain	WEST USSR • 250 kW
	†RFE-RL, Via Portugal	WEST USSR • 250 kW
	†WYFR-FAMILY RADIO, Okeechobee, Fl	(J) • S AMERICA • 100 kW
	USSR R TIKHIY OKEAN, Novosibirsk	(J) • E ASIA & PACIFIC • MARINERS • 200 kW
	RADIO MOSCOW, Novosibirsk	(J) • E ASIA • CHI, MONGOLIAN, ETC • 200 kW
11890	**DENMARK** †DANMARKS RADIO, Copenhagen	(D) • ATLANTIC & N AMERICA • DS • 50 kW
(con'd)		(D) Sa/Su • ATLANTIC & N AMERICA • DS • 50 kW

World Time 0–24: 0 Prime Time-Americas 6 Prime Time-E Asia 12 Prime Time-S Asia 18 Prime Time-Europe 24

SUMMER ONLY (J) WINTER ONLY (D) JAMMING / OR /\ EARLIEST HEARD ◁ LATEST HEARD ▷ NEW OR CHANGED FOR 1990 †

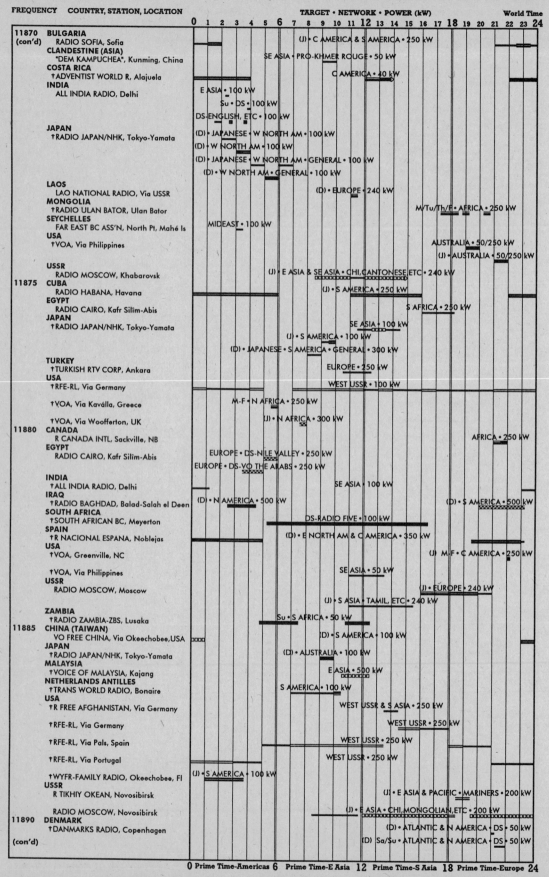

FREQUENCY | COUNTRY, STATION, LOCATION | TARGET • NETWORK • POWER (kW) | World Time

0 1 2 3 4 5 6 7 8 9 10 11 12 13 14 15 16 17 18 19 20 21 22 23 24

11890 (con'd) **GERMANY (DR)**
†R BERLIN INTL, Nauen
- N AMERICA • 100 kW
- S AMERICA • 100 kW

ICELAND
RIKISUTVARPID, Reykjavik
- (D) • ATLANTIC & E NORTH AM • DS-1 • 10 kW • USB
- Sa/Su • ATLANTIC & E NORTH AM • DS-1 • 10 kW • USB

OMAN
†RADIO OMAN, Sīb
- E AFRICA • DS • 50 kW

SPAIN
†R NACIONAL ESPANA, Noblejas
- N AFRICA & W AFRICA • 350 kW

USA
†VOA, Cincinnati, Ohio
- W AFRICA • 250 kW
- M-F • W AFRICA • 250 kW

†VOA, Greenville, NC
- C AMERICA • 500 kW
- (D) • C AMERICA • 500 kW
- (J) • C AMERICA • 500 kW
- (D) M-F • C AMERICA • 500 kW
- (J) M-F • C AMERICA • 250 kW
- Sa/Su • C AMERICA • 500 kW

USSR
†"RADIO MAGALLANES", Via R Moscow
- (J) • S AMERICA • 240 kW

RADIO MOSCOW, Kingisepp
- (J) • S ASIA • RUSSIAN, URDU • 240 kW

RADIO MOSCOW, Ryazan'
- (D) • EUROPE & W AFRICA • 240 kW
- (J) • E EUROPE • GREEK, ETC • 240 kW
- (D) • SE ASIA • VIETNAMESE, ETC • 240 kW

11895 **BRAZIL**
†R NOVA ESPERANÇA, Pôrto Alegre
- PORTUGUESE • DS • 5 kW

FRANCE
†R FRANCE INTL, Via Beijing, China
- SE ASIA • 120 kW

IRAN
†VO THE ISLAMIC REP, Tehrān
- (J) • EUROPE & MIDEAST • 500 kW

IRAQ
RADIO BAGHDAD
- (J)

SEYCHELLES
FAR EAST BC ASS'N, North Pt, Mahé Is
- S ASIA • 100 kW

SRI LANKA
†SRI LANKA BC CORP, Colombo-Ekala
- S ASIA • 35 kW

USA
†R FREE AFGHANISTAN, Via Portugal
- WEST USSR & S ASIA • 250 kW

†RFE-RL, Via Portugal
- E EUROPE & WEST USSR • 250 kW
- M-F • E EUROPE • 250 kW
- Sa/Su • WEST USSR • 250 kW

VOA, Greenville, NC
- C AMERICA & S AMERICA • 500 kW

11900 **ECUADOR**
HCJB-VO THE ANDES, Quito
- S AMERICA • 100 kW

SOUTH AFRICA
†RADIO RSA, Meyerton
- E AFRICA • 250 kW
- E AFRICA • 250/500 kW
- S AFRICA & W AFRICA • 250 kW
- (D) • S AFRICA • 250 kW
- (D) • S AFRICA & W AFRICA • 500 kW
- (J) • E AFRICA & MIDEAST • 250 kW

UNITED KINGDOM
†BBC, Via Zyyi, Cyprus
- (J) • WEST USSR • 250 kW

USA
VOA, Via Woofferton, UK
- (J) • WEST USSR • 300 kW

USSR
R TIKHIY OKEAN, Komsomol'sk 'Amure
- (D) • PACIFIC • MARINERS • 100 kW
- (D) Sa • PACIFIC • MARINERS • 100 kW
- (D) Su-F • PACIFIC • MARINERS • 100 kW

RADIO MOSCOW, Dushanbé
- (J) • S AMERICA • 240 kW
- (J) • N AFRICA & W AFRICA • 500 kW
- (J) • MIDEAST & N AFRICA • 240 kW

RADIO MOSCOW, Komsomol'sk 'Amure
- (D) • PACIFIC • 100 kW

RADIO MOSCOW, L'vov
- (D) • EUROPE • WS • 240 kW

RADIO MOSCOW, Tbilisi
- (J) • DS-2 • 100 kW

11905 **CANADA**
R CANADA INTL, Sackville, NB
- (J) • E NORTH AM & C AMERICA • 250 kW

CHINA (TAIWAN)
†CENTRAL BC SYSTEM, T'ai-pei
- PRC-1 • 100 kW
- PRC-6 • 100 kW

EGYPT
RADIO CAIRO, Abu Za'bal
- MIDEAST • DS-VO THE ARABS • 250 kW

RADIO CAIRO, Multiple Locations
- EUROPE & MIDEAST • DS-NILE VALLEY • 100/250 kW
- EUROPE & MIDEAST • DS-VO THE ARABS • 100/250 kW

GERMANY (FR)
†DEUTSCHE WELLE, Jülich
- N AFRICA • 100 kW
- (D) • WEST USSR • 100 kW
- E EUROPE • 100 kW
- (D) • E EUROPE • 100 kW

(con'd)

0 Prime Time-Americas 6 Prime Time-E Asia 12 Prime Time-S Asia 18 Prime Time-Europe 24

ENGLISH ▬ ARABIC ▩ CHINESE ▭ FRENCH ═ GERMAN ▬ RUSSIAN ═ SPANISH ▬ OTHER —

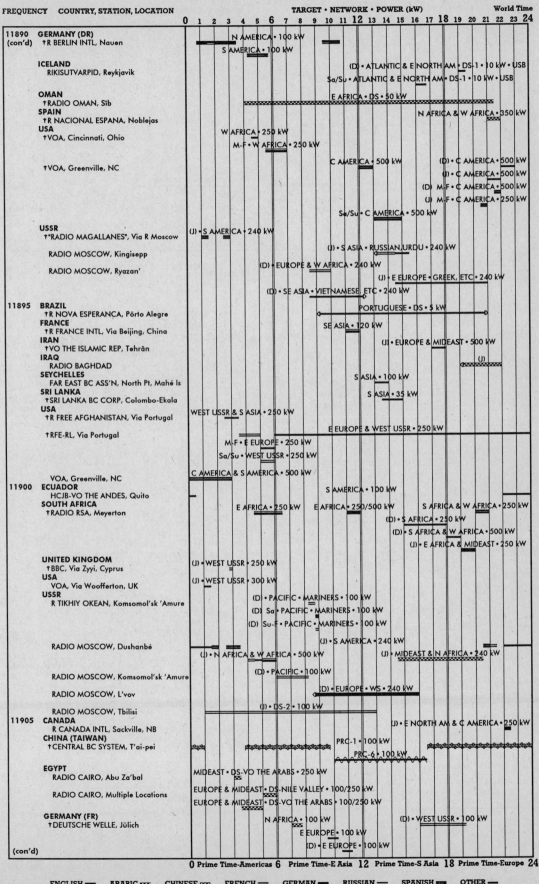

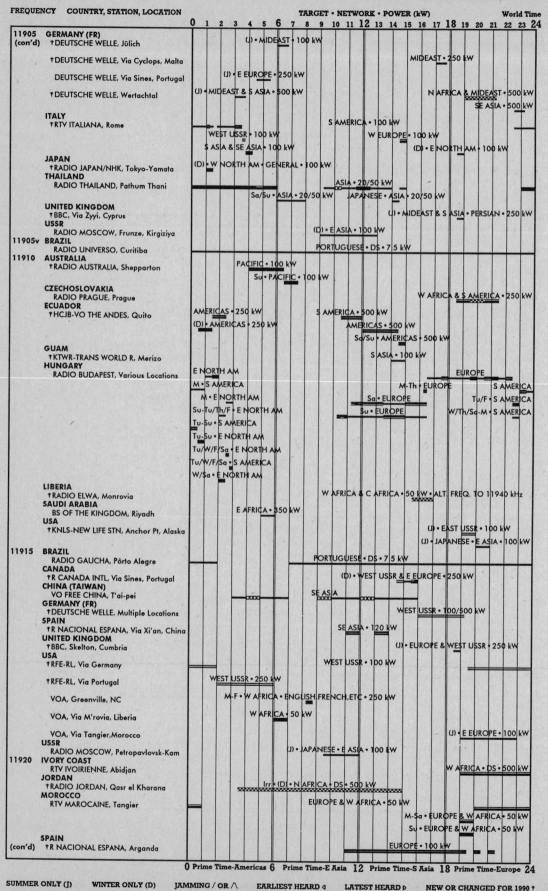

FREQUENCY	COUNTRY, STATION, LOCATION	TARGET • NETWORK • POWER (kW) — World Time 0–24
11905 (con'd)	**GERMANY (FR)** †DEUTSCHE WELLE, Jülich	(J) • MIDEAST • 100 kW
	†DEUTSCHE WELLE, Via Cyclops, Malta	MIDEAST • 250 kW
	DEUTSCHE WELLE, Via Sines, Portugal	(J) • E EUROPE • 250 kW
	†DEUTSCHE WELLE, Wertachtal	(J) • MIDEAST & S ASIA • 500 kW; N AFRICA & MIDEAST • 500 kW; SE ASIA • 500 kW
	ITALY †RTV ITALIANA, Rome	S AMERICA • 100 kW; WEST USSR • 100 kW; W EUROPE • 100 kW; S ASIA & SE ASIA • 100 kW; (D) • E NORTH AM • 100 kW
	JAPAN †RADIO JAPAN/NHK, Tokyo-Yamata	(D) • W NORTH AM • GENERAL • 100 kW
	THAILAND RADIO THAILAND, Pathum Thani	ASIA • 20/50 kW; Sa/Su • ASIA • 20/50 kW; JAPANESE • ASIA • 20/50 kW
	UNITED KINGDOM †BBC, Via Zyyi, Cyprus	(J) • MIDEAST & S ASIA • PERSIAN • 250 kW
	USSR RADIO MOSCOW, Frunze, Kirgiziya	(D) • E ASIA • 100 kW
11905v	**BRAZIL** RADIO UNIVERSO, Curitiba	PORTUGUESE • DS • 7.5 kW
11910	**AUSTRALIA** †RADIO AUSTRALIA, Shepparton	PACIFIC • 100 kW; Su • PACIFIC • 100 kW
	CZECHOSLOVAKIA RADIO PRAGUE, Prague	W AFRICA & S AMERICA • 250 kW
	ECUADOR †HCJB-VO THE ANDES, Quito	AMERICAS • 250 kW; (D) • AMERICAS • 250 kW; S AMERICA • 500 kW; AMERICAS • 500 kW; Sa/Su • AMERICAS • 500 kW
	GUAM †KTWR-TRANS WORLD R, Merizo	S ASIA • 100 kW
	HUNGARY RADIO BUDAPEST, Various Locations	E NORTH AM; EUROPE; M • S AMERICA; M-Th • EUROPE; S AMERICA; M • E NORTH AM; Sa • EUROPE; Tu/F • S AMERICA; Su-Tu/Th/F • E NORTH AM; Su • EUROPE; W/Th/Sa-M • S AMERICA; Tu-Su • S AMERICA; Tu-Su • E NORTH AM; Tu/W/F/Sa • E NORTH AM; Tu/W/F/Sa • S AMERICA; W/Sa • E NORTH AM
	LIBERIA †RADIO ELWA, Monrovia	W AFRICA & C AFRICA • 50 kW • ALT. FREQ. TO 11940 kHz
	SAUDI ARABIA BS OF THE KINGDOM, Riyadh	E AFRICA • 350 kW
	USA †KNLS-NEW LIFE STN, Anchor Pt, Alaska	(J) • EAST USSR • 100 kW; (J) • JAPANESE • E ASIA • 100 kW
11915	**BRAZIL** RADIO GAUCHA, Pôrto Alegre	PORTUGUESE • DS • 7.5 kW
	CANADA †R CANADA INTL, Via Sines, Portugal	(D) • WEST USSR & E EUROPE • 250 kW
	CHINA (TAIWAN) VO FREE CHINA, T'ai-pei	SE ASIA
	GERMANY (FR) †DEUTSCHE WELLE, Multiple Locations	WEST USSR • 100/500 kW
	SPAIN †R NACIONAL ESPANA, Via Xi'an, China	SE ASIA • 120 kW
	UNITED KINGDOM †BBC, Skelton, Cumbria	(J) • EUROPE & WEST USSR • 250 kW
	USA †RFE-RL, Via Germany	WEST USSR • 100 kW
	†RFE-RL, Via Portugal	WEST USSR • 250 kW
	VOA, Greenville, NC	M-F • W AFRICA • ENGLISH, FRENCH, ETC • 250 kW
	VOA, Via M'rovia, Liberia	W AFRICA • 50 kW
	VOA, Via Tangier, Morocco	(J) • E EUROPE • 100 kW
	USSR RADIO MOSCOW, Petropavlovsk-Kam	(J) • JAPANESE • E ASIA • 100 kW
11920	**IVORY COAST** RTV IVOIRIENNE, Abidjan	W AFRICA • DS • 500 kW
	JORDAN †RADIO JORDAN, Qasr el Kharana	Irr • (D) • N AFRICA • DS • 500 kW
	MOROCCO RTV MAROCAINE, Tangier	EUROPE & W AFRICA • 50 kW; M-Sa • EUROPE & W AFRICA • 50 kW; Su • EUROPE & W AFRICA • 50 kW
(con'd)	**SPAIN** †R NACIONAL ESPANA, Arganda	EUROPE • 100 kW

0 Prime Time-Americas 6 Prime Time-E Asia 12 Prime Time-S Asia 18 Prime Time-Europe 24

SUMMER ONLY (J) WINTER ONLY (D) JAMMING / OR /\ EARLIEST HEARD ◁ LATEST HEARD ▷ NEW OR CHANGED FOR 1990 †

FREQUENCY	COUNTRY, STATION, LOCATION	TARGET • NETWORK • POWER (kW)
11920 (con'd)	SPAIN	
	†R NACIONAL ESPANA, Arganda	(D) • EUROPE • 100 kW
		(J) • EUROPE • 100 kW
	†R NACIONAL ESPANA, Noblejas	(D) • EUROPE • 350 kW
		(J) • EUROPE • 350 kW
		(D) M-F • EUROPE • 350 kW
		(J) M-F • EUROPE • 350 kW
	UNITED KINGDOM	
	†BBC, Via Antigua	(J) • C AMERICA • 250 kW
	†BBC, Via Maṣīrah, Oman	MIDEAST & S ASIA • 100 kW
	†BBC, Via Singapore	SE ASIA & E ASIA • 100 kW
		S ASIA • 100 kW
		M-Sa • S ASIA • 100 kW
	USA	
	VOA, Via Philippines	E AFRICA • 250 kW
	USSR	
	RADIO MOSCOW, Novosibirsk	(J) • DS-2 • 100 kW
	RADIO MOSCOW, Tashkent	(J) • S AMERICA • 500 kW
		(J) M/W/Th/Sa • S AMERICA • 500 kW
		(J) Su/Tu/F • S AMERICA • 500 kW
11925	BRAZIL	
	RADIO BANDEIRANTES, São Paulo	PORTUGUESE • DS • 10 kW
		Irr • PORTUGUESE • DS • 10 kW
	CHINA (PR)	
	CENTRAL PEOPLES BS, Beijing	TAIWAN-1 • 50 kW
	ECUADOR	
	HCJB-VO THE ANDES, Quito	AUSTRALIA & PACIFIC • 100 kW
	FINLAND	
	†RADIO FINLAND, Pori	(J) • E EUROPE & WEST USSR • 250 kW
	FRANCE	
	†R FRANCE INTL, Via Xi'an, China	(J) • S ASIA • 150 kW
	INDIA	
	†ALL INDIA RADIO, Delhi	(D) • E ASIA • 100 kW
	MALTA	
	†VO MEDITERRANEAN, Cyclops	EUROPE, N AFRICA & MIDEAST • 250 kW
	PHILIPPINES	
	RADIO VERITAS ASIA, Malolos	SE ASIA • 100 kW
	SOUTH AFRICA	
	†RADIO RSA, Meyerton	S AFRICA • 250 kW
		E AFRICA • 250 kW
		S AFRICA • 250/500 kW
	TURKEY	
	†TURKISH RTV CORP, Ankara	TURKISH • WEST USSR • 250 kW
	UNITED KINGDOM	
	†BBC, Skelton, Cumbria	(J) • E EUROPE & MIDEAST • 250 kW
		(J) M-Sa • E EUROPE & MIDEAST • 250 kW
	USA	
	†RFE-RL, Via Germany	WEST USSR • 250 kW
	†VOA, Via Kavála, Greece	(J) • MIDEAST & S ASIA • 250 kW
	†VOA, Via Philippines	E ASIA • 250 kW
	VOA, Via Woofferton, UK	(D) • EUROPE • GREEK • 300 kW
	USSR	
	RADIO MOSCOW, Krasnoyarsk	(D) • E ASIA & SE ASIA • 500 kW
11930	CUBA	
	RADIO HABANA, Havana	(J) • C AMERICA • 50 kW
	FRANCE	
	†R FRANCE INTL, Issoudun-Allouis	(D) • AFRICA • 500 kW
	HOLLAND	
	†RADIO NEDERLAND, Flevoland	(D) • W EUROPE • 500 kW
	IRAN	
	†VO THE ISLAMIC REP, Tehrān	(J) • EUROPE & C AMERICA • 100 kW
	NETHERLANDS ANTILLES	
	†TRANS WORLD RADIO, Bonaire	N AMERICA • 100 kW
		Su/M • N AMERICA • 100 kW
		Tu-Sa • C AMERICA • 100 kW
	SRI LANKA	
	†SRI LANKA BC CORP, Colombo-Ekala	S ASIA • 35 kW
	SWAZILAND	
	†TRANS WORLD RADIO, Manzini	(J) • E AFRICA • 100 kW
	USA	
	KNLS-NEW LIFE STN, Anchor Pt, Alaska	(J) • E ASIA • 100 kW
	RADIO MARTI, Greenville, NC	C AMERICA • 500 kW
	VOA, Via Philippines	EAST USSR • 250 kW
		SE ASIA • 250 kW
	†WSHB, Cypress Creek, SC	C AMERICA • 500 kW
		M-F • C AMERICA • 500 kW
		Sa/Su • C AMERICA • 500 kW
(con'd)		

World Time: 0 Prime Time-Americas 6 Prime Time-E Asia 12 Prime Time-S Asia 18 Prime Time-Europe 24

ENGLISH ▬ ARABIC ▭ CHINESE ▫ FRENCH ═ GERMAN ═ RUSSIAN ═ SPANISH ═ OTHER —

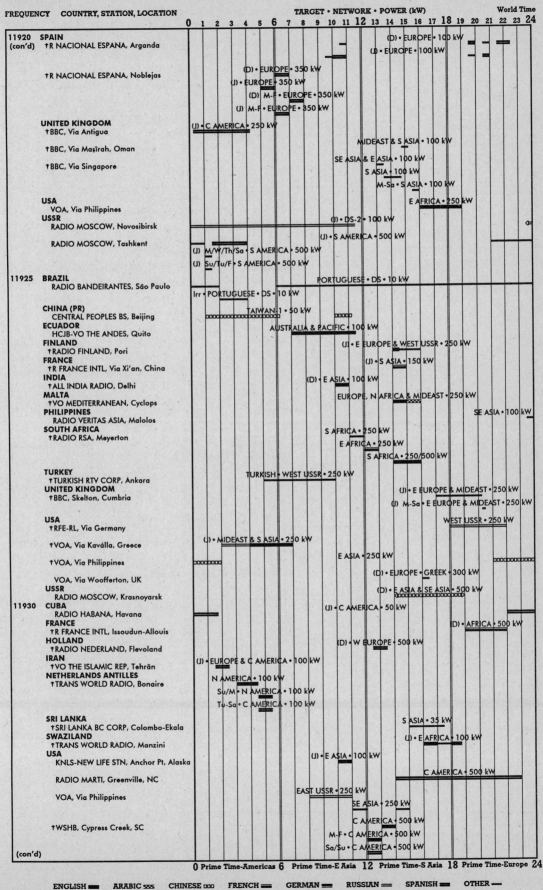

FREQUENCY	COUNTRY, STATION, LOCATION	TARGET • NETWORK • POWER (kW)
11930 (con'd)	**USSR** RADIO MOSCOW, Armavir	(D) • DS-1 • 100 kW
	RADIO MOSCOW, Ashkhabad	(J) • C AMERICA & S AMERICA • 100 kW
		(J) • EUROPE • 500 kW
11935	**ALBANIA** RADIO TIRANA, Lushnjë	SE ASIA • INDONESIAN • 100 kW
	CANADA †R CANADA INTL, Via United Kingdom	(D) • EUROPE & WEST USSR • 300 kW
		(J) • EUROPE & WEST USSR • 300 kW
	HOLLAND RADIO NEDERLAND, Flevoland	EUROPE, N AFRICA & MIDEAST • 500 kW
	INDIA ALL INDIA RADIO, Aligarh	WEST USSR • 250 kW
	ALL INDIA RADIO, Delhi	DS-ENGLISH, ETC • 20 kW
		E AFRICA & S AFRICA • 100 kW
	JAPAN RADIO JAPAN/NHK, Tokyo-Yamata	(D) • S ASIA & E AFRICA • 100 kW
		(D) • JAPANESE • S ASIA • GENERAL • 100 kW
		(D) • S ASIA • GENERAL • 100 kW
	SWITZERLAND RED CROSS BC SVC, Schwarzenburg	Irr • (D) M/Th • E ASIA • 150 kW
	†SWISS RADIO INTL, Schwarzenburg	(D) • E ASIA • 150 kW
	USA †RFE-RL, Via Pals, Spain	WEST USSR • 250 kW
	†VOA, Greenville, NC	S AMERICA • 500 kW
11937.7	**CAMBODIA** VO THE PEOPLE, Phnom Penh	SE ASIA • 50 kW
11940	**ALBANIA** RADIO TIRANA, Lushnjë	WEST USSR • 100 kW
	CANADA †R CANADA INTL, Sackville, NB	S AMERICA • 250 kW
		Su/M • S AMERICA • 250 kW
		Tu-Sa • S AMERICA • 250 kW
		(D) • S AMERICA • 250 kW
		M-F • S AMERICA • 250 kW
		Sa/Su • S AMERICA • 250 kW
	GABON AFRIQUE NUMERO UN, Moyabi	W AFRICA • 250 kW
	JORDAN †RADIO JORDAN, Qasr el Kharana	MIDEAST & E AFRICA • DS • 500 kW
	LIBERIA †RADIO ELWA, Monrovia	Alternative Frequency to 11910 kHz
	ROMANIA †RADIO BUCHAREST, Bucharest	AMERICAS • 250 kW
		AUSTRALIA • 250 kW
		EUROPE • 120 kW
		(D) • AFRICA • 250 kW
		(D) • E AFRICA & S AFRICA • 250 kW
		MIDEAST & S ASIA • 250 kW
		(D) • N AFRICA & W AFRICA • 250 kW
		(J) • MIDEAST & S ASIA • 250 kW
		(D) Su • AFRICA • MARINERS • 250 kW
		(J) • EUROPE • 120 kW
		(J) Su • W EUROPE & ATLANTIC • MARINERS • 250 kW
	SINGAPORE SINGAPORE BC CORP, Jurong	SE ASIA & PACIFIC • DS-1 • 50 kW
	UNITED ARAB EMIRATES UAE RADIO, Dubai	C AMERICA • 300 kW
	UNITED KINGDOM †BBC, Via Maseru, Lesotho	S AFRICA • 100 kW • ALT. FREQ. TO 9515 kHz
		F-Su • S AFRICA • 100 kW • ALT. FREQ. TO 9515 kHz
	USSR RADIO MOSCOW, Blagoveshchensk	(J) • E ASIA & SE ASIA • 240 kW
	RADIO MOSCOW, Simferopol'	(J) • DS-1 • 100 kW
11944.8	**PARAGUAY** †RADIO ENCARNACION, Encarnación	DS • 0.5 kW
11945	**CANADA** R CANADA INTL, Sackville, NB	(D) • EUROPE • 250 kW
		(J) • EUROPE • 250 kW
		(D) M-F • EUROPE • 250 kW
		(D) Sa/Su • EUROPE • 250 kW
	CHINA (PR) RADIO BEIJING, Baoding	W NORTH AM • CHINESE, CANTONESE • 240 kW
	RADIO BEIJING, Xi'an	SE ASIA • 150 kW
	FINLAND †RADIO FINLAND, Pori	(D) • E NORTH AM & C AMERICA • 500 kW
		(J) • E ASIA • 500 kW • ALT. FREQ. TO 11845 kHz
		(D) M-F • E NORTH AM & C AMERICA • 500 kW
		(D) Sa/Su • E NORTH AM & C AMERICA • 500 kW
	GERMANY (FR) DEUTSCHE WELLE, Via Sri Lanka	SE ASIA & AUSTRALIA • 250 kW
	DEUTSCHE WELLE, Wertachtal	(J) • S ASIA • 500 kW
(con'd)	**IRAQ** †RADIO BAGHDAD, Balad-Salah el Deen	(J) • N AMERICA • 500 kW

World Time: 0 1 2 3 4 5 6 7 8 9 10 11 12 13 14 15 16 17 18 19 20 21 22 23 24

0 Prime Time-Americas 6 Prime Time-E Asia 12 Prime Time-S Asia 18 Prime Time-Europe 24

SUMMER ONLY (J) WINTER ONLY (D) JAMMING / OR /\ EARLIEST HEARD ◁ LATEST HEARD ▷ NEW OR CHANGED FOR 1990 †

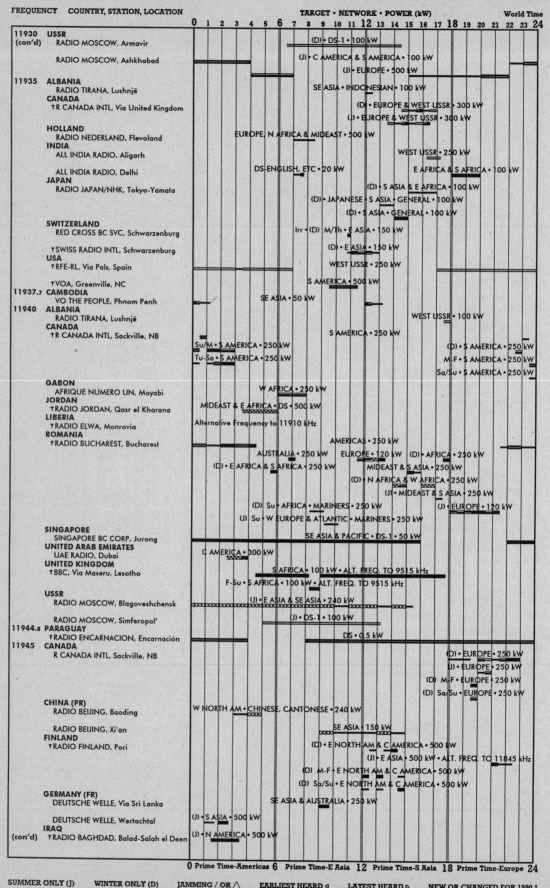

FREQUENCY	COUNTRY, STATION, LOCATION	TARGET • NETWORK • POWER (kW)
11945 (con'd)	**SPAIN** †R NACIONAL ESPANA, Noblejas	(D) • S AMERICA • 350 kW
	UNITED KINGDOM †BBC, Rampisham	(J) • WEST USSR • 500 kW
	†BBC, Skelton, Cumbria	(J) • E EUROPE & MIDEAST • 250 kW
		(J) M-F • E EUROPE & MIDEAST • 250 kW
		(J) M-Sa • E EUROPE & MIDEAST • 250 kW
	†BBC, Various Locations	WEST USSR • 100/500 kW
	†BBC, Via Hong Kong	E ASIA • 250 kW
		(J) • E ASIA • 250 kW
	†BBC, Via Zyyi, Cyprus	(D) • E EUROPE • 250 kW
		(J) • E EUROPE • 250 kW
		(D) M-Sa • E EUROPE • 250 kW
		(J) M-Sa • E EUROPE • 250 kW
		(D) Su • E EUROPE • 250 kW
		(J) Su • E EUROPE • 250 kW
	USA VOA, Via Kavála, Greece	(D) • MIDEAST & S ASIA • 250 kW
	USSR RADIO MOSCOW, Orcha	(J) • DS-3 • 50 kW
	†TATAR RADIO, Kazan'	DS-RUSSIAN, TATAR
11950	**BRAZIL** †RADIO MEC, Rio de Janeiro	PORTUGUESE • DS • 7.5 kW
	CUBA RADIO HABANA, Havana	S AMERICA • 50/250 kW
		(J) • W EUROPE & N AFRICA • 50/500 kW
	GERMANY (FR) DEUTSCHE WELLE, Various Locations	MIDEAST • 250/500 kW
	†DEUTSCHE WELLE, Via Sines, Portugal	(D) • E EUROPE • 250 kW
	DEUTSCHE WELLE, Wertachtal	AFRICA • 500 kW
	HOLLAND †RADIO NEDERLAND, Flevoland	Alternative Frequency to 11730 kHz
	USA †VOA, Cincinnati, Ohio	Alternative Frequency to 13740 kHz
	USSR KAZAKH RADIO, Alma-Ata	Sa • DS-1 • 100 kW
		Sa-M • DS-1 • 100 kW
		Su-F • DS-1 • 100 kW
		Tu-F • DS-1 • 100 kW
		DS-1/RUSSIAN, ETC • 100 kW
	RADIO MOSCOW	(J) • EUROPE • WS • 240/500 kW
	RADIO MOSCOW, Tula	(J) • MIDEAST & E AFRICA • 250 kW
11955	**ANGOLA** RADIO NACIONAL, Luanda	S AFRICA • 100 kW
	CANADA R CANADA INTL, Sackville, NB	Su • E NORTH AM & C AMERICA • 250 kW
	†R CANADA INTL, Via Xi'an, China(PR)	S ASIA • 120 kW
	JORDAN †RADIO JORDAN, Qasr el Kharana	(J) • E EUROPE & WEST USSR • DS • 500 kW
	LIBERIA RADIO ELWA, Monrovia	N AFRICA • 50 kW
	SWITZERLAND RED CROSS BC SVC, Schwarzenburg	Irr • M/Th • AFRICA • ENGLISH, FRENCH • 150 kW
	SWISS RADIO INTL, Schwarzenburg	AFRICA • 150 kW
		M-Sa • AFRICA • 150 kW
		Su • AFRICA • 150 kW
	TURKEY TURKISH RTV CORP, Ankara	MIDEAST • 250 kW
		TURKISH • MIDEAST • 250 kW
	UNITED ARAB EMIRATES †UAE RADIO, Dubai	(D) • E NORTH AM • 300 kW
	UNITED KINGDOM †BBC, Various Locations	S ASIA • 100/250 kW
	†BBC, Via Maşīrah, Oman	(D) • MIDEAST & S ASIA • 100 kW
	†BBC, Via Singapore	(J) • E ASIA & AUSTRALIA • 100/125 kW
		(D) • ASIA • 125 kW
		SE ASIA & AUSTRALIA • 250 kW
		E ASIA & AUSTRALIA • 100/125 kW
		E ASIA & SE ASIA • 250 kW
		SE ASIA • 250 kW
		(J) M-F • S ASIA • 100 kW
(con'd)	†BBC, Via Zyyi, Cyprus	(J) • WEST USSR • 250 kW

World Time: 0 Prime Time-Americas 6 Prime Time-E Asia 12 Prime Time-S Asia 18 Prime Time-Europe 24

ENGLISH ▬ ARABIC ▒ CHINESE ▭ FRENCH ═ GERMAN ▬ RUSSIAN ═ SPANISH ▬ OTHER —

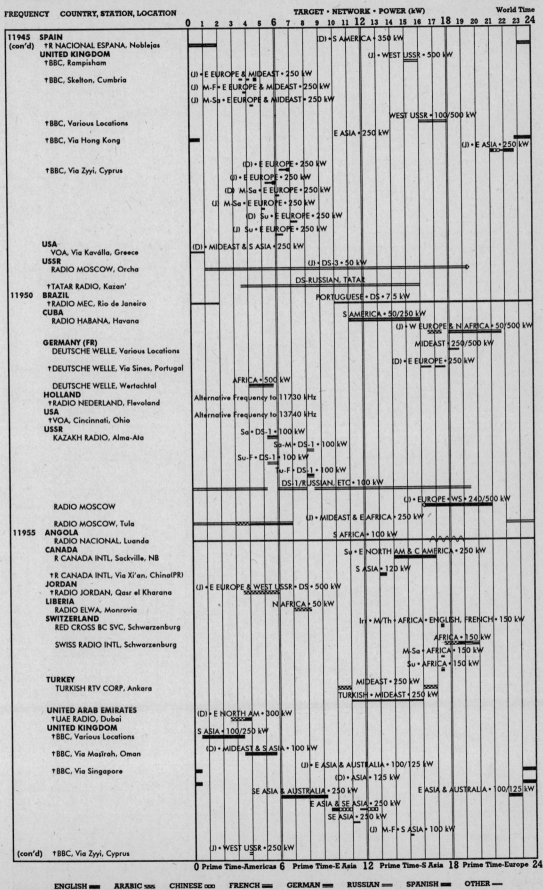

FREQUENCY	COUNTRY, STATION, LOCATION	TARGET • NETWORK • POWER (kW)
11955 (con'd)	**USA**	
	VOA, Via Philippines	E ASIA • 250 kW
	USSR	
	RADIO MOSCOW, Ivano-Frankovsk	(J) • W AFRICA • WS • 240 kW
	VATICAN STATE	
	†VATICAN RADIO, Sta Maria di Galeria	S ASIA • 500 kW • ALT. FREQ. TO 11960 kHz
11960	**ALBANIA**	
	RADIO TIRANA, Lushnjë	EUROPE • GREEK • 50 kW
	ECUADOR	
	†HCJB-VO THE ANDES, Quito	AMERICAS • 100 kW
	GERMANY (FR)	
	†DEUTSCHE WELLE, Jülich	(J) • E EUROPE • 100 kW
	†DEUTSCHE WELLE, Via Sines, Portugal	(J) • E EUROPE • 250 kW
	LAOS	
	LAO NATIONAL RADIO, Via USSR	(J) • EUROPE • 240 kW
	USA	
	VOA, Via Ismaning, GFR	(D) • WEST USSR • 100 kW
	†VOA, Via Kaválla, Greece	(J) • WEST USSR • 250 kW
	VOA, Via Rhodes, Greece	(D) • MIDEAST & E AFRICA • 50 kW
	VOA, Via Tangier,Morocco	(D) • WEST USSR • 35 kW
	USSR	
	RADIO MOSCOW, Armavir	(J) • E AFRICA & S AFRICA • ENGLISH, ETC • 500 kW
	RADIO MOSCOW, Krasnoyarsk	(J) • JAPANESE • E ASIA • 500 kW
	RADIO MOSCOW, Orcha	(J) • EUROPE • 200 kW
	RADIO MOSCOW, Serpukhov	(J) • EUROPE & ATLANTIC • 240 kW
	VATICAN STATE	
	†VATICAN RADIO, Sta Maria di Galeria	Alternative Frequency to 11955 kHz
11960v	**MALI**	
	RTV MALIENNE, Bamako	Irr • DS-FRENCH, ETC • 50 kW
		Irr • Su • DS-FRENCH, ETC • 50 kW
11965	**BRAZIL**	
	RADIO RECORD, São Paulo	Irr • PORTUGUESE • DS • 7.5 kW
		PORTUGUESE • DS • 7.5 kW
	FRANCE	
	†R FRANCE INTL, Issoudun-Allouis	S AMERICA • 100 kW
		(D) • S AMERICA • 100 kW
		(D) • W AFRICA • 500 kW
		(J) • S AMERICA • 100 kW
		(J) • W AFRICA • 500 kW
	GERMANY (FR)	
	†DEUTSCHE WELLE, Via Antigua	(D) • SE ASIA & AUSTRALIA • 250 kW
	DEUTSCHE WELLE, Via Kigali, Rwanda	(J) • C AFRICA & S AFRICA • 250 kW
	GUAM	
	†KTWR-TRANS WORLD R, Merizo	(D) • E ASIA • 100 kW
	UNITED ARAB EMIRATES	
	†VOICE OF THE UAE, Abu Dhabi	EUROPE • 500 kW
		(D) • E NORTH AM • 500 kW
	USA	
	†KNLS-NEW LIFE STN, Anchor Pt, Alaska	(J) • E ASIA • 100 kW
	†VOA, Via Philippines	EAST USSR • 250 kW
		S ASIA • 250 kW
		E ASIA • 250 kW
		(D) • AUSTRALIA • 250 kW
	WRNO WORLDWIDE, New Orleans, La	(J) • E NORTH AM • 100 kW
		E NORTH AM • ENGLISH, ETC • 100 kW
	USSR	
	†RADIO TASHKENT, Tashkent	(J) • MIDEAST • 100 kW
11965v	**PAKISTAN**	
	RADIO PAKISTAN, Islamabad	(D) • BANGLA • S ASIA • 100 kW
	RADIO PAKISTAN, Karachi	E AFRICA • 50 kW
11970	**CUBA**	
	RADIO HABANA, Havana	(D) • W EUROPE & N AFRICA • 500 kW
	GERMANY (DR)	
	†R BERLIN INTL, Leipzig	(D) • C AMERICA • 100 kW
		(D) • EUROPE & N AFRICA • 100 kW
	IRAQ	
	†RADIO BAGHDAD, Balad-Salah el Deen	(J) • N AFRICA • 500 kW
	ROMANIA	
	†RADIO BUCHAREST, Bucharest	(J) • EUROPE • 250 kW
	USA	
	†RFE-RL, Via Germany	WEST USSR • 20 kW
	†RFE-RL, Via Pals, Spain	WEST USSR • 250 kW
	†RFE-RL, Via Portugal	WEST USSR • 250 kW
	USSR	
	RADIO MOSCOW, Irkutsk	(J) • E ASIA • 240 kW
11975	**CHINA (PR)**	
	†RADIO BEIJING	(J) • S ASIA
		(J) • MIDEAST & S ASIA
		(J) • E AFRICA
(con'd)	**EGYPT**	
	RADIO CAIRO, Abu Za'bal	E AFRICA & S AFRICA • 100 kW

World Time 0–24: 0 Prime Time-Americas 6 Prime Time-E Asia 12 Prime Time-S Asia 18 Prime Time-Europe 24

SUMMER ONLY (J) WINTER ONLY (D) JAMMING / OR /\ EARLIEST HEARD ◁ LATEST HEARD ▷ NEW OR CHANGED FOR 1990 †

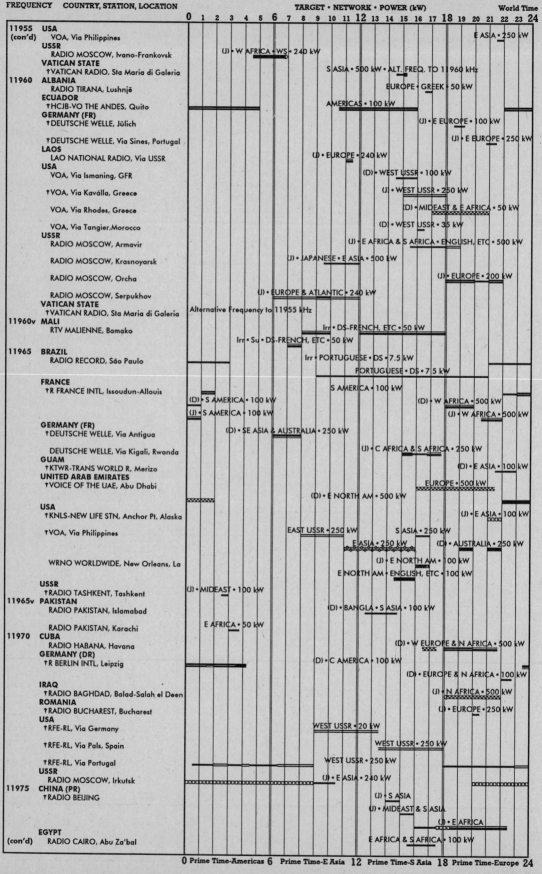

FREQUENCY	COUNTRY, STATION, LOCATION	TARGET • NETWORK • POWER (kW)
11975 (con'd)	USSR RADIO MOSCOW, Khar'kov	(J) • MIDEAST • 240 kW
		(J) • MIDEAST • WS • 240 kW
11980	CHINA (PR) RADIO BEIJING, Baoding	(D) • S AMERICA • 240 kW
	†RADIO BEIJING, Beijing	(D) • WEST USSR • 120 kW
	†RADIO BEIJING, Jinhua	(D) • W NORTH AM • 500 kW
	EGYPT RADIO CAIRO, Abu Za'bal	N AFRICA • DS-PALESTINE RADIO • 100 kW
		N AFRICA • DS-VO THE ARABS • 100 kW
		MIDEAST & N AFRICA • DS-VO THE ARABS • 250 kW
	RADIO CAIRO, Kafr Silîm-Abis	
	GUAM †ADVENTIST WORLD R, Agat	E ASIA • 100 kW
		JAPANESE • E ASIA • 100 kW
		S ASIA • 100 kW
	NORTHERN MARIANA IS KFBS-FAR EAST BC, Saipan Island	SE ASIA • 100 kW
	USA †WSHB, Cypress Creek, SC	C AMERICA • 500 kW
		M-F • C AMERICA • 500 kW
		Sa/Su • C AMERICA • 500 kW
	USSR RADIO MOSCOW, Tbilisi	(J) • C AMERICA & W EUROPE • 500 kW
		(J) • W EUROPE & W AFRICA • 240 kW
	RADIO MOSCOW, Vinnitsa	
11985	ALBANIA RADIO TIRANA, Lushnjë	S AMERICA • 100 kW
		WEST USSR • 100 kW
		EUROPE • 100 kW
		SE ASIA & AUSTRALIA • ENGLISH,INDONESIAN • 100 kW
	BELGIUM †BELGISCHE RADIO TV, Wavre	(D) • AFRICA • 100/250 kW
		(J) • AFRICA • 100/250 kW
		(D) M-Sa • AFRICA • 100/250 kW
		(J) M-Sa • AFRICA • 100/250 kW
	UNITED ARAB EMIRATES †VOICE OF THE UAE, Abu Dhabi	(J) • E NORTH AM • 500 kW
11990	CZECHOSLOVAKIA RADIO PRAGUE, Pieštány-Velké k'y	AMERICAS • 250 kW
	RADIO PRAGUE, Prague	AFRICA • 120 kW
		M-F • S ASIA • 120 kW
	KUWAIT RADIO KUWAIT, Jadādīyah	MIDEAST & N AFRICA • DS-MAIN PROGRAM • 500 kW
	USSR RADIO MOSCOW, Komsomol'sk 'Amure	DS-2 • 100 kW
	RADIO MOSCOW, Tula	(J) • W AFRICA • 100 kW
11995	FRANCE †R FRANCE INTL, Issoudun-Allouis	E AFRICA • 100 kW
		(D) • E EUROPE • 100 kW
		(D) • E AFRICA • 100 kW
		(J) • E EUROPE • 100 kW
		S AMERICA • 500 kW
	†R FRANCE INTL, Via French Guiana	
	PAKISTAN RADIO PAKISTAN, Islamabad	BANGLA • S ASIA • 100 kW
		(J) • BANGLA • S ASIA • 100 kW
	PHILIPPINES FAR EAST BC CO	SE ASIA • 50/100 kW
	USSR †RADIO TASHKENT, Tashkent	(J) • MIDEAST • 100 kW
12000	USSR RADIO MOSCOW, Armavir	(J) • S ASIA • WS • 100 kW
	RADIO MOSCOW, Kazan'	DS-2 • 100 kW
	†RADIO TASHKENT, Tashkent	(D) • MIDEAST • 100 kW
12005	PAKISTAN RADIO PAKISTAN, Islamabad	MIDEAST • 100 kW
	TUNISIA †RTV TUNISIENNE, Sfax	Irr • DS-RAMADAN • 100 kW
		DS • 100 kW
	USSR BELORUSSIAN RADIO, Minsk	Alternative Frequency to 7210 kHz
	RADIO MOSCOW, Petropavlovsk-Kam	WS • 100 kW
12010	AUSTRIA †RADIO AUSTRIA INTL, Vienna	MIDEAST • 100 kW
12015	CHINA (PR) RADIO BEIJING, Xi'an	SE ASIA • 120 kW
	MONGOLIA †RADIO ULAN BATOR, Ulan Bator	E ASIA • 250 kW
		Tu/F • JAPANESE • E ASIA • 250 kW
		W/Th/Sa-M • E ASIA • 250 kW
(con'd)		

World Time 0–24: 0 Prime Time-Americas 6 Prime Time-E Asia 12 Prime Time-S Asia 18 Prime Time-Europe 24

ENGLISH ▬ ARABIC ▨ CHINESE ▭▭▭ FRENCH ═ GERMAN ▬ RUSSIAN ═ SPANISH ═ OTHER —

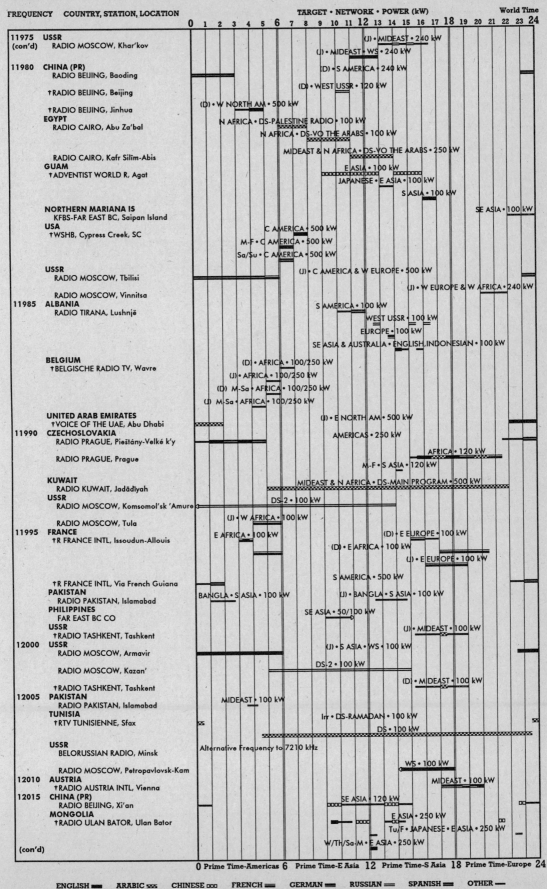

FREQUENCY	COUNTRY, STATION, LOCATION	TARGET • NETWORK • POWER (kW)
12015 (con'd)	**PAKISTAN**	
	RADIO PAKISTAN, Islamabad	MIDEAST • 250 kW
	USSR	
	RADIO MOSCOW, Yerevan	E AFRICA & S AFRICA • 100 kW
		E AFRICA & S AFRICA • AFRICAN • 100 kW
		E AFRICA & S AFRICA • WS • 100 kW
12020	**USSR**	
	RADIO MOSCOW, Chita	S ASIA • 240 kW
	RADIO MOSCOW, Kenga	DS-1(FEEDER) • 100 kW • LSB
	RADIO MOSCOW, Riga	EUROPE, ATLANTIC & S AMERICA • 100 kW
	VIETNAM	
	VOICE OF VIETNAM, Hanoi	(D) • 30 kW
		(D) • JAPANESE • 30 kW
12025	**IRAQ**	
	†RADIO BAGHDAD, Balad-Salah el Deen	(J) • E AFRICA • 500 kW
	MONACO	
	†TRANS WORLD RADIO, Monte Carlo	(D) • MIDEAST & WEST USSR • 500 kW
		(D) F/Sa • MIDEAST & WEST USSR • 500 kW
		(J) F/Sa • MIDEAST & WEST USSR • 500 kW
		(J) • MIDEAST & WEST USSR • 500 kW
		(D) Tu-Su • MIDEAST & WEST USSR • 500 kW
		(J) Tu-Su • MIDEAST & WEST USSR • 500 kW
	NORTHERN MARIANA IS	
	†KFBS-FAR EAST BC, Saipan Island	E ASIA • 100 kW
		(J) • E ASIA • 100 kW
	PHILIPPINES	
	FAR EAST BC CO, Iba	E ASIA • 100 kW
	USA	
	†KNLS-NEW LIFE STN, Anchor Pt, Alaska	(J) • E ASIA • 100 kW
12030	**SWITZERLAND**	
	†SWISS RADIO INTL, Sarnen	EUROPE & N AFRICA • 250 kW
	SWISS RADIO INTL, Schwarzenburg	W AFRICA • 150 kW
	USSR	
	R TIKHIY OKEAN, Petropavlovsk-Kam	(J) • PACIFIC • MARINERS • 100 kW
		(J) Sa • PACIFIC • MARINERS • 100 kW
		(J) Su-F • PACIFIC • MARINERS • 100 kW
	RADIO MOSCOW, Petropavlovsk-Kam	W NORTH AM • N AMERICAN • 100 kW
		(J) • W NORTH AM • 100 kW
		(J) • JAPANESE • E ASIA • 100 kW
	RADIO MOSCOW, Tula	(J) • N AFRICA & W AFRICA • 240 kW
12035	**SPAIN**	
	R NACIONAL ESPANA, Noblejas	EUROPE • SPANISH, ETC • 100 kW
		EUROPE • SPANISH, ETC • 350 kW
	SWITZERLAND	
	RED CROSS BC SVC, Schwarzenburg	Irr • Tu/F • E NORTH AM & C AMERICA • 150 kW
		Irr • Tu/F • N AMERICA • 150 kW
	†RED CROSS BC SVC, Via Moyabi,Gabon	Irr • M/Th • S AMERICA • 500 kW
	SWISS RADIO INTL, Schwarzenburg	E NORTH AM & C AMERICA • 150 kW
		N AMERICA • 150 kW
		M • E NORTH AM & C AMERICA • 150 kW
		M • N AMERICA • 150 kW
		Tu-Sa • E NORTH AM & C AMERICA • 150 kW
		Tu-Sa • N AMERICA • 150 kW
	†SWISS RADIO INTL, Via Moyabi,Gabon	S AMERICA • 500 kW
12039v	**VIETNAM**	
	VOICE OF VIETNAM, Hanoi	E ASIA • 30 kW
12040	**UNITED KINGDOM**	
	†BBC, Rampisham	(D) • E EUROPE • 500 kW
		(J) • E EUROPE • 500 kW
		(D) Su • E EUROPE • 500 kW
		(J) Su • WEST USSR • 500 kW
		(J) Su • E EUROPE • 500 kW
	USSR	
	RADIO MOSCOW, Sverdlovsk	(J) • E ASIA • CHINESE,KOREAN,ETC • 50 kW
		(J) • EUROPE • SPANISH,ITAL'N,ETC • 50 kW
12045	**GREECE**	
	FONI TIS HELLADAS, Kaválla	(D) • GREEK • AFRICA • 250 kW
		(D) • AFRICA • 250 kW
	NEW ZEALAND	
	†RADIO NEW ZEALAND, Wellington	Alternative Frequency to 11780 kHz
		(J) • SE ASIA • ENGLISH, ETC • 7.5 kW
(con'd)	**USSR**	
	RADIO MOSCOW, Kenga	EUROPE • 240/500 kW

World Time 0–24: 0 Prime Time-Americas 6 Prime Time-E Asia 12 Prime Time-S Asia 18 Prime Time-Europe 24

SUMMER ONLY (J) WINTER ONLY (D) JAMMING / OR /\ EARLIEST HEARD ◁ LATEST HEARD ▷ NEW OR CHANGED FOR 1990 †

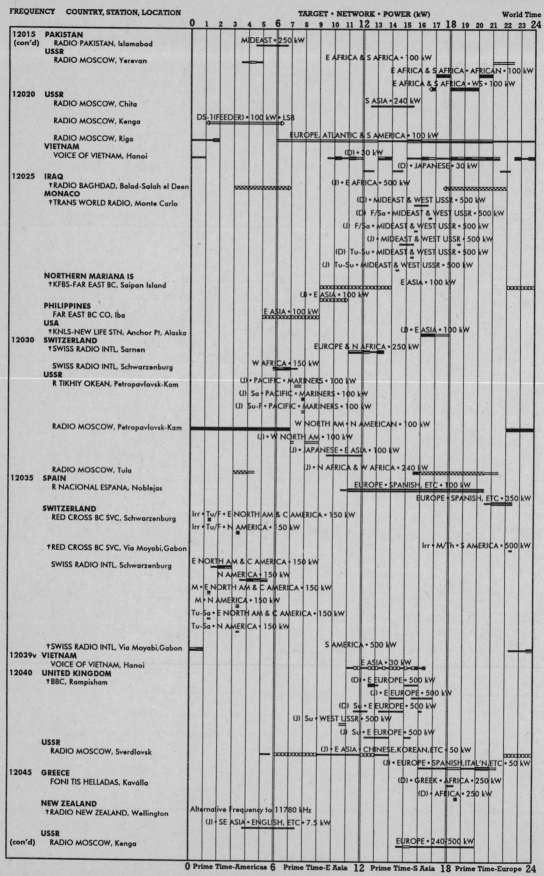

FREQUENCY	COUNTRY, STATION, LOCATION	TARGET • NETWORK • POWER (kW)
12045 (con'd)	**USSR** RADIO MOSCOW, Kenga	EUROPE • WS • 240/500 kW
	RADIO MOSCOW, Voronezh, RSFSR	DS-1 • 50 kW
12050	**EGYPT** RADIO CAIRO, Multiple Locations	DS-GENERAL • 100/250 kW
	MONGOLIA †RADIO ULAN BATOR, Ulan Bator	EUROPE • 250 kW
	USSR R TIKHIY OKEAN, Khabarovsk	(J) • PACIFIC & W NORTH AM • MARINERS • 100/240 kW
		(J) Sa • PACIFIC & W NORTH AM • MARINERS • 100/240 kW
		(J) Su-F • PACIFIC & W NORTH AM • MARINERS • 100/240 kW
	RADIO MOSCOW, Frunze, Kirgiziya	(J) • SE ASIA • 100 kW
	RADIO MOSCOW, Khabarovsk	PACIFIC & W NORTH AM • WS, N AMERICAN • 100/240 kW
		PACIFIC & W NORTH AM • 100/240 kW
		(J) • PACIFIC & W NORTH AM • N AMERICAN • 100/240 kW
	RADIO MOSCOW, Tbilisi	(J) • W AFRICA & ATLANTIC • 240 kW
	RADIO YEREVAN, Tbilisi	(J) • S AMERICA • ARMENIAN, SPANISH • 240/500 kW
12055	**CHINA (PR)** RADIO BEIJING, Xi'an	S AMERICA • 120 kW
	USSR RADIO MOSCOW, Armavir	AFRICA & ATLANTIC • 120 kW
		AFRICA & ATLANTIC • WS • 120 kW
12060	**USSR** RADIO MOSCOW, Sverdlovsk	(J) • EUROPE • POLISH • 100 kW
	RADIO MOSCOW, Vinnitsa	(J) • E NORTH AM & C AMERICA • N AMERICAN • 500 kW
	RADIO MOSCOW, Voronezh, RSFSR	DS-2 • 240 kW
12065	**AFGHANISTAN** †RADIO AFGHANISTAN, Via USSR	(J) • MIDEAST
	USSR RADIO MOSCOW, Armavir	(J) • E AFRICA & S AFRICA • SOMALI, ETC • 500 kW
12070	**USSR** R TIKHIY OKEAN, Khabarovsk	(J) • PACIFIC • MARINERS • 100 kW
		(J) Sa • PACIFIC • MARINERS • 100 kW
		(J) Su-F • PACIFIC • MARINERS • 100 kW
	RADIO MOSCOW, Khabarovsk	DS-1 • 100 kW
		(J) • DS-1 • 100 kW
	RADIO MOSCOW, L'vov	ATLANTIC • MARINERS • 240/500 kW
		(J) • EUROPE & W AFRICA • WS, MARINER, SPANISH • 240/500 kW
12075	**USSR** RADIO MOSCOW, Alma-Ata	SE ASIA & AUSTRALIA • WS • 500 kW
	RADIO MOSCOW, Novosibirsk	DS-2 • 50 kW
	RADIO MOSCOW, Sverdlovsk	MIDEAST • 100 kW
		MIDEAST • WS • 100 kW
12077v	**ISRAEL** †KOL ISRAEL, Tel Aviv	(D) • E NORTH AM & C AMERICA • 300 kW
		(D) • HEBREW • E NORTH AM & C AMERICA • 300 kW
		(D) • WEST USSR • 50 kW
		(J) Sa/Su • WEST USSR & E EUROPE • 300 kW
		(J) • EUROPE • 300 kW
		(J) • EUROPE & E NORTH AM • 300 kW
		(J) • EUROPE, N AFRICA & C AMERICA • 300 kW
12085	**SYRIA** †SYRIAN BC SERVICE, Adhra	(D) • S AMERICA • 500 kW
		(D) • EUROPE • 500 kW
		(D) • AUSTRALIA • 500 kW
		DS • 500 kW
		(J) • DS • 500 kW
		(D) • C AMERICA & S AMERICA • 500 kW
12095	**UNITED KINGDOM** †BBC, Daventry	(D) • C AMERICA • 100 kW
	†BBC, Multiple Locations	(D) • E EUROPE & MIDEAST • 100 kW
		(J) • EUROPE & W AFRICA • 250/300/500 kW
		(D) • EUROPE, N AFRICA & MIDEAST • 100/300 kW
		(D) • EUROPE & N AFRICA • 100/300/500 kW
		(D) • EUROPE, MIDEAST & W AFRICA • 100/250/500 kW
		(J) • EUROPE & WEST USSR • 100/300 kW
		(J) • EUROPE & N AFRICA • 250/300/500 kW
		(J) • EUROPE & N AFRICA • 100/250/300 kW
	†BBC, Rampisham	(J) • E NORTH AM • 500 kW
12100	**USSR** †RADIO MOSCOW	(D) • (FEEDER) • USB
12110	**CHINA (PR)** †RADIO BEIJING, Kunming	SE ASIA • 50 kW
12120	**CHINA (PR)** CENTRAL PEOPLES BS	DS-1
		W-M • DS-1

World Time: 0 Prime Time-Americas 6 Prime Time-E Asia 12 Prime Time-S Asia 18 Prime Time-Europe 24

ENGLISH ARABIC CHINESE FRENCH GERMAN RUSSIAN SPANISH OTHER

FREQUENCY	COUNTRY, STATION, LOCATION	TARGET • NETWORK • POWER (kW)
12175	**USSR** RADIO MOSCOW, Moscow	Irr • DS-1(FEEDER) • 20 kW • LSB
12200	**CHINA (PR)** CENTRAL PEOPLES BS, Beijing	DS-2 • 15 kW Th/Sa-Tu • DS-2 • 15 kW
12205	**USSR** RADIO MOSCOW, Alma-Ata	Irr • DS-2(FEEDER) • 15 kW • LSB
12230	**CLANDESTINE (ASIA)** "VOICE OF UNITY", Abu Za'bal, Egypt	MIDEAST & S ASIA • PRO-AFGHAN REBELS • 100 kW
13605	**UNITED ARAB EMIRATES** †VOICE OF THE UAE, Abu Dhabi	(J) • N AMERICA • 500 kW (J) • N AFRICA • DS • 500 kW
	USSR RADIO MOSCOW, Khabarovsk	(J) • W NORTH AM • N AMERICAN SVC • 100 kW
13610	**GERMANY (DR)** †R BERLIN INTL, Leipzig	(J) • C AMERICA • 100 kW MIDEAST & E AFRICA • 100 kW AFRICA • 100 kW (J) • EUROPE & N AFRICA • 100 kW
13615	**USSR** RADIO MOSCOW	SE ASIA (J) • E ASIA • CHINESE, CANTONESE
	RADIO MOSCOW, Nikolayev	(J) • W AFRICA • 500 kW
13625	**USSR** RADIO MOSCOW	E ASIA (J) • (FEEDER) • USB
13630	**USSR** RADIO MOSCOW	(J) • DS-1
13635	**SWITZERLAND** †RED CROSS BC SVC, Sottens	Irr • M/Th • AUSTRALIA • 500 kW Irr • M/Th • S ASIA & SE ASIA • 500 kW
	†SWISS RADIO INTL, Sottens	AUSTRALIA • 500 kW S ASIA & SE ASIA • 500 kW M-Sa • S ASIA & SE ASIA • 500 kW Su • S ASIA & SE ASIA • 500 kW
	†SWISS RADIO INTL, Various Locations	AFRICA • 125/500 kW
13645	**USSR** †RADIO KIEV, Khabarovsk	W NORTH AM • 100 kW
	†RADIO MOSCOW, Khabarovsk	W NORTH AM • 100 kW
	RADIO VILNIUS, Khabarovsk	W NORTH AM • 100 kW
	RADIO YEREVAN, Khabarovsk	W NORTH AM • 100 kW
13650	**CANADA** †R CANADA INTL, Sackville, NB	EUROPE & WEST USSR • 250 kW EUROPE • 250 kW
	KOREA (DPR) RADIO PYONGYANG, Kujang-dong	C AMERICA • 400 kW SE ASIA • 100 kW
13651.3	**USA** †AFRTS-US MILITARY, Via Barford, UK	Irr • ATLANTIC • DS-ABC/CBS/NBC/NPR(FEEDER) • 4 kW • LSB
13655	**JORDAN** †RADIO JORDAN, Qasr el Kharana	(J) • EUROPE & E NORTH AM • 500 kW Irr • (J) • EUROPE & E NORTH AM • 500 kW
13660	**CANADA** †R CANADA INTL, Sackville, NB	(J) • EUROPE • 100 kW
	IRAQ †RADIO BAGHDAD, Balad-Salah el Deen	(J) • EUROPE • 500 kW
13663v	**COSTA RICA** †RADIO FOR PEACE, Ciudad Colón	Tu-Sa • C AMERICA • 2/5 kW Sa/Su • C AMERICA • 2/5 kW
13665	**IRAQ** †RADIO BAGHDAD, Balad-Salah el Deen	(J) • EUROPE & C AMERICA • 500 kW • ALT. FREQ. TO 15230 kHz
	USSR RADIO MOSCOW	N AMERICAN SVC
13665v	**PAKISTAN** RADIO PAKISTAN, Karachi	(J) • MIDEAST • 50 kW
13670	**CANADA** †R CANADA INTL, Sackville, NB	(D) • AFRICA • 100 kW (D) M-F • AFRICA • 100 kW (D) Sa/Su • AFRICA • 100 kW
	KOREA (REPUBLIC) RADIO KOREA, In-Kimjae	EUROPE • 250 kW KOREAN • EUROPE • 250 kW
13675v	**PAKISTAN** RADIO PAKISTAN, Karachi	(J) • MIDEAST • 50 kW
13680	**CANADA** †R CANADA INTL, Sackville, NB	(J) • AFRICA • 100 kW (J) M-F • AFRICA • 100 kW (J) Sa/Su • AFRICA • 100 kW
	CHINA (PR) †RADIO BEIJING, Via French Guiana	S AMERICA • 500 kW
(con'd)	**IRAQ** †RADIO BAGHDAD, Balad-Salah el Deen	(D) • EUROPE & N AFRICA • 500 kW

World Time: 0 Prime Time-Americas 6 Prime Time-E Asia 12 Prime Time-S Asia 18 Prime Time-Europe 24

SUMMER ONLY (J) WINTER ONLY (D) JAMMING / OR /\ EARLIEST HEARD ◁ LATEST HEARD ▷ NEW OR CHANGED FOR 1990 †

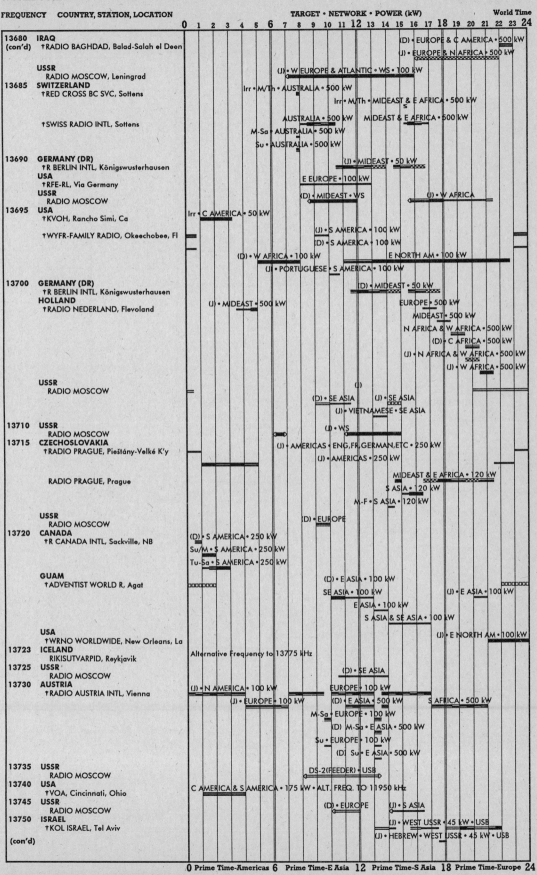

FREQUENCY	COUNTRY, STATION, LOCATION	TARGET • NETWORK • POWER (kW)
13680 (con'd)	IRAQ †RADIO BAGHDAD, Balad-Salah el Deen	(D) • EUROPE & C AMERICA • 500 kW (J) • EUROPE & N AFRICA • 500 kW
	USSR RADIO MOSCOW, Leningrad	(J) • W EUROPE & ATLANTIC • WS • 100 kW
13685	SWITZERLAND †RED CROSS BC SVC, Sottens	Irr • M/Th • AUSTRALIA • 500 kW Irr • M/Th • MIDEAST & E AFRICA • 500 kW
	†SWISS RADIO INTL, Sottens	AUSTRALIA • 500 kW MIDEAST & E AFRICA • 500 kW M-Sa • AUSTRALIA • 500 kW Su • AUSTRALIA • 500 kW
13690	GERMANY (DR) †R BERLIN INTL, Königswusterhausen	(J) • MIDEAST • 50 kW
	USA †RFE-RL, Via Germany	E EUROPE • 100 kW
	USSR RADIO MOSCOW	(D) • MIDEAST • WS (J) • W AFRICA
13695	USA †KVOH, Rancho Simi, Ca	Irr • C AMERICA • 50 kW
	†WYFR-FAMILY RADIO, Okeechobee, Fl	(J) • S AMERICA • 100 kW (D) • S AMERICA • 100 kW (D) • W AFRICA • 100 kW E NORTH AM • 100 kW (J) • PORTUGUESE • S AMERICA • 100 kW
13700	GERMANY (DR) †R BERLIN INTL, Königswusterhausen	(D) • MIDEAST • 50 kW
	HOLLAND †RADIO NEDERLAND, Flevoland	(J) • MIDEAST • 500 kW EUROPE • 500 kW MIDEAST • 500 kW N AFRICA & W AFRICA • 500 kW (D) • C AFRICA • 500 kW (J) • N AFRICA & W AFRICA • 500 kW (J) • W AFRICA • 500 kW
	USSR RADIO MOSCOW	(J) (D) • SE ASIA (J) • SE ASIA (J) • VIETNAMESE • SE ASIA
13710	USSR RADIO MOSCOW	(J) • WS
13715	CZECHOSLOVAKIA †RADIO PRAGUE, Pieštány-Velké K'y	(J) • AMERICAS • ENG,FR,GERMAN,ETC • 250 kW (J) • AMERICAS • 250 kW
	RADIO PRAGUE, Prague	MIDEAST & E AFRICA • 120 kW S ASIA • 120 kW M-F • S ASIA • 120 kW
	USSR RADIO MOSCOW	(D) • EUROPE
13720	CANADA †R CANADA INTL, Sackville, NB	(D) • S AMERICA • 250 kW Su/M • S AMERICA • 250 kW Tu-Sa • S AMERICA • 250 kW
	GUAM †ADVENTIST WORLD R, Agat	(D) • E ASIA • 100 kW SE ASIA • 100 kW (J) • E ASIA • 100 kW E ASIA • 100 kW S ASIA & SE ASIA • 100 kW
	USA †WRNO WORLDWIDE, New Orleans, La	(J) • E NORTH AM • 100 kW
13723	ICELAND RIKISUTVARPID, Reykjavik	Alternative Frequency to 13775 kHz
13725	USSR RADIO MOSCOW	(D) • SE ASIA
13730	AUSTRIA †RADIO AUSTRIA INTL, Vienna	(J) • N AMERICA • 100 kW EUROPE • 100 kW (J) • EUROPE • 100 kW (D) • E ASIA • 500 kW S AFRICA • 500 kW M-Sa • EUROPE • 100 kW (D) M-Sa • E ASIA • 500 kW Su • EUROPE • 100 kW (D) Su • E ASIA • 500 kW
13735	USSR RADIO MOSCOW	DS-2(FEEDER) • USB
13740	USA †VOA, Cincinnati, Ohio	C AMERICA & S AMERICA • 175 kW • ALT. FREQ. TO 11950 kHz
13745	USSR RADIO MOSCOW	(D) • EUROPE (J) • S ASIA
13750 (con'd)	ISRAEL †KOL ISRAEL, Tel Aviv	(J) • WEST USSR • 45 kW • USB (J) • HEBREW • WEST USSR • 45 kW • USB

World Time: 0 Prime Time-Americas 6 Prime Time-E Asia 12 Prime Time-S Asia 18 Prime Time-Europe 24

ENGLISH ARABIC CHINESE FRENCH GERMAN RUSSIAN SPANISH OTHER

FREQUENCY	COUNTRY, STATION, LOCATION	TARGET • NETWORK • POWER (kW) — World Time 0–24
13750 (con'd)	**ISRAEL** †RASHUTH HASHIDUR, Tel Aviv	(J) • HEBREW • EUROPE • DS-B • 20 kW
		(J) Su-F • HEBREW • EUROPE • DS-B • 20 kW
	KOREA (DPR) RADIO PYONGYANG, Kujang-dong	SE ASIA • 200 kW
13755	**USSR** RADIO MOSCOW, Simferopol'	ATLANTIC • MARINERS • 240 kW
13760	**GERMANY (FR)** †DEUTSCHE WELLE, Via Cyclops, Malta	(D) • E ASIA • 250 kW
	†DEUTSCHE WELLE, Wertachtal	(D) • JAPANESE • E ASIA • 500 kW
	USA †WORLD HARVEST R, Noblesville, Indiana	(D) • E NORTH AM & W EUROPE • 100 kW
		(J) • ENGLISH, SPANISH & PORTUGUESE • E NORTH AM & W EUROPE • 100 kW
		E NORTH AM & W EUROPE • ENGLISH, ETC • 100 kW
	†WRNO WORLDWIDE, New Orleans, La	(D) • E NORTH AM • 100 kW
	†WSHB, Cypress Creek, SC	S AMERICA • 500 kW
		W NORTH AM • 500 kW
		C AMERICA • 500 kW
		M-F • W NORTH AM • 500 kW
		M • S AMERICA • 500 kW
		Sa/Su • W NORTH AM • 500 kW
		M • C AMERICA • 500 kW
		M-F • C AMERICA • 500 kW
		M-Sa • S AMERICA • 500 kW
		Sa/Su • C AMERICA • 500 kW
		Su • S AMERICA • 500 kW
		Tu-Su • S AMERICA • 500 kW
		Tu-Su • C AMERICA • 500 kW
13770	**HOLLAND** RADIO NEDERLAND, Flevoland	S ASIA • 500 kW
		MIDEAST • 500 kW
	ICELAND RIKISUTVARPID, Reykjavik	(J) • ATLANTIC & EUROPE • DS • 10 kW • USB
	USA †WYFR-FAMILY RADIO, Okeechobee, Fl	(J) • EUROPE • 100 kW
13775	**ICELAND** RIKISUTVARPID, Reykjavik	(D) • ATLANTIC & EUROPE • DS-1 • 10 kW • USB • ALT FREQ. TO 13723 kHz
	USA †VOA, Greenville, NC	C AMERICA & S AMERICA • 250 kW
		M-F • S AMERICA • 500 kW
		Sa/Su • C AMERICA & S AMERICA • 250 kW
	USSR RADIO MOSCOW	(J) • E ASIA • CHINESE, KOREAN, ETC
13780	**GERMANY (FR)** †DEUTSCHE WELLE, Jülich	(D) • SE ASIA & AUSTRALIA • 100 kW
	†DEUTSCHE WELLE, Multiple Locations	E EUROPE & MIDEAST • 100/250 kW
	†DEUTSCHE WELLE, Various Locations	MIDEAST • 100/250 kW
	†DEUTSCHE WELLE, Wertachtal	(D) • E ASIA • 500 kW
		(D) • N AMERICA & C AMERICA • 500 kW
13785	**USSR** RADIO MOSCOW	(J) • W AFRICA & C AFRICA
13790	**GERMANY (FR)** †DEUTSCHE WELLE, Jülich	W AFRICA • 100 kW
	†DEUTSCHE WELLE, Various Locations	(J) • C AMERICA & S AMERICA • 100/250 kW
	†DEUTSCHE WELLE, Wertachtal	(D) • C AFRICA & S AFRICA • 500 kW
	USSR RADIO MOSCOW	(D) • JAPANESE • E ASIA
		(D) • EUROPE & E NORTH AM • WS
13810	**USSR** KAZAKH TELEGRAPH, Alma-Ata	M/W/F • DS-DICTATION NEWS • 15 kW
	KAZAKH TELEGRAPH, Alma-ata	M/W/F • DS-DICTATION NEWS • 15 kW
14305v	**CLANDESTINE (AFRICA)** †"VO BROAD MASSES", Ethiopia	E AFRICA • PLF OF ERITREA
14398	**USA** †VOA, Delano, California	SE ASIA • (FEEDER) • 50 kW • ISL
		SE ASIA • (FEEDER) • 50 kW • ISU
14410	**USSR** RADIO MOSCOW, Moscow	Irr • DS-1(FEEDER) • 15 kW • USB
14500	**UNITED NATIONS** UNITED NATIONS R, Via Switzerland	Alternative Frequency to 7443 kHz
14526	**USA** †VOA, Greenville, NC	(D) • EUROPE & MIDEAST • (FEEDER) • 40 kW • ISU
		(D) • EUROPE & MIDEAST • (FEEDER) • 40 kW • ISL
		(J) • EUROPE & MIDEAST • (FEEDER) • 40 kW • ISU
		(J) • EUROPE & MIDEAST • (FEEDER) • 40 kW • ISL
		Tu/F • EUROPE & MIDEAST • (FEEDER) • 40 kW • ISL
14802	**KIRIBATI** †RADIO KIRIBATI, Betio	Alternative Frequency to 14917.7 kHz

0 Prime Time-Americas 6 Prime Time-E Asia 12 Prime Time-S Asia 18 Prime Time-Europe 24

SUMMER ONLY (J) WINTER ONLY (D) JAMMING / OR /\ EARLIEST HEARD ◁ LATEST HEARD ▷ NEW OR CHANGED FOR 1990 †

FREQUENCY | COUNTRY, STATION, LOCATION | TARGET • NETWORK • POWER (kW) | World Time

0 1 2 3 4 5 6 7 8 9 10 11 12 13 14 15 16 17 18 19 20 21 22 23 24

14850 USSR
RADIO MOSCOW, Moscow
DS-1(FEEDER) • 20 kW • ISU
Irr • DS-3(FEEDER) • 20 kW • ISL

14917.7 KIRIBATI
†RADIO KIRIBATI, Betio
Irr • DS-ENGLISH, ETC(FEEDER) • 10 kW • USB • ALT. FREQ. TO 14802 kHz
M-Sa • DS-ENGLISH, ETC(FEEDER) • 10 kW • USB • ALT. FREQ. TO 14802 kHz
Sa • DS-ENGLISH, ETC(FEEDER) • 10 kW • USB • ALT. FREQ. TO 14802 kHz

15000 USA
WWV, Ft Collins, Colorado
WEATHER/WORLD TIME • 10 kW
WWVH, Kekaha, Hawaii
WEATHER/WORLD TIME • 10 kW

15010v VIETNAM
VOICE OF VIETNAM, Ha Son Binh
(J) • SE ASIA • 30 kW
(J) • E ASIA & AMERICAS • 30 kW
(J) • JAPANESE • E ASIA & AMERICAS • 30 kW

15030 CHINA (PR)
CENTRAL PEOPLES BS
DS-2
Th/Sa-Tu • DS-2

15039.5 CLANDESTINE (N AMER)
"VOICE OF TOMORROW, Virginia, USA
Irr • E NORTH AM • NEO-NAZI PARTY

15045 PIRATE (EUROPE)
†"WEEKEND MUSIC R", Scotland
Irr • Su • W EUROPE • 0.1 kW

15055 TURKEY
†TURKISH RTV CORP, Ankara
Alternative Frequency to 15200 kHz

USA
FAMILY RADIO, Via Taiwan
S ASIA • 250 kW

15060 SAUDI ARABIA
BS OF THE KINGDOM, Riyadh
MIDEAST • 350 kW
W AFRICA • 350 kW
N AFRICA • DS-GENERAL • 350 kW

15070 UNITED KINGDOM
†BBC, Daventry
(J) • N AFRICA & W AFRICA • 100 kW
†BBC, Multiple Locations
EUROPE, MIDEAST & W AFRICA • 100/250/500 kW
(J) • EUROPE, MIDEAST & W AFRICA • 100/250/500 kW
E EUROPE & MIDEAST • 250 kW
(J) • S AMERICA • 250 kW
†BBC, Skelton, Cumbria
(D) • E EUROPE & MIDEAST • 250 kW

15084 IRAN
†VO THE ISLAMIC REP, Tehrān
PERSIAN • EUROPE, E NORTH AM & C AMERICA • 250 kW
EUROPE, E NORTH AM & C AMERICA • 250 kW

15090 VATICAN STATE
†VATICAN RADIO, Sta Maria di Galeria
S ASIA • 100 kW

15090v PAKISTAN
RADIO PAKISTAN, Karachi
(J) • MIDEAST • 50 kW

15095 ISRAEL
†KOL ISRAEL, Tel Aviv
(D) • E EUROPE & WEST USSR • 300 kW
(J) • EUROPE • 20 kW
(D) Sa/Su • E EUROPE & WEST USSR • 300 kW
(D) • HEBREW • E EUROPE & WEST USSR • DS-B • 300 kW
†RASHUTH HASHIDUR, Tel Aviv
(J) • HEBREW • EUROPE • DS-B • 20 kW

SYRIA
†SYRIAN BC SERVICE, Adhra
DS • 500 kW
EUROPE • 500 kW
(J) • C AMERICA & S AMERICA • 500 kW • ALT. FREQ. TO 17810 kHz

15100 CHINA (PR)
†RADIO BEIJING
(J) • N AFRICA
RADIO BEIJING, Baoding
W NORTH AM, C AMERICA & S AMERICA • 240 kW

CLANDESTINE (M EAST)
†"IRAN FREEDOM FLAG, Egypt
PERSIAN • MIDEAST • ANTI-IRANIAN GOVT • 100 kW

15105 ALBANIA
†RADIO TIRANA, Lushnjë
E ASIA • 50 kW

GERMANY (FR)
†DEUTSCHE WELLE, Jülich
(J) • SE ASIA & AUSTRALIA • 100 kW
(J) • JAPANESE • E ASIA • 100 kW
†DEUTSCHE WELLE, Multiple Locations
MIDEAST & S ASIA • 100/250 kW
(D) • E ASIA • 100/500 kW
S AMERICA • 250 kW
DEUTSCHE WELLE, Via Antigua
†DEUTSCHE WELLE, Via Cyclops, Malta
(J) • E NORTH AM & C AMERICA • 250 kW
DEUTSCHE WELLE, Via Sri Lanka
(J) • E AFRICA • 250 kW

MOROCCO
RTV MAROCAINE, Tangier
EUROPE & N AFRICA • DS • 50 kW

TURKEY
†TURKISH RTV CORP, Ankara
(D) • TURKISH • MIDEAST & S ASIA • 250 kW
(J) • WEST USSR • 250 kW

UNITED KINGDOM
†BBC, Rampisham
(J) • W AFRICA • 500 kW
†BBC, Skelton, Cumbria
(J) • W AFRICA • 250 kW
(J) • EUROPE & W AFRICA • 250 kW
†BBC, Via Ascension
W AFRICA • 250 kW
C AFRICA • 250 kW
(J) • S AFRICA • 250 kW
S AFRICA • 250 kW

(con'd)

0 Prime Time-Americas 6 Prime Time-E Asia 12 Prime Time-S Asia 18 Prime Time-Europe 24

ENGLISH ▬ ARABIC ▭ CHINESE ▫ FRENCH ═ GERMAN ▬ RUSSIAN ═ SPANISH ▬ OTHER —

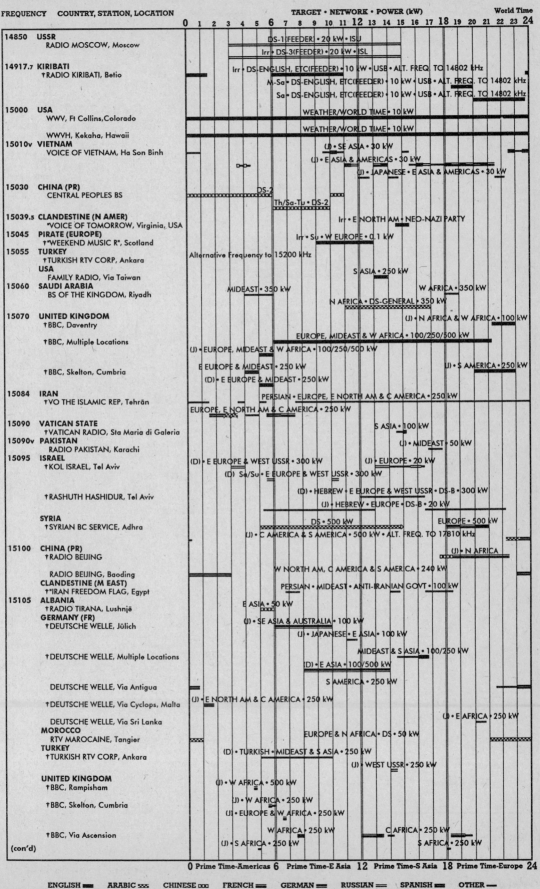

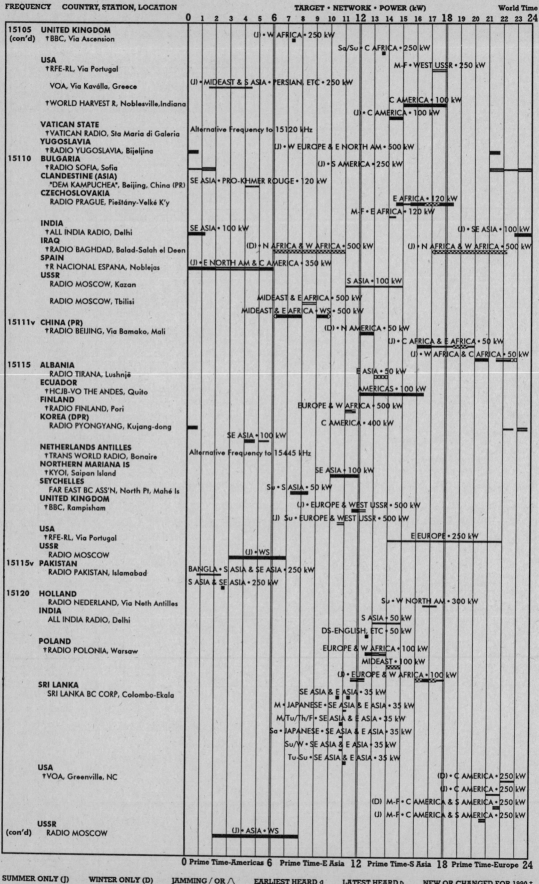

FREQUENCY	COUNTRY, STATION, LOCATION	TARGET • NETWORK • POWER (kW)
15105 (con'd)	**UNITED KINGDOM** †BBC, Via Ascension	(J) • W AFRICA • 250 kW
		Sa/Su • C AFRICA • 250 kW
	USA †RFE-RL, Via Portugal	M-F • WEST USSR • 250 kW
	VOA, Via Kaválla, Greece	(J) • MIDEAST & S ASIA • PERSIAN, ETC • 250 kW
	†WORLD HARVEST R, Noblesville, Indiana	C AMERICA • 100 kW
		(J) • C AMERICA • 100 kW
	VATICAN STATE †VATICAN RADIO, Sta Maria di Galeria	Alternative Frequency to 15120 kHz
	YUGOSLAVIA †RADIO YUGOSLAVIA, Bijeljina	(J) • W EUROPE & E NORTH AM • 500 kW
15110	**BULGARIA** †RADIO SOFIA, Sofia	(J) • S AMERICA • 250 kW
	CLANDESTINE (ASIA) "DEM KAMPUCHEA", Beijing, China (PR)	SE ASIA • PRO-KHMER ROUGE • 120 kW
	CZECHOSLOVAKIA RADIO PRAGUE, Piešťány-Velké K'y	E AFRICA • 120 kW
		M-F • E AFRICA • 120 kW
	INDIA †ALL INDIA RADIO, Delhi	SE ASIA • 100 kW
		(J) • SE ASIA • 100 kW
	IRAQ †RADIO BAGHDAD, Balad-Salah el Deen	(D) • N AFRICA & W AFRICA • 500 kW
		(J) • N AFRICA & W AFRICA • 500 kW
	SPAIN †R NACIONAL ESPANA, Noblejas	(J) • E NORTH AM & C AMERICA • 350 kW
	USSR RADIO MOSCOW, Kazan	S ASIA • 100 kW
	RADIO MOSCOW, Tbilisi	MIDEAST & E AFRICA • 500 kW
		MIDEAST & E AFRICA • WS • 500 kW
15111v	**CHINA (PR)** †RADIO BEIJING, Via Bamako, Mali	(D) • N AMERICA • 50 kW
		(J) • C AFRICA & E AFRICA • 50 kW
		(J) • W AFRICA & C AFRICA • 50 kW
15115	**ALBANIA** RADIO TIRANA, Lushnjë	E ASIA • 50 kW
	ECUADOR †HCJB-VO THE ANDES, Quito	AMERICAS • 100 kW
	FINLAND †RADIO FINLAND, Pori	EUROPE & W AFRICA • 500 kW
	KOREA (DPR) RADIO PYONGYANG, Kujang-dong	C AMERICA • 400 kW
		SE ASIA • 100 kW
	NETHERLANDS ANTILLES †TRANS WORLD RADIO, Bonaire	Alternative Frequency to 15445 kHz
	NORTHERN MARIANA IS †KYOI, Saipan Island	SE ASIA • 100 kW
	SEYCHELLES FAR EAST BC ASS'N, North Pt, Mahé Is	Su • S ASIA • 50 kW
	UNITED KINGDOM †BBC, Rampisham	(J) • EUROPE & WEST USSR • 500 kW
		(J) Su • EUROPE & WEST USSR • 500 kW
	USA †RFE-RL, Via Portugal	E EUROPE • 250 kW
	USSR RADIO MOSCOW	(J) • WS
15115v	**PAKISTAN** RADIO PAKISTAN, Islamabad	BANGLA • S ASIA & SE ASIA • 250 kW
		S ASIA & SE ASIA • 250 kW
15120	**HOLLAND** RADIO NEDERLAND, Via Neth Antilles	Su • W NORTH AM • 300 kW
	INDIA ALL INDIA RADIO, Delhi	S ASIA • 50 kW
		DS-ENGLISH, ETC • 50 kW
	POLAND †RADIO POLONIA, Warsaw	EUROPE & W AFRICA • 100 kW
		MIDEAST • 100 kW
		(J) • EUROPE & W AFRICA • 100 kW
	SRI LANKA SRI LANKA BC CORP, Colombo-Ekala	SE ASIA & E ASIA • 35 kW
		M • JAPANESE • SE ASIA & E ASIA • 35 kW
		M/Tu/Th/F • SE ASIA & E ASIA • 35 kW
		Sa • JAPANESE • SE ASIA & E ASIA • 35 kW
		Su/W • SE ASIA & E ASIA • 35 kW
		Tu-Su • SE ASIA & E ASIA • 35 kW
	USA †VOA, Greenville, NC	(D) • C AMERICA • 250 kW
		(J) • C AMERICA • 250 kW
		(D) M-F • C AMERICA & S AMERICA • 250 kW
		(J) M-F • C AMERICA & S AMERICA • 250 kW
(con'd)	**USSR** RADIO MOSCOW	(J) • ASIA • WS

World Time: 0 Prime Time-Americas 6 Prime Time-E Asia 12 Prime Time-S Asia 18 Prime Time-Europe 24

SUMMER ONLY (J) WINTER ONLY (D) JAMMING / OR /\ EARLIEST HEARD ◁ LATEST HEARD ▷ NEW OR CHANGED FOR 1990 †

FREQUENCY	COUNTRY, STATION, LOCATION	TARGET • NETWORK • POWER (kW)
15120 (con'd)	**VATICAN STATE** †VATICAN RADIO, Sta Maria di Galeria	E EUROPE & WEST USSR • 100 kW
		E AFRICA & MIDEAST • 100 kW
		Su • E EUROPE & WEST USSR • 100 kW
		AFRICA • 100 kW
		(J) • JAPANESE • ASIA & AUSTRALIA • 100 kW • ALT. FREQ. TO 15105 kHz
		(J) • ASIA & AUSTRALIA • 100 kW • ALT. FREQ. TO 15105 kHz
		Su • AFRICA • 100 kW
		M-Sa • ENGLISH, FRENCH & SPANISH • AFRICA • 100 kW
15125	**CHINA (PR)** †RADIO BEIJING	(J) • SE ASIA
		(J) • S ASIA
	GERMANY (DR) †R BERLIN INTL, Königswusterhausen	(J) • S AMERICA • 100 kW
		(J) • N AMERICA • 100 kW
	GUAM †ADVENTIST WORLD R, Agat	SE ASIA • 100 kW
	SPAIN R NACIONAL ESPANA, Noblejas	(J) • C AMERICA & S AMERICA • 350 kW
	UNITED KINGDOM †BBC, Via Maṣīrah, Oman	SE ASIA • 100 kW
		(J) • MIDEAST & S ASIA • 100 kW
	†BBC, Via Zyyi, Cyprus	(J) • N AFRICA • 100 kW
	USA †VOA, Via Philippines	SE ASIA • 250 kW
	USSR RADIO MOSCOW, Moscow	EUROPE • 250 kW
		EUROPE • WS • 250 kW
15125v	**PAKISTAN** RADIO PAKISTAN, Islamabad	(D) • E AFRICA • 100 kW
	RADIO PAKISTAN, Karachi	(D) • E AFRICA & S AFRICA • 50 kW
15130	**CHINA (TAIWAN)** VO FREE CHINA, Via Okeechobee, USA	S AMERICA • 100 kW
	USA †RFE-RL, Via Pals, Spain	WEST USSR • 250 kW
	†RFE-RL, Via Portugal	WEST USSR • 250 kW
	†WYFR-FAMILY RADIO, Okeechobee, Fl	S AMERICA • 100 kW
		C AMERICA • 50 kW
		(D) • PORTUGUESE • S AMERICA • 100 kW
		(D) • S AMERICA • 100 kW
		(J) • S AMERICA • 100 kW
15130v	**CHINA (PR)** †RADIO BEIJING, Via Bamako, Mali	(J) • N AMERICA • 50 kW
		(D) • C AFRICA & E AFRICA • 50 kW
		(D) • E NORTH AM & C AMERICA • 50 kW
15135	**CHINA (PR)** †RADIO BEIJING, Kunming	SE ASIA • 120 kW
	FRANCE †R FRANCE INTL, Issoudun-Allouis	E AFRICA • 100 kW
		(D) • E AFRICA • 100 kW
		(J) • E AFRICA • 100 kW
	UNITED ARAB EMIRATES †VOICE OF THE UAE, Abu Dhabi	EUROPE • DS • 500 kW
	UNITED KINGDOM †BBC, Skelton, Cumbria	(J) • E EUROPE & MIDEAST • TURKISH • 250 kW
	USA VOA, Greenville, NC	(D) • E AFRICA • 500 kW
	†VOA, Via Philippines	(J) • SE ASIA • 250 kW
	USSR RADIO MOSCOW, Via Plovdiv, Bulgaria	E NORTH AM • WS • 500 kW
15135v	**PAKISTAN** RADIO PAKISTAN, Karachi	(J) • E AFRICA & S AFRICA • 50 kW
15136	**PAKISTAN** RADIO PAKISTAN, Islamabad	(J) • E AFRICA • 100 kW
15140	**AUSTRALIA** RADIO AUSTRALIA, Carnarvon	SE ASIA • 100 kW
	CANADA R CANADA INTL, Sackville, NB	(D) • EUROPE • 250 kW
	JAPAN †RADIO JAPAN/NHK, Tokyo-Yamata	(J) • JAPANESE • SE ASIA • GENERAL • 100 kW
	PORTUGAL †R PORTUGAL INTL, Lisbon-S Gabriel	Sa/Su • S AMERICA • 100 kW
	SAUDI ARABIA BS OF THE KINGDOM, Jiddah	WEST USSR • DS-GENERAL • 50 kW
	UNITED KINGDOM †BBC, Via Singapore	SE ASIA & AUSTRALIA • 50/100 kW
		Su • AUSTRALIA • 100 kW
	†BBC, Via Zyyi, Cyprus	MIDEAST • 250 kW
	USSR RADIO MOSCOW, Ryazan'	S ASIA & SE ASIA • WS, LAO, RUSSIAN, ETC • 240 kW
		(J) • S ASIA & SE ASIA • WS, LAO, RUSSIAN, ETC • 240 kW
(con'd)	RADIO MOSCOW, Tbilisi	(J) • W AFRICA • 500 kW

World Time: 0 1 2 3 4 5 6 7 8 9 10 11 12 13 14 15 16 17 18 19 20 21 22 23 24

0 Prime Time-Americas 6 Prime Time-E Asia 12 Prime Time-S Asia 18 Prime Time-Europe 24

ENGLISH — ARABIC — CHINESE — FRENCH — GERMAN — RUSSIAN — SPANISH — OTHER —

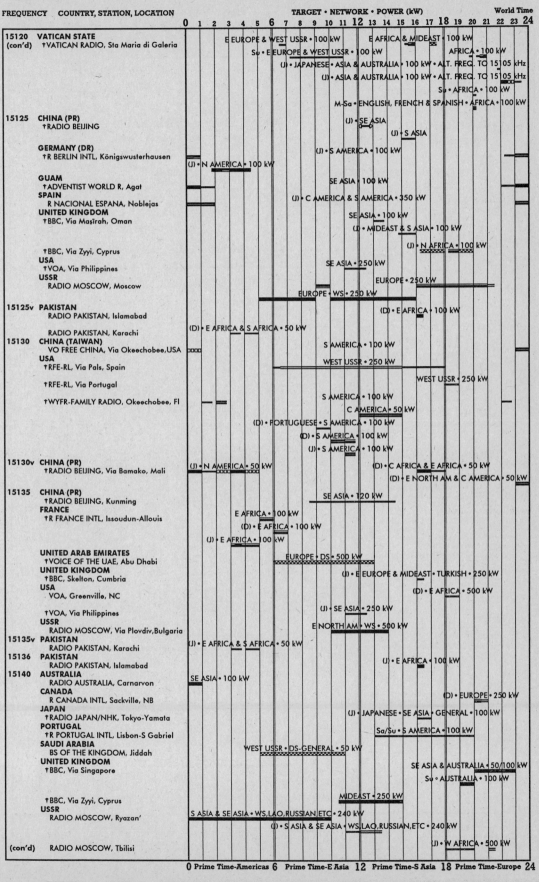

FREQUENCY	COUNTRY, STATION, LOCATION	TARGET • NETWORK • POWER (kW)
15140 (con'd)	**USSR** RADIO MOSCOW, Tbilisi	(J) • W AFRICA • AFRICAN • 500 kW
15140v	**CHILE** †RADIO NACIONAL, Santiago	Irr • AMERICAS • 100 kW
		AMERICAS • 100 kW
15145	**GERMANY (DR)** R BERLIN INTL, Nauen	E AFRICA & MIDEAST • 500 kW
	USA †RFE-RL, Via Germany	WEST USSR • 100 kW
	†RFE-RL, Via Portugal	E EUROPE • 250 kW
	WINB-WORLD INTL BC, Red Lion, Pa	S AMERICA • ENG, SPAN, PORT • 50 kW
		EUROPE & N AFRICA • ENGLISH,FRENCH,ETC • 50 kW
	†WYFR-FAMILY RADIO, Okeechobee, Fl	C AMERICA • 100 kW
		(J) • C AMERICA • 100 kW
	USSR RADIO MOSCOW	(J) • SE ASIA • WS
15150	**CANADA** R CANADA INTL, Sackville, NB	AFRICA • 250 kW
	CHINA (PR) †RADIO BEIJING	(J) • SE ASIA
	HOLLAND †RADIO NEDERLAND, Via Madagascar	S ASIA & SE ASIA • 300 kW • ALT. FREQ. TO 11735 kHz
	†RADIO NEDERLAND, Via Neth Antilles	S AMERICA • 300 kW
	IRAQ †RADIO BAGHDAD, Balad-Salah el Deen	(D) • W AFRICA • 500 kW
		(J) • EUROPE & N AFRICA • 500 kW
	NEW ZEALAND †RADIO NEW ZEALAND, Wellington	PACIFIC • 7.5 kW • ALT. FREQ. TO 15485 kHz
		(D) • PACIFIC • 7.5 kW • ALT. FREQ. TO 11780 kHz
		PACIFIC • 7.5 kW
		M-F • PACIFIC • 7.5 kW • ALT. FREQ. TO 15485 kHz
		Sa • PACIFIC • 7.5 kW • ALT. FREQ. TO 15485 kHz
		Sa-Su • PACIFIC • 7.5 kW • ALT. FREQ. TO 15485 kHz
	SWAZILAND †TRANS WORLD RADIO, Manzini	S ASIA • 100 kW
	USA VOA, Via Philippines	(J) M-F • C AFRICA & E AFRICA • 250 kW
	VOA, Via Rhodes, Greece	MIDEAST & E AFRICA • 50 kW
	USSR RADIO MOSCOW, Minsk	EUROPE, E NORTH AM & C AMERICA • 100 kW
		EUROPE, E NORTH AM & C AMERICA • WS • 100 kW
	RADIO MOSCOW, Multiple Locations	E AFRICA & EUROPE • 240/500 kW
		E AFRICA & EUROPE • WS • 240/500 kW
15150v	**INDONESIA** †VOICE OF INDONESIA, Jakarta	Alternative Frequency to 11744v kHz
15154.5	**INDONESIA** †RRI, Jakarta, Jawa	DS • 100/250 kW
15155	**CHINA (TAIWAN)** †VO FREE CHINA, T'ai-pei	(J) • MIDEAST • 250 kW
	CUBA RADIO HABANA, Havana	(J) • EUROPE • 100 kW
	CZECHOSLOVAKIA RADIO PRAGUE, Prague	E AFRICA • 120 kW
		M-F • E AFRICA • 120 kW
	ECUADOR †HCJB-VO THE ANDES, Quito	N AMERICA & C AMERICA • 100 kW
		(J) • N AMERICA & C AMERICA • 100 kW
		(J) • JAPANESE • N AMERICA & C AMERICA • 100 kW
	EGYPT RADIO CAIRO, Abu Za'bal	E AFRICA • 100 kW
	FRANCE †R FRANCE INTL, Issoudun-Allouis	(J) • E AFRICA • 100 kW
		E EUROPE & WEST USSR • 100 kW
		(D) • E AFRICA • 100 kW
		(J) • E EUROPE & WEST USSR • 100 kW
	†R FRANCE INTL, Multiple Locations	E AFRICA & S AFRICA • 100/250 kW
	GERMANY (FR) DEUTSCHE WELLE, Via Sines, Portugal	(J) • E EUROPE • 250 kW
	INDIA †ALL INDIA RADIO, Aligarh	E ASIA • 250 kW
	USA †FAMILY RADIO, Via Taiwan	E ASIA • 250 kW
	†VOA, Via Philippines	Alternative Frequency to 15160 kHz
	USSR RADIO MOSCOW, Kazan'	(J) • S ASIA • WS, TAMIL, ETC • 250 kW
15160	**ALGERIA** RTV ALGERIENNE, Bouchaoui	EUROPE • 100 kW
		EUROPE • DS-3 • 100 kW
	AUSTRALIA †RADIO AUSTRALIA, Shepparton	PACIFIC • 100 kW
	BULGARIA †RADIO SOFIA, Sofia	(J) • AFRICA • 250 kW
(con'd)	**CANADA** R CANADA INTL, Via Sines, Portugal	(J) • E EUROPE & WEST USSR • 250 kW

World Time 0–24: 0 Prime Time-Americas 6 Prime Time-E Asia 12 Prime Time-S Asia 18 Prime Time-Europe 24

SUMMER ONLY (J) WINTER ONLY (D) JAMMING / OR ⋀ EARLIEST HEARD ◁ LATEST HEARD ▷ NEW OR CHANGED FOR 1990 †

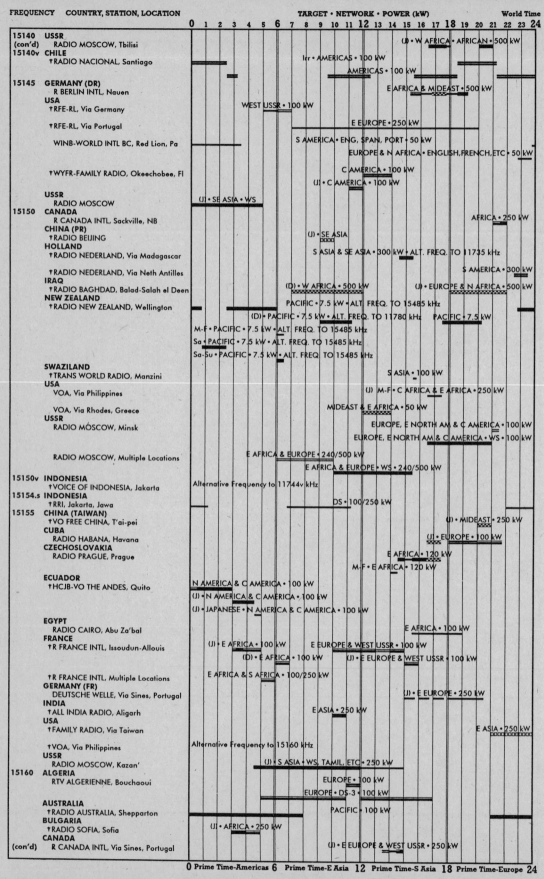

FREQUENCY · COUNTRY, STATION, LOCATION · TARGET • NETWORK • POWER (kW) · World Time 0–24

15160 (con'd) **ECUADOR**
HCJB-VO THE ANDES, Quito
C AMERICA & W NORTH AM • 100 kW

HUNGARY
RADIO BUDAPEST, Various Locations
E NORTH AM
EUROPE
M • S AMERICA
M/Th • EUROPE
S AMERICA
M • E NORTH AM
Sa • EUROPE
Tu/F • S AMERICA
Su-Tu/Th/F • E NORTH AM
Su • EUROPE
W/Th/Sa-M • S AMERICA
Tu-Su • S AMERICA
Tu-Su • E NORTH AM
Tu/W/F/Sa • E NORTH AM
Tu/W/F/Sa • S AMERICA
W/Sa • E NORTH AM

KOREA (DPR)
RADIO PYONGYANG, Kujang-dong
C AMERICA • 400 kW
SE ASIA • 200 kW
E ASIA & S ASIA • 100 kW

MEXICO
LV AMERICA LATINA, México City
Irr • DS • 10 kW

TURKEY
†TURKISH RTV CORP, Ankara
N AFRICA • 250 kW
F • TURKISH • N AFRICA • 250 kW

USA
†VOA, Via Kaválla, Greece
(J) • S ASIA • 250 kW

†VOA, Via Philippines
E ASIA • 50 kW • ALT. FREQ. TO 15155 kHz
E ASIA • 50/250 kW

VOICE OF THE OAS, Cincinnati, Ohio
C AMERICA & S AMERICA • 250 kW

15165 **CHINA (PR)**
†RADIO BEIJING
(J) • E AFRICA & S AFRICA
(J) • C AFRICA & W AFRICA
(J) • EUROPE

†RADIO BEIJING, Xi'an
SE ASIA • 150 kW
S ASIA • 150 kW
AUSTRALIA • CHINESE, CANTONESE • 150 kW

CZECHOSLOVAKIA
RADIO PRAGUE, Prague
(J) • MIDEAST • 120 kW

DENMARK
†DANMARKS RADIO, Copenhagen
(J) • S AMERICA • 50 kW
(D) • E NORTH AM • 50 kW
(J) • E NORTH AM • 50 kW
(J) • N AMERICA • 50 kW
(D) • MIDEAST & E AFRICA • 50 kW
(J) • ATLANTIC & N AMERICA • DS • 50 kW
(J) • E ASIA & AUSTRALIA • 50 kW
(J) • C AMERICA & S AMERICA • 50 kW
(D) • ATLANTIC & N AMERICA • DS • 50 kW

INDIA
ALL INDIA RADIO, Bombay
E AFRICA • 100 kW

†ALL INDIA RADIO, Delhi
(J) • SE ASIA • 50 kW

NORWAY
†RADIO NORWAY INTL, Kvitsøy
(D) • E ASIA & AUSTRALIA • 500 kW

†RADIO NORWAY INTL, Sveio
(J) • W NORTH AM • 500 kW
(J) M-Sa • PACIFIC • 500 kW
(J) Su • PACIFIC • 500 kW
(J) Su • W NORTH AM & PACIFIC • 500 kW

SOUTH AFRICA
†RADIO RSA, Meyerton
(J) • EUROPE • 250 kW

UNITED KINGDOM
†BBC, Via Zyyi, Cyprus
(J) • MIDEAST & E AFRICA • 100 kW

USA
†VOA, Via Philippines
(J) • E AFRICA • 250 kW

15170 **AUSTRALIA**
RADIO AUSTRALIA, Various Locations
E ASIA & SE ASIA • 250/300 kW

SAUDI ARABIA
BS OF THE KINGDOM, Jiddah
C AFRICA • DS-HOLY KORAN • 50 kW

USA
†RFE-RL, Via Portugal
E EUROPE • 250 kW

†WYFR-FAMILY RADIO, Okeechobee, Fl
(J) • C AMERICA • 100 kW
S AMERICA • 100 kW
C AMERICA • 50/100 kW
(D) • S AMERICA • 100 kW

USSR
RADIO MOSCOW, Irkutsk
SE ASIA • WS • 50 kW
(J) • SE ASIA • WS • 50 kW

15170.8 **SOCIETY ISLANDS**
†RFO-TAHITI, Papeete
PACIFIC • DS-FRENCH,TAHITIAN • 20 kW

15175 **DENMARK**
†DANMARKS RADIO, Copenhagen
(J) • ATLANTIC & N AMERICA • DS • 50 kW
(J) Sa/Su • ATLANTIC & N AMERICA • DS • 50 kW

EGYPT
(con'd) RADIO CAIRO, Abu Za'bal
MIDEAST • DS-GENERAL • 100 kW

0 Prime Time-Americas 6 Prime Time-E Asia 12 Prime Time-S Asia 18 Prime Time-Europe 24

ENGLISH · ARABIC · CHINESE · FRENCH · GERMAN · RUSSIAN · SPANISH · OTHER

FREQUENCY	COUNTRY, STATION, LOCATION	TARGET • NETWORK • POWER (kW)
15175 (con'd)	**EGYPT** RADIO CAIRO, Kafr Silîm-Abis	MIDEAST & S ASIA • 250 kW
	HOLLAND †RADIO NEDERLAND, Via Madagascar	(D) • E AFRICA • 300 kW
	INDIA ALL INDIA RADIO, Aligarh	SE ASIA • 250 kW
	NORWAY †RADIO NORWAY INTL, Kvitsøy	(J) • E AFRICA • 500 kW
	SEYCHELLES FAR EAST BC ASS'N, North Pt, Mahé Is	F • MIDEAST & E AFRICA • 25 kW
	UNITED KINGDOM †BBC, Via Brasília	(J) • S AMERICA • 250 kW
	USSR RADIO MOSCOW, Armavir	(J) • W EUROPE • 500 kW
		(J) • EUROPE & ATLANTIC • MARINERS • 500 kW
		(J) • W EUROPE • WS • 500 kW
	YUGOSLAVIA †RADIO YUGOSLAVIA, Bijeljina	(J) • WEST USSR • 500 kW
15180	**FRANCE** †R FRANCE INTL, Issoudun-Allouis	E EUROPE & WEST USSR • 500 kW
		(D) • E EUROPE & WEST USSR • 500 kW
		(J) • E EUROPE & WEST USSR • 500 kW
	KOREA (DPR) RADIO PYONGYANG, Kujang-dong	SE ASIA • 200 kW
		E ASIA & S ASIA • 100 kW
	NORWAY †RADIO NORWAY INTL, Kvitsøy	(J) • S ASIA • 500 kW
		(D) • AUSTRALIA • 500 kW
		(D) M-Sa • AUSTRALIA • 500 kW
		(D) Su • AUSTRALIA • 500 kW
	UNITED KINGDOM †BBC, Daventry	E EUROPE & MIDEAST • 300 kW
	†BBC, Rampisham	(D) • N AFRICA • 100 kW
	†BBC, Skelton, Cumbria	EUROPE & W AFRICA • 250 kW
		(J) • EUROPE & W AFRICA • 250 kW
	USA †VOA, Via Philippines	Alternative Frequency to 15185 kHz
	USSR †AZERBAIJANI RADIO	DS-2
	†RADIO KIEV, Komsomol'sk 'Amure	W NORTH AM • 100 kW
	†RADIO MOSCOW, Komsomol'sk 'Amure	W NORTH AM • 100 kW
		E ASIA • 100 kW
		(J) • E ASIA • 100 kW
		(J) • E ASIA • CHI, CANTONESE, ETC • 100 kW
		(J) • W NORTH AM • MARINERS • 100 kW
	†RADIO VILNIUS, Komsomol'sk 'Amure	W NORTH AM • 100 kW
	†RADIO YEREVAN, Komsomol'sk 'Amure	W NORTH AM • 100 kW
	VATICAN STATE †VATICAN RADIO, Sta Maria di Galeria	S AMERICA • 250 kW
		(J) • E NORTH AM • 250 kW
15185	**ALBANIA** RADIO TIRANA, Lushnjë	SE ASIA & AUSTRALIA • 100 kW
	FINLAND †RADIO FINLAND, Pori	(J) • AMERICAS • 500 kW
		(D) • MIDEAST & E AFRICA • 500 kW
		(J) • MIDEAST & E AFRICA • 500 kW
		(J) • EUROPE & W AFRICA • 500 kW
		(J) • EUROPE & W AFRICA • 250 kW
	GERMANY (FR) †DEUTSCHE WELLE, Jülich	(J) • WEST USSR • 100 kW
	DEUTSCHE WELLE, Various Locations	JAPANESE • E ASIA • 100/500 kW
		E ASIA • 100/500 kW
		SE ASIA • 100/500 kW
	DEUTSCHE WELLE, Via Brasília, Brazil	S AMERICA & C AMERICA • 250 kW
	†DEUTSCHE WELLE, Wertachtal	(J) • W AFRICA • 500 kW
	NORWAY †RADIO NORWAY INTL, Kvitsøy	(J) M-Sa • E ASIA & AUSTRALIA • 500 kW
	UNITED KINGDOM †BBC, Skelton, Cumbria	(J) • EUROPE & WEST USSR • 250 kW
	USA †VOA, Greenville, NC	M-F • C AMERICA & S AMERICA • 250 kW
	†VOA, Via Philippines	SE ASIA & PACIFIC • 50 kW
		(D) • S ASIA • 250 kW
		S ASIA • 250 kW
		SE ASIA & PACIFIC • 50 kW • ALT. FREQ. TO 15180 kHz
(con'd)	WINB-WORLD INTL BC, Red Lion, Pa	EUROPE & N AFRICA • 50 kW

World Time: 0 Prime Time-Americas 6 Prime Time-E Asia 12 Prime Time-S Asia 18 Prime Time-Europe 24

SUMMER ONLY (J) WINTER ONLY (D) JAMMING / OR ∧ EARLIEST HEARD ◁ LATEST HEARD ▷ NEW OR CHANGED FOR 1990 †

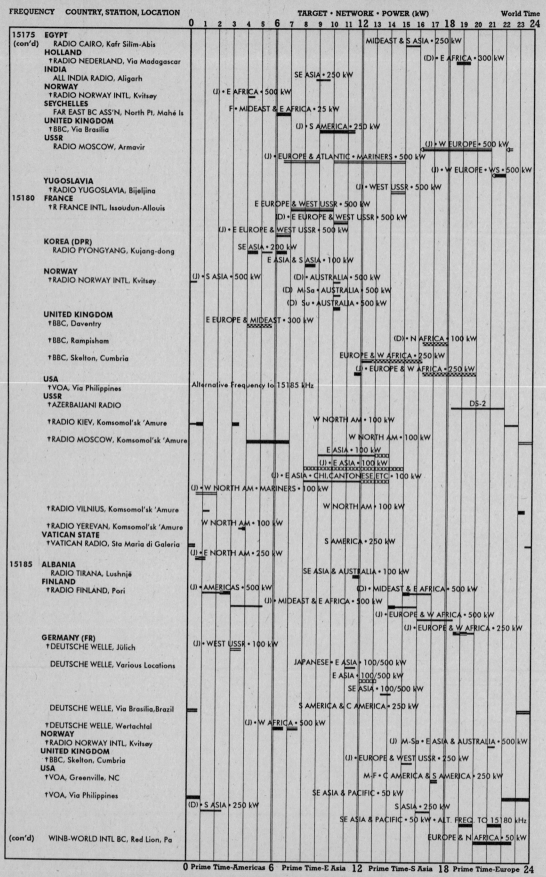

FREQUENCY	COUNTRY, STATION, LOCATION	TARGET • NETWORK • POWER (kW)
15185 (con'd)	**USSR** RADIO MOSCOW, Zhigulevsk	S ASIA • 240 kW
		DS-1 • 240 kW
	VATICAN STATE †VATICAN RADIO, Sta Maria di Galeria	Alternative Frequency to 15190 kHz
15190	**FRANCE** †R FRANCE INTL, Issoudun-Allouis	E EUROPE & WEST USSR • 100/500 kW
		(D) • E EUROPE & WEST USSR • 100/500 kW
		(J) • S AMERICA • 100/500 kW
		(J) • E EUROPE & WEST USSR • 100/500 kW
	LAOS LAO NATIONAL RADIO, Via USSR	(D) • EUROPE • 240 kW
	NORWAY †RADIO NORWAY INTL, Kvitsøy	(D) M-Sa • S ASIA & AUSTRALIA • 500 kW • ALT. FREQ. TO 15195 kHz
		(D) Su • S ASIA & AUSTRALIA • 500 kW • ALT. FREQ. TO 15195 kHz
	†RADIO NORWAY INTL, Sveio	(J) M-Sa • E NORTH AM & C AMERICA • 500 kW
		(J) Su • E NORTH AM & C AMERICA • 500 kW
	SWEDEN †RADIO SWEDEN, Hörby	(D) • USSR • 350 kW
		(D) • SWEDISH • E ASIA • 350 kW
		(D) • E ASIA • 350 kW
	USSR RADIO MOSCOW, Khabarovsk	(J) • E ASIA & SE ASIA • 100 kW
	VATICAN STATE †VATICAN RADIO, Sta Maria di Galeria	E AFRICA & MIDEAST • 100 kW
		(D) • E ASIA & SE ASIA • 250 kW
		E ASIA & SE ASIA • 250 kW
		M-Sa • AFRICA • 500 kW
		M-Sa • W AFRICA • 500 kW • ALT. FREQ. TO 15185 kHz
		(D) M-Sa • JAPANESE • E ASIA • 250 kW
		(D) M-Sa • E ASIA & SE ASIA • 250 kW
		(D) Su • E ASIA • 250 kW
15190v	**BRAZIL** R INCONFIDENCIA, Belo Horizonte	PORTUGUESE • DS • 5 kW
15191	**PAKISTAN** RADIO PAKISTAN, Islamabad	(J) • BANGLA • S ASIA • 100 kW
15195	**BANGLADESH** †RADIO BANGLADESH, Dhaka	EUROPE • 250 kW
	CHINA (PR) †RADIO BEIJING	(J) • WEST USSR
	†RADIO BEIJING, Baoding	(J) • S AMERICA • 240 kW
	†RADIO BEIJING, Jinhua	(J) • W NORTH AM • 500 kW
	FRANCE †R FRANCE INTL, Issoudun-Allouis	E EUROPE & WEST USSR • 100 kW
		(D) • E EUROPE & WEST USSR • 100 kW
		(J) • E EUROPE & WEST USSR • 100 kW
	JAPAN †RADIO JAPAN/NHK, Tokyo-Yamata	(J) • JAPANESE • PACIFIC & W NORTH AM • 100 kW
		E ASIA • GENERAL • 100 kW
		(J) • PACIFIC & W NORTH AM • 100 kW
		(J) • E ASIA • GENERAL • 100 kW
		JAPANESE • E ASIA • GENERAL • 100 kW
		(D) • E ASIA • GENERAL • 100 kW
		(J) • JAPANESE • E ASIA • GENERAL • 100 kW
		(D) • JAPANESE • E ASIA • GENERAL • 100 kW
		(J) • JAPANESE • PACIFIC & N AMERICA • GENERAL • 100 kW
		(J) • PACIFIC & N AMERICA • GENERAL • 100 kW
	NORWAY †RADIO NORWAY INTL, Kvitsøy	Alternative Frequency to 15190 kHz
	PAKISTAN RADIO PAKISTAN, Karachi	(J) • S ASIA • 50 kW
	USA VOA, Greenville, NC	W AFRICA & C AFRICA • 500 kW
	VOA, Via Rhodes, Greece	(D) • MIDEAST & E AFRICA • 50 kW
	†VOA, Via Tangier, Morocco	E EUROPE & MIDEAST • 100 kW
		(D) • E EUROPE & MIDEAST • 100 kW
	†VOA, Via Wertachtal, GFR	(J) • MIDEAST • 500 kW
	USSR RADIO MOSCOW	(J) • WS
15200	**FRANCE** †R FRANCE INTL, Via French Guiana	S AMERICA • 500 kW
		C AMERICA • 500 kW
	GABON †AFRIQUE NUMERO UN, Moyabi	Alternative Frequency to 17630 kHz
	IRAQ †RADIO BAGHDAD, Balad-Salah el Deen	(D) • S AMERICA • 500 kW
	TURKEY †TURKISH RTV CORP, Ankara	TURKISH • EUROPE • 500 kW • ALT. FREQ. TO 15055 kHz
	USSR RADIO MOSCOW, Kalach	S ASIA • 240 kW

World Time: 0 1 2 3 4 5 6 7 8 9 10 11 12 13 14 15 16 17 18 19 20 21 22 23 24

0 Prime Time-Americas 6 Prime Time-E Asia 12 Prime Time-S Asia 18 Prime Time-Europe 24

ENGLISH ARABIC CHINESE FRENCH GERMAN RUSSIAN SPANISH OTHER

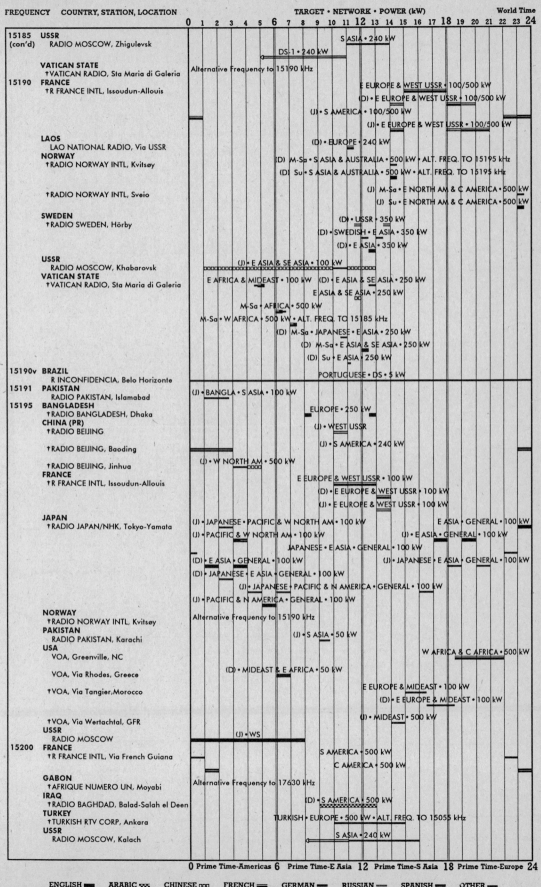

FREQUENCY	COUNTRY, STATION, LOCATION	TARGET • NETWORK • POWER (kW)
15205	**FRANCE**	
	†R FRANCE INTL, Via Beijing, China	SE ASIA • 120 kW
	GERMANY (FR)	
	DEUTSCHE WELLE, Via Antigua	S AMERICA • 250 kW
	†DEUTSCHE WELLE, Via Cyclops, Malta	(J) • E NORTH AM & C AMERICA • 250 kW
	UNITED KINGDOM	
	†BBC, Via Zyyi, Cyprus	(J) • WEST USSR • 250 kW
		(J) Su • WEST USSR • 250 kW
	USA	
	†VOA, Greenville, NC	C AMERICA & S AMERICA • 500 kW
		Tu-Sa • C AMERICA & S AMERICA • 500 kW
	†VOA, Via Kavála, Greece	MIDEAST & S ASIA • 250 kW
		(J) • MIDEAST & S ASIA • 250 kW
	VOA, Via Tangier, Morocco	(J) • EUROPE, N AFRICA & MIDEAST • 35/100 kW
	†VOA, Via Woofferton, UK	EUROPE & WEST USSR • 300 kW
		(D) • EUROPE & WEST USSR • 300 kW
15205v	**ALGERIA**	
	"VO PALESTINE", Via RTV Algerienne	N AFRICA & MIDEAST • 100 kW
	RTV ALGERIENNE, Bouchaoui	N AFRICA & MIDEAST • DS • 100 kW
		MIDEAST & N AFRICA • DS • 100 kW
15210	**CANADA**	
	†R CANADA INTL, Via Xi'an, China(PR)	(D) • SE ASIA • 120 kW
	EGYPT	
	RADIO CAIRO, Abu Za'bal	N AFRICA & W AFRICA • DS-GENERAL • 100 kW
	RADIO CAIRO, Kafr Silîm-Abis	W AFRICA • 250 kW
		N AFRICA, MIDEAST & EUROPE • DS-GENERAL • 250 kW
	PORTUGAL	
	†R PORTUGAL INTL, Lisbon-S Gabriel	M-F • MIDEAST & S ASIA • 100 kW
		M-Sa • MIDEAST & S ASIA • 100 kW
	USA	
	†VOA, Via Philippines	(J) • S ASIA • 250 kW
		(D) • SE ASIA • 50 kW
	USSR	
	RADIO MOSCOW	(J) • SE ASIA
		(D) • SE ASIA
	RADIO MOSCOW, Moscow	(J) • MIDEAST • WS, PERSIAN, TURKISH • 240 kW
15215	**CHINA (TAIWAN)**	
	VO FREE CHINA, Via Okeechobee, USA	S AMERICA • 100 kW
	FRANCE	
	†R FRANCE INTL, Via Tokyo, Japan	E ASIA • 300 kW
	JAPAN	
	†RADIO JAPAN/NHK, Tokyo-Yamata	(J) • E ASIA • 100 kW
	PHILIPPINES	
	RADIO VERITAS ASIA, Malolos	S ASIA & SE ASIA • ENG, CHI, TAMIL, ETC • 50 kW
	USA	
	†RFE-RL, Via Portugal	E EUROPE • 250 kW
	†VOA, Via Philippines	S ASIA & SE ASIA • 250 kW
		SE ASIA • 50/250 kW
		(D) • S ASIA & SE ASIA • 250 kW
	†WYFR-FAMILY RADIO, Okeechobee, Fl	S AMERICA • 100 kW
		W NORTH AM • 100 kW
		(J) • W NORTH AM • 100 kW
	USSR	
	RADIO MOSCOW	(J) • WS
15215v	**ALGERIA**	
	"VO FREE SAHARA", Via RTV Algerienne	W AFRICA & S AMERICA • POLISARIO FRONT • 100 kW
	RTV ALGERIENNE, Bouchaoui	W AFRICA & S AMERICA • DS-3 • 100 kW
		W AFRICA & S AMERICA • 100 kW
15220	**ECUADOR**	
	HCJB-VO THE ANDES, Quito	S AMERICA • 100 kW
	EGYPT	
	RADIO CAIRO, Kafr Silîm-Abis	C AMERICA & S AMERICA • 250 kW
	HUNGARY	
	RADIO BUDAPEST, Various Locations	EUROPE
		M-Th • EUROPE
		Sa • EUROPE
		Su • EUROPE
	NORWAY	
	†RADIO NORWAY INTL, Fredrikstad	(J) Su • EUROPE • 350 kW
	†RADIO NORWAY INTL, Kvitsøy	(D) • EUROPE & AFRICA • 500 kW
		(J) • MIDEAST • 500 kW
	SOUTH AFRICA	
	†RADIO RSA, Meyerton	(D) • C AFRICA • 500 kW
		(D) • S AFRICA & W AFRICA • 500 kW
	UNITED KINGDOM	
	†BBC, Skelton, Cumbria	(J) • W AFRICA • 100 kW
	USSR	
(con'd)	RADIO MOSCOW, Dushanbé	(J) • SE ASIA • WS, VIETNAMESE, ETC • 500 kW

World Time: 0 Prime Time-Americas 6 Prime Time-E Asia 12 Prime Time-S Asia 18 Prime Time-Europe 24

SUMMER ONLY (J) WINTER ONLY (D) JAMMING / OR ⋀ EARLIEST HEARD ◃ LATEST HEARD ▹ NEW OR CHANGED FOR 1990 †

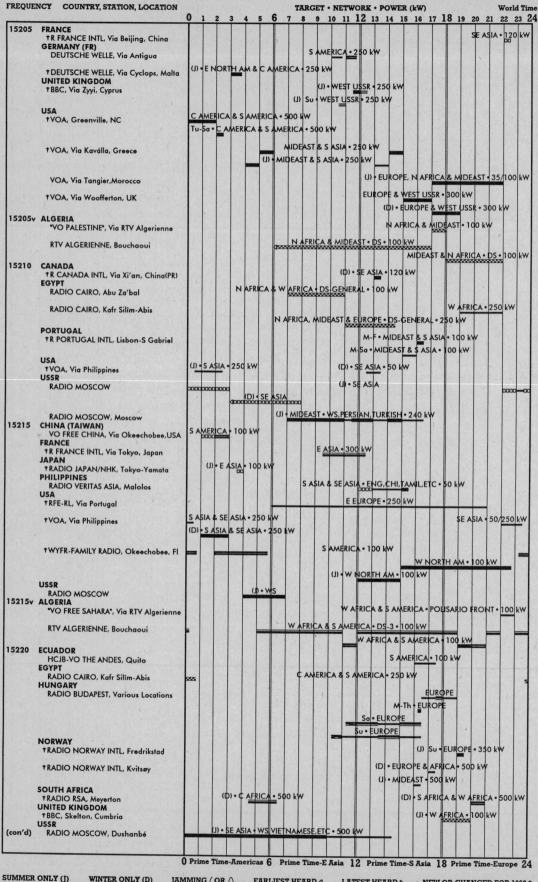

FREQUENCY	COUNTRY, STATION, LOCATION	TARGET • NETWORK • POWER (kW) — World Time 0–24
15220 (con'd)	**USSR** RADIO MOSCOW, Zhigulevsk	(D) • S ASIA • WS, URDU, ETC • 240 kW
15225	**CANADA** †R CANADA INTL, Via United Kingdom	(J) M-F • MIDEAST • 300 kW
	GUAM †ADVENTIST WORLD R, Agat	(J) • E ASIA • 100 kW
		Sa/Su • E ASIA • 100 kW
	NORWAY †RADIO NORWAY INTL, Kvitsøy	MIDEAST & E AFRICA • 500 kW
		(D) M-Sa • AFRICA • 500 kW
		(D) Su • AFRICA • 500 kW
	PHILIPPINES RADIO VERITAS ASIA, Malolos	SE ASIA • VIETNAMESE, ETC • 100 kW
	PORTUGAL †R PORTUGAL INTL, Lisbon-S Gabriel	M-F • SE ASIA • 100 kW
		Sa/Su • SE ASIA • 100 kW
	UNITED KINGDOM †BBC, Daventry	(J) • E EUROPE & MIDEAST • 300 kW
	BBC, Rampisham	(J) • WEST USSR • 500 kW
	USA KUSW, Salt Lake City,Utah	E NORTH AM • 100 kW
		Su • E NORTH AM • 100 kW
	†VOA, Greenville, NC	M-F • C AMERICA • 250 kW
	VOA, Via Kaválla, Greece	(J) • MIDEAST & S ASIA • 250 kW
	VOA, Via Woofferton, UK	(D) • WEST USSR • 250 kW
		(J) • WEST USSR • 250 kW
15230	**BRAZIL** RADIO NACIONAL, Brasília	EUROPE & W AFRICA • 250 kW
	CUBA RADIO HABANA, Via USSR	(J) • W EUROPE & W AFRICA • 120 kW
	ECUADOR †HCJB-VO THE ANDES, Quito	(J) • AMERICAS • 250 kW
	INDIA ALL INDIA RADIO, Aligarh	SE ASIA • 250 kW
	IRAQ †RADIO BAGHDAD, Balad-Salah el Deen	Alternative Frequency to 13665 kHz
	JAPAN †RADIO JAPAN/NHK, Tokyo-Yamata	(D) • JAPANESE • SE ASIA • GENERAL • 100 kW
		(D) • SE ASIA • GENERAL • 100 kW
		(J) • SE ASIA • GENERAL • 100 kW
	NORWAY †RADIO NORWAY INTL, Kvitsøy	(J) • S ASIA • 500 kW
	USSR RADIO MOSCOW, Alma-Ata	(J) • SE ASIA • WS, VIETNAMESE, ETC • 100 kW
15235	**CANADA** †R CANADA INTL, Sackville, NB	(J) • C AMERICA & S AMERICA • 250 kW
		(J) Su/M • C AMERICA & S AMERICA • 250 kW
		M-F/F • C AMERICA & S AMERICA • 250 kW
		(J) Tu-Sa • C AMERICA & S AMERICA • 250 kW
		(J) Sa/Su • C AMERICA & S AMERICA • 250 kW
	CHINA (PR) †RADIO BEIJING, Beijing	S AMERICA • 120 kW
	GERMANY (FR) †DEUTSCHE WELLE, Wertachtal	(J) • S ASIA & SE ASIA • 500 kW
	INDIA ALL INDIA RADIO, Delhi	DS-ENGLISH, ETC • 100 kW
	JAPAN †RADIO JAPAN/NHK, Via Moyabi, Gabon	(D) • EUROPE & N AFRICA • 500 kW
	LIBYA RADIO JAMAHIRIYA, Tripoli	S AMERICA • 500 kW
	UNITED KINGDOM †BBC, Rampisham	(D) • E EUROPE • 500 kW
		(J) • E EUROPE • 500 kW
		(D) Su • E EUROPE • 500 kW
		(J) Su • E EUROPE • 500 kW
	†BBC, Via Maşīrah, Oman	(D) • MIDEAST • 100 kW
		(J) • E AFRICA • 100 kW
	†BBC, Via Zyyi, Cyprus	(J) • MIDEAST & E AFRICA • 100 kW
	†BBC, Woofferton	(D) Su • WEST USSR • 300 kW
	USA VOA, Via Kaválla, Greece	(J) • WEST USSR • 250 kW
	VOA, Via Tangier,Morocco	(J) • E EUROPE • 100 kW
	†VOA, Via Woofferton, UK	N AFRICA • 300 kW
		WEST USSR • 250/300 kW
		(D) • WEST USSR • 300 kW
		(J) • WEST USSR • 250/300 kW
15240	**AUSTRALIA** RADIO AUSTRALIA, Multiple Locations	PACIFIC & SE ASIA • 100/250 kW
	RADIO AUSTRALIA, Shepparton	Su • PACIFIC • 50 kW
		PACIFIC • 50 kW
		PACIFIC & SE ASIA • 50/100 kW
(con'd)		

0 Prime Time-Americas 6 Prime Time-E Asia 12 Prime Time-S Asia 18 Prime Time-Europe 24

ENGLISH — ARABIC — CHINESE — FRENCH — GERMAN — RUSSIAN — SPANISH — OTHER —

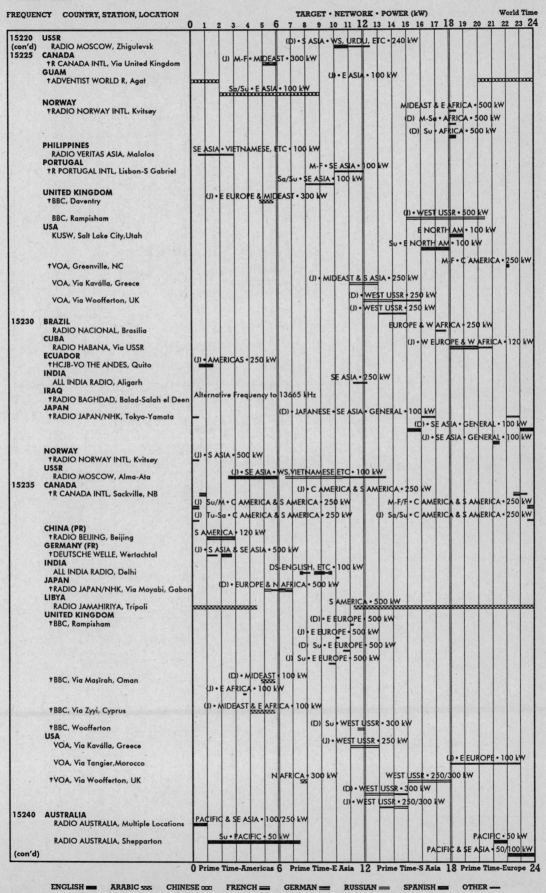

FREQUENCY	COUNTRY, STATION, LOCATION	TARGET • NETWORK • POWER (kW)
15240 (con'd)	**GERMANY (DR)** †R BERLIN INTL, Königswusterhausen	(J) • C AMERICA • 100 kW; S ASIA & SE ASIA • ENGLISH, HINDI • 100 kW
	†R BERLIN INTL, Nauen	MIDEAST & N AFRICA • 500 kW; S ASIA & SE ASIA • 500 kW
	GUAM KTWR-TRANS WORLD R, Merizo	SE ASIA • 100 kW
	PHILIPPINES RADIO VERITAS ASIA, Malolos	SE ASIA • INDONESIAN • 50 kW
	SOUTH AFRICA †RADIO RSA, Meyerton	(D) • EUROPE • 250 kW
	USSR †GEORGIAN RADIO	DS-1
15245	**FINLAND** RADIO FINLAND, Pori	E ASIA • 500 kW
	GERMANY (FR) †DEUTSCHE WELLE, Via Sines, Portugal	EUROPE & WEST USSR • 250 kW
	ITALY †RTV ITALIANA, Rome	(J) • S AMERICA • 100 kW; (J) • C AMERICA & S AMERICA • 100 kW; (J) • MIDEAST • 100 kW
	UNITED KINGDOM BBC, Via Maṣīrah, Oman	S ASIA • 100 kW
	†BBC, Via Zyyi, Cyprus	MIDEAST • 250 kW; (J) • MIDEAST • 250 kW; Sa/Su • MIDEAST • 250 kW
	USA VOA, Greenville, NC	N AFRICA • 500 kW
	VOA, Via Tangier, Morocco	(D) • WEST USSR • 35 kW
	USSR RADIO MOSCOW, Irkutsk	(J) • SE ASIA • 500 kW
	RADIO MOSCOW, Petropavlovsk-Kam	(J) • W NORTH AM • WS • 120 kW
	ZAIRE LA VOIX DU ZAIRE, Kinshasa	Irr • DS-FRENCH, ETC • 100 kW
15250	**ECUADOR** HCJB-VO THE ANDES, Quito	S AMERICA • 250 kW
	GERMANY (FR) †DEUTSCHE WELLE, Via Sri Lanka	(D) • E ASIA • 250 kW
	INDIA ALL INDIA RADIO, Delhi	DS-ENGLISH, ETC • 50 kW
	NORTHERN MARIANA IS †KYOI, Saipan Island	AUSTRALIA • 100 kW
	PORTUGAL †R PORTUGAL INTL, Lisbon-S Gabriel	E AFRICA & S AFRICA • 100 kW; M-F • E AFRICA & S AFRICA • 100 kW; Sa/Su • E AFRICA & S AFRICA • 100 kW
	ROMANIA †RADIO BUCHAREST, Bucharest	(D) • SE ASIA & AUSTRALIA • 250 kW; (D) • W EUROPE • 250 kW; (D) • MIDEAST • 250 kW; (J) • MIDEAST • 250 kW; (J) • W EUROPE & N AFRICA • 250 kW
	USA VOA, Via Philippines	SE ASIA • 50/250 kW; (J) • SE ASIA • 250 kW
	†VOA, Via Sri Lanka	S ASIA • 35 kW
15255	**AFGHANISTAN** †RADIO AFGHANISTAN, Via USSR	(J) • S ASIA • ALT. FREQ. TO 21600 kHz; (J) • S ASIA • DS-1 • ALT. FREQ. TO 21600 kHz; (J) • S ASIA • DS-2 • ALT. FREQ. TO 21600 kHz
	EGYPT RADIO CAIRO, Abu Za'bal	E AFRICA • 100 kW
	GERMANY (DR) †R BERLIN INTL, Nauen	(D) • W AFRICA • 500 kW
	PHILIPPINES RADIO VERITAS ASIA, Malolos	SE ASIA & S ASIA • CHI,INDO,TAMIL,ETC • 50 kW
	ROMANIA †RADIO BUCHAREST, Bucharest	(J) • W EUROPE & N AFRICA • 250 kW
	USA †RFE-RL, Via Portugal	E EUROPE • 250 kW
15260	**CANADA** R CANADA INTL, Sackville, NB	AFRICA • 250 kW; M-F • AFRICA • 250 kW; Sa/Su • AFRICA • 250 kW
	CHINA (PR) RADIO BEIJING, Xi'an	SE ASIA • 150 kW
	UNITED KINGDOM †BBC, Via Ascension	S AMERICA • 250 kW
	BBC, Via Sackville, Can	N AMERICA • 250 kW; Sa/Su • N AMERICA • 250 kW
(con'd)	**USA** VOA, Via Kavála, Greece	(J) • MIDEAST • 250 kW

World Time: 0 Prime Time-Americas 6 Prime Time-E Asia 12 Prime Time-S Asia 18 Prime Time-Europe 24

SUMMER ONLY (J) WINTER ONLY (D) JAMMING / OR ∧ EARLIEST HEARD ◁ LATEST HEARD ▷ NEW OR CHANGED FOR 1990 †

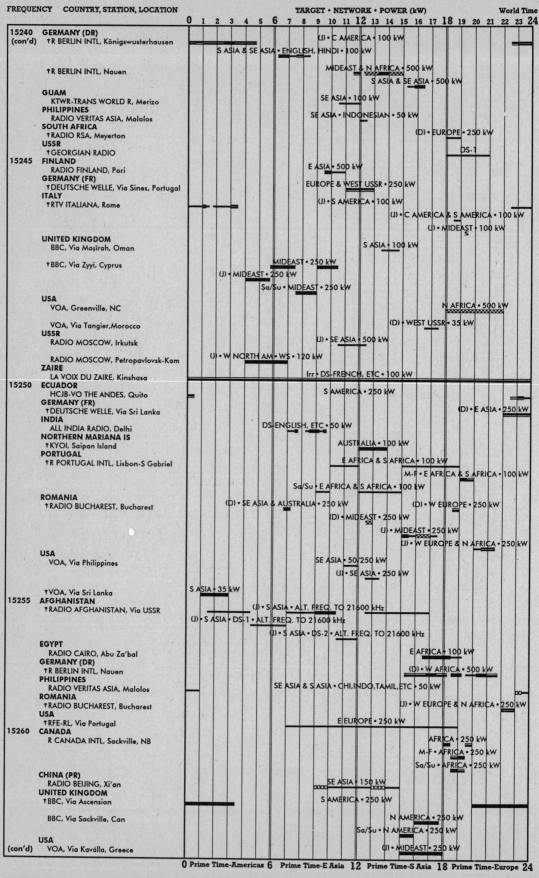

FREQUENCY	COUNTRY, STATION, LOCATION	TARGET • NETWORK • POWER (kW)
15260 (con'd)	**USSR** RADIO MOSCOW, Baku	(J) • EUROPE • WS • 240 kW
	RADIO MOSCOW, Kiev	(D) • EUROPE • 100 kW
		(D) M-Sa • EUROPE • 100 kW
	RADIO YEREVAN, Kiev	(D) Su • EUROPE • 100 kW
15265	**BRAZIL** RADIO NACIONAL, Brasília	EUROPE • 250 kW
	FRANCE †R FRANCE INTL, Via Moyabi, Gabon	(D) • MIDEAST • 250 kW
	GERMANY (FR) †DEUTSCHE WELLE, Wertachtal	(J) • C AFRICA & S AFRICA • 500 kW
	GUAM †KTWR-TRANS WORLD R, Merizo	E ASIA • 100 kW
	NORWAY †RADIO NORWAY INTL, Fredrikstad	(J) • MIDEAST • 350 kW
	†RADIO NORWAY INTL, Kvitsøy	(J) Su • E ASIA • 500 kW
	†RADIO NORWAY INTL, Sveio	(J) • S AMERICA • 500 kW
		(D) M-Sa • N AMERICA • 500 kW
		(D) Su • N AMERICA • 500 kW
	PORTUGAL †R PORTUGAL INTL, Lisbon-S Gabriel	(D) • E AFRICA & S AFRICA • 100 kW
		Sa/Su • E AFRICA & S AFRICA • 100 kW
	USA †VOA, Greenville, NC	M-F • S AMERICA • 500 kW
		Sa/Su • C AMERICA & S AMERICA • 500 kW
	†VOA, Via Philippines	Alternative Frequency to 21475 kHz
		(D) • S ASIA • 250 kW
	USSR RADIO MOSCOW, Chita	(J) • S ASIA & SE ASIA • WS • 100 kW
		(J) • S ASIA • HINDI, URDU • 100 kW
15265.6	**QATAR** QATAR BC SERVICE, Doha	N AFRICA • DS • 250 kW
15270	**CANADA** †R CANADA INTL, Via Tokyo, Japan	E ASIA & SE ASIA • 300 kW
	CHINA (TAIWAN) †CHINA BC CORP, T'ai-pei	E ASIA • DS
	VO FREE CHINA, T'ai-pei	SE ASIA • 100 kW
	ECUADOR †HCJB-VO THE ANDES, Quito	EUROPE • 500 kW
		(D) • EUROPE • 500 kW
		M-F • EUROPE • 500 kW
		Sa/Su • EUROPE • 500 kW
	GERMANY (FR) DEUTSCHE WELLE, Via Kigali, Rwanda	W AFRICA & AMERICAS • 250 kW
	JAPAN †RADIO JAPAN/NHK, Tokyo-Yamata	AUSTRALIA • 100 kW
		(J) • AUSTRALIA • GENERAL • 100 kW
		AUSTRALIA • GENERAL • 100 kW
		(J) • SE ASIA • 100 kW
		JAPANESE • AUSTRALIA • GENERAL • 100 kW
		(J) • JAPANESE • AUSTRALIA • GENERAL • 100 kW
	PAKISTAN RADIO PAKISTAN, Islamabad	(J) • EUROPE • 250 kW
	PHILIPPINES RADIO VERITAS ASIA, Malolos	JAPANESE • E ASIA • 100 kW
	ROMANIA †RADIO BUCHAREST, Bucharest	Alternative Frequency to 15365 kHz
		(D) • AFRICA • 250 kW
		(J) • EUROPE • 250 kW • ALT. FREQ. TO 15405 kHz
	UNITED KINGDOM †BBC, Via Zyyi, Cyprus	(D) • WEST USSR • 100 kW
		(D) Su • WEST USSR • 250 kW
	USA †VOA, Via Tangier, Morocco	(J) • WEST USSR • 100 kW
	†VOA, Via Wertachtal, GFR	(J) • WEST USSR • 500 kW
	†VOA, Via Woofferton, UK	(J) • WEST USSR • 300 kW
15275	**CANADA** †R CANADA INTL, Via Vienna, Austria	(J) • MIDEAST • 300 kW
		(J) M-F • MIDEAST • 300 kW
		(J) Sa-Su • MIDEAST • 300 kW
	FRANCE †R FRANCE INTL, Via Beijing, China	S ASIA • 120 kW
	GERMANY (FR) †DEUTSCHE WELLE, Jülich	C AFRICA & S AFRICA • 100 kW
		MIDEAST • 100 kW
		(J) • MIDEAST • 100 kW
	†DEUTSCHE WELLE, Multiple Locations	MIDEAST • 100/500 kW
		AFRICA • 100/500 kW
		MIDEAST & S ASIA • 100/500 kW
(con'd)		

World Time 0–24

0 Prime Time-Americas 6 Prime Time-E Asia 12 Prime Time-S Asia 18 Prime Time-Europe 24

ENGLISH ARABIC CHINESE FRENCH GERMAN RUSSIAN SPANISH OTHER

FREQUENCY	COUNTRY, STATION, LOCATION	TARGET • NETWORK • POWER (kW)
15275 (con'd)	**GERMANY (FR)** DEUTSCHE WELLE, Wertachtal	(J) • MIDEAST & S ASIA • 500 kW
	INDIA †ALL INDIA RADIO, Aligarh	(J) • SE ASIA • 250 kW
	NORTHERN MARIANA IS †KYOI, Saipan Island	SE ASIA • 100 kW
	SAUDI ARABIA BS OF THE KINGDOM, Riyadh	E AFRICA & S AFRICA • 350 kW
15280	**HOLLAND** RADIO NEDERLAND, Flevoland	W EUROPE & W AFRICA • 500 kW
	INDIA ALL INDIA RADIO, Bombay	E AFRICA • 100 kW
	SPAIN †R NACIONAL ESPANA, Arganda	(J) • EUROPE • 100 kW
	UNITED KINGDOM †BBC, Via Hong Kong	E ASIA • 250 kW
		(J) Su • E ASIA • 250 kW
		JAPANESE • E ASIA • 250 kW
		(J) • E ASIA • 250 kW
	USA KGEI-VO FRIENDSHIP, Redwood City,Ca	C AMERICA & S AMERICA • 50 kW
	†VOA, Via Tangier,Morocco	(J) • E EUROPE & WEST USSR • 100 kW
	VOA, Via Woofferton, UK	(D) • WEST USSR • 250 kW
		(J) • WEST USSR • 300 kW
	USSR RADIO MOSCOW, Armavir	(J) • W EUROPE & ATLANTIC • 500 kW
	RADIO MOSCOW, Serpukhov	(J) • S ASIA • WS • 240 kW
15285	**CANADA** †R CANADA INTL, Via Xi'an, China(PR)	(J) • SE ASIA • 120 kW
	EGYPT RADIO CAIRO, Abu Za'bal	MIDEAST • DS-NILE VALLEY • 100 kW
		MIDEAST • DS-PALESTINE RADIO • 100 kW
		MIDEAST • DS-VO THE ARABS • 100 kW
	FRANCE †R FRANCE INTL, Via Beijing, China	SE ASIA & AUSTRALIA • 120 kW
	PORTUGAL †R PORTUGAL INTL, Lisbon-S Gabriel	Sa/Su • E NORTH AM • 100 kW
	USSR RADIO MOSCOW, Irkutsk	E ASIA • 240 kW
	RADIO MOSCOW, Serpukhov	S ASIA • WS • 100 kW
15290	**BULGARIA** †RADIO SOFIA, Plovdiv	(J) • E NORTH AM & C AMERICA • 500 kW
		(J) • EUROPE • 500 kW
	CHINA (PR) RADIO BEIJING, Xi'an	(J) • E NORTH AM, C AMERICA & S AMERICA • 300 kW
	ICELAND RIKISUTVARPID, Reykjavik	Sa/Su • ATLANTIC & EUROPE • DS-1 • 10 kW • USB
	USA †RFE-RL, Via Pals, Spain	WEST USSR • 250 kW
	†RFE-RL, Via Portugal	WEST USSR • 50 kW
	VOA, Via Philippines	E ASIA • 100/250 kW
	USSR †RADIO KIEV, Via Plovdiv,Bulgaria	(J) • E NORTH AM & C AMERICA • 500 kW
	†RADIO MOSCOW, Via Plovdiv,Bulgaria	(J) • E NORTH AM & C AMERICA • 500 kW
15295	**CUBA** RADIO HABANA, Via USSR	(J) • MIDEAST & E AFRICA • 200 kW
	ECUADOR HCJB-VO THE ANDES, Quito	S AMERICA • 100 kW
		JAPANESE • S AMERICA • 100 kW
	MALAYSIA VOICE OF MALAYSIA, Kajang	AUSTRALIA • 500 kW
		MIDEAST • 500 kW
	MOZAMBIQUE †RADIO MOCAMBIQUE, Maputo	PORTUGUESE • DS • 100 kW
	USA WINB-WORLD INTL BC, Red Lion, Pa	EUROPE & N AFRICA • ENGLISH, ETC • 50 kW
	USSR RADIO MOSCOW, Voronezh, RSFSR	S ASIA • 240 kW
		S ASIA • WS • 240 kW
15296	**PAKISTAN** RADIO PAKISTAN, Islamabad	(J) • BANGLA • S ASIA • 100 kW
15300	**FRANCE** †R FRANCE INTL, Issoudun-Allouis	AFRICA • 100/500 kW
		(J) • MIDEAST • 100 kW
		(J) • AFRICA • 100/500 kW
	†R FRANCE INTL, Multiple Locations	(J) • AFRICA • 100/250/500 kW
	JAPAN †RADIO JAPAN/NHK, Tokyo-Yamata	SE ASIA • 100 kW
		(D) • SE ASIA • 100 kW
		(J) • JAPANESE • S AMERICA • GENERAL • 300 kW
	SEYCHELLES FAR EAST BC ASS'N, North Pt, Mahé Is	E AFRICA & MIDEAST • 100 kW
		F • E AFRICA & MIDEAST • 100 kW
(con'd)		

World Time: 0 Prime Time-Americas 6 Prime Time-E Asia 12 Prime Time-S Asia 18 Prime Time-Europe 24

SUMMER ONLY (J) WINTER ONLY (D) JAMMING / OR /\ EARLIEST HEARD ◁ LATEST HEARD ▷ NEW OR CHANGED FOR 1990 †

FREQUENCY	COUNTRY, STATION, LOCATION	TARGET • NETWORK • POWER (kW)
15300 (con'd)	**SEYCHELLES** FAR EAST BC ASS'N, North Pt, Mahé Is	Su/F • E AFRICA & MIDEAST • 100 kW
	UNITED ARAB EMIRATES †UAE RADIO, Dubai	EUROPE & E NORTH AM • 300 kW
	USA †WCSN, Scotts Corners, Me	W AFRICA & S AFRICA • 500 kW
		M-F • W AFRICA & S AFRICA • 500 kW
		Sa • W AFRICA & S AFRICA • 500 kW
		Sa/Su • W AFRICA & S AFRICA • 500 kW
		Su-F • W AFRICA & S AFRICA • 500 kW
	USSR RADIO MOSCOW, Novosibirsk	(J) • E ASIA • 500 kW
15305	**CANADA** †R CANADA INTL, Sackville, NB	(J) • E EUROPE & WEST USSR • 250 kW
	†R CANADA INTL, Via Sines, Portugal	(J) • E EUROPE & WEST USSR • 250 kW
	INDIA ALL INDIA RADIO, Delhi	Su • DS • 50 kW
		DS-ENGLISH, ETC • 50 kW
	MONGOLIA †RADIO ULAN BATOR, Ulan Bator	E ASIA • 250 kW
	NORTHERN MARIANA IS KFBS-FAR EAST BC, Saipan Island	S ASIA & SE ASIA • 100 kW
	USA †VOA, Via Philippines	E ASIA & AUSTRALIA • 35 kW
	VOA, Via Rhodes, Greece	(J) • MIDEAST & E AFRICA • 50 kW
	USSR RADIO MOSCOW, Tbilisi	(D) • EUROPE & ATLANTIC • MARINERS • 100 kW
15310	**BULGARIA** †RADIO SOFIA, Sofia	S AMERICA • 250 kW
		AFRICA • 250 kW
	GUAM †ADVENTIST WORLD R, Agat	(J) • JAPANESE • E ASIA • 100 kW
	IRAQ †RADIO BAGHDAD, Balad-Salah el Deen	E AFRICA • 500 kW
		(J) • E AFRICA • 500 kW
	NORWAY †RADIO NORWAY INTL, Fredrikstad	(J) • W NORTH AM & PACIFIC • 350 kW
		(D) • MIDEAST • 350 kW
	†RADIO NORWAY INTL, Sveio	(J) • S AMERICA • 500 kW
		N AMERICA • 500 kW
		(J) • W NORTH AM • 500 kW
		(D) • E NORTH AM & C AMERICA • 500 kW
		(D) • N AMERICA • 500 kW
		(D) M-Sa • W NORTH AM • 500 kW
		(J) M-Sa • N AMERICA • 500 kW
		(D) Su • W NORTH AM • 500 kW
		(J) Su • N AMERICA • 500 kW
	UNITED KINGDOM †BBC, Via Maṣīrah, Oman	S ASIA & SE ASIA • 100 kW
	†BBC, Via Singapore	S ASIA & SE ASIA • 100 kW
	†BBC, Via Zyyi, Cyprus	(J) • MIDEAST • 250 kW
15315	**AUSTRALIA** †RADIO AUSTRALIA, Shepparton	Alternative Frequency to 15320 kHz
	CANADA R CANADA INTL, Via Sines, Portugal	(D) • E EUROPE & WEST USSR • 250 kW
	FRANCE †R FRANCE INTL, Issoudun-Allouis	W AFRICA • 100/500 kW
		(J) • W AFRICA • 500 kW
		(D) • W AFRICA • 500 kW
	HOLLAND †RADIO NEDERLAND, Via Neth Antilles	S AMERICA • 300 kW
		E NORTH AM • 300 kW
	UNITED KINGDOM †BBC, Skelton, Cumbria	(J) • E EUROPE • 250 kW
	USA VOA, Via M'rovia, Liberia	W AFRICA & C AFRICA • 250 kW
	USSR RADIO MOSCOW, Irkutsk	(J) • E ASIA & SE ASIA • 500 kW
		(D) • E ASIA & SE ASIA • 500 kW
15320	**AUSTRALIA** †RADIO AUSTRALIA, Shepparton	PACIFIC & N AMERICA • 100 kW
		PACIFIC & E AFRICA • 100 kW • ALT. FREQ. TO 15315 kHz
	CANADA †R CANADA INTL, Sackville, NB	(J) M-F • C AMERICA & S AMERICA • 250 kW
	CHINA (PR) RADIO BEIJING, Xi'an	SE ASIA • 150 kW
	GERMANY (FR) †DEUTSCHE WELLE, Wertachtal	MIDEAST • 500 kW
	INDIA ALL INDIA RADIO, Delhi	DS-ENGLISH, ETC • 50 kW
	UNITED ARAB EMIRATES †UAE RADIO, Dubai	EUROPE • 300 kW • ALT. FREQ. TO 17865 kHz
		EUROPE & E NORTH AM • 500 kW
	USA VOA, Via M'rovia, Liberia	C AFRICA & S AFRICA • 250 kW
		M-F • C AFRICA & S AFRICA • 250 kW
(con'd)		

World Time 0 1 2 3 4 5 6 7 8 9 10 11 12 13 14 15 16 17 18 19 20 21 22 23 24

0 Prime Time-Americas 6 Prime Time-E Asia 12 Prime Time-S Asia 18 Prime Time-Europe 24

ENGLISH ▬ ARABIC ▭ CHINESE ▫▫▫ FRENCH ═ GERMAN ═ RUSSIAN ═ SPANISH ═ OTHER —

FREQUENCY	COUNTRY, STATION, LOCATION	TARGET • NETWORK • POWER (kW)
15320 (con'd)	**USSR**	
	RADIO MOSCOW, Kingisepp	(J) • MIDEAST • WS • 100 kW
	RADIO MOSCOW, Orcha	MIDEAST • WS, PERSIAN • 100 kW
15325	**CANADA**	
	†R CANADA INTL, Sackville, NB	(D) • EUROPE & WEST USSR • 250 kW
		(J) • EUROPE & WEST USSR • 250 kW
		(D) M-F • EUROPE & WEST USSR • 250 kW
		(J) M-F • EUROPE & WEST USSR • 250 kW
		(D) Sa/Su • EUROPE & WEST USSR • 250 kW
		(J) Sa/Su • EUROPE & WEST USSR • 250 kW
	†R CANADA INTL, Via Sines, Portugal	(D) • EUROPE & WEST USSR • 250 kW
	†R CANADA INTL, Via United Kingdom	(J) • EUROPE & WEST USSR • 300 kW
	FINLAND	
	†RADIO FINLAND, Pori	EUROPE & W AFRICA • 100 kW • USB
	JAPAN	
	†RADIO JAPAN/NHK, Tokyo-Yamata	(D) • EUROPE • 300 kW
		(D) • EUROPE • GENERAL • 300 kW
		(D) • JAPANESE • EUROPE • GENERAL • 300 kW
	†RADIO JAPAN/NHK, Via French Guiana	(J) • C AMERICA • 500 kW
		(J) • JAPANESE • C AMERICA • GENERAL • 500 kW
	NORWAY	
	†RADIO NORWAY INTL, Kvitsøy	(J) • N AMERICA • 500 kW
	†RADIO NORWAY INTL, Sveio	(D) • N AMERICA • 500 kW
		M-Sa • N AMERICA • 500 kW
		Su • N AMERICA • 500 kW
	SEYCHELLES	
	FAR EAST BC ASS'N, North Pt, Mahé Is	S ASIA • 25/50/100 kW
		M-Sa • S ASIA • 50 kW
		Sa/Su • S ASIA • 25 kW
	USA	
	VOA, Via Philippines	EAST USSR • 250 kW
	YUGOSLAVIA	
	†RADIO YUGOSLAVIA, Bijeljina	(D) • E NORTH AM • 500 kW
	†VARIOUS LOCAL STNS, Bijeljina	(D) Sa/Su • E ASIA & AUSTRALIA • DS • 500 kW
15330	**BULGARIA**	
	†RADIO SOFIA, Sofia	(J) • EUROPE • 250 kW
	CHINA (PR)	
	RADIO BEIJING, Beijing	SE ASIA • 120 kW
	HOLLAND	
	RADIO NEDERLAND, Via Madagascar	SE ASIA • 300 kW
	†RADIO NEDERLAND, Via Neth Antilles	C AMERICA • 300 kW
	ITALY	
	†RTV ITALIANA, Rome	S ASIA & SE ASIA • 100 kW
		(J) • E ASIA • 100 kW
		E AFRICA & MIDEAST • 100 kW
		(J) Su • AUSTRALIA • 100 kW
		AUSTRALIA • 100 kW
		SE ASIA & AUSTRALIA • 100 kW
		(J) • WEST USSR • 100 kW
		(J) • E AFRICA & MIDEAST • 100 kW
	MOROCCO	
	RTV MAROCAINE, Tangier	MIDEAST, EUROPE & N AFRICA • DS • 50 kW
	PHILIPPINES	
	RADIO VERITAS ASIA, Malolos	S ASIA & SE ASIA • ENGLISH, BENGAL, ETC • 100 kW
	USA	
	VOA, Via M'rovia, Liberia	(D) • S AMERICA • 250 kW
		(J) • S AMERICA • 250 kW
	VOA, Via Philippines	E AFRICA • 250 kW
		M-F • E AFRICA • 250 kW
	USSR	
	†RADIO MOSCOW	(J)
	RADIO MOSCOW, Kursk	(J) • W AFRICA & C AFRICA • AF SCE, PORT, ETC • 100 kW
	RADIO MOSCOW, Tashkent	(D) • S ASIA & SE ASIA • CHI, VIET, URDU, ETC • 100 kW
		(D) • SE ASIA • CHI, VIET, URDU, ETC • 100 kW
		(J) • E ASIA • CHINESE, KOREAN, ETC • 500 kW
15335	**EGYPT**	
	RADIO CAIRO, Kafr Silim-Abis	W AFRICA • 250 kW
	INDIA	
	ALL INDIA RADIO, Aligarh	AUSTRALIA • 250 kW
		SE ASIA • 250 kW
	ALL INDIA RADIO, Madras	S ASIA & SE ASIA • 100 kW
	MOROCCO	
	RTV MAROCAINE, Tangier	EUROPE & W AFRICA • DS • 100 kW
(con'd)	**PAKISTAN**	
	RADIO PAKISTAN, Karachi	(D) • S ASIA • 50 kW

World Time 0 1 2 3 4 5 6 7 8 9 10 11 12 13 14 15 16 17 18 19 20 21 22 23 24

0 Prime Time-Americas 6 Prime Time-E Asia 12 Prime Time-S Asia 18 Prime Time-Europe 24

SUMMER ONLY (J) WINTER ONLY (D) JAMMING / OR /\ EARLIEST HEARD ◁ LATEST HEARD ▷ NEW OR CHANGED FOR 1990 †

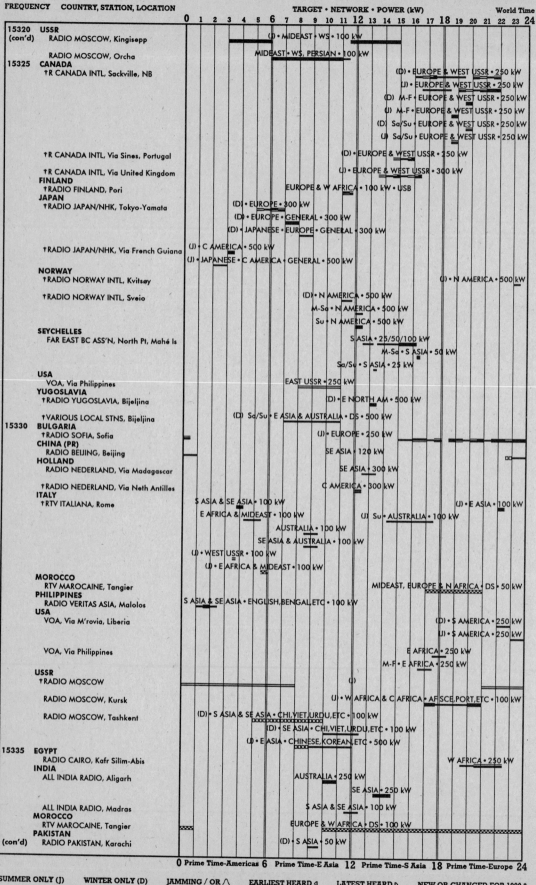

FREQUENCY COUNTRY, STATION, LOCATION TARGET • NETWORK • POWER (kW) World Time

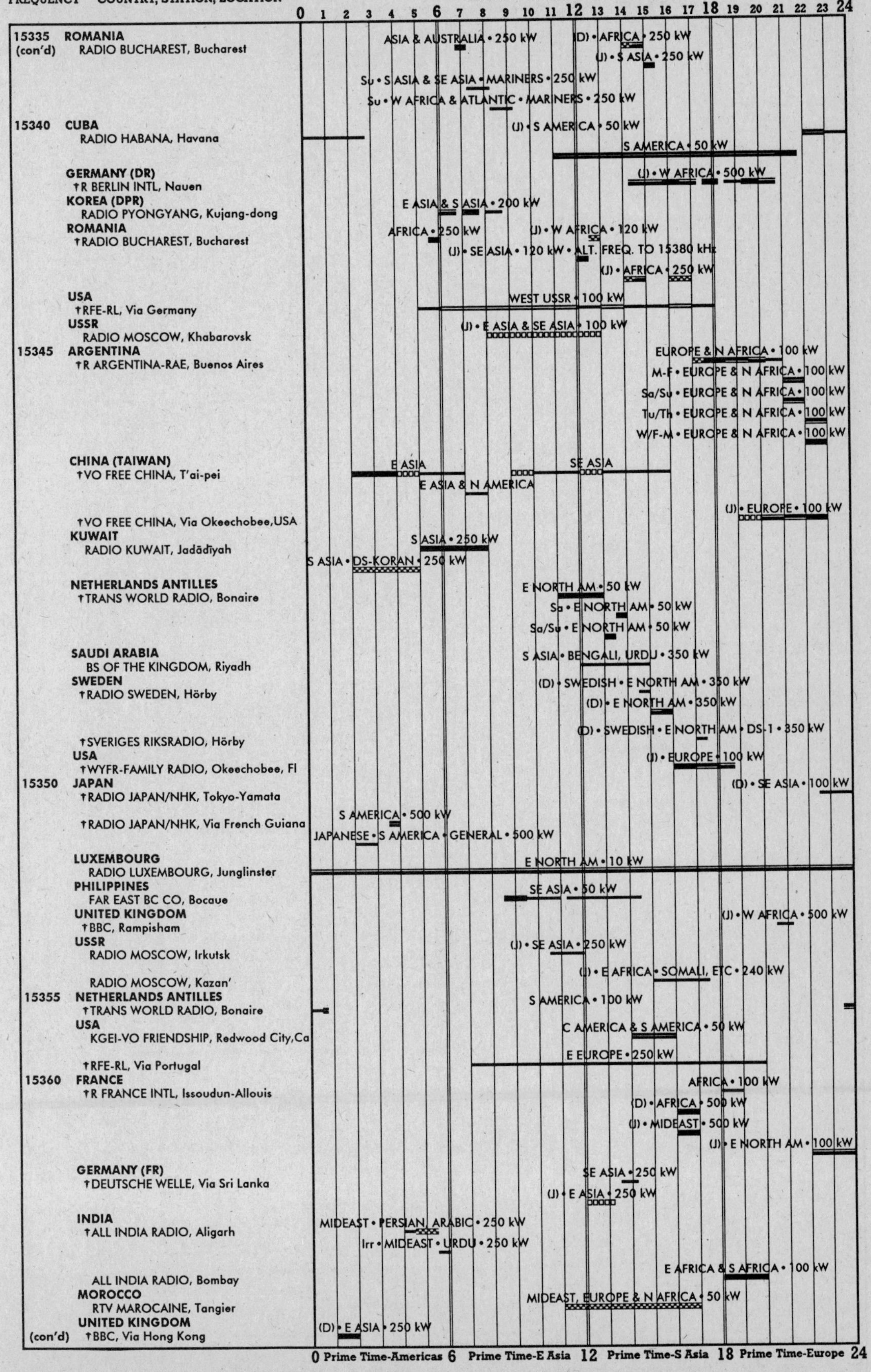
0 1 2 3 4 5 6 7 8 9 10 11 12 13 14 15 16 17 18 19 20 21 22 23 24
15335 (con'd) ROMANIA
RADIO BUCHAREST, Bucharest
ASIA & AUSTRALIA • 250 kW
(D) • AFRICA • 250 kW
(J) • S ASIA • 250 kW
Su • S ASIA & SE ASIA • MARINERS • 250 kW
Su • W AFRICA & ATLANTIC • MARINERS • 250 kW
15340 CUBA
RADIO HABANA, Havana
(J) • S AMERICA • 50 kW
S AMERICA • 50 kW
GERMANY (DR)
†R BERLIN INTL, Nauen
(J) • W AFRICA • 500 kW
KOREA (DPR)
RADIO PYONGYANG, Kujang-dong
E ASIA & S ASIA • 200 kW
ROMANIA
†RADIO BUCHAREST, Bucharest
AFRICA • 250 kW
(J) • W AFRICA • 120 kW
(J) • SE ASIA • 120 kW • ALT. FREQ. TO 15380 kHz
(J) • AFRICA • 250 kW
USA
†RFE-RL, Via Germany
WEST USSR • 100 kW
USSR
RADIO MOSCOW, Khabarovsk
(J) • E ASIA & SE ASIA • 100 kW
15345 ARGENTINA
†R ARGENTINA-RAE, Buenos Aires
EUROPE & N AFRICA • 100 kW
M-F • EUROPE & N AFRICA • 100 kW
Sa/Su • EUROPE & N AFRICA • 100 kW
Tu/Th • EUROPE & N AFRICA • 100 kW
W/F-M • EUROPE & N AFRICA • 100 kW
CHINA (TAIWAN)
†VO FREE CHINA, T'ai-pei
E ASIA
SE ASIA
E ASIA & N AMERICA
†VO FREE CHINA, Via Okeechobee, USA
(J) • EUROPE • 100 kW
KUWAIT
RADIO KUWAIT, Jadādīyah
S ASIA • 250 kW
S ASIA • DS-KORAN • 250 kW
NETHERLANDS ANTILLES
†TRANS WORLD RADIO, Bonaire
E NORTH AM • 50 kW
Sa • E NORTH AM • 50 kW
Sa/Su • E NORTH AM • 50 kW
SAUDI ARABIA
BS OF THE KINGDOM, Riyadh
S ASIA • BENGALI, URDU • 350 kW
SWEDEN
†RADIO SWEDEN, Hörby
(D) • SWEDISH • E NORTH AM • 350 kW
(D) • E NORTH AM • 350 kW
(D) • SWEDISH • E NORTH AM • DS-1 • 350 kW
†SVERIGES RIKSRADIO, Hörby
USA
†WYFR-FAMILY RADIO, Okeechobee, Fl
(J) • EUROPE • 100 kW
15350 JAPAN
†RADIO JAPAN/NHK, Tokyo-Yamata
(D) • SE ASIA • 100 kW
S AMERICA • 500 kW
†RADIO JAPAN/NHK, Via French Guiana
JAPANESE • S AMERICA • GENERAL • 500 kW
LUXEMBOURG
RADIO LUXEMBOURG, Junglinster
E NORTH AM • 10 kW
PHILIPPINES
FAR EAST BC CO, Bocaue
SE ASIA • 50 kW
UNITED KINGDOM
†BBC, Rampisham
(J) • W AFRICA • 500 kW
USSR
RADIO MOSCOW, Irkutsk
(J) • SE ASIA • 250 kW
RADIO MOSCOW, Kazan'
(J) • E AFRICA • SOMALI, ETC • 240 kW
15355 NETHERLANDS ANTILLES
†TRANS WORLD RADIO, Bonaire
S AMERICA • 100 kW
USA
KGEI-VO FRIENDSHIP, Redwood City, Ca
C AMERICA & S AMERICA • 50 kW
†RFE-RL, Via Portugal
E EUROPE • 250 kW
15360 FRANCE
†R FRANCE INTL, Issoudun-Allouis
AFRICA • 100 kW
(D) • AFRICA • 500 kW
(J) • MIDEAST • 500 kW
(J) • E NORTH AM • 100 kW
GERMANY (FR)
†DEUTSCHE WELLE, Via Sri Lanka
SE ASIA • 250 kW
(J) • E ASIA • 250 kW
INDIA
†ALL INDIA RADIO, Aligarh
MIDEAST • PERSIAN, ARABIC • 250 kW
Irr • MIDEAST • URDU • 250 kW
ALL INDIA RADIO, Bombay
E AFRICA & S AFRICA • 100 kW
MOROCCO
RTV MAROCAINE, Tangier
MIDEAST, EUROPE & N AFRICA • 50 kW
(con'd) UNITED KINGDOM
†BBC, Via Hong Kong
(D) • E ASIA • 250 kW
0 Prime Time-Americas 6 Prime Time-E Asia 12 Prime Time-S Asia 18 Prime Time-Europe 24

ENGLISH ▬ ARABIC ▭ CHINESE ▫▫▫ FRENCH ═ GERMAN ▬ RUSSIAN ═ SPANISH ▬ OTHER —

FREQUENCY | COUNTRY, STATION, LOCATION | TARGET • NETWORK • POWER (kW) | World Time

0 1 2 3 4 5 6 7 8 9 10 11 12 13 14 15 16 17 18 19 20 21 22 23 24

15360 (con'd) **UNITED KINGDOM**
†BBC, Via Singapore — E ASIA & SE ASIA • 100 kW; E ASIA & AUSTRALIA • 125 kW

USSR
RADIO MOSCOW, Moscow — S ASIA • 240 kW

15365 **AUSTRALIA**
RADIO AUSTRALIA, Darwin — SE ASIA • 250 kW

FRANCE
†R FRANCE INTL, Issoudun-Allouis — (D) • E NORTH AM & C AMERICA • 100 kW; (J) • E NORTH AM & C AMERICA • 100 kW
†R FRANCE INTL, Via French Guiana — C AMERICA & W NORTH AM • 500 kW

INDIA
†ALL INDIA RADIO, Aligarh — SE ASIA • 250 kW; E ASIA • CHINESE, CANTONESE • 250 kW

ROMANIA
†RADIO BUCHAREST, Bucharest — N AFRICA • 120 kW • ALT. FREQ. TO 15370 kHz; (J) • EUROPE • 120 kW • ALT. FREQ. TO 15270 kHz; (J) • EUROPE • 120 kW; (J) • AFRICA • 250 kW

SOUTH AFRICA
†RADIO RSA, Meyerton — AFRICA • 250 kW; E AFRICA & S AFRICA • 500 kW; (D) • S AFRICA & W AFRICA • 250 kW; (D) • AFRICA & W EUROPE • 500 kW

15370 **CHINA (TAIWAN)**
†VO FREE CHINA, T'ai-pei — SE ASIA • 50 kW; S AFRICA; AUSTRALIA

PHILIPPINES
RADIO VERITAS ASIA, Malolos — S ASIA & SE ASIA • ENGLISH, BENGAL, ETC • 50 kW

ROMANIA
†RADIO BUCHAREST, Bucharest — Alternative Frequency to 15365 kHz; (J) • MIDEAST • 120 kW; Su • MIDEAST • MARINERS • 120 kW

USA
†RFE-RL, Via Germany — WEST USSR • 250 kW

USSR
RADIO MOSCOW, Novosibirsk — MIDEAST • 500 kW

15375 **EGYPT**
RADIO CAIRO, Abu Za'bal — W AFRICA • 100 kW

KOREA (REPUBLIC)
RADIO KOREA, In-Kimjae — E ASIA • 100 kW; KOREAN • E ASIA • 100 kW

NORTHERN MARIANA IS
KFBS-FAR EAST BC, Saipan Island — SE ASIA • 100 kW

SPAIN
†R NACIONAL ESPANA, Noblejas — W AFRICA & S AFRICA • 350 kW

USSR
RADIO MOSCOW, Kenga — E ASIA • 100 kW

15380 **AUSTRALIA**
RADIO AUSTRALIA, Carnarvon — SE ASIA • 250 kW

NETHERLANDS ANTILLES
†TRANS WORLD RADIO, Bonaire — S AMERICA • 50 kW • ALT. FREQ. TO 15385 kHz

ROMANIA
†RADIO BUCHAREST, Bucharest — Alternative Frequency to 15340 kHz; AFRICA • 250 kW; (D) • W AFRICA • 250 kW; (J) • AMERICAS • 250 kW; (J) • C AFRICA & E AFRICA • 250 kW

UNITED KINGDOM
†BBC, Via Singapore — S ASIA & SE ASIA • 250 kW; (D) • S ASIA & SE ASIA • 250 kW; (D) Tu-Sa • S ASIA & SE ASIA • 250 kW
†BBC, Via Zyyi, Cyprus — (J) • MIDEAST & S ASIA • 250 kW

USA
†RFE-RL, Via Pals, Spain — WEST USSR • 250 kW

YUGOSLAVIA
†RADIO YUGOSLAVIA, Bijeljina — (D) • E ASIA & AUSTRALIA • 500 kW

15385 **BULGARIA**
†RADIO SOFIA, Plovdiv — (D) • MIDEAST • 500 kW; (J) • MIDEAST • ARABIC, TURKISH, ETC • 500 kW

ITALY
†RTV ITALIANA, Rome — E AFRICA & MIDEAST • 100 kW; AFRICA • 100 kW; (D) • E NORTH AM • 100 kW

NETHERLANDS ANTILLES
†TRANS WORLD RADIO, Bonaire — Alternative Frequency to 15380 kHz

NORTHERN MARIANA IS
†KYOI, Saipan Island — S ASIA • 100 kW

USSR
RADIO MOSCOW, Chita — (D) • E ASIA • CHINESE, MONGOLIAN • 240 kW
RADIO MOSCOW, Novosibirsk — (J) • E ASIA • CHINESE, KOREAN, ETC • 240 kW

15390 (con'd) **CHINA (PR)**
†CENTRAL PEOPLES BS, Beijing — DS-1 • 50 kW

0 Prime Time-Americas 6 Prime Time-E Asia 12 Prime Time-S Asia 18 Prime Time-Europe 24

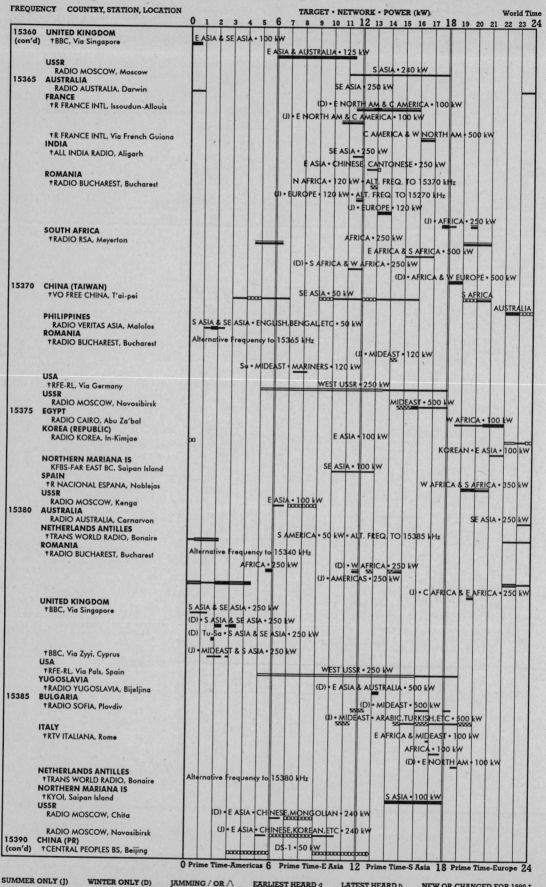

FREQUENCY | COUNTRY, STATION, LOCATION | TARGET • NETWORK • POWER (kW) | World Time

0 1 2 3 4 5 6 7 8 9 10 11 12 13 14 15 16 17 18 19 20 21 22 23 24

15390 (con'd)

CHINA (PR)
†CENTRAL PEOPLES BS, Beijing
- W-M • DS-1 • 50 kW

GERMANY (FR)
†DEUTSCHE WELLE, Jülich
- W AFRICA • 100 kW

ROMANIA
†RADIO BUCHAREST, Bucharest
- (J) • W AFRICA • 120 kW
- (J) • AFRICA • 120 kW

SWEDEN
†RADIO SWEDEN, Hörby
- (J) • S ASIA & SE ASIA • 350 kW • ALT. FREQ. TO 15405 kHz
- (J) • WEST USSR • 350 kW • ALT. FREQ. TO 15405 kHz
- (J) • SWEDISH • S ASIA & SE ASIA • 350 kW • ALT. FREQ. TO 15405 kHz

†SVERIGES RIKSRADIO, Hörby
- M-F • SWEDISH • AFRICA • DS-1 • 350 kW
- M-Sa • SWEDISH • AFRICA • DS-1 • 350 kW
- Su • SWEDISH • AFRICA • DS-1 • 350 kW
- SWEDISH • AFRICA • DS-1/DS-3 • 350 kW
- Sa/Su • SWEDISH • AFRICA • DS-1/DS-3 • 350 kW

UNITED KINGDOM
†BBC, Daventry
- (J) • E EUROPE • 300 kW
- (J) Su • E EUROPE • 300 kW

†BBC, Rampisham
- (D) • E EUROPE • 500 kW
- (J) • E EUROPE • 500 kW
- (D) Su • E EUROPE • 500 kW
- (J) Su • E EUROPE • 500 kW

†BBC, Via Ascension
- S AMERICA • 250 kW • ALT. FREQ. TO 15420 kHz
- (D) • S AMERICA • 250 kW
- (J) • S AMERICA • 250 kW
- (D) M-F • E EUROPE • 250 kW
- (J) M-F • S AMERICA • 250 kW
- (D) Sa/Su • S AMERICA • 250 kW
- (J) Sa/Su • S AMERICA • 250 kW

†BBC, Woofferton
- (J) Su • MIDEAST • TURKISH • 300 kW

USA
†WSHB, Cypress Creek, SC
- (J) • E NORTH AM • 500 kW
- (J) M-F • E NORTH AM • 500 kW
- (J) Sa • E NORTH AM • 500 kW
- (J) Sa/Su • E NORTH AM • 500 kW
- (J) Su-F • E NORTH AM • 500 kW

15395

AUSTRALIA
†RADIO AUSTRALIA, Carnarvon
- SE ASIA • 250 kW
- (J) • SE ASIA • 300 kW

RADIO AUSTRALIA, Shepparton
- PACIFIC & N AMERICA • 100 kW

QATAR
QATAR BC SERVICE, Doha
- (D) • N AFRICA • DS • 250 kW

SPAIN
†R NACIONAL ESPANA, Arganda
- EUROPE • 100 kW
- MIDEAST • 100 kW
- N AFRICA & W AFRICA • 100 kW
- (D) • EUROPE • 100 kW
- (J) • EUROPE • 100 kW

†R NACIONAL ESPANA, Noblejas
- (J) M-F • EUROPE • 350 kW

UNITED ARAB EMIRATES
†VOICE OF THE UAE, Abu Dhabi
- (D) • AUSTRALIA • DS • 500 kW

USA
†VOA, Via Philippines
- E ASIA • 250 kW

VOA, Via Sri Lanka
- S ASIA • 35 kW

USSR
RADIO MOSCOW, Kazan'
- S ASIA • 240 kW

RADIO MOSCOW, Tashkent
- E ASIA • 100 kW
- (J) • E ASIA • CHI, CANTONESE, ETC • 100 kW

15400

CHINA (PR)
†RADIO BEIJING
- (J) • SE ASIA

FINLAND
†RADIO FINLAND, Pori
- E NORTH AM & C AMERICA • 500 kW
- M-F • E NORTH AM & C AMERICA • 500 kW
- Sa/Su • E NORTH AM & C AMERICA • 500 kW

GERMANY (FR)
†DEUTSCHE WELLE, Jülich
- (D) • JAPANESE • E ASIA • 100 kW

†DEUTSCHE WELLE, Via Cyclops, Malta
- (D) • E ASIA • 250 kW

IRAQ
†RADIO BAGHDAD, Baghdad
- E AFRICA • 250 kW
- (J) • E AFRICA • 250 kW

UNITED KINGDOM
†BBC, Via Ascension
- W AFRICA & S AFRICA • 125/250 kW
- W AFRICA • 250 kW
- Sa/Su • W AFRICA & S AFRICA • 125 kW

(con'd)

0 Prime Time-Americas 6 Prime Time-E Asia 12 Prime Time-S Asia 18 Prime Time-Europe 24

ENGLISH — ARABIC — CHINESE — FRENCH — GERMAN — RUSSIAN — SPANISH — OTHER —

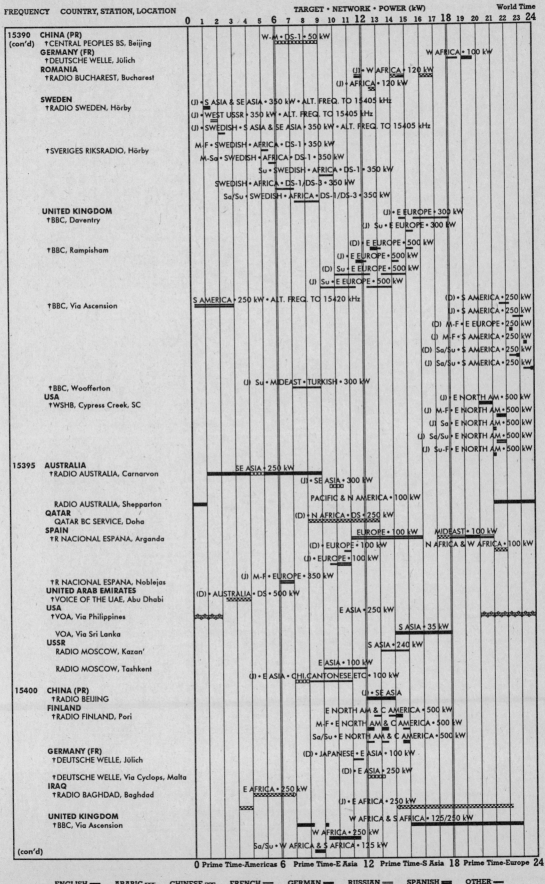

FREQUENCY	COUNTRY, STATION, LOCATION	TARGET • NETWORK • POWER (kW)
15400 (con'd)	**USA** VOA, Greenville, NC	C AMERICA & S AMERICA • 250/500 kW
15405	**ALBANIA** RADIO TIRANA, Lushnjë	S AFRICA • 100 kW
	GERMANY (FR) †DEUTSCHE WELLE, Jülich	WEST USSR • 100 kW
		(D) • WEST USSR • 100 kW
		(J) • WEST USSR • 100 kW
	NORTHERN MARIANA IS KYOI, Saipan Island	E ASIA • 100 kW
	ROMANIA †RADIO BUCHAREST, Bucharest	Alternative Frequency to 15270 kHz
	SEYCHELLES FAR EAST BC ASS'N, North Pt, Mahé Is	MIDEAST & E AFRICA • 100 kW
		Su/Th/F • MIDEAST & E AFRICA • 100 kW
	SWEDEN †RADIO SWEDEN, Hörby	Alternative Frequency to 15390 kHz
	TURKEY †TURKISH RTV CORP, Ankara	(J) • WEST USSR • 250 kW
		(J) • TURKISH • WEST USSR • 250 kW
	USSR RADIO MOSCOW, Armavir	E AFRICA • 100 kW
		E AFRICA • WS • 100 kW
	RADIO MOSCOW, Frunze, Kirgiziya	(J) • S ASIA • WS, TAMIL, ETC • 500 kW
	VATICAN STATE †VATICAN RADIO, Sta Maria di Galeria	S AMERICA • 250 kW
		C AMERICA • 250 kW
15410	**AUSTRIA** †RADIO AUSTRIA INTL, Vienna	MIDEAST • 100 kW
	GERMANY (FR) †DEUTSCHE WELLE, Via Antigua	(J) • S AMERICA • 250 kW
	†DEUTSCHE WELLE, Via Kigali, Rwanda	W AFRICA • 250 kW
		C AFRICA & E AFRICA • 250 kW
	DEUTSCHE WELLE, Via Sri Lanka	MIDEAST & S ASIA • 250 kW
	JAPAN †RADIO JAPAN/NHK, Tokyo-Yamata	(J) • S ASIA & E AFRICA • 100 kW
	USA VOA, Greenville, NC	W AFRICA • 500 kW
	VOA, Via Philippines	E ASIA • 250 kW
	USSR RADIO MOSCOW, L'vov	W EUROPE & ATLANTIC • MARINERS • 120 kW
15415	**AUSTRALIA** RADIO AUSTRALIA, Carnarvon	S ASIA & SE ASIA • 250 kW
	IRAQ †RADIO BAGHDAD, Balad-Salah el Deen	(D) • EUROPE • 500 kW
		(J) • EUROPE • 500 kW
	USSR RADIO MOSCOW, Kenga	(J) • S ASIA • 500 kW
		(J) • S ASIA • WS • 500 kW
15415v	**LIBYA** †RADIO JAMAHIRIYA, Tripoli	Alternative Frequency to 6120v kHz
15420	**CHINA (PR)** †RADIO BEIJING	(J) • JAPANESE • E ASIA
	†RADIO BEIJING, Beijing	(J) • E NORTH AM, C AMERICA & S AMERICA • 500 kW
	EGYPT †RADIO CAIRO, Abu Za'bal	S AMERICA • 100 kW
	GUAM †KTWR-TRANS WORLD R, Merizo	SE ASIA • 100 kW
	LAOS LAO NATIONAL RADIO, Via USSR	(J) • EUROPE • 100 kW
	SWITZERLAND SWISS RADIO INTL, Schwarzenburg	W AFRICA • 150 kW
	UNITED KINGDOM †BBC, Via Ascension	Alternative Frequency to 15390 kHz
	†BBC, Via Seychelles	E AFRICA • 250 kW
		(D) • E AFRICA • 250 kW
		S AFRICA • 250 kW
		(J) • E AFRICA • 250 kW
		E AFRICA & S AFRICA • 250 kW
		M-Sa • E AFRICA • 250 kW
		Sa/Su • E AFRICA • 250 kW
	†BBC, Via Zyyi, Cyprus	M-F • E AFRICA • 100/250 kW
		E AFRICA • 250 kW
	USA WRNO WORLDWIDE, New Orleans, La	E NORTH AM • 100 kW
		(D) • E NORTH AM • 100 kW
	USSR RADIO MOSCOW	(D) • S ASIA
	RADIO MOSCOW, Frunze, Kirgiziya	(D) • AUSTRALIA • WS • 500 kW
	RADIO MOSCOW, Serpukhov	(J) • EUROPE • 100 kW
		(J) • EUROPE • WS • 100 kW
15425 (con'd)	**AUSTRALIA** AUSTRALIAN BC CORP, Perth	DS • 50 kW

World Time: 0 1 2 3 4 5 6 7 8 9 10 11 12 13 14 15 16 17 18 19 20 21 22 23 24

0 Prime Time-Americas 6 Prime Time-E Asia 12 Prime Time-S Asia 18 Prime Time-Europe 24

SUMMER ONLY (J) WINTER ONLY (D) JAMMING / OR /\ EARLIEST HEARD ◁ LATEST HEARD ▷ NEW OR CHANGED FOR 1990 †

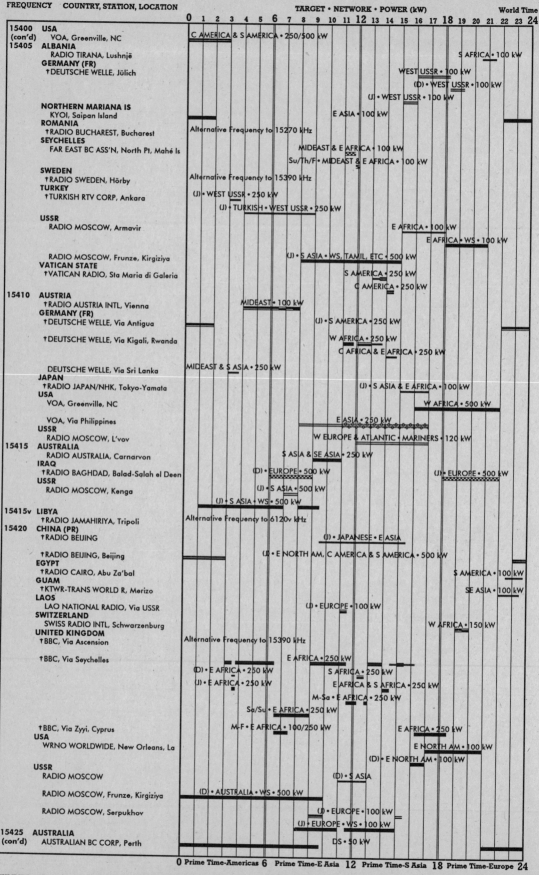

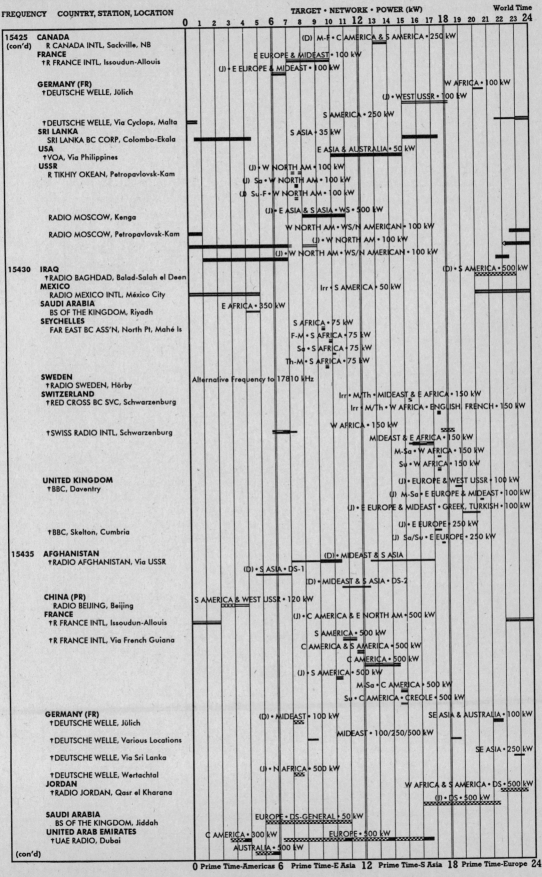

TARGET • NETWORK • POWER (kW)

World Time

0 1 2 3 4 5 6 7 8 9 10 11 12 13 14 15 16 17 18 19 20 21 22 23 24

15425
(con'd) **CANADA**
  R CANADA INTL, Sackville, NB (D) • M-F • C AMERICA & S AMERICA • 250 kW
  FRANCE
    †R FRANCE INTL, Issoudun-Allouis E EUROPE & MIDEAST • 100 kW
    (J) • E EUROPE & MIDEAST • 100 kW

  GERMANY (FR)
    †DEUTSCHE WELLE, Jülich W AFRICA • 100 kW
    (J) • WEST USSR • 100 kW

    †DEUTSCHE WELLE, Via Cyclops, Malta S AMERICA • 250 kW
  SRI LANKA S ASIA • 35 kW
    SRI LANKA BC CORP, Colombo-Ekala
  USA E ASIA & AUSTRALIA • 50 kW
    †VOA, Via Philippines
  USSR
    R TIKHIY OKEAN, Petropavlovsk-Kam (J) • W NORTH AM • 100 kW
    (J) • Sa • W NORTH AM • 100 kW
    (J) • Su-F • W NORTH AM • 100 kW

    RADIO MOSCOW, Kenga (J) • E ASIA & S ASIA • WS • 500 kW

    RADIO MOSCOW, Petropavlovsk-Kam W NORTH AM • WS/N AMERICAN • 100 kW
    (J) • W NORTH AM • 100 kW
    (J) • W NORTH AM • WS/N AMERICAN • 100 kW

15430 **IRAQ**
    †RADIO BAGHDAD, Balad-Salah el Deen (D) • S AMERICA • 500 kW
  MEXICO
    RADIO MEXICO INTL, México City Irr • S AMERICA • 50 kW
  SAUDI ARABIA
    BS OF THE KINGDOM, Riyadh E AFRICA • 350 kW
  SEYCHELLES
    FAR EAST BC ASS'N, North Pt, Mahé Is S AFRICA • 75 kW
    F-M • S AFRICA • 75 kW
    Sa • S AFRICA • 75 kW
    Th-M • S AFRICA • 75 kW

  SWEDEN
    †RADIO SWEDEN, Hörby Alternative Frequency to 17810 kHz
  SWITZERLAND
    †RED CROSS BC SVC, Schwarzenburg Irr • M/Th • MIDEAST & E AFRICA • 150 kW
    Irr • M/Th • W AFRICA • ENGLISH, FRENCH • 150 kW

    †SWISS RADIO INTL, Schwarzenburg W AFRICA • 150 kW
    MIDEAST & E AFRICA • 150 kW
    M-Sa • W AFRICA • 150 kW
    Su • W AFRICA • 150 kW

  UNITED KINGDOM
    †BBC, Daventry (J) • EUROPE & WEST USSR • 100 kW
    (J) • M-Sa • E EUROPE & MIDEAST • 100 kW
    (J) • E EUROPE & MIDEAST • GREEK, TURKISH • 100 kW

    †BBC, Skelton, Cumbria (J) • E EUROPE • 250 kW
    (J) • Sa/Su • E EUROPE • 250 kW

15435 **AFGHANISTAN**
    †RADIO AFGHANISTAN, Via USSR (D) • MIDEAST & S ASIA
    (D) • S ASIA • DS-1
    (D) • MIDEAST & S ASIA • DS-2

  CHINA (PR)
    RADIO BEIJING, Beijing S AMERICA & WEST USSR • 120 kW
  FRANCE
    †R FRANCE INTL, Issoudun-Allouis (J) • C AMERICA & E NORTH AM • 500 kW
    S AMERICA • 500 kW
    †R FRANCE INTL, Via French Guiana C AMERICA & S AMERICA • 500 kW
    C AMERICA • 500 kW
    (J) • S AMERICA • 500 kW
    M-Sa • C AMERICA • 500 kW
    Su • C AMERICA • CREOLE • 500 kW

  GERMANY (FR)
    †DEUTSCHE WELLE, Jülich (D) • MIDEAST • 100 kW   SE ASIA & AUSTRALIA • 100 kW
    †DEUTSCHE WELLE, Various Locations MIDEAST • 100/250/500 kW
    †DEUTSCHE WELLE, Via Sri Lanka SE ASIA • 250 kW
    †DEUTSCHE WELLE, Wertachtal (J) • N AFRICA • 500 kW
  JORDAN
    †RADIO JORDAN, Qasr el Kharana W AFRICA & S AMERICA • DS • 500 kW
    (J) • DS • 500 kW

  SAUDI ARABIA
    BS OF THE KINGDOM, Jiddah EUROPE • DS-GENERAL • 50 kW
  UNITED ARAB EMIRATES
    †UAE RADIO, Dubai C AMERICA • 300 kW   EUROPE • 500 kW
    AUSTRALIA • 500 kW

(con'd)

0 Prime Time-Americas 6   Prime Time-E Asia 12   Prime Time-S Asia 18   Prime Time-Europe 24

FREQUENCY	COUNTRY, STATION, LOCATION	TARGET • NETWORK • POWER (kW)
15435 (con'd)	**UNITED KINGDOM** †BBC, Rampisham	WEST USSR • 500 kW
		Su • WEST USSR • 500 kW
	USA VOA, Via Kaválla, Greece	S ASIA & MIDEAST • 250 kW
		(J) • S ASIA & MIDEAST • 250 kW
	USSR RADIO MOSCOW, Frunze, Kirgiziya	SE ASIA & E ASIA • 500 kW
		(J) • SE ASIA & E ASIA • 240 kW
15440	**CANADA** R CANADA INTL, Sackville, NB	(J) M-F • C AMERICA & S AMERICA • 250 kW
	†R CANADA INTL, Via Tokyo, Japan	SE ASIA • 300 kW
	CHINA (PR) RADIO BEIJING, Kunming	AUSTRALIA • 120 kW
	CHINA (TAIWAN) †VO FREE CHINA, Via Okeechobee, USA	(D) • EUROPE • 100 kW
	FRANCE †R FRANCE INTL, Via French Guiana	C AMERICA • 500 kW
	GERMANY (DR) R BERLIN INTL, Königswusterhausen	(J) • S ASIA & SE ASIA • ENGLISH, HINDI • 100 kW
	USA †WYFR-FAMILY RADIO, Okeechobee, Fl	(D) • C AMERICA • 100 kW
		(D) • EUROPE • 100 kW
		(J) • C AMERICA • 50 kW
	USSR RADIO MOSCOW, Ryazan'	MIDEAST & E AFRICA • 120/500 kW
		MIDEAST & E AFRICA • AFRICAN • 120/500 kW
		MIDEAST & E AFRICA • WS • 120/500 kW
15445	**GERMANY (DR)** †R BERLIN INTL, Königswusterhausen	(D) • S ASIA & SE ASIA • ENGLISH, HINDI • 100 kW
	NETHERLANDS ANTILLES †TRANS WORLD RADIO, Bonaire	S AMERICA • 100 kW • ALT. FREQ. TO 15115 kHz
	NORTHERN MARIANA IS †KYOI, Saipan Island	SE ASIA • 100 kW
	PHILIPPINES FAR EAST BC CO, Bocaue	S ASIA & SE ASIA • 50 kW • ALT. FREQ. TO 15480 kHz
	UNITED KINGDOM †BBC, Skelton, Cumbria	(J) • E EUROPE & MIDEAST • 250 kW
		(J) Sa • E EUROPE & MIDEAST • 250 kW
	USA †R FREE AFGHANISTAN, Via Portugal	WEST USSR & S ASIA • 250 kW
	†RFE-RL, Via Portugal	WEST USSR • 250 kW
	VOA, Via M'rovia, Liberia	W AFRICA & C AFRICA • 250 kW
15450	**AUSTRIA** †RADIO AUSTRIA INTL, Vienna	AUSTRALIA • 500 kW
		(D) • E NORTH AM • 100 kW
		(J) • E ASIA • 500 kW
		M-Sa • AUSTRALIA • 500 kW
		(J) M-Sa • E ASIA • 500 kW
		Su • AUSTRALIA • 500 kW
		(J) Su • E ASIA • 500 kW
	CHINA (PR) †RADIO BEIJING	(J) • PACIFIC
	LIBYA †RADIO JAMAHIRIYA, Tripoli	Alternative Frequency to 7245 kHz
	TUNISIA †RTV TUNISIENNE, Sfax	DS • 100 kW
	USSR RADIO MOSCOW, Serpukhov	(J) • S ASIA • TAMIL, ETC • 100 kW
15455	**CHINA (PR)** †RADIO BEIJING, Jinhua	(D) • W NORTH AM • 500 kW
	USSR †RADIO KIEV, Petropavlovsk-Kam	W NORTH AM • 240 kW
	†RADIO MOSCOW, Petropavlovsk-Kam	W NORTH AM • 240 kW
	†RADIO TASHKENT, Tashkent	(D) • S ASIA • 100 kW
	RADIO VILNIUS, Petropavlovsk-Kam	(J) • W NORTH AM • 240 kW
	RADIO YEREVAN, Petropavlovsk-Kam	(J) • W NORTH AM • 240 kW
15460	**FRANCE** †R FRANCE INTL, Issoudun-Allouis	E AFRICA • 100 kW
		(D) • E AFRICA • 100 kW
		(D) • SE ASIA • 500 kW
		(J) • E AFRICA • 100 kW
	USSR RADIO MOSCOW, Krasnoyarsk	DS-1 • 50 kW
	RADIO MOSCOW, Moscow	(D) • S ASIA • WS • 100 kW
	RADIO TASHKENT, Tashkent	(J) • S ASIA • 100 kW
15465 (con'd)	**PHILIPPINES** FAR EAST BC CO, Bocaue	S ASIA & SE ASIA • 50 kW

World Time: 0 Prime Time-Americas 6 Prime Time-E Asia 12 Prime Time-S Asia 18 Prime Time-Europe 24

SUMMER ONLY (J) WINTER ONLY (D) JAMMING / OR /\ EARLIEST HEARD ◁ LATEST HEARD ▷ NEW OR CHANGED FOR 1990 †

FREQUENCY	COUNTRY, STATION, LOCATION	TARGET • NETWORK • POWER (kW) — World Time 0–24
15465 (con'd)	**PHILIPPINES** FAR EAST BC CO, Bocaue	Sa/Su • S ASIA • 50 kW
	USSR RADIO MOSCOW	(J) • W AFRICA & S AMERICA
15470	**GERMANY (FR)** †DEUTSCHE WELLE, Via Sines, Portugal	(D) • E EUROPE • 250 kW
	USSR RADIO MOSCOW	(J) • E ASIA
	RADIO MOSCOW, Dushanbé	(J) • SE ASIA • 100 kW
	RADIO MOSCOW, Vladivostok	(D) • SE ASIA • MARINERS • 100 kW; (J) • SE ASIA • WS • 100 kW
15475	**GABON** †AFRIQUE NUMERO UN, Moyabi	W AFRICA & E NORTH AM • 250 kW
	USSR †"RADIO MAGALLANES", Via R Moscow	(J) • S AMERICA; (J) Su-Tu/Th/F • S AMERICA
	RADIO KIEV	(J) • W EUROPE & E NORTH AM
	†RADIO MOSCOW	(J) W/Sa • S AMERICA; AFRICA • WS, FRENCH; (J) • W EUROPE & E NORTH AM • WS,UK N AM SVCS
15476	**ANTARCTICA** †R NACIONAL-LRA36, Base Esperanza	S AMERICA • DS • 1.5 kW; Irr • S AMERICA • DS • 1.5 kW
15480	**PHILIPPINES** FAR EAST BC CO, Bocaue	Alternative Frequency to 15445 kHz
	USSR RADIO MOSCOW, Khar'kov	MIDEAST • 120 kW; MIDEAST • WS • 120 kW
15485	**ISRAEL** †KOL ISRAEL, Tel Aviv	(J) Sa/Su • WEST USSR • 20 kW; (D) • USSR • 300 kW; (J) • WEST USSR • 20 kW; (J) • HEBREW • WEST USSR • 20 kW; (D) M/Tu/Th-Sa • USSR • 300 kW; (J) M/Tu/Th-Sa • USSR • 20 kW; (D) Su/W • USSR • 300 kW; (J) Su/W • USSR • 20 kW
	NEW ZEALAND †RADIO NEW ZEALAND, Wellington	Alternative Frequency to 15150 kHz
	USSR RADIO MOSCOW, Kiev	W EUROPE & W AFRICA • 100 kW
	RADIO MOSCOW, Simferopol'	W EUROPE & W AFRICA • 240 kW; (D) • W EUROPE & W AFRICA • 240 kW
	RADIO YEREVAN, Simferopol'	(D) Su • W EUROPE & W AFRICA • 240 kW; (J) Su • W EUROPE & W AFRICA • 240 kW
15490	**USSR** RADIO MOSCOW	(J) • W AFRICA & S AMERICA
	RADIO MOSCOW, Irkutsk	DS-1(FEEDER) • 15 kW • USB
	RADIO MOSCOW, Minsk	MIDEAST • WS • 100 kW
	RADIO MOSCOW, Moscow	(J) • E AFRICA & S AFRICA • 240 kW
	RADIO MOSCOW, Tula	(J) • S ASIA & SE ASIA • 240 kW; S ASIA & SE ASIA • WS • 240 kW; (J) • S ASIA & SE ASIA • WS • 240 kW
15495	**KUWAIT** RADIO KUWAIT, Jadādīyah	Irr • SE ASIA & AUSTRALIA • DS-RAMADAN • 500 kW; SE ASIA & AUSTRALIA • DS-HOLY KORAN • 500 kW; SE ASIA & AUSTRALIA • DS-MAIN PROGRAM • 500 kW
	USSR RADIO MOSCOW, Kiev	W EUROPE & W AFRICA • 100 kW
15500	**CHINA (PR)** CENTRAL PEOPLES BS, Beijing	DS-2 • 120 kW; Th/Sa-Tu • DS-2 • 120 kW
	USSR RADIO MOSCOW, Frunze	SE ASIA • 100 kW
	RADIO MOSCOW, Frunze, Kirgiziya	(J) • SE ASIA • WS,VIETNAMESE,ETC • 100 kW
	RADIO MOSCOW, Moscow	(J) • MIDEAST • WS • 240 kW; (D) • MIDEAST • WS, PERSIAN • 240 kW
	RADIO MOSCOW, Yerevan	(J) • E AFRICA & S AFRICA • AFRICAN SCE,WS,ETC • 120 kW
15505	**KUWAIT** RADIO KUWAIT, Jadādīyah	Irr • DS-RAMADAN • 250 kW; (J) • EUROPE • 250 kW
(con'd)	**USSR** RADIO MOSCOW	EUROPE

0 Prime Time-Americas 6 Prime Time-E Asia 12 Prime Time-S Asia 18 Prime Time-Europe 24

ENGLISH ARABIC CHINESE FRENCH GERMAN RUSSIAN SPANISH OTHER

FREQUENCY | COUNTRY, STATION, LOCATION | TARGET • NETWORK • POWER (kW) | World Time

0 1 2 3 4 5 6 7 8 9 10 11 12 13 14 15 16 17 18 19 20 21 22 23 24

15505 (con'd) **USSR**
RADIO MOSCOW, Kazan' — S ASIA • 240 kW

15510 **AFGHANISTAN**
†RADIO AFGHANISTAN, Via USSR — (J) • EUROPE

BELGIUM
†BELGISCHE RADIO TV, Wavre — (D) • AFRICA • 250 kW
(D) M-Sa • AFRICA • 250 kW
(D) Su • AFRICA • 250 kW

GERMANY (FR)
†DEUTSCHE WELLE, Jülich — E EUROPE • 100 kW
(J) • E EUROPE • 100 kW
†DEUTSCHE WELLE, Via Cyclops, Malta — (J) • S ASIA • 250 kW

USSR
†"RADIO MAGALLANES", Via R Moscow — (J) • S AMERICA • 100 kW
RADIO MOSCOW, Frunze, Kirgiziya — (J) • S ASIA & SE ASIA • CHINESE, VIET, ETC • 100 kW
†RADIO MOSCOW, Zhigulevsk — (J) • S AMERICA • 100 kW
RADIO YEREVAN, Yerevan — Su • EUROPE • 100 kW
(J) • EUROPE • 100 kW
(J) M-Sa • EUROPE • 100 kW
(J) Su • EUROPE • 100 kW

15515 **BELGIUM**
†BELGISCHE RADIO TV, Wavre — (J) • AFRICA • 250 kW
(D) M-Sa • EUROPE • 100 kW

USSR
RADIO MOSCOW, Tashkent — S ASIA & SE ASIA • WS • 100 kW

15520 **AFGHANISTAN**
RADIO AFGHANISTAN, Via USSR — (J) • MIDEAST

USSR
†"RADIO MAGALLANES", Via R Moscow — (J) • S AMERICA
†RADIO MOSCOW — (J) • W AFRICA & S AMERICA
(J) • S AMERICA
WS
MIDEAST & S ASIA

15525 **SWITZERLAND**
RED CROSS BC SVC, Sottens — Irr • M/Th • MIDEAST & E AFRICA • ENGLISH, FRENCH • 500 kW
†SWISS RADIO INTL, Schwarzenburg — (J) • W AFRICA • 500 kW
†SWISS RADIO INTL, Sottens — MIDEAST & E AFRICA • 500 kW
M-Sa • MIDEAST & E AFRICA • 500 kW
Su • MIDEAST & E AFRICA • 500 kW

USSR
†RADIO MOSCOW — (J) • E ASIA
RADIO MOSCOW, Kenga — DS-1 • 100 kW

15530 **USSR**
RADIO MOSCOW, Moscow — (J) • E AFRICA & S AFRICA • WS, SWAHILI, ETC • 100/240 kW
RADIO MOSCOW, Novosibirsk — (D) • E ASIA • 100 kW

15535 **USSR**
RADIO MOSCOW — (J) • MARINERS
(J) • SE ASIA • VIETNAMESE, ETC
RADIO MOSCOW, Frunze, Kirgiziya — (J) • E EUROPE & W AFRICA • AFRICAN SCE, WS • 500 kW
(J) • E EUROPE & W AFRICA • GREEK, HAUSA, ETC • 500 kW

15540 **BELGIUM**
†RT BELGE FRANCAISE, Wavre — (D) • AFRICA • 100 kW
(J) • AFRICA • 100 kW
(D) Sa/Su • AFRICA • 100 kW
(J) W/Sa/Su • AFRICA • 100 kW

CZECHOSLOVAKIA
†RADIO PRAGUE, Pieštány-Velké K'y — (J) • AMERICAS • 250 kW

USSR
RADIO MOSCOW, Minsk — MIDEAST • 100 kW
MIDEAST • WS • 100 kW
(D) • MIDEAST • WS • 100 kW
(J) • MIDEAST • WS, PERSIAN • 100 kW

15545 **USSR**
RADIO MOSCOW — E ASIA
(D) • E ASIA
(J) • E ASIA

15550 **CHINA (PR)**
CENTRAL PEOPLES BS, Beijing — DS-1 • 15 kW
W-M • DS-1 • 15 kW

USSR
RADIO MOSCOW, L'vov — (D) • MIDEAST & S ASIA • 500 kW
(J) • S ASIA • 500 kW
MIDEAST & S ASIA • PERSIAN, TAMIL, ETC • 500 kW

15555 **CLANDESTINE (M EAST)**
†"IRAN FREEDOM FLAG, Egypt — PERSIAN • MIDEAST • ANTI-IRANIAN GOVT • 100 kW

UNITED ARAB EMIRATES
†UAE RADIO, Dubai — (J) • E NORTH AM • 500 kW
EUROPE & E NORTH AM • 500 kW

15560 **CLANDESTINE (M EAST)**
†"IRAN FREEDOM FLAG, Egypt — (J) • PERSIAN • MIDEAST • ANTI-IRANIAN GOVT • 100 kW

HOLLAND
(con'd) †RADIO NEDERLAND, Flevoland — W EUROPE • 500 kW
(D) • C AFRICA • 500 kW

0 Prime Time-Americas 6 Prime Time-E Asia 12 Prime Time-S Asia 18 Prime Time-Europe 24

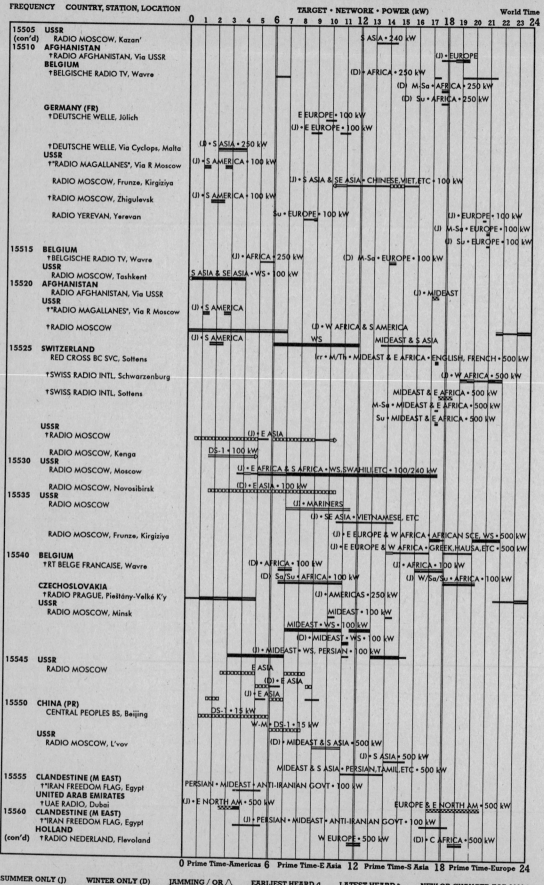

FREQUENCY   COUNTRY, STATION, LOCATION

TARGET • NETWORK • POWER (kW)   World Time

0 1 2 3 4 5 6 7 8 9 10 11 12 13 14 15 16 17 18 19 20 21 22 23 24

15560 HOLLAND
(con'd)   †RADIO NEDERLAND, Flevoland
- (J) • E EUROPE & MIDEAST • 500 kW
- MIDEAST • 500 kW
- (D) • W EUROPE • 500 kW
- (J) • W AFRICA • 500 kW
- (D) • SE ASIA • 500 kW
- (D) • S ASIA • 500 kW
- (J) • EUROPE & MIDEAST • 500 kW
- Su • MIDEAST • 500 kW

   †RADIO NEDERLAND, Via Madagascar
- W AFRICA & C AFRICA • 300 kW
- (D) • W AFRICA • 300 kW
- (J) • E AFRICA • 300 kW

   †RADIO NEDERLAND, Via Neth Antilles
- (J) • S AMERICA • 300 kW
- S AMERICA • 300 kW

USSR
   RADIO MOSCOW, Khabarovsk
- (J) • E ASIA • JAPANESE, KOREAN • 100 kW
- (J) • JAPANESE • E ASIA • JAPANESE, KOREAN • 100 kW

15565 PAKISTAN
   RADIO PAKISTAN, Islamabad
- MIDEAST • 100 kW

   RADIO PAKISTAN, Karachi
- (J) • SE ASIA • 50 kW

15566 USA
   †WYFR-FAMILY RADIO, Okeechobee, Fl
- (J) • S AMERICA • 100 kW
- W AFRICA & S AFRICA • 100 kW
- EUROPE • 100 kW
- (D) • PORTUGUESE • W AFRICA & S AFRICA • 100 kW
- (J) • EUROPE • 100 kW
- (J) • W AFRICA & S AFRICA • 100 kW

15570 HOLLAND
   †RADIO NEDERLAND, Flevoland
- (J) • C AFRICA • 300 kW

   †RADIO NEDERLAND, Via Madagascar
- E AFRICA • 300 kW
- (D) • S ASIA • 300 kW
- (J) • E AFRICA • 300 kW

SWITZERLAND
   RED CROSS BC SVC, Schwarzenburg
- Irr • M/Th • E ASIA & AUSTRALIA • 150 kW
- Irr • M/Th • S ASIA & SE ASIA • 150 kW

   SWISS RADIO INTL, Schwarzenburg
- E ASIA & AUSTRALIA • 150 kW
- S ASIA & SE ASIA • 150 kW
- M-Sa • S ASIA & SE ASIA • 150 kW
- Su • S ASIA & SE ASIA • 150 kW

   †SWISS RADIO INTL, Sottens
- (D) • W AFRICA • 500 kW

USSR
   RADIO MOSCOW
- (J) • MIDEAST • WS
- (J) • MIDEAST

   RADIO MOSCOW, Khabarovsk
- E ASIA • 100 kW

   RADIO MOSCOW, Tashkent
- (D) • SE ASIA • WS

15575 KOREA (REPUBLIC)
   RADIO KOREA, In-Kimjae
- E NORTH AM • 250 kW
- KOREAN • E NORTH AM • 250 kW
- EUROPE • 250 kW
- MIDEAST & AFRICA • 250 kW
- KOREAN • AFRICA • 250 kW
- AFRICA • 250 kW

15580 PAKISTAN
   RADIO PAKISTAN, Karachi
- SE ASIA • 50 kW
- (D) • SE ASIA • 50 kW

USA
   KUSW, Salt Lake City, Utah
- Tu-Su • E NORTH AM • 100 kW
- M-Sa • E NORTH AM • 100 kW

   VOA, Greenville, NC
- W AFRICA & S AFRICA • 250 kW

USSR
   †RADIO MOSCOW
- (J) • SE ASIA

15585 USSR
   †"RADIO MAGALLANES", Via R Moscow
- (J) • S AMERICA

   †P & PROGRESS
- (J) • S AMERICA

   †RADIO MOSCOW
- (J) • S AMERICA

   RADIO MOSCOW, L'vov
- W AFRICA & ATLANTIC • MARINERS • 200 kW
- W AFRICA • WS • 200 kW

   †RADIO YEREVAN
- (J) • S AMERICA

15590 CHINA (PR)
   CENTRAL PEOPLES BS, Beijing
- DS-1 • 15 kW
- W-M • DS-1 • 15 kW

USSR
   †RADIO MOSCOW
- (J) • SE ASIA
- (J)

15595 GERMANY (FR)
   †DEUTSCHE WELLE, Jülich
- (J) • JAPANESE • E ASIA • 100 kW

(con'd) †DEUTSCHE WELLE, Various Locations
- S ASIA • 100/500 kW

0 Prime Time-Americas   6   Prime Time-E Asia   12   Prime Time-S Asia   18   Prime Time-Europe   24

ENGLISH ▬   ARABIC ▨   CHINESE ▢▢▢   FRENCH ▬   GERMAN ▬   RUSSIAN ═   SPANISH ▬   OTHER ▬

FREQUENCY	COUNTRY, STATION, LOCATION	TARGET • NETWORK • POWER (kW)
15595 (con'd)	USSR †RADIO MOSCOW	WS
		(J) • N AFRICA
15600	CHINA (PR) †RADIO BEIJING	SE ASIA
		(D) • SE ASIA
	USA †VOA, Via M'rovia, Liberia	W AFRICA • 250 kW
		M-F • W AFRICA & S AFRICA • ENGLISH, FRENCH, ETC • 250 kW
	USSR RADIO MOSCOW	DS-1 (FEEDER) • 15 kW • USB
15605v	PAKISTAN RADIO PAKISTAN, Islamabad	MIDEAST • 250 kW
		EUROPE • 250 kW
		(J) • MIDEAST • 250 kW
15610	USA †WCSN, Scotts Corners. Me	(J) • EUROPE • 500 kW
		(J) M-Sa • EUROPE • 500 kW
		(J) Sa • EUROPE • 500 kW
		(J) Su-F • EUROPE • 500 kW
		(J) Su • EUROPE • 500 kW
	†WSHB, Cypress Creek, SC	(D) • W NORTH AM • 500 kW
		M-F • W NORTH AM • 500 kW
		(D) Sa • W NORTH AM • 500 kW
		(D) Sa/Su • W NORTH AM • 500 kW
		(D) Su-F • W NORTH AM • 500 kW
15615	ISRAEL †KOL ISRAEL, Tel Aviv	(D) • E NORTH AM • 50/300 kW
		(J) • E NORTH AM & C AMERICA • 300 kW
		(J) • S AMERICA • 300 kW
		(J) • W EUROPE & E NORTH AM • 300 kW
		(J) • HEBREW • W EUROPE & E NORTH AM • 300 kW
		(J) • HEBREW • E NORTH AM & C AMERICA • 300 kW
		(J) M/Tu/Th-Sa • W EUROPE & E NORTH AM • 300 kW
		(J) Su/W • W EUROPE & E NORTH AM • 300 kW
	†RASHUTH HASHIDUR, Tel Aviv	HEBREW • EUROPE & E NORTH AM • DS-B • 50/300 kW
		Su-F • HEBREW • EUROPE & E NORTH AM • DS-B • 50/300 kW
15625	GREECE FONI TIS HELLADAS, Athens	Alternative Frequency to 15630 kHz
15630	GREECE FONI TIS HELLADAS, Athens	GREEK • AUSTRALIA • 100 kW • ALT. FREQ. TO 15625 kHz
		AFRICA • 100 kW
		AUSTRALIA • 100 kW • ALT. FREQ. TO 15625 kHz
		GREEK • E ASIA • 100 kW
		E ASIA • 100 kW
		GREEK • N AMERICA & EUROPE • 100 kW
		N AMERICA & EUROPE • 100 kW
		GREEK • AFRICA • 100 kW
		(J) • GREEK • WEST USSR • GREEK, RUSSIAN • 100 kW
		(J) • WEST USSR • GREEK, RUSSIAN • 100 kW
15640	ISRAEL †KOL ISRAEL, Tel Aviv	(J) • E NORTH AM & C AMERICA • 300 kW
		(J) • HEBREW • E NORTH AM & C AMERICA • 300 kW
		(J) Sa/Su • EUROPE & E NORTH AM • 300 kW
15650	CLANDESTINE (M EAST) "RADIO IRAN", Abu Za'bal, Egypt	PERSIAN • MIDEAST • ANTI-KHOMEYNI • 100 kW
	ISRAEL †KOL ISRAEL, Tel Aviv	S ASIA & SE ASIA • 300 kW
		(D) Sa/Su • USSR • 300 kW
		(D) • WEST USSR • 300 kW
		(J) • WEST USSR • 300 kW
		(J) • HEBREW • WEST USSR • 300 kW
		(D) M/Tu/Th-Sa • WEST USSR • 300 kW
		(J) M/Tu/Th-Sa • WEST USSR • 300 kW
		(D) Su/W • WEST USSR • 300 kW
		(J) Su/W • WEST USSR • 300 kW
	USA †KUSW, Salt Lake City, Utah	M-Sa • E NORTH AM • 100 kW
15660	USSR †RADIO MOSCOW	(J) • (FEEDER) • USB
15662	ICELAND RIKISUTVARPID, Reykjavik	(J) • ATLANTIC & EUROPE • DS • 10 kW • USB
15670	CHINA (PR) CENTRAL PEOPLES BS, Kunming	DS-MINORITIES • 50 kW
15685	CLANDESTINE (ASIA) "VOICE OF UNITY", Abu Za'bal, Egypt	MIDEAST & S ASIA • PRO-AFGHAN REBELS • 100 kW
15690	USA †WWCR, Nashville, Tennessee	ENGLISH, FRENCH & SPANISH • E NORTH AM & EUROPE • 100 kW • ALT. FREQ. TO 7520 kHz
15710	CHINA (PR) CENTRAL PEOPLES BS, Beijing	TAIWAN-1 • 10 kW

World Time: 0 Prime Time-Americas 6 Prime Time-E Asia 12 Prime Time-S Asia 18 Prime Time-Europe 24

SUMMER ONLY (J) WINTER ONLY (D) JAMMING / OR /\ EARLIEST HEARD ◁ LATEST HEARD ▷ NEW OR CHANGED FOR 1990 †

FREQUENCY	COUNTRY, STATION, LOCATION	TARGET • NETWORK • POWER (kW)
15720	USSR †RADIO MOSCOW	(J) • (FEEDER) • USB
15750	USSR †RADIO MOSCOW	(J) • DS-1(FEEDER) • USB
15780	ARGENTINA †RADIO DEL PLATA, Buenos Aires	Irr • DS(FEEDER) • 10 kW • ISL
		Irr • DS(FEEDER) • 10 kW • ISU
	†RADIO RIVADAVIA, Buenos Aires	
15880	CHINA (PR) CENTRAL PEOPLES BS, Beijing	TAIWAN-2 • 15 kW
		Th-Tu • TAIWAN-2 • 15 kW
16041.3	USA †AFRTS-US MILITARY, Via Barford, UK	Irr • ATLANTIC • DS-ABC/CBS/NBC/NPR(FEEDER) • 4 kW • LSB
16065	USA †RFE-RL, Via Holzkirchen,GFR	W EUROPE • (FEEDER) • 10 kW • ISL
		W EUROPE • (FEEDER) • 10 kW • ISU
		(J) • W EUROPE • (FEEDER) • 10 kW • ISL
		(J) • W EUROPE • (FEEDER) • 10 kW • ISU
16230	ALBANIA RADIO TIRANA, Lushnjë	E ASIA • 50 kW
16454.3	USA †AFRTS-US MILITARY, Via Barford, UK	Irr • ATLANTIC • DS-ABC/CBS/NBC/NPR(FEEDER) • 4 kW • LSB
17387	INDIA ALL INDIA RADIO, Delhi	E ASIA • 50/100 kW
		SE ASIA • 50/100 kW
17533	CHINA (PR) †RADIO BEIJING, Kunming	(D) • S AMERICA • CHINESE, CANTONESE • 120 kW
	CLANDESTINE (ASIA) "DEM KAMPUCHEA", Kunming, China	(J) • SE ASIA • PRO-KHMER ROUGE • 50 kW
17540	CLANDESTINE (ASIA) †"VOICE OF UNITY", Abu Za'bal, Egypt	(J) • MIDEAST & S ASIA • PRO-AFGHAN REBELS • 100 kW
17545v	ISRAEL †RASHUTH HASHIDUR, Tel Aviv	HEBREW • W EUROPE & E NORTH AM • DS-B • 50/300 kW
		(J) • HEBREW • W EUROPE & E NORTH AM • DS-B • 50/300 kW
17555	BELGIUM †BELGISCHE RADIO TV, Wavre	E NORTH AM & C AMERICA • 100/250 kW • ALT. FREQ. TO 17560 kHz
		M-Sa • E NORTH AM & C AMERICA • 100/250 kW • ALT. FREQ. TO 17560 kHz
	USA †WSHB, Cypress Creek, SC	C AMERICA • 500 kW; S AMERICA • 500 kW
		M-F • C AMERICA • 500 kW
		M-Sa • S AMERICA • 500 kW
		Sa • S AMERICA • 500 kW
		Sa/Su • C AMERICA • 500 kW
		Su • S AMERICA • 500 kW
		Su-F • S AMERICA • 500 kW
17558	ICELAND RIKISUTVARPID, Reykjavik	(J) • ATLANTIC & E NORTH AM • DS-1 • 10 kW • USB
17560	BELGIUM †BELGISCHE RADIO TV, Wavre	Alternative Frequency to 17555 kHz
	GERMANY (FR) †DEUTSCHE WELLE	(J) • JAPANESE • E ASIA
		(J) • E ASIA
		(J) • S ASIA
	USSR RADIO MOSCOW	(J) • SOVIETS ABROAD
17565	GREECE FONI TIS HELLADAS, Athens	(J) • GREEK • AUSTRALIA • 100 kW
		(J) • AUSTRALIA • 100 kW
17570	SWITZERLAND SWISS RADIO INTL, Sottens	AFRICA • 500 kW
	USSR RADIO MOSCOW	(J) • WS
17575	HOLLAND †RADIO NEDERLAND, Via Madagascar	S ASIA • 300 kW
		SE ASIA • 300 kW
		E ASIA • 300 kW
	†RADIO NEDERLAND, Via Neth Antilles	(J) • N AFRICA & W AFRICA • 300 kW
17575v	ISRAEL †KOL ISRAEL, Tel Aviv	(D) • E EUROPE & WEST USSR • 300 kW
		(J) • W EUROPE & E NORTH AM • 300 kW
		(J) • HEBREW • W EUROPE & E NORTH AM • 300 kW
		(D) Sa/Su • E EUROPE & WEST USSR • 300 kW
		(J) • E NORTH AM & C AMERICA • 300 kW
		(D) M/Tu/Th-Sa • E EUROPE & WEST USSR • 300 kW
		(J) M/Tu/Th-Sa • W EUROPE & E NORTH AM • 300 kW
		(J) Sa/Su • W EUROPE & E NORTH AM • 300 kW
		(D) Su/W • E EUROPE & WEST USSR • 300 kW
		(J) Su/W • W EUROPE & E NORTH AM • 300 kW
17580	USSR RADIO MOSCOW	E AFRICA • WS, FRENCH
17585 (con'd)	BELGIUM †RT BELGE FRANCAISE, Wavre	(D) • AFRICA • 100/250 kW

World Time 0–24: 0 Prime Time-Americas 6 Prime Time-E Asia 12 Prime Time-S Asia 18 Prime Time-Europe 24

ENGLISH ▬ ARABIC ▭ CHINESE ▫▫▫ FRENCH ═ GERMAN ═ RUSSIAN ═ SPANISH ▬ OTHER —

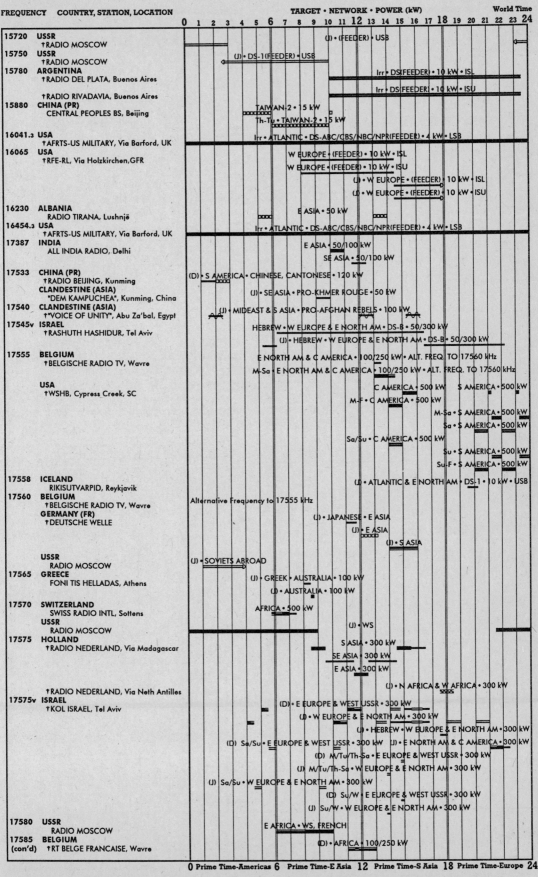

FREQUENCY	COUNTRY, STATION, LOCATION	TARGET • NETWORK • POWER (kW) — World Time 0–24
17585 (con'd)	BELGIUM †RT BELGE FRANCAISE, Wavre	(D) Su • AFRICA • 100/250 kW
17590	ISRAEL †KOL ISRAEL, Tel Aviv	(J) • EUROPE & N AMERICA • 250 kW
		(J) • W EUROPE & E NORTH AM • 300 kW
		(J) Sa/Su • EUROPE & N AMERICA • 250 kW
	†RASHUTH HASHIDUR, Tel Aviv	(J) • HEBREW • EUROPE & N AMERICA • DS-B • 250 kW
	USSR †RADIO MOSCOW	(J) • E AFRICA
		(D) • S ASIA • WS, RUSSIAN
17595	BELGIUM †BELGISCHE RADIO TV, Wavre	(D) • AFRICA • 100/250 kW
		(D) M-F • AFRICA • 100/250 kW
		(J) • AFRICA • 100/250 kW
		(D) M-Sa • AFRICA • 100/250 kW
		(J) M-Sa • AFRICA • 100/250 kW
		(D) Sa/Su • AFRICA • 100/250 kW
		(J) Su • AFRICA • 100/250 kW
		(D) Su • AFRICA • 100/250 kW
	EGYPT RADIO CAIRO, Kafr Silîm-Abis	S ASIA & SE ASIA • 250 kW
	MOROCCO RTV MAROCAINE, Tangier	EUROPE & W AFRICA • 50 kW
		M-F • EUROPE & W AFRICA • 50 kW
		Sa/Su • EUROPE & W AFRICA • 50 kW
	USSR †P & PROGRESS	(J) • W AFRICA & S AMERICA
	†RADIO MOSCOW	(J) • W AFRICA & S AMERICA
	†RADIO YEREVAN	(J) • W AFRICA & S AMERICA
17600	USSR RADIO MOSCOW	(D) • SE ASIA
		(J) • S ASIA & SE ASIA • WS,BENGALI,ETC
17605	CHINA (PR) CENTRAL PEOPLES BS, Beijing	DS-1 • 15 kW
		W-M • DS-1 • 15 kW
	HOLLAND †RADIO NEDERLAND, Flevoland	SE ASIA • 500 kW
		(D) • MIDEAST • 500 kW
		(D) • W AFRICA • 500 kW
		(J) • SE ASIA • 500 kW
		(J) • S ASIA • 500 kW
		(J) • MIDEAST • 500 kW
		(J) • N AFRICA & W AFRICA • 500 kW
		Su • W AFRICA • 500 kW
	†RADIO NEDERLAND, Via Neth Antilles	W AFRICA • 300 kW
		S AMERICA • 300 kW
		(D) • N AFRICA • 300 kW
		Su • E NORTH AM • 300 kW
		(D) Su • S AMERICA • 300 kW
	USSR †R TIKHIY OKEAN	(J) • W NORTH AM
		(J) Sa • W NORTH AM
		(J) Su-F • W NORTH AM
	†RADIO MOSCOW	(J) • W NORTH AM
17610	SYRIA †SYRIAN BC SERVICE, Adhra	Alternative Frequency to 17710 kHz
	TUNISIA †RTV TUNISIENNE, Sfax	(J) • DS • 100 kW
	USSR RADIO MOSCOW	S ASIA
		(J) • S ASIA
17612.5	CHINA (TAIWAN) VO FREE CHINA, Via Okeechobee,USA	(J) • EUROPE • 100 kW
	USA †WYFR-FAMILY RADIO, Okeechobee, Fl	(J) • S AMERICA • 100 kW
		S AMERICA • 100 kW
		(D) • W AFRICA • 100 kW
		(J) • EUROPE • 100 kW
17615	USSR RADIO MOSCOW	(D) • ASIA
17620	FRANCE †R FRANCE INTL, Issoudun-Allouis	AFRICA • 100/500 kW
		(J) • AFRICA • 100/500 kW
	R FRANCE INTL, Via French Guiana	(J) • S AMERICA • 500 kW
17625	USSR RADIO MOSCOW	(J) • E AFRICA • WS,SOMALI,ETC

0 Prime Time-Americas 6 Prime Time-E Asia 12 Prime Time-S Asia 18 Prime Time-Europe 24

SUMMER ONLY (J) WINTER ONLY (D) JAMMING / OR /\ EARLIEST HEARD ◃ LATEST HEARD ▹ NEW OR CHANGED FOR 1990 †

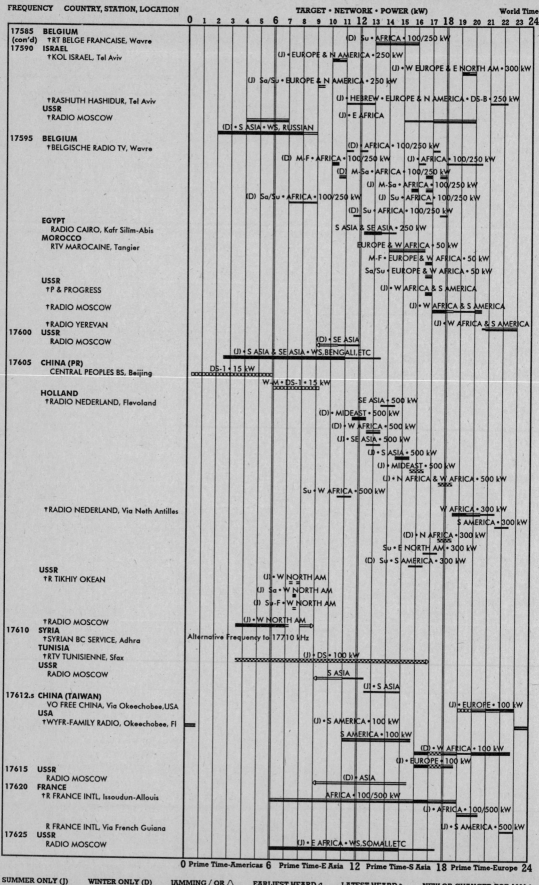

FREQUENCY   COUNTRY, STATION, LOCATION

TARGET • NETWORK • POWER (kW)

World Time

0 1 2 3 4 5 6 7 8 9 10 11 12 13 14 15 16 17 18 19 20 21 22 23 24

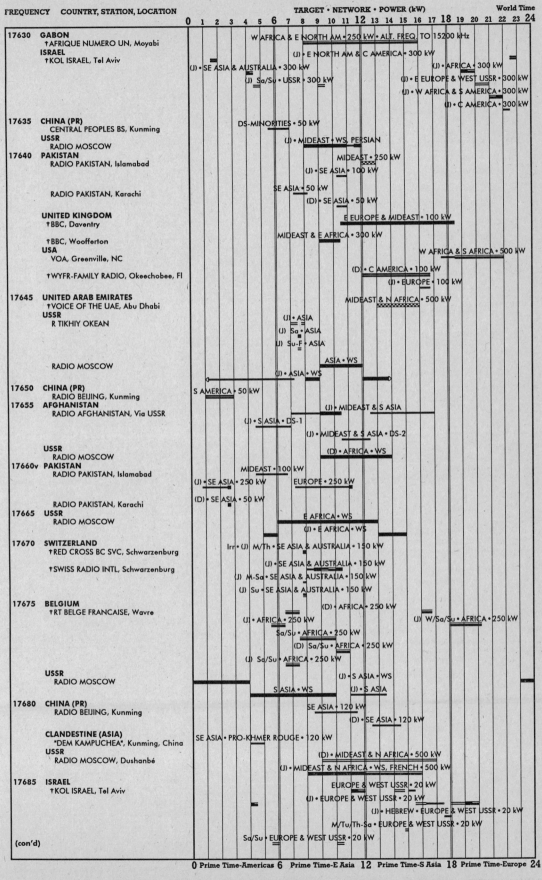

17630 GABON
†AFRIQUE NUMERO UN, Moyabi — W AFRICA & E NORTH AM • 250 kW • ALT. FREQ. TO 15200 kHz
ISRAEL
†KOL ISRAEL, Tel Aviv — (J) • E NORTH AM & C AMERICA • 300 kW
(J) • SE ASIA & AUSTRALIA • 300 kW   (J) • AFRICA • 300 kW
(J) Sa/Su • USSR • 300 kW   (J) • E EUROPE & WEST USSR • 300 kW
(J) • W AFRICA & S AMERICA • 300 kW
(J) • C AMERICA • 300 kW

17635 CHINA (PR)
CENTRAL PEOPLES BS, Kunming — DS-MINORITIES • 50 kW
USSR
RADIO MOSCOW — (J) • MIDEAST • WS, PERSIAN
17640 PAKISTAN
RADIO PAKISTAN, Islamabad — MIDEAST • 250 kW
(J) • SE ASIA • 100 kW
RADIO PAKISTAN, Karachi — SE ASIA • 50 kW
(D) • SE ASIA • 50 kW
UNITED KINGDOM
†BBC, Daventry — E EUROPE & MIDEAST • 100 kW
†BBC, Woofferton — MIDEAST & E AFRICA • 300 kW
USA
VOA, Greenville, NC — W AFRICA & S AFRICA • 500 kW
†WYFR-FAMILY RADIO, Okeechobee, Fl — (D) • C AMERICA • 100 kW
(J) • EUROPE • 100 kW

17645 UNITED ARAB EMIRATES
†VOICE OF THE UAE, Abu Dhabi — MIDEAST & N AFRICA • 500 kW
USSR
R TIKHIY OKEAN — (J) • ASIA
(J) Sa • ASIA
(J) Su-F • ASIA
RADIO MOSCOW — ASIA • WS
(J) • ASIA • WS

17650 CHINA (PR)
RADIO BEIJING, Kunming — S AMERICA • 50 kW
17655 AFGHANISTAN
RADIO AFGHANISTAN, Via USSR — (J) • MIDEAST & S ASIA
(J) • S ASIA • DS-1
(J) • MIDEAST & S ASIA • DS-2
USSR
RADIO MOSCOW — (D) • AFRICA • WS
17660v PAKISTAN
RADIO PAKISTAN, Islamabad — MIDEAST • 100 kW
(J) • SE ASIA • 250 kW   EUROPE • 250 kW
RADIO PAKISTAN, Karachi — (D) • SE ASIA • 50 kW
17665 USSR
RADIO MOSCOW — E AFRICA • WS
(J) • E AFRICA • WS

17670 SWITZERLAND
†RED CROSS BC SVC, Schwarzenburg — Irr • (J) M/Th • SE ASIA & AUSTRALIA • 150 kW
†SWISS RADIO INTL, Schwarzenburg — (J) • SE ASIA & AUSTRALIA • 150 kW
(J) M-Sa • SE ASIA & AUSTRALIA • 150 kW
(J) Su • SE ASIA & AUSTRALIA • 150 kW

17675 BELGIUM
†RT BELGE FRANCAISE, Wavre — (D) • AFRICA • 250 kW
(J) • AFRICA • 250 kW   (J) W/Sa/Su • AFRICA • 250 kW
Sa/Su • AFRICA • 250 kW
(D) Sa/Su • AFRICA • 250 kW
(J) Sa/Su • AFRICA • 250 kW
USSR
RADIO MOSCOW — (J) • S ASIA • WS
S ASIA • WS   (J) • S ASIA

17680 CHINA (PR)
RADIO BEIJING, Kunming — SE ASIA • 120 kW
(D) • SE ASIA • 120 kW
CLANDESTINE (ASIA)
"DEM KAMPUCHEA", Kunming, China — SE ASIA • PRO-KHMER ROUGE • 120 kW
USSR
RADIO MOSCOW, Dushanbé — (D) • MIDEAST & N AFRICA • 500 kW
(J) • MIDEAST & N AFRICA • WS, FRENCH • 500 kW

17685 ISRAEL
†KOL ISRAEL, Tel Aviv — EUROPE & WEST USSR • 20 kW
(J) • EUROPE & WEST USSR • 20 kW
(J) • HEBREW • EUROPE & WEST USSR • 20 kW
M/Tu/Th-Sa • EUROPE & WEST USSR • 20 kW
Sa/Su • EUROPE & WEST USSR • 20 kW

(con'd)

0 Prime Time-Americas 6 Prime Time-E Asia 12 Prime Time-S Asia 18 Prime Time-Europe 24

ENGLISH ▬▬   ARABIC ⌇⌇⌇   CHINESE □□□   FRENCH ▬▬   GERMAN ▬▬▬   RUSSIAN ══   SPANISH ▬▬   OTHER ──

FREQUENCY	COUNTRY, STATION, LOCATION	TARGET • NETWORK • POWER (kW)
17685 (con'd)	**ISRAEL**	
	†KOL ISRAEL, Tel Aviv	Su/W • EUROPE & WEST USSR • 20 kW
	USSR	
	RADIO MOSCOW, Irkutsk	(J) • E ASIA & SE ASIA • WS • 500 kW
17690	**EGYPT**	
	RADIO CAIRO, Kafr Silîm-Abis	S ASIA • 250 kW
	USSR	
	RADIO MOSCOW	(D) • AFRICA
17695	**FRANCE**	
	†R FRANCE INTL, Issoudun-Allouis	(D) • SE ASIA • 500 kW
		(J) • SE ASIA • 500 kW
	UNITED KINGDOM	
	†BBC, Daventry	(D) • WEST USSR • 300 kW
		(D) Su • WEST USSR • 300 kW
	†BBC, Rampisham	(J) Su • E EUROPE & MIDEAST • 500 kW
	†BBC, Skelton, Cumbria	(J) • N AFRICA & W AFRICA • 250 kW
	†BBC, Various Locations	(J) • E EUROPE • 250/500 kW
		(J) Su • E EUROPE • 250/300/500 kW
	†BBC, Woofferton	(D) Su • E EUROPE & MIDEAST • 300 kW
	USSR	
	R TIKHIY OKEAN	(J) • ASIA
		(J) Sa • ASIA
		(J) Su-F • ASIA
	RADIO MOSCOW	(J) • ASIA
17700	**CHINA (PR)**	
	CENTRAL PEOPLES BS, Beijing	DS-2 • 50 kW
		Th/Sa-Tu • DS-2 • 50 kW
	SOUTH AFRICA	
	†RADIO RSA, Meyerton	Alternative Frequency to 17735 kHz
	USSR	
	RADIO MOSCOW	WS
		(D) • MIDEAST • WS,RUSSIAN,PERSIAN
	RADIO MOSCOW, L'vov	(J) • E AFRICA & S AFRICA • 240 kW
		(J) • C AFRICA • 240 kW
17705	**CZECHOSLOVAKIA**	
	RADIO PRAGUE, Pieštány-Velké K'y	Alternative Frequency to 17730 kHz
	FRANCE	
	†R FRANCE INTL, Via Tokyo, Japan	E ASIA & SE ASIA • 300 kW
	GERMANY (FR)	
	†DEUTSCHE WELLE, Via Sines, Portugal	(J) • E EUROPE • 250 kW
	INDIA	
	ALL INDIA RADIO, Delhi	DS-ENGLISH, ETC • 50 kW
	NEW ZEALAND	
	†RADIO NEW ZEALAND, Wellington	PACIFIC • 7.5 kW
		M-F • PACIFIC • 7.5 kW
		Sa • PACIFIC • 7.5 kW
		Sa/Su • PACIFIC • 7.5 kW
	SWEDEN	
	†RADIO SWEDEN, Hörby	Alternative Frequency to 17740 kHz
	UNITED ARAB EMIRATES	
	†VOICE OF THE UAE, Abu Dhabi	(D) • AUSTRALIA • DS • 500 kW
		(D) • E ASIA • DS • 500 kW
	UNITED KINGDOM	
	†BBC, Various Locations	W AFRICA • 100/250 kW
	USA	
	VOA, Via M'rovia, Liberia	W AFRICA & S AFRICA • 250 kW
		W AFRICA & C AFRICA • 250 kW
		(D) M-F • C AFRICA & E AFRICA • 250 kW
	†VOA, Via Tangier,Morocco	(J) • E EUROPE • 35 kW
17708v	**COLOMBIA**	
	RADIO NACIONAL, Bogotá	Alternative Frequency to 17840v kHz
17710	**CHINA (PR)**	
	†RADIO BEIJING	(J) • AUSTRALIA
	CUBA	
	RADIO HABANA, Via USSR	(J) • E AFRICA & S AFRICA • 240 kW
	FRANCE	
	†R FRANCE INTL, Via Tokyo, Japan	SE ASIA • 300 kW
	SYRIA	
	†SYRIAN BC SERVICE, Adhra	(J) • C AMERICA & S AMERICA • 500 kW
		(J) • EUROPE • 500 kW • ALT. FREQ. TO 17610 kHz
		(J) • AUSTRALIA • 500 kW
	USA	
	†VOA, Greenville, NC	M-F • C AMERICA & S AMERICA • 250 kW
	USSR	
	RADIO MOSCOW, L'vov	(D) • C AFRICA • 240 kW
		(J) • C AFRICA • 240 kW
	RADIO MOSCOW, Moscow	S ASIA • MARINERS • 240 kW
	RADIO MOSCOW, Novosibirsk	E ASIA • 100 kW
17714v	**BANGLADESH**	
	†RADIO BANGLADESH, Dhaka	EUROPE • 250 kW

World Time: 0 1 2 3 4 5 6 7 8 9 10 11 12 13 14 15 16 17 18 19 20 21 22 23 24

0 Prime Time-Americas 6 Prime Time-E Asia 12 Prime Time-S Asia 18 Prime Time-Europe 24

SUMMER ONLY (J) WINTER ONLY (D) JAMMING / OR /\ EARLIEST HEARD ◁ LATEST HEARD ▷ NEW OR CHANGED FOR 1990 †

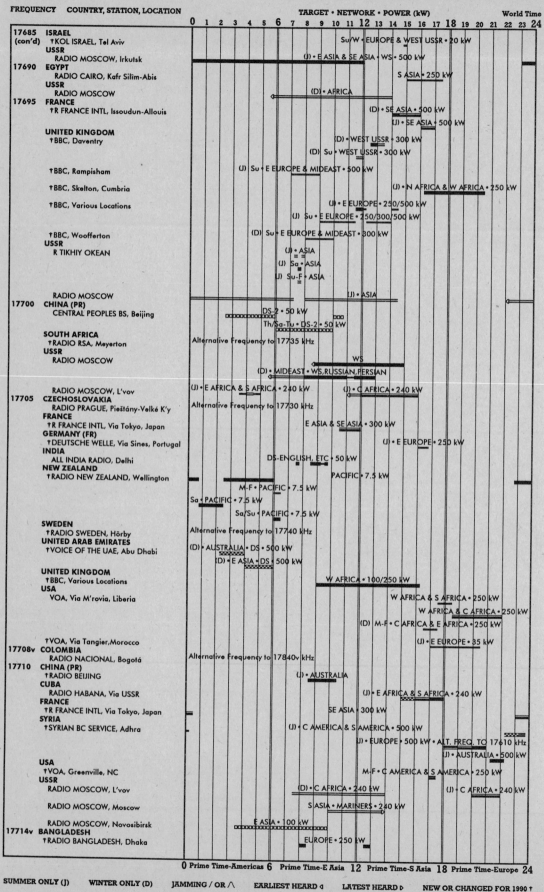

FREQUENCY | COUNTRY, STATION, LOCATION | TARGET • NETWORK • POWER (kW) | World Time 0 1 2 3 4 5 6 7 8 9 10 11 12 13 14 15 16 17 18 19 20 21 22 23 24

17715 AUSTRALIA
†RADIO AUSTRALIA, Darwin — E ASIA • 250 kW

GERMANY (FR)
†DEUTSCHE WELLE, Jülich — C AFRICA & S AFRICA • 100 kW
DEUTSCHE WELLE, Via Antigua — AMERICAS • 250 kW
DEUTSCHE WELLE, Via Cyclops, Malta — (J) • JAPANESE • E ASIA • 250 kW
†DEUTSCHE WELLE, Wertachtal — MIDEAST • 500 kW

SPAIN
†R NACIONAL ESPANA, Noblejas — (J) • S AMERICA • 350 kW
(J) • C AMERICA & S AMERICA • 350 kW

UNITED KINGDOM
†BBC, Skelton, Cumbria — W AFRICA • 100 kW
(J) • W AFRICA • 100 kW

USA
VOA, Via M'rovia, Liberia — M-F • W AFRICA & S AFRICA • ENGLISH,FRENCH,ETC • 250 kW

17715v CHINA (PR)
†RADIO BEIJING, Via Bamako, Mali — (D) • E NORTH AM • 50 kW
(J) • E NORTH AM & C AMERICA • 50 kW

17720 AFGHANISTAN
†RADIO AFGHANISTAN, Via USSR — (D) • MIDEAST & S ASIA
(J) • MIDEAST & S ASIA
(D) • MIDEAST & S ASIA • DS-1
(J) • MIDEAST & S ASIA • DS-1
(D) • MIDEAST & S ASIA • DS-2
(J) • MIDEAST & S ASIA • DS-2

CHINA (TAIWAN)
VO FREE CHINA, T'ai-pei — SE ASIA • 50/100 kW

EGYPT
RADIO CAIRO, Kafr Silîm-Abis — S AMERICA • 250 kW

FRANCE
†R FRANCE INTL, Issoudun-Allouis — E NORTH AM & C AMERICA • 100 kW
(J) • E NORTH AM & C AMERICA • 100 kW
R FRANCE INTL, Via French Guiana — C AMERICA • 500 kW

GERMANY (FR)
†DEUTSCHE WELLE, Via Cyclops, Malta — S AMERICA • 250 kW

IRAQ
†RADIO BAGHDAD, Balad-Salah el Deen — (J) • N AFRICA & W AFRICA • 500 kW

ROMANIA
†RADIO BUCHAREST, Bucharest — AFRICA • 250 kW; S ASIA • 250 kW
AUSTRALIA • 250 kW
Su • MIDEAST & S ASIA • MARINERS • 250 kW
Su • S AFRICA • MARINERS • 250 kW

USSR
RADIO MOSCOW, Khabarovsk — (J) • PACIFIC • 100 kW

17725 INDIA
†ALL INDIA RADIO, Delhi — (J) • SE ASIA • 50 kW

PAKISTAN
RADIO PAKISTAN, Karachi — E AFRICA • 50 kW; (J) • S ASIA • 50 kW
(J) • SE ASIA • 50 kW

USA
†RFE-RL, Via Portugal — E EUROPE & WEST USSR • 250 kW

17730 CZECHOSLOVAKIA
RADIO PRAGUE, Piešťány-Velké K'y — AFRICA • 250 kW • ALT. FREQ. TO 17705 kHz
M-F • AFRICA • 250 kW • ALT. FREQ. TO 17705 kHz

IRAQ
†RADIO BAGHDAD, Balad-Salah el Deen — (D) • S AMERICA • 500 kW

SOUTH AFRICA
†RADIO RSA, Meyerton — (J) • S ASIA & E ASIA • 250 kW

SPAIN
†R NACIONAL ESPANA, Noblejas — (J) • EUROPE • 350 kW

SWITZERLAND
RED CROSS BC SVC, Via Brasília,Brazil — Irr • Tu/F • C AMERICA & W NORTH AM • 250 kW
SWISS RADIO INTL, Via Brasília,Brazil — C AMERICA & W NORTH AM • 250 kW
M • C AMERICA & W NORTH AM • 250 kW
Tu-Su • C AMERICA & W NORTH AM • 250 kW

USA
†VOA, Cincinnati, Ohio — M-F • C AMERICA & S AMERICA • 250 kW
(D) M-F • C AMERICA & S AMERICA • 250 kW
(J) M-F • C AMERICA & S AMERICA • 250 kW
†VOA, Greenville, NC — Sa/Su • C AMERICA & S AMERICA • 250 kW

USSR
†KAZAKH RADIO — DS-2
RADIO MOSCOW, Serpukhov — (D) • SE ASIA • WS, THAI • 250 kW

VATICAN STATE
†VATICAN RADIO, Sta Maria di Galeria — E AFRICA & MIDEAST • 250 kW
M-Sa • AFRICA • 250 kW
M-Sa • W AFRICA • 250 kW

0 Prime Time-Americas 6 Prime Time-E Asia 12 Prime Time-S Asia 18 Prime Time-Europe 24

ENGLISH ▬ ARABIC ▭ CHINESE ▯▯▯ FRENCH ═ GERMAN ═ RUSSIAN ═ SPANISH ═ OTHER —

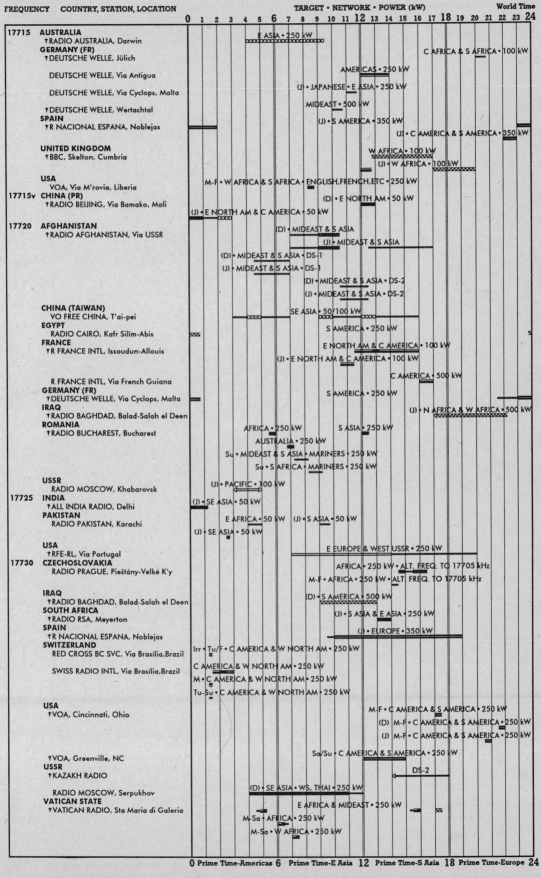

FREQUENCY	COUNTRY, STATION, LOCATION	TARGET • NETWORK • POWER (kW)
17735	**OMAN** †RADIO OMAN, Thamarīt	MIDEAST & N AFRICA • DS • 100 kW
		(J) • MIDEAST & N AFRICA • DS • 100 kW
	SOUTH AFRICA †RADIO RSA, Meyerton	W EUROPE • 500 kW • ALT. FREQ. TO 17700 kHz
	USA †RFE-RL, Via Portugal	E EUROPE & WEST USSR • 250 kW
	†VOA, Via Philippines	S ASIA • 250 kW
		AUSTRALIA • 250 kW
	USSR RADIO MOSCOW, Kazan'	(J) • E AFRICA • 240 kW
17740	**DENMARK** †DANMARKS RADIO, Copenhagen	(D) • S ASIA & AUSTRALIA • 50 kW
	INDIA †ALL INDIA RADIO, Aligarh	SE ASIA • 250 kW
		(J) • E ASIA • 250 kW
	ITALY †RTV ITALIANA, Rome	Alternative Frequency to 17780 kHz
	PORTUGAL †R PORTUGAL INTL, Lisbon-S Gabriel	(J) • E AFRICA & S AFRICA • 100 kW
	SAUDI ARABIA BS OF THE KINGDOM, Riyadh	EAST USSR & E ASIA • DS-HOLY KORAN • 350 kW
	SWEDEN †RADIO SWEDEN, Hörby	(J) • SWEDISH • S ASIA & SE ASIA • 350 kW • ALT. FREQ. TO 17705 kHz
		(J) • S ASIA & SE ASIA • 350 kW • ALT. FREQ. TO 17705 kHz
		(J) • USSR • 350 kW • ALT. FREQ. TO 17705 kHz
	UNITED KINGDOM †BBC, Via Zyyi, Cyprus	(J) • N AFRICA • 100 kW
		E AFRICA • 100 kW
		(J) • E AFRICA • 100 kW
	USA VOA, Greenville, NC	N AFRICA • 250 kW
	VOA, Via M'rovia, Liberia	M-F • W AFRICA & C AFRICA • 250 kW
	VOA, Via Philippines	E AFRICA • 250 kW
		M-F • E AFRICA • 250 kW
	USSR RADIO MOSCOW, Ashkhabad	(J) • SE ASIA • WS, VIETNAMESE, ETC • 100 kW
		(D) • SE ASIA • WS • 100 kW
	VATICAN STATE VATICAN RADIO, Sta Maria di Galeria	C AMERICA • 100 kW
	YUGOSLAVIA †RADIO YUGOSLAVIA, Bijeljina	(J) • E NORTH AM • 500 kW
17745	**ALGERIA** RTV ALGERIENNE, Algiers	E AFRICA • 100 kW
		E AFRICA • DS-3 • 100 kW
	EGYPT †RADIO CAIRO, Kafr Silîm-Abis	MIDEAST • 250 kW
	ROMANIA †RADIO BUCHAREST, Bucharest	(J) • AMERICAS • 250 kW
		(J) • MIDEAST & S ASIA • 250 kW
		(J) Su • S ASIA & SE ASIA • MARINERS • 250 kW
	SOUTH AFRICA †RADIO RSA, Meyerton	Alternative Frequency to 17755 kHz
		(J) Su • E AFRICA • 500 kW
		AFRICA • 250/500 kW
	USSR RADIO MOSCOW, Frunze, Kirgiziya	(D) • SE ASIA • MARINERS • 100 kW
17750	**AUSTRALIA** †RADIO AUSTRALIA, Darwin	SE ASIA • 250 kW
	IRAQ †RADIO BAGHDAD, Balad-Salah el Deen	(J) • N AFRICA & W AFRICA • 500 kW
	USA †RFE-RL, Via Germany	WEST USSR • 250 kW
	†WYFR-FAMILY RADIO, Okeechobee, Fl	(D) • EUROPE • 100 kW
		(J) • EUROPE • 100 kW
17755	**JAPAN** †RADIO JAPAN/NHK, Via Moyabi, Gabon	(D) • S AMERICA • 500 kW
		(D) • JAPANESE • S AMERICA • GENERAL • 500 kW
	SOUTH AFRICA †RADIO RSA, Meyerton	W AFRICA • 250 kW • ALT. FREQ. TO 17745 kHz
		(D) • W AFRICA • 500 kW
		(D) • EUROPE • 500 kW
	SURINAME †R SURINAME INTL, Via Brasília, Brazil	(J) M-F • EUROPE • ENGLISH, DUTCH • 250 kW • ALT. FREQ. TO 17765 kHz
	UNITED KINGDOM †BBC, Via Zyyi, Cyprus	(J) • N AFRICA • 250 kW
	USA †VOA, Via Philippines	(J) • E AFRICA • 250 kW
17760	**TURKEY** †TURKISH RTV CORP, Ankara	(J) • TURKISH • SE ASIA • 500 kW
		(J) • SE ASIA • 500 kW
	UNITED KINGDOM †BBC, Via Antigua	S AMERICA • 250 kW
	USA †RFE-RL, Via Germany	WEST USSR • 100 kW

World Time 0–24: 0 Prime Time-Americas 6 Prime Time-E Asia 12 Prime Time-S Asia 18 Prime Time-Europe 24

SUMMER ONLY (J) WINTER ONLY (D) JAMMING / OR /\ EARLIEST HEARD ◁ LATEST HEARD ▷ NEW OR CHANGED FOR 1990 †

FREQUENCY	COUNTRY, STATION, LOCATION	TARGET • NETWORK • POWER (kW)
17765	**GERMANY (FR)**	
	†DEUTSCHE WELLE, Multiple Locations	(D) • SE ASIA & AUSTRALIA • 100/500 kW
	†DEUTSCHE WELLE, Via Sri Lanka	E AFRICA & S AFRICA • 250 kW
	†DEUTSCHE WELLE, Wertachtal	C AFRICA & E AFRICA • 500 kW
		W AFRICA • 500 kW
		W AFRICA & S AFRICA • 500 kW
	JAPAN	
	†RADIO JAPAN/NHK, Tokyo-Yamata	JAPANESE • E ASIA • GENERAL • 300 kW
		E ASIA • GENERAL • 300 kW
		(J) • JAPANESE • E ASIA • GENERAL • 300 kW
		(J) • E ASIA • GENERAL • 300 kW
	SURINAME	
	†R SURINAME INTL, Via Brasília, Brazil	Alternative Frequency to 17755 kHz
	USA	
	†VOA, Via Philippines	(J) • E ASIA • 250 kW
	USSR	
	RADIO MOSCOW, Armavir	(J) • S ASIA & SE ASIA • WS,HINDI,URDU,ETC • 500 kW
	RADIO MOSCOW, Tula	(D) • S ASIA & SE ASIA • WS,HINDI,URDU • 240 kW
17765v	**MEXICO**	
	RADIO MEXICO INTL, México City	Irr • W NORTH AM • 10 kW
17770	**EGYPT**	
	†RADIO CAIRO, Abu Za'bal	DS-GENERAL • 100 kW
	RADIO CAIRO, Kafr Silîm-Abis	SE ASIA • 250 kW
	GERMANY (FR)	
	†DEUTSCHE WELLE	(J) • S ASIA
	OMAN	
	RADIO OMAN, Thamarīt	E AFRICA & S AFRICA • DS • 100 kW
	SPAIN	
	†R NACIONAL ESPANA, Noblejas	M-Sa • MIDEAST • 350 kW
		Th • MIDEAST • LADINO • 350 kW
	UNITED KINGDOM	
	†BBC, Daventry	(J) • WEST USSR • 300 kW
		(J) Su • WEST USSR • 300 kW
	USA	
	†R FREE AFGHANISTAN, Via Germany	WEST USSR & S ASIA • 100 kW
	†RFE-RL, Via Pals, Spain	WEST USSR • 250 kW
	†RFE-RL, Via Portugal	WEST USSR • 250 kW
17775	**FRANCE**	
	†R FRANCE INTL, Issoudun-Allouis	M-Sa • E AFRICA • MEDIAS FRANCE • 100 kW
	GERMANY (DR)	
	†R BERLIN INTL, Königswusterhausen	W AFRICA • 100 kW
	UNITED ARAB EMIRATES	
	†UAE RADIO, Dubai	AUSTRALIA • 300 kW
		EUROPE • 300 kW
	USA	
	†KVOH, Rancho Simi, Ca	C AMERICA • 50 kW
		(J) M-Sa • C AMERICA • 50 kW
		(J) Tu-Sa • C AMERICA • 50 kW
		M-F • C AMERICA • 50 kW
		M-Sa • C AMERICA • 50 kW
		Sa/Su • C AMERICA • 50 kW
		Su • C AMERICA • 50 kW
	USSR	
	RADIO MOSCOW, Frunze, Kirgiziya	S ASIA & SE ASIA • 100 kW
		(J) • S ASIA & SE ASIA • 100 kW
		(J) • E AFRICA • WS • 500 kW
17780	**GERMANY (FR)**	
	DEUTSCHE WELLE, Multiple Locations	SE ASIA & AUSTRALIA • 100/500 kW
	†DEUTSCHE WELLE, Via Sri Lanka	MIDEAST & S ASIA • 250 kW
	ITALY	
	†RTV ITALIANA, Rome	AUSTRALIA • 100 kW • ALT. FREQ. TO 17740 kHz
		(J) • E NORTH AM • 100 kW
		E AFRICA • 100 kW
	NORTHERN MARIANA IS	
	KYOI, Saipan Island	E ASIA • 100 kW
	NORWAY	
	†RADIO NORWAY INTL, Kvitsøy	(J) • E ASIA • 500 kW
	†RADIO NORWAY INTL, Sveio	W AFRICA & S AMERICA • 500 kW
		(J) • E NORTH AM & C AMERICA • 500 kW
		(J) • W NORTH AM • 500 kW
		(J) M-Sa • E NORTH AM & C AMERICA • 500 kW
		(J) M-Sa • W NORTH AM • 500 kW
		(J) Su • E NORTH AM & C AMERICA • 500 kW
		(J) Su • W NORTH AM • 500 kW
	SEYCHELLES	
	FAR EAST BC ASS'N, North Pt, Mahé Is	Su • S ASIA • 75/100 kW
	UNITED KINGDOM	
	†BBC, Rampisham	(J) • WEST USSR • 500 kW
		(J) Su • WEST USSR • 500 kW
(con'd)		

World Time 0–24: 0 Prime Time-Americas 6 Prime Time-E Asia 12 Prime Time-S Asia 18 Prime Time-Europe 24

ENGLISH ▬ ARABIC ▧ CHINESE ▭ FRENCH ═ GERMAN ═ RUSSIAN ═ SPANISH ═ OTHER —

FREQUENCY	COUNTRY, STATION, LOCATION	TARGET • NETWORK • POWER (kW)
17780 (con'd)	USA †VOA, Via Kavála, Greece	(D) • WEST USSR • 250 kW
		(J) • WEST USSR • 250 kW
	VOA, Via Woofferton, UK	(J) • WEST USSR • 300 kW
17785	FRANCE R FRANCE INTL, Issoudun-Allouis	AFRICA • MEDIAS FRANCE • 500 kW
		(J) M-Sa • AFRICA • MEDIAS FRANCE • 500 kW
	INDIA †ALL INDIA RADIO, Aligarh	MIDEAST • PERSIAN, ARABIC • 250 kW
		SE ASIA • 250 kW
		Irr • MIDEAST • URDU • 250 kW
	SOUTH AFRICA †RADIO RSA, Meyerton	(D) Su • E AFRICA • 250 kW
	TURKEY †TURKISH RTV CORP, Ankara	(D) • MIDEAST & S ASIA • 500 kW
		(J) • E ASIA • 500 kW
		(J) • MIDEAST & S ASIA • 500 kW
	UNITED KINGDOM †BBC, Via Zyyi, Cyprus	(J) • MIDEAST • 250 kW
	USA VOA, Greenville, NC	W AFRICA & S AFRICA • 500 kW
	†VOA, Via Philippines	S ASIA • 250 kW
17790	ECUADOR †HCJB-VO THE ANDES, Quito	EUROPE • 500 kW
		(J) • EUROPE • 500 kW
	ROMANIA †RADIO BUCHAREST, Bucharest	S AFRICA • 250 kW
		Su • MIDEAST & S ASIA • MARINERS • 250 kW
		Su • W AFRICA • MARINERS • 250 kW
	SOUTH AFRICA †RADIO RSA, Meyerton	(J) • EUROPE • 500 kW
	SWEDEN †RADIO SWEDEN, Hörby	Alternative Frequency to 17800 kHz
	UNITED KINGDOM †BBC, Via Ascension	(D) • S AFRICA • 250 kW
		(J) • C AFRICA • 250 kW
	†BBC, Via Maşīrah, Oman	(D) • S ASIA & SE ASIA • 100 kW
17795	AUSTRALIA †RADIO AUSTRALIA, Shepparton	PACIFIC & N AMERICA • 100 kW
	CANADA †R CANADA INTL, Sackville, NB	(J) M-Sa • EUROPE & WEST USSR • 250 kW
	FINLAND †RADIO FINLAND, Pori	(D) • SE ASIA & AUSTRALIA • 500 kW
		(J) • SE ASIA & AUSTRALIA • 500 kW • ALT. FREQ. TO 17800 kHz
		(J) • E ASIA • 500 kW • ALT. FREQ. TO 17800 kHz
	FRANCE †R FRANCE INTL, Issoudun-Allouis	(D) M-Sa • W AFRICA • MEDIAS FRANCE • 500 kW
		E AFRICA • 100 kW
		E AFRICA • MEDIAS FRANCE • 100 kW
	GERMANY (FR) †DEUTSCHE WELLE, Via Antigua	AMERICAS • 250 kW
	DEUTSCHE WELLE, Wertachtal	(J) • USSR • 500 kW
	ITALY RTV ITALIANA, Rome	(J) • S ASIA & SE ASIA • 100 kW
		(J) • E AFRICA • 100 kW
		(J) • MIDEAST • 100 kW
	SOUTH AFRICA †RADIO RSA, Meyerton	(D) • W EUROPE • 250 kW
		(D) • E AFRICA & MIDEAST • 250 kW
	UNITED KINGDOM †BBC, Via Maşīrah, Oman	(J) • S ASIA & SE ASIA • 100 kW
	USSR RADIO MOSCOW, Tashkent	(J) • SE ASIA • VIETNAMESE, ETC • 500 kW
17800	EGYPT RADIO CAIRO, Kafr Silîm-Abis	C AFRICA & S AFRICA • 250 kW
	FINLAND †RADIO FINLAND, Pori	Alternative Frequency to 17795 kHz
	FRANCE †R FRANCE INTL, Issoudun-Allouis	(J) • MIDEAST & E AFRICA • 500 kW
		E AFRICA • 100 kW
		(D) • E AFRICA • 100 kW
		(J) • E AFRICA • 100 kW
	GERMANY (FR) †DEUTSCHE WELLE, Via Kigali, Rwanda	W AFRICA • 250 kW
	†DEUTSCHE WELLE, Via Sri Lanka	MIDEAST & S ASIA • 250 kW
	ITALY †RTV ITALIANA, Rome	E NORTH AM • 100 kW
		Su • E NORTH AM • 100 kW
	PAKISTAN RADIO PAKISTAN, Islamabad	(J) • E AFRICA • 100 kW
(con'd)	SWEDEN †RADIO SWEDEN, Hörby	(J) • SE ASIA & AUSTRALIA • 350 kW • ALT. FREQ. TO 17790 kHz

World Time: 0 1 2 3 4 5 6 7 8 9 10 11 12 13 14 15 16 17 18 19 20 21 22 23 24

0 Prime Time-Americas 6 Prime Time-E Asia 12 Prime Time-S Asia 18 Prime Time-Europe 24

FREQUENCY	COUNTRY, STATION, LOCATION	TARGET • NETWORK • POWER (kW) — World Time 0–24
17800 (con'd)	**SWEDEN** †RADIO SWEDEN, Hörby	(J) • USSR • 350 kW • ALT. FREQ. TO 17790 kHz
		(J) • SWEDISH • SE ASIA & AUSTRALIA • 350 kW • ALT. FREQ. TO 17790 kHz
	USA VOA, Cincinnati, Ohio	W AFRICA & S AFRICA • 250 kW
17805	**CHINA (TAIWAN)** †VO FREE CHINA, Via Okeechobee, USA	S AMERICA • 100 kW
	INDIA ALL INDIA RADIO, Aligarh	E AFRICA • 250 kW
	ROMANIA †RADIO BUCHAREST, Bucharest	AUSTRALIA • 250 kW
		(J) • MIDEAST • 250 kW
		(J) • W AFRICA • 250 kW
		(J) • AFRICA • 250 kW
	USA †RFE-RL, Via Portugal	E EUROPE • 250 kW
	WYFR-FAMILY RADIO, Okeechobee, Fl	S AMERICA • 100 kW
17810	**CANADA** †R CANADA INTL, Via Tokyo, Japan	E ASIA & SE ASIA • 100 kW
	GERMANY (FR) DEUTSCHE WELLE, Via Antigua	AMERICAS • 250 kW
	†DEUTSCHE WELLE, Wertachtal	C AFRICA & E AFRICA • 500 kW
		W AFRICA • 500 kW
	JAPAN †RADIO JAPAN/NHK, Tokyo-Yamata	(J) • SE ASIA • 100 kW
		JAPANESE • SE ASIA & S AMERICA • GENERAL • 300 kW
		SE ASIA & S AMERICA • GENERAL • 300 kW
		SE ASIA & S AMERICA • GENERAL • 100 kW
		(J) • JAPANESE • SE ASIA & S AMERICA • GENERAL • 100 kW
		(J) • SE ASIA & S AMERICA • GENERAL • 100 kW
	SWEDEN †RADIO SWEDEN, Hörby	(D) • USSR • 350 kW • ALT. FREQ. TO 15430 kHz
		(D) • SWEDISH • S ASIA & SE ASIA • 350 kW • ALT. FREQ. TO 15430 kHz
		(D) • S ASIA & SE ASIA • 350 kW • ALT. FREQ. TO 15430 kHz
	SYRIA †SYRIAN BC SERVICE, Adhra	Alternative Frequency to 15095 kHz
	UNITED KINGDOM †BBC, Rampisham	(J) • W AFRICA • 500 kW
	BBC, Skelton, Cumbria	N AFRICA & W AFRICA • 250 kW
	†BBC, Various Locations	W AFRICA & C AFRICA • 250/500 kW
	†BBC, Via Ascension	S AMERICA • 250 kW
		(D) M-F • S AMERICA • 250 kW
		(J) M-F • S AMERICA • 250 kW
	USA †VOA, Via Ascension	M-F • S AMERICA • 250 kW
	USSR †TATAR RADIO, Kazan'	DS-RUSSIAN, TATAR
17815	**BRAZIL** RADIO CULTURA, São Paulo	PORTUGUESE • DS • 7.5 kW
	MOROCCO RTV MAROCAINE, Tangier	EUROPE & W AFRICA • 50 kW
		M-Sa • EUROPE & W AFRICA • 50 kW
		Su • EUROPE & W AFRICA • 50 kW
	ROMANIA †RADIO BUCHAREST, Bucharest	(J) • W AFRICA • 250 kW
	SPAIN †R NACIONAL ESPANA, Noblejas	Su • C AMERICA & S AMERICA • 350 kW
		(J) Su • C AMERICA & S AMERICA • 350 kW
	UNITED KINGDOM †BBC, Via Hong Kong	E ASIA • 250 kW
		(J) Su • E ASIA • 250 kW
		(J) • E ASIA • 250 kW
	USSR RADIO MOSCOW, Frunze, Kirgiziya	(D) • E ASIA & SE ASIA • 100 kW
		(J) • S ASIA & SE ASIA • WS • 100 kW
17820	**CANADA** R CANADA INTL, Sackville, NB	AFRICA • 250 kW
		(D) • EUROPE & WEST USSR • 250 kW
		(J) • EUROPE & WEST USSR • 250 kW
		M-F • AFRICA • 250 kW
		(D) M-F • C AMERICA & S AMERICA • 250 kW
		(J) M-F • C AMERICA & S AMERICA • 250 kW
		(D) M-Sa • EUROPE & WEST USSR • 250 kW
		(J) M-Sa • EUROPE & WEST USSR • 250 kW
		Sa/Su • AFRICA • 250 kW
		(D) Su • C AMERICA & S AMERICA • 250 kW
		(J) Su • C AMERICA & S AMERICA • 250 kW
(con'd)		

0 Prime Time-Americas 6 Prime Time-E Asia 12 Prime Time-S Asia 18 Prime Time-Europe 24

ENGLISH ▬ ARABIC ▭ CHINESE ▫▫▫ FRENCH ═ GERMAN ▬ RUSSIAN ═ SPANISH ▬ OTHER —

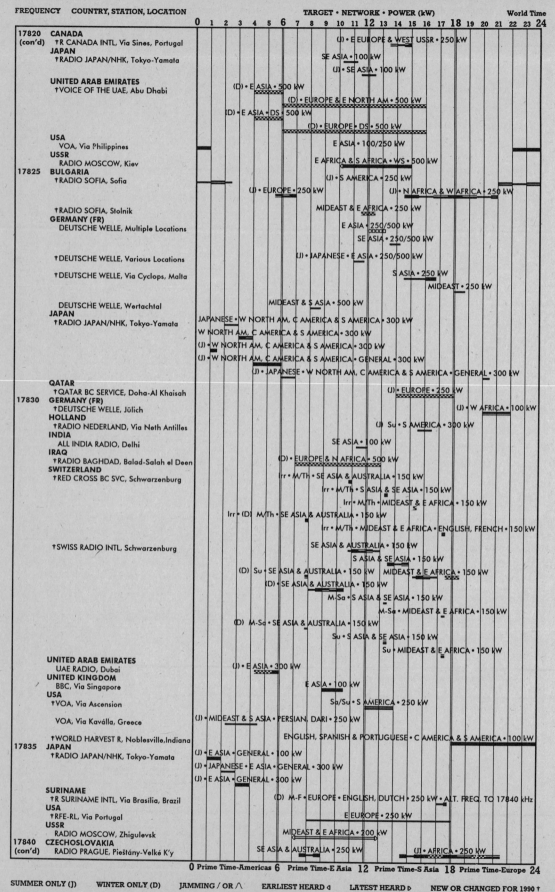

FREQUENCY	COUNTRY, STATION, LOCATION	TARGET • NETWORK • POWER (kW)
17820 (con'd)	**CANADA** †R CANADA INTL, Via Sines, Portugal	(J) • E EUROPE & WEST USSR • 250 kW
	JAPAN †RADIO JAPAN/NHK, Tokyo-Yamata	SE ASIA • 100 kW
		(J) • SE ASIA • 100 kW
	UNITED ARAB EMIRATES †VOICE OF THE UAE, Abu Dhabi	(D) • E ASIA • 500 kW
		(D) • EUROPE & E NORTH AM • 500 kW
		(D) • E ASIA • DS • 500 kW
		(D) • EUROPE • DS • 500 kW
	USA VOA, Via Philippines	E ASIA • 100/250 kW
	USSR RADIO MOSCOW, Kiev	E AFRICA & S AFRICA • WS • 500 kW
17825	**BULGARIA** †RADIO SOFIA, Sofia	(J) • S AMERICA • 250 kW
		(J) • EUROPE • 250 kW
		(J) • N AFRICA & W AFRICA • 250 kW
	†RADIO SOFIA, Stolnik	MIDEAST & E AFRICA • 250 kW
	GERMANY (FR) DEUTSCHE WELLE, Multiple Locations	E ASIA • 250/500 kW
		SE ASIA • 250/500 kW
	†DEUTSCHE WELLE, Various Locations	(J) • JAPANESE • E ASIA • 250/500 kW
	†DEUTSCHE WELLE, Via Cyclops, Malta	S ASIA • 250 kW
		MIDEAST • 250 kW
	DEUTSCHE WELLE, Wertachtal	MIDEAST & S ASIA • 500 kW
	JAPAN †RADIO JAPAN/NHK, Tokyo-Yamata	JAPANESE • W NORTH AM, C AMERICA & S AMERICA • 300 kW
		W NORTH AM, C AMERICA & S AMERICA • 300 kW
		(J) • W NORTH AM, C AMERICA & S AMERICA • 300 kW
		(J) • W NORTH AM, C AMERICA & S AMERICA • GENERAL • 300 kW
		(J) • JAPANESE • W NORTH AM, C AMERICA & S AMERICA • GENERAL • 300 kW
	QATAR †QATAR BC SERVICE, Doha-Al Khaisah	(J) • EUROPE • 250 kW
17830	**GERMANY (FR)** †DEUTSCHE WELLE, Jülich	(J) • W AFRICA • 100 kW
	HOLLAND †RADIO NEDERLAND, Via Neth Antilles	(J) Su • S AMERICA • 300 kW
	INDIA ALL INDIA RADIO, Delhi	SE ASIA • 100 kW
	IRAQ †RADIO BAGHDAD, Balad-Salah el Deen	(D) • EUROPE & N AFRICA • 500 kW
	SWITZERLAND †RED CROSS BC SVC, Schwarzenburg	Irr • M/Th • SE ASIA & AUSTRALIA • 150 kW
		Irr • M/Th • S ASIA & SE ASIA • 150 kW
		Irr • M/Th • MIDEAST & E AFRICA • 150 kW
		Irr • (D) M/Th • SE ASIA & AUSTRALIA • 150 kW
		Irr • M/Th • MIDEAST & E AFRICA • ENGLISH, FRENCH • 150 kW
	†SWISS RADIO INTL, Schwarzenburg	SE ASIA & AUSTRALIA • 150 kW
		S ASIA & SE ASIA • 150 kW
		(D) Su • SE ASIA & AUSTRALIA • 150 kW
		MIDEAST & E AFRICA • 150 kW
		(D) • SE ASIA & AUSTRALIA • 150 kW
		M-Sa • S ASIA & SE ASIA • 150 kW
		M-Sa • MIDEAST & E AFRICA • 150 kW
		(D) M-Sa • SE ASIA & AUSTRALIA • 150 kW
		Su • S ASIA & SE ASIA • 150 kW
		Su • MIDEAST & E AFRICA • 150 kW
	UNITED ARAB EMIRATES UAE RADIO, Dubai	(J) • E ASIA • 300 kW
	UNITED KINGDOM BBC, Via Singapore	E ASIA • 100 kW
	USA †VOA, Via Ascension	Sa/Su • S AMERICA • 250 kW
	VOA, Via Kavála, Greece	(J) • MIDEAST & S ASIA • PERSIAN, DARI • 250 kW
	†WORLD HARVEST R, Noblesville, Indiana	ENGLISH, SPANISH & PORTUGUESE • C AMERICA & S AMERICA • 100 kW
17835	**JAPAN** †RADIO JAPAN/NHK, Tokyo-Yamata	(J) • E ASIA • GENERAL • 100 kW
		(J) • JAPANESE • E ASIA • GENERAL • 300 kW
		(J) • E ASIA • GENERAL • 300 kW
	SURINAME †R SURINAME INTL, Via Brasília, Brazil	(D) M-F • EUROPE • ENGLISH, DUTCH • 250 kW • ALT. FREQ. TO 17840 kHz
	USA †RFE-RL, Via Portugal	E EUROPE • 250 kW
	USSR RADIO MOSCOW, Zhigulevsk	MIDEAST & E AFRICA • 200 kW
17840 (con'd)	**CZECHOSLOVAKIA** RADIO PRAGUE, Piešťány-Velké K'y	SE ASIA & AUSTRALIA • 250 kW
		(J) • AFRICA • 250 kW

World Time: 0 Prime Time-Americas 6 Prime Time-E Asia 12 Prime Time-S Asia 18 Prime Time-Europe 24

SUMMER ONLY (J) WINTER ONLY (D) JAMMING / OR /\ EARLIEST HEARD ◁ LATEST HEARD ▷ NEW OR CHANGED FOR 1990 †

FREQUENCY	COUNTRY, STATION, LOCATION	TARGET • NETWORK • POWER (kW) — World Time 0–24
17840 (con'd)	CZECHOSLOVAKIA RADIO PRAGUE, Pieštány-Velké K'y	M-F • S ASIA • 120 kW Sa/Su • SE ASIA & AUSTRALIA • 250 kW
	DENMARK †DANMARKS RADIO, Copenhagen	(J) • S ASIA & AUSTRALIA • 50 kW
	NORWAY †RADIO NORWAY INTL, Kvitsøy	(J) • MIDEAST • 500 kW (J) • AUSTRALIA • 500 kW M-Sa • E ASIA & AUSTRALIA • 500 kW Su • E ASIA & AUSTRALIA • 500 kW (J) • E NORTH AM & C AMERICA • 500 kW
	†RADIO NORWAY INTL, Sveio	
	SAUDI ARABIA BS OF THE KINGDOM, Riyadh	E AFRICA • 350 kW
	SURINAME †R SURINAME INTL, Via Brasília, Brazil	Alternative Frequency to 17835 kHz
	USSR RADIO MOSCOW, Frunze, Kirgiziya	(D) • SE ASIA • 500 kW
	VATICAN STATE †VATICAN RADIO, Sta Maria di Galeria	E AFRICA & MIDEAST • 100 kW AFRICA • 250 kW M-Sa • E AFRICA & MIDEAST • 250 kW Su • E AFRICA & MIDEAST • 250 kW
17840v	COLOMBIA RADIO NACIONAL, Bogotá	Irr • DS • 25 kW • ALT. FREQ. TO 17708v kHz
17845	CHINA (TAIWAN) †VO FREE CHINA, Via Okeechobee, USA	S AMERICA • 100 kW
	FRANCE †R FRANCE INTL, Issoudun-Allouis	(D) • E AFRICA & S AFRICA • 500 kW
	GERMANY (FR) †DEUTSCHE WELLE, Multiple Locations	S ASIA & SE ASIA • 100/500 kW MIDEAST & S ASIA • 100/500 kW
	DEUTSCHE WELLE, Wertachtal	SE ASIA & AUSTRALIA • 500 kW
	JAPAN RADIO JAPAN/NHK, Tokyo-Yamata	JAPANESE • S ASIA • GENERAL • 300 kW S ASIA • GENERAL • 300 kW
	SPAIN †R NACIONAL ESPANA, Noblejas	C AMERICA & S AMERICA • 350 kW (D) • C AMERICA & S AMERICA • 350 kW
	USA †WYFR-FAMILY RADIO, Okeechobee, Fl	(J) • S AMERICA • 100 kW S AMERICA • 100 kW (D) • EUROPE • 100 kW (D) • C AMERICA • 100 kW (J) • W AFRICA • 100 kW
17850	DENMARK †DANMARKS RADIO, Copenhagen	(D) • MIDEAST & E AFRICA • 50 kW
	FRANCE †R FRANCE INTL, Issoudun-Allouis	AFRICA • 500 kW (J) • AFRICA • 500 kW Su • AFRICA • 500 kW AFRICA • MEDIAS FRANCE • 500 kW M-Sa • AFRICA • MEDIAS FRANCE • 500 kW
	KUWAIT RADIO KUWAIT, Jadādīyah	C AFRICA • DS-MAIN PROGRAM • 250 kW
	ROMANIA †RADIO BUCHAREST, Bucharest	(J) • W EUROPE • 250 kW
	SRI LANKA SRI LANKA BC CORP, Colombo-Ekala	SE ASIA • 35 kW M • JAPANESE • SE ASIA • 35 kW M/Tu/Th/F • SE ASIA • 35 kW Sa • JAPANESE • SE ASIA • 35 kW Su/W • SE ASIA • 35 kW Tu-Su • SE ASIA • 35 kW
	USSR RADIO MOSCOW, Khabarovsk	(J) • SE ASIA & AUSTRALIA • WS • 100 kW
17855	CHINA (PR) †RADIO BEIJING, Jinhua	(J) • E NORTH AM, C AMERICA & S AMERICA • 500 kW (J) • W NORTH AM & C AMERICA • 500 kW
	†RADIO BEIJING, Shijiazhuang	(J) • E NORTH AM, C AMERICA & S AMERICA • 500 kW
	NORTHERN MARIANA IS †KYOI, Saipan Island	SE ASIA • 100 kW AUSTRALIA • 100 kW
	SEYCHELLES FAR EAST BC ASS'N, North Pt, Mahé Is	F • MIDEAST & E AFRICA • 100 kW
	UNITED KINGDOM †BBC, Woofferton	(D) Su • WEST USSR • 300 kW
	USA VOA, Via Tangier, Morocco	(D) • MIDEAST & WEST USSR • 35/100 kW (J) • E EUROPE & WEST USSR • 35/100 kW
(con'd)	VOA, Via Woofferton, UK	(D) • WEST USSR • 300 kW

0 Prime Time-Americas 6 Prime Time-E Asia 12 Prime Time-S Asia 18 Prime Time-Europe 24

ENGLISH ARABIC CHINESE FRENCH GERMAN RUSSIAN SPANISH OTHER

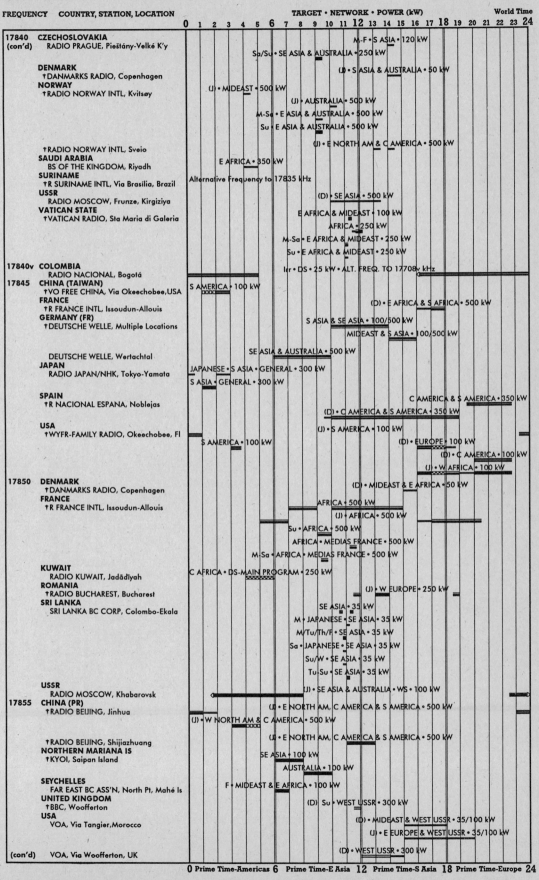

FREQUENCY	COUNTRY, STATION, LOCATION	TARGET • NETWORK • POWER (kW)
17855 (con'd)	**USA** VOA, Via Woofferton, UK	(J) • WEST USSR • 300 kW
		(J) • MIDEAST & WEST USSR • 300 kW
	†WSHB, Cypress Creek, SC	(J) • C AMERICA & AUSTRALIA • 500 kW
		(J) M-F • C AMERICA & AUSTRALIA • 500 kW
		(J) Sa/Su • C AMERICA & AUSTRALIA • 500 kW
	USSR RADIO MOSCOW, Simferopol'	(D) • E AFRICA • WS • 100 kW
17860	**FRANCE** †R FRANCE INTL, Via French Guiana	C AMERICA & S AMERICA • 500 kW
		S AMERICA • 500 kW
	GERMANY (FR) †DEUTSCHE WELLE, Via Antigua	S AMERICA • 250 kW
	†DEUTSCHE WELLE, Via Kigali, Rwanda	W AFRICA & C AMERICA • 250 kW
	ROMANIA †RADIO BUCHAREST, Bucharest	(J) • AFRICA • 250 kW
	SOUTH AFRICA †RADIO RSA, Meyerton	(J) • W AFRICA • 500 kW
	SWEDEN †RADIO SWEDEN, Hörby	(D) • SWEDISH • E NORTH AM • 350 kW
		(D) • E NORTH AM • 350 kW
	USSR RADIO MOSCOW, Chita	(J) • AUSTRALIA • WS • 500 kW
	RADIO MOSCOW, Kursk	(D) • EUROPE • 240 kW
	RADIO MOSCOW, Vladivostok	(D) • PACIFIC & S AMERICA • 240 kW
17865	**DENMARK** †DANMARKS RADIO, Copenhagen	(J) • MIDEAST & E AFRICA • 50 kW
		(J) M-F • EUROPE & W AFRICA • DS • 50 kW
	NORTHERN MARIANA IS †KYOI, Saipan Island	SE ASIA • 100 kW
	UNITED ARAB EMIRATES †UAE RADIO, Dubai	Alternative Frequency to 15320 kHz
	UNITED KINGDOM †BBC, Rampisham	(D) Su • WEST USSR • 500 kW
	USA †RFE-RL, Via Pals, Spain	WEST USSR • 250 kW
	†VOA, Via Kavála, Greece	(D) • WEST USSR & MIDEAST • 250 kW
		(J) • WEST USSR & MIDEAST • 250 kW
	VOA, Via Philippines	EAST USSR • 50/250 kW
	VATICAN STATE †VATICAN RADIO, Sta Maria di Galeria	E ASIA • 500 kW
		SE ASIA • 500 kW
		M-Sa • JAPANESE • E ASIA • 500 kW
		M-Sa • E ASIA • 500 kW
		Su • E ASIA • 500 kW
		Su • E ASIA • 100 kW
17870	**AUSTRIA** †RADIO AUSTRIA INTL, Vienna	(J) • E NORTH AM • 100 kW
	USA VOA, Via M'rovia, Liberia	W AFRICA & S AFRICA • 250 kW
	USSR RADIO MOSCOW, Chita	(D) • E ASIA & SE ASIA • 500 kW
		(J) • E ASIA & SE ASIA • 250 kW
	VATICAN STATE †VATICAN RADIO, Sta Maria di Galeria	S AMERICA • 250 kW
		C AMERICA • 250 kW
		S ASIA • 250 kW
17875	**CANADA** †R CANADA INTL, Sackville, NB	(D) • EUROPE • 250 kW
		(J) • EUROPE • 250 kW
		(D) M-F • EUROPE • 250 kW
		(J) M-F • EUROPE • 250 kW
		(D) Sa/Su • EUROPE • 250 kW
		(J) Sa/Su • EUROPE • 250 kW
	ECUADOR †HCJB-VO THE ANDES, Quito	S AMERICA • 100 kW
		JAPANESE • S AMERICA • 100 kW
		(J) • S AMERICA • 100 kW
	GERMANY (FR) DEUTSCHE WELLE, Via Sri Lanka	MIDEAST • 250 kW
		(J) • SE ASIA & AUSTRALIA • 250 kW
		(J) • JAPANESE • E ASIA • 250 kW
		(J) • E ASIA • 250 kW
	†DEUTSCHE WELLE, Wertachtal	AFRICA • 500 kW; (J) • MIDEAST • 500 kW
(con'd)		MIDEAST & S ASIA • 500 kW

World Time: 0 Prime Time-Americas 6 Prime Time-E Asia 12 Prime Time-S Asia 18 Prime Time-Europe 24

SUMMER ONLY (J) WINTER ONLY (D) JAMMING / OR /\ EARLIEST HEARD ◁ LATEST HEARD ▷ NEW OR CHANGED FOR 1990 †

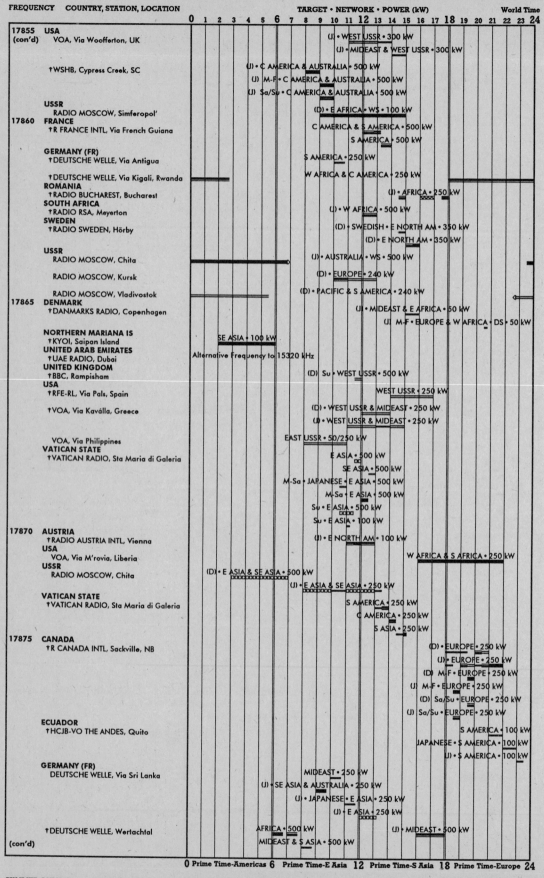

FREQUENCY	COUNTRY, STATION, LOCATION	TARGET • NETWORK • POWER (kW)
17875 (con'd)	**QATAR** QATAR BC SERVICE, Doha	(J) • EUROPE • DS • 250 kW
	SEYCHELLES FAR EAST BC ASS'N, North Pt, Mahé Is	MIDEAST & E AFRICA • 100 kW Su/Th/F • MIDEAST & E AFRICA • 100 kW
	UNITED KINGDOM †BBC, Via Hong Kong	E ASIA • 250 kW (D) • E ASIA • 250 kW (J) • E ASIA • 250 kW
	†BBC, Via Singapore	(J) • MIDEAST & S ASIA • 100 kW (J) Tu-Sa • MIDEAST & S ASIA • 100 kW
	USA †VOA, Via Kavála, Greece	MIDEAST & S ASIA • 250 kW (J) • MIDEAST & S ASIA • 250 kW
	USSR RADIO MOSCOW, Yerevan	(J) • W AFRICA • WS • 100 kW
17880	**GERMANY (DR)** †R BERLIN INTL, Nauen	S ASIA & SE ASIA • 500 kW S ASIA & SE ASIA • 100 kW
	NORTHERN MARIANA IS KFBS-FAR EAST BC, Saipan Island	(J) • S ASIA & SE ASIA • 100 kW
	SWEDEN †RADIO SWEDEN, Hörby	(J) • SWEDISH • N AMERICA • 350 kW (J) • N AMERICA • 350 kW
	UNITED KINGDOM †BBC, Via Ascension	(J) • S AFRICA • 250 kW
	USSR RADIO MOSCOW, Irkutsk	SE ASIA • WS • 500 kW
	RADIO MOSCOW, Kiev	W AFRICA • 500 kW (D) • W AFRICA • 500 kW (J) • W AFRICA • 500 kW
17885	**KUWAIT** RADIO KUWAIT, Jadādīyah	E ASIA • DS-MAIN PROGRAM • 250 kW
	UNITED KINGDOM †BBC, Via Ascension	S AFRICA • 250 kW (D) • S AFRICA • 250 kW
	†BBC, Via Seychelles	S AFRICA • 250 kW E AFRICA • 250 kW Sa/Su • E AFRICA • 250 kW
	†BBC, Via Zyyi, Cyprus	(J) • E AFRICA • 250 kW M-F • E AFRICA • 100 kW
	USA †RFE-RL, Via Pals, Spain	WEST USSR • 250 kW
17890	**ECUADOR** HCJB-VO THE ANDES, Quito	N AMERICA & C AMERICA • 100 kW S AMERICA • 100 kW
	GABON ADVENTIST WORLD R, Moyabi	Su • W AFRICA • VIA AFRIQUE NR UN • 500 kW
	JAPAN †RADIO JAPAN/NHK, Tokyo-Yamata	(J) • AUSTRALIA • 100 kW (J) • SE ASIA • 100 kW (J) • AUSTRALIA • GENERAL • 100 kW
	PAKISTAN RADIO PAKISTAN, Islamabad	SE ASIA • 100 kW (D) • SE ASIA • 100 kW
	SPAIN †R NACIONAL ESPANA, Noblejas	AFRICA • 350 kW (D) • AFRICA • 350 kW (J) • AFRICA • 350 kW
	UNITED ARAB EMIRATES UAE RADIO, Dubai	E NORTH AM & C AMERICA • 300 kW
	USA †VOA, Via Philippines	(J) • E ASIA • 100 kW
	USSR RADIO MOSCOW, Moscow	SE ASIA • WS • 250 kW
17895	**KUWAIT** RADIO KUWAIT, Jadādīyah	S ASIA • DS-MAIN PROGRAM • 250 kW S ASIA • 250 kW
	SAUDI ARABIA BS OF THE KINGDOM, Riyadh	SE ASIA • 350 kW ASIA • DS-HOLY KORAN • 350 kW
	USA †RFE-RL, Via Germany	WEST USSR • 100 kW
	†RFE-RL, Via Pals, Spain	WEST USSR • 250 kW
	†RFE-RL, Via Portugal	WEST USSR • 50 kW
	†WYFR-FAMILY RADIO, Okeechobee, Fl	(D) • C AMERICA • 100 kW
	ZAMBIA †RADIO ZAMBIA-ZBS, Lusaka	Su • S AFRICA • 50 kW
18050	**PAKISTAN** RADIO PAKISTAN, Islamabad	EUROPE • 100 kW
18137.5	**USA** †VOA, Delano, California	Alternative Frequency to 18525 kHz

World Time: 0 Prime Time-Americas 6 Prime Time-E Asia 12 Prime Time-S Asia 18 Prime Time-Europe 24

ENGLISH ▬ ARABIC ▨ CHINESE ▭ FRENCH ═ GERMAN ▬ RUSSIAN ═ SPANISH ▬ OTHER —

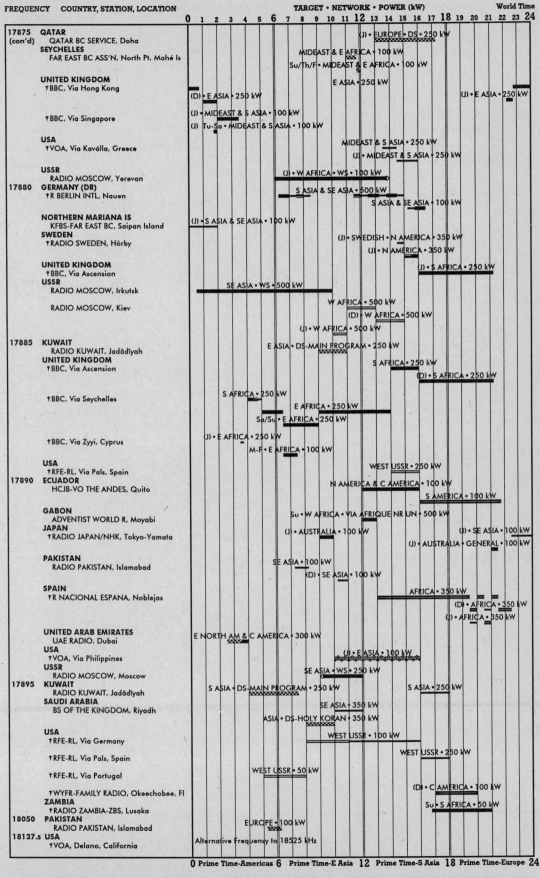

FREQUENCY	COUNTRY, STATION, LOCATION	TARGET • NETWORK • POWER (kW)
18157	USA †VOA, Delano, California	Alternative Frequency to 18511 kHz
18175	USSR RADIO MOSCOW, Moscow	MARINERS (FEEDER) • 20 kW • USB
18275	USA †VOA, Greenville, NC	(D) • EUROPE • (FEEDER) • 50 kW • ISL
		(D) • EUROPE • (FEEDER) • 50 kW • ISU
		(J) • EUROPE • (FEEDER) • 50 kW • ISL
		(J) • EUROPE • (FEEDER) • 50 kW • ISU
18402	USSR †RADIO MOSCOW	(J) • (FEEDER) • USB
18460	USSR †RADIO MOSCOW	(J)
18511	USA †VOA, Delano, California	SE ASIA • (FEEDER) • 50 kW • ISL • ALT. FREQ. TO 18157 kHz
		SE ASIA • (FEEDER) • 50 kW • ISU • ALT. FREQ. TO 18157 kHz
18525	USA †VOA, Delano, California	SE ASIA • (FEEDER) • 50 kW • ISU • ALT. FREQ. TO 18137.5 kHz
		SE ASIA • (FEEDER) • 50 kW • ISL • ALT. FREQ. TO 18137.5 kHz
18605	USA †VOA, Greenville, NC	Tu/F • EUROPE & N AFRICA • (FEEDER) • 40 kW • USB
19261.5	USA †VOA, Cincinnati, Ohio	N AFRICA • (FEEDER) • 50 kW • ISU
		(J) • N AFRICA • (FEEDER) • 50 kW • ISL
		M-F • N AFRICA • (FEEDER) • 50 kW • ISU
19480	USA VOA, Cincinnati, Ohio	W AFRICA • (FEEDER) • 50 kW • ISL
		W AFRICA • (FEEDER) • 50 kW • ISU
		M-F • W AFRICA • (FEEDER) • 50 kW • ISU
20280	USSR †RADIO MOSCOW	(J) • (FEEDER) • USB
21450	CZECHOSLOVAKIA †RADIO PRAGUE, Prague	(J) • MIDEAST • 120 kW
		(J) M-F • MIDEAST • 120 kW
21455	USA †RFE-RL, Via Germany	WEST USSR • 100 kW
	†RFE-RL, Via Portugal	WEST USSR • 250 kW
21460	BELGIUM †RT BELGE FRANCAISE, Wavre	(J) • AFRICA • 250 kW
	QATAR †QATAR BC SERVICE, Doha-Al Khaisah	N AFRICA & MIDEAST • 250 kW • ALT. FREQ. TO 21525 kHz
	SPAIN †R NACIONAL ESPANA, Noblejas	(J) • E NORTH AM • 350 kW
21465	GERMANY (DR) R BERLIN INTL, Leipzig	S ASIA & SE ASIA • 100 kW
		Sa/Su • E ASIA • 100 kW
21470	UNITED KINGDOM †BBC, Via Zyyi, Cyprus	E AFRICA • 250 kW
		Sa/Su • E AFRICA • 250 kW
		S AFRICA • 250 kW
21470.5	ECUADOR †HCJB-VO THE ANDES, Quito	(J) • EUROPE • 80 kW
		(J) M-F • EUROPE • 80 kW
		(J) Sa/Su • EUROPE • 80 kW
21475	PAKISTAN RADIO PAKISTAN, Karachi	SE ASIA • 50 kW
		(J) • SE ASIA • 50 kW
	USA †VOA, Via Philippines	(J) • S ASIA • 250 kW • ALT. FREQ. TO 15265 kHz
21480	HOLLAND †RADIO NEDERLAND, Flevoland	(J) • SE ASIA • 300 kW
	†RADIO NEDERLAND, Via Madagascar	E ASIA • 300 kW • ALT. FREQ. TO 21485 kHz
		SE ASIA • 300 kW
		(D) • SE ASIA • 300 kW
		(J) • S ASIA • 300 kW
21485	HOLLAND †RADIO NEDERLAND, Via Madagascar	Alternative Frequency to 21480 kHz
		SE ASIA & N AFRICA • 300 kW
		E ASIA • 300 kW
		SE ASIA • 300 kW
	USA VOA, Via M'rovia, Liberia	W AFRICA • 15 kW
		M-F • E AFRICA & S AFRICA • 50 kW
	VATICAN STATE †VATICAN RADIO, Sta Maria di Galeria	AFRICA • 100 kW
		S AMERICA • 500 kW
		C AMERICA • 500 kW
		M-Sa • AFRICA • 100 kW
		Su • AFRICA • 100 kW
21490 (con'd)	AUSTRIA †RADIO AUSTRIA INTL, Vienna	AUSTRALIA • 100 kW

World Time: 0 1 2 3 4 5 6 7 8 9 10 11 12 13 14 15 16 17 18 19 20 21 22 23 24

0 Prime Time-Americas 6 Prime Time-E Asia 12 Prime Time-S Asia 18 Prime Time-Europe 24

SUMMER ONLY (J) WINTER ONLY (D) JAMMING / OR /\ EARLIEST HEARD ◁ LATEST HEARD ▷ NEW OR CHANGED FOR 1990 †

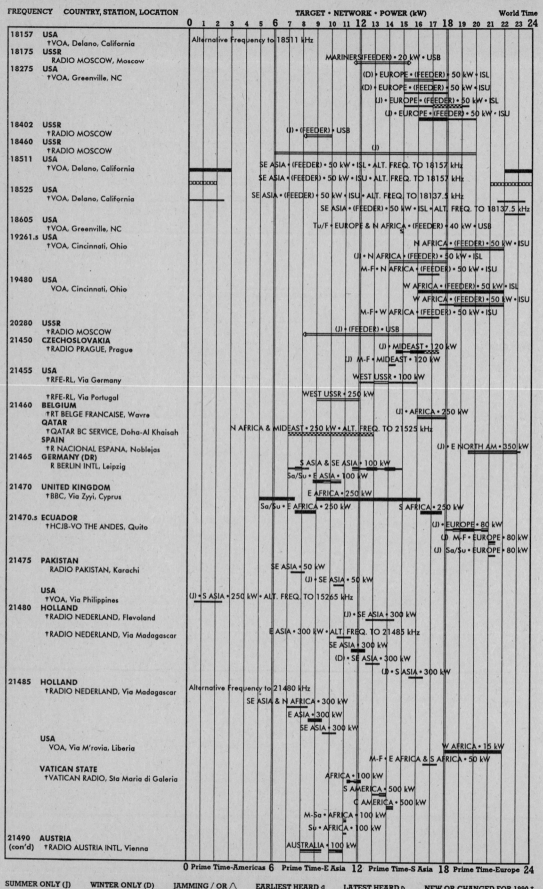

FREQUENCY	COUNTRY, STATION, LOCATION	TARGET • NETWORK • POWER (kW)
21490 (con'd)	**AUSTRIA** †RADIO AUSTRIA INTL, Vienna	W EUROPE & W AFRICA • 100 kW
		M-Sa • AUSTRALIA • 100 kW
		M-Sa • W EUROPE & W AFRICA • 100 kW
		Su • AUSTRALIA • 100 kW
		Su • W EUROPE & W AFRICA • 100 kW
	FRANCE †R FRANCE INTL, Via Moyabi, Gabon	(D) • MIDEAST • 250 kW
	UNITED KINGDOM †BBC, Skelton, Cumbria	(J) • MIDEAST • 250 kW
	†BBC, Via Ascension	S AMERICA • 250 kW
		(D) M-F • S AMERICA • 250 kW
		(J) M-F • S AMERICA • 250 kW
	USA †VOA, Via Ascension	M-F • S AMERICA • 250 kW
		Sa/Su • S AMERICA • 250 kW
	USSR †RADIO MOSCOW, Irkutsk	(J) • SE ASIA • DS-2 • 250 kW
21495	**SAUDI ARABIA** †BS OF THE KINGDOM, Riyadh	Alternative Frequency to 21670 kHz
	SPAIN †R NACIONAL ESPANA, Noblejas	(J) • S AMERICA • 350 kW
21500	**JAPAN** †RADIO JAPAN/NHK, Tokyo-Yamata	(J) • EUROPE • 300 kW
		(J) • EUROPE • GENERAL • 500 kW
		(J) • JAPANESE • EUROPE • GENERAL • 500 kW
	USA VOA, Via M'rovia, Liberia	M-F • AFRICA • ENGLISH, FRENCH, ETC • 50 kW
21505	**CZECHOSLOVAKIA** †RADIO PRAGUE, Prague	MIDEAST & E AFRICA • 120 kW
		(J) • MIDEAST & E AFRICA • 120 kW
		M-F • MIDEAST & E AFRICA • 120 kW
	SAUDI ARABIA †BS OF THE KINGDOM, Riyadh	(J) • N AFRICA • 350 kW
21510	**SAUDI ARABIA** †BS OF THE KINGDOM, Riyadh	(J) • 350 kW
	USA †RFE-RL, Via Germany	WEST USSR • 250 kW
21515	**ITALY** RTV ITALIANA, Rome	(J) Su • E AFRICA • 100 kW
	UNITED ARAB EMIRATES †VOICE OF THE UAE, Abu Dhabi	AUSTRALIA • DS • 500 kW
		E ASIA • DS • 500 kW
		(J) • EUROPE • DS • 500 kW
	USA †VOA, Via Philippines	S ASIA & SE ASIA • 50 kW
	USSR †RADIO MOSCOW, Frunze, Kirgiziya	(J) • E ASIA • 50 kW
	VATICAN STATE †VATICAN RADIO, Sta Maria di Galeria	(J) • E ASIA • 500 kW
		(J) • SE ASIA • 500 kW
		(J) M-Sa • JAPANESE • E ASIA • 500 kW
		(J) M-Sa • E ASIA • 500 kW
		(J) Su • E ASIA • 500 kW
21520	**FRANCE** †R FRANCE INTL, Multiple Locations	(J) • MIDEAST & E AFRICA • 100/250 kW
	†R FRANCE INTL, Via Moyabi, Gabon	S AFRICA • 250 kW
		(D) • S AFRICA • 250 kW
	HOLLAND †RADIO NEDERLAND, Flevoland	S ASIA • 500 kW • ALT FREQ. TO 21615 kHz
		C AFRICA • 500 kW
	USA VOA, Via Kavàlla, Greece	(J) • S ASIA • 250 kW
21525	**AUSTRALIA** †RADIO AUSTRALIA, Carnarvon	Sa • S ASIA • 300 kW
		Sa/Su • S ASIA • 300 kW
	QATAR †QATAR BC SERVICE, Doha-Al Khaisah	Alternative Frequency to 21460 kHz
	USA WYFR-FAMILY RADIO, Okeechobee, Fl	W AFRICA & S AFRICA • 100 kW
21530	**USA** †R FREE AFGHANISTAN, Via Portugal	WEST USSR & S ASIA • 250 kW
	†RFE-RL, Via Portugal	WEST USSR • 250 kW
21535	**SOUTH AFRICA** †RADIO RSA, Meyerton	(J) • EUROPE & W AFRICA • 500 kW
		W • EUROPE • 250 kW
21540	**GERMANY (DR)** R BERLIN INTL, Nauen	S ASIA & SE ASIA • 500 kW
		E ASIA & AUSTRALIA • 500 kW
(con'd)	**HOLLAND** RADIO NEDERLAND, Via Neth Antilles	Su • S AMERICA • 300 kW

World Time 0 1 2 3 4 5 6 7 8 9 10 11 12 13 14 15 16 17 18 19 20 21 22 23 24

0 Prime Time-Americas 6 Prime Time-E Asia 12 Prime Time-S Asia 18 Prime Time-Europe 24

ENGLISH ▬ ARABIC ▦ CHINESE ▭ FRENCH ═ GERMAN ▬ RUSSIAN ═ SPANISH ▬ OTHER —

FREQUENCY	COUNTRY, STATION, LOCATION	TARGET • NETWORK • POWER (kW)
21540 (con'd)	**ISRAEL** †KOL ISRAEL, Tel Aviv	Alternative Frequency to 21550 kHz
21545	**CANADA** †R CANADA INTL, Sackville, NB	EUROPE & WEST USSR • 250 kW
		M-Sa • EUROPE & WEST USSR • 250 kW
21550	**FINLAND** †RADIO FINLAND, Pori	(J) • SE ASIA & AUSTRALIA • 500 kW
		(J) • N AMERICA & C AMERICA • 500 kW
		(J) M-F • N AMERICA & C AMERICA • 500 kW
		(J) Sa/Su • N AMERICA & C AMERICA • 500 kW
	ISRAEL †KOL ISRAEL, Tel Aviv	(J) • HEBREW • W EUROPE & E NORTH AM • DS-B • 50 kW • ALT. FREQ. TO 21540 kHz
	SWITZERLAND †SWISS RADIO INTL, Schwarzenburg	(J) • S ASIA & SE ASIA • 150 kW
	UNITED KINGDOM †BBC, Via Maṣīrah, Oman	(J) • SE ASIA • 100 kW
	USSR RADIO MOSCOW	(D) • MIDEAST
		(D) • PERSIAN • MIDEAST
21555	**SPAIN** †R NACIONAL ESPANA, Noblejas	(J) • C AMERICA & S AMERICA • 350 kW
	YUGOSLAVIA †RADIO YUGOSLAVIA, Bijeljina	(J) • E ASIA & AUSTRALIA • 500 kW
	†VARIOUS LOCAL STNS, Bijeljina	(J) Sa/Su • E ASIA & AUSTRALIA • DS • 500 kW
21560	**GERMANY (FR)** †DEUTSCHE WELLE, Jülich	SE ASIA & AUSTRALIA • 100 kW
		(J) • S ASIA • 100 kW
		S ASIA & SE ASIA • 100 kW
	†DEUTSCHE WELLE, Via Cyclops, Malta	(J) • C AMERICA • 250 kW
	†DEUTSCHE WELLE, Via Sri Lanka	AFRICA • 250 kW
	†DEUTSCHE WELLE, Wertachtal	(J) • E ASIA • 500 kW
	ITALY †RTV ITALIANA, Rome	(J) • E AFRICA • 100 kW
		E NORTH AM • 100 kW • ALT. FREQ. TO 21690 kHz
		(J) • E NORTH AM • 100 kW
21566v	**COSTA RICA** †RADIO FOR PEACE, Ciudad Colón	Tu-Sa • N AMERICA • 2/5 kW
		N AMERICA • 2/5 kW
		M-F • N AMERICA • 2/5 kW
21570	**SPAIN** †R NACIONAL ESPANA, Noblejas	C AMERICA & S AMERICA • 350 kW
	SWEDEN †RADIO SWEDEN, Hörby	SWEDISH • SE ASIA & AUSTRALIA • 350 kW
		SE ASIA & AUSTRALIA • 350 kW
		(D) • USSR • 350 kW
		(J) • USSR • 350 kW
	USA VOA, Via Tangier, Morocco	(J) • MIDEAST & WEST USSR • 35 kW
21580	**FRANCE** †R FRANCE INTL, Issoudun-Allouis	AFRICA • 500 kW
		(J) • AFRICA • 500 kW
	USA †VOA, Greenville, NC	C AMERICA & S AMERICA • 250 kW
		Sa/Su • C AMERICA & S AMERICA • 250 kW
21585	**USA** †VOA, Via Philippines	(J) • E ASIA • 250 kW
	USSR RADIO MOSCOW, Dushanbé	(J) • SE ASIA • WS, INDONESIAN • 100 kW
21590	**GERMANY (FR)** DEUTSCHE WELLE, Via Sri Lanka	(J) • E ASIA • 250 kW
	SOUTH AFRICA †RADIO RSA, Meyerton	EUROPE & AFRICA • 250/500 kW
		(D) • EUROPE & AFRICA • 500 kW
		(D) • EUROPE & W AFRICA • 500 kW
		(D) Su • EUROPE & AFRICA • 500 kW
		(D) • W EUROPE & W AFRICA • 250 kW
		(J) • EUROPE & AFRICA • 500 kW
		(J) • E AFRICA & S AFRICA • 250 kW
		(J) • S ASIA & E ASIA • 250 kW
		(J) Su • EUROPE & AFRICA • 500 kW
		(J) • W EUROPE • 250 kW
	USA †VOA, Cincinnati, Ohio	M-F • S AMERICA • 250 kW
21595	**SPAIN** †R NACIONAL ESPANA, Noblejas	MIDEAST • 350 kW
		(D) • MIDEAST • 350 kW
		(J) • MIDEAST • 350 kW
21600	**AFGHANISTAN** †RADIO AFGHANISTAN, Via USSR	Alternative Frequency to 15255 kHz
	GERMANY (FR) †DEUTSCHE WELLE, Jülich	AFRICA • 100 kW
	†DEUTSCHE WELLE, Via Sri Lanka	MIDEAST & S ASIA • 250 kW
	DEUTSCHE WELLE, Wertachtal	AFRICA • 500 kW

World Time: 0 1 2 3 4 5 6 7 8 9 10 11 12 13 14 15 16 17 18 19 20 21 22 23 24

0 Prime Time-Americas 6 Prime Time-E Asia 12 Prime Time-S Asia 18 Prime Time-Europe 24

SUMMER ONLY (J) WINTER ONLY (D) JAMMING / OR /\ EARLIEST HEARD ◃ LATEST HEARD ▹ NEW OR CHANGED FOR 1990 †

FREQUENCY	COUNTRY, STATION, LOCATION	TARGET • NETWORK • POWER (kW)
21605	UNITED ARAB EMIRATES	
	†UAE RADIO, Dubai	EUROPE • 300 kW
		(J) • EUROPE • 300 kW
21610	ITALY	
	RTV ITALIANA, Rome	Su • AUSTRALIA • 100 kW
	JAPAN	
	†RADIO JAPAN/NHK, Tokyo-Yamata	JAPANESE • PACIFIC & S AMERICA • 100 kW
		(J) • SE ASIA • GENERAL • 100 kW
		PACIFIC & S AMERICA • 100 kW
		(J) • JAPANESE • SE ASIA • GENERAL • 100 kW
	SWEDEN	
	†RADIO SWEDEN, Hörby	(J) • USSR • 350 kW
		(J) • SWEDISH • E ASIA & AUSTRALIA • 350 kW
		(J) • E ASIA & AUSTRALIA • 350 kW
		(J) • SWEDISH • E NORTH AM • 350 kW
		(J) • E NORTH AM • 350 kW
	†SVERIGES RIKSRADIO, Hörby	(J) • SWEDISH • E NORTH AM • DS-1 • 350 kW
	USA	
	†VOA, Greenville, NC	Sa/Su • C AMERICA & S AMERICA • 250 kW
	VOA, Via Kaválla, Greece	(J) • MIDEAST & S ASIA • 250 kW
21615	HOLLAND	
	RADIO NEDERLAND, Flevoland	Alternative Frequency to 21520 kHz
	ITALY	
	RTV ITALIANA, Rome	AUSTRALIA • 100 kW
	USA	
	†WYFR-FAMILY RADIO, Okeechobee, Fl	EUROPE • 100 kW
		(J) • EUROPE • 100 kW
	USSR	
	RADIO MOSCOW, Tashkent	S ASIA & SE ASIA • 100 kW
21620	FRANCE	
	†R FRANCE INTL, Issoudun-Allouis	E AFRICA & MIDEAST • 100 kW
		(J) • E AFRICA & MIDEAST • 100 kW
21625	USA	
	†VOA, Via Wertachtal, GFR	(J) • WEST USSR • 500 kW
21630	GERMANY (FR)	
	DEUTSCHE WELLE, Jülich	(J) • MIDEAST • 100 kW
	†DEUTSCHE WELLE, Via Cyclops, Malta	C AMERICA • 250 kW
	†DEUTSCHE WELLE, Via Sri Lanka	MIDEAST • 250 kW
	SWITZERLAND	
	†RED CROSS BC SVC, Schwarzenburg	Irr • M/Th • MIDEAST • 150 kW
	†SWISS RADIO INTL, Schwarzenburg	MIDEAST • 150 kW
	USSR	
	RADIO MOSCOW, Star'obel'sk	(J) • MIDEAST & E AFRICA • WS • 100 kW
21635	FRANCE	
	†R FRANCE INTL, Issoudun-Allouis	(J) • E NORTH AM
	JAPAN	
	†RADIO JAPAN/NHK, Via Moyabi, Gabon	(J) • S AMERICA • 500 kW
		(J) • JAPANESE • S AMERICA • GENERAL • 500 kW
	USSR	
	RADIO MOSCOW, Kalinin	SE ASIA • WS, INDONESIAN • 240 kW
21640	GERMANY (FR)	
	†DEUTSCHE WELLE, Via Sri Lanka	SE ASIA & AUSTRALIA • 250 kW
		E ASIA • 250 kW
	JAPAN	
	†RADIO JAPAN/NHK, Via Moyabi, Gabon	JAPANESE • EUROPE & N AFRICA • GENERAL • 500 kW
	UNITED KINGDOM	
	†BBC, Rampisham	(D) • WEST USSR • 500 kW
		(D) Su • WEST USSR • 500 kW
	†BBC, Various Locations	W AFRICA • 250/300/500 kW
	USA	
	†WCSN, Scotts Corners, Me	AFRICA • 500 kW
		M-F • AFRICA • 500 kW
		Sa • AFRICA • 500 kW
		Sa/Su • AFRICA • 500 kW
		Su-F • AFRICA • 500 kW
21645	FRANCE	
	†R FRANCE INTL, Issoudun-Allouis	C AMERICA • 500 kW
		C AMERICA & N AMERICA • 500 kW
		(J) • C AMERICA • 500 kW
	†R FRANCE INTL, Via French Guiana	C AMERICA • 500 kW
		M-Sa • C AMERICA • 500 kW
		Su • C AMERICA • CREOLE • 500 kW
21650	GERMANY (FR)	
	†DEUTSCHE WELLE, Jülich	MIDEAST & S ASIA • 100 kW
		(J) • MIDEAST • 100 kW
		SE ASIA & AUSTRALIA • 100 kW
	†DEUTSCHE WELLE, Multiple Locations	JAPANESE • E ASIA • 250/500 kW
		SE ASIA • 100/250/500 kW
(con'd)		

World Time: 0 Prime Time-Americas 6 Prime Time-E Asia 12 Prime Time-S Asia 18 Prime Time-Europe 24

ENGLISH ▬ ARABIC ▩ CHINESE ▭ FRENCH ═ GERMAN ▬ RUSSIAN ═ SPANISH ▬ OTHER —

World Time: 0 1 2 3 4 5 6 7 8 9 10 11 12 13 14 15 16 17 18 19 20 21 22 23 24

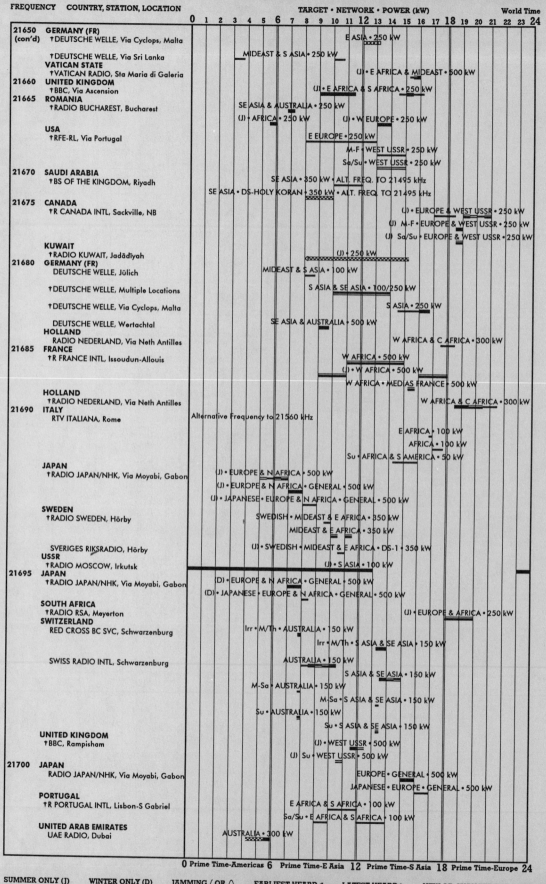

FREQUENCY	COUNTRY, STATION, LOCATION	TARGET • NETWORK • POWER (kW)
21650 (con'd)	**GERMANY (FR)** †DEUTSCHE WELLE, Via Cyclops, Malta	E ASIA • 250 kW
	†DEUTSCHE WELLE, Via Sri Lanka	MIDEAST & S ASIA • 250 kW
	VATICAN STATE †VATICAN RADIO, Sta Maria di Galeria	(J) • E AFRICA & MIDEAST • 500 kW
21660	**UNITED KINGDOM** †BBC, Via Ascension	(J) • E AFRICA & S AFRICA • 250 kW
21665	**ROMANIA** †RADIO BUCHAREST, Bucharest	SE ASIA & AUSTRALIA • 250 kW
		(J) • AFRICA • 250 kW
		(J) • W EUROPE • 250 kW
	USA †RFE-RL, Via Portugal	E EUROPE • 250 kW
		M-F • WEST USSR • 250 kW
		Sa/Su • WEST USSR • 250 kW
21670	**SAUDI ARABIA** †BS OF THE KINGDOM, Riyadh	SE ASIA • 350 kW • ALT. FREQ. TO 21495 kHz
		SE ASIA • DS-HOLY KORAN • 350 kW • ALT. FREQ. TO 21495 kHz
21675	**CANADA** †R CANADA INTL, Sackville, NB	(J) • EUROPE & WEST USSR • 250 kW
		(J) M-F • EUROPE & WEST USSR • 250 kW
		(J) Sa/Su • EUROPE & WEST USSR • 250 kW
	KUWAIT †RADIO KUWAIT, Jadādīyah	(J) • 250 kW
21680	**GERMANY (FR)** DEUTSCHE WELLE, Jülich	MIDEAST & S ASIA • 100 kW
	†DEUTSCHE WELLE, Multiple Locations	S ASIA & SE ASIA • 100/250 kW
	†DEUTSCHE WELLE, Via Cyclops, Malta	S ASIA • 250 kW
	DEUTSCHE WELLE, Wertachtal	SE ASIA & AUSTRALIA • 500 kW
	HOLLAND RADIO NEDERLAND, Via Neth Antilles	W AFRICA & C AFRICA • 300 kW
21685	**FRANCE** †R FRANCE INTL, Issoudun-Allouis	W AFRICA • 500 kW
		(J) • W AFRICA • 500 kW
		W AFRICA • MEDIAS FRANCE • 500 kW
	HOLLAND †RADIO NEDERLAND, Via Neth Antilles	W AFRICA & C AFRICA • 300 kW
21690	**ITALY** RTV ITALIANA, Rome	Alternative Frequency to 21560 kHz
		E AFRICA • 100 kW
		AFRICA • 100 kW
		Su • AFRICA & S AMERICA • 50 kW
	JAPAN †RADIO JAPAN/NHK, Via Moyabi, Gabon	(J) • EUROPE & N AFRICA • 500 kW
		(J) • EUROPE & N AFRICA • GENERAL • 500 kW
		(J) • JAPANESE • EUROPE & N AFRICA • GENERAL • 500 kW
	SWEDEN †RADIO SWEDEN, Hörby	SWEDISH • MIDEAST & E AFRICA • 350 kW
		MIDEAST & E AFRICA • 350 kW
	SVERIGES RIKSRADIO, Hörby	(J) • SWEDISH • MIDEAST & E AFRICA • DS-1 • 350 kW
	USSR †RADIO MOSCOW, Irkutsk	(J) • S ASIA • 100 kW
21695	**JAPAN** †RADIO JAPAN/NHK, Via Moyabi, Gabon	(D) • EUROPE & N AFRICA • GENERAL • 500 kW
		(D) • JAPANESE • EUROPE & N AFRICA • GENERAL • 500 kW
	SOUTH AFRICA †RADIO RSA, Meyerton	(J) • EUROPE & AFRICA • 250 kW
	SWITZERLAND RED CROSS BC SVC, Schwarzenburg	Irr • M/Th • AUSTRALIA • 150 kW
		Irr • M/Th • S ASIA & SE ASIA • 150 kW
	SWISS RADIO INTL, Schwarzenburg	AUSTRALIA • 150 kW
		S ASIA & SE ASIA • 150 kW
		M-Sa • AUSTRALIA • 150 kW
		M-Sa • S ASIA & SE ASIA • 150 kW
		Su • AUSTRALIA • 150 kW
		Su • S ASIA & SE ASIA • 150 kW
	UNITED KINGDOM †BBC, Rampisham	(J) • WEST USSR • 500 kW
		(J) Su • WEST USSR • 500 kW
21700	**JAPAN** RADIO JAPAN/NHK, Via Moyabi, Gabon	EUROPE • GENERAL • 500 kW
		JAPANESE • EUROPE • GENERAL • 500 kW
	PORTUGAL †R PORTUGAL INTL, Lisbon-S Gabriel	E AFRICA & S AFRICA • 100 kW
		Sa/Su • E AFRICA & S AFRICA • 100 kW
	UNITED ARAB EMIRATES UAE RADIO, Dubai	AUSTRALIA • 300 kW

0 Prime Time-Americas 6 Prime Time-E Asia 12 Prime Time-S Asia 18 Prime Time-Europe 24

SUMMER ONLY (J) WINTER ONLY (D) JAMMING / OR /\ EARLIEST HEARD ◁ LATEST HEARD ▷ NEW OR CHANGED FOR 1990 †

FREQUENCY	COUNTRY, STATION, LOCATION	TARGET • NETWORK • POWER (kW)
21705	**CZECHOSLOVAKIA** RADIO PRAGUE, Piešťány-Velké K'y	SE ASIA & AUSTRALIA • 250 kW
		Sa/Su • SE ASIA & AUSTRALIA • 250 kW
	NORWAY †RADIO NORWAY INTL, Kvitsøy	AUSTRALIA • 500 kW
		(J) Su • AFRICA • 500 kW
		S ASIA & AUSTRALIA • 500 kW • ALT. FREQ. TO 21710 kHz
		(J) • AUSTRALIA • 500 kW
		(J) M-Sa • S ASIA & AUSTRALIA • 500 kW • ALT. FREQ. TO 21710 kHz
		(J) Su • E ASIA • 500 kW
		(J) Su • S ASIA & AUSTRALIA • 500 kW • ALT. FREQ. TO 21710 kHz
		S AMERICA • 500 kW
	†RADIO NORWAY INTL, Sveio	(J) • W AFRICA & AUSTRALIA • 500 kW
21710	**NORWAY** †RADIO NORWAY INTL, Kvitsøy	Alternative Frequency to 21705 kHz
	UNITED KINGDOM †BBC, Daventry	(J) • N AFRICA & W AFRICA • 100 kW
		N AFRICA & W AFRICA • 100/250 kW
	†BBC, Multiple Locations	
21720	**USA** †RFE-RL, Via Portugal	E EUROPE & WEST USSR • 250 kW
21725	**NORWAY** †RADIO NORWAY INTL, Kvitsøy	M-Sa • MIDEAST • 500 kW
		Su • MIDEAST • 500 kW
	USSR RADIO MOSCOW, Tbilisi	(D) • W AFRICA • WS • 100 kW
21730	**FRANCE** †R FRANCE INTL, Issoudun-Allouis	M-Sa • E AFRICA • MEDIAS FRANCE • 100 kW
	NORWAY †RADIO NORWAY INTL, Kvitsøy	S ASIA & AUSTRALIA • 500 kW
		(J) M-Sa • E AFRICA • 500 kW
		(J) • AUSTRALIA • 500 kW
		(J) Su • E AFRICA • 500 kW
		M-Sa • AUSTRALIA • 500 kW
		Su • AUSTRALIA • 500 kW
	†RADIO NORWAY INTL, Sveio	(J) • S AMERICA • 500 kW
21735	**UNITED ARAB EMIRATES** †VOICE OF THE UAE, Abu Dhabi	(D) • EUROPE • DS • 500 kW
	USA †WYFR-FAMILY RADIO, Okeechobee, Fl	EUROPE • 100 kW
21740	**AUSTRALIA** †RADIO AUSTRALIA, Shepparton	PACIFIC • 50 kW
21745	**USA** †RFE-RL, Via Portugal	E EUROPE & WEST USSR • 250 kW
21750	**USSR** †RADIO MOSCOW	(J) • MIDEAST
21760	**ISRAEL** †KOL ISRAEL, Tel Aviv	(J) • W EUROPE & E NORTH AM • 300 kW
		(D) • HEBREW • W EUROPE & E NORTH AM • DS-B • 50/300 kW
21770	**FRANCE** †R FRANCE INTL, Issoudun-Allouis	(J) • SE ASIA • 500 kW
21780	**ISRAEL** †KOL ISRAEL, Tel Aviv	(D) • E EUROPE & WEST USSR • 300 kW
		(D) M/Tu/Th-Sa • E EUROPE & WEST USSR • 300 kW
		(D) Sa/Su • E EUROPE & WEST USSR • 300 kW
		(D) Su/W • E EUROPE & WEST USSR • 300 kW
	USA †WCSN, Scotts Corners, Me	EUROPE • 500 kW
		M-F • EUROPE • 500 kW
		Sa • EUROPE • 500 kW
		Su • EUROPE • 500 kW
21785	**USSR** †RADIO MOSCOW	(J) • E AFRICA
21790	**USSR** †RADIO MOSCOW	(J)
21795	**USSR** †RADIO MOSCOW	(J)
21800	**USSR** †RADIO MOSCOW	(J) • E AFRICA
21810	**BELGIUM** †BELGISCHE RADIO TV, Wavre	(D) • AFRICA • 100/250 kW
		(J) • AFRICA • 100/250 kW
		(D) M-F • AFRICA • 100/250 kW
		(J) M-F • AFRICA • 100/250 kW
		(D) M-Sa • AFRICA • 100/250 kW
		(J) M-Sa • AFRICA • 100/250 kW
		(J) Sa/Su • AFRICA • 100/250 kW
		(D) Su • AFRICA • 100/250 kW
		(J) Su • AFRICA • 100/250 kW
21815	**BELGIUM** †BELGISCHE RADIO TV, Wavre	(J) M-F • SE ASIA • 250 kW
		(D) • SE ASIA • 250 kW
		(J) • SE ASIA • 250 kW

(con'd)

World Time: 0 Prime Time-Americas 6 Prime Time-E Asia 12 Prime Time-S Asia 18 Prime Time-Europe 24

ENGLISH ▬ ARABIC ▬ CHINESE ▬ FRENCH ▬ GERMAN ▬ RUSSIAN ▬ SPANISH ▬ OTHER ▬

FREQUENCY	COUNTRY, STATION, LOCATION	TARGET • NETWORK • POWER (kW)
21815 (con'd)	**BELGIUM** †BELGISCHE RADIO TV, Wavre	(D) M-F • SE ASIA • 250 kW
		(D) M-Sa • SE ASIA • 250 kW
		(J) M-Sa • SE ASIA • 250 kW
21820	**USSR** †RADIO MOSCOW	(J)
21840	**USA** †WORLD HARVEST R, Noblesville, Indiana	(J) • E NORTH AM & W EUROPE • ENGLISH, ETC • 100 kW
25645	**BELGIUM** †RT BELGE FRANCAISE, Wavre	(J) • AFRICA • 250 kW
		(J) Su • AFRICA • 250 kW
25670	**UNITED ARAB EMIRATES** †VOICE OF THE UAE, Abu Dhabi	(J) • AUSTRALIA • DS • 500 kW
		(J) • E ASIA • DS • 500 kW
25730	**NORWAY** †RADIO NORWAY INTL, Fredrikstad	(D) • S AMERICA • 350 kW
		(J) • E AFRICA • 500 kW
	†RADIO NORWAY INTL, Kvitsøy	(D) • AUSTRALIA • 500 kW
		(D) • AFRICA • 500 kW
		(D) • S ASIA & SE ASIA • 500 kW
		(J) • W AFRICA & S AMERICA • 500 kW
		(J) M-Sa • W AFRICA & S AMERICA • 500 kW
		(J) Su • W AFRICA & S AMERICA • 500 kW
	†RADIO NORWAY INTL, Sveio	(D) • N AMERICA • 500 kW
		(J) • S AMERICA • 500 kW
25740	**GERMANY (FR)** †DEUTSCHE WELLE	(J) • SE ASIA & AUSTRALIA
	†DEUTSCHE WELLE, Jülich	(D) • S ASIA & SE ASIA • 100 kW
	NORWAY †RADIO NORWAY INTL, Fredrikstad	(D) • C AMERICA • 350 kW
25750	**UNITED KINGDOM** †BBC, Daventry	AFRICA & MIDEAST • 50 kW
		(J) • AFRICA & MIDEAST • 50 kW
25780	**USSR** †RADIO MOSCOW	(J) • E AFRICA • ENGLISH, SWAHILI
25790	**SOUTH AFRICA** †RADIO RSA, Meyerton	E AFRICA & MIDEAST • 250 kW
25795	**YUGOSLAVIA** †RADIO YUGOSLAVIA, Bijeljina	(J) • SE ASIA • 500 kW
25820	**DENMARK** †DANMARKS RADIO, Copenhagen	(J) • MIDEAST & E AFRICA • 50 kW
	FRANCE †R FRANCE INTL, Issoudun-Allouis	E AFRICA • 100 kW
		Su • E AFRICA • 100 kW
		E AFRICA • MEDIAS FRANCE • 100 kW
		M-Sa • E AFRICA • MEDIAS FRANCE • 100 kW
25850	**DENMARK** †DANMARKS RADIO, Copenhagen	(D) • EUROPE & W AFRICA • 50 kW
		(D) • AUSTRALIA • 50 kW
		(J) • ASIA • 50 kW
		(J) • EUROPE & W AFRICA • 50 kW
25900	**UNITED ARAB EMIRATES** †VOICE OF THE UAE, Abu Dhabi	(J) • N AFRICA • DS • 500 kW
		(J) • EUROPE • DS • 500 kW
25945v	**COSTA RICA** †RADIO FOR PEACE, Ciudad Colón	M-F • N AMERICA • 2/5 kW
26050	**BELGIUM** †BELGISCHE RADIO TV, Wavre	(J) • AFRICA • 250 kW
		(J) M-F • AFRICA • 250 kW
		(J) M-Sa • AFRICA • 250 kW
		(J) Su • AFRICA • 250 kW

World Time: 0 1 2 3 4 5 6 7 8 9 10 11 12 13 14 15 16 17 18 19 20 21 22 23 24

0 Prime Time-Americas 6 Prime Time-E Asia 12 Prime Time-S Asia 18 Prime Time-Europe 24

SUMMER ONLY (J) WINTER ONLY (D) JAMMING / OR /\ EARLIEST HEARD ◁ LATEST HEARD ▷ NEW OR CHANGED FOR 1990 †

GLOSSARIES AND GUIDES

Terms and Abbreviations Used in World Band Radio

A wide variety of terms and abbreviations is used in world band radio. Some are specialized and need explanation; a few are foreign words that need translation; and yet others are simply adaptations of common usage. Here, then, is *Passport's* guide to what's what in world band terminology and abbreviations—including what each one means. For a thorough writeup on what determines how well a world band radio performs, please see the *RDI White Paper*, "How to Interpret Receiver Specifications and Lab Tests."

Adjacent-Channel Rejection. *See* Selectivity.

AGC. *See* Automatic Gain Control.

Alt. Alternative frequency or channel. Frequency or channel that may be used irregularly or unexpectedly in place of the regularly scheduled frequency or channel.

Amateur Radio. *See* Hams.

AM Band. The local radio band, which currently runs from 520 to 1,611 kHz (530–1700 kHz in North America as of mid-1990), within the Medium Frequency (MF) range. In many countries it is called the mediumwave (MW) band.

Artificial Intelligence. The ability of a computer to operate similarly to the human brain.

Audio Quality, Audio Fidelity. *See* High Fidelity.

Automatic Gain Control. Smoothes out the fluctuations in signal strength brought about by fading, a common occurrence with world band signals.

AV. A Voz—Portuguese for Voice of.

Bandwidth. One of the variables that determines selectivity (*see*), bandwidth is the amount of radio signal a set will let pass through. With world band channel spacing at 5 kHz, the best single bandwidths are usually in the vicinity of 3-6 kHz. Better radios offer two or more selectable bandwidths: one of 5-7 kHz or so for when a station is "in the clear," and one or more others between 2-4 kHz for when a station is hemmed in by other stations next to it.

BC, BS. Broadcasting, Broadcasting Company, Broadcasting Corporation, Broadcasting Station, Broadcasting Service.

Broadcast. A radio or TV transmission meant for the general public. *Compare* Utility Stations.

Cd. Ciudad—Spanish for City.

Channel. An everyday term to indicate where a station is supposed to be located on the dial. World band channels are exactly 5 kHz apart. Stations operating outside this norm are "off channel" (for these, *Passport* provides resolution to better than one kHz to aid in station identification). Measured in units of 5 kHz; that is, world band channels, unlike some other radio/TV channels, aren't assigned sequentially, like street numbers, in an $n+1$ fashion.

Cl. Club, Clube.

Cu, Cult. Cultura, Cultural, Culture.

(D). Frequency operates at this time winters only. Not heard summers.

Digital Channel Display, Digital Frequency Display, Digital Tuning Display. *See* Synthesizer.

DS. Domestic Service—Broadcasting intended for audiences in the broadcaster's home country. *Compare* ES.

DXers. From an old telegraph term "to DX"; that is, to communicate over a great distance. Thus, "DXers" are those who specialize in finding distant or exotic stations.

Dynamic Range. The ability of a set to handle weak signals in the presence of strong competing signals within the same world band segment (*see* World Band Spectrum). Sets with inferior dynamic range sometimes "overload," causing a mishmash of false signals mixed together up and down—and even beyond—the band segment being received.

Earliest Heard (or **Latest Heard**). See the key at the bottom of each "Blue Page." If the *Passport* monitoring team cannot establish the definite sign-on (or sign-off) time of a station, the earliest (or latest) time the station could be traced is indicated, instead, by a triangular "flag." This means that the station almost certainly operates beyond the time shown by that "flag." It also means that, unless you live relatively close to the station, you're unlikely to be able to hear it beyond that "flagged" time.

Ed, Educ. Educational, Educação, Educadora.

Em. Emissora, Emisora, Emissor, Emetteur—In effect, station in various languages.

EP. Emissor Provincial—Portuguese for Provincial Station.

ER. Emissor Regional—Portuguese for Regional Station.

Ergonomics. How handy and comfortable a set is to operate, especially hour after hour.

ES. External Service—Broadcasting intended for foreign audiences. *Compare* DS.

F. Friday.

Feeder. A "utility" station that transmits programs from the broadcaster's home country to a relay site abroad. Although these stations are not intended to be received by the general public, many world band radios can handle these quasi-broadcasts anyway. Feeders operate in lower sideband (LSB), upper sideband (USB) or independent sideband (termed ISL if heard on the lower side, ISU if heard on the upper side) modes. *See* Single Sideband.

FR. Federal Republic.

Frequency. The standard term to indicate where a station is located on the dial—regardless whether it's "on-channel" or "off-channel" (*see* channel). Measured in kilohertz (kHz) or Megahertz (MHz).

GMT. Greenwich Mean Time—*See* UTC.

Hams. Government-licensed amateur radio hobbyists that communicate with each other by radio for pleasure within special "amateur bands."

High Fidelity, Enhanced Fidelity. World band reception is ordinarily of only fair audio quality, or fidelity, with some stations sounding even worse. Advanced radios with good audio performance and certain high-tech circuits already can improve on this, and radios of the 21st century are expected to provide genuine high fidelity; i.e., smooth wideband audio and freedom from distortion.

Independent Sideband. *See* Single Sideband.

1000
25 x1000
5000
25000

Interference. Sounds from other stations that are disturbing the station you're trying to hear.
Ionosphere. *See* Propagation.
Irr. Irregular operation or hours of operation; i.e., schedule tends to be unpredictable.
(J). Frequency operates at this time summers only. Not heard winters.
Jamming. Deliberate interference to a transmission with the intent of making reception impossible.
kHz. Kilohertz, the most common unit for measuring where a station is on the dial. Formerly known as "kilocycles/second." 1,000 kilohertz equals one Megahertz.
kW. Kilowatt(s), the most common unit of measurement for transmitter power (*see*).
Loc. Local.
Location. The physical location of the station's transmitter, which may be different from the studio location. Transmitter location is useful as a guide to reception quality. For example, if you're in Eastern North America and wish to listen to Radio Moscow, a transmitter located in the Western USSR will almost certainly provide better reception than one located in Siberia, and one located in Cuba will probably be better yet.
LV. La Voix, La Voz—French and Spanish for The Voice.
M. Monday.
Mediumwave Band. *See* AM Band.
Meters. The unit of measurement used for individual world band segments of the shortwave spectrum. The frequency range covered by a given meters designation—also known as "wavelength"—can be gleaned from the following formula: frequency (kHz) = 299,792/meters. Thus, 49 meters comes out to a frequency of 6118 kHz—well within the range of frequencies included in that segment (*see* World Band Spectrum). Inversely, meters can be derived from the following: meters = 299,792/frequency (kHz).
MHz. Megahertz, a common unit to measure where a station is on the dial. Formerly known as "Megacycles/second." One Megahertz equals 1,000 kilohertz.
N. New, Nueva, Nuevo, Nouvelle, Nacional, National.
Nac. Nacional.
Narrow-Band Facsimile Video. A technique in which pictures can be transmitted without taking up a great deal of radio spectrum space.
Nat, Natl. National, Nationale.
Other. Programs are in a language *other* than one of the world's primary languages.
Overloading. *See* Dynamic Range.
PBS. People's Broadcasting Station.
Power. Transmitter power *before* amplification by the antenna, expressed in kilowatts (kW). The present range of world band powers is 0.01 to 600 kW.
PR. People's Republic.
Programmable Channel Memory. Allows you to push one button, as on a car radio, to select a station.
Propagation. World band signals travel, like a basketball, up and down from the station to your radio. The "floor" below is the earth's surface, whereas the "player's hand" on high is the *ionosphere*, a gaseous layer that envelops the earth. While the earth's surface remains pretty much the same from day-to-day, the ionosphere—nature's own satellite—varies in how it propagates radio signals, depending on how much sunlight hits the "bounce points."

This is why some world band segments do well mainly by day, whereas others are best by night. During winter there's less sunlight, so the "night bands" become unusually active, while the "day bands" become correspondingly less useful (*see* World Band Spectrum). Day-to-day changes in the sun's weather also cause short-term changes in world band radio reception; this explains why some days you hear rare signals. Additionally, the 11-year sunspot cycle has a long-term effect on propagation. It's now peaking, so the high bands should be even better than usual through about 1993.
PS. Provincial Station, Pangsong.
Pto. Puerto, Pôrto.
QSL. A card or letter from a station verifying that a listener indeed heard that particular station.
R. Radio, Radiodiffusion, Radiodifusora, Radiodifusão, Radiofonikos, Radiostansiya, Radyo, Radyosu, and so forth.
Receiver. Synonym for a radio. In practice, "receiver" is often used to designate a set—usually a tabletop model—with superior ability to ferret out weak, hard-to-hear signals.
Reg. Regional.
Relay. A retransmission facility—shown in **bold** in "Worldwide Broadcasts"—located outside the broadcaster's country. Relay signals, being closer to the target audience, usually provide superior reception. *See* Feeder.
Rep. Republic, République, República.
RN. *See* R and N.
RS. Radio Station, Radiostantsiya, Radiofonikos Stathmos.
RT, RTV. Radiodiffusion Télévision, Radio Télévision, and so forth.
S. San, Santa, Santo, São, Saint.
Sa. Saturday.
Selectivity. The ability of a set to ignore strong signals next to the one being heard. *See* Bandwidth.
Sensitivity. The ability of a set to receive weak signals.
Shortwave Spectrum. The shortwave spectrum—also known as the High Frequency (HF) spectrum—is, strictly speaking, that portion of the radio spectrum from 3-30 MHz (3,000-30,000 kHz). However, common usage places it between 2-30 MHz (2,000-30,000 kHz). It includes not only world band stations, but also "utility" stations and "hams." *See* World Band Spectrum, Utility Stations and Hams.
Single Sideband, Independent Sideband. Spectrum-conserving modes of transmission commonly used by "utility" stations and "hams." Very few broadcasters—world band or other—use these modes, but this is expected to change early in the 21st century. Many world band radios are already capable of receiving single sideband transmissions, and some can even receive independent sideband transmissions. *See* Feeder.
St, Sta, Sto. Saint.
Su. Sunday.
Synchronous Detector. World band radios are increasingly coming equipped with this hightech circuit that improves adjacent-channel rejection (*see*).
Synthesizer. Simple radios use ordinary needle-and-dial tuning that makes it difficult to find a desired channel, or to tell what you are hearing, except by ear. Advanced models utilize a digital frequency *synthesizer* to tune in signals without your having to "hunt and peck." Among other things, synthesizers allow for pushbutton tuning and display the exact frequency digitally—two plusses that make tuning in the world much easier.
Target. Where a transmission is beamed if it is intended to be heard outside the country.
Th. Thursday.
Tu. Tuesday.
Universal Time. *See* UTC.
UTC. Coordinated Universal Time, also known as World Time, Greenwich Mean Time and Zulu. With 161 countries on world band radio, if each announced its own local time you would need a calculator to figure it all out. To get around this, a single international time—UTC—is used. The difference between UTC and local time is determined simply by listening to UTC time checks given on the hour by world band broadcasters. A 24-hour clock is used, so "1800 UTC" means 6:00 PM UTC. If you're in North America, Eastern Time is five hours behind UTC winters and four hours behind UTC summers, so 1800 UTC would be 1:00 PM EST or 2:00 PM EDT. The easiest solution is to use a 24-hour clock set to UTC. Many radios already have these built in, and UTC clocks are also available as accessories.
"Utility" Stations. Most signals within the shortwave spectrum are not world band stations. Rather, they are professional "utility" stations—radio telephones, ships at sea, aircraft and the like—that transmit point-to-point and are not intended to be heard by the general public. *Compare* Broadcast, Hams and Feeders.
v. Variable frequency; i.e., one that is unstable or drifting

because of a transmitter malfunction.

Vo. Voice of.

W. Wednesday.

Wavelength. *See* Meters.

World Band Radio. Similar to regular AM band and FM band radio, except that world band broadcasts can be heard for enormous distances and thus often carry programs created especially for audiences abroad. Hundreds of millions of people on every continent now listen to world band radio.

World Band Spectrum. The collected segments of the shortwave spectrum set aside by the International Telecommunication Union (ITU) for broadcasting. The ITU also allows some world band broadcasting to take place outside these segments. The official world band segments—along with, when appropriate, the "real world" segments [in brackets]— follow, with general guides as to when reception may be best. Remember, these are only *general* guides—actual reception will vary according to your location, the station's location, the time of year, and other factors (*see* Propagation).

Weak Reception Winter Nights

***120 Meters:**
2300-2498 kHz (Tropical Domestic Stations)

***90 Meters:**
3200-3400 kHz (Tropical Domestic Stations)

Fair Reception Winter Nights

***75 Meters:**
3900-3950 kHz (Asia & Pacific only)
3950-4000 kHz (except Americas)

***60 Meters:**
4750-5060 kHz [4600-5100 kHz] (Tropical Domestic Stations)

Strong Nighttime Reception

49 Meters:
5950-6200 kHz [5850-6250 kHz]

***41 Meters:**
7100-7300 kHz [7100-7600 kHz]

Strong Night and Day Reception

31 Meters:
9500-9975 kHz [9300-9995 kHz]

25 Meters:
11700-11975 kHz [11500-12100 kHz]

Strong Daytime Reception

22 Meters:
[13600-13800 kHz]

19 Meters:
15100-15450 kHz [15005-15700 kHz]

16 Meters:
17700-17900 kHz [17500-17900 kHz]

13 Meters:
21450-21750 kHz [21450-21850 kHz]

Fair Daytime Reception

11 Meters:
25670-26100 kHz**

World Time. *See* UTC.

WS. World Service.

**Shared with other radio services, such as "utility" stations and "hams."*

***Provides interference-free reception briefly many days.*

Termes et abréviations

Il existe, dans le domaine de la radiodiffusion par bandes internationales, une multiplicité de termes techniques et d'abréviations: acceptions spécialisées à définir, locutions étrangères à traduire, expressions usuelles à préciser. Pour rendre accessible ce vocabulaire international nous avons dressé la liste des termes couramment employés.

GUIDE DE WORLDSCAN

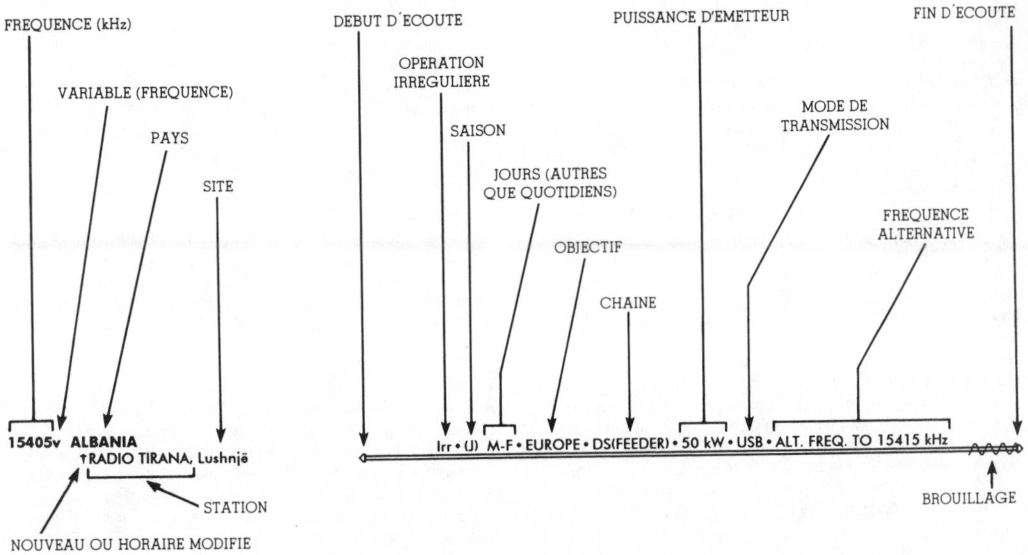

Alt. Fréquence alternative. Fréquence qui s'emploie de façon irrégulière ou exceptionnellement à la place d'une fréquence régulière.
AV. A Voz—portugais: Voix de.
BC, BS. Radiodiffusion, Société de Radiodiffusion, station de radiodiffusion, service de radiodiffusion.
Cd. Ciudad—espagnol: ville.
Cl. Club, clube.
Cu, Cult. Cultura, Cultural, Culture.
(D). Fréquence en opération à l'heure indiquée seulement en hiver.
DS. Service interne—radiodiffusion à l'intention de l'auditoire national, *v.* ES.
Earliest Heard (or **Latest Heard**). Début d'Ecoute (ou Fin d'Ecoute). V. en bas de la page bleue. Dans le cas où notre équipe de contrôle ne réussissait pas à établir, de façon définitive, le début ou la fin d'une émission, l'heure de la première réception captée est indiquée au moyen d'un triangle. Il faut en déduire que la station émet probablement en dehors de l'heure indiquée au triangle et, qu'à moins d'habiter à proximité de la station d'émission, on ne peut la capter en dehors de l'heure indiquée au triangle.
Ed, Educ. Educational, Educação, Educadora—éducatif.
Em. Emissora, Emisora, Emissor, Emetteur—équivalence dans plusieurs langues de "station."
EP. Emissor Provincial—portugais: Station provinciale.
ER. Emissor Regional—portugais: Station régionale.
ES. Service externe—radiodiffusion à l'intention d'auditoires étrangers, *v.* DS.
F. Vendredi.
Feeder. Station réservée à l'intention de certains usagers diffusant des programmes du pays d'origine vers un site de relais situé à l'étranger. Bien que ces émissions ne s'adressent pas à des auditoires généraux, il est cependant possible de les capter au moyen de postes récepteurs à gammes mondiales. Les lignes d'alimentation opèrent en différents modes: bandes latérales inférieures LSB), bandes latérales supérieures (USB), bandeslatérales indépendantes (désignées ISL dans le cas des bandes inférieures, ISU dans le cas des bandes supérieures.)
FR. République Fédérale.
Frequency. Fréquence: terme normalement employé pour indiquer la position exacte au cadran d'une station, et qui se mesure en kilohertz (kHz.) or Mégahertz (MHz.).
Irr. Heures d'écoute irrégulières, c'est-à-dire que l'horaire tend à changer d'une façon imprévisible.
Jamming. Brouillage intentionnellement afin de perturber la réception d'une station.
kHz. Kilohertz: l'unité de mesure la plus employée pour indiquer au cadran la situation exacte d'une station. Autrefois se calculait en "kilocycles/seconde." 1 000 kilohertz égale un Mégahertz.
kW. Kilowatt(s): l'unité normalement employée pour mesurer la puissance d'émetteur.
Loc. Local.
Location. Le lieu où est situé l'émetteur d'une station et qui n'est pas nécéssairement celui des studios de programmation. Il existe entre le site de l'émetteur et la qualité de réception une corrélation certaine. Par exemple, si l'on est en Europe et que l'on veut écouter Radio Moscou, la réception assurée par un émetteur situé à l'ouest de l'URSS sera sans doute meilleure que celle en provenance de la Sibérie, et celle en provenance de la Bulgarie sera encore mieux.
LV. La Voix, La Voz (Espagnol).
M. Lundi.
Meters. L'unité de mesure utilisée pour désigner des segments de bandes du spectre ondes courtes. La gamme des fréquences désignée par un certain nombre de mètres donnés—ou longueur d'onde—se déduit d'après la formule suivante: fréquence (kHz.) = 299 792/mètres. Par conséquent, 49 mètres répond à une fréquence de 6 118 kHz.—étant bien dans la gamme des fréquences comprises dans ce segment. (*V.* World Band Spectrum). A l'opposé, on peut calculer la fréquence en mètres d'après la formule suivante: mètres = 299 792/fréquence (kHz.).
N. New, Nueva, Nuevo, Nouveau, Nouvelle, Nacional, National.
Nac. Nacional.
Nat., Natl. National, Nationale.
Other. Programmes diffusés dans une langue *autre* qu'une des langues universelles.
PBS People's Broadcasting Station: Station de Radiodiffusion Populaire.
Power. Puissance d'émetteur *avant* l'amplification par antenne, exprimée en kilowatts (kW.). Le spectre actuel des gammes mondiales se situe entre 0,01 et 600 kW.
PR. People's Republic: République Populaire.
PS. Station Provinciale, Pangsong.
Pto. Puerto, Pôrto.
R. Radio, Radiodiffusion, Radiodifusora, Radio-difusão, Radiofonikos, Radiostansiya, Radyo, Radyosu, et cetera.
Reg. Régional.
Relay. Installation de radiodiffusion—indiquée en **caractères gras** dans "Worldwide située à létranger. Les signaux de relais, étant plus proches des auditeurs ciblés, assurent généralement une meilleure réception. *V.* Feeder.
Rep. Republic, République, Republica.
RN. *V.* R. et N.
RS. Station de Radio, Radiostantsiya, Radiofonikos Stathmos.
RT, RTV. Radiodiffusion Télévision, Radio Televisión, et cetera.
S. Saint, San, Santo, Santa, São.
Sa. Samedi.
Shortwave Spectrum. Spectre Ondes Courtes. Le spectre ondes courtes ou spectre à hautes fréquences (HF) correspond à la partie du spectre située entre 3 et 30 MHz. (3 000–30 000 kHz.). Les fréquences normalement employées, cependant, se situent entre 2 et 30 MHz. (2 000- 30 000 kHz.). Cette gamme comporte non seulement les bandes ondes courtes captées à traverle monde mais aussi les stations réservées à certains usagers dans les domaines de la radiotéléphonie, des services maritimes, de la radio amateur, et cetera.
St., Sta., Sto. Saint.
Su. Dimanche.
Target. Région-cible. Pays vers lequel une émission est diffusée à l'intention d'un auditoire étranger.
Th. Jeudi.
Tu. Mardi.
Universal Time. *V.* UTC.
UTC. Heure Universelle Coordonnée. Si chacun des 161 pays à diffuser sur bandes mondiales annonçait l'heure locale, l'auditeur aurait à faire, sans cesse, des calculs compliqués. Pour résoudre ce problème, on a recours à l'emploi d'une heure universelle coordonnée. Afin de déterminer la différence entre l'heure universelle coordonnée et l'heure locale, il suffit simplement D'écouter les annonces de vérification régulièrement programmées au début de chaque heure par les Chaînes Internationales Radiodiffusion. On utilise l'horloge de 24 heures. Ainsi par "1800 UTC" il faut comprendre 6:00 du soir UTC. Pour l'auditeur de Paris l'heure locale, l'hiver, avance d'une heure sur celle d'UTC, tandis que, l'été, l'heure locale avance de deux heures sur celle d'UTC. Ainsi, 1800 UTC serait l'équivalence, en hiver, de 7:00 du soir, heure locale, et de 8:00 du soir, heure locale, en été. Pour effectuer cetter conversion il est possible de se servir d'horloges munies d'un cadran 24-heures réglé sur l'UTC. Il existe de nombreux récepteurs prémunis de ces cadrans qui peuvent également s'acheter comme accessoires.
v. Fréquence variable; c'est-à-dire peu stable ou fluctuante à cause du fonctionnement défectueux d'un émetteur.
Vo. Voix de.
W. Mercredi.
World Band Radio. Semblable à la radiodiffusion sur ondes moyennes (AM) et en modulation de fréquence (FM), sauf que la radiodiffusion à gammes mondiales peut être captée à longue distance et diffuse donc des programmes destinés à des auditoires étrangers. Des millions d'auditeurs dans tous les continents écoutent à présent des émissions à gammes mondiales.

World Band Spectrum. L'ensemble des bandes du spectre ondes courtes attribuées à la radiodiffusion universelle par l'Union Internationale de Télécommunication (ITU). L'ITU autorise également la diffusion de certaines émissions en dehors des bandes prévues. La liste des bandes universelles conférées—et, s'il y a lieu, des bandes réservées à des usagers spécialisés [entre parenthèses]—s'accompagne de recommandations quant aux meilleures heures d'écoute. Il ne faut pas oublier qu'il s'agit simplement d'indications générales et que la qualité de réception varie suivant le lieu de réception, la situation géographique de la station, la saison de l'année, et d'autres facteurs encore.

Réception de nuit médiocre en hiver

***120 Mètres:**
2300-2498 kHz. (Stations Tropicales Internes)
***90 Mètres:**
3200-3400 kHz. (Stations Tropicales Internes)

Réception de nuit satisfaisante en hiver

***75 Mètres:**
3900-3950 kHz. (Asie et Pacifique exclusivement)
***60 Mètres:**
4750-5060 kHz. [4600-5100 kHz.] (Stations Tropicales Internes)

Réception de nuit excellente

49 Mètres:
5950-6200 kHz. [5850-6250 kHz.]
***41 Mètres:**
7100-7300 kHz. [7100-7600 kHz.]

Réception de nuit et de jour excellente

31 Mètres:
9500-9900 kHz. [9000-9100 & 9300-10100 kHz.]
25 Mètres:
11760-12050 kHz. [11500-12100 kHz.]

Réception de jour excellente

22 Mètres:
[13600-13800 kHz.]
19 Mètres:
15100-15450 kHz. [15005-15700 kHz.]
16 Mètres:
17700-17900 kHz. [17500-17900 kHz.]
13 Mètres:
21450-21750 kHz. [21450-21850 kHz.]

Réception de jour satisfaisante

11 Mètres:
25670-26100 kHz.**

World Time. *V.* UTC.

WS. World Service: service mondial.

**Bandes réparties entre plusieurs services: stations réservées aux usagers spécialisés et aux amateurs.*
***Permet une réception sans interférence pendant de courtes périodes. Les meilleures conditions d'écoute se produiront d'ici vers 1993.*

Terminos y abreviaturas

Se utiliza una amplia gama de términos y abreviaturas en este libro. Algunos son especializados y necesitan un explicación; otros son de procedencia extranjera y requieren una traducción; y algunos son adaptaciones de uso común. Lo que sigue es una guía de las abreviaturas y terminología utilizadas, incluyendo las explicaciones correspondientes.

COMO UTILIZAR EL WORLDSCAN

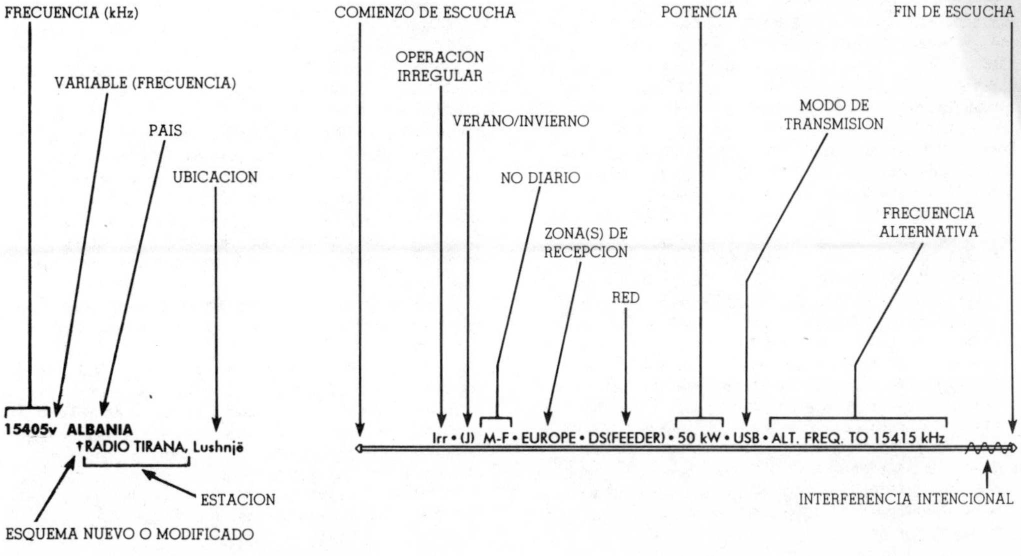

Alt. Frecuencia alternativa; una frecuencia cuyo uso sea imprevisto o irregular y en lugar de la frecuencia asignada.
AV. A Voz.
BC, BS. Broadcasting, Broadcasting Company, Broadcasting Corporation; Broadcasting Station, Broadcasting Service.
Cd. Ciudad.
Cl. Club, Clube.
Cu, Cult. Cultura, Cultural, Culture.
(D). Indica que los detalles refieren solamente al período 'D' que corresponde al invierno en el hemisferio del norte y al verano en los países del sur.
DS. Domestic Service (Servicio Doméstico).
Earliest Heard (or **Latest Heard**). Vease la clave al pie de cada 'Hoja Azul'. Si el equipo de monitores del *Passport* no puede establecer definitivamente el comienzo (o fin) de una transmisión, se entra en cambio la hora más temprana (o tarde) en que pudo rastrearse la estación, indicándola con una banderita triangular.
Ed, Educ. Educational, Educação, Educadora.
Em. Emisora, Emissor, Emissora, Emetteur.
EP. Emissor Provinical.
ER. Emissor Regional.
ES. External Service (Servicio al Exterior).
F. Friday (Viernes).
Feeder. Una transmisión de servicio fijo (punto a punto) usualmente en modo de banda lateral única o independiente, dirigida a la estación de redifusión desde el país de origen de la transmisión. Aunque no destinadas para la recepcióngeneral, las transmisiones de eslabón de onda corta a veces proporcionan la mejor o única oportunidad para la recepción de una emisora determinada a una hora dada. Por esta razón se incluyen en el *Passport* datos sobre este tipo de transmisión, aunque el uso no sea regular. Los modos de transmisión para los eslabones de onda corta son:
- LSB—Banda lateral inferior (señal banda lateral única)
- ISL—Banda lateral inferior (de una señal banda lateral independiente)
- USB—Banda lateral superior (señal banda lateral única)
- ISU—Banda lateral superior (de una señal banda lateral independiente)

FR. Federal Republic (República Federal).
Frequency. Frecuencia. La medida más ampliamente aceptada para indicar la ubicación de una estación dentro de la gama radial. La frecuencia se expresa en kilohertz (kHz) o Megahertz (MHz).
Irr. Operación irregular; horas de recepción irregulares.
(J.) Indica que los detalles refieren solamente al período 'J' que corresponde al verano en el hemisferio del norte y al invierno en los países del sur.
Jamming. Interferencia intencional a una transmisión con el propósito de hacer imposible la recepción de la misma.
kHz. Kilohertz. Anteriormente conocido como 'kilociclo(s) por segundo'. *Vease* 'Frequency'.
kW. Kilovatio(s) (*vease* 'Power').
Loc. Local.
Location La ubicación física del complejo transmisor/antena. Esta ubicación pudiera no corresponder a la de los estudios donde se preparan los programas.
LV. La Voix, La Voz.
M. Monday (Lunes).
Meters. Metros. La unidad para definir segmentos determinados de la gama de onda corta. La gama de frecuencias cubierta por una designación en metros (también conocida como 'longitud de onda') puede calcularse de la siguiente fórmula: frecuencia (kHz) = 299.792/metros. Así 49 metros corresponde a la frecuencia de 6118 kHz—bien dentro de la gama de frecuencias incluidas en ese segmento (*vease* 'World Band Spectrum'). Inversamente, metros pueden derivarse de la fórmula: metros = 299.792/ frecuencia.
MHz. Megahertz. Anteriormente conocido como 'Megaciclo(s) por segundo'. Un Megahertz equivale a 1.000 kilohertz.
N. New, Nouvelle, Nova, Novo, Nueva, Nuevo; Nacional, National, Nationale.
Nac. Nacional.
Nat, Natl. National, Nationale.
Network. La red o el servicio de una emisión. Transmisiones de servicios domésticos son indicadas por 'DS'.
Other. Otro. Cualquier idioma fuera de los principales idiomas del mundo.
PBS. People's Broadcasting Station (Estación de Radiodifusión del Pueblo).
Power. La potencia de salida de RF (radiofrecuencia)—eso es, antes de la amplificación—expresado en kilovatios. La gama actual de potencias de emisoras de onda corta es 0.01-600kW.
PR. People's Republic (República Popular).
PS. Provincial Station, Pangsong.
Pto. Puerto, Pôrto.
R. Radio, Radiodiffusion, Radiodifusora, Radiodifusão, Radioemisora, Radiofonikos, Radiostantsiya, Radyo, Radyosu, etc.
Reg. Regional.
Relay Instalaciones transmisoras extraterritoriales que retransmiten programas recibidos por satélite, eslabón de onda corta, o en forma de grabación.
Rep. Republic, República, République.
RN. *Vease* 'R' y 'N'.
RS. Radio Station, Radiostantsiya, Radiofonikos Stathmos.
RT, RTV. Radiodiffusion Télévision, Radio Televisión, etc.
n, Santa, Santo, São.
Sa. Saturday (Sábado).
Shortwave Spectrum. Gama de onda corta. Estrictamente hablando, la gama de onda corta (o alta frecuencia) es esa porción de la gama radial que se encuentra entre 3 y 30 MHz (3.000-30.000 kHz). Sin embargo, de ordinario se ubica la gama de onda corta entre 2 y 30 MHz aproximadamente, e incluye no solo estaciones de radiodifusión sino también radioaficionados y servicios utilitarios tal como radiotelefonía y radioteletipo.
St. Saint.
Sta, Sto. Santa; Santo.
Su. Sunday (Domingo).
Target. Adonde se dirige una transmisión, con tal que está destinada fuera del país de origen.
Th. Thursday (Jueves).
Tu. Tuesday (Martes).
Universal Time. *Vease* 'UTC'.
UTC. Hora Universal Coordinada. Con unos 160 países transmitiendo sus programas en onda corta, es necesario utilizar una hora única para evitar confusión entre las emisoras y sus oyentes. Esta referencia internacional de 24 horas para la radiodifusión se llama UTC. La diferencia entre UTC y la hora local puede determinarse escuchando los avisos rutinarios de la hora UTC transmitidos por emisoras internacionales. Si uno está en Madrid, la hora local de invierno es UTC + 1, y de verano, UTC + 2. Así 1800 UTC sería las siete de la noche en invierno, y ocho de la noche en verano.
v. Frecuencia variable, eso es, una que es inestable.
Vo. Voice of (Voz de).
W. Wednesday (Miércoles).
Wavelength. Longitud de onda (*vease* 'Meters').
World Band Radio. Similar a onda media y frecuencia modulada, con la excepción de que las emisiones pueden ser captadas sobre enormes distancias. Por eso las transmisiones contienen a menudo programas creados especialmente para audiencias en el exterior. Hoy en día cientos de millones de gente en todos los continentes escuchan estas emisiones.
World Band Spectrum. Todos los segmentos de la gama de onda corta autorizados por la Unión Internacional de Telecomunicaciones (UIT) para la radiodifusión. La UIT también permite el uso de algunas frecuencias fuera de estos segmentos. Los segmentos oficialmente autorizados—junto con los segmentos actualmente utilizados [entre paréntesis rectangular]—siguen, con algunas sugerencias generales para indicar cuando la recepción podría ser óptima. Conviene recordar que estas sugerencias son generales ya que la recepción variará de acuerdo a la ubicación de la emisora, la estación del año, y otros factores.

Recepción débil, noches de invierno

***120 Metros:**
2300-2498 kHz (Emisoras domésticas tropicales)
***90 Metros:**
3200-3400 kHz (Emisoras domésticas tropicales)
***75 Metros:**
3900-3950 kHz (Asia & Pacífico solamente)
3950-4000 kHz (excepto las Américas)
***60 Metros:**
4750-5060 kHz [4600-5100 kHz] (Emisoras domésticas tropicales)

Buena recepción nocturna

49 Metros:
5950-6200 kHz [5850-6250 kHz]
***41 Metros:**
7100-7300 kHz [7100-7600 kHz]

Buena recepción, día y noche

31 Metros:
9500-9775 kHz [9300-9995 kHz]
25 Metros:
11700-11975 kHz [11500-12100 kHz]

Buena recepción diurna

22 Metros:
[13600-13800 kHz]
19 Metros:
15100-15450 kHz [15000-15700 kHz]
16 Metros:
17700-17900 kHz [17500-17900 kHz]
13 Metros:
21450-21750 kHz [21450-21850 kHz]

Recepción diurna regular

11 Metros:
25670-26100 kHz**

**Compartido con otros servicios radiofónicos, tal como estaciones utilitarias y radioaficionados.*
***Proporciona breves períodos de recepción sin interferencia durante muchos días, con los mejores resultados desde ahora hasta 1993 aproximadamente.*

Begriffe und Abkuerzungen die im Weltbandradio vorkommen

Im Weltbandradio wird eine große Anzahl technischer, ausländischer und aus der Allgemeinsprache übernommene Begriffe verwendet. Der folgende Glossar dient als Orientierungshilfe für den *Passport* Benützer.

Alt. Alternative frequency: Alternative Frequenz die abwechselnd an Stelle der regelmäßigen Frequenz verwendet werden kann.
AV. A Voz: Portugiesisch für Stimme von.
BC. Broadcasting, Broadcasting Company, Broadcasting Corporation: Rundfunksendung, Rundfunkgesellschaft.
BS. Broadcasting Station, Broadcasting Service: Rundfunksender, Rundfunkdienst.
Cd. Ciudad: Spanisch für Stadt.
Cl. Club, Clube: Klub.
Cu. Cult., Cultura, Culture, Cultural: Kultur, kulturell.
(D). Frequenz kann zur Zeit nur im Winter empfangen werden. Empfang im Sommer nicht möglich.
DS. Domestic Service: Rundfunkdienst fürs Inland. *Vergleiche* ES.
Earliest Heard (or **Latest Heard**). Hineinschwinden (oder Herausschwinden). Siehe Schlüssel am unteren Rande der „Blue Pages." Falls das *Passport*-Rundfunkerfasserteam den Anfang oder das Ende einer Sendung nicht genau bestimmen kann, wird die früheste (oder späteste) mögliche Empfangszeit durch ein schwarzes Dreieck (,) angegeben. Das heißt, die Rundfundsendug kann nur mit aller Wahrscheinlichkeit über die mit dem schwarzen Dreieck angegebene Zeit hinaus empfangen werden, wenn man in unmittelbarer Nähe des Rundfunksenders wohnt.
Ed., Educ. Educational, Educação, Educadora: Bildungsprogramm.
Em. Emissora, Emisora, Emissor, Emetteur: Begriff für Sender in verschiedenen Sprachen.
EP. Emissor Provincial: Portugiesisch für Landkreis-Sender.
ER. Emissor Regional: Portugiesisch für Regional-Sender.
ES. External Service: Rundfunkdienst fürs Ausland. *Siehe* DS.
F. Friday: Freitag.
Feeder. Versorger: Eine „Versorgungsstation" die Programme vom Rundfunkdienst im Inland an eine Relaisstelle im Ausland sendet. Obwohl der Empfang dieser Stationen für die öffentlichkeit nicht beabsichtigt ist, können viele der Weltbandradios diese Neo-Rundfunksendungen auf jeden Fall empfangen. „Feeder" Sendearten sind:
1. Unteres Seitenband (LSB—Lower Sideband)
2. Oberes Seitenband (USB—Upper Sideband)
3. Unabhängiges Seitenband (Independent Sideband)
   a. Unteres (ISL—lower)
   b. Oberes (ISU—upper)

FR. Federal Republic: Bundesrepublik.
Frequency. Frequenz: Das Standardmaß um die Lage einer Sendung im Radiospektrum anzugeben. Wird in Kilohertz (kHz) oder Megahertz (MHz) ausgedrückt.
Irr. Irregular Operation or Hours of Operation: Unregelmäßige Sendung, das heißt Sendeprogramm ist nicht vorhersagbar.
(J). Frequenz kann zur Zeit nur im Sommer empfangen werden. Empfang im Winter nicht möglich.
Jamming. Störung durch andere Sender: Der Empfang einer Sendung wird mit Absicht gestört.
kHz. Kilohertz: Allgemeine Maßeinheit um die Lage einer Sendung im Radiospektrum anzugeben. Früher bekannt als „Kilocycles/second." 1000 kHz = 1 MHz.
kW. Kilowatt(s): Allgemeine Maßeinheit der Senderleistung.
Loc. Local: örtlich.
Location. Standort des Radiosenders, der mit dem Standort des Studios nicht übereinstimmen muß. Der Standort des Radiosenders ist für die Empfangsqualitätwichtig. Z.B. ist der Empfang Radio Moskaus in Europa bei einem Senderstandort im Westen der Sowjetunion wahrscheinlicher als bei einem Senderstandort in Sibirien. Ein Standort in Bulgarien wäre günstiger.
LV. La Voix, La Voz: Französisch und Spanisch für Die Stimme.
M. Monday: Montag.
Meters. Maßeinheit für einzelne Weltbandabschnitte des Kurzwellenspektrums. Der Frequenzbereich gemessen in Meter, auch als Wellenlänge bekannt, kann mit folgender Formel errechnet werden: Frequenz (kHz) = 299,792/Meter. D.h. 49 m = Frequenz von 6118 kHz liegt mit Sicherheit im Kurzwellenbereich (*siehe* Weltbandspektrum). Umgekehrt, können Meter errechnet werden: Meter = 299,792/Frequenz (kHz).

MHz. Megahertz: Allgemeine Maßeinheit um die Lage einer Sendung im Radiospektrum anzugeben. Früher bekannt als „Megacycles/second." 1 MHz = 1000 kHz.
N. New, Nueva, Nuevo, Novelle: Neu.
Nac. Nacional: National.
Nat. Natl., National, Nationale: National.
Other. Andere. Programme in anderen Sprachen als Weltsprachen.
PBS. People's Broadcasting Station: Volksrundfunkstation.
Power. Kraft. Senderleistung vor der Amplifikation durch die Antenne, ausgedrückt in Kilowatt (kW). Der Empfangsbereich des Weltbandradios liegt z.Zt. zwischen 0.01 und 600 kW.
PR. People's Republic: Volksrepublik.
PS. Provincial Station, Pangsong: Landkreis-Sender.
Pto. Puerto, Pôrto: Hafen.
R. Radio, Radiodiffusion, Radiodifusora, Radiodifusão, Radiofonikos, Radiostansiya, Radyo, Radyosu, usw.: Radio
Reg. Regional: Regional.
Relay. Relais. Eine zusätzliche Sendestation (fettgedruckt im „Worldwide Broadcasts") im Ausland. Relaissignale in der Nähe des Empfängers ermöglichen einen besseren Empfang. (*Siehe* Feeder.)
Rep. Republic, République, Republica: Republik.
RN. *Siehe* R. und N.
RS. Radio Station, Radiostansiya, Radiofonikos Stathmos: Radiostation.
RT, RTV. Radiodiffusion Télévision, Radio Television, etc.: Radio und Fernsehen.
S. San, Santa, Santo, São, Saint: Sankt (St.).
Sa. Saturday: Samstag.
Shortwave Spectrum. Kurzwellenspektrum. Das Kurzwellenspektrum, auch als Hochfrequenzspektrum (HF) bekannt, liegt genau gesagt zwischen 3 und 30 MHz (3,000–30,000 kHz) im Radiospektrum. Die allgemeine Empfangsmöglichkeit liegt jedoch zwischen 2 und 30 MHz (2,000–30,000 kHz). Enthalten sind nicht nur die Weltbandstationen, sondern auch die Versorgerstationen („Feeder")—Radiotelephone, Schiffe auf See, usw.—und Radioamateure.
St., Sta., Sto. Saint: Sankt (St.).
Su. Sunday: Sonntag.
Target. Zielgebiet einer Sendung, wenn sie außerhalb des Landes gehört werden soll.
„Targets" sind:
Africa: Afrika
Americas: Die amerikanischen Kontinente
Australia & New Zealand: Australien & Neuseeland
Asia: Asien
Atlantic Ocean & Islands: Atlantischer Ozean & Inseln
Central America, Caribbean, & Mexico: Mittelamerika, Karibik, & Mexiko
Central Africa: Zentralafrika
East Africa: Ostafrika
East Asia: Ostasien
Eastern Europe: Osteuropa
Eastern North America: Ostnordamerika
Europe: Europa
Eastern USSR: UdSSR (Ost)
Middle East: Nahost
North America: Nordamerika
North Africa: Nordafrika
Pacific Ocean & Islands: Pazifischer Ozean & Inseln
South America: Südamerika
Southern Africa: Südliches Afrika
South Asia: Südasien
Southeast Asia: Südostasien
Soviet Union: Sowjetunion
West Africa: Westafrika
Western Europe: Westeuropa
Western North America: Westnordamerika
Western USSR: UdSSR (West)
Th. Thursday: Donnerstag.
Tu. Tuesday: Dienstag.
Universal Time. Universalzeit. *Siehe* UTC.
UTC. Coordinated Universal Time: Koordinierte Universalzeit. 161 Länder der Welt beteiligen sich am Weltbandradio. Wenn jedes Land seine Ortszeit angeben würde, so müßte der Empfänger einen Rechner benützen um seine Zeit zu kalkulieren. Um das zu vermeiden wird eine internationale Zeit—UTC—verwendet. Stündliche UTC-Zeitansagen im Weltbandrundfunk geben die Differenz zwischen UTC und der jeweiligen Ortszeit an. Eine 24-Stunden-Uhr wird verwendet, d.h. „1800" UTC = 6:00 PM UTC. Die deutsche Winter/Sommerzeit is 1 bzw. 2 Stunden später als UTC-Zeit. (D.h. 1800 UTC = 7:00 PM Winterzeit und 8:00 PM Sommerzeit). Am einfachsten ist es eine 24-Stunden-Uhr auf UTC-Zeit einzustellen. Bei vielen Radios ist diese schon eingebaut und außerdem sind UTC-Uhren als Zusatz erhältlich.
v. Variable frequency: Variierende Frequenz. D.h. eine Frequenz die wegen Funktionsstörung des Senders unstabil oder schwankend ist.
Vo. Voice of: Stimme von.

WORLDSCAN: GEBRAUCHSANWEISUNG

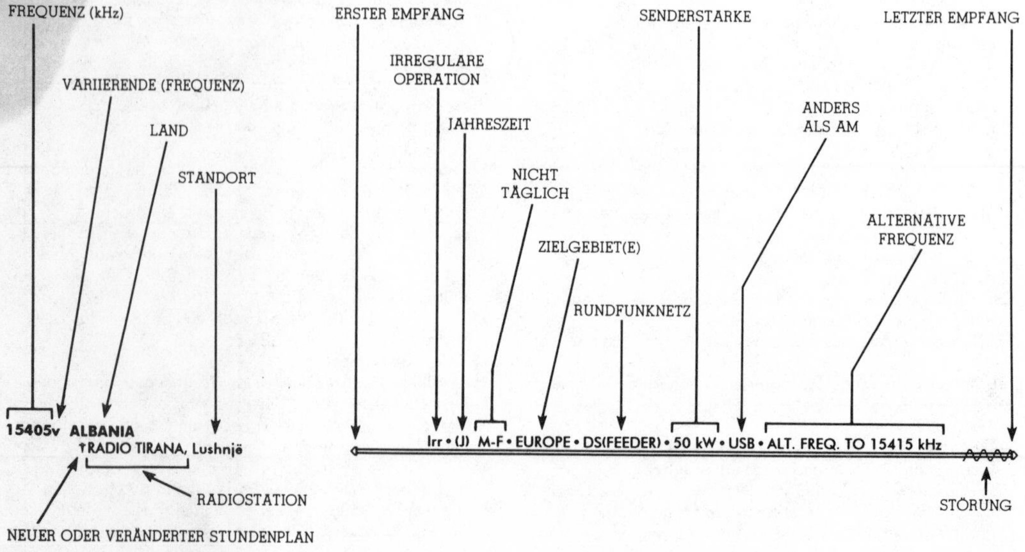